Fourth Edition

TRANSFORMING THE SCHOOL COUNSELING PROFESSION

Bradley T. Erford
Loyola University Maryland

PEARSON

Boston   Columbus   Indianapolis   New York   San Francisco   Upper Saddle River
Amsterdam   Cape Town   Dubai   London   Madrid   Milan   Munich   Paris   Montreal   Toronto
Delhi   Mexico City   Sao Paulo   Sydney   Hong Kong   Seoul   Singapore   Taipei   Tokyo

Vice President and Editorial Director: Jeffery W. Johnston
Senior Acquisitions Editor: Meredith Fossel
Editorial Assistant: Janelle Criner
Vice President, Director of Marketing: Margaret Waples
Senior Marketing Manager: Darcy Betts Prybella
Production Project Manager: Jennifer Gessner
Development Project Management: Aptara®, Inc.
Procurement Specialist: Patricia Tonneman
Senior Art Director: Jayne Conte
Cover Designer: Karen Salzbach
Cover Photo: © Laurentiu Lordache/Fotolia
Media Project Manager: Noelle Chun
Full-Service Project Management: Mohinder Singh/Aptara®, Inc.
Composition: Aptara®, Inc.
Printer/Binder: Courier/Kendallville
Cover Printer: Lehigh-Phoenix/Hagerstown
Text Font: Minion Pro

Credits and acknowledgments for material borrowed from other sources and reproduced, with permission, in this textbook appear on the appropriate page within the text.

Every effort has been made to provide accurate and current Internet information in this book. However, the Internet and information posted on it are constantly changing, so it is inevitable that some of the Internet addresses listed in this textbook will change.

Library of Congress Cataloging-in-Publication Data
Transforming the school counseling profession / [edited by] Bradley T. Erford, Loyola University, Maryland.
—Fourth edition.
    pages cm
ISBN-13: 978-0-13-335189-7
ISBN-10: 0-13-335189-0
1. Educational counseling—United States—Handbooks, manuals, etc. I. Erford, Bradley T.
LB1027.5.T65 2015
371.4—dc23

                                                                                    2013039781

V011
10 9 8 7 6 5 4 3 2 1

PEARSON

ISBN 10:   0-13-335189-0
ISBN 13: 978-0-13-335189-7

This effort is dedicated to The One: the Giver of energy, passion, and understanding; Who makes life worth living and endeavors worth pursuing and accomplishing; the Teacher of love and forgiveness.

PREFACE

Myriad societal changes have created significant academic, career, and personal/social developmental challenges for today's students. A short list of these challenges includes high academic standards; suicide; substance abuse; technological changes recasting future labor-force needs; violence in schools, homes, and communities; and high-stakes testing. The prominence of these and many other challenges that confront the children and youth of today makes professional school counselors more essential than ever to the missions of schools.

In the past, many educators have viewed school counseling as an ancillary service. More recently, due to national school reform and accountability initiatives, school counselor leaders have encouraged professional school counselors in the field to dedicate their programs to the schools' mission objectives, which typically focus on academic performance and the achievement of high academic standards by all students. Without question, school counseling programs with curricula emphasizing affective skills associated with academic performance help students become motivated to perform, "learn how to learn," and cope with the challenges of our diverse and changing world. Historically, professional school counselors have focused on career and personal/social needs as ends in themselves.

This new focus on academic performance in support of a school's educational mission is necessary to win the respect of school reform advocates and achievement-focused educators. Thus, professional school counselors must ensure that comprehensive, developmental school counseling programs address career and personal/social issues with the end goal of removing barriers to, and improving, educational performance. To accomplish this goal, however, professional school counselors must develop programs offering a broad range of services aimed at the increasingly diverse needs of systems, educators, families, and students. *Transforming the School Counseling Profession*, Fourth Edition, was written to help to accomplish this goal.

Designed as an introduction to the school counseling profession, this book may also serve as a school counseling program development resource. Its goal is to inform the reader about how the seemingly diverse roles of the professional school counselor fit together in a comprehensive manner. Some topics are treated more thoroughly than others. Whereas most school counselor educational programs offer entire courses on some of these topics, others are barely touched on before students encounter them in the field. This book will help school counselors in training

to prepare for their entry into a career as a professional school counselor and to avoid mistakes. Experienced professional school counselors and counselor supervisors interested in new ideas may also find the book stimulating in its offering of new perspectives and detailed descriptions aiding program development. At times both idealistic and futuristic, the authors attempt to be realistic and practical as well, while pointing out more effective methods. Although our goal is primarily to educate the reader, we also seek to provoke discussion among professional school counselors, school counselors in training, school counselor educators and supervisors, and the broader educational community.

ORGANIZATION OF THE TEXT

Transforming the School Counseling Profession, Fourth Edition, begins with a concise synopsis of the history of the profession, highlights issues that will determine its future course, and concludes with an explanation of 10 roles emerging from the current school counseling literature that must be considered to effectively implement a comprehensive school counseling program. In Chapter 2, I summarize the *ASCA National Model* (2012), its various components, and its application to school counseling. Chapter 3 offers a glimpse of current barriers to effective implementation of a school counseling program and presents a vision for the 21st century. Patricia J. Martin of the College Board and formerly of the Education Trust's Transforming School Counseling Initiative presents some interesting perspectives on how to remove barriers to academic performance. This is followed in Chapter 4 by Vivian V. Lee of the College Board and Gary E. Goodnough of Plymouth State University, who summarize the planning and implementation of a systemic data-driven school counseling program.

Chapters 5 and 6 focus the reader's attention on discovering what works in school counseling. Chapter 5 explores the many facets of school counseling accountability, including needs assessment, program evaluation, service assessment, outcomes evaluation, and performance appraisal. School reform movements around the country have made accountability a critical element in all educational components, and professional school counselors are wise to become knowledgeable leaders in this area. In Chapter 6, Susan C. Whiston, Rachel Feldwisch, and Barbara James of Indiana University provide a concise summary of school counseling outcomes research, concluding that, although little research is available, existing research is generally supportive of school counseling services.

Section II provides foundational support for understanding ethical, legal, and advocacy issues in school counseling. In Chapter 7, Lynn Linde of Loyola University Maryland focuses on the importance of ethical, legal, and professional issues related to the practice of school counseling. In Chapter 8, Cheryl Holcomb-McCoy of the Johns Hopkins University and Stuart F. Chen-Hayes of CUNY–Lehman bring their unique scholarly perspectives to bear on answering the question, "What does a multiculturally competent school counselor look like?" The cases and questionnaire provided are certain to provoke interesting classroom discussions! In Chapter 9, Stuart F. Chen-Hayes and Yvette Q. Getch of the University of Georgia provide practical, down-to-earth advice on leadership in the schools and how to advocate, and teach others to advocate, for academic success and social equity. This chapter focuses on the professional school counselor as leader and as academic and social advocate and is an exciting addition to school counseling literature and practice.

Beginning with Chapter 10, the "how-to" of comprehensive and data-driven school counseling programs takes shape. Gary E. Goodnough, Rachelle Pérusse, and I expand on the curriculum development and implementation processes in Chapter 4 and extend into the classroom guidance component of a developmental program. Chapter 11, authored by Stuart Chen-Hayes and Melissa Ockerman, is a new chapter to this edition and focuses on school counselor competencies to promote academic and college access for every K–12 student. We need to promote access to rigorous academic coursework from the early years of elementary school to ensure that every student is college- and career-ready by graduation. In Chapter 12, Patrick Akos of UNC–Chapel Hill, Hyoyeon In of Penn State University, and Spencer (Skip) G. Niles of the College of William and Mary expand on the career-planning component of a comprehensive program that, although historically a focus in high school, has received greater emphasis recently in K–8 curricula. Chapter 13 provides a basic introduction to the individual and group counseling components of a comprehensive program, and Chapter 14 reviews the importance of consultation and collaboration, setting the stage for systemic collaboration and parent/community outreach.

Section IV reviews some of the essential and emerging issues in education and school counseling. No discussion of school counseling would be complete without some attention to violence and bullying in the school and community and to students with complex problems. Chapter 15, authored by myself, Vivian V. Lee, and Elana

Rock, focuses on systemic solutions, as well as assessing and counseling youth with complex problems through just such systemic solutions, while also addressing the development of conflict resolution and peer mediation programs in schools to combat violence and enhance interpersonal communication and problem solving.

Elana Rock of Loyola University Maryland and Erin H. Leff, a lawyer who specializes in education law, provide an exceptionally comprehensive look in Chapter 16 at the professional school counselor's role in meeting the needs of students with disabilities, providing sufficient justification to protect the counselor from being overused in the special education process, while providing enough information to allow professional school counselors to advocate for the needs of these students. Finally, an excellent introduction to mental and emotional disorders is provided in Chapter 17. Although professional school counselors may not diagnose these conditions in their workplace, knowledge of the medical model and characteristics of mental and emotional disorders will surely facilitate appropriate referrals, liaising with mental health practitioners, and integration of students with mental and emotional disorders into the school environment.

Transforming the School Counseling Profession seeks to be more than just an introductory text. Its purpose is to strike a chord with professional school counselors and school counselors in training all around the world and to lead the professional practice of school counseling in new and exciting directions that will benefit students, educators, parents, and the entire community. Professional school counselors can and must provide advocacy, leadership, and support in the school reform and accountability movements, helping to ensure that no student falls through the cracks.

WHAT'S NEW IN THIS EDITION

The school counseling profession is changing rapidly, and the purpose of this revision is to accurately reflect these changes in practice and the extant literature, as well as providing direction and leadership for future practice and scholarship. In this Fourth Edition of *Transforming the School Counseling Profession*, readers and instructors will note the following changes:

- Chapter 11, "Academic Development and Planning for College and Career Readiness K–12," is new to this edition and focuses on school counselor competencies to promote academic and college access for every K–12 student.
- Major revisions have been made to Chapter 2, "The ASCA National Model: Developing a Comprehensive, Developmental School Counseling Program," which

provides an overview of the third edition of the *ASCA National Model* (ASCA, 2012) and how it can be applied to practice in the schools; Chapter 4, "Systemic, Data-Driven School Counseling Practice and Programming for Equity," to reflect evolutionary changes in systemic school counseling program and practice philosophy; and Chapter 9, "Leadership and Advocacy for Every Student's Achievement and Opportunity."

- Nearly every chapter has incorporated a new feature called "Cultural Reflections," which provides reflective questions aimed at getting counselor trainees to consider how every topic in this book requires culturally sensitive modifications and consideration in implementing the transformed role.
- Nearly every chapter has incorporated a new feature called "Theory into Practice," which provides brief passages written by professional school counselors that demonstrate real-life examples of practitioners applying the theory and concepts covered in the chapter to actual practice venues, thus providing students with concrete applications.
- Revisions have been made to the PowerPoint® slides available to instructors and the test questions provided in the Instructor's Manual.
- As a result of updating the literature, more than 70% of the Fourth Edition's references are as recent as 2005, and about one third are as recent as 2010.

SUPPLEMENTAL INSTRUCTIONAL FEATURES

Supplemental to this book are pedagogical tools helpful to school counselor educators choosing to use this book as a course textbook. The companion Instructor's Manual contains at least 50 multiple-choice questions, 20 essay questions, and 15 classroom or individual activities per chapter. In addition, a comprehensive Microsoft PowerPoint® presentation is available from the publisher for counselor educators to use or modify for classroom presentations. Case studies included in the text can stimulate lively classroom discussions.

ACKNOWLEDGMENTS

This book is dedicated to the tens of thousands of professional school counselors and school counselors in training who struggle daily to meet the seemingly ever-expanding needs of the students, families, educational colleagues, and communities they serve. This dedication extends to the thousands of counselor educators and supervisors who have devoted their lives to their profession, colleagues, and students. Thank you for making this a profession to be proud of! I especially want to thank the authors who contributed their perspectives and words of wisdom. They are all true experts in their specialty areas and are truly dedicated to the betterment of the profession. It is an honor to work closely with such an august group of scholars. Meredith Fossel and Krista Slavicek of Pearson deserve special mention for their stewardship during the editing of this book. I am also grateful to the following reviewers for their helpful and supportive comments: Stephanie Eberts, Texas State University; Eric Green, UNT Dallas; Vivian V. Lee, University of Maryland; Lynn Leonard, University of Missouri–Kansas City; Leann M. Morgan, University of Texas at Tyler; and Zark VanZandt, University of Southern Maine. Finally, I am forever grateful to my family, whose tolerance for my periodic quest of solitude makes projects such as this possible.

ABOUT THE EDITOR

Bradley T. Erford, Ph.D., LCPC, NCC, LPC, LP, LSP, is a professor in the school counseling program of the Education Specialties Department in the School of Education at Loyola University Maryland. He was President of the American Counseling Association (ACA) for 2012–2013. He is the recipient of the ACA Research Award, ACA Extended Research Award, ACA Arthur A. Hitchcock Distinguished Professional Service Award, ACA Professional Development Award, and ACA Carl D. Perkins Government Relations Award. He was also inducted as an ACA Fellow. In addition, he has received the Association for Assessment in Counseling and Education (AACE) AACE/MECD Research Award, AACE Exemplary Practices Award, AACE President's Merit Award, the Association for Counselor Education and Supervision's (ACES) Robert O. Stripling Award for Excellence in Standards, Maryland Association for Counseling and Development (MACD) Maryland Counselor of the Year, MACD Counselor Advocacy Award, MACD Professional Development Award, and MACD Counselor Visibility Award. He is the editor of numerous texts, including: *Orientation to the Counseling Profession* (Pearson Merrill, 2010, 2014), *Crisis Intervention and Prevention* (Pearson Merrill, 2010, 2014), *Group Work in the Schools* (Pearson Merrill, 2010), *Group Work: Process and Applications* (Pearson Merrill, 2011), *Transforming the School Counseling Profession* (Pearson Merrill, 2003, 2007, 2011, 2015), *Professional School Counseling: A Handbook of Principles, Programs and Practices* (PRO-ED, 2004, 2010), *Assessment for Counselors* (Cengage, 2007, 2013), *Research and Evaluation in Counseling* (Cengage, 2008, 2014), and *The Counselor's Guide to Clinical, Personality and Behavioral Assessment* (Cengage, 2006); and coauthor of four more books: *Mastering the NCE and CPCE* (Pearson Merrill, 2011, 2015), *35 Techniques Every Counselor Should Know* (Merrill/Prentice Hall, 2010), *Educational Applications of the WISC-IV* (Western Psychological Services, 2006), and *Group Activities: Firing Up for Performance* (Pearson Merrill, 2007). He is also the General Editor of *The American Counseling Association Encyclopedia of Counseling* (ACA, 2009). His research specialization falls primarily in development and technical analysis of psychoeducational tests and has resulted in the publication of more than 60 refereed journal articles, 100 book chapters, and a dozen published tests. He was a representative to the ACA Governing Council and the ACA 20/20 Visioning Committee. He is a past president and past treasurer of AACE; past chair and parliamentarian of the American Counseling Association—Southern (U.S.) Region; past-chair of ACA's Task Force on High Stakes Testing; past chair of ACA's Standards for Test Users Task Force; past chair of ACA's Interprofessional Committee; past chair of the ACA Public Awareness and Support Committee (co-chair of the National Awards Sub-committee); chair of the Convention and past chair of the Screening Assessment Instruments Committees for AACE; past president of the Maryland Association for Counseling and Development (MACD); past president of Maryland Association for Measurement and Evaluation (MAME); past president of Maryland Association for Counselor Education and Supervision (MACES); and past president of the Maryland Association for Mental Health Counselors (MAMHC). He was also an associate editor of the *Journal of Counseling and Development.* Dr. Erford has been a faculty member at Loyola since 1993 and is a Licensed Clinical Professional Counselor, Licensed Professional Counselor, Nationally Certified Counselor, Licensed Psychologist, and Licensed School Psychologist. Prior to arriving at Loyola, Dr. Erford was a school psychologist/counselor in the Chesterfield County (VA) Public Schools. He maintains a private practice specializing in assessment and treatment of children and adolescents. A graduate of The University of Virginia (Ph.D.), Bucknell University (M.A.), and Grove City College (B.S.), he teaches courses in Testing and Measurement, Lifespan Development, Research and Evaluation in Counseling, School Counseling, and Stress Management.

ABOUT THE AUTHORS

Patrick Akos is a professor in the school counseling program in the School of Education at the University of North Carolina at Chapel Hill. His research involves strengths-based school counseling (SBSC) and, in particular, centers on how school counselors can promote development and build strengths in students during early adolescence. A primary focus of his research is on school transitions (e.g., elementary to middle, middle to high school) and how school counselors and schools can promote optimal developmental paths and strengths-enhancing environments.

Stuart F. Chen-Hayes is an associate professor of counselor education/school counseling at Lehman College of the City University of New York. He has worked in middle school counseling, college student affairs, addictions, sexuality counseling, couple and family counseling, and mental health settings. He is the coauthor of 55 refereed publications, including *101 Solutions for School Counselors and Leaders in Challenging Times* (Corwin). Dr. Chen-Hayes works as an equity-focused school counseling program consultant in school districts in Delaware, New Jersey, New York, and Pennsylvania through the University of Pennsylvania's Graduate School of Education Leadership and Equity Initiatives. He has also taught at National-Louis University in Chicago and National Changhua University of Education in Taiwan and chaired a school counseling dissertation in Oregon State University's hybrid doctoral program. He has led the infusion of transformed school counseling, ASCA National Model/Standards, and NOSCA 8 Components of College and Career Counseling at Lehman in coursework and fieldwork. He co-chairs a monthly national teleconference meeting of the Association for Counselor Education and Supervision (ACES) Transformed School Counseling/College Access Interest Network. He is a past-president of Counselors for Social Justice, the North Atlantic Region of Counselor Educators and Supervisors, and the Illinois Counseling Association. He is on the editorial boards of the *Journal of Gay, Lesbian, Bisexual, and Transgender Issues in Counseling, Journal of Counselor Preparation and Supervision*, and *Journal of International Counselor Education*.

Rachel P. Feldwisch, MA, MS, is a licensed professional school counselor, licensed mental health counselor, and registered art therapist. She was an elementary and middle school counselor in a metropolitan school district and conducted research with the Center for Urban and Multicultural Education in Indianapolis. She is currently a student in the counseling psychology Ph.D. program at Indiana University, where she teaches undergraduate counseling courses.

Yvette Q. Getch is the Executive Director of the Suzanne Vitale Clinical Education Complex and associate professor at Western Kentucky University. Before accepting her current position, she was an associate professor at the University of Georgia. She earned a B.S. in social work at Florida State University, an M.Ed. in rehabilitation counseling from the University of Arkansas, and a Ph.D. in rehabilitation education and research from the University of Arkansas. Her primary areas of research include advocacy skills development for students who have disabilities or chronic illnesses, the impact of a child's chronic illness on the family, and accommodations for children with chronic illness and disabilities in schools and the community.

Gary E. Goodnough, NCC, is the chair of the Counselor Education and School Psychology Department at Plymouth State University, New Hampshire. He received a Ph.D. in counselor education from the University of Virginia in 1995 and is a National Certified Counselor and state-licensed clinical mental health counselor. A former high school director of guidance, he has coedited a book on school counseling, written several articles and book chapters, and made numerous regional and national professional presentations.

Cheryl Holcomb-McCoy received her Ph.D. in counseling and educational development from the University of North Carolina at Greensboro in 1996. She is currently Professor and Vice Dean of Academic Affairs at Johns Hopkins University's School of Education. Prior to her appointment at Johns Hopkins, Dr. Holcomb-McCoy was an associate professor in the Department of Counseling and Personnel Services at the University of Maryland, College Park. She also served as the director of the school counseling program at Brooklyn College of the City University of New York. Her areas of research specialization include the measurement of multicultural self-efficacy in school counseling, the measurement of school college-going culture, and best practices in urban school counselor preparation.

Hyoyeon In is a Ph.D. candidate in counselor education and supervision at Pennsylvania State University. Prior to entering the doctoral program, she developed and implemented employee training programs at the Human Resource Development center of POSCO, a multinational steel corporation headquartered in South Korea. She completed her M.A. in educational counseling at Seoul National University in Korea. Her work focuses on career development for diverse populations. As a member of the Hope-Centered Model of Career Development (HCMCD) research team, she has been involved in various research projects, publications, and presentations on the HCMCD. She also has been committed to helping students with their career needs in Penn State's Career Services as a career counseling graduate assistant.

Barbara N. James is a doctoral student in counseling and educational psychology at Indiana University. Prior to entering the doctoral program, she served as a professional school counselor for 10 years in both public and private P-12 school settings. Barbara is very interested in the effectiveness of school counseling interventions and is currently involved in outcomes evaluations of middle school career development interventions as part of her dissertation project at Indiana University.

Vivian V. Lee is associate professor of transcultural counseling at University of Malta, Malta. She is the former Senior Director at the National Office for School Counselor Advocacy of the College Board. She is a former teacher, secondary school counselor, director of school counseling, and counselor educator. She continues to teach school counseling courses as an adjunct at the University of Maryland at College Park. Her work includes research in the area of school counselor professional development, she has served as trainer with the Education Trust's National Center for Transforming School Counseling Initiative, and she has published articles and book chapters on developing school counseling programs, conflict resolution and violence, and group counseling. She worked in public education for 24 years before joining the College Board and received her master's and doctoral degrees from the University of Virginia.

Erin H. Leff is an attorney, mediator, and retired master's-level psychologist who has worked in special education for over 30 years. She earned an M.S. in educational psychology from the University of Wisconsin–Madison and a J.D. from Rutgers–Camden. She has worked as an attorney and as a psychologist as well as a program administrator in multiple states. She has been a special education due process hearing officer, appeals officer, and mediator. She has provided training on various topics in special education

and mediation. She also has provided instruction on special education law and process at the graduate level.

Lynn E. Linde is an assistant professor of education and the director of clinical programs in the school counseling program at Loyola University Maryland. She received her master's degree in school counseling and her doctorate in counseling from George Washington University. She was previously the chief of the Student Services and Alternative Programs Branch at the Maryland State Department of Education, the state specialist for school counseling, a local school system counseling supervisor, a middle and high school counselor, and a special education teacher. She has made numerous presentations, particularly in the areas of ethics and legal issues for counselors and public policy and legislation, over the course of her career. Dr. Linde is an American Counseling Association (ACA) Fellow and the recipient of the ACA Carl Perkins Award, the Association for Counselor Education and Supervision's (ACES) Program Supervisor Award, the Southern Association for Counselor Education and Supervision's (SACES) Program Supervisor Award, and a 2013 ACA President's Award as well as numerous awards from the Maryland state counseling association and from the state of Maryland for her work in student services and youth suicide prevention. She has held a number of leadership positions in the ACA and its entities and was the 2009–2010 president and the 2012–13 treasurer of the ACA.

Patricia J. Martin is a nationally recognized leader in the reform of school counseling and efforts to design training opportunities to help practicing counselors become an integral part of the primary mission for schools. She holds a B.A. in mathematics and an M.A. in school counseling from Our Lady of the Lake College in San Antonio, Texas. She has more than 30 years of experience as a public school educator, having worked as a teacher, professional school counselor, district supervisor of counselors, high school principal, chief educational administrator, and assistant superintendent of schools in Prince George's County, Maryland. In her work as the senior program manager at the Education Trust, she provided the leadership and technical expertise that solidly launched the National Transforming School Counseling Initiative, which was underwritten by the DeWitt Wallace Foundation. She is currently an assistant vice president at the College Board, leading the National Office for School Counselor Advocacy (NOSCA) in Washington, D.C. In this capacity, she continues working to establish a national presence in education reform for school counselors as they seek to advance the academic agenda for all students.

At NOSCA, under her leadership, the College Board has become a nationally recognized force in advocating for school counselors, providing research, publications, tools, and training for school counselor practitioners to enhance their skills in College and Career Readiness Counseling.

Spencer G. Niles is Dean for the School of Education at The College of William & Mary and previously served as a Distinguished Professor and Department Head for Educational Psychology, Counseling, and Special Education at Pennsylvania State University. He is also Director of the Center for the Study of Career Development and Public Policy. Dr. Niles is the recipient of the National Career Development Association's (NCDA) Eminent Career Award, a Fellow of the American Counseling Association (ACA) and NCDA, the recipient of ACA's President's Award, David Brooks Distinguished Mentor Award, Extended Research Award, the Thomas J. Sweeney Visionary Leadership and Advocacy Award, and the University of British Columbia's Noted Scholar Award. He served as president for the National Career Development Association, Editor for both *The Career Development Quarterly* and *Journal of Counseling & Development,* and serves on six additional editorial boards for national and international journals. He is also on the advisory board for the International Centre for Career Development and Public Policy. He has authored or coauthored approximately 120 publications and delivered over 125 presentations on career development theory and practice.

Melissa S. Ockerman is an assistant professor in the counseling program at DePaul University. A proud Buckeye, she graduated with an M.A. in school counseling and Ph.D. in counselor education from The Ohio State University. She has established a strong research agenda focusing on school counselor leadership, the efficacy of school counseling interventions and systemic antibullying and school safety strategies. As such, she appeared before the Congressional Black Caucus in Washington, D.C., to discuss bipartisan antiviolence policies. She is a frequent presenter at local, state, and national conferences. In 2012, she was named the *Illinois Counselor Educator of the Year.* She currently holds executive positions in national and state professional organizations, including Co-Chair of the Association for Counselor Education and Supervision (ACES) *Transformed School Counseling & College Access Network* and Vice President, Counselor Education of the Illinois School Counseling Association. In addition, she is the Chair of the school counseling committee for the Illinois Safe Schools Alliance, a National Center for Transforming School

Counseling (NCTSC) Counselor Educator Coalition fellow, and is proud to be an Advisory Council member for the Evidence-Based Practice in School Counseling conference. She is currently coauthoring a school counseling text with colleagues Drs. Stuart Chen-Hayes and Erin Mason published by Corwin Press. Her passion for educating the next generation of transformed school counselors is matched only by her strong desire to dismantle the pervasive achievement gap in schools through innovative and effective evidence-based school counseling interventions.

Rachelle Pérusse, NCC, NCSC, has been an associate professor in the counseling program at the University of Connecticut since the fall of 2004. Prior to this appointment, she was a tenured associate professor and the school counseling coordinator at Plattsburgh State University in Plattsburgh, New York, from 1997 to 2004. She received a Ph.D. in counselor education from Virginia Polytechnic Institute in 1997. Before becoming a school counselor educator, she worked with poor and minority youth as a high school counselor in a rural school district in Georgia. Professionally, she has served as secretary for the North Atlantic Regional Association for Counselor Education and Supervision (2000–2002), secretary for the Association of Counselor Education and Supervision (2005–2006), and president of the North Atlantic Regional Association for Counselor Education and Supervision (2007–2008). Since 2002, she has been a consultant with the Education Trust's National Transforming School Counseling Initiative. She has published numerous articles about national trends in school counselor education and has coedited two books: *Critical Incidents in Group Counseling* and *Leadership, Advocacy, and Direct Service Strategies for Professional School Counselors.*

Elana Rock is an associate professor of special education in the Education Specialties Department at Loyola University Maryland. Her responsibilities include teaching undergraduate and graduate special education courses, developing and revising curriculum, and assessing the personnel preparation needs of local schools. She earned a B.A. from the University of Pennsylvania, an M.A. in teaching children with emotional disturbance from New York University, and an Ed.D. in special education from Johns Hopkins University. Dr. Rock has served as expert research consultant to the U.S. District Court's Special Master overseeing special education service delivery in the Baltimore City Public Schools and continues to consult with schools and school districts on special education issues. Her research publications and presentations focus on children with concomitant high-prevalence disorders, the evaluation of service delivery in special education, and special education teacher education. Prior to earning her doctorate, she taught elementary and secondary students with learning disabilities and emotional/behavioral disorders.

Susan C. Whiston is a professor at Indiana University in the Department of Counseling and Educational Psychology. She has been teaching counseling courses since 1986 and has published many articles concerning the empirical support for school counseling. She has been on the editorial boards of *Career Development Quarterly, Journal of Career Assessment, Journal of Counseling Psychology,* and was associate editor for research for the *Journal of Counseling and Development.* In 2010, she received the Best Practices Award from the American Counseling Association. Prior to receiving her doctorate from the University of Wyoming, she worked in secondary schools as a counselor for low-income students.

BRIEF CONTENTS

CONTENTS

Chapter 4   Systemic, Data-Driven School Counseling Practice and Programming for Equity   66

Vivian V. Lee and Gary E. Goodnough

Chapter 9 Leadership and Advocacy for Every Student's Achievement and Opportunity   194

Stuart F. Chen-Hayes and Yvette Q. Getch

Becoming a Professional School Counselor: Current Perspectives, Historical Roots, and Future Challenges

Bradley T. Erford*

Editor's Introduction: It has been said that to know who you are, you must understand where you came from. When attempting to discern the future, historical events provide intriguing perspectives. Likewise, when beginning a journey of professional transformation, it is essential to understand the profession's roots and key developmental events. This chapter offers insights into current models by which to explain and understand what professional school counselors do, a synopsis of the historical roots of the school counseling profession, and from these perspectives, a peek at some of the profession's current and future challenges.

ON BECOMING A PROFESSIONAL SCHOOL COUNSELOR: YOUR DESTINY

Welcome to an exciting career—and adventure! Among the many important components of a school counseling program and the functions of the professional school counselor, the professionals authoring the chapters of this book will advocate for the development of systemic, data-driven and comprehensive developmental school counseling programs, evidence-based and outcomes-based procedures, and the establishment of school–community partnerships. We will underscore the importance of social advocacy in removing systemic barriers to student academic performance and career and personal/social development. Much of the philosophical and practical underpinnings of this approach will be covered in detail in Chapters 2 through 6. And we will make clear that professional school counselors must attain and maintain a high degree of skill and competence in the various components of a comprehensive program to ensure that all students succeed.

Transformations are visible at both surface and deeper levels. The lessons of this text will be wasted if readers simply make cosmetic changes to program and profession. The transformations advocated in this text cut to the core of our mission, indeed to the very essence of why we wanted to become professional school counselors. Most professional school counselors enter the profession because they love to work with children or adolescents, want to make an important difference in students' daily lives, and believe in the power of education as an equalizing social force. Welcome to a profession in which you can do all that and more! But before you begin that journey, take a moment to visualize, in your mind's eye, what you see yourself doing as a professional school counselor.

Some professional school counselors-in-training picture themselves counseling a student in a one-on-one setting or, perhaps, a small group of students. Although this is certainly part of what a professional school counselor does, it is but a single facet.

---

*I wish to acknowledge the contributions of Dr. Edwin Herr to the first two editions of this chapter.

The American Counseling Association (ACA) School Counseling Task Force (2013), building on the definition of counseling passed by the 20/20 Committee: A Vision for the Future of Counseling, provided the following definition:

> Counseling is a professional relationship that empowers diverse individuals, families, and groups to accomplish mental health, wellness, education and career goals. Using counseling theories and techniques, school counselors accomplish these goals by fostering educational and social equity, access, and success. The professional school counselor serves as a leader and an assertive advocate for students, consultant to families and educators, and team member to teachers, administrators and other school personnel to help each student succeed.

The professional school counselor provides a comprehensive school counseling program that is very broad and very deep—so broad and so deep that many counselor educators struggle to prepare professional school counselors who can "do it all." From a realistic perspective, this may not be possible for all counselors (or perhaps any). The job of the professional school counselor is complex and involves a complicated interplay of what the school community's needs are and the strengths and weaknesses of the individual counselor.

As you make your way through this text, try to picture yourself performing the described practices and implementing the suggested strategies. It is likely that your strengths and weaknesses as a counselor and learner, as well as your past life experiences, will make some practices feel natural, whereas others may feel uncomfortable. This is the normal developmental process of becoming a professional school counselor.

Please do enjoy your wondrous journey in becoming a professional school counselor and transforming the school counseling profession—a journey on which hundreds of thousands have preceded you, but which will be as distinct and fulfilling a path as you choose to make it. Enjoy the struggles. Serve the students, their families, your colleagues, and the community. But most of all, always remember in your heart why you wanted to become a professional school counselor!

THE RISE OF PROFESSIONAL SCHOOL COUNSELING IN THE UNITED STATES

Knowledge of the history of the school counseling profession provides essential context for where we have been and often provides insights into mistakes made and future opportunities. Generally, historical overviews are far from exhilarating, but as you read the next dozen or so pages, consider all the changes your predecessors have experienced; how you will likely need to undergo a number of changes over the course of your career; and how you will need to continuously transform as a practicing school counselor to keep up with the changes of society, education, your students, and the counseling profession.

It can be argued that school counseling is the earliest form of intentional or systematic counseling in the United States or, perhaps, in the world. It also can be argued that many of the philosophical ideas and process methods incorporated into what professional school counselors now do could be traced in a fragmented way into ancient history (Dumont & Carson, 1995; Miller, 1961; Murphy, 1955; Williamson, 1965) as elders, teachers, or mentors engaged in dialogues intended to provide guidance to young people. Throughout history, every society has found methods beyond the family by which to provide selected young people direction and support as they grapple with questions of who they might become and how to achieve such goals. In some instances, the persons who delivered such guidance were philosophers, physicians, priests or other clerics, medicine men or shamans, teachers, or masters of apprentices. But such "guidance" or "counseling" was neither equally available to all young people nor planned and systematic.

Given this context, it is fair to suggest that the pervasive, formal, and systematic provision of guidance and counseling in schools is an American invention. Although notions that arose in European research laboratories about individual differences, assessment techniques, and psychological classifications and explanations for behavior were conceptually important in shaping some of the content and methods of school counseling, they were not the stimuli that caused school counseling to come into being.

Like other major social institutions, guidance and counseling in schools did not arise spontaneously, nor did they occur in a vacuum. Although there were visionaries, scholars, and early practitioners of guidance and counseling who were critical to the implementation of school counseling, the historical moment had to be right for the ingredients of change to take root and begin to flourish. In the last quarter of the 19th century in the United States, political and social conditions converged to prod the nation to initiate education reform and to sensitize it to emerging issues of human dignity and the exploitation of children in the workplace, to the dynamics of massive immigration, and to the demands for human resources by the burgeoning Industrial Revolution.

Various authors during the 20th century have identified the different conditions that gave rise to guidance and counseling in U.S. schools. Brewer (1942) contended that four of the most important conditions were the division of labor, the growth of technology, the extension of vocational education, and the spread of modern forms of democracy. Traxler and North (1966) contended that the guidance movement in schools could be traced to five divergent sources: "philanthropy or humanitarianism, religion, mental hygiene, social change, and the movement to know pupils as individuals" (p. 6).

Clearly, many background or contextual variables influenced the rise of school counseling at the end of the 19th and the beginning of the 20th century. But there is general consensus that the beginnings of school counseling in the 20th century lay in vocational guidance. It also is clear that many of the concerns that gave rise to school counseling were focused on the quality and utility of existing educational processes. Embedded in the emerging concepts of both vocational guidance and education reform were issues of individual freedom of choice and dignity. These three factors, interacted and intertwined as philosophies and models of school guidance or counseling, were introduced by various pioneers in the field.

Different persons can be described as early visionaries or practitioners of school guidance and counseling. History has failed to record the names of many of them. But among those about whom we know, several persons have been worthy of special note: George Merrill, who in 1895 developed the first systematic vocational guidance program in San Francisco; Jesse B. Davis, who in 1898 began working as a counselor in Central High School in Detroit and in 1908 organized a program of vocational and moral guidance in the schools of Grand Rapids, Michigan; and Eli W. Weaver, principal of a high school in Brooklyn, who authored *Choosing a Career* in 1908. Although each made important contributions to the founding of vocational guidance, the person generally regarded as the primary architect of vocational guidance in the United States, the man who has come to be known as the "father of vocational guidance," is Frank Parsons.

Parsons was a man with multiple interests and a social conscience. Trained as a civil engineer and as a lawyer, throughout much of his adult life Parsons was heavily involved in the activities of settlement houses in central Boston and in other cities along the eastern seaboard. It was there that he learned firsthand about the plight of immigrants and others trying to survive physically and find appropriate access to the rapidly growing occupational structure of the cities to which they had come. Such experiences fueled Parsons's concerns about the need to deal with what he viewed as the excesses of the free enterprise system and the management of industrial organizations that led, in his view, to the debasement of individual dignity.

As these experiences grew, Parsons turned his attention to strengthening industrial education and creating the process of vocational guidance. His perception was that too many people, especially the immigrants from Europe, were not able to effectively use their abilities and to prosper economically and socially because of the haphazard way they found work and made the transition to the specialized world of the factory. Parsons created not only a counseling approach, which will be described later, but also what to him was a moral and social imperative to value and facilitate the effective use of human resources. In this sense, Parsons's initiatives in vocational guidance were congruent with the growing emphasis of the time on vocational guidance as the "conservation of human resources" (Spaulding, 1915), the effort to avoid the waste of human talent by identifying and maximizing its use.

After several years of experience in providing vocational guidance and counseling, Parsons founded the Vocations Bureau of the Civic Services in Boston in January 1908, serving as the director and vocational counselor. The setting was not a school, but rather the Civic Service House (Miller, 1961), with branch offices in the Young Men's Christian Association (YMCA), the Economic Club, and the Women's Educational and Industrial Union in Boston. Unfortunately, Parsons died only a few months after founding the Vocations Bureau. His legacy to the field of vocational guidance was captured in his major work, *Choosing a Vocation*, which was published posthumously in 1909. This extraordinary book laid out the principles and methods of implementing vocational guidance, collecting and publishing occupational information, conducting a group study of occupations, carrying on individual counseling, and processing individual assessment. Perhaps Parsons's most famous contribution was what became known as a *trait and factor approach*: his articulation of the three broad factors or steps of the vocational guidance process. The trait and factor approach called for the following:

> First, a clear understanding of yourself, aptitudes, abilities, interests, resources, limitations, and other qualities. Second, a knowledge of the requirements and conditions of success, advantages and disadvantages, compensation, opportunities and prospects in different lines of work. Third, true reasoning on the relations of these two groups of facts. (Parsons, 1909, p. 5)

Following Parsons's death, the work of the Vocations Bureau was extended to the Boston schools, and training of vocational counselors was undertaken. During the years following the publication of *Choosing a Vocation*, many leaders in American education began to recognize the social significance of and adapt to Parsons's paradigm of vocational guidance (Bloomfield, 1915). This process was compatible with the growing calls for educational reform in the nation's schools. Parsons himself, among many observers of the time, attacked the public schools for their specialization in book learning and advocated that "book work should be balanced with industrial education; and working children should spend part time in culture classes and industrial science" (Stephens, 1970, p. 39).

Such views, targeted on the public schools, and particularly those in the cities, reflected both the rising issues of child labor—children ages 8, 10, or 12 years working in coal mines and factories and not receiving the opportunity to go to school—and the dynamics of the Industrial Revolution that served as the backdrop for concerns about social and education reform. In the late 1800s and early 1900s, the United States was in the midst of making the transition from a national economy that was, in general, agriculturally based to one that was increasingly based in manufacturing and industrial processes. As this transition ensued, urbanization and occupational diversity increased, as did national concerns about strengthening industrial education as a way to prepare young people to take advantage of the growing opportunities in the workforce. To play out such goals effectively required information about how persons could identify and get access to emerging jobs. By the turn of the 20th century, particularly in urban areas, such information was so differentiated and comprehensive that families or local neighborhoods could no longer be the primary sources of occupational information or of the allocation of jobs. This set the stage for more formal mechanisms, including vocational guidance in the schools.

The issues of vocational guidance in the schools and elsewhere in society became confounded by the changing demographics of the potential workforce. At the beginning of the 20th century, large numbers of immigrants from nations with poor economic opportunities were coming to the United States seeking new lives and options for themselves and for their children. Likewise, people within the United States were migrating from rural to urban areas, spurred by the concentration of large plants producing steel, furniture, automobiles, and other capital goods.

Such social and economic phenomena as industrialization, urbanization, and immigration stimulated concerns about whether existing forms of education were appropriate in a rapidly growing industrial society, how to meet the need for less bookish and more focused industrial education, how to bridge the gap between schooling and the realities of the adult world, how to make the school-to-work transition, and how to adapt the new educational theories being advanced (e.g., Progressive Education, the concepts of John Dewey) for use in the schools.

Stephens (1970), a historian, spoke about the relationship between industrial or vocational education and vocational guidance, indicating that, in this context, vocational education and vocational guidance were seen as a partnership. Certainly, as one of the major roots of the professional school counselor's role, engaging in vocational guidance was seen as a significant emphasis. However, other forces were also at work shaping the role of the professional school counselor at the beginning of the 20th century. For example, Cremin (1964), also a historian, suggested that the clearest reminder in the schools of the impact of the Progressive Education movement, spanning the latter quarter of the 19th century and the first 50 years of the 20th century, is the guidance counselor. Although these events shaped the profession nearly 100 years ago, notice how similar the challenges were to those we encounter today: economic/technological changes, oppression/justice issues, diversity/cultural issues, and the call for school personnel to address these changes.

THE ROLE OF THE PROFESSIONAL SCHOOL COUNSELOR IN THE 1920s, 1930s, AND 1940s

As the layers of expertise expected of the vocational counselor began to be defined in the 1880s and 1890s and in the first decades of the 1900s, debates about approaches to the philosophy and the role of counselors continued to occur in the 1920s, 1930s, and 1940s. These issues tended to be affected by other forces coming to prominence in schools and in educational philosophy at the same time. Some of these forces directly affected the extant perspectives about school counseling; others were more indirect. Hutson (1958) suggested that, in addition to the importance of vocational guidance as a powerful force shaping the guidance counselor's role, there were five others: student personnel administration; psychologists, working as researchers and clinicians; personnel work in industry; social work; and mental health and psychiatry. Each deserves further comment.

Student Personnel Administration

This concept originated in higher education, where it essentially related to the identification of a specific official, often called the Dean of Students, whose responsibility was dealing with the personal and disciplinary problems of students. In time, this person would be expected to administer or provide leadership to all the nonacademic services that facilitate the progress of the students through the institution. Included were such services as admissions, counseling, student orientation, financial aid, and placement.

The functions of the vocational counselor took on an increasingly large array of responsibilities. Perhaps more important, this concept foreshadowed the creation of positions now commonly titled Director of Guidance Services or Director of Pupil Personnel Services or, in some larger school districts, Assistant Superintendent of Pupil Personnel Services.

Psychologists, Working as Researchers and Clinicians

The content and methodology of school counseling owe much to psychology as the major discipline providing insights into student development, cognition, behavior classification and analysis, and effective interventions. In his observations, Hutson (1958) referred to two particular contributions of psychologists. The first had to do with psychologists' research into the development of objective instruments for measuring human behavior (e.g., interest inventories, aptitude and achievement tests, diagnostic tests), without which many would see the role of the vocational counselor as nothing more than "organized common sense." But the availability of these tools and their use gave vocational counselors areas of expertise and information that enriched their ability to engage in vocational guidance and increased their professional credibility. The second contribution of psychologists in a clinical sense was to provide specialized services to specific groups of students experiencing particular learning or behavioral problems.

Personnel Work in Industry

As personnel work in industry grew during the first 50 years of the 20th century, it provided job requirement specifications, motivation studies, and tests for job application and vocational guidance purposes. Personnel work in industry also broadened the application of counseling to specific job-related problems such as meeting job requirements, getting along with fellow workers, and other factors that could interfere with a worker's job efficiency. Such information helped to broaden the content and processes of vocational guidance in schools.

Social Work

Starting with the visiting teacher movement that originated in 1906 and 1907 in settlement houses or civic associations and involved working with problem pupils and their parents, school social work was taking on its own identity in the 1930s and 1940s. School social workers represented an official liaison among the school, the home, and community social agencies. The introduction of social workers to school staffs replaced the former concepts of

law and punishment of problem or delinquent children by truant officers with such emphases as diagnosis, understanding, and adjustment. As school social workers became available to deal with specific problem children—those who were habitually truant and whose behavior was being monitored by legal or family services—the role of the school social worker also affected the role of the vocational counselor. Where social workers were available, counselors tended to be less directly involved with home visits or with community social agencies. The social worker tended to be the community liaison; the counselor was more school bound. In addition, as the school social worker and community agencies provided interventions for children with specific problems, the professional school counselor could focus more fully on the children who needed primarily educational and vocational guidance.

Mental Health and Psychiatry

With the rise in psychiatric attention to schools, beginning in the early decades of the 20th century, the National Association for Mental Hygiene and related organizations disseminated the principles of mental health and information about various types of personality maladjustment and advocated that the development of wholesome personalities "is the most important purpose of education" (Hutson, 1958, p. 13). In the 1920s and subsequent decades, psychiatry focused on combating juvenile delinquency and sought to establish "child guidance clinics" for the psychiatric study and treatment of problem children in the schools. Although the direct impact of guidance clinics on problem children was small, the insights about maladaptive behavior and the principles of treatment subtly affected how professional school counselors were prepared, whom they referred to community agencies for treatment, and how they viewed the fostering of mental health as part of their role.

Each of these influences or forces shaped perspectives on why counselors were important in schools; how they needed to differ from, but be collaborators with, psychologists, social workers, and psychiatric specialists; and what functions they could serve in schools and with what groups of students. Such perspectives extended the analysis of the relationship of counselors to schools per se to why schools should appoint counselors. Cowley (1937) reported three areas of emphasis that were evolving in the public schools: (a) guidance as the personalization of education, (b) guidance as the integration of education, and (c) guidance as the coordination of student personnel services. Like so many issues and possibilities for action that occurred as guidance and counseling were taking root in the schools, these three areas continue to influence contemporary issues.

Guidance as the Personalization of Education

Cowley (1937) suggested that of most importance, "counselors have been appointed to counteract the deadening mechanical limitations of mass education" (p. 220). He decried the depersonalization of both higher and secondary education, the growing lack of close relationships between teachers and students, the lack of a personal touch in education, and the decreased concern on the part of administrators about student problems. All these factors led Cowley to argue:

> No matter how expert personnel people may be as technically trained psychological testers or diagnosticians, the real test of a personnel program is the extent to which it makes the student feel that he individually is important—that he is not being educated in a social vacuum. (1937, p. 221)

In more contemporary terms, guidance as personalization of education continues, with different language, to be embedded in statements about the professional school counselor's role as one in which the student is helped to achieve academic development (American School Counselor Association [ASCA], 2012).

Guidance as the Integration of Education

Cowley (1937) was particularly concerned with the explosion of knowledge and the rapid growth of curricular offerings: the movement away from a fixed curriculum, which all students took advantage of in elective courses, and toward the compartmentalization of knowledge and the specialization of instruction. Cowley saw the professional school counselor as the person who would help each student facing such challenges to effectively sort through the educational options and create for himself or herself a unified course of instruction—that is, as the person who would discover each student's talents and motivations and bring the resources of the institution to bear on developing these talents and motivations.

Guidance as the Coordination of Student Personnel Services

Although Cowley saw educational counseling as the most important function that professional school counselors undertook, he felt it was necessary to coordinate the counseling function with the other functions professional school counselors engaged in, in relation to the roles of other mental health workers (e.g., psychologists, social workers, psychiatrists). He was concerned that a student could be "chopped up," seen as a person with a specific problem rather than as a whole person. Thus, Cowley argued that the guidance counselor should be responsible for coordinating all the specialist services available to students and for integrating those findings into a coordinated set of directions and support.

Arthur J. Jones provided additional perspectives on the needs of students and schools for counselors. In his classic work, *Principles of Guidance* (Jones, 1934), he summarized both the need for providing guidance and the significance of the schools offering the guidance. He advocated for the need for guidance from the standpoint of the individual and the significance of providing guidance to enhance the school climate and support the school mission. In other words, school counselors should align their services with school mission and reform efforts—just like today.

By the mid-1930s, when Jones was discussing the status of school guidance and counseling in the nation (Jones, 1934), the approach to school counseling often, but not always, followed a trait and factor, or directive, approach. Tests had increasingly become available, although the range of behavior they assessed was still limited primarily to intelligence, aptitude, achievement, and interests. There were not yet any major theories of school counseling per se. Philosophies and principles of school counseling were being shaped by the Progressive Education movement, by psychiatry, and by other emerging theories. Jones also described "methods of guiding students," which in his view included counseling; homeroom guidance and group guidance; educational guidance with regard to choices of courses, schools, and colleges; "stay in school" campaigns; vocational guidance (beginning in the elementary school), including instruction, tryout, exploration, choice, placement, and follow-up relative to occupations; leadership guidance; and leisure-time guidance. Jones also explicitly stated that it is necessary to distinguish between counseling and the other activities that the counselor does:

> This distinction is not a trivial one. . . . Counselors are now so burdened with other work as to make it impossible to do counseling well. If we can focus the attention upon counseling as the center and core of the work, we shall do much to relieve the situation. (Jones, 1934, p. 273)

If this sounds familiar, it should. To this day, noncounseling responsibilities continue to impede ASCA's (2012) recommendation that professional school counselors spend at least 80% of their time in delivery of services. Thus, professional school counselors continue to struggle with similar role diffusion and overload. Focusing on the comprehensive and important work of Jones illustrates that many contemporary issues related to counseling versus guidance and the role of the professional school counselor have antecedents that have not yet been brought to closure. Support for and refinement of the techniques, the tools, and the philosophies of school counseling continued throughout the 1920s, 1930s, and 1940s. Space is not available here to analyze the continuing support for school counseling or the additional techniques made available to the counselor through these three decades. Suffice it to say that during the 1920s, concerns about the dignity and rights of children flourished, as did concerns for greater emphasis on mental hygiene in the schools in which professional school counselors would be important players. In 1926, New York became the first state to require certification for guidance workers and, in 1929, the first state to have full-time guidance personnel in the State Department of Education, providing leadership to school systems for the integration of professional school counselors in schools.

Again, an economic crisis pointed to the need for counseling services in schools and society in general. Given the growing deterioration of the national economy, the need to certify and train people in school counseling was overshadowed by the need for the techniques and processes associated with vocational guidance counseling. These included the creation, during the Great Depression of the 1930s, of a national occupational classification system, which resulted in the 1939 publication of the first edition of the *Dictionary of Occupational Titles* by the U.S. Department of Labor, and establishment, in 1940, of the U.S. Bureau of Labor Statistics. In 1933, the Wagner-Peyser Act established the U.S. Employment Service, and several laws enacted during the 1930s provided fiscal support for vocational guidance activities. In 1938, a Guidance and Personnel Branch was created in the Division of Vocational Education in the U.S. Office of Education. That's correct—the U.S. government recognized the importance of counseling services way back in the 1930s! This unit continued until 1952 as the only federal office dealing with guidance in the schools, but restricting the federal emphasis to vocational guidance. The major issues of technological unemployment during the Great Depression tended to focus on vocational guidance as a placement activity, causing some debate about whether school counselors or vocational educators should undertake the vocational guidance activities funded by the federal government.

The 1940s were a period in which the use of testing grew dramatically in response to the armed forces' need for worker classification as World War II ensued and,

later, as veterans returned to society and were provided guidance services through schools, colleges, and community agencies. The *Occupational Outlook Handbook* was first published by the U.S. Bureau of Labor Statistics in 1948 (U.S. Department of Labor, 1949). During this period, federal support continued for vocational guidance and counseling in schools in support of vocational education.

In 1942, Carl Rogers published *Counseling and Psychotherapy*, which defined the counseling process as that concerned with other than traditional medical models, disease entities, and psychoanalytic approaches in which the counselor was a directive authority. Rogers's book heralded the beginning of client-centered counseling in which the counselor and client were seen as collaborators. Such perspectives were incorporated into the expansion of guidance techniques and increasingly eclectic models of what school counseling might be.

SCHOOL COUNSELING COMES INTO ITS OWN: THE 1950s AND 1960s

In a sense, all the important strides made in support of counseling and guidance in schools during the first 50 years of the 20th century were a prelude to the major events of the 1950s and 1960s. These were the watershed years of legislation and professional development that essentially defined the importance of school counseling for the remaining decades of the 20th century.

Until the 1950s, there were relatively few school counselors across the United States; the opportunities for the professional preparation of school counselors were relatively limited; the advocacy for professional school counselors by professional organizations was not systematic; and the legislative support for school counseling, other than for vocational guidance, was largely nonexistent. All these conditions changed in the 1950s and 1960s.

Among the extraordinarily important indicators of support for school counseling in the 1950s was the founding of the American School Counselor Association (ASCA) in 1952 and its becoming, in 1953, a division of the American Personnel and Guidance Association (APGA; now known as the American Counseling Association [ACA]), formed in 1952 by the merger of the National Vocational Guidance Association, the American College Personnel Association, the National Association of Guidance Supervisors and Counselor Trainers, and the Student Personnel Association for Teacher Education.

It is important to note that the perspectives that the founding organizations brought to the creation of the APGA shaped for the ensuing several decades the language and the emphases within which professional school counselors were evolving. For example, the term *guidance*, not *counseling*, was the accepted term for all that counselors did (Sweeney, 2001)—school counselors were often called guidance counselors in the decades immediately before and after the founding of APGA. Frequently, what professional school counselors did was called personnel work. The term *guidance* was widely viewed as conveying the notion that the professional school counselor was primarily involved in a directive form of advice giving to the students. Personnel work suggested that the professional school counselor was engaged primarily in administrative tasks related to maintaining student records about their schedules and progress. Although these terms lost favor by the early 1980s, their residual effects were to distort the images of professional school counselors. Indeed, one could argue that many, if not most, of the members of the four founding organizations were themselves administrators, not counselors. For example, to this day, the American College Personnel Association is composed primarily of deans of students and related administrative personnel. The same was true of the Student Personnel Association for Teacher Education before it was renamed and significantly changed in purpose in 1974, when it became the Association for Humanistic Education and Development, and again in 1999, when it changed its name to the Counseling Association for Humanistic Education and Development (C-AHEAD).

Nevertheless, this federation of professional organizations speaking for counseling in K–12 schools, in institutions of higher education, and in workplaces gave credibility to and advocated for standards, ethical guidelines, and training for professional counselors working with various populations and in various settings. In 1953, *School Counselor* was created as the professional journal of the ASCA. Also in 1953, the Pupil Personnel Services Organization of the Division of State and Local School Systems was created in the U.S. Office of Education, a move that significantly broadened the view of school counseling as more than vocational guidance.

In 1957, the APGA created the American Board for Professional Standards in Vocational Guidance. In 1959, the National Association of Guidance Supervisors and Counselor Trainers undertook a 5-year project designed to build a set of standards for education in the preparation of secondary school counselors.

In 1959, James B. Conant, the former president of Harvard, wrote *The American High School Today*, an influential analysis of the need for strengthened secondary school education. In the book, Conant argued for 1 full-time counselor (or guidance officer) for every 250 to 300 pupils in each American high school, a criterion that has been used frequently, even though such a ratio of school

counselors to students has rarely been met at the elementary or middle school level.

The National Defense Education Act, 1958–1968

By the 1930s, nearly every city of 50,000 or more inhabitants had some formal guidance work in the schools and professional school counselors employed to carry it out. Courses to train professional school counselors had been developed and were being offered in several universities (e.g., Harvard University; Teachers College, Columbia University; the University of Pennsylvania; Stanford University), and textbooks were being written to identify the techniques by and assumptions on which such work could be undertaken (Jones, 1934). Guidance work in the schools continued to grow, and the number of professional school counselors multiplied through the 1940s and 1950s. But the major stimulus to the education and implementation of school counseling clearly was the National Defense Education Act (NDEA) of 1958 (Herr, 1979).

Although not often considered in this vein, the NDEA, like the legislation on vocational education and vocational guidance that preceded it, identified professional school counselors as sociopolitical instruments to achieve national goals. In the case of the NDEA, professional school counselors became indirect participants in the Cold War between the United States and the Soviet Union. To be more specific, in 1957, the Soviet Union launched *Sputnik I*, the first human-made object to orbit the earth. As a result, although the United States was close to launching its own space vehicle, the Soviet launch precipitated a major national outpouring of news articles suggesting that the United States had lost the space race; that our science and engineering capabilities were inferior to those of the Russians; and that, once again, American schools had failed to produce students whose scientific and mathematical skills were competitive with those of students in the Soviet Union. The NDEA was the result. Passed by the U.S. Congress in 1958, the NDEA required states to submit plans of how they would test secondary school students so that academically talented students could be identified and encouraged to study the "hard sciences" in high school and go on to higher education, emphasizing courses of study in the sciences, engineering, and mathematics. These legislative goals were not altruistic or concerned with the self-actualization of students. They were designed to increase the scientific capacity of the United States as it competed in the Cold War.

Central to the provisions of the NDEA were the training of large numbers of professional secondary school counselors and their placement in schools primarily to test students, to identify those capable of entering higher education in the sciences, and to encourage them to do so. Title V of the NDEA provided funds for school systems to hire and provide resources (e.g., tests, occupational and educational materials) to professional secondary school counselors and to reeducate existing secondary school counselors, as well as funds for universities to prepare professional school counselors in full-time, year-long guidance and counseling institutes or to offer more specialized programs (e.g., pre-college guidance) in summer guidance and counseling institutes. The 1964 amendments to the NDEA emphasized guidance and counseling for all students, giving impetus to professional elementary school counseling and to counseling in technical institutes and other nonbaccalaureate postsecondary educational institutions.

It is not possible to discuss all the effects of the NDEA, but there are several obvious results. With the full force of federal legislation behind the preparation and employment of professional secondary school counselors, the number of these counselors and the high schools employing them exploded. So did the number of colleges and universities providing preparation programs. Literature on professional school counseling became more comprehensive, as did the state certification requirements for counselors. The programs were transformed from simply taking courses on a piecemeal basis until one had completed what was needed for certification to full-time, more systematic and integrated curricula, usually leading to a master's degree. Certainly, many more students in the United States were being served by professional school counselors in the 1960s and beyond than ever before; some state departments of education mandated that schools maintain specific counselor-to-student ratios to receive state funding. As the large amounts of federal support ended in the late 1960s, professional school counselors had become embedded in schools and were engaged in initiatives that went beyond the expectations of the NDEA. Even though the responsibility for funding school guidance and counseling programs shifted from the federal government to local school districts, by the end of the 1960s professional school counselors were vital participants in achieving the multiple missions of schools (e.g., dropout prevention, academic scheduling, educational and career guidance, crisis intervention).

The Great Society Legislation of the 1960s

As the impact of the NDEA legislation unfolded during the late 1950s and throughout the 1960s, other major legislation was developed to address the Civil Rights Movement, the beginnings of technological impact on the occupational structure, rising unemployment, poverty,

and other social ills. In many of these legislative acts, education was viewed as the instrument to restructure society, and again, professional school counselors were supported. For example, the Elementary and Secondary Education Act (ESEA) of 1965 designated funds for guidance and counseling. The 1969 amendments to the ESEA combined funds from the NDEA's Title V-B with funds from the ESEA's Title III into one appropriation for guidance. The Vocational Education Act Amendments of 1968 advocated for career guidance programs; responses to people who were disadvantaged and people with disabilities; and the expansion of a broadened concept of guidance and counseling, including its extension into the elementary schools. These pieces of legislation stimulated a large number of national and state conferences on guidance and counseling and innovative projects in career guidance, counseling, and placement.

THE YEARS OF CONSOLIDATION AND REFINEMENT: THE 1970s AND BEYOND

The outpouring of federal legislation that specifically focused on guidance and counseling in the schools essentially reached its zenith in the 1960s. However, there were important legislative initiatives in the 1970s, 1980s, and 1990s and into the first decade of the third millennium. Much of the legislation in the 1970s focused on vocational education and career education. For example, career education was seen as a school reform initiative as it developed in the early 1970s and as it was reflected in the Career Education Incentive Act of 1976. Career education indirectly institutionalized career guidance in schools and infused its concepts and experiences as part of the teaching and learning process. The educational amendments—the ESEA—of 1976 included major support for guidance and counseling in schools, a major emphasis on vocational guidance in schools, and the implementation of an administrative unit in the U.S. Office of Education. The purpose of this administrative unit was to coordinate legislative efforts in the Congress on behalf of guidance and counseling and to serve in a consultative capacity with the U.S. Commissioner of Education about the status and needs of guidance and counseling in the nation's schools.

During this period, a large amount of theory building took place, leading to the development of materials on decision making, career education, drug abuse prevention, and self-development, which became available for specialists in guidance and counseling. Fears of economic crisis and concerns about widespread unemployment among youth continued to spur development of career guidance initiatives. The impact of the Civil Rights and Women's

Liberation Movements, as well as legislation effectively mainstreaming all special education students, refocused the attention of professional school counselors to diversity in schools and the needs of special populations for guidance and counseling.

Multicultural Diversity

It is important to note that beginning in the 1960s, federal legislation and state and local educational initiatives began to incorporate responses to multicultural diversity in the schools. The civil rights legislation had essentially banned segregated schools and caused municipalities throughout much of the United States to embark on policies and tactics by which to integrate African-American children into schools with White children. Such policies struck down notions of "separate but equal schools" and expected that children of all ethnic and racial backgrounds would be in the same classrooms and courses, on the same athletic teams, in the same musical groups, and at the same social events. Children of different racial backgrounds and genders and those having other special characteristics could no longer be the target of discrimination or segregation.

Schools and communities used many methods to integrate schools. The busing of children from one part of town to another or from one town to another to change the demographic mix of students in a particular school was a frequently used method. In many schools, professional school counselors were given responsibility to develop plans of action and to work with culturally diverse groups of students in classrooms, in group counseling, and in other settings to help them to learn more about each other, to air their fears and concerns about integration, and to learn to respect each other and reduce conflict.

Part of the problem at the time was a lack of attention to issues of cultural diversity in counseling theory and counseling practice. A major challenge to counseling processes in a culturally diverse world was that for most of its history in the United States, counseling, in both its assumptions and its techniques, had ignored cultural differences or treated them as unimportant (Clark, 1987). Theories of counseling did not acknowledge the cultural distinctiveness of most people in the United States or the racial and ethnic traditions that shaped their behavior and affected their approaches to learning and decision making (Herr, 1998). Too often, culturally different students were treated as deficient, inferior, or abnormal, rather than as distinct in their socialization. In response to such inappropriate behavior toward cultural differences, Vontress (1970), among others, talked about the issues involved when White counselors counseled African-American students, and how cultural differences affect the establishment of rapport between counselors and students.

During the ensuing decades, growing attention has been directed to embedding scholarship about ethnic and racial differences into counseling theory and practice. Such perspectives do not embrace deficit models; rather, they provide affirmations of the worldviews of different cultural groups and the implications of these for counseling process. Virtually all counselor education programs now have one or more courses, practicum experiences, or other methods by which to prepare professional school counselors to work effectively and sensitively in a culturally diverse world. Professional school counselor training now includes studies of how appraisal, ethics, interventions, and counseling competencies/standards are affected by cultural diversity (e.g., Sue, Arredondo, & McDavis, 1992). The refinement and application of these perspectives will

| **VOICES FROM THE FIELD 1.1** | **SERVING A DIVERSE AND CHANGING STUDENT POPULATION** |

Today's world is growing ever smaller, thanks to modern advances in technology. But it is also growing smaller because of the diversity that continues to add to the depth of our communities and bring types of people who rarely interacted previously into the same sphere. In my experience at a suburban Baltimore public high school, the importance of keeping up with cultural changes and the growth that is occurring is critical to our field. Those cultural changes are not only ethnic or racial group changes, but also socioeconomic differences and family structure, among others. As professional school counselors, it is imperative that we understand our stakeholders and the perspectives from which they are coming in the best ways that we can in order to understand how to help them most effectively.

When a school's demographics begin to change, many structural implications need to be considered. For example, my school has a rising need for interpreters and for persons who can translate documents into different languages. In order to most effectively communicate with some students and many parents, we need to do so in their native language. There are many complex and detailed educational issues of which parents/guardians and students need to be aware. It is particularly challenging to tell a parent/guardian about a student's academic difficulties or behavioral concerns if the parent/guardian is better versed in a different academic structure or has different expectations of the school's role compared to the parent's role and, on top of that, speaks a different language. It may not be necessary to know the details of other countries' school structures, but it is essential to keep in mind that a family may have very different expectations of your role as a professional school counselor than you do.

Socioeconomic changes within a school's population also require sensitivity and continued growth on the part of professional school counselors. If a school becomes less affluent, new issues such as residency concerns, homelessness, and the need for students to have jobs are important for counselors to keep in mind. If a community becomes more affluent, other issues, like access to cars, drugs, and career opportunities or connections, need to be considered. All of these issues affect our students in unique ways, but if counselors do not learn about the community being served, students and families may not receive needed services.

Changing family structure is another factor that must be taken into consideration by counselors. Today, family structures are diverse—and often different from the "one mother, one father" model. In many instances, counties or districts have policies about which parents have access to student records and who is able to make educational decisions, so professional school counselors need to be aware of the changes students' families undergo. Counselors must also be sensitive to those differences and learn about how those changes affect the students.

It is critical for professional school counselors to be aware of diverse student characteristics so adjustments can be made in our buildings to best serve students. Cultural proficiency requires that counselors *not* treat everyone exactly the same and *not* be blind to the differences or the changes. Instead, cultural proficiency requires professional school counselors to be aware of and sensitive to changes and differences while working to always serve students and their families in ways that will be most beneficial.

Source: Kami Wagner, Professional School Counselor, Mt. Hebron High School, Howard County Public School System, Maryland

---

be a constant presence in the training of professional school counselors throughout the 21st century.

The Latter Decades of the 20th Century

During the 1980s and into the 1990s, much of the legislative activity in the nation did not directly address school counseling; it focused instead on the need for professional school counselors to deal with issues such as child abuse, drug abuse prevention, and dropout prevention. Legislation supporting career guidance continued under new guises as well. Among the major legislation defining school guidance and counseling, with a primary emphasis on career guidance, was the Carl D. Perkins Vocational Education Act of 1984, the Carl D. Perkins Vocational and Applied Technology Act of 1990, and the subsequent amendments to these acts. These were the major federal sources of funding for guidance and counseling in the schools through the 1980s and early 1990s. In 1994, Congress passed the School to Work Opportunities Act, which reinforced the importance of career guidance and counseling as students contemplate their transition from school to employment. Throughout the 1980s and 1990s, the National Occupational Information Coordinating Committee (NOICC), created by congressional legislation as a joint effort of the U.S. Departments of Education, Defense, and Labor, provided career development and guidance program information and resources to elementary, middle, and secondary schools. Unfortunately, the NOICC was disbanded in 2000.

However, in 2003, the National Career Development Guidelines Project was commissioned by the U.S. Department of Education's Office of Vocational and Adult Education. By 2005, the Guidelines Revision Project had reconceived the original NOICC Career Development Guidelines, aligned them with the goals of the No Child Left Behind (NCLB) Act, and created a website by which information on the new guidelines; learning activities; and strategies for K–12 students, teachers, counselors, parents, and administrators and the business community could be delivered.

In 1995, the Elementary School Counseling Demonstration Act, which was expanded and reauthorized in 1999, represented the first major legislative departure in more than a decade from the emphasis on career guidance and related topics. This legislation, providing $20 million, assisted schools in making counseling services more accessible and in creating a more positive ratio of professional school counselors to students. Given the reduction of direct support for school counseling during the 1980s and 1990s at the state and national levels, the current statistics indicate that, rather than a ratio of 1 counselor to every 250 students, as recommended by the ACA and the ASCA, in 2012 the ratio across the United States averaged 1 professional school counselor to every 471 students. The state with the lowest counselor-to-student ratio was Wyoming (1:200), whereas the highest ratio was in California, where there is 1 professional school counselor per 1,015 students (ACA, 2013). There were, however, some hopeful signs that more professional school counselors and innovative counseling programs were developing.

For example, by the beginning of the 21st century, the Elementary School Counseling Demonstration Act had been expanded to include secondary schools, and the word *Demonstration* was dropped. The Elementary and Secondary School Counseling Program is a discretionary program administered by the U.S. Department of Education to provide competitive grants to school districts that demonstrate the greatest need for new or additional counseling services or the greatest potential for replication or dissemination or that propose the most innovative program. For fiscal year 2013, some $50 million in federal funds were expended to meet the goals of the act. The more wide-ranging affirmation of the need for professional school counselors is embedded in NCLB, signed into law in January 2002. This comprehensive legislation required that states adopt a specific approach to testing and accountability to lead to higher achievement for all children, take direct action to improve poorly performing schools, raise the qualifications of teachers, and make many other changes in schools to make them accountable for student achievement. The need for and support of school counseling is evident in many parts of the legislation relating to dropout prevention, career counseling, drug and alcohol counseling, safe and drug-free schools, facilitation of the transition of students from correctional institutions back to community schools, identification of and services for gifted and talented students, and children who are neglected or delinquent or otherwise at risk of academic and social failure. These many legislative actions suggest the importance of counseling as a process that complements and is integral to the success of instructional methods and goals and, as such, allows, if not encourages, school districts to have professional school counselors engage in many complex tasks. A time line of significant events in the history of school counseling is provided in Table 1.1.

CULTURAL REFLECTION 1.1

Given the historical overview so far, how might students, parents, and educators from diverse cultural backgrounds view the school counseling profession's track record on achievement, access, and opportunity for all students? What cultural barriers and access points might exist?

TABLE 1.1   A School Counseling Historical Time Line

Year	Event
1895	George Merrill developed the first systemic guidance program in San Francisco.
1908	Jesse B. Davis organized a program of vocational and moral guidance in the schools of Grand Rapids, Michigan.
1908	Eli W. Weaver, a high school principal in Brooklyn, New York, authored *Choosing a Career*.
1908	Frank Parsons founded the Vocational Bureau of the Civic Services, a vocational counseling program that was soon expanded to schools in Boston.
1908	Clifford Beers, a former patient in a mental institution, wrote *A Mind That Found Itself*, which helped illuminate the plight of patients with mental disorders.
1909	Parsons's book *Choosing a Vocation* was published posthumously; it established the principles and methods counselors should follow to provide vocational guidance in schools.
1913	The National Vocational Guidance Association (NVGA) was founded at a meeting in Grand Rapids, Michigan. The NVGA became the first professional counseling organization and later became one of the four founding divisions of the American Counseling Association. Today, the NVGA is known as the National Career Development Association (NCDA).
1920s	This decade saw the rise of the student personnel, social work, children's rights, mental health, measurement, and Progressive Education movements.
1926	William Henry Burnham became a pioneering advocate for elementary school counseling by publishing *Great Teachers and Mental Health*.
1926	New York became the first state to require certification for guidance workers.
1929	New York became the first state to have full-time guidance personnel in the State Department of Education.
1930	Arthur J. Jones wrote *Principles of Guidance*.
1938	The Vocational Education Division in the U.S. Office of Education established the Guidance and Personnel Branch.
1939	The *Dictionary of Occupational Titles* (*DOT*) was published.
1942	Carl Rogers published *Counseling and Psychotherapy*.
1948	The *Occupational Outlook Handbook* was published by the U.S. Bureau of Labor Statistics.
1952	The American Personnel and Guidance Association (APGA) was established. Today, the APGA is known as the American Counseling Association (ACA).

Year	Event
1952	The American School Counseling Association (ASCA) was founded.
1953	The ASCA became the fifth division of APGA.
1953	The Pupil Personnel Services Organization was created in the U.S. Office of Education.
1953	*School Counselor* was created as the journal of the ASCA.
1957	The APGA created the American Board for Professional Standards in Vocational Guidance.
1957	The Soviet Union launched *Sputnik I*, the first human-made satellite to orbit the earth.
1958	The National Defense Education Act passed, expanding the training and hiring of school counselors.
1959	James B. Conant authored *The American High School Today*, suggesting a ratio of 1 school counselor for every 250–300 students.
1962	C. Gilbert Wrenn published *The Counselor in a Changing World*, which influenced the school counseling profession in the years to follow.
1964	NDEA Title A was passed, which extended counseling to elementary schools.
1976	The Career Education Act integrated career education into schools.
1988	Gysbers and Henderson published *Developing and Managing Your School Guidance Program*, which focused the profession on comprehensive, developmental school counseling programs.
1994	The School to Work Act was passed, reinforcing career guidance and counseling.
1995	The Elementary School Counseling Demonstration Act was passed to assist elementary schools in providing counseling services.
1995	The Education Trust's Transforming School Counseling Initiative began.
1996	The new scope of work was released by the Education Trust (leadership, advocacy, assessment, use of data, counseling, and coordination).
1997	The ASCA published *The National Standards for School Counseling Programs*, providing benchmarks for school counseling programs to promote student competency in the academic, career, and personal/social domains.
Late 1990s	The original six schools received significant grants from the Education Trust to restructure their school counseling training programs based on the original eight essential elements. Additional universities became companion schools for transformation.
2002	The No Child Left Behind Act was signed into law.
2003	*ASCA National Model: A Framework for School Counseling Programs* was published. It was revised in 2005, and a third edition was released in 2012.
2006	The 20/20 Committee: A Vision for the Future of Counseling convenes for the first time at the ACA conference in Montreal.
2010	The 20/20 committee agrees to the following consensus definition of counseling: Counseling is a professional relationship that empowers diverse individuals, families, and groups to accomplish mental health, wellness, education and career goals.
2010	Common Core State Standards are introduced.
2013	The 20/20 Committee ends work after reaching consensus on principles that promote professional unity, a definition of counseling, model licensure title (Licensed Professional Counselor), and scope of practice. The Committee was unable to reach consensus on model educational training standards for licensure.
2013	The ACA School Counseling Task Force promoted the following definition related to school counseling, building on the 20/20 definition of counseling: Counseling is a professional relationship that empowers diverse individuals, families, and groups to accomplish mental health, wellness, education and career goals. Using counseling theories and techniques, school counselors accomplish these goals by fostering educational and social equity, access, and success. The professional school counselor serves as a leader and an assertive advocate for students, consultant to families and educators, and team member to teachers, administrators and other school personnel to help each student succeed.

As a retired school counselor and teacher of graduate school students in school counseling, I often look back at my 30-year journey in school counseling and try to find things of value to share with my students. In the mid-1970s, I started out in high school counseling. At that time, the main focus was on career exploration and crisis counseling and whatever else the administration of the school wanted counselors to pursue. I was ever so lucky to have supervisors in the counseling department that encouraged all their counselors to become part of counseling associations and to attend programs that would help in our professional growth. At the same time, various grants were pursued, so school counselors could get all types of resources for their schools. In the summer, counselors were encouraged to work on various curriculum writing projects that could be shared with other counselors from the county school system.

As I observed the school environment in which I worked, I realized that there were many needs of the students not being met by our current counseling program. I was given the opportunity by my principal and supervisor to visit other schools in other school districts in order to bring back ideas that might be usable at our site. After some of the counselors in the county heard about this experience, they also wanted to be a part of it. So began a different type of professional development that proved beneficial to many schools and counselors. At the same time, many counselors were attending annual conferences and were bringing back ideas from other states and countries.

Society as a whole was changing during the 1980s, and more and more materials were being published on career activities, decision making, drug abuse, diversity, and, oh yes, accountability. We also saw a push from our administrations to be more precise in our child abuse reporting and to develop ways of charting dropouts and the prevention methods we were using. This, of course, brought about the question of what uniform evaluation methods we could use across the school system.

Workshops were developed in our county to produce a uniform school counseling program given to all students, while also addressing the diverse needs of students within schools. It was a wonderful time for counseling. Principals and staff were seeing how a sequential program in a school could elevate the level of learning for all students, while helping individual students to develop a plan that would make them more successful in everyday life. School counselors were given financial support in order to develop programs and to train students to help others in their school (e.g., peer facilitators).

During the 1990s, not only did the counseling profession change, but also the school administrative profession changed. This caused a paradigm shift in the counseling profession. In Maryland, more and more counties were embracing site-based management. This gave principals more power to direct the programs in their schools. School counselors then had to present their program to the principal and see how that program fit in with the school's mission. It was also the age in middle schools of "Teams!" This was very positive, in that the counselor was a part of the "Team" and therefore a major player in presenting counseling curriculum to a whole grade level. It initiated a collaborative environment with the staff of the schools that promoted counseling. In the high schools, however, counseling staffs often were more focused on counting credits, registering students, and completing other tasks that took them away from the classroom and other counseling-related programs.

When the ASCA's *National Standards* and *National Model* came to the forefront in the late 1990s and the first decade of 2000, principals began to look at their school's counseling program to see how it could become a program that could have a more detailed role in the achievement and success of all students. Again, across the nation, principals could see a more uniform method of delivering counseling objectives. Principals especially liked the data-driven methods of evaluation because they could use them in reports and put them in various aspects of the school program. Technological innovations helped show the impact of the counseling program. Principals also could see a yearly plan from their counselors that would allow principals to see how important counselor time was and to make a case for not assigning counselors to non-counseling duties.

Society is continually changing, and today professional school counselors are facing many challenges. Every year new administrators and counselors are coming into the schools, each with their own ideas and feelings about counseling. In our schools today, we have many different generations, each with its own perspectives on how school counseling should move forward. The following challenges are a few of the issues that should be looked at by our associations, advocates, and legislative representatives:

1. As economic difficulties arise, more and more pressure will be put on principals to determine what the staffing in a counseling program will be.
2. More and more, counselors will need to affect the "climate of the school" in a positive manner, showing the importance of the program.
3. New students going into counseling need to recognize the impact they can have and convey to students that the future is full of hope and possibilities.

As I look back on my experience in counseling, I see how far school counselors have come and how hard they must work to not slide back to where we were in the 1970s, given the frequent pendulum swings of educational changes. Professional school counselors and their programs have a great deal to offer a society in need of transformation and direction.

Source: Mary Keene, Retired Professional School Counselor, Baltimore County Public Schools, Maryland; Affiliate Professor, School Counseling Program, Loyola University Maryland

CONTINUING AND FUTURE ISSUES FOR THE SCHOOL COUNSELING PROFESSION

Space limitations prohibit a comprehensive analysis of all the trends cited in each of the decades discussed. For example, the use of computers in guidance and counseling began in the 1960s, with the first computer-assisted career guidance system becoming operational in 1965. In 1964, the Association for Counselor Education and Supervision (ACES) published the *ACES Standards for Counselor Education in the Preparation of Secondary School Counselors*, the forerunner to standards developed by the Council for the Accreditation of Counseling and Related Educational Programs (CACREP). In the 1970s, pressure mounted for accountability in guidance and counseling. During the 1970s and 1980s, models were developed that envisioned school guidance and counseling as an integrated, planned, and systematic K–12 program, rather than a loosely connected set of services (Gysbers & Henderson, 2012; Herr, 2002).

Such efforts were designed, among other reasons, to clarify the expected results or outcomes of guidance and counseling programs in the schools. To that end, in 1997, ASCA published *The National Standards for School Counseling Programs* (Campbell & Dahir, 1997). These standards argued that school counseling programs should facilitate three broad areas of student development: academic development, career development, and personal/social development. Within these three areas are nine standards, each of which includes a list of student competencies or desired learning outcomes that define the specific types of knowledge, attitudes, and skills students should obtain as a result of effective school counseling programs. Among their other purposes, the *National Standards* were intended to clarify appropriate and inappropriate aspects of the counselor role. The basic point was that the role of school counselors needs to be focused on addressing student needs, not performing noncounseling quasi-administrative tasks. Further, implementation of the *National Standards* and, more specifically, the three broad areas of student development—academic, career, and personal/social development—requires counselor competencies that are important assets in furthering student development and in achieving educational goals. These counselor competencies should not be ignored or misused if local programs are to be comprehensive, professional, and provided for all students (ASCA, 2012).

In 2003, the ASCA published *ASCA National Model: A Framework for School Counseling Programs* to help professional school counselors implement the *National Standards* and focus school counseling programs on four primary areas: foundation, management, delivery, and accountability. The *National Model* was published in a second edition in 2005 and a third edition in 2012 and is expanded upon in far greater detail in Chapter 2. The *National Model* has served to focus both what goals professional school counselors across the United States accomplish and how they do so through systemic and comprehensive developmental programs.

In the quest for clarity, professionalism, and accountability of professional school counselors, in addition to the substantial program of content and delivery identified in the *National Standards* and *National Model*, the National Career Development Guidelines, briefly mentioned previously, have provided another source of program content and delivery, particularly for the career development segment of the ASCA's *National Standards*. The National Career Development Guidelines also address three broad areas of student development: personal/social development, educational achievement and lifelong learning, and career management. The three domains organize the content of the guidelines in 11 goals and in three learning stages: knowledge acquisition, application, and reflection (www.acrnetwork.org). These guideline domains, goals, indicators, and learning stages can be the basis for a K–12 or K–adult career development program, its delivery, and its evaluation.

Causal to these efforts, in 1995 the Education Trust began the Transforming School Counseling Initiative (TSCI). The next year, the new scope of work was released by the Education Trust (leadership, advocacy, assessment, use of data, counseling and coordination), establishing the original foundation for essential transformation conversations. Later in the 1990s, the original six universities received significant grants from the Education Trust to restructure their school counseling training programs based on the original eight (and now 10) essential elements. Universities that did not receive grants were invited to become EdTrust companion schools for transformation. The TSCI movement was successful in changing the national conversation about school counseling to focus on leadership and advocacy and the use of data to equitably serve students of color and students from low-income backgrounds in ways they had not been served before. The focus was on equity in educational outcomes and opening opportunities for historically underserved populations. These principles became the foundation of the *ASCA National Model* (ASCA, 2012).

In 2010, the National Governors Association and the Council of Chief State School Officers introduced the Common Core State Standards. These standards set high quality expectations for all students in the areas of math and language arts to prepare graduates to compete in the global economy. Although our understanding of the scope and reach of the common core are still developing, almost every state has adopted the standards. Table 1.2 provides a top 10 listing of what school counselors should know about the Common Core State Standards (ACA, 2013).

The school counseling profession continues to grow and develop through the daily efforts of tens of thousands of professional school counselors; professional counseling associations, such as the ASCA, ACA, and ACES; private, nonprofit organizational initiatives, such as the Education Trust and College Board; and governmental programs. But the school counseling profession is not without current and future issues and challenges.

TABLE 1.2   Common Core State Standards: Essential Information for School Counselors (ACA, 2013)

— Top Ten Things to Know —

1. How did Common Core come about?

As of today, forty-five states, the District of Columbia, four territories, and the Department of Defense Education Activity have adopted the Common Core State Standards. These rigorous standards were developed by state leaders through the National Governors Association and the Council of Chief State School Officers. Other groups such as parents, teachers, administrators, researchers, Achieve, ACT, and the College Board also participated in the creation of the standards. School counselor representation has not been included in the process.

2. What is it? (And what is it not?)

The Common Core State Standards have become a national movement, setting high quality academic expectations in English language arts (ELA) and mathematics. Each standard has been created with keeping students on track for success in college and career in mind. They define what skills and knowledge every student should have at the end of each grade. These state-driven standards are said to be research and evidence-based and internationally benchmarked. Beginning in 2014, assessments that are aligned with the Common Core standards should be integrated into participating schools. These assessments will determine if students are college and career ready, as defined by these rigorous standards. Many educators caution that scores on these assessments will initially be lower than current assessments, because of the material being tested. (This was the case in a pilot study in Kentucky.)

This is not policy enacted by Congress or run by the Department of Education. The standards are also not specific curriculum for teachers to follow. They are designed to allow flexibility for how the standards are taught and enable teachers to embrace diversification in their planning.

3. Definition of college and career readiness and the role of the school counselor.

The Career Readiness Partnership Council has recognized that college readiness is only part of the issue; what is needed is a comprehensive strategy that links education with workforce preparation and includes all aspects of preparation and support. The Council defines a career ready person as someone who "effectively navigates pathways that connect education and employment to achieve a fulfilling, financially-secure and successful career (p.2)." The emphasis is on life-long learning; adaptability to change; knowledge, skills, and career dispositions. The school counseling program drives college-and-career readiness through programs that address areas such as social and interpersonal skills, organizational skills, and problem solving skills.

To help students become career-ready, schools must begin in elementary school and coordinate and collaborate throughout all grades to create opportunities for all students to gain the knowledge and skills needed for their futures. Counselors understand that to accomplish these goals they must address the academic barriers through a focus on social and emotional learning as part of their unique function in the schools.

4. What a professional school counselor needs to know.

Professional school counselors need to become familiar with the Common Core standards, its implementation in their district and school, and how student's achievement will be measured under Common Core. Counselors must also understand how their comprehensive, development counseling program integrates with Common Core, that is how the components of their program support student outcomes and help students become college-and career-ready. Lastly, they must understand Common Core components and implementation so that they may facilitate the inclusion of all students as appropriate and advocate for those who might be excluded from activities needed for their success.

For counselors the implementation of the Common Core State Standards will bring increased focus to their career development and college awareness activities. This includes becoming knowledgeable about the world of work, post-secondary opportunities, and financial aid and college admissions. They will also need to design programs that ensure all students have access to information about these areas and the support they need to become successful.

5. Why professional school counselors are critical to discussions about Common Core.

Leading initiatives and removing barriers surrounding college and career access, professional school counselors are typically the gate keepers of college and career pathways. Common Core State Standards are designed to determine the degree to which students are on-track or off-track for college and career readiness. As Common Core is integrated into standard testing practices within schools, it's likely its outcomes will drive interventions meant to safeguard on-track performance, and prevent and intervene in off-track performance. Student outcomes on the Common Core State Standards will most likely become a part of early warning systems identifying student performance gaps; therefore, school counselors should be prepared to discuss how Common Core data could drive discussions around scheduling and student placement, college and career selection (entrance exams), as well as what types of remedial and student support services will effectively intervene, getting students back 'on track'. As a student advocate and leader of college and career readiness within the school community, it's imperative that school counselors are familiar with the language, theories, and data surrounding Common Core Standards, allowing them to effectively consult, counsel, and collaborate with students, parents, and school stakeholders, removing barriers to ALL students college and career success.

6. How will these standards impact your role?

The Common Core standards will impact the roles of the professional school counselor in a number of ways. Counselors, working in schools at all levels:

may need to adjust the content of classroom guidance and career development activities to align with the outcomes for their school and grade. They may also need to increase their focus on career development initiatives if they are not already a significant component of their program;

must advocate to ensure that all students are served under college-and-career ready initiatives, particularly those who have traditionally been underserved by college-readiness programs; and

help students and parents understand the changes effected by the Common Core Standards and the implications for students.

7. What does Common Core means for students?

Common Core State Standards provide a much desired comprehensive vision of what it means to be college and career ready. A national yardstick, students will be able to measure their readiness against national standards for entry into college

and career pathways. While not all students will perform adequately, it's important that students do not internalize their performance as a final determination of their ability; rather assessment outcomes should act as a tool to initiate conversations in which students can comprehend their performance level, deficit areas, and explore interventions and support services that will bridge their achievement gaps. School counselors' holistic perspective of education, allows them to frame these discussions with encouragement, motivating students, parents, and school stakeholders to implement effective interventions resulting in higher student achievement levels and outcomes, fostering a college and career going culture.

8. What do parents need to know about Common Core?

A significant shift in how we measure student achievement, it's important that parents understand what the Common Core measures, how the indicators are determined, and in what ways the assessment outcomes will impact their students' educational trajectory. The influence assessment outcomes will have on students' educational experience may vary from school to school, and perhaps from school system to school system; nonetheless it's imperative that parents are educated on the concepts and implications Common Core Assessment could have on their students' education, as they are partners in our work of advocating for student success. We highly recommend collaborating with your administration to establish effective ways in which you will educate parents about the Common Core State Standards and what it means to their students education.

9. How Common Core will impact your collaboration with your school administration?

As with most systemic initiatives, school counselors will need to collaborate with administration to successfully implement Common Core State Standards in ways that will drive student performance outcomes. As schools implement programs and develop systems of support, school counselors will be a critical voice at the table, safeguarding students' personal/social wellbeing, and advocating for systems that support and promote ALL students. School counselors will identify student performance barriers and equity gaps by assessing disaggregated testing data and making recommendations to their school leadership team(s) on how to effectively infuse interventions to fill performance gaps. School Counselors also play a significant role in managing school wide policies that stem from student performance outcomes (i.e., scheduling and placement, remedial supports, tutoring, etc.), and should work to ensure they're a part of their schools leadership team and discussions. Administrators, teachers, parents, and students will seek their advisement and consult on this topic; therefore it's important that they are well versed in Common Core subject matter, and prepared to implement and manage effective interventions and support systems in

(Continued)

TABLE 1.2   Common Core State Standards: Essential Information for School Counselors (ACA, 2013) (*Continued*)

comprehensive and data driven ways. Common Core data will most likely drive School Counseling Program Plans; another collaborative tool counselors use with principals to align goals and outcomes.

10. Where can I find more information on Common Core Standards?

Common Core State Standards Webpage: *ww.CoreStandards.org*

Common Core Works: *www.CommonCoreWorks.org*

National Governors Association's Center for Best Practices: *http://www.nga.org/cms/home/nga-center-for-best-practices/center-issues/pageedu-issues/col2-content/main-content-list/common-core-state-standards.html*

The following website for CASEL addresses implementing Social Emotional Learning standards and practices into the school:*http://casel.org/in-schools/implementation/implementation-guidance/*

The following website for the Center for Mental Health in the Schools, housed at the University of California Los Angeles, includes information specific to the integration of specialized support services in Common Core:

http://www.smhp.psych.ucla.edu/pdfdocs/commoncore.pdf. The Career Readiness Partnership Council has created a definition of what it means to be career ready. This information can be found at *http://www.careerreadynow.org/*

The National Council of La Raza (NCLR) provides Common Core State Standards information for families and educators of Latino students. Handouts are in English and Spanish. Two great resources from this organization are 1) an implementation guide for educators called Raising the Bar: Implementing Common Core State Standards for Latino Student Success and 2) a report called Access to Common Standards for All: An Advocacy Tool Kit for Supporting Success. These can be found at *www.nclr.org*

Counseling is a professional relationship that empowers diverse individuals, families, and groups to accomplish mental health, wellness, education and career goals. Using counseling theories and techniques, professional school counselors accomplish these goals by fostering educational and social equity, access, and success. The professional school counselor serves as a leader, an assertive advocate for students, consultant to families and educators, and team member to teachers, administrators and other school personnel to help each student succeed.

Reprinted from American Counseling Association, Task Force on School Counseling. (2013). *Common core standards: Essential information for school counselors*. Retrieved from http://www.counseling.org/docs/resources---school-counselors/common-core-standards.pdf?sfvrsn=2. Reprinted with permission. No further reproduction authorized without written permission from the American Counseling Association.

Despite the important contributions to the nation's schools and to its students made by professional school counselors, there continue to be basic issues that confront professional school counselors and school counseling programs. Herr (1998) has suggested that the future role of professional school counselors is based on several pivotal concerns. Admittedly, different school counseling programs and the regulations of different state departments of education promote or require different approaches to address these issues. Herr's concerns, as prescient today as in 1998, are presented in abridged form with added commentary.

1. *The degree to which school counseling programs are systematically planned; tailored to the priorities, demographics, and characteristics of a particular school district or building; and clearly defined in terms of the results to be achieved rather than the services to be offered.*

   The ASCA (2012) and, indeed, other blue-ribbon panels and national organizations have increasingly advocated for planned programs of school counseling. Such

planned programs are intended to clarify the expected outcomes and how these outcomes will be achieved, to maximize the efficient use of resources committed to school counseling, to prevent or modify student risk factors and promote social and educational competence, and to provide a structure by which to assess whether professional programs of school counseling are meeting the goals assigned to them. The development of the *ASCA National Model* is a large step forward in addressing this and other issues.

2. *The degree to which school counseling programs [that] begin in the elementary school or in the secondary school [are] truly . . . longitudinal (K to 12) and systematically planned.*

   For much of the latter part of the 20th century, as both secondary school counselors and, increasingly, elementary school counselors have been employed in schools, there has been support in the professional literature for longitudinal (i.e., vertically articulated) programs of school counseling. Essentially, the advocates of such approaches have argued that students at every educational level have concerns, problems, and environmental circumstances that affect their behavior and productivity in school. Although the issues and tasks that students experience vary developmentally from kindergarten through grade 12, they are important at each developmental level and deserve the attention of professional school counselors and planned programs tailored to their needs.

3. *The degree to which school counseling programs are seen as responsible for the guidance of all students or for only some subpopulations of students, such as those at risk.*

A debate that has recurred throughout the history of professional school counseling has focused on whether school counseling programs should serve all students or only selected groups of students (e.g., college-bound youth, potential dropouts, those in crisis, those who are disruptive and act out). This issue has to do with how best to use the limited number of professional school counselors and to maximize their positive effects on students. The subquestions focus on whether all students need the attention and support of professional school counselors and whether subgroups of students who would benefit most from such services can be identified. Among the underlying assumptions are that many students can get along effectively without the help of professional school counselors, that many students receive positive support and resources from their parents or other persons in their environment that replace the need for a professional school counselor, and that a school should direct its resources to those students who cannot get adequate guidance outside school or who are most in need of such support. On the other hand, more recent initiatives insist that school counselors become achievement, access, and opportunity advocates for all students to ensure all students are college and career ready.

4. *The degree to which school counseling programs include teachers, other mental health specialists, community resources, parent volunteers, and families as part of the delivery system.*

Because the ratio of professional school counselors to students is so high (e.g., almost 1:500 nationally) in many schools, it is necessary to broaden the network of persons who can augment the work of professional school counselors. Thus, in many schools, teachers, parents, and others are trained to perform specific functions (e.g., completing academic scheduling, coordinating a career resource center, helping students use educational and career resources, providing group guidance topics or workshops) that free professional school counselors to deal with student problems for which they, specifically among school employees, are qualified (e.g., individual counseling, group work). In such situations, professional school counselors coordinate community resources and train and support other persons who augment and extend the outreach of their functions.

5. *The degree to which school counseling programs are focused on precollege guidance and counseling; counseling in and for vocational education and the school-to-work transition; counseling for academic achievement; and counseling for students with special problems such as bereavement, substance abuse, antisocial behavior, eating disorders, and family difficulties (single parents, stepparents, blended family rivalries).*

The issue here is whether the school counseling program in a particular school offers a range of interventions that address the academic, career, and personal/social needs of all students or whether the program emphasis is on a restricted range of students or topics (e.g., college-bound students, students in crisis).

6. *The degree to which professional school counselors should be generalists or specialists; members of teams or independent practitioners; and proactive or reactive with regard to the needs of students, teachers, parents, and administrators.*

This issue has to do with how professional school counselors should be educated and how they should function in a school. Should they be trained to view children or adults in holistic terms and thus be prepared to deal with any type of problem students experience? Or should counselors be trained in a subspecialty (e.g., career, discipline, family, testing, substance abuse) and melded into a team of specialists who can combine to serve the needs of a particular individual? A further question is whether professional school counselors should be essentially passive and wait for students, parents, or teachers to come to them or be assertive in marketing their program and providing services, workshops, and so forth in multiple and visible forms and potentially outside counselors' offices.

7. *The degree to which professional school counselors employ psychoeducational models or guidance curricula as well as individual forms of intervention to achieve goals.*

As professional school counseling has evolved during the past 100 years, so has the range of techniques available for use. In addition, the knowledge bases that students need to acquire for purposes of self-understanding, educational and career planning, interpersonal effectiveness, conflict resolution, and decision making have expanded. The question is, given pressures for efficiency and accountability, can such knowledge, and the associated attitudes and skills, be best conveyed to students by individual counseling? Or are these types of knowledge best conveyed through group work or a guidance curriculum (e.g., workshops, units in classrooms) that is likely to disseminate this information more evenly to all students?

8. *The degree to which the roles of professional school counselors can be sharpened and expanded while not holding counselors responsible for so many expectations that their effectiveness is diminished and the outcomes they affect are vague.*

Clearly, the role of professional school counselors is complex and comprehensive. The range of concerns and problems that professional school counselors are expected to address continues to grow as the dynamics of the larger society affect the readiness and behavior of students in schools. Thus, these questions must be addressed: What can counselors do best? For what outcomes should they be held accountable? How should their workload be balanced and to what end? Which current duties should be eliminated and which emphasized? How can the responsibilities of professional school counselors be made explicit and achievable?

9. *The degree to which professional school counselors have a reasonable student load, 250 or less, so that they can know these students as individuals and provide them personal attention.*

If one of the important aspects of professional school counselors' role is to help students personalize their education and make individual plans pertinent to their abilities, interests, and values, how is that best done when a professional school counselor is responsible for 400 to 1,000 students? Is the answer providing more group work; making more use of technology; shifting selected functions of professional school counselors to other persons in the school or community, such as teachers, parents, or mental health specialists; limiting the responsibilities of professional school counselors to a specific and defined set of functions; or lowering the counselor-to-student ratio to the recommended 1:250?

One possible response, now lost in the history of professional school counseling, is the Carnegie Foundation for the Advancement of Teaching's book *High School: A Report on Secondary Education in America* (Boyer, 1983). This report was unequivocal in its support of guidance services and student counseling as critical needs in American high schools. According to the report's conclusions,

> The American high school must develop a more adequate system of student counseling. Specifically, we recommend that guidance services be significantly expanded; that no counselor should have a caseload of more than 100 students. Moreover, we recommend that school districts provide a referral service to community agencies for those students needing more frequent and sustained professional assistance. (Boyer, 1983, p. 306)

This very important, but long overlooked, recommendation has increased urgency in today's school environment, which is fraught with pressures for students and for those who teach and counsel them. It suggests that the needs of many students go beyond the capacity of the school to address and that there is a communitywide responsibility to coordinate and use all of the mental health resources available on behalf of the needs of the student population.

10. *The degree to which professional school counselors effectively communicate their goals and results to policy makers and the media both to clarify their contributions to the mission of the school and to enhance their visibility as effective, indeed vital, components of positive student development.*

This issue relates to how professional school counselors should use knowledge about what interventions work effectively, for which student problems, and under what conditions to help policy makers understand more fully their role. In this sense, professional school counselors must be advocates for the profession, spokespersons for their field, able to interpret their goals, use their skills, and promote an awareness of the added value they bring to positive student development and to the mission of the school.

VOICES FROM THE FIELD 1.3   **A 30-YEAR PERSPECTIVE ON SCHOOL COUNSELING**

In the early 1970s, when I completed my Masters of Education program in what was then "Guidance and Counseling" and entered the profession of "Guidance Counseling," my primary goal was "How do I get students who are upset to come see me?" The answer was "visibility, connections, and relationships." With that in mind, my first year as a "guidance counselor" began. I remained in my first school placement for eight years, during which time there was a growing awareness that simply providing responsive services to students who requested them was clearly not enough. In a school, one can see trends (e.g., developmental, seasonal, social, societal, economic) that can be addressed through a developmental and comprehensive plan of action. Therefore, after a couple of years, I began to assess the needs of the school community to ensure that I could deliver activities to all students that met those needs. This began to change my view of how to implement "guidance and counseling" in a school setting. Prevention became important in the delivery of services. Classroom guidance and group counseling took on new meanings as I began to see how a proactive approach could change the climate in a school.

Over the years, various models were constructed that answered the needs of professional school counselors who shared the vision that school counseling is for all students. These models included a data-driven, needs-based program, allowing a wide variety of delivery methods; the incorporation of counseling, coordination, and consultation; a focus on specific goals; and a system of accountability that gave school counselors the needed framework on which to build. I began to look at all of the day-to-day things in which I was involved and realized that all of these activities supported the three overall domains crafted by the ASCA (Campbell & Dahir, 1997). The ASCA's *National Model* (2012) has provided a more organized structure and identified the professional school counselor as having an integral role in the achievement and success of all students.

This paradigm shift did not come without obstacles. Some of these challenges were as follows: (1) If schools are solely for student learning, how can a professional school counselor convince others that what they do has a direct impact on student achievement? (2) If a school counseling program is based on data and evaluated using data, what data should we be collecting, how are the data tied to student achievement, and how can they be measured? (3) How can a school counseling program be marketed to principals and the public in order to ensure "our seat at the table" as a contributing, indispensable educator? None of these answers has come easily. There is a constant need to educate other professionals regarding the role of the professional school counselor. Other professionals continue to judge counselors based solely on *how many students they see, how many students went to college*, and the like. That professional school counselors contribute to students, staff, and the school climate is not easily observed—and not easily measured.

The barriers that school counselors remove to ensure students can learn often go unnoticed. Hence, marketing and accountability continue to be a need for professional school counselors, as they continue to make a difference in schools. It is difficult at times for school counseling interns to implement a comprehensive school counseling program, since often they work with only a limited percentage of the student population, and their part-time schedule precludes daily follow-up. In such cases, I recommend that interns create a mini-program for a smaller group of students with whom they work. Often, it is easier to see the results of your efforts with that smaller group.

One of the programs that has strongly influenced my thinking as an educator and professional school counselor over the years is Positive Behavioral Interventions and Support (PBIS), a school-wide behavior system based on the theory of response to intervention (RTI). It is an approach or framework for redesigning and establishing teaching and learning environments. RTI was designed primarily to address the academic needs of students with disabilities, but it is really an approach for addressing the behavioral needs of all students. Both RTI and PBIS offer a range of interventions that are systematically applied to students based on their demonstrated level of need and address the role of the environment as it applies to development and improvement of behavior problems. Both approaches implement their programs through a system of tiered interventions. This tiered-intervention approach has been extremely helpful to me as I implement a comprehensive school counseling program. Each approach delimits critical elements to be in place at each tier. There are three tiers:

- Tier 1, or the universal tier, includes programs and interventions that address *all* students;
- Tier 2, or the targeted tier, includes programs and interventions for students in smaller groups who have demonstrated the need for additional supports; and
- Tier 3, or the intensive tier, includes a more in-depth analysis of the data on and individual interventions for students who have not responded to tier 1 or tier 2.

This model also fits well as school counselors implement the ASCA *National Model*. The universal tier (tier 1) includes all of the activities and programs developed for all students. Prevention, psychoeducation, advisement, and coordination of programs are included in this tier. The targeted tier (tier 2) includes counseling and consultation for students who need additional supports. The intensive tier (tier 3) involves systemic interventions and includes the coordination of wraparound services with other interventionists to meet the needs of students who require individual services in and outside of the school. A pictorial representation of the tiered approach is shown in Figure 1.1. I share this model because it has helped me to visualize my program around a graphic organizer, and it reminds me daily that I need to be creating a plan that addresses all students and includes a differentiated approach for a variety of issues.

(Continued)

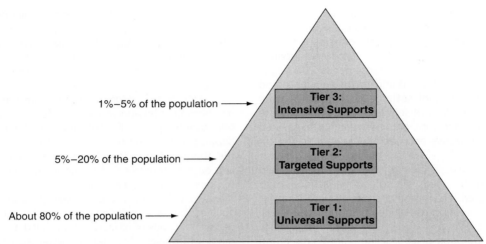

FIGURE 1.1   A model for understanding a professional school counselor's responsibilities to all students in a comprehensive school counseling program.

In summary, I consider the delivery of a school counseling program to be as much about a philosophy as about an approach. Once you begin to see how the school counseling program positively affects a school, you begin to recognize how indispensable a comprehensive,

developmental school counseling program is in helping to fulfill the mission and vision of the school.

Source: Marcia Lathroum, retired school counselor and School Counselor Specialist, Maryland State Department of Education; Affiliate Faculty, School Counseling Program, Loyola University Maryland

TRADITIONAL AND EMERGING PRACTICES

The work of the transformed professional school counselor is multifaceted and stems from several essential "realizations," which are discussed next. Following the realizations are 10 current and emerging practice areas that influence the implementation of school counseling services in various parts of the country. It is essential to note that, depending on the school community's needs and the skills of the professional school counselor, some of these "roles" may predominate in a given school or even at certain times of the school year. However, necessary boundaries must be in place to ensure that no single role or service predominates universally. A comprehensive, developmental school counseling program requires substantial attention to balance to meet the needs of *all* students.

Realizations Guiding the Transformation of the Professional School Counselor

The first important realization is that, of all the education professionals, professional school counselors receive the most extensive specialized training in consultation and collaboration and in team and relationship building. It follows therefore that professional school counselors are among those most able and qualified not only to build collaborative relationships to fully implement a comprehensive,

developmental school counseling program, but also to move school reform work and task groups in positive directions, leading to changes that will benefit all students. That is, professional school counselors are in an excellent position to facilitate systemic changes that will eliminate barriers to student academic, career, and personal/social success, and advocate for achievement, access and opportunity for all students.

Over the past several decades, many professional school counselors and counselor educators have come to realize that the job descriptions and role responsibilities, coupled with the work and caseload realities, are overwhelming for all but the superhuman. Add to this the challenge professional school counselors face in taking a leadership role in school reform, and experienced professionals would justifiably throw up their hands.

This leads to the second realization: Professional school counselors can't do it all alone. Societal problems are creating developmental and clinical problems for children and youth in record numbers, and most citizens and stakeholders are expecting school personnel to effectively address these issues. Children are developing serious psychological problems at younger ages and in greater numbers; teachers are leaving the field in droves, and fewer college students are choosing teaching as a professional career; professional school counselor caseloads and workloads are expanding;

and governments and citizens demand improved test scores in high-stakes testing programs. In addition, school violence is all too common, technology is changing rapidly, and the challenges stemming from an increasingly diverse student population are growing. How can one person, a professional school counselor, possibly do it all?

One person can't do it all—and shouldn't be expected to. For too long, the "lone ranger" attitude has pervaded the profession. In transforming the profession, counselors must think systemically and look to resources beyond themselves: community agencies, local business partners, teachers, parents, grandparents, and, yes, even the students themselves, among many other possible partners. If school conflict and violence are increasing, professional school counselors can partner with students, teachers, and organizations to implement a teacher- or student-led developmental conflict resolution curriculum and peer mediation program, while also tapping community organizations to provide workshops on personal safety. If substance abuse is a problem, professional school counselors can partner with community mental health and substance abuse professionals, teachers, parents, and students to implement a substance abuse curriculum taught by teachers. Counselors can run groups for students who abuse substances and for children of alcoholics and can harness the resources of local businesses and organizations such as the local Mothers Against Drunk Driving chapter to offer continuing programs to help parents and their children cope with substance abuse. If children's reading scores are below expectations, professional counselors can partner with community organizations, grandparents, parents, and educators to hold book drives to procure books for use by preschoolers and school-aged children; organize community "read-ins" at local bookstores or the school or public library; facilitate coordination of a parent and grandparent volunteer reading program; and even ask older students to volunteer some time before or after school to listen to and help a younger child read.

The common denominator is that someone has to take the initiative to think systemically and get things started, and the professional school counselor has the systemic, collaborative, and human relationship skills to do it. Many traditional thinkers will reflexively argue that these are not the kinds of things that professional school counselors do—or should do. But think about it: Which of the partnering examples mentioned does not fit perfectly into the goals of a comprehensive, developmental school counseling program? The key is that the examples describe different ways to achieve the goals, rather than having a professional school counselor counsel one child at a time or go into the classroom to teach one or several guidance lessons on these topics. Although these traditional interventions

are effective in their own way, the partnering plans use the gifts and talents of many other people who are more than willing to help, if invited to do so.

The third realization guiding the transformation of the professional school counselor's role is that well-organized and well-run, comprehensive, developmental school counseling programs are greatly needed in today's schools and do work (see Chapter 6 for outcomes studies on school counselor interventions). Furthermore, if a professional school counselor fails to implement a comprehensive program in a school, no one else will. Establishing such a program must become the professional school counselor's top priority. Some schools lack a comprehensive program because of poorly trained and unmotivated counselors or counselors who believe their job is merely to put out fires, provide long-term individual therapy for a select group of students in need, or complete office work. When a counselor spends nearly all his or her time providing one type of service, a comprehensive program does not exist. The exception is when a school has multiple professional school counselors engaging in specialties, but even in this case, professional school counselors expend a lot of effort integrating and coordinating their services in a comprehensive manner.

This leads to the fourth realization: All professional school counselors have strengths and weaknesses and therefore may provide services of varying levels of quality to varying populations. Thus, in many ways, specialization makes sense and is most efficient, but only if the remaining portions of a comprehensive, developmental school counseling program are provided by other qualified individuals. It is here that the argument recycles to the discussion of partnering, including other professional school counselors, school personnel, or community resources. For professional school counselors, the key is to know what they are good at and to specialize in those areas without upsetting the balance of the school counseling program. Counterbalancing is provided by counselor, school, and community collaboration.

The fifth and final realization is that many students are not getting what they need from our educational and mental health systems (Substance Abuse and Mental Health Services Administration [SAMHSA], 2008). Some professional school counselors view their role as something like "triage," which in medical terms means to sort, prioritize, or allocate the treatment of patients. Although this holds true in most instances, like it or not, professional school counselors will encounter many students for whom they are the last and only hope. This is why school counselor training is so broad and comprehensive and includes topics such as human and career development, counseling techniques and multicultural issues, appraisal, and special services. If counselors do not have the skills and knowledge to help those students, those students will likely not get help. This is also why professional school counselors need to become social advocates and members of their local, state, and national professional organizations. Oftentimes, working with an individual who has nowhere else to turn is like sticking a finger in the dike. A look to the left and right will often show other professionals using their fingers to plug a hole. By joining with other professional counselors in the same area, state, and nation and speaking with a united voice in advocating for the needs of students, professional school counselors are seeking solutions not only for the students they are working to help, but also for all students—those whom colleagues are seeking to serve and those who will seek help in the future. The counseling profession is based on the belief that all human beings have worth and dignity (ACA, 2005). Professional school counselors seek to create systemic solutions for students who are oppressed and marginalized so that their paths of development will also lead to successful life opportunities.

Although many of the services provided by professional school counselors are well known and accepted, others are gaining wider acceptance in various parts of the country and world. The purpose of this text is to explore not only what professional school counselors *do*, but also what they *could do*. A number of important roles and practices appear to have value to the transformation of school counseling. These 10 practices or initiatives will be reviewed briefly here and serve as a prelude to the chapters that follow.

The School Counselor as a Professional

By now, you have noticed the use of the term *professional school counselor*. This is the term preferred by the ASCA (1999) and adopted by numerous counselor educators and professional school counselors around the world. It means something! Professional school counselors are first and foremost representatives of their profession. How one professional school counselor behaves, good or bad, reflects on all professional school counselors.

Professional school counselors practice as professionals in three major ways. First, professional school counselors are aware of the history of guidance and counseling, as well as the pressing issues guiding future transformations. When one is trying to know where one is going, it is generally helpful to know where one has been. Second, professional school counselors use effective techniques and practices implemented through legal, ethical, and professional means. Belonging to a profession requires one to adhere to the highest standards of that profession.

Third, professional school counselors maintain membership in professional organizations at the local, state, and national levels. At the national level, the ACA and the ASCA are the professional and political forces supporting the mission of professional school counselors. Each of these has branches or divisions in most states, and many local areas have affiliated chapters. All are ready to welcome professional school counselors and students-in-training into the profession, but it is the counselors' responsibility to join and support these efforts. It is estimated that almost 90% of doctors belong to the American Medical Association (AMA), and 70% of licensed psychologists join the American Psychological Association (APA). Each organization has a powerful political and professional voice. Less than 20% of eligible counselors belong to either the ACA or the ASCA. Until counselors develop an allegiance to the profession to a degree commensurate with that of psychologists and doctors, their political and professional voices will remain background noise. Being a professional school counselor means committing to the mission of the professional organizations. The dues money contributed annually to these organizations is small compared to the professional and political gains benefiting students and colleagues. It is no stretch to conclude that the job you seek in the near future exists because of the groundwork laid by professional organizations—and that the strength of the professional organizations will determine how long that job will exist in the future! Join today, and stay a member throughout the remainder of your career.

The Professional School Counselor as an Agent of Diversity and Multicultural Sensitivity

Referred to as the Fourth Wave, multicultural (systemic) counseling and development is a strong influence on the counseling field today. With U.S. demographic projections estimating that the trend toward a more diverse U.S. population will continue for decades, the demographics of teachers and professional school counselors, who are mainly White and female, will most likely also shift. Regardless, current professional school counselors must retool, and future professional school counselors must enter the field prepared to address the developmental and counseling needs of a diverse student population. Although professional school counselors are, by and large, ahead of other education professional groups, the multicultural counseling movement is helping professional school counselors lead the way toward a more diverse, tolerant, and sensitive educational environment. Chapter 8 addresses this essential area of practice, and multicultural issues are infused throughout the other chapters of this book.

The Professional School Counselor as a Leader and Advocate for Academic and Social Justice

In some ways, this entire text is about preparing the professional school counselor to be an advocate for social justice, but Chapters 3, 4, 8, and 9 specifically address the issue. Professional school counselors have an ethical responsibility to help students minimize or eliminate barriers to educational performance and career and personal/social development, to advocate for achievement, access, and opportunity for all students. Sometimes these barriers and inequities exist in federal and state laws, regulations, and funding mechanisms; sometimes in the policies and procedures of local school systems; and sometimes in the hearts and minds of students, their parents, the community, and, yes, even teachers, administrators, and professional school counselors. Professional school counselors seek to address barriers and inequities, wherever they may exist, for the benefit of all. If a single student is oppressed and treated unfairly, no one in that society can claim equity.

The Professional School Counselor as a Developmental Classroom Guidance Specialist

Professional school counselors are aware of recent national (ASCA, 2012), state, and local standards that guide implementation of a comprehensive, developmental school counseling program. They have specialized expertise in planning and evaluating comprehensive programs. Although many have not been teachers before entering the profession, professional school counselors provide developmental educational and guidance instruction to classes and other large groups and prepare their lessons much as classroom teachers do. This means they write measurable objectives and plan interesting activities to meet the diverse learning needs of the students. Perhaps most important, professional school counselors must assess the effectiveness of their instruction and evaluate the outcomes of the comprehensive program. Chapters 2, 4, 5, 6 and 10 address these issues in detail.

The Professional School Counselor as a Provider of Individual and Group Counseling Services

Although it may come as no shock to hear that the professional school counselor will continue to provide specialized group and individual counseling in the schools, the nature of the problems that bring students to counseling today differs from in years past. Today, students are much more likely to need assistance with special issues, exhibit clinical symptoms, or show resistance, all requiring a different approach.

Chapter 13 briefly reviews the developmental facets so essential to the implementation of individual counseling and group work within a comprehensive approach to school counseling. Chapter 17 focuses on what professional school counselors need to know about clinical disorders and psychopathology to help ensure their students get appropriate help. Some view professional school counselors of the future as serving in a school-based clinical role; undoubtedly, some professional school counselors are providing services to clinically diagnosed students already. Other school systems have hired licensed clinicians to provide counseling services (often receiving third-party reimbursement in the process), confining professional school counselors to those "noncounseling" functions of their role or, in a few instances, cutting school counseling positions altogether. Although many professional school counselors, having received appropriate education, experience, and supervision, are licensed to provide clinical counseling services by state licensing boards, the practice of what some see as mental health counseling in the schools is likely to remain a professional issue receiving much attention and discussion. While striving to implement systemic solutions to complex student problems, school counselors should not abandon the provision of mental health counseling in schools to other helping professions.

The Professional School Counselor as a Career Development and Educational Planning Specialist

Many states now require that individual educational and career plans be developed for every high school student to serve as a guide for college and career readiness. School counseling claims career development as its roots, and many professional secondary school counselors become specialists in career and lifestyle development. The trend is for elementary, middle, and secondary school counselors to provide more emphasis in this area as well. Chapters 11 and 12 provide an overview of the important developmental issues requiring attention. School reform and accountability movements in the United States demand that professional school counselors focus on academic performance, achievement, access and opportunity. This is commensurate with the *ASCA National Model: A Framework for School Counseling Programs* (ASCA, 2012) and the goals of a comprehensive developmental school counseling program.

The Professional School Counselor as a School and Community Agency Consultation/Collaboration Specialist

Chapter 14 addresses the basics of consultation/collaboration models used with individuals and organizations, as well as how to engage parents in the educational process. Consultation has long been a part of the professional school counselor's role, but collaboration makes the professional school counselor a more active and vested participant in the problem-solving process, whether working with individuals or organizations. In the future, working hand in hand with parents will become more important to all education professionals because supportive parents are more likely to have successful students. For example, students who have at least one parent actively involved in their academic life are more likely to get high grades and less likely to get suspended. More than half of all Americans believe parents encounter circumstances when help is needed to raise their children. Interestingly, the parents are not viewed as irresponsible so much as overwhelmed at the time (U.S. Department of Education, Office of Educational Research and Improvement, 2008).

The Professional School Counselor as a School Reform and Accountability Expert

Another topic addressed throughout the text is the professional school counselor as an agent of school reform. School reform hinges on an understanding of what is and isn't working—a process called accountability. Chapter 5 introduces the topics of needs assessment and program evaluation, and Chapter 6 provides a synopsis of counseling and guidance outcomes research. Although one can take heart in knowing that there is validation for much of what professional school counselors do, what amazes many experienced counselors is the relative dearth of outcomes studies related to school counseling. For example, in comparison with other functions outlined in this text, outcomes assessment has traditionally received the least attention, although recent efforts are addressing this problem. This becomes another essential task for your generation of professional school counselors. Much more outcomes research and results evaluation of school counseling activities and services are greatly needed to determine the effectiveness of what is currently done and to lead the school counseling field in new directions.

The Professional School Counselor as a Safe Schools, Violence Prevention, At-Risk Specialist

Recent sensational news stories have created powerful "safe schools" and "at-risk" movements in the United States, and

professional school counselors are positioned to play a pivotal role. Chapter 15 addresses the professional school counselors' responsibility in counseling students at risk. It is hard to underestimate the importance of these components in the future of school counseling. Conflict and violence are prevalent in schools and society, and the developmental and intervention components of a comprehensive school counseling program can address these problems on multiple levels.

The Professional School Counselor as an Advocate for Students with Special Needs

Over five million students ages 6 to 21 years receive special education services in the public schools (U.S. Department of Education, 2005a). The inclusion movement returned numerous students with significant emotional and learning problems to the regular education classroom to be taught by regular teachers with little or no training to instruct children with special needs. Though the research has demonstrated neutral to positive outcomes for special education students, the impact on regular education students and teachers is largely unknown.

Professional school counselors are often the designated (and sometimes lone) advocates for children with special needs and their parents in an intricate and often intimidating education bureaucracy. It follows that the more professional school counselors know about testing and special programs, including special education and the requirements of Section 504 of the Rehabilitation Act, the more effective the school counselor's advocacy will be.

It is essential that professional school counselors know all there is to know about school system standardized testing programs, the child study process, special education eligibility procedures and planning, Section 504 eligibility procedures and modifications, and group and individual assessment procedures and interpretation strategies. Professional school counselors who know the laws, ethics, policies, procedures, and loopholes serve as effective advocates for students, families, and schools. Chapter 16, which focuses on special education, serves as a primer on this subject.

LIVING THE TRANSFORMED ROLE

The question becomes not whether the role of the professional school counselor will continue its transformation, but what shape this transformation will involve. This text focuses on the importance of a systemic perspective, a comprehensive developmental program, and some important areas of professional practice, each of which has a great deal to offer a school community. But for a professional school counselor alone in a school to focus on only one of these practice areas would result in an ineffective program, or at least a program that is not comprehensive and that will not address many student needs. Likewise, professional school counselors who attempt to focus on all practice areas will probably become overwhelmed. No one can do it all. School counseling services involve a complex interplay of student and school community needs with counselor strengths. Balance is needed, and it is quite possible that a professional school counselor who is "unsuccessful" in one school venue can be very successful in another venue in need of his or her particular strengths and talents. Thus, the transformed role of the professional school counselor will be multifaceted, but flexible and practical.

It is helpful to think of the transformed role in terms of the confluence of rivers. When two or more rivers join, the resulting flow is dependent on a complex interplay of factors, including the volume of water (e.g., school, societal, and individual needs) and topographical features (e.g., services and resources). If the water volume of various rivers is heavy and the topography flat and featureless, a messy flood occurs! However, if the topography allows for channeling and measures of control such as deep collecting pools, which make for calm appearances, or even steep, narrow walls with a rock–strewn path, which can lead to an appearance of controlled turbulence, the situation can be managed. In many ways, skilled, competent professional school counselors can make a huge difference in very important ways. Likewise, professional school counselors who partner with stakeholders to provide a pool of resources and services can often calm the flow or at least channel the flow in some positive directions. Either way, the needs of many students, parents, educators, and citizens will be addressed in a proactive manner.

Another helpful way of looking at this complex interplay is through the metaphor of nets of various sizes. Systemic interventions and a comprehensive, developmental school counseling program with its focus on large-group guidance and prevention-based programs is the first and highest net attempting to catch students and keep them on track developmentally. But as fate would have it, some students' needs are more complex, serious, and not necessarily developmental in nature, thus requiring intervention services. The next level of netting attempting to catch students in need may be group counseling with students or consultation or collaboration with parents and teachers. Although many students are put back on track through effective implementation of these services, some require additional interventions (nets) that are more individualized. Individual counseling or referral to qualified mental health professionals when lack of time or skill requires it serves as that next level of netting. However, even after individualized services, some students will still present with unmet needs. These students are the ones who in the past have been described as "falling through the cracks" (or nets) and require a more systemic service delivery approach. This is where school–community–agency partnering, additional systemic interventions, and social and academic advocacy come in. These systemic interventions (nets) are essential to ensure that the needs of all children in our society are addressed.

CULTURAL REFLECTION 1.2

How might professional school counselors-in-training from diverse cultural backgrounds view the myriad approaches to school counseling presented in this chapter as each relates to enhancing children's educational achievement, access, and opportunity? How might students, parents, and educators from diverse backgrounds view the myriad approaches to school counseling presented in this chapter as each relates to enhancing children's educational achievement, access, and opportunity? What cultural barriers and access points might exist?

Summary/Conclusion

Professional school counseling in the United States rests on a rich heritage of ideas, techniques, and implementation approaches. The profession has evolved in response to institutional changes such as immigration; national defense; social and school reform; economic circumstances, such as poverty and programs for the economically disadvantaged; the integration of culturally diverse students who had been previously segregated in some parts of the nation; and growing knowledge about student development—changes that have shaped concepts of education and the role of school counseling.

The historical roots that have spawned the need for counselors in schools and the future issues that remain to be fully resolved at the beginning of the 21st century suggest that the role of the professional school counselor is not a rigid and static set of functions. Rather, it is a role in a constant state of transformation in response to the changing demands on American schools and the factors and influences that affect the growth and development of America's children and youth.

Across the 100 years or so that make up the history of school counseling in the United States, the questions and issues have changed. However, there is no longer a question of whether professional school counseling will survive or whether it is relevant to the mission of the school. The questions today are how to make its contribution more explicit, how to distribute its effects more evenly across school and student groups, and how to deploy these precious professional resources in the most efficient and effective manner. These are the challenges that this generation of professional school counselors faces.

Activities

1. Interview a school social worker, school psychologist, or community-based mental health worker to find out what role his or her profession plays in student development.
2. Research a culture different from your own, and brainstorm possible counseling issues someone from this culture may experience.
3. Talk to a professional school counselor or a school administrator to find out some of the noncounseling tasks counselors are often asked to perform in a school. Develop a plan of action to advocate for using counselor time for counseling and not for non-counseling-related tasks.

2

The *ASCA National Model*: Developing a Comprehensive, Developmental School Counseling Program

Bradley T. Erford

Editor's Introduction: A comprehensive, developmental school counseling program is an essential part of any K–12 educational program and has been effectively addressing developmental and prevention needs for several decades. It is responsible for supporting student educational performance and forms the foundation for career and college readiness and personal/social development. The ASCA *National Standards* and *National Model* are reviewed in this chapter, as are practical program implementation issues, including other school personnel partners. A thorough understanding of a comprehensive, developmental school counseling program sets the stage for comprehending the role of the varied professional school counselor services presented in subsequent chapters.

THE ASCA *NATIONAL STANDARDS* AND *NATIONAL MODEL*

In 1997, the American School Counselor Association (ASCA) published *The National Standards for School Counseling Programs* (Campbell & Dahir, 1997) to provide a standardized basis for the creation of comprehensive, developmental, and preventive school counseling services. The nine standards, three each in the domains of academic, career, and personal/social development, were accompanied by suggested student competencies (i.e., knowledge and skills to be acquired) and led to the development of comprehensive, developmental school counseling curricula by school systems around the country. The ASCA *National Standards* were a historical landmark that gave direction to a profession floundering for a unified identity and role in school reform. Although the *National Standards* can be implemented through nearly any component of the school counseling program, many professional school counselors today implement much of this developmental model through developmental classroom guidance lessons, which are covered in depth in Chapter 10, and responsive services, covered in Chapter 13. School counselors in training should peruse the ASCA *National Standards* and become well acquainted with these domains, standards, and competencies. They likely will form the basis of your school counseling program whether you work in an elementary, middle, or high school.

Shortly after publication of the ASCA *National Standards* (Campbell & Dahir, 1997), leaders in the school counseling field realized that producing curricular standards and competencies was only the first step in transforming the school counseling profession. A developmental curriculum is essential to educating students and provides the "what," but it falls short of the "how." At the same time, the Education Trust's Transforming School Counseling Initiative was gaining steam in school counselor education and public school venues. This initiative emphasized systemic, data-driven services and programs to address achievement disparities, particularly between racial or socioeconomic subpopulations, as well as more specific attention to issues of social advocacy and justice (see Chapters 3 and 4). To expand on and integrate the ASCA *National Standards* into a comprehensive framework that addressed the "how" of school counseling, the ASCA (2003) published *ASCA National Model: A Framework for School Counseling Programs*, which was followed by a second edition (ASCA, 2005), and is now in its third edition (ASCA, 2012). This model focused professional school counselors on a more comprehensive, systemic approach to four core elements or mechanisms for student success—foundation, delivery, management, and accountability—and four infused themes—leadership, advocacy, systemic change, and collaboration and teaming, which will be covered exhaustively later in various chapters of this book. The *ASCA National Model* borrowed heavily from several existing and effective approaches (e.g., Education Trust, 2013; Gysbers & Henderson, 2012; Myrick, 2003a). In doing so, professional school counselors were encouraged to switch from the traditional focus on services for some select needy students to program-centered services for every student in the school and, by extension, for their families and community.

THEMES OF THE *ASCA NATIONAL MODEL*

The *ASCA National Model* (2012) encouraged professional school counselors to focus on local student needs and on the local political context and to use data to identify and meet these needs, as well as to document program effectiveness. It emphasized four important themes: leadership, advocacy, collaboration and teaming, and systemic change. *Leadership* describes the activities of professional school counselors within the school and beyond to enact systemwide changes to facilitate student success. Professional school counselors work diligently to ensure that all students have access to rigorous academic programs and to close achievement gaps among student groups, particularly minorities and the materially poor.

Advocacy involves the systematic identification of student needs and accompanying efforts to ensure that those needs are met. Professional school counselors help every student to achieve academic success by setting high expectations, providing needed support, and removing systemic barriers to success. Chapter 9 provides in-depth information on how professional school counselors can develop leadership and advocacy skills.

Collaboration and teaming require that professional school counselors work with a wide array of stakeholders within the school, school system, and community. Collaborative efforts should focus on providing students access to rigorous academic programs and on other factors leading to academic success. Teaming with parents, educators, and community agencies to develop effective working relationships is critical to this goal. Chapter 14 addresses collaboration and consultation in depth.

Systemic change encompasses schoolwide changes in expectations, instructional practices, support services, and philosophy with the goal of raising achievement levels and creating opportunity and access for all students. A focus on data-driven programming allows professional school counselors to identify areas in need of improvement, leading to alterations in systemic policies and procedures that empower students and lead to higher performance and greater opportunities for postsecondary success. Chapter 4 provides professional school counselors with a primer on creating systemic changes in schools. These four themes are woven throughout the *ASCA National Model* (2012), but the heart of a comprehensive, developmental school counseling program is the four primary program components: foundation, delivery, management, and accountability.

CULTURAL REFLECTION 2.1

How might professional school counselors from diverse cultural backgrounds view the various components of the *ASCA National Model* as it relates to children's educational achievement, access, and opportunity? How might students, parents, and educators from diverse backgrounds view the leadership role of the professional school counselor in implementing the various components of the *ASCA National Model*? What cultural barriers and access points might exist?

FOUNDATION

The program *foundation*, the "what" of a comprehensive school counseling program, makes clear what every student will know and be able to do and includes emphases on the school counseling program's vision statement that stems from a school counselor's beliefs and philosophies, mission, student competencies (i.e., academic, career, personal/social), and professional competencies (ASCA, 2012). The student competencies, including the domains and standards, are amply described in the ASCA *National Standards* (Campbell & Dahir, 1997) and form the foundation of a comprehensive, developmental school counseling program.

Likewise, an important focus of Chapter 4 is the systemic changes reflected in a school system's and school counseling program's beliefs, philosophy, and mission. The school counseling program must be based on a set of principles and beliefs that will direct the implementation of program components and services. Through collaboration and teamwork, professional school counselors help build a consensus among stakeholders on the principles and beliefs that will guide the program through construction of a vision statement. The purpose and vision of a program are then operationalized through development of a program mission statement, which aligns with the overall mission of the school system, as well as those of the individual schools. Again, these facets of program foundation will be expanded on in Chapter 4.

Finally, professional competencies comprise the attitudes, knowledge, and skills that school counselors need to develop to efficiently and effectively implement a comprehensive school counseling program (see Appendix H of the *National Model* [ASCA, 2012]). Ongoing *professional development* congruent with the needs of the school community is critical. Relevant skill development and knowledge updating prepare the professional school counselor to continuously facilitate the implementation of a comprehensive school counseling program. Professional development encompasses in-service training, postgraduate education, and membership in professional associations.

THEORY INTO PRACTICE 2.1

IMPLEMENTING A COMPREHENSIVE, DEVELOPMENTAL SCHOOL COUNSELING PROGRAM AT THE ELEMENTARY SCHOOL

A comprehensive, developmental guidance program is the cornerstone of an effective school counseling program and includes delivering a school guidance curriculum, individual student planning and counseling services, responsive counseling services, and systems support services. The total guidance program must be able to show the results of that program, not just serve as a list of what I accomplish on a day-to-day basis. A comprehensive, developmental school counseling program allows me to be in touch with *each student* in each class at least every other week. In addition to allowing me time to teach the students specific concepts and skills identified by my school system, it allows students the opportunity to set a time to meet with me regarding any issues they may be experiencing. It allows me to be approachable and accessible to all students, parents, and staff members.

In my school system, the Elementary Guidance Essential Curriculum, which drives my classroom guidance program, was developed by current professional school counselors. Its purpose is to provide all students, K through 5, with the knowledge and skills appropriate to each grade's developmental level. The three domains identified by the ASCA—academic, personal/social, and career—are embedded in the curriculum. Beginning with kindergarten and continuing through fifth grade, identified ASCA competencies and concepts are scheduled to be taught at specific times in the school calendar based on the developmental assets (strengths) and abilities of students in each grade. Each grade level builds upon the previous grade level (vertical articulation) in terms of the concepts taught. For example, the personal safety topic taught in kindergarten is "Stranger Safety and Teasing." In first grade, the personal safety concept taught in September is "Teasing and Bullying"; then personal safety is revisited in April with the concept of "Good and Bad Secrets and Touches," when students are deemed to be more developmentally ready to handle this topic. In the fourth and fifth grades, personal safety concepts include "Internet Safety," "Sexual Harassment," "Peer Pressure," and "Child Sexual Abuse," all developmentally advanced, but age-appropriate concepts.

This continuum within each grade and across grades K–5 provides all students the content necessary to attain the knowledge, attitudes, and skills related to each ASCA domain in a systematic and systemic manner (meaning a child can move within our county and still be aligned with the next concept being taught in the classroom by the school counselor). Each professional school counselor then creates lessons based on the developmental levels within each class, allowing us to differentiate classroom guidance instruction much like classroom teachers differentiate content area instruction, while addressing students with special needs or learning disabilities and even the personality of the class and classroom teacher. If I need to revisit a particular concept or skill, I am able to do so. At a teacher's or an administrator's request, I can develop a lesson to help that particular class with any concepts needing to be strengthened in order to prevent future problems or to address current concerns. Our school also has an annual, supplemental focus (e.g., Character Education, Habits of Mind, Keys to Success), which I am able to either embed into lessons that are part of the existing Elementary Guidance Essential Curriculum or include as part of my comprehensive, developmental guidance program. Finally, as part of the classroom guidance program, I must always assess the effectiveness of my lessons. I do this by consulting with teachers to see that overall student progress is noted. This service definitely allows me to get "the biggest bang for the buck" in terms of having face-to-face time with each student.

The two biggest challenges in delivering the Elementary Guidance Essential Curriculum are limited amounts of time and the need to keep parents informed of the concepts being taught in classroom guidance so that they can reinforce these skills at home. I insist on

(Continued)

being part of the Cultural Arts schedule in that it *guarantees* me a scheduled time each week in each classroom. I request that classroom teachers remain in the classroom during my lesson so that they can supplement the lesson and so that, as teachable moments arise in the classroom, they can reflect back on my lesson with the class. I consider it a loose form of "co-teaching," but an effective one. In order to keep parents informed of the concepts being taught in classroom guidance, I include a brief description of the concept being covered with each grade level in our monthly school newsletter. I also purchased a stamp with my name and "Guidance Lesson" imprinted on it. Each paper I use as part of the classroom guidance lesson is imprinted with this stamp so that parents know that that particular paper was part of my lesson.

Individual student planning and counseling services assist students in establishing personal goals and developing future plans. At the beginning of each marking period, I issue a needs assessment to the teachers as a form of data collection on children and needs they may have. I usually know of students and their particular needs, but the needs assessment brings students to my attention whom I may not be aware of as having problems. At the elementary level, I meet with students struggling academically, behaviorally, or socially. Sometimes I meet with the students individually or with those students experiencing the same types of issues in a small group. We discuss the problems the students are experiencing and list ways they can work on the problems. Goals are set and revisited within an established time. With elementary-aged students, I find that putting problems, possible solutions, and goals on paper helps them to remember what they are to be working on and provides teachers and parents with information on what the students are working on. Contracts are often developed as a way to keep the students, the parents, and the teacher "in the loop" in terms of expectations and progress. Each time we meet, the worksheet or contract provides us a "talking point" on which to focus. Often, older students and I will review tests, benchmark assessments, and even state test scores to help establish the most meaningful goals for each particular student. In order for this service delivery model to be effective, the students and their progress must be monitored in a consistent manner, and communication with the teacher and the home is imperative.

Responsive counseling services include consulting with teachers, parents/guardians, other professional school staff (e.g., special educators, administrators), and community resource groups to identify ways to best help students and their families. Such services also include small-group counseling, where, again through a needs assessment and my knowledge of the student

body, small groups are developed and services are delivered based on similar student needs. Each small group runs between 6 and 8 weeks, once permission is obtained from the parent/guardian. I survey the teachers, parents, and students (if developmentally appropriate) to see which skills students in the small group would *benefit most* from acquiring. Small-group lessons are then developed based on this information and other skills I deem necessary. Small groups are run according to traditional group counseling methods. After the completion of the group, students self-assess, and teachers and parents/guardians are again surveyed to see if growth has taken place. I then reflect on what went well with the group as a whole, what didn't work well, and what I would repeat again. This reflection piece is critical in moving forward with small-group counseling. Again, the challenge in delivering this service comes with scheduling. Whenever possible, I schedule groups during lunch so that students do not miss instruction or recess. I have also scheduled groups that deal with academic needs during reading instructional time as part of a three-group rotation.

Responsive counseling services also include crisis counseling as needed to provide staff and students and their families with support during emergencies. It may be short term or long term in nature and is based on the presented emergency. I also make referrals to outside agencies/resources as needed and follow up frequently with the person or family involved in the emergency. Referrals to other resources also fall into the responsive services delivery model for concerns such as depression, suicide ideation, academic difficulties, and other individual or family issues.

The final cornerstone of my comprehensive, developmental guidance program is systems support services. These include seeking ways to continue my personal professional development and growth through taking postgraduate classes, attending workshops/in-services, participating in professional learning communities, and being a member of professional associations (local and national). It also includes my providing staff and parents with up-to-date information and workshops on topics that are helpful to those two groups (based on a needs assessment distributed during fall parent–teacher conferences or administrative directive). Finally, systems support services include consulting, collaborating, and teaming with all stakeholders for the students in my school, including teachers, support staff members, parents/guardians, and outside community members and agencies.

Source: Kim K. Baicar, National Board Certified School Counselor, Broadneck Elementary School, Anne Arundel County Public Schools, Maryland

DELIVERY

Delivery is the "how" of the comprehensive, developmental school counseling program. As professional school counselors implement their programs, they use delivery systems that include attention to the school counseling core curriculum (e.g., systematic, developmental classroom guidance lessons, parent workshops), individual student planning (i.e., assistance in establishing personal goals and future plans), responsive services (i.e., individual or small-group counseling, crisis response, consultation, peer facilitation, referrals), and systems support (i.e., program maintenance through professional development, systemic consultation/collaboration, management functions). These delivery systems are often called program components.

Program components provide methods of service delivery that operationalize program goals. Each program component can include direct and indirect services. *Direct services* are frequently targeted to students. Typical direct service activities are individual counseling, small-group counseling, and classroom guidance. *Indirect services* support direct services and are the foundation of a system-focused school counseling program. Typical indirect services include consultation, coordination, team building, leadership, and advocacy. This system focus puts into action the "new vision of school counseling" (see Chapter 3).

For effective service delivery of a comprehensive school counseling program, professional school counselors must possess the knowledge and skills to implement both the direct and the indirect services detailed for each program component (school counselor competencies). For example, group counseling is one method of service delivery within the responsive services program component. This service delivery method is frequently used to address recurring needs identified in individual sessions, needs assessments, and consultations with parents and/or teachers. Planning and implementing group counseling services requires a cadre of group leadership knowledge and skills in such areas as teamwork, coordination, consultation, group skill building, and organizational skills. If any of these skills or knowledge bases is not developed, even the best-intended small-group counseling services might go awry. Therefore, in planning activities in each program component area, it is critical for professional school counselors to carefully inventory their knowledge and skills. Deficits in knowledge and skills are opportunities for professional development. In this way, service delivery within the comprehensive school counseling program reflects student needs and will not be compromised by limited professional school counselor knowledge or skills.

Moreover, professional school counselor knowledge and skills development should not be limited to service delivery that is primarily counseling related, where the professional school counselor provides direct service to students. The professional school counselor needs to possess knowledge and skills, even in areas where the primary service to students is indirect and focused on classroom and academic performance. Consultation with teachers on issues of curriculum development, classroom management, and classroom assessment is critical, even though professional school counselors' primary role is not teaching in the classroom all day. The professional school counselor's knowledge and competence in these skill areas, applied through consultation services, delivers a direct service to teachers and an indirect service to students. This also broadens the school counselor's skill base to facilitate delivery of curriculum in both the classroom and other large-group settings.

Thus, within the framework of a comprehensive school counseling program, various components provide multiple levels of service that build on and connect with each other. The professional school counselor is involved in both direct and indirect service activities that target the developmental needs of the school community.

Gysbers and Henderson's (2012) enumeration of comprehensive school counseling program components is widely used and consists of four program components: guidance curriculum, individual student planning, responsive services, and systems support. Each program component encompasses both direct and indirect service delivery.

The remainder of this section elaborates on these four program components as adopted by the *ASCA National Model*. For each program component, suggestions are shared on both "how to do it" (techniques/strategies for successful implementation) and "why do it" (expected benefits).

School Counseling Core Curriculum

The school counseling core curriculum provides services to large groups. For example, classroom instruction and activities (guidance) consists of units on age-appropriate topics presented by either the professional school counselor or the classroom teacher in consultation with the professional school counselor. Each unit typically consists of multiple classroom lessons. Coordination and facilitation of peer helper programs may be related to the school counseling core curriculum, as may parent workshops.

Classroom instructional units are not independent; they may be linked to classroom guidance units at other grade levels and/or integrated into the school's core curriculum. Scope and sequence across grade levels is an important classroom guidance consideration. For example, self-esteem is a common classroom guidance unit. An effective, comprehensive school counseling program articulates self-esteem classroom lessons at various grade levels, increasing in cognitive and affective complexity in the upper grade levels. A self-esteem unit in one grade level builds and expands on the content presented at the previous grade level. Classroom guidance also includes activities specific to one grade level, such as senior-year events and transition orientation (e.g., for kindergarten students and incoming ninth graders).

An advantage of classroom guidance is that it enables service delivery to a large number of individuals that addresses topics in a preventive manner. Many professional school counselors report that school counseling classroom instruction and activities provide the opportunity to "get to know" students. This eases the transition when professional school counselors need to intervene for individual student issues. Implementation of the school counseling core curriculum through developmental classroom guidance (instruction and activities) is reviewed in detail in Chapter 10.

Individual Student Planning

Individual student planning addresses the need for all students to plan and monitor their academic progress. Individual or small-group appraisal includes using test information and other student data to help develop goals and plans. The comprehensive school counseling program offers an integrated and holistic method for students to assess and become knowledgeable about their abilities, interests, skills, and achievement. Test information is linked with other data to help students develop immediate goals and plans (e.g., course selection), as well as long-range goals and plans (e.g., college, career).

During *individual advisement*, the professional school counselor helps students plan for and realize their goals. Students need direction in understanding, applying, and analyzing self-appraisal information in conjunction with social, career, and labor market information. This will help them plan for and realize their educational, career, and personal goals.

Responsive Services

Effective, comprehensive school counseling programs incorporate both direct and indirect services within the program component of *responsive services*. These services address both proactive and reactive goals. The methods of service delivery for responsive services are individual counseling, group counseling, consultation, referral, crisis response, and peer facilitation.

INDIVIDUAL COUNSELING Individual counseling sessions meet both proactive and reactive student needs. Given the complex and wide-ranging issues confronting students today, expertise in individual counseling is required, as is continuous updating of one's knowledge and skill repertoire through professional development. Some professional school counselors may overrely on individual counseling because it is often easier to provide, deliver, and/or schedule individual counseling sessions than various other interventions. This view may be shared by others in the school community, who assert that individual counseling is more sensitive to both the classroom routine and the overall school schedule.

The perspective on individual counseling promoted by the "new vision" of school counseling is that, if professional school counselors spend too much time with a few students, they will be perceived as "therapists" and probably shortchange most of the student body. Extensive time devoted to individual counseling means less time for services included in program components that can address common needs of a larger proportion of the student body. Professional school counselors need to effectively collaborate with community mental health professionals without engaging in the role of "therapist at school." A large proportion of a professional school counselor's day needs to be spent outside of or beyond the school counseling office. Individual counseling as an effective intervention is addressed in Chapter 13.

SMALL-GROUP COUNSELING Small-group activities respond both proactively and reactively to student needs (see Chapter 13). *Group counseling and psychoeducational counseling* services offer a variety of small-group experiences on relevant topics or issues such as study skills, effective relationships, bereavement, and postsecondary planning. Group counseling allows professional school counselors to address issues common to several students at one time, and comprehensive group counseling services can be offered throughout the academic year. This can help students perceive participating in group counseling as a "normal" or expected school experience.

Each group counseling activity consists of several sessions with a small group of students who explore their ideas, attitudes, feelings, and behaviors. Student insight and/or learning can come from group leaders, other group members, and/or the synergy of the group. Outcomes research studies document that small-group counseling frequently is effective, especially when focused on academic or personal development topics. Professional school counselors also conduct group counseling services for others in the school community, such as parenting groups or new teacher support groups. Because one group serves several individuals, group counseling is a time- and cost-efficient method of service delivery.

CRISIS RESPONSE *Crisis response* to critical and acute situations that require immediate intervention is an important counselor function. Crisis situations usually call for such immediate intervention because of their sudden onset. Crisis counseling interventions include individual counseling, group counseling, and/or the managing and coordinating of the services of others. The purpose of crisis response interventions is to diffuse a situation, serve school community members affected by the situation, and initiate a healing process. This may require direct services by the professional school counselor. However, professional school counselors may not be the only service providers in a crisis situation. Therefore, they may also need to coordinate the efforts of others.

Professional school counselors may lead or contribute to a committee review and update of the school's crisis response plan to ensure it is current and accurate. Many school administrators rely on the professional school counselor to annually lead a discussion on crisis situation roles and responsibilities among members of the school community.

In crisis situations, professional school counselors may also provide indirect services such as collaboration and referral. Often, crisis response also involves additional resources and individuals beyond the school counseling department staff.

CONSULTATION AND COLLABORATION *Consultation and collaboration* are indirect responsive services in which professional school counselors consult and collaborate with administrators, teachers, or parents to help them with student issues or concerns. Consultation and collaboration are cooperative processes in which the professional school counselor (serving in the role of consultant) helps others in the school community to think through problems and to develop skills that make them more effective in working with students. Thus, consultation is a process of directly working with a second party (the consultee) to indirectly help a third party (the student). Each of these processes will be explained in much greater detail in Chapter 14.

When consulting with administrators, professional school counselors most typically discuss program or curriculum planning, academic or behavioral interventions for students, and school climate and work-related concerns. Common consultation activities with teachers include presenting in-service programs and working with an individual student's or a class's difficulties. When parents are the consultees, concerns about a student's academic, behavioral, or social development typically are shared. Assuming that professional school counselors cannot meet each and every one of the intense, complex counseling needs of students today, an effective consulting relationship with referral agency personnel is critical.

When serving as a consultant, professional school counselors need to follow all the steps of the consultation process: identify a purpose, establish a goal, plan strategies to meet that goal, and assign responsibilities to carry out that goal. No matter who is the target of the consultation, the goal of a consultation intervention is the same: Consultees will learn information and enhance skills that they can use to interact more effectively with others, especially with students.

Collaboration and advocacy themes are frequently implemented through partnering with parents, educators, and community organizations, as well as through participating on school district committees, on community advisory councils, and in parent and community outreach activities. As mentioned earlier with regard to responsive services, consultation and collaboration with parents, teachers, and others support the school system mission by facilitating feedback on student, system, and community needs.

REFERRAL *Referral* enlists the services of other professionals to assist school counselors. Many students today are confronted with complex issues compounded by family, peer pressure, developmental, and societal situations; it is not practical for professional school counselors to be the sole service provider for these students. As a result, professional school counselors enlist the services of other school personnel (e.g., school psychologist, school nurse, school social worker) and/or community agency personnel to address some student issues.

VOICES FROM THE FIELD 2.1   **COUNSELING IN AN INDEPENDENT/PRIVATE SCHOOL**

The presence of professional school counselors in private and independent schools is a relatively new phenomenon. With its roots in career and vocational assessment and placement, school counseling was once thought to be the realm of the public sector because the perception among educators at independent schools often is "all our students are going to college." Although there is a longer tradition of college counseling in independent schools, counseling for personal/social issues in independent schools traditionally was more often left to coaches, advisors, and teachers. With smaller class sizes and mandatory athletics, teachers and coaches did have a lot of contact with students. What teachers and coaches did not have was professional counseling training, and as the psychosocial issues facing students and schools have become more complex, more and more independent schools have hired professional school counselors.

One of the advantages of being a professional school counselor in an independent school setting is that students and educators actually require less unlearning of what counselors *used to* do because, for the most part, there did not *used to* be a counselor. If an independent school did employ a counselor, it was often as a "therapist in residence," so the first challenge in implementing the new vision is to help

(Continued)

the administration and the school community understand the professional school counselor's role in serving the whole community, rather than a few students with special needs who are better served by outside mental health professionals. Because the needs of the whole community are so great, I have found independent school communities to be very open to a broader understanding of the school counselor's role across the curriculum. Some of this work is directly with students through classroom guidance, group and individual counseling, peer education, parenting programs, and so on. But much of the work is often indirect—helping those teachers, advisors, and coaches who already do have significant access to students learn the skills that can make those relationships more productive and beneficial. In this sense, the "new vision" of counseling supports the old model of helping the teachers and coaches develop the skills they need to help the students of today. Although there are certainly crises that counselors need to react to in independent schools, our primary focus is definitely proactive, preventive, and focused on early intervention.

Like public school counselors, independent school counselors are not sitting in their offices waiting to react to the next crisis or for a "client" to wander in. Professional school counselors are very visible in the halls, lunchrooms, and classrooms. As packed as students' and teachers' schedules are in independent schools, much of our "checking in" happens between classes. During class times, counselors visit classes with a very proactive and developmental curriculum. Our middle school counselor visits small health classes quarterly with a developmental curriculum that mixes group guidance and counseling. In my lower school, the counselor supports teachers with character education programs and presents various counseling units to various grades. Our upper school counselor trains 11th-grade peer educators who teach a guidance curriculum to younger students. The counselors sponsor annual mandatory parent–student dialogue evenings for students and parents in grades 4–12 on topics ranging from bullying to substance abuse to healthy relationships. Although we have done much with transitions from lower school and middle school, this year we introduced a 4-day, 3-night senior retreat program designed to help students with the personal and emotional transition from high school to college and beyond.

As you look toward a career in school counseling, remember the fertile ground that independent schools offer for building, sometimes from the ground up, a truly developmental and comprehensive counseling program. Being truly independent of state and local curricula and expectations really does give professional school counselors in independent schools freedom to shape school counseling as it ought to be. Graduate students in my introductory-level course often ask if this new vision of counseling really happens in schools because that has not always been their experience in the public sector. I say that I can speak only for my school, but, yes, it really happens, and it really works.

Source: John Mojzisek, Director of Counseling, The Gilman School; Affiliate Professor, School Counseling Program, Loyola University Maryland

MANAGEMENT

The *management* system element accounts for the "when," "why," and "on what authority" of a comprehensive school counseling program (ASCA, 2012). It comprises school counselor competencies assessments (see earlier discussion and Appendix H of the *National Model* [ASCA, 2012]), school counseling program assessments (formerly known as a program audit; see school counseling program assessment in Chapter 5), use of time assessments (see service assessment in Chapter 5) of which 80% of a school counselor's time is supposed to go toward service delivery, the annual agreements (i.e., what accomplishments professional school counselors are accountable for during the school year), the advisory council, the use of data (for student monitoring and the closing of achievement/social disparities), annual results data (e.g., process data, perceptions data, outcome data; see Chapter 5), action plans, lesson plans (see Chapter 10), and the school counseling program calendar.

Annual Agreement

The use of *annual agreements* (formerly known as management agreements) is somewhat controversial, but such agreements are meant to help both professional school counselors and school administrators to understand the goals of a school counseling program and to remove barriers to effective implementation of services to meet those goals. The ASCA (2012, pp. 64–65) provided a template sample annual management agreement. These agreements are short and to the point, but they represent a basic understanding of responsibilities and program management.

Advisory Council

Advisory councils provide a mechanism for input, feedback, and evaluation of the school counseling program's activities for a wide range of individuals. The community advisory council, also known as the *school counseling program advisory committee (SCPAC)*, serves as a sounding board and steering committee. The most important factor to consider when constituting an SCPAC is influence. The professional school counselor must seek to include individuals who can influence and hold the confidence of school and school system decision makers, generally the principal and central office administrators. Including influential members on the SCPAC will ease the way in obtaining necessary programmatic changes as well as resources.

From a personnel perspective, it is essential for the principal to be a member of the SCPAC. The principal can hear firsthand the ideas and planning that go into recommendations for improvement, as well as the rationale for any additional funding that may be needed. In addition to the professional school counselor(s), at least several influential teachers and parents should be included. Political linkages to parent–teacher organizations often play to the advantage of a professional school counselor, as these members can serve as conduits to and from the organizations. The members can inform the SCPAC of various constituencies' concerns and provide information back to those constituencies regarding actions recommended by the SCPAC or the blockage of the recommended actions.

To round out the committee, an influential school resource person (e.g., school psychologist, special education teacher, reading specialist) and influential community organization and business leaders should be included. Individuals from community organizations and businesses are useful for providing an external perspective, as well as partnerships and external funding and resources.

The SCPAC should convene at least twice annually— and more frequently if the program is new or undergoing major changes. The primary role of the SCPAC is to review the results of needs assessments, make recommendations for program development, review accountability data and outcome research generated by staff, and locate internal and external funding sources for program development. Locating funding sources often requires the cooperation of the building principal; this is where it pays off to include the principal on the committee, as well as other individuals who can influence the principal's decision making. Thus, the SCPAC can serve a practical and political function, making it a top priority on the professional school counselor's agenda.

Use of Data

Professional school counselors monitor student progress and collect and disaggregate data to identify systemic issues that interfere with equity in achievement. School counselors also collect, analyze, and disseminate program evaluation and "closing the gap" data and analyses. Data collection, analysis, and program evaluation procedures will be covered in much greater detail in Chapter 5.

Action Plans

Action plans are detailed strategies for achieving important outcomes. The ASCA (2012) outlines the components of both school guidance curriculum action plans and closing the gap action plans. School guidance curriculum action plans contain the following information (p. 53):

- Goals to be addressed
- Domain(s), standard(s), and competencies that are consistent with school and program goals
- Description of school counseling activities to be delivered
- Title of any packaged or created curriculum that will be used
- Timeline for completion of activities
- Name of person(s) responsible for each activity
- Methods of evaluating student success using process, perception and outcome data
- Expected result for students stated in terms of what will be demonstrated by the student

School counselors should know how to complete curriculum action plans, small-group action plans, and closing-the-gap action plans, which are generated from a data-driven approach that identifies some existing discrepancy in students' achievement.

Calendars

Planning is an essential component of any program management system. Indeed, if one does not plan for something to occur, it usually won't! Thus, professional school counselors are strongly encouraged to produce weekly, monthly, and annual calendars. Annual calendars should contain "school counseling classroom lessons, back-to-school night, open house, student/parent/teacher meeting days, standardized test dates, career or college nights, evening activities provided through the school and the community," whereas weekly calendars should contain "classroom lessons, group and individual counseling, meetings with students, collaboration and advocacy, data analysis, committee and fair-share responsibilities" (p. 57).

THEORY INTO PRACTICE 2.2

USING THE SCHOOL COUNSELING CALENDAR

The school counseling office creates a basic annual calendar for all counselors in the county according to level. I add pertinent information, send a copy back to the office, and provide one to my principal as well. Counselors are also provided with an Essential Curriculum, which outlines the monthly classroom guidance topics from pre-kindergarten through 12th grade. These tools provide the basic foundation for my school counseling program, and I

(Continued)

have the flexibility to make adjustments to fit the needs of my school.

My elementary school includes 26 classrooms from pre-K to fifth grade (just over 600 students). We are expected to grow to 655 students and 28 classrooms next year. The staffing includes my principal and a half-time assistant principal. In addition to being the sole school counselor in the building, I am the PBIS Team Leader, Attendance Committee Chair, Volunteer Liaison, and a member of the SIT, EMT, and Equity teams. I teach two lessons per month in grades 1–5, about 1.5 lessons per month in kindergarten, and an occasional lesson in pre-K. Therefore the majority of my time is reserved for classroom lessons.

I distribute my schedule to each grade level with times blocked off for duties and appointments. Once the teachers sign up for their lessons, I schedule times for small-group sessions, individual counseling, communication (phone calls, e-mails, website updates), collaboration, committee responsibilities, and program support activities.

At the end of each week I e-mail my proposed schedule to the teachers to give them a chance to make any changes, and I copy the e-mail to my administrator. I make a photocopy for the secretaries in the front office so they know where to find me in case of an emergency. Although I do not publish a weekly schedule for parents, I provide descriptions and materials from my monthly lessons on our school website. I include tips for parents to transfer the skills learned in class to the home environment. Publishing my weekly and monthly calendars would be easier if I used an online calendar to schedule lessons and small groups rather than the paper-and-pencil version I currently use, but my staff is not quite ready for that yet!

April Planning Notes

County Calendar Notes:

Essential Curriculum

K—Career Awareness

1—Jobs That Help

2—Jobs and Tools

3—My Interests, Future Possibilities

4—My Skills, Career Exploration

5—Career Interests and Categories

Activities

Work with Targeted Intervention Plan students

Meet with 4th grade on Academic Plans

Identify Back to School Program students

Important Dates:

2 Spring Break ends

10-May 4 MSA Science

11 Cluster meeting

25 report card distribution

30 TIP data due

Data Considerations:

Attendance

Discipline

Achievement

TIP

Monthly Calendar—April

Sun	Mon	Tue	Wed	Thu	Fri	Sat
	1 No school	2 PBIS evaluation	3	4 PBIS mtg.	5	6
7	8 Student of the Month	9 MSA Science PTO mtg.	10 MSA Science	11 Cluster mtg.	12 Volunteer data due 2 hr. ED	13
14	15 Volunteer Appreciation Week	16 Instructional Rounds EMT	17	18	19	20
21	22	23 SIT	24	25 Report card distribution	26 PBIS monthly event	27
28	29	30 TIP data due	May 1 Grandparents' Day 2 hr. ED			

Weekly Calendar

Time	Monday	Tuesday	Wednesday	Thursday	Friday PBIS Event Day
8:00-8:30	Collaboration, Check-In, Check-Out (CICO)			8:00 RST meeting	
8:30-9:00	Academic Groups 4th & 5th				
9:00-9:30	Walk-through	3rd—I Love My Job	Middle school forms 5th grade	K—Job Clues	3rd—A Picture's Worth 1,000 Careers
9:30-10:00	Individual counseling	Communication	3rd—A Picture's Worth 1,000 Careers	K—Job Clues	Next week's schedule
10:00-10:30		5th—Learning Styles, Holland Codes in lab	5th—Campus Tours, computer lab	5th—Campus Tours, computer lab	Communication
10:30-11:00	Communication		K—Job Clues	Walk-through	
11:00-11:30	Program support	4th—Career Interest Areas	Communication	Individual counseling	4th—Career Interest Areas
11:30-12:00		Walk-through			Duty
12:00-12:30	Small group	Individual counseling	Duty	RST meeting Parent conference	1st—Career Bingo
12:30-1:00		Duty	1st—Career Bingo		
1:00-1:30	Student observation	Communication	1st—Career Bingo	Student observation	2nd—Career Clusters
1:30-2:00	Individual counseling			2nd—Career Clusters	Walk-through
2:00-2:30	2nd—Career Clusters	2nd—Career Clusters	Assembly		5th grade benchmark accommodation
2:30-3:00	Committee data	IEP team report		4th—You're the Boss	
3:00-4:20	CICO Duty Communication	SIT, share PBIS data	Communication	Duty Program Support	PBIS/TIP data Student of the Month

Source: Holly J. Kleiderlein, NBCT, Oak Hill Elementary School, Anne Arundel County Public Schools.

Use of Time

How much time do professional school counselors spend providing various services or implementing components of the school counseling program? How much time should they spend? These are questions of use of time, ordinarily answered through what is commonly known as a service assessment or through collection of a time log. Service assessment is reviewed in greater detail in Chapter 5. ASCA recommends that professional school counselors should spend at least 80% of their time in direct service activities. *"Fair share" responsibilities*, the final facet of program management, acknowledge that professional school counselors are full participants on the school's educational team and, as such, equitably participate in necessary responsibilities, even though these responsibilities may not be part of counselor training. For example, teachers and administrators often have "bus duty," so counselors should also contribute a fair share of their time to such activities. The *National Model* also identifies appropriate responsibilities that professional school counselors should engage in and inappropriate activities that they should avoid (ASCA, 2012, p. 45). For example, ASCA designates the following activities as inappropriate: "coordinating paperwork and data entry of all new students . . . teaching classes when teachers are absent . . . computing grade-point averages . . . maintaining student records . . . keeping clerical records . . . assisting with duties in the principal's office . . . serving as a data entry clerk."

Planning and administrative tasks support the activities of a comprehensive school counseling program. These may include securing and allocating resources, providing for staffing needs and training, and dealing with facility constraints. Coordination activities frequently draw on the leadership and advocacy dimensions of the professional school counselor's role as counselors plan and coordinate numerous services and initiatives. Professional school counselors also serve as the liaison between the school and community agencies. Effective coordination in a comprehensive school counseling program requires interfacing with the entire school community.

ACCOUNTABILITY SYSTEM

Accountability answers the all-important question of "How are students different as a result of the program?" Accountability is provided by professional school counselors through data analysis (e.g., a school data profile analysis, use of time analysis), program results (e.g., curriculum results analysis, small-group results analysis, closing-the-gap analysis), and evaluation and improvement studies (e.g., school counselor competencies assessment analysis, program assessment analysis, school counselor performance appraisal). *Program results* comprise outcomes assessments that document changes in students and other stakeholders through systematic analysis of their performance within various program components. An example might be academic performance changes as a result of participation in a study skills small-group experience. Monitoring changes in perceptions, processes, and attitudes can also provide helpful evidence of professional school counselor effectiveness. *Performance appraisal* for professional school counselors includes all local job and program expectations that help to assess one's skill in implementing a comprehensive, developmental school counseling program. *Program assessment analyses* (formerly known as program audits) are conducted to ensure that a school's comprehensive developmental program aligns with some set of standards, whether at the local or state level,

or with the *ASCA National Model*. Such alignment is deemed critical in addressing the needs of all students. All these accountability processes are aimed at program evaluation and continuous quality improvement. Each of these facets of program accountability is explained in detail in Chapter 5.

Data analysis is a key facet of program accountability and involves analysis of student achievement data and use-of-time (service) assessments (see Chapter 5). Through program results studies, professional school counselors are particularly interested in identifying gaps in student achievement, sharing the data and information with colleagues, and developing individual and systemic interventions to address these needs.

Applications of the *ASCA National Model* (2012) and its facets can be seen in every chapter in this text. The *National Model* presents professional school counselors with a cogent starting point for implementing comprehensive, developmental programs that will benefit all students and with a solid framework on which to build responsive, proactive, comprehensive, developmental school counseling programs. These programs ensure that all students are exposed to rigorous academic curricula, treated equitably and with dignity, and held to high academic standards that enhance postsecondary career opportunities (Table 2.1).

But the *ASCA National Model* is not without its critics. Some of this criticism is based on the lack of outcomes data supporting the model. That is not to say that the model is not effective, just that studies supporting its use have yet to emerge. Counseling researchers will continue to strive for resolution of this concern over the next decade or so. Regardless, keep in mind that implementation of the model is above all a team effort; students, parents, and education professionals all have their roles to play. The final section in this chapter reviews some of the school professionals and staff members with whom the professional school counselor often partners.

TABLE 2.1   Summary of the *ASCA National Model*

- Themes: Leadership, advocacy, collaboration, and systemic change
- Foundation: Program focus, student competencies, and professional competencies
- Management: Assessments (competencies, program, and use-of-time) and tools (advisory council, calendars, lesson and action plans)
- Delivery: Direct (responsive services, core curriculum, and student planning) and indirect (referrals, consultation, and collaboration) services
- Accountability: Data analysis, program results, evaluation and improvement

THE EFFECTS OF IMPLEMENTING THE ASCA *NATIONAL STANDARDS* AND *ASCA NATIONAL MODEL* SYSTEMWIDE

The ASCA *National Standards* and *ASCA National Model* have played an important role in my work as the Coordinator of School Counseling in Howard County Public Schools in Maryland. Until late 1997, I was a school counselor at the elementary and middle school levels when I applied for the Coordinator of School Counseling position. By this time, I had worked in two different counties in Maryland and never felt that I had been clear on what an effective school counseling program should entail. I believe it was fate that led me to be asked to read a draft version of the ASCA *National Standards* 2 weeks before my interview for the new position. This draft helped provide a framework for all the elements that I wanted to bring to the interview, and I am sure it was a factor in the awarding of this supervisory position to me. So, of course, when the ASCA *National Standards* were officially published in 1997, and the *ASCA National Model* in 2003, both gave me the vision and tools for the school counseling program in the Howard County Public Schools.

In my opinion, the *ASCA National Model* has brought many positive changes to school counseling. In a time of tight budgets, limited resources, and accountability, the *ASCA National Model* helped school counseling align with school improvement efforts and made the school counselor an integral player in these efforts. The following are some of the changes in Howard County, Maryland, that were the result of using the *ASCA National Model* as our framework:

1. **A Focus on Quality Instead of Quantity** Many school systems, including Howard County, had school counselors collecting tally-mark data to show how many students they met with each day, how many groups they ran, how many classrooms they visited, and so on. Although this gives quantitative data, it did nothing to show the effectiveness of the school counseling program. We immediately began to make a shift toward using effectiveness data to drive our programs. It doesn't matter if the school counselor sees every single student in the building if the counselor isn't effective in the interaction.
2. **Essential Curriculum in School Counseling** A team of counselors developed an essential curriculum in school counseling that focused on academic, career, and personal/social development. They used the *ASCA National Model* as the basis for their work. This essential curriculum helped us change the focus

from what the counselor does to what students should know and be able to do as a result of the school counseling program. It also gave consistent goals and objectives for students, regardless of the school they attended.
3. **Program Planning** Counselors were asked to create a yearly plan that showed how their school counseling program aligned with the school improvement efforts. All school counseling programs have some similar elements, but each program is unique based on the needs of the school. Each plan contains milestones and evaluation components to measure program effectiveness.
4. **The Use of Data** This was one of the biggest changes that resulted from our use of the *ASCA National Model*. Counselors were asked to use data to make decisions about their programs. The data included pre- and postactivity surveys, attendance data, office referral data, suspension data, and test scores. We challenged counselors to develop more strategies to help improve academic achievement in our students.
5. **Professional Development** An increased importance was placed on professional development to help train our counselors. With all the changes in our school counseling program, there were many opportunities for professional development. The counselors in Howard County are fortunate that monthly professional development meetings are part of the culture in our county. These meetings are critical in helping counselors to integrate the components of the *ASCA National Model* into their work.
6. **A Reduction in Noncounseling Duties** Because our school counselors now had a written yearly plan to show what students should know and be able to do and data to show their effectiveness, it became easier to show that they didn't have the time to do some of the noncounseling duties they had typically been assigned. Our counselors were relieved of their duties as accountability coordinators for testing, which had traditionally taken a large chunk of time from their school counseling program.

Has it been easy to implement the *ASCA National Model* in our school counseling program? Yes and no. I have found that like most initiatives, it takes time and consistent effort to develop the buy-in among the school counselors. Those counselors who were trained in counseling programs where the *ASCA National Model* was taught generally come in and hit the ground running. The counselors who were trained before the *ASCA National Model* was developed fall into two categories: those who embrace the change and move forward and those who resist the change and hope it will go away. Although those in the last group are a challenge, they have had no choice but to join the new way of school counseling because the *ASCA National Model* has increased the importance of having an effective school counseling program in each of our schools.

Source: Lisa Boarman, Coordinator of School Counseling, Howard County Public Schools, Maryland

ROLES OF OTHER SCHOOL PERSONNEL IN THE COMPREHENSIVE SCHOOL COUNSELING PROGRAM

Although a great deal of this book focuses on the role of the professional school counselor, it is important to emphasize that the counselor is but one player in a team effort. Without collaborative partnerships with other school personnel and community agencies, it is quite likely that a professional school counselor trying to stand alone will fall flat on his or her face. Although establishing viable community partnerships is an important and evolving role of the professional school counselor and will be explored further in Chapter 14, this section will focus on school-based personnel who can become valuable partners in the comprehensive school counseling program.

Teachers

Few people can make or break the school counseling program like classroom teachers can. Teachers can serve as valuable allies of professional school counselors in many ways. First, teachers are often the implementers of developmental guidance lessons, and in large part, their competence and enthusiasm can determine the fate of numerous goals and learning objectives. Therefore, it becomes necessary to properly prepare and motivate teachers to help students to reach the established competencies. An unmotivated teacher can block access to students and derail a comprehensive program. Therefore, a golden rule of school counseling is "Always treat your teachers with respect and kindness (especially when they don't reciprocate)." Failing to do so will affect not only your relationship with that teacher, but also often your access to that teacher's students.

Teachers also serve as excellent referral sources for children in need of counseling services. Teachers not only see their students daily, but also see the friends of students in need. A tuned-in teacher misses little and can effectively encourage troubled youth to seek needed help. In addition, teachers are a valuable source of information for needs assessments and program evaluations. Their input is vital to understanding the needs of a school community, as well as the effectiveness of the school counseling program interventions.

It may seem strange to start this section off with teachers, rather than the principal, but although principals often have more policy-making authority at the school level, teachers hold the power over what does and does not happen in the classroom. A seasoned professional school counselor understands this and seeks to bond strongly with all teachers. In summary, if you take good care of your teachers, your teachers will take good care of you.

Resource Teachers

Resource teachers take many forms in different states, but generally include special education teachers, reading specialists, speech and language pathologists, and behavior intervention specialists. Special education teachers are especially important to connect with in schools because special education students are often underserved by professional school counselors. Connecting with special education teachers is one way to ensure that *all* students receive comprehensive school counseling services. Students in need of special education often require specialized services related to social and study skills, and their teachers are often open to program-related suggestions to meet these needs. Like professional school counselors, resource teachers have special expertise that makes them invaluable consultants and referral sources. The experienced professional school counselor explores the specific strengths of these professionals and does not hesitate to call on them when the need arises.

Principals and Assistant Principals

Principals and their assistants contribute to many important facets of the comprehensive school counseling program. They frequently serve on the school counseling program advisory committee and provide support and leadership to that committee when necessary. The principal provides resources and contributes to the working environment, while defending the counselor from role diffusion and "noncounseling" tasks—although this is a bit like the fox guarding the henhouse.

Administrators can also play a vital role in facilitating needs assessments and evaluations of the comprehensive school counseling program, as well as communicating to the public the importance of a developmental program.

School Psychologists

School psychologists are specially trained to provide psychological services in a school environment. In many states, school psychologists are relegated to simply providing psychoeducational testing to determine a child's eligibility for special education or Section 504 services. However, many school systems have greatly expanded the school psychologist's role to allow for consultation with parents and school personnel, case management of special-needs children, and counseling with severely behavior-disordered or emotionally disturbed students. Developing a strong collaborative relationship with the school psychologist is an excellent strategy for beginning to address the needs of a school's most serious cases. School psychologists and counselors are often on the front lines together when it comes to intervening with dangerous and suicidal students.

School Social Workers (Visiting Teachers, Pupil Personnel Workers)

School social workers (sometimes called visiting teachers or pupil personnel workers, depending on the state or locale) often conduct sociological assessments for child study proceedings and work with needy families to secure social, financial, and medical services. They are frequently valuable sources of information on families and communities and serve as liaisons between the school and public heath facilities.

School Nurses

School nurses provide a wide range of health services, depending on the state. Nurses monitor the medications taken by students in school and often facilitate teacher feedback on the effectiveness of those medications when requested by physicians. Nurses also conduct hearing and vision screening and are a valuable ally of professional school counselors on developmental matters such as hygiene, personal safety, and physical and sexual development. School nurses also frequently come in contact with students with anxiety disorders, depression, eating disorders, reproductive issues, and phobias and can serve as valuable referral and information sources.

Secretaries

The climate of a school often rises and falls with the quality of the secretarial staff. Secretaries are usually the first contacts parents have with the school or school counseling program—and you never get a second chance to make a first impression. Experienced administrators and professional school counselors make clear their expectations for how secretaries and other staff are to treat the public—including the students. Secretaries are often among the first to encounter parents and students in crisis, and the respectfulness, sensitivity, and efficiency with which they handle these situations speak volumes about the school climate. Finally, one need not be employed in an office environment long to realize that a secretary can make you look very good—or very incompetent. Always treat your secretary with great respect.

CULTURAL REFLECTION 2.2

How might professional school counselors from diverse cultural backgrounds view the importance of collaboration with various school personnel as partners in enhancing children's educational achievement, access, and opportunity? How might students, parents, and educators from diverse backgrounds view various school personnel as partners enhancing children's educational achievement, access, and opportunity? What cultural barriers and access points might exist?

Summary/Conclusion

The ASCA *National Standards* and *ASCA National Model* have had a positive effect on the service delivery proficiency of professional school counselors. The *National Standards* provide a guide for implementing curricular goals and competencies across the domains of student academic, career, and personal/social development. The *National Model* provides a framework for describing, implementing, and evaluating a comprehensive developmental school counseling program. The model includes four themes that are infused throughout the program: leadership, advocacy, collaboration and teaming, and systemic change.

However, the heart of the program is the four primary program components: program foundation, delivery system, management system, and accountability. The program foundation, the "what" of a comprehensive school counseling program, makes clear what every student will know and be able to do as a result of the school counseling program and includes the program's beliefs and philosophies, mission, domains (i.e., academic, career, personal/social), standards, and competencies. The delivery system is the "how" of the comprehensive developmental school counseling program. As professional school counselors implement their programs, they include the guidance curriculum, individual student planning, responsive services (e.g., individual and group counseling, referral, consultation), and systems support (e.g., professional development, collaboration). The management system accounts for the "when," "why," and "on what authority" of program implementation and includes management agreements, school counseling program advisory committees (SCPACs), use of data, action plans, calendars, and use of time. The SCPAC is a diverse group of stakeholders and can be helpful in guiding the program in positive directions through understanding and meeting the needs of the school community. The SCPAC can also play an important role in securing resources and demonstrating accountability. Accountability answers the all-important question of "How are students different as a result of the program?" It includes results reports, performance standards, and program audits.

Finally, the roles of other school personnel as they have an impact on the comprehensive school counseling program were discussed. Professional school counselors should develop partnerships with teachers, resource teachers, administrators, school psychologists, school social workers, school nurses, and secretaries to help facilitate and smoothly implement the comprehensive school counseling program.

Activities

1. Survey the schools in your area, and find out how many of the school counseling programs follow *ASCA's National Model*. For those that do, how long did it take the school counselor to fully implement the model? How does ASCA's model compare to the program the school counselor had before? Summarize your findings.

2. Compose a hypothetical mission statement for a high school counseling program and draft a philosophical statement that includes your beliefs about student learning and the principles that would guide you in the creation of your school counseling program.

3. Using the *ASCA National Model*'s lists of appropriate and inappropriate activities for school counselors, interview local school counselors and determine how many appropriate and inappropriate activities they currently engage in. Summarize your findings.

4. Interview someone who works at a local school who is not a school counselor. Ask that person to describe his or her relationship with the school counselor. Do they collaborate? How often do they work together or consult with one another? What is his or her perception of the school counselor's role? Summarize your findings.

3

Transformational Thinking in Today's Schools

Patricia J. Martin*

E ditor's Introduction: Transforming school counseling involves changing its substance and appearance. The changes encouraged in this text are not cosmetic but deep, meaningful changes that encourage professional school counselors to become agents of education reform and social change. The effective professional school counselor seeks to remove barriers to educational, career, and personal/social development, whether for a single student or an entire society. Although professional school counselors are usually pursuing a common purpose, each one must understand and integrate the school's mission and goals, the needs of the school community, and his or her own strengths into a systemic, comprehensive, developmental school counseling program. Such an approach adds uniqueness to each program, while ensuring that needs are addressed in a comprehensive manner.

THE SCHOOL: THE PRIMARY WORKPLACE FOR SCHOOL COUNSELORS

The 21st century brings a new age in the profession of school counseling, one in which traditional methods must be transformed to meet current and future challenges. Professional school counseling must evolve into a model that will both fit the needs of the students in this rapidly changing society and conform to the demands of school reform and accountability mandates, as well as workforce demands. The national movement toward preparing all students to be college and career ready will require that professional school counselors develop and/or increase their capacity to work as leaders and advocates in schools to remove barriers to student success. Equitable educational outcomes for all student groups (broken down by race/ethnicity, gender, socioeconomic status, students with disabilities, students for whom English is a second language, etc.) measured by results like promotion and graduation rates, rates of participation and success in rigorous courses, academic course-taking patterns, as well as college-going rates have become benchmarks for school success.

The Context of Professional School Counseling

A system is an interconnected complex of functionally related components that work together to try to accomplish the aim of the system.

—W. Edwards Deming

---

*The first and second editions of this chapter were coauthored by Dr. Reese M. House, may he rest in peace. I wish to acknowledge the contributions of Stephanie G. Robinson to the third edition of this chapter.

Professional school counselors work in schools and therefore must be knowledgeable about the venue in which they must effectively practice. School counseling is one component of a complex education system that is being held accountable for educating today's students to a higher level of academic proficiency than ever before. School counselors must therefore exit from preservice training programs with the knowledge and skills that will prepare them to function effectively in systems with policies and practices that affect all participants. As a result, school counselor education must provide an understanding of the new mission of schools, how schools function, and the school counselor's accountability for helping schools achieve the mission—to educate all students to high levels so that they have the skills and knowledge that will enable them to lead a productive life in a democratic and global society.

Schools are systems undergoing reform. This reform effort is requiring an assessment of the inputs, processes, and outcomes of the schools' systemic components. Much attention has been given to the components of curriculum, teaching and learning, and assessment. There has been considerable emphasis on making sure that the inputs and processes of the systemic components are aligned with the new mission of schools to deliver the desired academic outcomes for students in these schools. Likewise, the transformed school counseling profession must align the inputs, processes, and outcomes of its programs for students with the new mission of schools. Preservice training for school counselors must prepare them with the knowledge and skills needed to align the goals of their comprehensive school counseling programs with the academic achievement goals of the school. In addition, this alignment must be done with an intentional focus on equitable outcomes and future postsecondary options for all students, especially underserved student populations. Success resulting from comprehensive school counseling programs must be measured in hard data elements that are consistent with the ones for which the whole school/district is being held accountable.

Schools are multifaceted institutional systems that operate according to a set of norms that govern the behavior of people within those systems. Each system—in this case, the school—is governed by both written and unwritten policies and practices that are implemented, maintained, and institutionalized by people who, for the most part, believe that these actions are necessary to achieve the results they seek for the students, families, and communities they serve.

> *When placed in the same system, people, however different, tend to produce similar results.*
> —Peter Senge

Professional school counselors are part of an educational system that has historically produced disparate results for different populations of students and has thus ensured unequal future life opportunities and choices for many young people. Changing the outcomes for underachieving student populations will require that the inputs and processes accepted and traditionally implemented by all professionals in the school system be examined, altered, reconstructed, or deleted.

Most important, the transforming school counseling movement must be an effort that adds value to school reforms designed to change the educational outcomes for students in schools today. School counseling is a critically important professional component among the many components that make schools work. The transformed school counselor must function in schools in an interdependent, interconnected fashion to meet the 21st-century goal of educating all students to higher levels of literacy, numeracy, and analytic functioning than ever before achieved. Consequently, the word *school* in the title *professional school counselor* has incredible significance for what is expected of the professionals who occupy this role in K–12 public schools today.

In this chapter, we discuss the forces driving change in schools and the implications of those changes for professional school counselors. The resulting changes in education policy and the implications for school counselors are discussed at length, as are the changes in practice that will be required for school counseling to remain a viable component of the educational system. Finally, we posit some changes that school counselor educators must make to ensure the viability of the profession.

FOUR FORCES DRIVING CHANGE IN SCHOOLS

Public schools have been "reforming" almost constantly since their inception. However, the impetus for change in the early 1990s was occasioned by several factors including, but not limited to, the following: (a) inequities in the educational system, (b) changes in the nation's demographics and school populations, (c) changes in the economy and the workplace, and (d) major changes in education public policy. Each of these will be explored in the following sections.

Inequities in the Educational System

In the 1980s, the nation's attention was directed to the inequities in the educational system by the seminal report *A Nation at Risk* (National Commission on Excellence in Education, 1983), which concluded that the educational system in the United States lagged behind those of other industrialized nations in meeting world-class educational standards. The report identified the decline in student performance in the United States as a function of curriculum content, expectations, time spent on academics, and teaching. The report decried the watered-down "cafeteria"-style high school curriculum and the migration of students from more rigorous courses to the "general" course track.

One of the significant observations in the report was that the United States' educational system lacked a set of coherent academic content standards to define what all students should know and be able to do as a result of their 12 years of public education. The report went on to recommend that the high school core curriculum be strengthened, along with stiffer graduation requirements. The *Nation at Risk* report also issued recommendations for strengthening science instruction and teacher education. The report, however, did not identify education inequities relative to race, gender, or disabiity in relation to differences in student performance.

Subsequent to this report, the Commission on Chapter 1 (1992)—a group of policy makers, education practitioners, researchers, and grantmakers—issued a seminal report, which identified structural inequities in the educational system that contributed to the problems cited in the *Nation at Risk* report. This commission's report highlighted the systemic barriers that contribute to (a) the poor achievement/underachievement of students of color and students from low-income families and (b) the achievement gap that exists between these students and their more affluent peers. According to the Commission on Chapter 1 (1992) and the Education Trust (2005), the achievement gap among students exists primarily because schools that serve poor students and large numbers of students of color consistently

- Expect and demand less in the way of academic performance of children of color and those from low-income families.
- Provide these same students with watered-down, weak curriculum that lacks academic content rigor.
- Assign inexperienced and the least-qualified teachers to students who have the most serious academic need.
- Provide fewer material resources to students who have the greatest needs. In fact, studies show that school-funding formulas too often shortchange the schools that serve the most educationally needy students.

In short, the educational system systematically and consistently provides less to students who have the greatest educational needs (Haycock, 2009). These deep, structural inequities went mostly unnoticed by the general public and many policy makers. In addition, these inequities were ignored by too many educators and school support personnel, including school counselors. Like the educators in the system, many professional school counselors acceded to the policies often without realizing the implications for their students. On the other hand, other school counselors, through herculean efforts, labored valiantly to save, push, and encourage individual students to achieve success, often by circumventing policy barriers. Even so, currently there remain too many schools across the nation where some groups of students (those who have been historically underserved) remain systematically excluded from the quality curriculum and instruction that would prepare them to be successful in the workplace and in postsecondary settings. The educational system that operates in this manner represents an inherently inequitable state of affairs that professional school counselors are obliged to address. As a profession, school counseling has prided itself on being in the forefront of issues related to social justice and competency in multicultural knowledge and practice. As education reform shifts its emphasis from implementing programmatic interventions for some students to patch up a broken system to making changes in the policies and practices that inhibit student and educator success, so, too, must the school counseling profession shift to systemic interventions. The school counseling profession must connect its actions to changing the systemic problems that contribute to student failure (Education Trust, 2005).

Changes in the Nation's Demographics and School Populations

This passage from the *Prospectus* (2001) of Teachers for a New Era captures some of the titanic changes occurring in the U.S. demography:

> There are today in the United States more adherents of Islam than there are Episcopalians. More than 70% of the pupils in the Los Angeles unified school district are immigrants from Latin America, as are more than 50% of the pupils in Dodge City, Kansas. In many of the nation's largest cities, some districts are composed by majorities of more than 90% of pupils whose parents are Americans with family histories hundreds of years old on this continent and of African descent. In many communities Asian families form an imposing majority, and everywhere a current tide of immigration from throughout the world is affecting the makeup of the nation's classrooms. (p. 2)

The implications of these changes for school counselor practice and school counselor education are discussed in a later section of this chapter.

The elementary and secondary school demographic changes occurring in the United States constitute another catalyst for change in the educational system, as Figure 3.1 indicates. Communities and schools are changing as a result of immigration, declining birthrates among some populations, and the general aging of the population. To maintain the nation's status as a world power and to protect and maintain the democratic way of life, it is imperative that the educational system educate all its citizens. We need an educated population for the United States to maintain its position as a world leader and an economic and social power and to maintain its thriving democratic society. Being "educated" in this society entails more than just acquiring the basic skills of reading (decoding) and writing. We need a population that is literate, able to think analytically, and scientifically and mathematically literate. We need citizens who are knowledgeable about world cultures, can make informed decisions based on data, and can think critically about the data they use. Given the demographic changes indicated in Figure 3.1, we must have an educational system where "all" means "all." Resources must be distributed equitably, based on student need (i.e., those who need more should get more) if we are to meet the mandate to educate all students to higher levels of academic proficiency.

Changes in the Economy and the Workplace

The global economy, technological advances, and the explosion of knowledge in science and related fields have resulted in major changes in the workplace, the way we work, and the requirements for success in the workplace. In the past, professional school counselors could support the placement of students into less-demanding courses, possibly without considering this action a severe detriment to the students' future life options. This is no longer the case because all students need to be provided with the opportunity to master challenging academic content to participate successfully in the local and global economies.

There have been significant increases in the skills and knowledge required for success at all levels in the 21st-century workplace—from entry-level to professional jobs. According to Achieve, Inc. (2004), an organization that has studied requirements for success in the workplace and college, the skills and knowledge needed for success in the 21st-century workplace are essentially the same as those needed for success in a postsecondary education setting. For example, building engineers (formerly known as building custodians) must master mathematics and technology because many functions required for building maintenance are computerized. Doctors must understand the latest scientific discoveries that affect medical advances. Twenty-first-century entry-level jobs require analytic and literacy skills and problem-solving competencies, as well as the ability to work successfully in teams.

As Figure 3.2 indicates, just when a more highly skilled workforce and more highly educated citizens are needed, the educational system is producing an over-abundance of high school graduates and a dearth of two-

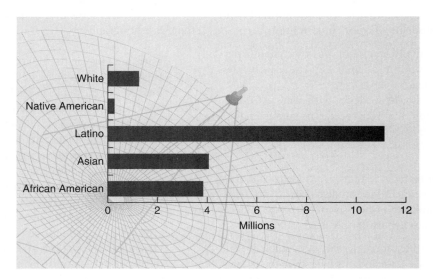

FIGURE 3.1   The demographics of the United States are changing rapidly: Projected increase in the population of 25- to 64-year-olds, 2000 to 2020.

Source: U.S. Census Bureau (2009). Retrieved from http://www.census.gov/population/www/projections/usinterimproj

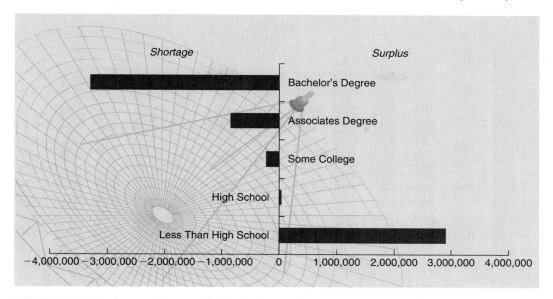

FIGURE 3.2 There is a growing need for higher levels of education: Projections of education shortages and surpluses in 2012.

Source: Analysis by Anthony Carnevale (2006) of Current Population Surveys (1992–2004) and U.S. Census population projection estimates.

and four-year college graduates. This mismatch of talent to the needs in the workplace is potentially disastrous to our country. This trend is a threat to our democracy and our economy and must be staunched by an educational system that teaches all students to achieve high levels of academic proficiency.

In the United States and in the global workplace, the economic demand for a more knowledgeable workforce equipped to work in an ever-expanding technological world is growing. Concurrent with these demands, school reform is being driven by data that indicate the student population is increasingly more diverse and now includes higher numbers of students of color, students from low-income families, and students who are English language learners living in urban and rural communities. These students need additional academic and social supports to succeed. Educational institutions have not served these populations well in the past and are faced with dire consequences if the job is not done better (Lee, 2005).

Concurrent with the need for more highly skilled workers, especially in the fields of science, engineering, and technology, the academic performance of U.S. students is being surpassed by the students in industrialized competitor countries (American Institutes for Research, 2005). Not only are these countries graduating higher percentages of students from high schools and college, but also the students typically have mastered rigorous science

and mathematics curricula. Many more of these students are graduating with the technical, mathematical, and scientific knowledge demanded by the 21st-century world job market than in the United States. Students in the United States consistently score lower on international assessments of mathematics and science than do students in other industrialized and even some nonindustrialized nations. Most distressing is that U.S. students' performance levels decrease as they move through the system, as indicated by Figures 3.3 and 3.4.

Major Changes in Education Public Policy

Changes in demographics and workplace skill requirements, as well as recognition of the inequities in the educational system, spurred significant education policy changes in the current school reform movement. In the early 1990s, American education began its not-yet-completed shift to a standards-based system of education. An agreed-upon set of content standards in the major academic subject areas would guide instruction for all students. Reforms in assessment and accountability were designed to produce a more equitable educational system.

The 1994 reauthorization of the *Elementary and Secondary Education Act* (ESEA)—also known as the Improving America's Schools Act—brought a sea change to the educational landscape. The ESEA required all schools to educate students from low-income families

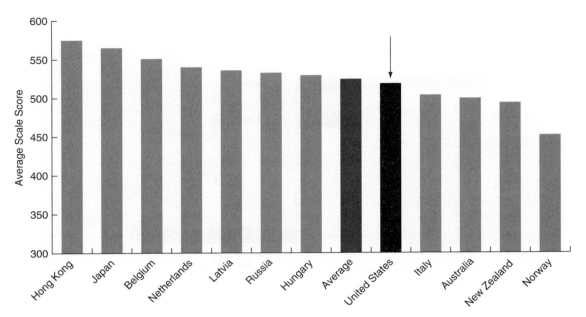

FIGURE 3.3 TIMSS grade 4 mathematics, 2003.
Source: American Institutes for Research (2005, November).

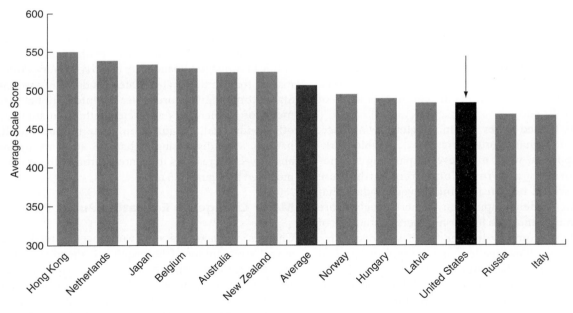

FIGURE 3.4 PISA mathematics, 15-year-olds, 2003.
Source: American Institutes for Research (2005, November).

according to the same challenging academic content stand- ards used by all other schools (i.e., schools serving students from affluent families). Under the new law, states were responsible for developing the challenging academic standards, aligning rigorous criterion-referenced assess- ments to the standards, and implementing accountability systems to measure progress of all groups of students

toward meeting the standards. Under these new policies, virtually all students would be expected to reach proficient levels on the challenging state academic standards.

The ESEA instituted another deep policy change, a change from a focus on measuring inputs to one on meas- uring success. For example, the previous focus may have assessed "*How many computers were purchased* with Title 1 funds?" whereas the current focus now measures results such as "*What have students learned* when they used the computers that were bought with Title 1 funds?" This change from using inputs to using the students' academic learning as the measure of success constituted an enormous change for educators. For the first time, public policy put the accountability for student learning (not just teaching) squarely on the shoulders of educators. Those accountable for student learning ranged from the classroom teacher to the superintendent. Schools and districts that consistently failed to raise student achievement had to improve or face consequences—all of this in the glare of public opinion. For many educators, the idea that they were accountable for successfully educating students whom they previously deemed unable to learn constituted a brand-new experience.

The requirement that state accountability plans document the progress that groups of students made toward attaining proficient levels on the state standards was another feature of the new law. States, districts, and schools had to measure the achievement gap that separated students from low-income families and students of color from their more affluent peers and identify how they would close that gap. In short, for the first time all states, districts, and schools receiving federal support from Title 1 of the ESEA would be accountable for the academic results of all students—both what students learned and their progress toward meeting proficiency levels on state standards.

The new accountability system was supported by a mandate to report disaggregated achievement data not only to educators, but also to parents and the public in an understandable format. Public reporting is still being worked on in many states. This mandate for public reporting of educational data was instituted so that states, districts, schools, and communities (and especially parents) could monitor the progress that groups of students made toward attaining proficiency on state academic standards. In other words, school systems must now expect all groups of students to achieve proficient levels of academic work, measure each group's progress toward proficiency, and provide public monitoring of the process. This sweeping policy change altered the landscape for educators, professional school counselors, and other support personnel in schools. For example, school counselors, working as ancillary professionals in schools and not directly connected to the new mandates for accountability for the school success of all students, sometimes found themselves being viewed as "would be nice to have, but not essential to the mission of schools."

With data more available to them than ever before, parents, community advocates, policy makers, and professional school counselors are equipped with the tools to measure student success and to develop and implement policies and practices that will promote academic success for all students. For the first time, professionals and parents had disaggregated data they could use to monitor more closely the progress of groups of students traditionally underserved by the system. These data revealed just how inequitable the system was in some cases.

As required by law, the ESEA was reauthorized in 2000 and came to be known as the No Child Left Behind (NCLB) Act. NCLB is a contiuation the 1994 reauthorization. It stregthened the accountability provisions of the orginal law because these requirements were being ignored for the most part by states and districts. NCLB, among other changes, requires states to set time lines for closing acheivement gaps and to set a 12-year time frame for getting all students to proficiency. Accountability was strengthened by adding a formula to track student progress. Schools had to make enough progress toward meeting standards, called adequate yearly progress (AYP), that all groups would meet proficient levels by a time certain—at most 12 years into the future. The outcry from educators was deafening, and as of this writing, the law is due for reauthorization, and changes are expected in the time frame. However, the basic concepts of high standards for all students, accountability of educators and educational systems for results, and public reporting of data will still hold. All these forces for change in schools have profound implications for school counselor training and practice. The accountability policies affect all the professionals in the educational system.

CULTURAL REFLECTION 3.1

How might professional school counselors-in-training, school students, parents, and educators from diverse backgrounds view these four factors driving change in American education as each relates to enhancing children's educational achievement, access, and opportunity? What cultural barriers and access points might exist?

EDUCATION REFORM

The College and Career Readiness Policy and School Reform

The policy to promote college-level learning for all students is a response to changes in the demographic and economic landscape. Over the last 15 years, educators, policy makers, community groups, and business leaders across the nation have worked in venues as diverse as boardrooms, legislative arenas, school districts, and universities,

FROM THE PRESIDENT

In a global economy where the most valuable skill you can sell is your knowledge, a good education is no longer just a pathway to opportunity—it is a prerequisite.... I ask every American to commit to at least one year or more of higher education or career training. This can be community college or a four-year school, vocational training or an apprenticeship. But whatever the training may be, every American will need to get more than a high school diploma.

—President Barack Obama

and even at kitchen tables, to reform K–16 education. Recently, these efforts received a very public boost when the National Governors Association (NGA) proclaimed high school reform in America a highest priority and declared that students must graduate from high school ready for college, work, and citizenship (Gates, 2005). Partly as a result of this attention, most states have increased their graduation requirements and are requiring students to complete a rigorous curriculum in the core courses of mathematics, science, English/language

arts, and foreign language. States have eliminated their "seat time" diploma in favor of a diploma that represents successful completion of such courses.

By 2010, the Common Core State Standards Initiative became the driver of the national movement toward preparing all students to graduate from high school being college and career ready. The Common Core State Standards Initiative, a state-led effort spearheaded by the National Governors Association (NGA) and the Council of Chief State School Officers (CCSSO) developed a set of robust standards for English Language Arts and Mathematics that has been adopted by 46 states and 3 territories. The Common Core State Standards made clear what K–12 students are expected to learn and what teachers should teach at each grade level. The standards made transparent what skills and knowledge students needed to become college and career ready, thereby becoming prepared for futures that would enable the students to compete successfully in a global society.

Policies moving the previous K–12 education outcomes expectations from simply graduating students from high school to making all graduating students college and career ready are quantum leaps given that educational systems previously had different curricular requirements for different students. The change is driven by the national need for the United States to continue its prominence as a world leader and workforce demands for a more educated workforce. Figure 3.5 shows the dramatic increase in

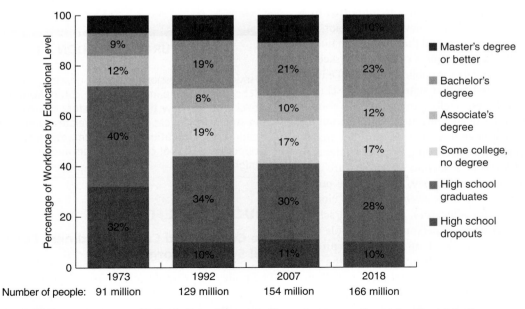

FIGURE 3.5 By 2018 two thirds of all employment will require some college education or better.
Source: Carnevale, A. P., Smith, N., & Strohl, J. (June 2010). *Help wanted projections of jobs and education requirements through 2018* (p. 14). Retrieved from http://www9.georgetown.edu/grad/gppi/hpi/cew/pdfs/FullReport.pdf

employment opportunities that require some postsecondary education or a college degree from 1973 to projections for 2018, where two thirds of all employment will require some postsecondary education or a college degree.

Later, this chapter will explore the significant implications these changes in policies have for the practice of school counseling and what school counselors need to know and do to be successful. To work effectively in today's schools, professional school counselors must be knowledgeable about the academic side of the education house and collaborate with other professionals in the school to ensure that policies are equitably implemented. Not only must all students be able to access challenging rigorous content, but also schools must have the support systems in place for those students who need them.

CHANGING TIMES, CHANGING DEMANDS

Maintenance workers in modern buildings, such as the newly constructed mega conference centers and office buildings, must be computer literate. Upon summoning a "janitor" to change the room temperature in one of these centers, we learned that he was the building engineer and that the room temperature was controlled by a central computer system, which he had to access to change the room temperature.

Teachers, students, and school administrators visited a car manufacturing plant owned by a foreign car company and built in a southern rural county of the United States. The visitors were stunned to learn that entry-level jobs (no postsecondary training) required mastery of trigonometry.

Policies That Promote College-Level Rigor for All Students Drive Changes in School Counselor Practice

As is so often the case in the initiation of sweeping education reforms, there is a lag between policy adoption and successful implementation. As noted earlier, systems and the people in them tend to perpetuate behavior even when the behavior is no longer appropriate. In other words, old habits die hard. For example, the practice of sorting students into those who are college bound and those who are not is proving very resistant to change. "Guiding" students into college-bound and non-college-bound education "tracks" seemed like the correct action to take as long as education policies supported the differentiated content in the two tracks. The sorting practice helped to perpetuate the multitiered curricular tracking system—the college-bound curriculum for some, the "general" curriculum for

others, and the technical and "business" tracks for still others. The movement toward college-level content for all students makes these tracking practices unnecessary. These changes requiring college-level rigorous coursework do not negate additional opportunities for students to take content courses in business, technology, and other technical fields. However, because of the mandated levels of academic proficiency, students pursuing these interest areas must not be tracked out of the rigorous courses. It is this rigorous course work that will enable students to reach required proficiency and keep their options open for postsecondary education and academic training beyond high school. Sadly, meeting the mandate for rigorous course work for all students in some schools across the nation, in the past, ended up being a pretense, giving a course a "rigorous" label such as Algebra 1, but providing content that is actually advanced basic arithmetic and bears little resemblance to the real algebra content needed for both college and work readiness. Because of the Common Core State Standards, this practice will no longer be easily continued, as shortcomings will be made apparent through the use of common assessments that will measure, with consistency across the nation, the skills and knowledge students are expected to acquire in rigorous classes.

Expecting all students to achieve at proficient levels makes obsolete the long-standing practice by school systems and counselors of sorting students into college-bound and non-college-bound categories. All students are now to be educated to academic levels that will allow them to make the choice to enter postsecondary training without the need for remediation—and succeed. Professional school counselors must turn their attention to helping all students succeed in a challenging curriculum and working to change policies and practices that are impediments. Professional school counselors also need to help develop and implement institutional policies to ensure that all students have access to the challenging curriculum.

The lines between college preparatory courses and other courses have blurred as far as content is concerned. All students must have the opportunity to learn challenging core academic subjects. The delivery of the content can vary greatly from "vocational" settings to community classrooms and laboratories, but under the new policy, the goal is for all students to receive the same rigorous academic experiences. If some students are not getting challenging work, professional school counselors must develop comprehensive plans to eliminate this type of barrier to school success. They can use academic standards to gauge whether or not all students are actually receiving the rigorous curriculum to which they are entitled and which school districts are obligated to provide. Academic content standards, when translated into documents that the public can understand, provide powerful tools to support advocacy efforts and a high-quality education to all students. When fully implemented, the Common Core State Standards, which call for teaching high-level academic content and stipulate college and career readiness outcomes for all students, will help make equity in educational outcomes a reality.

The transformed school counselor, while addressing the needs of individual students, will have an eye on the institutional policies and practices that impede student progress. For example, the professional school counselor may gather data on the achievement patterns of groups of students in different levels of academic classes to highlight differences in acheivement that may be the result of variations in the intensity of the curriculum to which the students are exposed, rather than their lack of ability. This difference in exposure to challeging content is a major contributor to the achievement gap.

Studies (Achieve, Inc., 2005; Johnson, Arumi, & Ott, 2006) have indicated that most students want to be challenged, and indeed, many feel their high school experiences are not challenging at all. Professional school counselors deal with the behavioral results of student malaise and boredom every day by applying programs to help these students change their behavior. In some instances, the behavior may be a reaction to an "unhealthy" school situation. School counselors have the skills to determine the reasons for student behavior and to develop comprehensive interventions to address the root causes of student failure.

An earlier discussion focused on how changes in the economy and changing demands in the workplace add to the notion that all students need to be prepared for success at the postsecondary level or in the workplace. As noted in Figure 3.6, the greatest growth in workers in the past two decades has been in workers with some postsecondary education. It is important for professional school counselors to know that 46 states and two territories have adopted the Common Core State Standards (CCSS) with the stated outcome for all students to graduate college and career ready. Transformed school counselors must focus on practices to ensure that this policy creates a stepping stone, rather than a barrier, to better opportunities in life for all students by ensuring that they get the academic, social, and emotional support they need to meet the new requirements.

TRANSFORMING THE SCHOOL COUNSELING PROFESSION

School Reforms Prompt the Transforming School Counseling Movement

Because of the many changes in schools and the world (e.g., demograhics of students enrolled in schools; public policies, including state and federal mandates for increases in student achievement; workplace demands for more educated workers and a better educated citizenry), all educational professionals must be involved in educating children

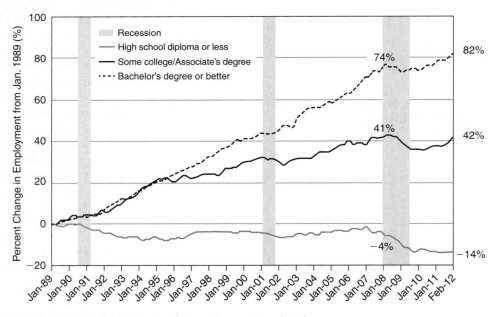

FIGURE 3.6 Employment growth over the past two decades.
Source: Georgetown Public Policy Institute, Georgetown Center on Education and the Workforce (August 2012). *The college advantage: Weathering the economic storm* (p. 10). Retrieved from http://www9.georgetown.edu/grad/gppi/hpi/cew/pdfs/CollegeAdvantage.FullReport.081512.pdf

for a new global economy. School counseling, along with all other components of the educational system, was subject to review, change, and/or reorganization. The stage was set for changes in school counseling that brought the profession from a position of ancillary support to one of leadership and advocacy, supporting school success for all students. The Education Trust, the American School Counselor Association (ASCA), and the College Board stepped forward with actions that were far reaching and are still pivotal in guiding the transformation of the profession.

> *Vision is the capacity to create and communicate a view of a desired state of affairs that induces commitment among those working in an organization.*
> —Thomas Sergiovanni

The Transforming School Counseling Initiative

The forces pushing for change in education and the resulting revisions in education policies cited earlier provided the impetus for the Transforming School Counseling Initiative (TSCI), which was developed at the Education Trust beginning in 1994 and is continuing its work to transform policies

and practices in the field. Supported by a grant from the DeWitt Wallace Foundation, the TSCI was built on the premise that school counseling, as a profession, had to move from a focus primarily on fixing individual students to one on removing the systemic barriers to student success for whole groups of students. Although still serving some individual students, to achieve equitable results for all students, the systemic barriers that hinder all students had to be addressed by the profession. Initially, TSCI worked to change preservice training of school counselors so that newly trained practitioners would enter the profession with the knowledge and skills needed to perform effectively in 21st-century schools, where accountability for students' academic success had become the focus of the nation.

The new vision for school counseling that was developed and distributed by the Education Trust (1996) through the TSCI emphasized changes that would align the school counselors' role with new educational changes and mandates for educators in schools (House & Martin, 1998). This new vision highlighted movement of the professional school counselor from engaging in traditional practice to being a proactive change agent and advocate who focuses on supporting and creating pathways that allow all students to have school success (see Table 3.1).

TABLE 3.1 Transformation of the Role of Professional School Counselor

Present Focus	New Vision
Mental health issues	Academic and student achievement
Individual student concerns and issues	Whole school and system concerns and issues
Clinical model focused on student deficits	Academic focus, building on student strengths
Providing service, one-to-one and small groups	Leading, planning, and developing programs
Primary focus on personal/social	Focus on academic counseling, learning and achievement, supporting student success
Ancillary support personnel	Integral members of educational team
Loosely defined role and responsibility	Focusing on mission and role identification
Record keeping	Using data to effect change
Sorting, selecting course placement process	Advocating inclusion in rigorous preparation for all, especially students from low-income and minority families
Work in isolation or with other counselors	Teaming and collaboration with all educators in school in resolving issues involving the whole school and community
Guarding the status quo	Acting as change agent, especially for educational equity for all students
Involvement primarily with students	Involvement with students, parents, education professionals, community, and community agencies
Little or no accountability	Full accountability for student success, use of data, planning and preparation for access to wide range of postsecondary options
Dependence on use of system's resources for helping students and families	Brokering services for parents and students from community resources/agencies, as well as school system's resources
Postsecondary planning with interested students	Creating pathways for all students to achieve high aspirations

This new vision created considerable upheaval, as well as a great deal of discussion, in the counseling field. Change in school counseling being posited by an organization that was virtually unknown by leaders in the counseling field was difficult to accept, even though in subsequent years many of the conceptual changes put forth by the Education Trust have been embraced by the ASCA, school leaders, and counselor educators.

Teaming, collaboration, advocacy, leadership, and use of data to effect change are the linchpins for the TSCI's structured changes in the way professional school counselors should be trained. The universities involved in the TSCI addressed changes in their pre-service training programs to align with the new vision. They also revised practices in the areas of candidate selection; curriculum content and structure and sequence of courses; methods of instruction, including field experiences and practice; practicum experiences; induction into the profession; and working relationships with community partnerships. In 1998, using a grant from the Met Life Foundation, the TSCI turned its attention to changing the way practicing counselors work and continued pushing for a focus on academic counseling, advocacy, and collaboration with colleagues in the educational system. Leadership, advocacy, teaming and collaboration, counseling and coordination, and assessments and use of data with accountability for results became the foundation for reforming practice and preservice training (see Table 3.2).

National Standards for School Counseling Programs

In 1997, the ASCA published *The National Standards for School Counseling Programs* (Campbell & Dahir, 1997), consisting of nine standards, three each in the domains of academic, career, and personal/social development. The *National Standards* provided a standardized basis for the creation of comprehensive, developmental guidance programs. The competencies (i.e., the knowledge and skills to be acquired) that accompanied the *National Standards* led the way to development of comprehensive school counseling curricula in school districts. The *National Standards* gave direction to a profession searching for ways to solidify an identity and role in standards-based school reform. They provided professional school counselors in districts across the nation with a common set of expectations for each of the three ASCA domains: academic, career, and personal/social development. Metrics for students' achievement of proficiency in accomplishing the *National Standards*, however, were not addressed, as the standards were not written in the format of course content standards with student outcomes. Nonetheless, the *National Standards* became unifying elements that helped professional school counselors find ways to respond affirmatively that school counseling was a discipline in schools with standards that resembled those of other content disciplines (e.g., math, science, social studies).

TABLE 3.2 New Vision for Professional School Counselors

Leadership	Advocacy and Systemic Change	Teaming and Collaboration	Counseling and Coordination	Assessment and Use of Data
Promoting, planning, and implementing prevention programs, career and college activities, course selection and placement activities, social/personal management, and decision-making activities	Making available and using data to help the whole school look at student outcomes	Participating in or consulting with teams for problem solving; ensuring responsiveness to equity and cultural diversity issues, as well as learning styles	Providing brief counseling of individual students, groups, and families	Assessing and interpreting student needs and recognizing differences in culture, languages, values, and backgrounds
Providing data snapshots of student outcomes, showing implications and achievement gaps, and providing leadership for school to view through equity lens	Using data to effect change; calling on resources from school and community	Collaborating with other helping agents (peer helpers, teachers, principal, community agencies, business)	Coordinating resources, human and other, for students, families, and staff to improve student achievement (community, school, home)	Establishing and assessing measurable goals for student outcomes from counseling programs, activities, interventions, and experiences

Leadership	Advocacy and Systemic Change	Teaming and Collaboration	Counseling and Coordination	Assessment and Use of Data
Arranging one-to-one relationships for students with adults in school setting for additional support and assistance in reaching academic success	Advocating student experiences and exposures that will broaden students' career awareness and knowledge	Collaborating with school and community teams to focus on rewards, incentives, and supports for student achievement	Working as key liaison with students and school staff to set high aspirations for all students and develop plans and supports for achieving these aspirations	Assessing building barriers that impede learning, inclusion, and/or academic success for students
Playing a leadership role in defining and carrying out the guidance and counseling function	Advocating student placement and school support for rigorous preparation for all students	Collaborating with school staff members in developing staff training on team responses to students' academic, social, emotional, and developmental needs	Coordinating staff training initiatives that address student needs on a schoolwide basis	Interpreting student data for use in whole school planning for change

The *ASCA National Model: A Framework for School Counseling Programs*

Subsequent to publishing the *National Standards*, the ASCA developed and published the *ASCA National Model: A Framework for School Counseling Programs* (2012), which represented a more comprehensive approach for integration of the *National Standards* into a school counseling program. The model addressed elements of program foundation, delivery, management, and accountability. The ASCA incorporated into the framework of its model the themes of leadership, advocacy, collaboration, and systemic change, themes that were foundational to the work of the TSCI at the Education Trust. The *National Model* is widely used by school counselors across the nation and has provided coherence to districtwide and individual school counseling programs.

A WORD FROM MAYA ANGELOU

Each one of us has the right and responsibility to assess the roads that lie ahead and those roads we have traveled. And if the future road looms ominous and unpromising and the roads back uninviting, then we need to gather our resolve and carrying only the necessary baggage, step off that road to a new direction.

(From *Wouldn't Take Nothing for My Journey Now,* by Maya Angelou)

IMPACT OF CHANGE ON SCHOOL COUNSELOR PRACTICE

Accountability in School Counselor Practice

Accountability, measurable evidence of a positive impact on student academic success, is a critical driver for school reform with far-reaching implications for school counseling practice. Practitioners' use of school data for identifying problems; developing programs and strategies for ameliorating disparities in students' educational access, achievement, and attainment outcomes; and ensuring and documenting equity in access and success for all students requires systemic approaches for solutions (College Board, 2008b). The fundamental work of professional school counselors in the development of school counseling program goals and the implementation of focused, data-driven strategies must align with the schools' goals. With significant emphasis in school reform being put on outcomes for students, as opposed to inputs, professional school counselors must transform and/or reframe the work they do to create concrete, measurable outcomes for students. Doing "good work" is now deemed less important than "doing work that produces student results." School counselors' work that supports the three ASCA domains (i.e., academic, career, and personal/social) is still applicable, but not essential to school reform if not aligned with or contributing to the schools' goals and driven by relevant school data, school culture/climate circumstances, and educational equity (Elam, McCloud, & Robinson, 2007).

Traditionally this has been seen as the responsibility of teachers, administrators, and central office personnel in charge of curriculum and instructional programs. In reality, accountability is the responsibility of everyone in the school setting, including professional school counselors, students, parents, and the community at large. Until recently, professional school counselors have been left out of discussions regarding school reform, student achievement, and accountability. This omission is deleterious to the accomplishment of the goals for 21st-century K–12 school reform. School reform that constitutes systemic change for all students will not occur without the involvement of all the critical players.

Professional school counselors need to integrate themselves into school reform by collaborating with all school staff instead of working as ancillary personnel removed from the instructional side of schools. For professional school counselors to work effectively in schools, they must design data-driven school counseling programs that fit into the mission of today's schools to provide rigorous standards and accountability for all students. Consider the typical challenges raised in Case Study 3.1.

CASE STUDY 3.1

Typical Academic Challenges Professional School Counselors Face in the World of Education Reform: High Standards and Accountability

Consider strategies for addressing each of the following challenges.

Challenge 1

Only a very small number of students of color are enrolled in rigorous academic classes. When pressed, the other students of color do not want to be placed in rigorous academic subjects. However, they still think they are going to college, and their parents want them to go and, in fact, think they are going. Both the students and the parents are clueless about what it takes to get into college and succeed.

Challenge 2

Over 50% of the students in your school are English language learners and/or students of color. Over 80% of the student body participates in the free and reduced lunch program. Their state basic test scores are low—less than 10% of the students are proficient in English/language arts and mathematics, according to the state tests, and the SAT/ACT scores are extremely low. Faced with the threat of state takeover for not meeting adequate yearly progress for the last 3 years, your school must show improved results immediately.

Challenge 3

Your school has been mandated to raise the average daily attendance rate. The school staff has not been able to do so in years past. However, it is now part of the school report card and one of the elements by which the principal will be evaluated at the end of the year. He is putting pressure on the whole staff to make it happen—constantly monitoring and documenting all departments' contributions to this goal.

Challenge 4

The building strategic plan calls for all educators to be part of the school plan to improve attendance, create a safe and orderly environment, increase test scores, get more students into Advanced Placement classes, and raise SAT/ACT scores. The principal is requiring each department to submit a plan for its work that will support these system goals.

Challenge 5

Of the students taking Algebra I in your school, 75% are earning Ds & Fs. Your math teachers have a reputation for being tough and openly state that this is a weeding-out class or that those students who fail should never have been in the classes in the first place. They see high failure rates as a sign of rigor. However, one teacher—one with low influence with other department members—seems to have success with her students. The parents in the community all want their children in this teacher's classes. The other math teachers think this teacher is too easy on the students. You can show that she is not by using data on continued success of her students in higher-level classes. The successful teacher appears to have a handle on how to engage students in the learning with hands-on activities and creativity.

Challenge 6

At Whitaker Elementary School over the last 3 years, there has been a rise in the number of students being referred for evaluation and placed in special education classes. The school counselor has become alarmed at the number of children who are put on the child study list for testing and placement. She suspects that most of the students being referred and placed are not really in need of this drastic change in school programming. She has no method of proving what she thinks, but is aware that the referrals are mostly African-American males.

Thus, successful school counselors in 21st-century schools will shift from focusing on fixing individual students to fixing the policies and practices in the educational system that contribute to academic failure of students. This shift is predicated on the assumption that a major source of academic failure for some students is the way the educational system is organized to deliver services to different groups of students (Commission on Chapter 1, 1992).

As we move further into the 21st century, it is critical for professional school counselors to move beyond their current role as "helper–responder" and become proactive leaders and advocates for the success of all students. To do this, professional school counselors must move out of the traditional mode of operation and begin collaborating with other school professionals to influence systemwide changes and become an integral part of their schools and school reform (House & Hayes, 2002). This approach requires counselors to examine and question inequitable practices that do not serve the interests of all students.

When professional school counselors operate under an ancillary model with programs that are peripheral to the major mission of the school, they focus on services addressing individual issues and concerns. Most often, those services have to do with social and emotional development. This role is often seen by decision makers as nonessential to teaching and learning. Indeed, when professional school counselors operate in this manner, it is often labeled an ineffective use of resources, as well as fiscal irresponsibility, by policy makers, school boards, and school system leaders who are being held accountable for increasing student achievement. This knowledge and state of affairs in school buildings do not mean that school counselors must relinquish their programs, goals, and activities that address the personal/social needs of

VOICES FROM THE FIELD 3.1

I have recently returned to high school counseling after spending the past year and a half in the district office. As I returned to a school I realized more than ever how important it is for counselors to act as leaders. Counselors serving on committees, such as Faculty Advisory or School Advisory Council, is important because we need to be a part of the "big picture."

—School counselor from Georgia

VOICES FROM THE FIELD 3.2

I have been closely involved in bringing professional learning communities to our school as well as analyzing data to decide the direction of both professional development and curriculum/instruction for our school. I have always been actively involved in writing the School Improvement Plan as well as presenting it to the district for approval. I find that working at a systemic level gives me the "big picture" and better enables me to communicate academic expectations to our parents and students. Collaborating weekly with the 8th grade teacher team as well as meeting weekly with the leadership team enables me to help lead the school toward fulfilling the most important goal we have, student learning. This involvement gives me a framework for underscoring my role of student support and advocacy. When I am working with students to remove the barriers that often prevent students from focusing on their education, I can begin to link their future education and career goals with the need for them to take advantage of their education now.

—Texas school counselor

their students. Nor does this mean that one-on-one counseling is removed from their repertoire of counseling strategies. It does mean, however, that if these activities subsume the bulk of school counselors' time without producing measurable student results that align with the system's primary goal of educating all students to high levels, then the value of having school counselors and counseling programs will be irreparably diminished. Quoting the title of a recent minister's sermon, "Without a presence, there is no absence" in todays' schools. Value in schools is now being defined in terms of student academic achievement and is driven and supported by federal law, the economy (i.e., lowered funding levels in constricted budgetary time periods), and business and industry roundtables seeking a better prepared workforce and hence the ability to continue to compete in a global marketplace. The confluence of these extremely powerful influencers is moving the educational agenda in schools across the nation. As one counselor educator stated, "The train has left the station, and we find ourselves running to jump onboard."

Advocacy in School Counseling Practice

Traditionally, professional school counselors have described themselves as advocates for their students and agents of change (ASCA, 2012). And, indeed, many counselors have performed in ways that help their students negotiate their way in an inherently inequitable system. Professional school counselors have provided services to individual students, changed the students' course schedules, responded to teacher and parent referrals regarding adjustments and behavior issues, worked with and made outside referrals for individual students with complex social and mental health needs that required extensive therapeutic interventions, and initiated group activities to help students improve organization, study, and test-taking skills—all laudable activities. Nonetheless, these supports have not been broad-based enough to support the bulk of the students in need of help, and professional school counselors have not been able to show they had measurable systemic impact in the school. Seemingly intractable school data continue to show that identifiable populations of students enter school with advantages that grow as they progress through the educational

---

THEORY INTO PRACTICE 3.1

THE NATIONAL OFFICE FOR SCHOOL COUNSELOR ADVOCACY (NOSCA)

In response to the national and state movements toward standards and raising student achievement for all students, the College Board launched the National Office for School Counselor Advocacy (NOSCA) in July 2003 with the expressed mission of advocating for and supporting the work of school counselors in getting all students, especially underserved populations, college and career ready. NOSCA envisioned every student participating in an education experience that provided them with the academic preparation and social capital needed to be college and career ready on graduating from high school. Using a systemic approach to carve out and institutionalize a national space for school counseling in education reform efforts, NOSCA advocates for school counselors, affirming the importance and value of their role in advancing school reform and student achievement. Building on the foundational work launched at the Education Trust in the Transforming School Counseling Initiative (TSCI), NOSCA focused on college and career readiness counseling using the following three priorities for national advocacy, training, research and public policy:

- Equity in college and career readiness counseling
- Leadership in systemic education reform
- Transformation of school counseling practice

NOSCA is the home of the "Own the Turf Campaign" a national effort to galvanize and mobilize school counselors to own the turf of college and career readiness counseling and to take the lead in establishing a college-going culture in their schools, districts, communities, and states. The roadmap for implementing the Own the Turf Campaign is NOSCA's Eight Components of College and Career Readiness Counseling, a framework for ensuring that all K–12 students receive the comprehensive planned support needed to be college and career ready when completing high school. These components can transform school counseling practices when implementation is informed by data, delivered systemically across all grade levels with equity and cultural sensitivity.

NOSCA provides training, publications, and tools for counselors' use in implementing comprehensive college and career readiness counseling. In addition, to inform national, state, and local policies for the work of school counselors that is critical to education reform success, NOSCA produces a national survey that captures the voices of school counselors regarding their roles, training and accountability.

system, whereas other populations suffer, fail to thrive, and even drop out. When schools' disaggregated data are reviewed, this latter group will most often represent disproportional numbers of students of color, students from low-income families, and students for whom English is a second language. These and other issues are the focus of the College Board's National Office for School Counselor Advocacy (NOSCA; see Theory into Practice 3.1).

For professional school counselors to work as leaders and advocates to affect systems change, it is of paramount importance that the school counselor role undergo a transformative change. To "transform" means to alter, to shift, or to change the way one works. For professional school counselors, it means moving away from a primary focus on mental health and individual changes to a focus on whole-school and systemic concerns that fit the schools' mission—academic achievement (see Table 3.1).

Through data-driven advocacy that purposefully highlights and focuses on marginalized populations, the scope of the professional school counselor's work will be expanded and transformed. Using data to strategically plan and measure their programs and practices allows professional school counselors to demonstrate accountability for their actions and to show they can make a difference in the academic success of all students. The results of these deliberate actions can be documented by "hard data" that move school counseling from the periphery of school business to a position front and center in constructing and supporting student success.

Professional school counselors are ideally positioned in schools to serve as conductors and transmitters of information to promote schoolwide success for all students. When professional school counselors aggressively support quality education for all students, they create a school climate where access and support for rigorous preparation is expected. In so doing, they give students who have not been served well in the past a chance at acquiring the skills necessary to unconditionally participate in the 21st-century economy.

A CALL FOR CHANGE IN SCHOOL COUNSELOR PREPARATION PROGRAMS

For the professional school counselor to assume the role of leader and advocate working to make systemic change to benefit all students, professional school counselor preparation programs will need to change practices. The Transforming School Counseling Initiative (Education Trust, 2005) suggested eight essential elements of change that would transform counselor education programs and, thus, the school counseling profession, including changes in admission and induction practices, the practicum

experience, certification requirements, and changes in the curriculum to include advocacy.

Since the 1960s, most professional school counselors have been taught the three "Cs"—counseling, consultation, and coordination—as a way of defining their role in schools. This role served the profession well over the years, but it is now too limiting and no longer provides enough breadth and depth of scope for professional school counselors to be effective. In addition, the older model does not provide a basis for serving all students. Instead of limiting professional school counselor training and practice to this role, counselor educators and practitioners must broaden their role to include leadership, advocacy and systemic change, teaming and collaboration, counseling and coordination, and assessment and use of data (see Table 3.2).

Teaching professional school counselors these new approaches broadens the scope of the work so that it is systemically more inclusive and thus helpful to more students. The model allows competent professional school counselors to work as leaders and team members with parents and members of the educational community to create supportive pathways that allow all students to succeed. Examples of school counselor preparation programs preparing students in this transformed model can be found at the Education Trust website (www.edtrust.org) under the Transforming School Counseling tab.

ACCOUNTABILITY: MAKING SCHOOL COUNSELING COUNT

Data that demonstrate positive results in students' school academic success and access to, and success in, substantial postsecondary future options have become the "coin of the realm" for defining school success in 21st-century schools. Designing comprehensive school counseling programs that are accountable for intentional student outcomes must be built around specific strategies using student data to create vision and targeted change. These strategies include clear indicators that the school counseling program is producing results. Using data to identify disparities in students' access to and success in rigorous academic courses of study is critical to aligning the work of school counselors to the district and/or school goals for increasing school achievement for all students. In this accountability model, professional school counselors are a key to removing barriers to learning and achievement and promoting success for all students. Removal of these barriers is critical to the future success of students and their families. Holding low expectations and believing that students cannot achieve due to life circumstances out of their control (i.e., born into families with low income and/or to families for whom English is a second language, living in communities with high rates of violence, being reared by a single parent or being a ward of the state) can cause irrevocable damage to their future life options. To act as agents of school and community change, professional school counselors must

1. Articulate and provide a well-defined developmental counseling program with attention to equity, access, and support services.
2. Routinely use data to analyze and improve access to, and success in, rigorous academic courses for all students, and especially underrepresented students.
3. Actively monitor the progress of underrepresented students in rigorous courses and provide assistance or interventions when needed.
4. Actively target and enroll underrepresented students into rigorous courses.
5. Develop, coordinate, and initiate support systems designed to improve the learning success of students experiencing difficulty with rigorous academic programs.

Leadership and Transformed School Counselor Practice

Advocating for high achievement for all students by serving as a leader and team member (see Table 3.1) in schools becomes the key role for counselors in this new approach to school counseling. It places professional school counselors at the center of the mission of school and school reform. In addition to having counseling skills, professional school counselors will need to

- Expect all students to achieve at a high level.
- Actively work to remove barriers to learning.
- Teach students how to help themselves (e.g., organization, study and test-taking skills).
- Teach students and their families how to successfully manage the bureaucracy of the school system (e.g., teach parents how to enroll their children in academic courses that will lead to college, make formal requests to school officials on various matters, and monitor the academic progress of their children).
- Teach students and their families how to access support systems that encourage academic success (e.g., inform students and parents about tutoring and academic enrichment opportunities and teach students and parents how to find resources on preparation for standardized tests).
- Use local, regional, and national data on disparities in resources and academic achievement to promote system change.

- Work collaboratively with all school personnel.
- Offer staff development training for school personnel that promotes high expectations and high standards for all students.
- Use data as a tool to challenge the deleterious effects of low-level and unchallenging courses.
- Highlight accurate information that negates myths about who can and cannot achieve success in rigorous courses.
- Organize community activities to promote supportive structures for high standards for all students (e.g., after-school tutoring programs at neighborhood religious centers).
- Help parents and the community organize efforts to work with schools to institute and support high standards for all children.
- Work as resource brokers within the community to identify all available resources to help students succeed.

What Prevents Professional School Counselors from Changing?

The call for change in the role of the professional school counselor is not new. Although professional school counselors are identified in educational literature as being important to the success of students in schools (Hayes, Dagley, & Horne, 1996), it seems that the profession has changed very slowly until recently. The following obstacles, or barriers, to changing the way professional school counselors practice may help explain why.

- There is sometimes an unwillingness to change resulting in maintenance of the status quo.
- Administrative practices can dictate the role of professional school counselors, even if the dictated role is different from counselor training.
- Professional school counselors can be pliable, often accepting responsibilities that are not part of their counseling role and function (e.g., bus duty and cafeteria duty).
- Pressure from special-interest groups may dictate the role of professional school counselors.
- Many counselor educators have little or no ongoing involvement with K–12 institutions, including little or no follow-up with recent graduates.
- Special education mandates for assessment, documentation, and ongoing services take too much of the counselor's time.
- Large numbers of practicing professional school counselors are functioning as highly paid clerical staff and/or quasi administrators.

- Professional school counselors sometimes function as inadequately trained therapeutic mental health providers with unmanageable client loads.
- The role of professional school counselors is frequently determined by others, rather than by the counselors developing their own purposeful, comprehensive programs.
- Little or no professional development is provided for professional school counselors.
- Crisis management on a day-to-day basis usurps too much of the professional school counselor's time.
- Professional school counselors may choose not to be involved in school reform efforts in school buildings.
- Professional school counselors may not see academic achievement as their goal or mission.
- Professional school counselors generally work to change the student, not the system in which the student functions. Thus, the student, not the system, is assumed to be the "problem."

Professional school counselors who continue to use these "excuses" to avoid change often serve as maintainers of the status quo, advocating for the school system, rather than for students and marginalized groups. They become "sorters and selectors," perpetuating the accepted placements and systemic barriers that cause an inequitable distribution between achievers and nonachievers based on race and socioeconomic status.

A Sense of Urgency Is Propelling Change

The sense of urgency to help all students be successful in school is propelling professional school counselors to change. Indeed, many professional school counselors are seizing the opportunity to be leaders in schools and work as advocates for students. School counselors are spearheading and successfully executing initiatives around improving schoolwide attendance rates, graduation rates, college-going rates, and access to and success in Advanced Placement and/or other college preparation courses for underserved student populations—all efforts that allow them to demonstrate their value using concrete school data. As schools and districts across the country assess and develop strategies to improve student outcomes for all students, they have begun to take a critical look at how budget funds support their systemwide goals for student outcomes. The business of making sure there are quantifiable returns on their investment in school counselors is a reality in schools today. Serving in a periphery capacity or focusing on activities that are misaligned with the school's/district's essential goals for student success is no longer a viable option for professional school counselors. Transforming school counseling practices with a laser focus on measureable positive outcomes for all students is the pathway to ensure that professional school counselors are integral to the success of education reform efforts of the 21st century and beyond.

CULTURAL REFLECTION 3.2

How might professional school counselors-in-training, students, parents, and educators from diverse backgrounds view the proposed transformative vision for school counseling as it relates to enhancing children's educational achievement, access, and opportunity? What cultural barriers and access points might exist? How can you overcome these barriers?

CASE STUDY 3.2

Application of New Vision: Transformed Practice Knowledge: Individual Students or Systemic Issues?

Many school counselors have felt that addressing systemic issues was beyond their purview—and at one point, it may have been. However, the transformed school counselor is now working in school districts that are held accountable for making sure that all students have an opportunity to achieve academic success in challenging curricula. Professional school counselors must maximize their capacity to have an impact on the greatest number of students in need of their help. The "transformed" school counselor must develop the capacity to determine when the intervention should be focused on helping individual students and when the intervention should be focused on changing the policies and practices being implemented by the system that are the source of student failure and/or student social distress.

(Continued)

Professional school counselors can make such a determination only by using data to understand patterns in student success and failure, analyzing the policies and practices for their impact on student success, and working with the adults in the system who are responsible for student success to maximize their capacity to work successfully together to fulfill the academic mission of the schools.

Professional school counselors must ask themselves if it is ethical to counsel a student to "adjust" to conditions in a school that may actually contribute to the antisocial behavior exhibited by the student. Should a school counselor continue to change classes for individual students from a particular teacher's class when the data reveal that the teacher has a disproportionately high failure rate with the group of students who have asked to change classes? Consider this scenario:

Mr. E is in his second year as a professional school counselor in a middle school in a first-ring suburb in a midwestern state. The community has undergone significant demographic changes, going from a predominately White, lower- to middle-income town to a multiethnic community with a large influx of non-native-English-speaking families, including a sizable population of students from Southeast Asia. In the last 10 years, the school demographics have changed from predominately White students to over 50% students of color who are from both low- and middle-income families. A small percentage of the families of color have resided in the community for years, but have not been notably visible. Now, these families of color, primarily African American, have become more visible in the community, and their children seem to have become more visible in the school community.

The school has a past reputation for being one of the "better" middle schools in the community. Their students feed into two high schools, one an "academic" high school and the other a "general" high school. High school placement is determined by grades and teacher recommendations. There is no written policy, and no data are consistently collected.

Over the past few years, the number of students attending the academic high school has declined. There are discussions among some parents that the students who attend the general high school are predominately students of color. They are concerned that their children are not being well prepared for postsecondary success, but have no organized effort to address the issues.

The principal has been at the school for the past 6 years and has come under increasing pressure to raise test scores. The teaching staff has remained stable, but is aging, and a significant percentage is or will be eligible for retirement in the next couple of years. The teaching staff is predominately White, whereas custodial and helping staff are persons of color. The staff increasingly feels that they are "under the gun" and being pressured to narrow their curriculum to get all students to pass the state tests.

Teachers complain that it is difficult to teach because of the increasing need to address the discipline problems caused (they say) mostly by the minority students or the "new" students. They argue that students are not prepared academically to do the level of work they expect and decry the lack of parental involvement.

Recently, the district's test scores have been published in the local paper. Current state policy requires that the scores to be disaggregated by race, socioeconomic status, and disability. The data show an achievement gap between the students of color and low-income students and their White and Asian peers.

In the past, professional school counselors have concentrated on getting students into the academic high school, helping students chart their high school courses, and keeping a lid on the discipline problems by providing group counseling programs, community mentoring, and after-school activities, which were voluntary and poorly attended. Staff members are demoralized, and morale in the school is low.

Discussion Questions

This scenario is designed to prompt a discussion about school counselor intervention strategies.

- How would the professional school counselor go about formulating an intervention plan to assist the school in closing the achievement gap?
- What issues should the professional school counselor address, and why?
- What data would the professional school counselor collect to construct an intervention plan?
- What are the major change dynamics operating in the scenario?
- How does understanding equity and being multiculturally competent come into play when considering solution finding in this case study?

Summary/Conclusion

The work of school counselors in schools today has been profoundly affected by forces that have driven all professionals in schools to change and/or ratchet up their contributions to raising student achievement, especially for students who have not had school success in the past. Schools as systems undergoing reformation have historically produced disparate results for different populations of students. School counseling, a critical working component of the system, has undergone, and is still undergoing, a transformation in which traditional inputs and processes are changing to support raising student achievement.

The vision for professional school counselors presented in this book is cutting edge, compelling, and essential to maintaining the profession in the 21st century and beyond. This vision puts professional school counselors in the middle of school reform and gives them an opportunity to demonstrate that they do make a difference in the success of students. Professional school counselors will be valued when they demonstrate effectiveness in making systemic changes that allow all students access to rigorous academic programs and support for success. Education is a substantial quality-of-life issue that determines the life options of students, their immediate and future families, and the economic viability of our nation, as well as our nation's position as a global leader. Professional school counselors who transform their practice as described in this text can be indispensable to schools in accomplishing the new mission of educating all students to high levels.

Activities

1. Research the schools in your local community. Find test scores, percentages of students who graduate, percentages of low-income students, and racial and ethnic breakdowns. Identify the most compelling student inequities/disparities in the data you find. How would the specifics of the schools in your area affect your focus as a professional school counselor in one of those schools?

2. Because the goals for education reform are about raising students' academic achievement and the Common Core State Standards require that all students graduate both college and career ready, how do these national, state, and local policies/practices affect comprehensive school counseling programs and practices?

3. Brainstorm ways that a professional school counselor could conduct and transmit information to an entire school to promote the success of all students. Design several activities or lessons a guidance department could implement to support student achievement for all.

4. Read the *ASCA National Model: A Framework for School Counseling Programs* (2012). What are some of the significant themes affecting change in the profession? How could you incorporate this model in a new program that you have been assigned to begin?

4

Systemic, Data-Driven School Counseling Practice and Programming for Equity

Vivian V. Lee and Gary E. Goodnough

Editor's Introduction: A systemic, data-driven school counseling program is essential to K–12 education. It is responsible for supporting student achievement and forms the foundation for effective career and personal/social development interventions.

IMPLEMENTING THE NEW VISION OF SCHOOL COUNSELING

The new vision of school counseling for the 21st century focuses on social justice, which intentionally increases the social and cultural capital for all students and aids in the attainment of equitable educational outcomes, especially for marginalized populations. Inherent in this vision is a scope of work that is systemic, data driven, and aligned and integrated with the educational program in such a way that it supports the mission of schools. This vision for school counseling is a response to the demands of today's schools, which are driven by federal and state mandates and focus on issues such as complying with No Child Left Behind (NCLB), reducing dropout rates, increasing graduation rates, getting more students into college, increasing student participation and performance in rigorous courses, and increasing scores on high-stakes testing. This new mission of schools is designed to close the access, attainment, and achievement gaps (Lee, 2005, 2006; Lee & Goodnough, 2006) between all student groups and the gap between achievement and academic standards set forth for all students.

To be integral to the mission of schools, school counseling programs need to be systemic, data driven, equity focused, and able to produce measurable results that support the educational success of all students, especially students from underrepresented populations. A full description of the new vision of school counseling is presented in Chapter 3, which outlines the new scope of the work for school counselors and school counseling programs. To complement the new vision, this chapter will present a process that uses the role of the transformed school counseling in the practice and programming of a systemic, data-driven school counseling program (see Figure 4.1).

To ensure clarity of message and purpose, this chapter describes school counseling practice and programming as data driven, equitable, and systemic. We believe that for change to truly occur and for gaps to be eliminated, school counselors must embrace these tenets. This is challenging and exciting work that requires a belief system rooted in equity and the courage necessary to be a culturally responsive leader and advocate. Figures 4.2 and 4.3 diagram the process of program development that is discussed in this chapter.

Program Vision—Commitment to Social Justice

Commitment to a vision of social justice and a mission of equitable educational outcomes for all students is a moral and ethical mandate for the school counseling profession. This mandate causes school counseling professionals to deeply examine their beliefs and how those beliefs affect behavior. In other words, it asks school counselors

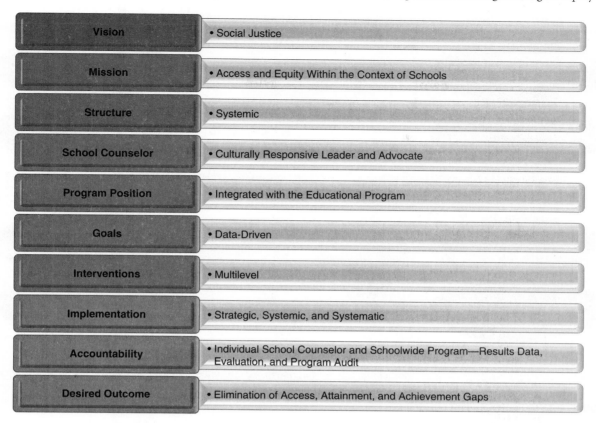

Vision	• Social Justice
Mission	• Access and Equity Within the Context of Schools
Structure	• Systemic
School Counselor	• Culturally Responsive Leader and Advocate
Program Position	• Integrated with the Educational Program
Goals	• Data-Driven
Interventions	• Multilevel
Implementation	• Strategic, Systemic, and Systematic
Accountability	• Individual School Counselor and Schoolwide Program—Results Data, Evaluation, and Program Audit
Desired Outcome	• Elimination of Access, Attainment, and Achievement Gaps

FIGURE 4.1 Systemic, data-driven school counseling programs.

to know what they believe in and to courageously lead and advocate through intentional behavior in their daily work on behalf of students, especially those who are traditionally marginalized and underserved. As President Barack Obama stated, the "fight for social and economic justice begins in the classroom." We would add that it also begins in the school counseling office, in the teachers' lounge, and in the hallways of any school in any district in the country. When school counselors hold these beliefs, they engage students and their parents/families and communities in ways that are meaningful and relevant. Some have questioned whether or not equity and social justice are the work of school counselors. But Lee and Hipolito-Delgado (2007, p. xiv) remind us that "improving society by challenging systemic inequities has always been a major objective of the counseling profession . . . to ensure that all individuals can participate fully in the life of a society." Indeed, such a commitment is ensconced in the preamble of the American School Counselor Association's (ASCA) *Ethical Standards for School Counselors* (2010). What would such a futuristic

and inclusive vision look like? At the Democratic National Convention in August 2008, then–presidential candidate Barack Obama gave us an idea that still holds true today of what that might mean. He stated, "Now is the time to finally meet our moral obligation to provide every child a world-class education, because it will take nothing less to compete in the global economy." The notion of a "world-class education" for all provides us with that visionary hope for the future.

Equity—A Working Definition

The complement to a vision of social justice is the striving for equity. Throughout the school counseling and educational literature, there is a resounding call for "equity" in student outcomes. However, most definitions don't actually describe what working in an equitable way means. After examining multiple definitions (Coalition of Essential Schools, 2008; College Board, 2008a), we have developed the following working definition of equity:

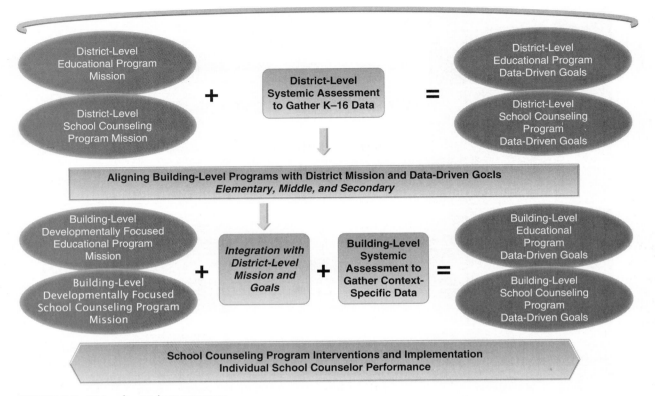

FIGURE 4.2 Vision for student outcomes.

Equity is the elimination of systemic barriers to create a culturally responsive school/district climate. In such a climate, policies and practices build social capital, shape high expectations, and ensure access to rigorous courses necessary for college readiness, extracurricular activities, and other educational experiences. Equity is measured by participation and performance outcomes that show minimal variance due to race, income, language status, gender, or other demographic variables.

This definition highlights the four tenets that define a systemic, data-driven school counseling program. First is a belief in equity. Although there is much talk about equity in school counseling and education, this reality still eludes us. Therefore, we use the word *create* in our definition to make clear that equity will not just happen: It requires action. We must intentionally become visionary leaders able to shed the bonds of "oppression[s that] restrict our ability to imagine new possibilities, [and become] transformational leaders [that can] hold a proxy vision for what may be that is radically different from what is" (Coalition of Essential Schools, 2008, p. 1). Part of that difference is a school counseling leader who possesses the *courage* and

persistence to reframe power structures through practice and programming to build social capital among those who are traditionally underrepresented.

Second, this definition makes explicit the systemic tenet. The systemic baseline or marker against which practice and programming can be measured moves school counseling away from a solely school-based endeavor to the wider district arena. This expansion allows professional school counselors to contextualize their work from a pre-K–12 perspective, as well as across a level—for example, all high schools or all middle schools.

The third tenet is data. This definition uses data to fuel equity by requiring outcomes in both participation and performance to be measured against the school/district demographic data as a baseline. In this way, data are the guiding force in identifying inequity, developing measurable goals, shaping interventions, and demonstrating accountability based on the context and demographics of a school.

Finally, each of the tenets described is executed by a culturally responsive school counselor, the last tenet. This means that professional school counselors simultaneously work to address existing disparity and take proactive measures to help prevent further inequity, especially for underserved or underrepresented populations such as students of color and those from lower socioeconomic backgrounds.

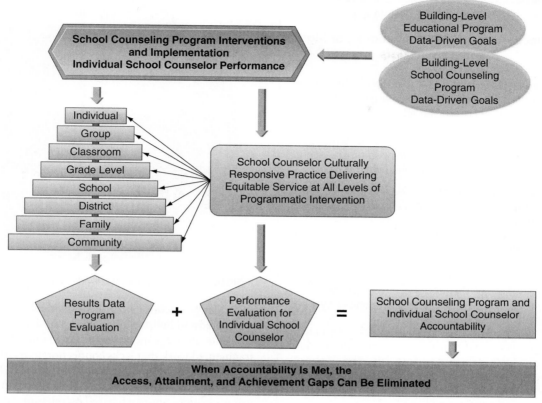

FIGURE 4.3   The systemic, data-driven school counseling process.

When this definition is actualized, the roles of leadership and advocacy gain primacy and direct the work of culturally responsive school counselors. Unfortunately, longitudinal data tell us that such equitable practice is not always the case in schools across our country. This ongoing unacceptable reality means that, when left to chance, equity and social justice can become hollow rhetoric. We believe that the lives of *all* students are equally worthy; therefore, this chapter makes explicit that achieving equity requires intentionality.

Program Structure—Making a Paradigm Shift to Systems

With the understanding of equity described earlier, the professional school counselor is poised to engage in "systems thinking" and action (Fullan, 2005). There is a real need for systemic, data-driven school counseling programs. Citing the Education Trust (1997), the *ASCA National Model* (2012) supports data-driven approaches through "closing the gap" activities and action plans. Although we support these activities and plans, the complexity and persistence of educational gaps, rooted as they are in social injustice, require a broader and more in-depth

response. Changing deeply grounded inequities requires a systems-focused program that reaches deep into and across the inner workings of the system and populations of a school district and each individual school. Essentially, it requires a school counseling program to be grounded in the applied principles of systems theory. If a program is not grounded in these principles in structure and delivery, we believe it is misleading to consider it systemic. It is equally misleading to consider *systemic* to be the same as *systematic*. According to *Merriam-Webster's Collegiate Dictionary* (2012), *systematic* is defined as a methodical or orderly process, and *system* is defined as the whole or universal. Thus, without attention to the principles of systems, school counseling programs can offer interventions in a systematic fashion that are not necessarily systemic. Moreover, even if a program is called systemic, if it is not structured according to a systems theory paradigm, it is systemic in name only. Systemic, data-driven programs intentionally intervene across the entire school, with outreach to other schools in the district, to parents and families, and to the larger community, using the principles of systems theory. All those conditions are necessary for a school counseling program to be systemic.

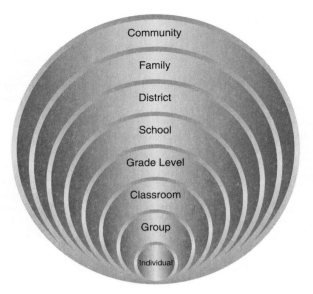

FIGURE 4.4 Programmatic levels of intervention.

UNDERSTANDING SYSTEMS IN SCHOOL COUNSELING

To begin, it is essential to first acknowledge that schools are systems (Rowley, Sink, & MacDonald, 2002). Thus, the most critical point in developing and implementing effective systemic school counseling programs is that *the system*, both the structures and all the people there, is as much the client as the individual student is (Green & Keys, 2001). A systemic focus is achieved by placing the individual at the center of the system and examining the relations between, and expectations of, larger subsystems that affect the individual, such as school, family, community, and society (see Figure 4.4). In addition, because systemic approaches highlight the interconnectedness and interdependence of all subsystems within a school, they are more likely to address policy and procedural barriers to access, achievement, and attainment. In today's school counseling literature, there is much written about school counselors working from both an individual and a systemic approach. This statement reflects limited understanding of systems theory. Based on the preceding definition, working

systemically is working for the individual as well—it is an integrated and holistic approach. A mind-set of working in two different ways increases the likelihood of isolated and fragmented work that lacks connection to the diverse contexts of a school environment. Moreover, when school counseling programs are developed and implemented using a systems approach based on relevant data, interventions become a strategic and intentional response to all students' academic, career, and personal/social needs and the ways in which these needs interface. Finally, a systemic, data-driven approach supports embedding school counseling interventions across multiple levels of the educational program.

The use of multilevel interventions (Lee & Goodnough, 2006; Ripley, 2001) across the school and community was found to be among the 10 elements critical in addressing complex educational, social, and cultural challenges in striving schools (College Board, 2008b). Multilevel interventions are also a basis for Response to Intervention (RTI) programs (see Chapter 16). Thus, systemic, data-driven school counseling programs provide a dynamic framework that easily interfaces with the structure of the school and the delivery of the educational program. Without a systemic approach that uses strategic interventions and multilevel approaches, school counseling programs struggle to align with the mission of schools and the educational program. For example, many environmental factors affecting student development and achievement are beyond student control. Among these are family influences and systemic intolerance. Systemic intolerance is often manifested in phenomena such as racism, sexism, and homophobia. These environmental factors may play a major role in shaping the attitudes, values, and behaviors of all members of a community—factors that can insidiously affect student educational success in the school environment. Consequently, professional school counselors need to address the negative effects of these environmental factors through systemic intervention.

Integrated Educational and School Counseling Programs

The educational success of all students is a school moral obligation and therefore part of the ethical and professional responsibility of all school personnel. Fulfilling this foundational responsibility requires the creation of a culturally responsive teaching and learning environment that encourages the dreams and aspirations of all students. In this way, the educational program and the school counseling program become collaborative and intertwined forces that share an overarching goal of equitable access, attainment, and achievement for all students. It also means both programs share complementary structures of delivery and reporting of results. More specifically, the systemic, data-driven school counseling program is essential to the mission of the schools by integrating its program goals, development, implementation, and evaluation with those aspects of the educational program. Thus, integration of the educational program and the school counseling program exemplifies a commitment to serve all students through mutually dependent goals, interventions, and desired outcomes. This mutuality has the advantage of also integrating the school counseling program into school improvement plans and initiatives, which, in turn, positions school counseling within educational reform. For example, in many schools across the country, the goal of increasing student participation and performance in rigorous courses is paramount. To achieve this goal, administrators, teachers, counselors, students, parents, and the community are all essential in changing expectations, increasing knowledge and skill for all populations, and fostering the structural changes necessary to attain this goal.

Understanding integration of the school counseling program with the educational program can be difficult. For successful integration to occur, professional school counselors need to be familiar with the academic goals and standards of their district and state and with any other established curriculum that is used in the school, such as reading programs and conflict resolution curricula. It is also essential to understand how the educational program is delivered, the multiple ways it is implemented, and how the results are measured and reported.

EDUCATIONAL PROGRAMS ARE DELIVERED AT MULTIPLE LEVELS Reflecting on the earlier discussion about systems, recall that schools are systems and that systems are made up of individuals. Within these systems, standards-based educational programs are delivered across the entire school using multilevel initiatives. More specifically, each academic discipline has standards and competencies implemented in the school, using multilevel initiatives. Standards and competencies are delivered not only in classrooms, but also through other initiatives such as tutoring, clubs, service learning projects, sports, student buddies, mentoring projects, honor societies, band, chorus, and fine arts initiatives. Parent contacts, collaborations with businesses, and outreach programs are all part of the overall educational program.

Significantly, the educational program is also delivered through the policies, practices, and procedures of the school. These aspects of the educational program affect the culture and climate of a school and serve as long-term environmental instructors that either promote or hinder achievement. For example, policies that affect discipline, course enrollment patterns, attendance, and participation in co- or extracurricular activities systemically affect the educational program—and therefore student outcomes. This means that to positively affect systems, purposeful interaction across all levels of the system, or *vertical integration*, is necessary to create coherence among the many unconnected and superficial innovations that can permeate a school in the name of making change (Fullan, 2005). School counseling programs, central as they are to schools achieving their academic mission, need to have a structure/delivery process that mirrors this system-level reality to fully engage this process.

SCHOOL COUNSELING PROGRAMS ARE DELIVERED AT MULTIPLE LEVELS The structure and delivery of a systemic, data-driven approach are conceptualized as *levels of programmatic intervention*. This perspective focuses on the eight levels of intervention introduced previously—individual, group, classroom, grade, school, district, home/family, and community/society—which are interdependent and interrelated. These levels of intervention can be viewed as concentric circles with individually based interventions in the middle. Each additional ring represents a larger and potentially more diverse population, including the larger society, as shown in Figure 4.4. The eight levels are points of intervention into the structure of the school and the community. The rationale behind this approach is that systemic transformation requires consistent and intentional intervention across all levels of the school and the community to affect persistent inequities. In other words, this approach is a pragmatic response to complex issues that require complex solutions.

Professional school counselors cannot do the work of equity and social justice alone. Therefore, this approach fully embraces collaboration within a systems theory perspective to mold and shape *constellations of interventions* across the eight levels that can saturate a system with a desired message, knowledge, and skill. Attributing systemic change to singular school counselor interventions, especially to just distal data elements, is questionable, especially in light of the scant school counseling research. Creating constellations of interventions (multilevel) around what we do empirically know may hold greater promise, as some research is beginning to show (College Board, 2009). In addition, these levels are basic structures for collecting and reporting data in the elementary, middle, and high schools and in the school system. Recently, this method of school counseling program delivery was adopted by the National Office for School Counselor Advocacy (NOSCA) of the College Board in their *School Counselor Guide* series for elementary, middle, and high school counselors to implement the NOSCA Eight Components of College and Career Readiness Counseling. Significant as college and career readiness is in today's schools for all students, multilevel interventions offer school counselors a new approach to "systemwide" impact (NOSCA, 2010). Thus, this method of implementation is appropriate for content that school counselors traditionally deliver and more cutting-edge college and career readiness content.

To deliver a program effectively, professional school counselors must possess the knowledge and skills to implement services at all levels of intervention so that program delivery is rigorous and is not compromised by limited professional school counselor knowledge or skill. This broader delivery of school counseling services exemplifies the systemic nature of the school counseling program.

Educational and school counseling integration is also essential from a goals and content perspective. This added dimension of integration requires professional school counselors to become familiar with the academic curriculum and to know the general aspects of the content and the specific sequence of the curriculum being taught. It does not mean that the professional school counselor teaches geometry and chemistry, but it does mean that he or she broadly knows the curriculum, as well as concepts and constructs that facilitate learning across the academic disciplines, such as critical thinking and problem solving. It also means that professional school counselors assist teachers with the delivery of the curriculum through *collaborative classroom instruction* in areas where counseling expertise can support and enhance student learning and development toward goal attainment.

For example, professional school counselors can contribute to student learning and development in specific disciplines. In civics, government, and history, issues of diversity, human rights, citizenship, conflict and war, oppression, and violence are prevalent. Professional school counselors do not have to be history experts to assist teachers with discussions and activities that help students explore these areas and relate them to their day-to-day lives. Second, language arts curricula often include consideration of careers, resume writing, alternative points of view, conflict resolution, relationships, and a host of human dramas and triumphs explored through literature. School counseling interventions that are integrated into the curriculum in these areas provide a holistic environment for learning. Third, the health curriculum is often replete with topics in which professional school counselors possess expertise. Issues such as healthy relationships, alcohol and drug prevention, sexuality, personal safety, family relationships, and wellness are all areas where professional school counselors and teachers can team and collaborate to achieve curricular goals. Fourth, although *collaborative classroom instruction* is the most obvious point of integration, integration that includes policy, practices, and procedures, as well as school-wide culture and climate, can have a significant effect on student outcomes. Finally, integration of the educational and school counseling programs also occurs around issues like attendance, promotion and retention, extracurricular activities, transitions, and graduation.

Outcomes/Results

The multilevel structures of school produce outcomes or results that are collected and reported systemically. In the assessment climate fostered by education reform initiatives, results are often reported at the following levels: group/subgroup, grade, school, and district. For example, individual state department of education websites provide links to school districts and individual school performance report card data (as does the Maryland Department of Education at msp.msde.state.md.us). A school counseling program that aligns with reporting categories provides a ready-made database to assist in conceptualizing and responding to the link between the educational program and the school counseling program. This linkage forms a collaborative and systemic integration in the accountability and results of both programs. When all school personnel team up and collaborate in these ways to reach collective goals, programs become integrated, and all stakeholders share in the responsibility and results. Engaging in this type of practice does require professional school counselors to ensure that they have both proximal and distal outcomes that highlight their work as they link to more whole-school data elements to avoid minimizing their contribution (Brown & Trusty, 2005c).

District and School Policies

District and school policies, both spoken and unspoken, govern and shape the day-to-day operations of a school district and individual schools. Policies are used to create a "way of doing things," set the tone for the culture and climate of the school, operationalize ethical and legal mandates, and implement goals. The practices and procedures used to implement policy, though assumed necessary and beneficial, can either advantage or disadvantage all or groups of students. For example, policies affecting school counselor activities can either promote equity for all students or inadvertently create or maintain access, attainment, and achievement barriers. Because student and community demographics are dynamic, an ongoing analysis of policies, practices, and procedures is essential to ensure that they promote access and equity for all students. In addition, school policies, practices, and procedures can be used to promote or mitigate environmental influences that affect students—from racism, classism, and violence to access to postsecondary opportunity.

District and school policies interface with the mission, goals, development, implementation, and evaluation of the systemic, data-driven school counseling program. Ongoing examination of school policy may point to needed revisions and changes, and professional school counselors need to be aware of the effects of policy on the school (Ripley & Goodnough, 2001). As part of the educational leadership teams in their schools, professional school counselors can be leaders and advocates who give voice to the day-to-day interpretation and application of school policy. Inequities in interpretation and application may be the result of oversights, outdated rules, or the values, attitudes, and beliefs of the policy makers that are translated into school policy and create barriers to educational access and equity. Although the role of the professional school counselor in the examination, influence, and revision of school policy is new, it is a moral imperative because it is unprofessional for counselors, as part of the school system, to ignore aspects of the school or school counseling program that hinder educational success for all students.

Understanding the Role of Data

During the past decade, as the accountability movement continued to dominate and reshape public education, data became central to the work of professional school counselors. During this time of transition, new catch-phrases emerged as part of a new language that provided a rationale for using data. One of those phrases was "data create the urgency for change." Despite the fact that this phrase has gained seemingly wide popularity, it can be misleading. Although data certainly are important and certainly should create an urgency that drives the work of school counselors, data are only a tool of discovery and a tool to monitor and report outcomes. Using data in powerful and transformative ways can happen only when those examining the data *believe that the inequities revealed are unacceptable*. Then urgency for change can become a reality. The inequities revealed in today's social and educational data are not new. Yet the struggle to respond to the data without blaming students and their families, and without using excuses that maintain stereotypes and resistance, still remains a challenge in some school counseling offices. Fortunately, many professional school counselors embrace the use of data as the guide for challenging long-standing inequity.

VOICES FROM THE FIELD 4.1   **USING DATA K–12**

It is imperative that all professional school counselors learn and understand how to use data; moreover how to disaggregate data, regardless of setting. Disaggregating data can reveal hidden inequities or reinforce harmful systemic practices that jeopardize student success. It can also assist school counselors in understanding the gap and identifying where and why services are needed. When we as school counselors fail to recognize and act upon these gaps, it can cause a ripple effect that impacts student achievement K–12. Using data can assist in effective and efficient college and career readiness counseling for all students. It can lead to changes in school district policies and practices and expose and create equity for those families who do not know how to advocate for their students.

School counselors must learn how to recognize data. We work with data every day; most of the time we see data in its raw form. It is important to capture data in its natural state and work with it, so that it can tell you a story; a story about whether students are being underserved, overlooked, misguided, or forgotten. Once the story unfolds, you have to be able to withstand the challenges to achieve the desired outcome. As school counselors we must deviate from the practice of providing obsolete counseling. By this I mean doing the same things over and over again because *"we have always"* done something the same way for the same groups of students. Our services need to be based on data, period, and there is no cookie-cutter approach to serving students. It looks different at every school because every school is different.

District school counseling offices provide the framework from which to counsel, but school counselors are the foot soldiers who implement the guidelines and have the ability to cater and/or make changes based on the needs of their students, needs that are reflected in data. The implementation of college and career readiness counseling involves equitable and culturally relevant choices and services that successfully use data to make positive systematic and systemic changes. Only when school counselors take on this task will true change occur for all students.

What does this look like for school counselors? As part of the state's initiative for Academic and Career Planning and new diploma requirements, school divisions have been charged with creating a protocol that allows for completion of a career interest survey and a 4-year academic plan highlighting career clusters that begins in the seventh grade. Our division implemented the academic and career plans (ACP) 3 years before the start date. We also begin the plan in fifth grade to introduce planning to elementary students regarding their middle school years.

- Elementary school counselors complete the K–5 career interest inventory on *VA Career View* during classroom guidance. Students then log their answers onto the ACP. During another lesson, the school counselors meet with fifth-grade students one-on-one, in small groups, or classroom guidance to review and select middle school courses based on teacher, parent, and student recommendations and preferences. The students, assisted by the school counselor, fill out the 3-year middle school plan based on the sequences of courses that begin in sixth grade. Career cluster, career aspirations, and postsecondary ideas are also noted on the plan. Once the plan is complete, a copy is sent home with the student for the family to review, and a copy is placed in the cumulative folder.

- Middle school counselors meet with seventh-grade students to complete the 6-8 career interest inventories on *VA Career View* or *VA Wizard*. The same process for completion of the elementary plan is used in middle school as well. In eighth grade, students complete a new high school ACP using the career interest information from seventh grade. Again, high school courses and their sequences are selected based on teacher, parent, and student recommendations and preferences, as well as revised career aspirations and postsecondary ideas and plans sent home to be reviewed.

- High school counselors meet with 9th- or 10th-grade students to complete the final ACP. Students complete the career interest inventory on *VA Wizard*. The same process ensues as with lower grades. The main difference here is that in high school the planning becomes more high stakes because completion of high school and graduation are key factors. By academic and career planning, school counselors can reduce the number of students who graduate from high school without formalized plans. This early awareness can assist with closing the postsecondary planning gap of students.

It is the role of all school counselors to use career interest inventory data to help place students in courses/programs that will aid in supporting their career aspirations. This means that school counselors ensure students take courses that will allow them to be college and career ready with the accurate number of courses in higher-level math and science, foreign language, and complete career and technical clusters so that they have the opportunity to possess industry certifications and not just complete myriad courses that on the surface appear to make one well rounded.

Source: Tracy L. Jackson, Coordinator of Guidance Services, Virginia Beach Public Schools

DATA SKILLS

The first step in using data for equity is to master the basics of data usage. Data skills are used at every step throughout the development, implementation, and outcome reporting in a school counseling program. Data skills allow the school counselor to reach into the past and present of a school and plan for the future. When used effectively, data allow the school counselor to see the school and its needs through the eyes of its diverse populations. Table 4.1 provides a list of the data skills that are essential for school counselors to master. A separate explanation of each of these skills is beyond the scope of this chapter; the process of program development based on these skills is integrated throughout the chapter.

Measuring Progress Toward Access, Attainment, and Achievement: Data and Nondata Elements

Measuring progress is a challenge because many school counselors do not have data skills and are overwhelmed by the sheer volume of data available in schools. To effectively manage data and maintain a focus on analyzing and interpreting it for equity, it is helpful to have a means to categorize or label types of data. What are these categories? Earlier in the chapter, we discussed access, attainment, and achievement gaps (Lee, 2005; Lee & Goodnough, 2006). For each of these gaps, there are specific corresponding data elements. Although each one of these categories holds specific types of data, they also reflect the interdependent

---

TABLE 4.1   Data Skills

The school counselor will know how to

- Identify and gain access to relevant data sources—students, school, district, state, national, and international.
- Collect relevant data.
- Analyze and interpret relevant data to identify inequity and trends using disaggregated and longitudinal data.
- Establish baseline data.
- Develop and prioritize measurable goals with benchmarks to drive the school counseling program and the work of the individual school counselor (individual, group, classroom, grade, school, district. family, and community).
- Align goals to the school improvement plan, district goals, and state and federal mandates.
- Develop feasible interventions that directly connect to measurable goals.
- Implement interventions and collect outcome data.
- Develop accountability reports and share them with stakeholders.

---

and interrelated nature of systems, as we shall see later in our discussion. In-depth understanding of these interrelationships is critical in strategic planning to address equity concerns and promote systemic change.

ACCESS DATA Access is about creating pathways to equitable engagement in the educational process for equitable outcomes. Without access, students who have traditionally not been equitably served by the educational system do not even have the chance to attain or achieve at higher levels. Thus, when attempting to close gaps, attention to the inequities in access data is a precursor. But access is multifaceted. There are both data and nondata elements of access. We will detour in this discussion to address the nondata elements of access before returning to the data elements of access, attainment, and achievement.

The nondata elements of access have direct bearing on the data elements of access. The nondata elements of access include, but are not limited to, (a) school/school counselor belief systems or cultural responsiveness and (b) school policies, practices, and procedures regarding information and student identification. These two aspects of access are highly interdependent and play a definitive role in determining whether or not school personnel (i.e., administrators, teachers, and other staff) and their school counselors *respond* to hard data elements when they reveal inequity. For example, a counselor's or teacher's or administrator's belief system about why the data look the way they do, who should or should not be in rigorous courses, or who goes to college is intertwined with his or her response to inequitable data. If counselors and other school personnel do not truly believe, deep in their hearts, that *all* students should be college and career ready, they will not behave in ways that promote equitable access to academic preparation by addressing corresponding policy issues. And it is likely that they will not engage in leadership, outreach, and

advocacy efforts to challenge the *status quo* regardless of the data. In those cases, a school counselor's low expectations and biasing beliefs will see the data as the outcomes expected from students incapable of meeting high standards. These beliefs create and support inequitable policies, practices, and procedures. Once these are put in place, the data will not move school counselors toward the elimination of the access, attainment, and achievement gaps regardless of the identified disparities. Thus, the nondata elements of access shape and mold the data elements of access. Moreover, the degree to which the nondata elements of access are equity focused can be considered a predictor of the outcome of the data elements of access. The data elements of access include, but are not limited to, course enrollment patterns (i.e., rigorous and nonrigorous courses) and availability of rigorous course, extracurricular, or enrichment opportunities.

ATTAINMENT DATA Attainment data measure the rate at which a behavior, event, or marker point is reached or completed. Often the term *achievement gap* is used to refer to gaps that are actually about attainment. For example, data elements that are often considered part of the achievement gap are course completion rates, graduation rates, college-going rates, and attendance rates. Each of these is a marker of *attainment*—a point or rate at which something is attained. Although they represent different data elements, attainment and achievement are not mutually exclusive.

ACHIEVEMENT DATA Achievement data are primarily about grades and scores. Achievement data indicate a test, class, or exam score or grade. Scores on state tests and end-of-course tests and even semester and marking period grades are all achievement data. Other well-known achievement data are grade point averages (GPAs) and PSAT, SAT, and ACT scores. But working for equity using data is not as simple as using data elements from one of these categories. As

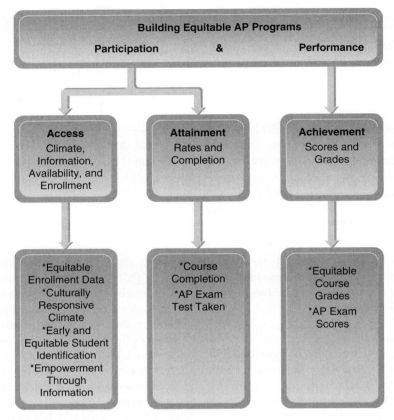

FIGURE 4.5 Building equitable AP programs.

mentioned earlier, the three data categories are intertwined. For example, even if all (100%) of the seniors in a class graduate, it is still very possible that an achievement gap exists. How is that possible? There are several ways. The most striking can be revealed in students' GPAs. If the GPAs of the graduating class are disaggregated and some groups of students consistently have higher GPAs than other groups, then the achievement gap is still present regardless of the fact that all of the seniors graduate, thereby closing the attainment gap. It is also possible that, although 100% of the seniors graduate, there are still remaining attainment gaps in other data elements. Figure 4.5 and Theory into Practice 4.1 demonstrate how gaps that affect equity can go unnoticed unless we are sharply focused on all three types of data that affect equity.

THEORY INTO PRACTICE 4.1

RIGOROUS HIGH SCHOOL COURSES

If a school counseling program wanted to work toward equity by closing the gaps among students in rigorous courses, there are several pieces of data to consider in addition to the nondata elements of access.

1. **Access**

   a. Consider the nondata elements—that is, whether the learning environments are culturally responsive, how students are identified for rigorous courses, and who receives information about rigorous courses and the policies that govern entrance.

  b. Review course enrollment patterns and disaggregate the data.

  c. Identify which students are or are not enrolled in rigorous classes.

2. **Attainment**

  a. Identify which students actually finish the course. Many counselors know that students who begin rigorous courses often do not finish those courses. Therefore, it is essential to examine not only the enrollment data, but also the course completion data. Participation has not increased until the course is completed.

  b. Disaggregate data on completion by teacher and course. Attainment data have equity implications around teacher quality, safety nets (especially for nontraditional students), culturally responsive teaching and learning environments, school peer group acceptance of rigorous course taking, and student academic preparedness.

3. **Achievement**

  a. Disaggregate course grades and/or end-of-course test scores. When disaggregated, the achievement data for those who finish the course shed light on the quality of teaching and learning that occurred in a course throughout the academic year. Ideally, the grade distribution should be equitable among all student groups and genders.

As you can see in Theory into Practice 4.1, to work toward equity in outcomes for students requires that all three gap categories be addressed. Professional school counselors can effectively employ this method of using data when they encounter a goal in schools to increase participation and performance in a given area. The example demonstrates that the gap in participation is closed through attention to access and attainment, whereas the gap in performance is closed with attention to achievement. The example of taking rigorous courses (see Theory into Practice 4.2 through 4.4) is often associated with high school. However, this process can also be applied to middle and elementary schools. For example, in middle school it is well known that Algebra I is a gatekeeping math course. Eighth-grade students who complete Algebra I are more likely to reach the point of taking AP courses in high school; thus, it serves to significantly assist students in becoming college and career ready.

In addition, determining equity needs requires inquiry, asking questions about the data and why the data looks the way it does. Inquiry can help reveal student need and inform the type of support needed for teachers to meet the diverse learning needs of all students. Following are three Theory into Practice examples (4.2–4.4) using inquiry that can assist school counselors in examining data to determine need and how equitable the teaching and learning environment is for all students. Table 4.2 provides insights into the whole-school data elements required to address access, attainment, and achievement gaps.

THEORY INTO PRACTICE 4.2

MIDDLE SCHOOL ALGEBRA I

The successful completion of Algebra I in eighth grade can significantly affect how far students will progress in math in high school, and completion of those higher-level math courses can determine eligibility into postsecondary institutions. Thus, careful examination into the data using inquiry can not only provide middle school students with more rigorous opportunities but it can also have a long-range impact on students' life options.

1. **Access**

  a. Who is enrolled in Algebra I, and is the enrollment representative of the demographics of the school? If the enrollment is not representative, which groups are missing?

  b. What policies, practices, and procedures determine entrance into Algebra I, and how might it

(Continued)

advantage or disadvantage different groups of students?

c. How is information disseminated about Algebra I to ensure all student groups get the same information?

d. Are there sufficient sections of Algebra I so that all students can take the class? If no, what needs to happen to ensure there are?

2. **Attainment**

a. Of the students who enroll in Algebra I, who finishes? This data should be disaggregated by group, gender, and teacher.

b. Of the students who take Algebra I, who takes an end-of-course test (as applicable), and who does not? This data should be disaggregated by group, gender, and teacher.

3. **Achievement**

a. Of the students who complete Algebra I, what is the grade distribution? This data should be disaggregated by group, gender, teacher, or other identifier.

b. Of the students who complete Algebra I, what are the end-of-course test scores disaggregated by group, gender, teacher, or other identifier?

THEORY INTO PRACTICE 4.3

HIGH SCHOOL AP COURSES

Use Figure 4.5. In high school, enrollment, completion, and performance in rigorous courses like advanced placement (AP) courses can also be examined by applying inquiry to the three types of data to determine equity. The goal here is to be of assistance so that all students who enter rigorous courses are successful and to examine trends where interventions may be needed.

1. **Access:**
   a. Are AP courses available?
   b. Are AP courses available that reflect the interests of students to meet their future career goals?
   c. Are AP courses open to all students?
   d. Do policies, practices, or procedures disadvantage some students and discourage them from taking AP?
   e. Is the enrollment in AP classes representative of the demographic enrollment of the school? For which groups is it representative, and for which groups is it not?

2. **Attainment:**
   a. Of those students who enter AP, which students complete the class, and which students do not? This data should be disaggregated by group and gender. Which classes do they leave? Who teaches those classes?
   b. Of the students who complete an AP class, who takes the AP exam, and who does not? This data should be disaggregated by group and gender. From which courses do students take the AP exam or not take the exam, and who are their teachers?

3. **Achievement**
   a. Of the students who complete an AP class, what is the grade distribution disaggregated by group and gender? Are there any inequities in grades; are those trends consistent over time? If yes, in which courses and with which teachers?
   b. For the students who took an AP exam, what is the distribution of scores disaggregated by group and gender for each course and each teacher?

THEORY INTO PRACTICE 4.4

ELEMENTARY SCHOOL GIFTED AND TALENTED

Now apply the process to the identification of students for the gifted and talented (GT) program at the elementary level.

1. **Access**
   a. Does the enrollment in the GT program represent the demographics of the school? For which

groups is it representative, and for which groups is it not?

b. How do the policies, practices, and procedures that guide entrance either advantage or disadvantage different groups of students?

c. How is information about the program disseminated to all student groups and their families?

2. Attainment

a. Of those students who participate in GT, who completes the program, and who does not? This

information should be disaggregated by group, grade, and gender.

3. Achievement

a. Of the students who participate in GT, how do their grades and test scores differ from those who do not?

TABLE 4.2   Whole-School Data Elements

Access

- Enrollment patterns in
  - Rigorous courses such as AP, International Baccalaureate (IB), honors, and college prep, and nonrigorous courses
  - Special education
  - Gifted and talented programs
  - English for speakers of other languages classes
  - Extracurricular and enrichment activities
  - Availability of courses, programs, and activities for all populations

Attainment

- Attendance rates
- Dropout rates
- Promotion and retention rates
- Graduation rates
- Passing rates for all subjects
- Completion rates in rigorous and nonrigorous courses
- Successful transitions to elementary, middle, and high school and to postsecondary options
- Proficiency rates in all subjects, especially math, reading, language arts, and science
- Discipline infraction rates, suspensions, and/or expulsions
- Parent participation rates in academic, college/postsecondary, and career activities
- Enrichment program completion rates
- College/postsecondary acceptance patterns
- College applications completed
- FAFSA completions
- Scholarship forms completed
- Test-taking rates for state assessments, college entrance exams, and career and interest inventories

Achievement

- Grade point averages
- Scores on state tests and end-of-course tests
- Scores on AP and IB exams
- SAT, ACT, and PSAT scores
- Career assessments and interest inventory scores
- Marking period, quarter, or semester grades

TABLE 4.3   Examples of Student and School Demographic Data, Culture and Climate Data, and Community Life Data

Student and School Demographic Data	Culture and Climate Data	Community Life Data
Whole-school enrollment data	Staff-to-staff relationships	Family issues and configurations
Disaggregated enrollment data by student gender, grade level, race/ethnicity, English language proficiency, and disability	Student-to-student relationships	
Socioeconomic data	Student-to-staff relationships	Neighborhood/community makeup
Mobility and stability of students and staff	Respect for diversity and equity agenda	Local employment patterns
Highly qualified teachers	Leadership styles	Environmental impact—military deployments, layoffs, unemployment
		Immigration populations
		Migrant populations
		Homelessness

Once school counselors understand how to use data for equity, as described earlier, they are better able to develop goals and interventions that address equity in a multifaceted manner. They no longer view reaching a goal as a singular event, but rather recognize the complexity of and interrelationship among various data elements in categories with gaps. Moreover, using data in this way complements a systems theory approach to school counseling, as it emphasizes the interdependent and interrelated nature of systems, hence the use of multilevel interventions. In addition to access, attainment, and achievement data, there is also *student and school demographic data*, *culture and climate data*, and *community life data*, referred to as part of the *Rubric of Data Elements*. These data elements can be collected in more informal ways and can substantially impact student success, as indicated in Table 4.3.

Systemic Assessment

With a solid grasp of data knowledge and skills, school counselors are positioned to create a program that equitably serves the entire school population. To do this school counselors conduct a **systemic assessment**, a process used to identify the needs of students and of the larger community by reaching every subsystem of that community. These subsystems include the various microsystems present (e.g., various subgroups of students, teachers, and administrators), as well as the relationships among the various microsystems. The goal of the systemic assessment is to ensure that relevant data are collected that represent the needs of diverse populations, as identified by those populations. The purpose of conducting a systemic assessment is to use the data to drive the school counseling program so that it is relevant and serves the dynamic and ever-changing needs of a community in a culturally responsive manner. In this way, the services of the school counseling program can be said to reflect the context and demographics of the school. When the school counseling program is relevant to the needs of the school, it more easily integrates or interfaces with the educational program and supports the mission of the school.

Systemic assessments employ multiple methods of data collection within the school and from external sources in the district. For example, data can be gathered by examining both school and district databases. Extending a systemic assessment to the district level allows counselors to understand the needs of their school in relation to the larger district. This perspective helps mold and shape goal development and the strategic planning process. Many data reports are available at the district level and can range from reports submitted to the state department of education on a yearly basis to more contextualized or in-house reports. Examples of these types of reports may include adequate yearly progress (AYP) reports, graduation reports, and college-going reports. More-qualitative methods such as surveys, focus groups, interviews, and observations can also be used to gather information and data.

When determining what types of data will be collected, it is essential that school counselors include access, attainment, and achievement data. By examining the various data elements in each of the three data categories, professional school counselors are more likely to get an in-depth understanding of student needs and the barriers that hinder the equitable outcomes. In addition to the data elements within access, attainment, and achievements listed earlier, student and school demographic, culture and climate, and community life data should be addressed in a systemic assessment. These areas can provide powerful information about the dynamic life of a community. Once data from the assessment are collected, they are disaggregated to provide a clear picture of the needs of all students and the school. Data can be disaggregated in many ways. Some of the most common ways to disaggregate data elements about student access, attainment, and achievement are by student group, grade, gender, socioeconomic level, English language proficiency, disability, and mobility. Once the needs are identified, data-driven goals can be developed for the systemic school counseling program. This process ensures that the school counseling program is reflective of student need.

Data-Driven Goals

The goals of a systemic, data-driven school counseling program represent a confluence of several points. First, goals represent the overall desired outcome for all students. Second, goals represent the attempt to close the gaps between student groups, as well as the difference between established standards and the reality of the data for all students in a school or district. Third, goals are influenced by national, state, district, and local school goals. National goals (e.g., AYP requirements) provide key mandates such as closing the access, attainment, and achievement gaps. For example, common goals include improving attendance and graduation rates and ensuring safe and drug-free schools. States consider these national goals in developing their strategic plans and add issues specific to their states. These state goals may originate in the state department of education, a board of regents, or gubernatorial mandates, depending on the state and those currently in political office. These additional mandates could put a focus on issues such as promoting African-American male achievement or promoting literacy or attending to the psychological repercussions of military deployments. School districts attend to these goals, while adapting them to the specific needs, contexts, and demographics of their populations. Individual schools add or adapt additional goals based on the needs identified by their data and their mission statement.

Within the context of national, state, district, and schoolwide goals and missions, professional school counselors analyze and interpret the data collected from the systemic assessment to create the specific goals on which the school counseling program is based. Goals are developed as general, data-based statements of a desired outcome. To ensure that goals are systemic and reflect district needs, professional school counselors can team and collaborate with counselors at feeder schools to develop goals that fortify students during transitions and identify potential trouble spots. The goals then guide program implementation and individual school counselor performance. Table 4.4 presents a host of student issues affected by school policies, practices, and procedures.

Goals are written so that they identify concrete measures for the results and can be aligned to other schoolwide measures of student access, attainment, and achievement. In this way, the results of the school counseling program address the needs and concerns within the delivery and outcomes of the educational program. Once goals are developed, they are prioritized and "sized" for feasibility of implementation. Goals and corresponding interventions that are relevant, feasible, and aligned with the needs of the educational program have a higher likelihood of contributing to the overall success of students. As the school's goals exist in the context of district, state, and national goals, it is appropriate that the goals of each

TABLE 4.4   Student Issues Affected by School Policies, Practices, and Procedures

Attendance	Student recognition
Discipline	Club membership
Tardiness	Release time from class for school-sponsored activities
Suspensions	Promotion and retention
Makeup work due to illness	Transitions from one level to another
Student recognition	Scholarships
Club membership	Testing practices
Decisions regarding placement in rigorous curricula	Communication with families and the community
Dissemination of academic and postsecondary information	College advising and application procedures

school counseling program reflect wider concerns such as the AYP status of the school. A school counseling program that is not supportive of and that fails to address these broader needs directly through its goals and interventions is not integral to the mission of the school (i.e., it is a marginal program). Such marginalized programs and services do not serve the needs of all students.

But how are goals actually written? Goals must contain certain components to be able to show the metrics on completion of the desired interventions. For example, a school that wants to increase successful transitions from elementary to middle school needs to think strategically and specifically about the needs of its students. First, the school needs to establish a baseline and determine criteria:

- What are the data elements that define a successful transition?
- Based on the criteria, how many students make a successful transition—and who are they?

Second, the school must disaggregate both longitudinal data and snapshot data, if available:

- What inequities are identified?

Third, based on the inequities identified, it must write a measurable goal in a metric format:

- What is the desired percentage increase or decrease in the identified data element?
- How many students and what percentage does that desired goal represent?

This means that the goal clearly states what percentage of increase or decrease will occur after the intervention. It is important to clarify the meaning of a percentage with the number of students the percentage represents because a given percentage in one school can mean something very different in another school in terms of actual numbers of students affected. For example, in School A, a 10% increase may involve 16 students, whereas in School B a 10% increase may involve 120 students—so School A is 10% ($n = 16$) and School B is 10% ($n = 120$).

A goal may be written in either of the following ways:

A broad, general goal: "Increase successful transitions between elementary and middle school by 10% ($n = 20$) for the new sixth-grade class of 2013."

A more specific goal: "Increase successful transitions for the incoming African-American male sixth-grade students by 15% ($n = 48$) beginning fall of 2013."

Essential to the more specific goal is the ability of school counselors to focus on those populations most in need of assistance.

After the goal is written, the next steps in the strategic planning process can be activated, including (a) determining the feasibility of goal implementation and revisions, if needed, (b) implementing the goal, (c) collecting data, and (d) promoting advocacy to both sustain and grow successful results.

| VOICES FROM THE FIELD 4.2 | DALLAS ISD SCHOOL COUNSELORS: OWN THE TURF ON COLLEGE AND CAREER READINESS |

The word "Data" was the new four-letter word for our school counselors. It was difficult for the counselors to understand why it was important for them to interpret and understand the data. Professional school counselors felt that the data was meant for administrators and did not have any part in their counseling program. It was very clear to me that counselors had to learn to identify the gaps, interpret results, and feel comfortable about working with the school's data. They had to be convinced that all educators, including school counselors, are responsible for improving student achievement. The journey started by demonstrating the impact and the significant role counselors played in student success. The focus was to design their counseling programs based on data-driven decisions.

Our journey started with the school counselors signing the Own the Turf pledge campaign. By signing and committing to the pledge, they agreed to become experts and leaders in college career counseling. This literally transformed the mind-set of the counselors. The acronym shift I would express to the counselors was NCLB (No Child Left Behind) really means No *Counselor* Left Behind. Our counselors had to commit to be learners, leaders, and data experts. Each school had different data elements to review and analyze. Some of the data elements reviewed by the counselors were increasing graduation rates, increasing attendance rates, reducing grade retentions, increasing AP enrollment, and many others. In addition, the district had specific districtwide goals on which the high schools were being measured. These goals became the driving force behind Own the Turf in college career counseling. The results confirmed the influence that the counselors had in designing a counseling program that positively impacts student achievement.

Example of the targeted goals met:

2012 Targeted Goals	Met Goals
80% Submitted College Applications	Yes—80%
60% Registered and took the SAT/ACT Exams	Yes—90%
50% Submitted FAFSA	Yes—51%
35% Scholarships Offered	Yes —41%

It was imperative to find a data tool to help counselors monitor and track their progress. This data tool had to be user friendly with minimal data entry. With the help of the Instructional Technology Department, the first tool developed was called The Counselor Tracking Form. This tool was simple to use, but required data entry by the counselors and did not have the reports that the counselors or my department needed. This evolved to our second version data tool called the College Ready Portal. This portal pulled data from our existing student management system and uploaded the specific targeted goals to the portal daily. Data such as SAT or ACT results, FAFSA results, college applications submitted, and so on were uploaded with no data entry from the school counselors. The data that had to be entered on the portal were the scholarships offered and received by the students. Summary reports of the overall district percentages by individual schools are created each 6 weeks from January to June. This report was shared with upper-level administration and principals. Sharing the summary results districtwide served two major purposes. First, the results shared painted a picture of how well one school is doing compared to another school in the district. Most principals or counselors do not like to see their school at the bottom of the list. Second, the data picture guided the counselors and the principals to pinpoint the challenges and started the conversations on what strategies were needed to increase the percentages of the college readiness goals.

The professional school counselor's mind-set changed from data as negative to using data to identify opportunities for improvement. It is important for school counselors to disaggregate the data, establish a baseline, develop a plan, educate stakeholders, and monitor progress frequently to sustain continuous improvement. The proof is in the data.

Strategies and interventions implemented are intentional. There is no room for professional school counselors to entertain the idea of "random acts of guidance." There is still much work ahead to learn about disaggregating and compiling the data, but the counselor who Owns the Turf understands the power behind the data.

Source: Sylvia Lopez, Director of Counseling Services, Dallas Independent School District, TX

PLANNING THE SCHOOL COUNSELING PROGRAM

Strategic Planning and Program Development

Throughout this chapter, we have discussed parts of a strategic plan and the use of data-driven strategic interventions as a way to match the needs of students and the community with program development and interventions for a desired outcome (Brown & Trusty, 2005a). The process of developing the program's structure, planning and delivering the program, and ensuring accountability is similar to that used for school improvement and educational reform. Moreover, using strategic interventions helps school counselors adopt a more proactive approach and focus on the outputs in the form of student success rather than on the input of the counseling program. It calls into account the relevance of any program or intervention to be directly focused on the identified needs of students. The steps in the process of planning and implementing a school counseling program are outlined here and modified and demonstrated in the example shown in Figure 4.6:

- Establish a vision and a mission.
- Determine the outcomes stated in the mission statement and how they are measured.
- Conduct a systemic assessment to collect data and identify need (this includes information from a gap analysis and program assessment).
- Engage in goal development, feasibility analysis, and prioritization.
- Select and develop interventions as constellations that include both proximal and distal data elements.
- Implement systemic interventions and monitor outcomes with established benchmarks, timelines, and responsibilities. Communicate the plan to all stakeholders.
- Collect data at both formative and summative points.
- Analyze and report findings to all stakeholders.
- Engage in advocacy efforts to translate gains into established practice codified in policy.
- Establish a strategic planning review and revision cycle at 1-, 3-, and 5-year intervals.

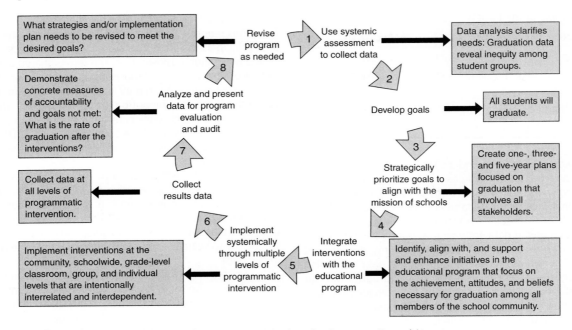

FIGURE 4.6   Vision: Social justice; Mission: Access and equity; Program: Data driven.

The Program Calendar

A calendar for the school counseling program is an essential tool that serves a variety of purposes. First, the calendar is the tool that is the visual representation of the interventions that a school counselor will use to reach data-driven goals. It serves as the written representation of the strategic plan and goals of the program. Second, the calendar format and structure demonstrate the systemic nature of the program in a monthly plan by outlining the multilevel interventions. Third, the calendar serves as a means of organizing interventions into a clear and intentional order. It defines the work of the counselor and presents a structure of professional activities similar to that used by other educational professionals in the school.

Calendars are organized by year, month, week, or day. Yearly calendars are global, so we recommend a monthly calendar as the format of choice for a school counseling department. The activities for each month can be laid out using the same template for each month, with the eight levels of intervention as a base. This ensures consistency of format in the delivery interventions from month to month. It also allows stakeholders to become familiar with the format of school counseling program delivery. See Table 4.5 for an outline of a calendar. Once the monthly calendar is established, individual counselors can then transfer their assignments to their own weekly and daily calendars.

IMPLEMENTATION AT MULTIPLE LEVELS OF PROGRAMMATIC INTERVENTION

As demonstrated in Figure 4.4, school counseling program implementation can occur at multiple levels, including individual, group, classroom, grade, school, district, family, and community to ensure success of data-driven goals. Implementation at each of these levels will be described in the following sections.

Individual

This level of intervention is used to respond to crisis situations and issues specific to individual students. Importantly, individual counseling is not the key target of school counseling program interventions. Issues identified at this level provide insight into issues in the larger school that can then be further examined using specific data elements. Interventions can be developed and delivered at other programmatic levels to address issues in a preventive, developmental, and even remedial fashion. Services at the individual level include personal and crisis counseling. Most often included in this area, referral represents collaborative interventions at the community level and therefore is not a singular intervention. In addition, issues at the individual level involve policies that are practiced schoolwide, such as policies around confidentiality, informed consent, duty to warn, and parental or guardian

TABLE 4.5   A Content Outline of Activities for a Calendar for a Systemic, Data-Driven School Counseling Program

Each Month
- Data driven goal(s) addressed
- Ongoing activities including team meetings
- Individual level
- Referrals
- IEP meetings
- Section 504 meetings
- Crisis counseling

Group (should indicate the grade level[s])
- Groups that are beginning, continuing, and/or ending this month
- Any other targeted group activities

Classroom (collaborative classroom instruction)
- Targeted interventions with classrooms in need

Grade
- Transitional interventions at a particular grade level
- Grade-specific interventions—preventive, developmental, remedial

School
- Data collection, analysis, presentation, planning, and revision of programs and policies
- Discipline policies
- Course enrollment patterns
- Attendance policies

- Interventions with all teachers
- In-service on learning styles
- Interventions focused on schoolwide culture and climate

District
- Vertical and horizontal activities to address pervasive needs

Family
- Parent/guardian groups
- Informational/skill-building workshops
- Advocacy activities for parents

Community
- Task force for equity
- Community advisory boards
- Collaborations to promote achievement
- Community educational and career mentors
- Special presenters
- Business sponsors for student needs
- School–community partnerships
- School-to-work initiatives

Professional Development Activities
- Conferences and in-house trainings
- School counselor building- and district-level meetings

Planning for Upcoming Events
- List the activities that need to be accomplished to ensure timely and thorough planning for each upcoming intervention

permission for counseling. Data around issues that necessitate the use of these policies (e.g., child abuse, substance abuse, self-injurious behaviors) can inform counselors about the health and wellness of the school population, which can also be addressed at other levels in a preventive fashion. Other data that are often collected at this level include the number of students a counselor meets with, although these data are sometimes limited in value because they do not address outcomes.

Group

Efficacious use of group interventions requires examination of data elements gleaned from a systemwide assessment. This level of intervention can be either developmental or remedial and responds to data that identify specific and targeted needs across all grade levels. Group interventions can focus on specific subgroups of students or can be offered across student groups, depending on the identified needs of students. In addition, group work is a critical level of intervention because it provides social modeling and peer support and promotes learning through a developmentally appropriate forum. Because this level of intervention serves only a small population of students, it

should be intentionally interrelated to corresponding services at other levels.

Classroom

Collaborative classroom instruction can be offered in one particular class, across several classes in the school, or as part of an interdisciplinary team effort. Data are used at this level to identify classrooms and teachers in need of specific and targeted assistance with transforming the culture and climate of the teaching and learning environment to deliver developmental and preventive interventions that result in specific student outcomes. For example, specific collaborative classroom instruction interventions can focus on learning styles, healthy classroom relationships, or the sharing of responsibility. Likewise, they can supplement an academic unit such as diversity in history, citizenship, careers in the curriculum, or any other area that affects student performance and attainment. This level of intervention is a powerful way for school counselors to connect their work to the educational program and academic curriculum in specific subjects. For example, school counselors can team with teachers in history or civics on issues of civil rights, conflicts and peace, and a wide range of the "isms." They can also team with language arts teachers around themes of relationships, personal triumphs, and challenges in novels that students are reading. Or they can even work with health teachers on issues of personal health and wellness such as healthy dating and friendship, areas of substance prevention and abuse, healthy nutrition, eating and exercise, or in any other class to infuse career information to help students mold and shape their future goals and aspirations. All these strategies can be linked to the data elements schools and counselors are trying to move to ensure healthy human growth and development for all students.

Grade

Grade-level interventions specifically attend to the context of grade-level experiences (e.g., sixth grade) and transitions at developmental benchmarks (e.g., entering and leaving kindergarten, middle school, and high school). An emphasis on examining policies that affect specific grade levels is essential at this level of intervention. Because of the broader reach of this level, intervention usually involves a number of other levels of service, such as the school and community levels, and may require long-term planning as for transition events or postsecondary planning events. The ability to analyze and use disaggregated data on postsecondary plans, promotions, course enrollment patterns, and retentions helps the professional school counselor discern the influence of grade-level and transition points on these processes. In addition, revision of grade-level policies that either support or hinder achievement is appropriate. Finally, grade-level data by subgroups (e.g., ethnicity, socioeconomic status, English language proficiency) are analyzed to develop interventions both within and between grade levels to promote achievement. An example of interventions at the grade level is transition activities—from elementary to middle school, from middle to high school, and from high school to postsecondary options. Other examples include senior activities such as college and career application completion, FAFSA completion, resume writing, and the scholarship process.

School

The school level of intervention has the greatest potential for removing systemic barriers and creating the conditions for learning at all other levels (Hayes, Nelson, Tabin, Pearson, & Worthy, 2002; House & Hayes, 2002). As far back as 1992, Gerler posited that the coordinating of systems-level interventions was the most important role of the professional school counselor. Now under accountability mandates, this level of intervention emphasizes reform as a whole-school challenge in which all stakeholders must be actively involved.

The potential of this level of intervention lies in examining the interrelatedness and interdependence of all school populations and the corresponding schoolwide disaggregated data. Interventions at this level involve the entire school, reflecting a data profile that includes policies and procedures, which are often the focus of these interventions. These interventions can also reflect areas of growth and development that are important to the entire school and focus on issues such as culture and climate. Interventions in these areas involve students, teachers, administrators, and all other school personnel to make the interventions strong collaborative initiatives. Finally, interventions at this level can provide the support necessary to ensure success of interventions at other levels. For example, policy change at this level can be the linchpin that helps more students enroll in rigorous courses at a particular grade level.

District

Interventions at the school district level focus on connecting the work of professional school counselors to the larger district in ways that respond to both vertical and lateral districtwide issues. In the same way that particular student needs can be pervasive in a school, those same needs can be pervasive throughout a district. Work at the district level can happen in several ways. First, student needs can be present across a district at elementary, middle, and high schools. For example, issues around attendance, discipline, or academic achievement and attainment can be pervasive and persistent. Second, sometimes issues can be more focused on one level, but involve all or some of the schools at that level. For example, in elementary schools, where students are more likely to be referred for special education than at other levels, it may be that there is disproportionate representation across the district of one student group over another. Although this is not solely an elementary school issue, a strong focus on the elementary level would be necessary to alter this situation. If there is a low college-going rate at multiple high schools across a district, it would be helpful for counselors to team and collaborate as they plan their interventions to increase the college-going rate among students. Such districtwide strategic interventions that pool the skill and resources of counselors in both vertical and horizontal teaming and collaboration can maximize time and efficiency and provide a broader perspective on the needs of students. To work effectively at this level, the professional school counselor must possess an understanding of the interrelationship between the needs of elementary, middle, and high school students and the factors that affect healthy growth and development, as well as a basic understanding of the functioning of schools at all levels. Data and gaps at this level can involve all three types: access, attainment, and achievement. The disaggregation of data at this level occurs across schools as well as within schools.

Family

The primary content of the interventions at the family level should include all the information, knowledge, and skills that school counselors impart to students delivered in ways that inform families. The goal is to ensure that families, parents, and guardians learn the skills that enable them to successfully navigate school and community services to gain access to resources for their children and assist their children in mastering the skills necessary for educational success. Intentional and culturally responsive outreach to marginalized parent and guardian populations can promote increased engagement of their children in the educational process and thus result in greater equity. It can also help parents and families take an active and empowered role in the school. This level of intervention uses data to intentionally assess need and involve families, parents, and guardians in the school counseling program as equal partners in promoting student educational success. Data at this level most often are collected by counting how many parents attend an activity. Although it is important to have data to demonstrate that increased numbers of families and parents participate, it is also important to collect data that can demonstrate that the knowledge and skill parents gained made a difference in the lives of their students through changes in targeted data elements.

Community

Interventions at the community level are used to actively involve all community stakeholders in creating broad-based partnerships for student success. This broad base can increase the likelihood that students will experience consistent expectations for success across the multiple contexts of their lives. These can include places of worship, libraries, sport and entertainment venues, and local businesses. Also important are even broader outreach and public relations efforts with local civic organizations, school boards, businesses, social services agencies, professional organizations, state departments of education, and federal bodies that contribute to the creation of standards, policies, and laws that affect schools, school counseling programs, and student achievement. Implementation of community-level interventions requires strategic planning over time. Careful planning, documentation, timely and clear communication, and shared decision making are essential. As with all other levels of intervention, using data to create urgency and drive decision making and using inquiry to continue to focus, evaluate, and revise interventions are essential and the hallmarks of a well-articulated data process. Administrative support and sanctioning (preferably codified in policy) of the collaborative efforts at this level of intervention can help prevent school counseling programs from becoming marginalized and superfluous to the mission of schools (Ripley & Goodnough, 2001).

THEORY INTO PRACTICE 4.5

AN EXAMPLE OF MULTILEVEL INTERVENTIONS AT THE HIGH SCHOOL LEVEL

This example primarily focuses on using data to increase participation in one school. However, the interventions used in this example could be used in different schools across a district. Or the strategies used in different schools to reach this goal may vary depending on student needs. It is important to examine the data and determine which interventions are most needed in a particular school.

Level: High school

Goal: Increase the number of students entering rigorous courses by 10% ($n = 40$)

The levels in action:

Individual: Provide individual counseling that focuses on building aspirations, addressing stereotypes, disseminating information, carrying out academic planning, carrying out career and college planning, and reviewing high school graduation requirements and college requirements.

Group: Carry out academic planning, conduct college and career groups, focus on building aspirations for the future, and review high school and college graduation requirements.

Classroom: Cover the same topics as at the group level, but focus them more on the educational aspect of the information around academic, college, and career planning. Make sure messaging is consistent with individual and group initiatives. Target classrooms where messages of educational equity are not readily accepted.

(Continued)

Grade: Target grade-level information and activities to ensure optimal enrollment in rigorous courses, provide information that outlines the opportunities at each grade level, and implement culture and climate initiatives around educational and career success. Address what each grade level needs to know.

School: Collect schoolwide data related to course enrollment and completion patterns, as well as grades, all of which should be disaggregated by group, grade, gender, English language proficiency, disability, and any other salient demographics. Conduct workshops with teachers on differentiated learning, cultural responsiveness, classroom management, and belief systems.

District: Engage in vertical teaming with middle school counselors to prepare students and parents for the transition to high school and the need to take rigorous courses as it relates to postsecondary choices; provide information on graduation requirements, course selection, career choice, and building aspirations. Consult with other high schools about their difficulties or successes in increasing student enrollment in rigorous courses.

Family: Conduct workshops and outreach for parents that address all the areas discussed earlier. Ensure the same information and messaging for parents along with the use of specific culturally responsive techniques that respond to multiple generational, ethnic, racial, religious, and language differences, to name a few. Engage in advocacy that opens the doors of empowerment for parents and families.

Community: Inform and engage community and business leaders in understanding the importance of equitable student participation and performance in rigorous courses and the impact successful participation has on their businesses and the community at large.

THEORY INTO PRACTICE 4.6

EXAMPLE OF A MULTILEVEL SYSTEMIC INTERVENTION TO INCREASE FAFSA COMPLETION

The goal is to increase the number of seniors who complete the FAFSA form by 10% ($n = 25$).

Individual: Meeting with students individually may be especially helpful for students who are first-generation college-going or for those students who do not qualify for federal student aid and who need more personalized assistance.

Group: For any underserved or first-generation students, groups can offer more personalized and customized assistance around postsecondary financial planning and FAFSA completion.

Classroom: Integrate content about postsecondary financial planning into math classes, civics and sociology classes, as well as specialty classes focused on career education.

Grade: Beginning in the ninth grade, structure opportunities for all students to learn how to fill out a FAFSA form; learn the documentation required, special circumstances, benefits, and consequences of not engaging in financial planning; identify financial opportunities for students who may not qualify for federal student aid; and show how to read a Student Aid Report (SAR).

School: Share updated information about postsecondary financial planning and FAFSA completion with all school personnel and help them outline their role in supporting students' FAFSA completion.

District: Use sites like Federal Student Aid and the FAFSA Completion by High School data (www.studentaid.ed.gov) to find the numbers of those submitted and completed across the district—by school—to determine need. Meet with school counselors at other high schools to share strategies and messaging aimed at FAFSA completion. Work with middle school counselors to continue and build on student learning they provided on postsecondary financial planning and the FAFSA.

Family: Engage in outreach to families to ensure that all the information taught to students about FAFSA and financial planning for postsecondary education is taught to parents and families as well. Help them learn their role and responsibilities in the financial planning process as well as the benefits and consequences of nonparticipation for their students. Conduct sessions both in the school and in the community. Develop relationships with parents and families that are leaders in their communities to assist in reaching a greater portion of the population. Make sure all services honor and respect the diversity of all parents and families.

Community: Locate and outreach to local businesses, organizations, and educational and faith-based institutions that have information, knowledge, and skill to help assist parents and families with the financial planning process, especially the FAFSA, for postsecondary education.

CULTURAL REFLECTION 4.2

A Reflection for Elementary, Middle, or High School Counselors

After engaging in a systemic assessment that included an examination of discipline referrals, suspensions, and expulsions you notice that not only are more students of color involved in discipline actions, but there is also an overrepresentation of male students. Inquiry with some of the teachers and administrators reveals a "what else do you expect" attitude and belief. Explanations such as where they live, their family makeup, socioeconomic status, societal influences as well as peer influence all paint a picture that says the data—which represents the lives of children and adolescents—is just a reflection of a reality that cannot change, and thus no direct action for change is occurring in the school.

- Do you believe the life circumstances of the students are an insurmountable barrier to school and life success?
- What is your belief?
- What is your response to the teachers' and administrators' assessment of the problem?
- What is happening in the school that helps perpetuate the belief expressed by the teachers and administrators?
- How does systemic and institutionalized oppression perpetuate low expectations and stereotypic images?
- How is it communicated to the students?
- How would internalized oppression be played out in this scenario?
- What do you believe a school community can do to help create a culture and climate where all students can thrive?
- What is your role as a school counselor?
- How and in what ways do you need to grow and develop as a culturally competent individual to respond to this situation?
- Where do you start?

EVALUATING THE SYSTEMIC, DATA-DRIVEN SCHOOL COUNSELING PROGRAM

Full and detailed attention to program evaluation and accountability, research, and best practices requires in-depth study. This brief discussion will focus on the importance of program evaluation and provide some clarification of terms. First, evaluation demonstrates accountability and establishes the credibility of professional school counselors and the school counseling program as viable contributors to the achievement of all students. This occurs when concrete measures can demonstrate that established goals were met and allows counselors to assess the effect of the program and the levels of programmatic interventions that were most successful. It also allows counselors to determine combinations of interventions that proved successful in goal attainment.

Second, evaluation demonstrates where goals were not met. Determining when goals are not met is equally as important as determining success. Unachieved goals highlight the need for further examination of needs, assessment methods, strategic planning, and selected intervention, as well as the skill level of all stakeholders involved in implementing the initiative. Also, it is important to not continue to engage in interventions that do not work.

Third, it is important to make the distinction between research and school counseling program evaluation. Carey and Dimmitt (2006) define evaluation as information that allows stakeholders to assess programs and interventions to make better decisions within the program context. The information gained by evaluating programs and interventions is designed to answer this question: "Did this work in our context?" These authors also define research as adding "knowledge to a field of study and . . . [contributing] to the growth of a theory" (p. 417). Many professional school counselors do not have the resources to conduct stringent research studies, but do have the ability to conduct evaluations. This is an important difference between research and evaluation.

Fourth, when school counselors do engage in evaluation, Carey (2006) suggests that it is ideal for programs and interventions to be evaluated within a framework of three types of relevant outcomes: immediate, proximal, and distal. Immediate outcomes address questions such as "Did students learn what was intended?" and include outcomes tied to learning objectives, such as comprehension or changes in knowledge. Proximal outcomes answer questions such as "Did students change in ways that predict long-term changes in school behavior and performance?" and include changes in test-taking skills, college search skills, and decision-making skills. Distal outcomes answer questions such as "Did students show long-term changes in behavior and/or performance?" and include changes in graduation rates, college placement data, achievement test scores, and discipline data. Data in all three areas are important to school counselor accountability and provide clarity about school counselor impact because data elements from distal outcomes alone can be difficult to link to school counselor actions (Brown & Trusty, 2005a). Finally, linking these kinds of outcomes to strategic interventions can benefit school counseling practice and assist in program development. Now, as a culminating activity for Chapter 4, apply what you have learned about systemic, data-driven school counseling program practices by addressing the issues raised in Case Studies 4.1–4.4.

CASE STUDY 4.1

You just started your first job as an elementary school counselor, and you are the only school counselor in the school. There are three other elementary schools in the district, and they all have one school counselor each. Your school is primarily a Title I school and is known for low achievement. Attendance and promotions rates are not as high as the rest of the schools in the district. Parent and family involvement is low, and teachers are not sure how to work with you to help students achieve. The school's goals are to increase attendance, promotions, and state test scores. How will you use these data, your skills of inquiry, and multilevel interventions to drive the creation of an equitable and culturally competent program that is customized to your population?

CASE STUDY 4.2

You are a middle school counselor in a school system where the new goal is to ensure all students graduate college and career ready with initiatives to begin in middle school. What five data elements would be most important for the school counselors in your school to examine to assist your students, and what inquiry would be needed to determine larger school needs? Discuss how the answers to these questions would inform practice to help make school counselors integral in this new district initiative.

CASE STUDY 4.3

You were just appointed the building-level director of school counseling in your school. You have a team of three other school counselors who mostly rely on using individual, group, and some grade-level initiatives to deliver school counseling services. You know that the work is not systemic, and thus not all students are receiving services. How will you explain systemic multilevel interventions and how to use data to drive those interventions to your colleagues to increase efficiency and address the equity needs of all students?

CASE STUDY 4.4

You are a school counselor in a school where you see data used in the aggregate form and without attention to the three types of data. As a result you are aware that equity issues are not being addressed despite the claims of initiatives to close the gaps in student outcomes. What information, knowledge, and skills are needed in the school and by whom to create a change in this building?

Summary/Conclusion

This chapter has offered a rationale, description, and tools useful in creating a systemic, data-driven school counseling program. To build this type of program, professional school counselors need to possess the values, attitudes, and beliefs implicit in the transformed role of the professional school counselor. In addition, professional school counselors who possess the awareness, knowledge, and skills necessary to develop and implement such programs will ensure that school counseling is integral to the mission of the school and demonstrate the value-added worth of school counseling through concrete measures of accountability. Most important, the implementation of systemic, data-driven school counseling programs can form the bedrock of an effort to ensure that the needs of all students are equitably met in a learning environment that encourages academic success with cultural integrity.

Creating systemic, data-driven school counseling programs is the ethical responsibility of all professional school counselors, including school-based directors of school counseling services and district directors of school counseling. Although the knowledge and skills needed to develop and implement systemic, data-driven programs are slowly becoming accepted practice for school counseling professionals, attaining these skills and others necessary to meet the needs of all students is an ethical responsibility regardless of the stage in one's career. Implicit in this statement is the recognition that professional school counselors are self-reflective practitioners who engage in ongoing professional development to ensure they are relevant. Such a commitment ensures professional school counselors will develop the competence to implement the systemic, data-driven programs that equitably meet the academic, personal/social and college and career needs of all students.

Activities

1. Reflecting on your graduate training thus far, identify areas in which you need to develop greater levels of awareness, knowledge, and skill to begin the career-long process of becoming a transformed school counselor. What do you need to do to improve those skills throughout the remainder of your training and after you graduate?

2. In which level(s) of program intervention do you feel most comfortable, and which level(s) are most challenging? Why? What do you need to do to improve those skills throughout the remainder of your training and after you graduate?

3. Using the Department of Education website for your state, locate the state report card or other student data. Determine if it is access, attainment, or achievement data. What other type of data may be needed to tell a more in-depth story about that data. For example, if it is access data, what other attainment or achievement data may be important?

4. Using the data in activity 3, apply the line of inquiry used earlier in the chapter to begin to determine what the equity issues may be around this data.

5. Create a goal using the method discussed earlier. Apply the Programmatic Levels of Intervention to implement a multilevel solution in a school.

CHAPTER

5

Accountability: Assessing Needs, Determining Outcomes, and Evaluating Programs

Bradley T. Erford

Editor's Introduction: Education reform movements have made accountability a central responsibility of all educators, including professional school counselors. But accountability is not just tallying the number of students seen for individual or group counseling or how much time has been spent in direct or indirect services. At its core, accountability addresses several issues: needs assessment, program (process) assessment, service assessment, outcomes studies, and performance appraisal. Each of these important facets of accountability is addressed in this chapter.

ACCOUNTABILITY IN SCHOOL COUNSELING

One of the cornerstones of the *ASCA National Model* (American School Counselor Association [ASCA], 2012) is accountability. Accountability involves responsibility for professional actions—in other words, for the effectiveness of one's actions. In the more specific context of school counseling program accountability, this may involve

- Identifying and collaborating with stakeholder groups (e.g., a school counseling program advisory committee, parents/guardians, teachers, students)
- Collecting data and assessing needs of students, staff, and community
- Setting goals and establishing objectives based on data and determined need
- Implementing effective interventions to address the goals and objectives
- Measuring the outcomes or results of these interventions
- Using these results for program improvement
- Sharing results with major stakeholder groups such as administration, teachers and staff, parents and guardians, students, school boards, community and business leaders, school counselors, and supervisors

It is undeniable that accountability and assessment have, in general, been given greater visibility in both the extant counseling literature and the day-to-day functioning of the average professional school counselor over the past 15 years. Indeed, calls for greater accountability from professional school counselors have been occurring since at least the mid-1970s (Nims, James, & Hughey, 1998). This increased focus on accountability is due to numerous contemporary factors, including the education reform movement, the rise in high stakes and other standardized testing programs, federal and state legislation (e.g., Reach for the Top, No Child Left Behind [NCLB] Act, Title I, the Individuals with Disabilities Education Improvement Act, Section 504 of the Rehabilitation Act), data-driven transformative initiatives, and outcomes-driven practice emphases. It is the professional and ethical responsibility of professional school counselors to ensure that the comprehensive school counseling services offered to stakeholder groups are truly effective. Given the impetus of school reform, professional

92

school counselors need to partner with administration and key stakeholders to promote accountability and provide effective services to ensure the academic success of all students.

The focus of this chapter is on the wide-ranging accountability functions of the professional school counselor, including needs assessment, program assessment, and interpretation of assessment results. The content of this chapter is among the most important in terms of understanding the needs of a school community and a school counseling program's effectiveness (i.e., answering that critical question, "Why do we need school counselors?"). This information will also allow professional school counselors to speak the language of decision makers, thus allowing social and academic advocacy for children with special needs or those encountering systemic barriers to academic, career, or personal/social success. Finally, every professional school counselor should be constantly asking and gathering information to answer the question, "Is what I'm doing working with this student?" As with nearly every counselor function, conducting accountability studies has its advantages and challenges (see Table 5.1). Consider these and others as you peruse the remainder of this chapter.

More to the point, accountability in the school counseling program must address five primary questions using the five accountability measures noted in parentheses following each question: (a) What are the needs of the school's student population when compared to these standards? (needs assessment); (b) Is a comprehensive, standards-based program in place? (program [process] assessment); (c) What services were implemented to address the identified needs and standards? (service assessment); (d) What was the result of the implemented services? (results or outcomes studies); and (e) How well is the professional school counselor performing? (performance evaluation/appraisal). This chapter will focus on each of these questions.

In this age of school reform and accountability, program evaluation is more important than ever. Traditionally, however, professional school counselors for many reasons have failed to hold their programs and services accountable or to provide evidence that activities undertaken were achieving intended results. Some complain that the nature of what school counselors do is so abstract and complicated that it renders the services and results unmeasurable. Others are so busy attempting to meet the needs of students that they shift time that should be spent in evaluation to responsive interventions. Some lack an

---

TABLE 5.1   Advantages and Challenges of Accountability Studies

Advantages

1. Data is almost always better than perception when it comes to guiding decision making about programs, practices, and interventions.

2. Accountability studies help demonstrate necessity, efficiency, and effectiveness of counseling services.

3. Accountability studies can help identify professional development and staff development needs.

4. Professional school counselors can network to share program results, thereby spreading the word about effective practices.

5. Conducting accountability studies is a professional responsibility and demonstrates one's commitment to personal and professional improvement.

6. Accountability results can serve a public relations function by informing educators and the public of a school counseling program's accomplishments.

Challenges

1. Outcome measures and surveys take some training and skill (sometimes including consultation with experts) to develop.

2. It takes time and resources to do quality outcomes research and evaluation, time and resources that could be dedicated to additional service delivery.

3. Many do not understand the nature and purpose of accountability (e.g., impact of school counseling program on student outcome data) because of misperceptions or previous "bad" experiences (e.g., evaluations by principals or others not skilled in counseling, having to "count" every minute or service).

4. Data are sometimes "overinterpreted" or given undue meaning (e.g., the facts may not support the conclusion). All studies have limitations that must be considered when arriving at conclusions.

5. Comprehensive evaluations are seldom conducted. More often, bits and pieces of evaluative information are collected, and the "big picture" is often incomplete.

CULTURAL REFLECTION 5.1

The Culture of Accountability Within the School

As school counselors we are trained to view schools from a systemic perspective and as an evolving culture. Schools are famous for testing students to see what they know and are able to do. But a huge part of accountability involves personal assessment and improvement. Developing a culture that values accountability involves challenging every faculty, staff, and administrator to provide evidence that what we are doing is resulting in positive changes in our students. Otherwise, we are just repeating rituals that do not help us to achieve the desired objectives and outcomes. How can the professional school counselor work collaboratively with faculty, staff, and administrators to develop a school culture that values accountability?

---

understanding of the methods and procedures needed to conduct accountability studies. Still others are unsure of the effectiveness of the services provided and shy away from accountability unless forced to do so by supervisors.

Whatever the reason, the end result is a glaring lack of accountability that poses dangers for the future of the profession. Each of the listed reasons contributes to a shirking of professional and ethical responsibility to ensure that the services provided to students, school personnel, and parents are of high quality and effective in meeting intended needs. Think about it from a business perspective. How long would a business last if it continued to engage in indiscernible or ineffective activities, the value of which was unknown to the business's consumers, managers, or employees? Such businesses are selected out for extinction! The same may hold true for professional school counselors. Without accountability data to back up service provision, school counseling services could be among the first "nonessential services" to go during budget cutbacks. The key is to document and determine the worth of all aspects of the comprehensive school counseling program. The evaluation of a comprehensive school counseling program involves needs assessment, program (process) assessment, service assessment, results (outcomes) evaluation, and personnel evaluation. Each component is essential in holding school counseling programs accountable.

NEEDS ASSESSMENT

At least two primary purposes underlie the use of a needs assessment in school counseling programs. First, needs assessment helps professional school counselors understand the needs of various subpopulations of a school community. These subpopulations may include teachers, parents, students, administrators, community organizations, local businesses, and the general citizenry. Subpopulations may also include groups of students experiencing achievement gaps or differential access to rigorous academic programming. Each of these groups holds a stake in the success of the total educational enterprise. Second, needs assessment helps establish the priorities that guide the construction of a comprehensive, developmental school counseling program, as well as continuous quality improvement of the program. In this way, a needs assessment assesses not only what currently is, but also what should be. Assessing the needs of a school community provides a trajectory for addressing what the community values and desires to pursue. Two types of needs assessments are commonly conducted within school counseling programs: data-driven needs assessments and perceptions-based needs assessments.

Data-Driven Needs Assessments

Data-driven decision making deals with demonstrated need and impact, not perceived needs. It begins with an analysis of school-based performance data. Given the prominence of high-stakes testing and large-scale testing programs required under NCLB, schools are frequently provided with aggregated and disaggregated performance results. *Aggregated* means that all student results are lumped together to show total grade-level or schoolwide (average) results. Aggregated data are helpful in understanding how the average student performs in a given class, grade, or school, but tell very little about the diversity of learner performance or needs and nothing about how various subgroups or subpopulations performed. In Table 5.2, the aggregated results are represented by the "Total Grade" line at the top for a school with 100 fifth graders.

To fully understand how to use school performance data, professional school counselors must become proficient in understanding norm-referenced and criterion-referenced score interpretation. Although a comprehensive explanation of score interpretation is beyond the scope of the text and typically encountered by counselors in an assessment or testing course, what follows can be considered a very basic primer on interpretation of norm-referenced scores.

Note that in the example in Table 5.2, the mean national percentile rank was 50. A percentile rank is most easily understood if one visualizes a lineup of 100 individuals, all with certain characteristics in common; in this case, they are all fifth-grade math students. Importantly, when interpreting percentile ranks, the first student in the line is the lowest-performing student, and the 100th student is the highest-performing student. A student's place indicates his

TABLE 5.2 Aggregated and Disaggregated Results From a Typical Large-Scale Math Achievement Test for a Total-School Fifth-Grade Level

	n	NPR	% in Quartile			
			Q_1	Q_2	Q_3	Q_4
Total Grade	100	50	19	31	26	24
Male	48	45	22	34	26	18
Female	52	56	10	31	31	28
Asian	8	72	0	25	38	38
Black	31	37	29	52	13	6
Hispanic	8	43	25	50	25	0
White	52	58	9	30	33	28
Other	1	44	0	100	0	0
Low SES	48	31	36	38	23	3
Non–Low SES	52	71	5	24	36	35
English (second language)	3	43	0	67	33	0
English (primary language)	97	51	19	30	27	24
Special Education	10	25	60	20	20	0
Non–Special Education	90	58	11	31	32	26

Note: n = number of students in sample; NPR = national percentile rank; "% in Quartile" means the percentage of the sample that performed in a given quartile; SES = Socioeconomic Status.

or her relative standing compared to other fifth-grade math students across the country (thus the term *national percentile rank*). For example, a student scoring at the 79th percentile performed better than 79% of the fifth graders in the national norm group or was the 79th student standing in the line of 100 students. Likewise, a student performing at the 5th percentile would be standing in the fifth place in line and has outperformed only 5% of the fifth graders in the nationwide norming group.

A *quartile* is a commonly used interpretive statistic that divides the percentile rank distribution into four segments. The first quartile includes percentile ranks ranging up to and including 25, the lowest quarter of a distribution and designated Q_1. The second quartile (Q_2) includes percentile ranks ranging from 26 to 50. The third quartile (Q_3) includes percentile ranks ranging from 51 to 75. The fourth quartile (Q_4) includes percentile ranks ranging from 76 and up, the highest quarter of the distribution. Some test publishers also use an interpretive statistic known as stanines. *Stanines*, short for "standard nine," divide a normal distribution into nine segments, although in a manner quite different from quartiles. Stanines actually represent one-half standard deviation units. So whereas each quartile represents 25% of the population, stanines may represent varying percentages of the population. The first stanine represents the lowest level of performance, and the ninth stanine represents

the highest level of performance. Importantly, parents, teachers, and students will understand performance most easily and most accurately when using percentile ranks. Other standardized scores can require some sophistication and may lead to errors in interpretation. Figure 5.1 provides a graphic of the normal curve and commonly used standardized scores the professional school counselor may encounter. Note that each of these standardized scores can be converted into percentile ranks for easy explanation to parents, teachers, and students. Erford (2013) provides a thorough explanation of standardized scores.

Disaggregated means the data have been broken down by subpopulations so that performance differences between and among groups can be analyzed. Usually, this analysis involves intergroup differences (e.g., male vs. female, race, ethnicity, special education vs. regular education status). Most test publishers can provide this information on request, broken down by school, by grade level, and even by individual classes. Differences can be determined using statistical methods or informal comparison. Seeing differences in disaggregated data helps professional school counselors to provide hard evidence of gaps in student performance, rather than relying on perceptions. It also provides direction for the types of strategies and interventions needed to close these achievement gaps. Returning to the data provided in Table 5.2, one can see several noticeable gaps in achievement. First, students

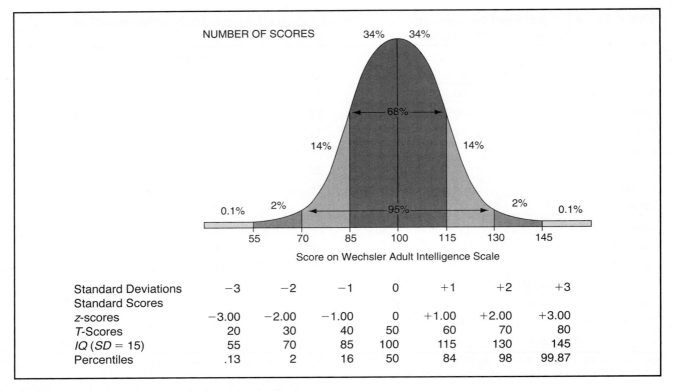

Standard Deviations	−3	−2	−1	0	+1	+2	+3
Standard Scores							
z-scores	−3.00	−2.00	−1.00	0	+1.00	+2.00	+3.00
T-Scores	20	30	40	50	60	70	80
IQ (SD = 15)	55	70	85	100	115	130	145
Percentiles	.13	2	16	50	84	98	99.87

FIGURE 5.1   The normal curve and related standardized scores.

CULTURAL REFLECTION 5.2

Demographic Differences?

Much debate has ensued around the "achievement gap" and how to close that gap. When viewing data like that presented in Table 5.2 it is important to keep in mind that averages can be both enlightening and deceiving. It is easy to conclude that average perform- ance differences are caused by systemic barriers and that one group or another may be advantaged or disad- vantaged. But always try to remember that averages are made up from the data of many individuals—and that every one of those individuals is a unique human being struggling to overcome a unique set of challenges. The multicultural counseling research repeatedly teaches us that the variance of within-group differences is much larger than the variance of between-group dif- ferences, and the overlap of the two groups is usually quite substantial. Thus, how to help one individual overcome an achievement issue may involve a very dif- ferent course of action than for another individual, even though the two individuals may share common demographic characteristics. What are some examples of how our understanding of perceived cultural differ- ences both enhance and detract from our abilities to solve human problems in school settings?

---

from the low socioeconomic status (SES) group performed at the 31st percentile rank, on average, whereas students from the non–low SES group performed at the 71st percentile rank, on average. Second, there is a noticeable difference between the average math performance for Black and Hispanic stu- dents (37th and 43rd percentile ranks, respectively), as com- pared to Asian and White students (72nd and 58th percentile ranks, respectively). Third, females outperformed males, on average (56th and 45th percentile ranks, respectively). From these comparisons of disaggregated data, discussions can ensue and strategies can be developed to decrease the math performance gap. But importantly, it all starts with the data— thus the name *data driven*. In this way, data provide the impe- tus and drive behind school improvement plans and responsive school counseling programs.

Perceptions-Based Needs Assessments

In contrast to a data-driven needs assessment, a more traditional approach to needs assessment is more content and perception driven. Professional school counselors are often interested in what teachers, parents, and students perceive as primary needs to be addressed in a developmental way.

FREQUENCY OF CONDUCTING A NEEDS ASSESSMENT
Although it may seem tempting to design and conduct a global needs assessment on an annual basis, such an

endeavor would be a massive administrative undertaking, likely resulting in findings being outdated by the time changes are made to the total program. It is probably best to follow a continuous cycle of assessing programmatic needs. This will allow ample time for program development and improvements over the course of the cycle. For example, the *ASCA National Model* (2012) designates the areas of academic, career, and personal/social development as cornerstones of a comprehensive, developmental guidance program; therefore, it makes sense that school community needs can be assessed according to these components on a rotating basis. For a new program or one undergoing tremendous renovations, years 1 and 2 of a 6-year cycle can be spent conducting needs assessment and implementing programmatic changes to address horizontal and vertical articulation issues surrounding student academic development. Years 3 and 4 can be spent addressing student career development needs; years 5 and 6 can focus on student personal/social issues. On the other hand, the 6-year cycle could rotate among the three domains, addressing half of the domain issues every three years (i.e., year 1: academic, year 2: career, year 3: personal/social, year 4: academic, year 5: career, year 6: personal/social). A program in good condition and requiring only fine-tuning may be put on a 3-year continuous improvement cycle. The main point here is that assessing needs is part of a much bigger endeavor—that of implementing curricular changes to continuously improve the comprehensive, developmental counseling program. Implementing curricular changes can be quite time intensive and simply a waste of time if not guided by accurate needs assessments and program outcomes research. An effective program uses this information to fine-tune its efforts in data-driven decision making.

POPULATIONS TO BE ASSESSED In the broadest sense, any stakeholder group can provide helpful information about the needs of a school community. However, it is most practical and efficient to seek out those who are informed and likely to respond. Teachers, administrators, students, and parents are the most likely to be informed about school issues and needs and, under most circumstances, will be the primary stakeholder groups surveyed during a needs assessment. Valuable information can be garnered from community organizations, local businesses, and the general citizenry as well. It is just more difficult to obtain a large representative sampling from these groups. Information from these stakeholders is probably best obtained through personal contacts and interviews.

Return rate is another factor in the needs assessment process. Return rate is the percentage of surveys returned of all those sent out. As in any research sampling procedure, the higher the return rate, the lower the sampling error; this leads to greater confidence in the accuracy of the results. In this way, counselors help control for nonresponse bias. Return rate is generally maximized when the participants are a "captive audience." For example, if a social skills needs assessment of fourth-grade students is conducted in the classroom, the response rate should be nearly 100%. On the other hand, if a needs assessment for parents is sent home, the professional school counselor may be lucky to receive 25% to 50% of the questionnaires back. Whenever possible, surveys should be distributed and collected immediately during faculty meetings, class meetings, and parent gatherings.

Triangulation of needs across populations should be attempted when possible; that is, the highest priority needs should be those agreed to by all or most populations assessed. This ensures that the school community's needs, not an individual's agenda, drive the developmental guidance curriculum. For instance, if a principal has decided to place a high priority on social skills, but teachers, parents, and students indicate this is a low priority—and far below other issues such as school safety, substance abuse, and study skills—the triangulated responses of the teachers, parents, and students can provide compelling evidence to guide the program's focus.

DESIGN ISSUES IN AN EFFICIENT NEEDS ASSESSMENT
Designing an efficient needs assessment is essential to meaningful results. Although some advocate for a comprehensive needs assessment simultaneously assessing all goals and topics associated with a comprehensive developmental guidance program, others have found it more helpful to focus the assessment on specifically defined topics or issues that are being updated or altered. This chapter will focus on the latter method.

In a classic treatise on the topic, Stone and Bradley (1994) recommended seven methods for determining needs: questionnaires and inventories, analysis of records, personal interviews, counseling statistics, classroom visits, use of outside consultants, and systematic evaluation of the guidance program. Perhaps what is most important is that the needs assessment use objective methods for data gathering and analysis. It is essential to understand that different questions are addressed by different methodologies. Although all these methods are important and useful, questionnaires (formal or informal surveys) are most commonly used and will be focused on here. Importantly, although open-ended questionnaires are generally easier to design and yield rich and diverse information, such questionnaires are usually more difficult to tabulate, interpret, and translate into goals and objectives. Also, consider that the younger a student is, the lower the demands must be for reading comprehension and written responses.

From a return-rate perspective, it is good practice to try to design a needs assessment that is only one or two pages in length and can be completed in less than 5 minutes. The content of the needs assessment should be topical (e.g., social skills, changing families, substance abuse, college application procedures), rather than service related (e.g., individual counseling, group counseling, consultation). As will be explained later, the professional school counselor should keep in mind that services are simply methods for meeting needs, not needs in themselves. The topics should be related to the program goals as described in the *ASCA National Model* (2012) and in local or state standards so that priority status can be given to addressing the most pressing needs of the school in comparison to these standards. A good needs assessment directly translates into program development.

In general, the following steps form the basis of an efficient needs assessment:

1. Decide what you need to know.
2. Decide on the best approach to derive what you need to know.
3. Develop the needs assessment instrument or method.
4. Enlist the support of colleagues and a few individuals from the target groups to review and try out items for understanding.
5. Implement the final version with the target groups.
6. Tabulate, analyze, and interpret the results.
7. Translate the results into programmatic goals and objectives.

The design of the scale itself deserves some mention. The survey should ask for the name of the individual completing the form (unless the form is to be completed anonymously). Teacher surveys may ask for the grade level, the number of students in class, or other pertinent information. Parent surveys should ask for the names of the parent's children in case their response to the survey requires contact by the counselor. Student surveys should ask for the student's grade and homeroom teacher's name. Questions or response stems should be short, to the point, and easily understood. The reading level of the items should also be appropriate for the target audience. Figures 5.2, 5.3, and 5.4 show examples of topic-focused needs assessments for teachers (student interpersonal skills), students (academic development), and parents (student tolerance for diversity of sexual orientation), respectively.

Substantial consideration also should be given to the response format. If the purpose of the survey is to determine the importance or frequency of a potential problem, it is generally best to use a multipoint scale with four to five choices. For example, Figure 5.2 asks about the frequency of display of interpersonal skills, so the response choices "Rarely," "Sometimes," "Frequently," "Most of the time,"

and "Almost always" are appropriate. Note that the response choices "Never" and "Always" do not appear. It is rare that behaviors never or always occur; to include these descriptors may force responses to the center of the distribution and truncate the range of results. Also notice how each category has a descriptor. Thankfully, gone are the days in survey construction when a survey listed the response categories of 0, "Rarely," and 4, "Almost always," and then provided the center points of 1, 2, and 3 with no accompanying descriptors. The reliability problems of such a scale are obvious: Will all respondents agree on what 1, 2, and 3 represent? Certainly not! All choice categories must be accompanied by verbal descriptors.

Figure 5.4 asks parents to rate the importance of seven sexual orientation tolerance items. Notice that the scale responses move from "Not important" (because in this case it is possible that a parent may perceive a total absence of importance) to "Very important." Such a scaling choice format allows parents to register incremental perceptions of importance. Alternatively, the scaling choice format could have simply stated "Yes" or "No," but to do so would have significantly truncated parent perceptions and forced an all-or-nothing response, thus complicating rather than simplifying the interpretation of the needs assessment.

Another important response component of a needs assessment is a frequency count. Suppose a professional school counselor would want to not only assess the importance of an issue, but also determine how many students were likely in need of services to address the problems stemming from the issue. When possible, the needs assessment should be designed to include an indication of whether the student should be targeted for intervention. In Figure 5.3, notice how the far right-hand column asks for a "Yes" or "No" response to the statement "I need help with this." An affirmative response targets the student for intervention to address a self-perceived weakness.

Figure 5.2 asks teachers, "About how many of your students need help in this area?" The teachers' responses will indicate the type of intervention required. For example, if the teacher determines that 25 out of 26 students require intervention, the professional school counselor may decide to implement a series of group guidance lessons or consult with the teacher in this regard. If only a handful of students in each of several classes requires intervention, the counselor may opt for a small-group counseling program to address the needs. If only one or a few individuals are identified, the counselor may attempt to address the difficulties through teacher or parent consultation or through time-limited individual counseling services.

Finally, Figure 5.4 asks for a frequency count of those students who parents believe could benefit from a program dealing with tolerance for diversity of sexual

Grade you teach _____   Number of students in your homeroom _____   Teacher's name _____

Please place an X in the boxes that you agree with. Do the students in your class:

	Rarely	Sometimes	Frequently	Most of the time	Almost always	About how many of your students need help in this area?
1. Complain of others teasing them?						
2. Complain about problems on the playground?						
3. Complain about problems with others during less structured class time?						
4. Work well in cooperative groups?						
5. Show respect for other students?						
6. Show respect for adults?						
7. Identify feelings of frustration with other students?						
8. Express feelings of frustration with other students?						
9. Have trouble making friends?						
10. Have trouble keeping friends?						

Thank you for taking the time to complete this!

FIGURE 5.2   Elementary teacher needs assessment of interpersonal skills.

orientation. Such information gives impetus for a schoolwide program that is either developmental or preventive in nature.

Tallying or computing the information from a needs assessment is simple and has been alluded to in the preceding paragraphs. Tallying simply involves counting the number of students who may benefit from intervention.

Computing the results of a needs assessment is probably best accomplished by assigning a number value to each response category and averaging all responses for a given item. In Figure 5.3, assume that the response categories are assigned the following values: "Almost never" = 0, "Seldom" = 1, "Sometimes" = 2, "Often" = 3, and "Almost always" = 4. For item 1, "Are you an active participant in

	Almost never	Seldom	Sometimes	Often	Almost always	I need help with this	
						Yes	No
Are you an active participant in class discussions and activities?							
Do you look forward to going to class every day?							
Do you double-check assignments before turning them in for a grade?							
Do you complete lengthy assignments on time?							
Do you ask for help as soon as you don't understand an assignment?							
Do you use a variety of learning strategies when performing school tasks?							
Do you take immediate responsibility for your actions, whether positive or negative?							
Do you enjoy working independently in class?							
Do you enjoy working in cooperative groups in class?							
Do you willingly share what you have learned with your peers when they don't seem to know or understand?							

Student Name and Grade: _____

Below is a series of questions. Answer these questions by placing a check mark in the appropriate boxes.

Thanks for your help!

FIGURE 5.3   Secondary-level student needs assessment for academic development.

class discussions and activities?" simply add all student response values and divide by the number of responses. Therefore, if 25 students completed the needs assessment and 2 students marked "Almost never" ($2 \times 0 = 0$), 4 students marked "Seldom" ($4 \times 1 = 4$), 10 students marked "Sometimes" ($10 \times 2 = 20$), 5 students marked "Often" ($5 \times 3 = 15$), and 4 students marked "Almost always" ($4 \times 4 = 16$), simply sum the points ($0 + 4 + 20 + 15 + 16 = 55$)

My child is in (check one) ☐ 9th grade ☐ 10th grade ☐ 11th grade ☐ 12th grade	Very important	Important	Somewhat important	A little important	Not important
1. How important is it to be aware of the school's mission statement as it pertains to tolerance for students who are gay or lesbian?					
2. How important is it for students to exhibit tolerance for students who are gay or lesbian?					
3. How important is it that diversity in sexual orientation not be a cause of verbal conflict in the school?					
4. How important is it that diversity in sexual orientation not be a cause of physical conflict in the school?					
5. How important is it that "jokes" regarding sexual orientation be eliminated from the school community?					
6. How important is it that slang words and other inappropriate references to students who are gay or lesbian be eliminated in the school community?					
7. How important is it that students who are gay or lesbian feel safe and secure in the school community?					
8. I believe my child could benefit from a program on this topic.				Yes _____	No _____
9. I believe other students could benefit from a program on this topic.				Yes _____	No _____
10. I believe parents could benefit from a program on this topic.				Yes _____	No _____

FIGURE 5.4 Parent needs assessment of tolerance for diversity of sexual orientation in the student body (Targeted group: Parents of sophomore students).

and divide by the number of student responses (sum of 55 divided by 25 students = 2.20) to compute the average frequency rating (2.20). Although this assumes a ratio scale and is somewhat nebulous from a statistical interpretation perspective (i.e., what does a 2.20 really mean?), it does offer a reasonable estimate of the average frequency of a behavior, or importance of an issue, in comparison with the other issues under study.

CONVERTING NEEDS TO PROGRAM GOALS AND OBJECTIVES If the needs assessment was designed correctly, translating the results into goals and learning objectives is relatively easy. The first step is to prioritize the needs in order of their importance and their relation to existing components of the program. Prioritization can be accomplished most easily by using the tallying, computing, and triangulation strategies mentioned. Next, the needs should be matched with, or translated into, the goals included in the *ASCA National Model* (2012) or in state and local standards. Finally, the goals are operationalized

---

THEORY INTO PRACTICE 5.1

NEEDS ASSESSMENTS

When I was a school counseling intern at the middle school level, needs assessments were crucial in the development of my counseling interventions. Using a combination of perception-based needs assessments and data-driven needs assessments, I sought to better understand the critical areas of need within the school. While I believe the perceptions of teachers and administrators are important, I initially strive to understand the students' point of view before narrowing my focus through staff feedback. I have found that this approach helps foster rapport and a sense of empowerment with the students, as they are able to directly communicate their concerns and feel they are contributing to the development of the counseling program.

Within the first few weeks of the school year, the other counselors and I administered needs assessments in the form of surveys to every student in the school. This was done during students' study hall periods, so as to not detract from their academics. Needs assessments were color coded according to grade level so data could be disaggregated. The surveys were one page in length and asked students to check off areas of need from the personal/social, academic, and career domains aligned with the ASCA Model. Students were asked to identify three things they felt the counselor should know about them and to select items from a checklist of topics they felt they needed further assistance with. Checklist topics included needs such as study skills/organization, changing families, understanding and managing feelings, and loss and grief. Additional space was provided for students to include topics they would like help with that were not listed.

The open-ended responses allowed us as school counselors to learn more about the students, communicated to students that the school counselors were interested in what they had to share, and in many cases shed light on significant events that warranted further examination on the part of the professional school counselor (i.e., issues at home, abuse, self-injury, suicidal ideation). The qualitative responses were analyzed for recurring themes and grouped accordingly. Responses from the checklist were tallied and the frequency of each topic noted.

Once analysis of the needs assessments was complete, I selected the three topics with the highest frequencies for each grade level. The findings indicated that across the board, study skills/organization, loss and grief, and peer conflict/bullying were the most pressing issues according to students' perceptions. From there, I e-mailed teachers from every grade level with the findings and asked for specific names of students who they felt could benefit from small-group counseling in those areas. A pool of potential small-group candidates was collected from the teachers' feedback and from student responses in the surveys.

In addition, I examined existing data for each topic to narrow my scope. For example, I looked at Maryland State Assessment scores and interim grade reports for information on which students to target for the study skills/ organization group because such an overwhelming number of students and teachers indicated this was an area of need. Interim reports largely indicated that sixth graders were consistently unprepared for the middle school standards of organization and study skills. Furthermore, teacher comments on interims and low grades narrowed the scope of potential small-group candidates. After integrating my findings from the hard data, self-referrals from student surveys, and teacher feedback, I had a solid group of students to establish a sixth-grade study skills/organizational group.

The data collected during the needs assessments were integral in developing an initial plan of action for the school year. Numerous small groups were developed, students were identified for individual counseling, and topics for classroom guidance were unveiled. In addition, the data used in this process were used when writing goals, objectives, and pretest evaluations. Needs assessments, whether perception based or data driven, are essential components to the development of a comprehensive school counseling program. Although still in the beginning stages of my career as a professional school counselor, I understand the value of needs assessments and will continue to refine my use of such tools to ensure accountability within my profession.

Source: Caitlin J. Eckert, Professional School Counselor, Frederick County Public Schools, Maryland

through development of learning objectives. (See Chapter 10 for an excellent nuts-and-bolts discussion of how to write learning objectives.)

A reasonable goal stemming from the needs assessment shown in Figure 5.2 would be "To increase students' interpersonal and friendship skills." Notice how the wording of a goal is nebulous and not amenable to measurement as stated. In developing learning objectives related to goals, particular emphasis is given to specific actions that are measurable. For example, a possible objective stemming from this goal could be "After reading *Frog and Toad* by Arnold Lobel and answering discussion questions, 80% of the students will be able to recognize at least two qualities (describing words) to look for in a friend." Another possible objective might be "After reading *Frog and Toad* by Arnold Lobel and answering discussion questions, 80% of the students will be able to identify at least one issue that may cause problems among friends." Notice how the objectives designate the audience, the stated behavior, how the behavior will be measured, and the level of expected performance.

A reasonable goal from the assessment shown in Figure 5.4 might be "To create a school environment that is accepting of gay and lesbian students." A possible learning objective stemming from this goal might be "After participating in a series of class sessions focusing on school policies and respect for sexual diversity, 85% of the students will recognize that acceptance of gay and lesbian students is an integral part of a school's mission and essential to harassment-free life at school." Again, notice how the objective designates the audience, the stated behavior, how the behavior will be measured, and the level of expected performance.

PROGRAM (PROCESS) ASSESSMENT

Program assessment (also sometimes called process evaluation or program auditing) is akin to the measurement concept of content validity (which is a systematic examination of a test's content) in that it is a systematic examination of a program's content. In short, the assessment of a program involves determining whether there is written program documentation and whether the program is being implemented appropriately. A program assessment provides an analysis of each facet of the comprehensive school counseling program. Auditing the program will often point to areas of programmatic strengths and weaknesses. The *ASCA National Model* (2012, pp. 59–62) provided a school counseling program assessment aligning with model components; for example, whether the program "Addresses the school counselor's role as an advocate for every students [sic]" and "Promotes achievement, attendance, behavior and/or school safety"

(p. 59). The ASCA suggested that program criteria be evaluated using the following response choices: "No" meaning not in place; "In Progress" meaning perhaps begun, but not completed; and "Yes" meaning fully implemented. In practice, a program assessment should be conducted as the program is being planned and implemented, and then annually near the end of each academic year after the professional school counselor has had an opportunity to see the program run a full annual cycle. Reports derived from the school counseling program assessment should address program strengths, areas in need of improvement, and long- and short-term improvement goals. The areas in need of improvement and goals also may be derived from a needs assessment. These areas and goals then drive program development procedures and activities during subsequent years.

SERVICE ASSESSMENT

Service assessments are sometimes requested by guidance supervisors and demanded by superintendents and school boards to document how counselors are spending their time. Two types of service assessments are commonly used: event–topic counts and time logs. Event–topic counts involve the professional school counselor documenting each time an individual is contacted or provided with a counseling service and the nature of the topic addressed. In this way, professional school counselors can keep a weekly or monthly tally of the number of students seen not only for global individual counseling, but also specifically for individual counseling for depression, anxiety, behavior, changing family, social skills, anger management, or conflict resolution issues. Such data are quite impressive when aggregated and presented to a school board to indicate that "38,961 individual counseling sessions were held with students last year."

A time log is sometimes kept by professional school counselors to document the amount of time spent in various counseling and non-counseling-related activities. For example, some administrators may wish to know the percentage of time counselors actually spend doing group counseling or teacher consultation at the high school level. Time logs require professional school counselors to document and categorize their activities for every minute of the workday. In states with mandates for providing direct service activities (e.g., elementary professional counselors must spend at least 50% of their time in the direct service activities of individual counseling, group counseling, and group guidance), time logs may be necessary to document compliance for funding purposes.

Although service assessments do a wonderful job of telling what or how much a professional school counselor is doing, such assessments give no information about the quality or effectiveness of counselor interventions. The important question becomes "What happens as a result of professional school counselors choosing to use their time this way?" After all, what will a professional school counselor who spends 80% of his or her time doing group and individual counseling, but has ineffective counseling skills, really accomplish? For this kind of information, we must conduct outcomes studies.

RESULTS OR OUTCOMES EVALUATION

Results evaluation (sometimes called outcomes evaluation) answers the question of whether students are different as a result of school counselor prevention and intervention services. There is much confusion in the field regarding what program assessment is and what it isn't. Table 5.3 shows a list of some of these issues. Most important among these is the ongoing, cyclical nature of evaluation. The

---

VOICES FROM THE FIELD 5.1   ALL THAT I DID

The shift from "all that I do" to "the results of my interventions are demonstrated by . . ." is one of the toughest issues facing professional school counselors in public education. How is it that highly trained professionals have been taught to measure their professional worth by naming activities and tasks, but failing to speak of the impact of their programs and services? This shift, I believe, is the most critical to ensure that school counseling programs and services truly support all children's success in school.

The misconception that data, numbers, and bottom-line measurements don't mix with school counseling is largely an antiquated mind-set that is dampening the forward movement of the profession. Professional school counselors continue to resist articulating the value of their services by ignoring the absolute necessity of bottom-line results. The benefits of school counseling services are quantifiable and not a mystery that can be understood only through feelings and abstract representations.

As a system-level school counseling supervisor, I see the resistance to accountability in my day-to-day work. Shifting from tools that count activities and hours to measurable outcomes has created discomfort, as school counselors are anxious about not reporting all that they do. Further, the idea of linking results data to performance evaluations has not been received easily. As I grapple with why this is so unnatural for a group of professionals that pride themselves on being change agents, I wonder how much is fear and how much can be attributed to systemic influences. Specifically, I often consider how much reinforcement the system provides for school counselors to continue business as usual. Clearly, educational institutions can be resistant to changes and have established rigid hierarchies, rules, and policies to protect the status quo. For professional school counselors, this means doing business as usual and not fully involving themselves in the accountability measures associated with school reform efforts. It is tough to negotiate the system norms and work in new ways, while maintaining important relationships within the schools.

Perhaps one solution is assisting professional school counselors in negotiating systems successfully and teaching advocacy and leadership skills to drive needed changes. This can be accomplished through continuous professional development and mentoring from peers and supervisors. Some strategies that have been useful in transforming the work of school counselors in my experience include informal mentoring sessions (individual and small group), leadership courses designed for professional school counselors, data training workshops, and weekly electronic announcements across the system to convey a vision that includes high levels of accountability. These strategies must be coordinated, strategic, and linked to systemwide goals and rating tools. Although none of the identified strategies is highly effective in isolation, layering strategies and building a pool of competent advocates drive the needed energy to shift to a more accountable culture. It takes a refreshed culture to shift the paradigm to one that embraces accountability as a natural and healthy aspect of school counseling.

I hold an idealistic view that professional school counselors will serve all children well as accountability is embraced by all those working in the profession. Measuring the actual results of interventions will ensure that targeted interventions are effective and allow the school counselor to acknowledge, in tangible terms, the payoff. Further, effectively measuring outcomes allows interventions to be adjusted for optimal results. In other words, no longer is it enough to just "do an intervention" because it was planned; rather, the current question is whether to continue an intervention because the data support that it is working. It is no longer enough to do what we do and talk about all that we've done; it is time to assess what we've done and use that information to inform and modify our future work!

Source: Gayle Cicero, Director of Student Services and former Coordinator of School Counseling, Anne Arundel County Public Schools, Maryland

TABLE 5.3 The "Is" and "Isn't" of Assessment

Assessment of school counseling programs is

- A way to answer important program-related questions.
- The responsibility of an accountable professional school counselor.
- A cooperative endeavor with other SCPAC members and stakeholders.
- Ongoing and evolving.
- A means to a better end—better education for *all* students.

Assessment of school counseling programs isn't

- The evaluation of an individual professional school counselor.
- An assault on the professional school counselor's freedom.
- A mandate for standardized tests or curricula.
- All figured out.

assessment loop shown in Figure 5.5 provides a helpful way to visually conceptualize program evaluation and how outcome studies can be used to improve programs.

Many educators view assessment as a discrete component, but it is actually an integrated part of a continuous process for program improvement. All assessment procedures must have the institution's mission in mind because the institutional values and needs will determine the focus of study. Questions of worth and effectiveness are derived from a confluence of values, needs, goals, and mission, and these questions lead to the determination of what evidence must be collected. For example, consider an elementary school counseling program that recently implemented a study skills curriculum in grades 3–5 using classroom guidance lessons. A reasonable research question might be "How is student academic performance/achievement different as a result of the new study skills curriculum?" The

elementary school counselor and teachers may collect several types of evidence to answer this question (performance data on tests, homework completion, parent survey of amount of time spent, or work and study habit improvements). Likewise, a high school counseling team may be interested in knowing "Is the recently modified educational and career planning curriculum using small psychoeducational groups and individual planning sessions over a 3-year period accomplishing the ASCA career domain competencies?" Again, the counseling team would plan for the collection of evidence to answer this question.

Evidence may exist in many places, but it is typically derived using preplanned measures or from the performances or products students engage in during program activities. Once information has been gathered, it must then be interpreted, and conclusions must be drawn from it regarding the program's or activity's worth, strengths, and weaknesses. Finally, the interpretations and conclusions must be used to change the program or parts of the program to improve it.

Notice how the loop in Figure 5.5 never stops—it represents a continuous process in which assessment results are interpreted and fed back into the improvement process. As assessment information is used to prompt programmatic changes, so goal-setting and the posing of new questions about the revised program begin anew. Most professional school counselors fail in the assessment loop because they gather evidence and then stop, believing that the program has been evaluated and the job finished. Why spend valuable time collecting evidence and not use it to improve what you are doing?

Important Assessment Terms

A number of terms associated with research and evaluation are important to understand. *Evaluation* is the measurement of worth and indicates that a judgment will be made regarding the effectiveness of a program. The experienced researcher knows that being very specific about what you are measuring and how you are measuring it is the key to successful results. This is made clear in the section on writing learning objectives in Chapter 10. Too often, professional school counselors are not specific about what they are trying to accomplish and become frustrated when they fail to measure what they may or may not have achieved. If a person doesn't know where she is heading, she must either get specific directions (write a specific, measurable objective) or be satisfied with wherever she ends up (perhaps an ineffective program)!

Evidence is any data that will help make judgments or decisions and can be quantitatively or qualitatively derived. *Formative evaluation* is evaluative feedback that occurs during the implementation of a program, whereas

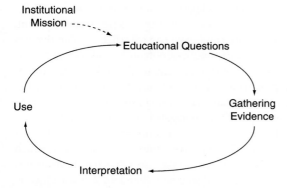

FIGURE 5.5 The assessment cycle.

summative evaluation is feedback collected at a specified endpoint in an evaluation process. Although summative evaluation is conducted most frequently, formative evaluation has the advantage of allowing corrective action to occur if an implemented program is shown to be off course. This makes sense when you consider that some programs are expensive (in time and money) to implement. If you know after one third of the program has been implemented that desired results are not occurring, then midcourse corrections can be made to tailor the program to the audience and desired outcomes.

A *stakeholder* is anyone involved in or potentially benefiting from the school counseling program (Erford, 2014). Stakeholders may include students, parents, teachers, professional school counselors, administrators, community organizations, and local businesses, among others. A *baseline* is any data gathered to establish a starting point. It is essential to know where students are so you can tailor interventions to help facilitate their development. *Inputs* are any resources (e.g., personnel, material) that go into a program; *outcomes* are what stakeholders can do as a result of the program.

A *pretest* is a measure administered before a program is implemented, and a *posttest* is a measure administered after the program or intervention has been completed (Erford, 2014). If a study calls for both a pretest and a posttest, usually there is tremendous overlap in their content because the goal is to determine changes in the individual or group as a result of participating in the program. Any changes that occur in the examinee between administration of the pretest and the posttest are usually attributed to the program activities.

Sources of Evidence

Both people and products merit discussion as potential sources of evidence. Almost anyone—students, teachers, staff, administration, parents, employers, graduates, community resource people, and so on—can serve as a helpful source of evidence. Numerous products from data collection methods can also be used. A short list includes portfolios, performances, use of ratings from external judges or examiners, observations, local tests, purchased tests, student self-assessments, surveys, interviews, focus groups, and student work. Each of these sources or products can produce helpful evaluative data, but what is collected will result from the specific question to be answered.

Practical Program Evaluation Considerations

Erford (2014) provided practical guidelines for conducting accountability studies. To be of practical value, assessment must be connected to real program concerns, as well as the core values of the school or program. Avoid overwhelming the data collectors, focus on only one or several important questions at a time, and always select measures that will yield reliable and valid scores for the purposes under study. Oftentimes, ineffective program outcomes stem from poor or inappropriate measurement rather than faulty programming. Be sure to involve the relevant stakeholders, and use a variety of approaches. Perhaps most important, do not reinvent the wheel—use what you are already doing to generate useful data about program effectiveness. Also, don't be afraid to call on outside experts to consult on the development and evaluation of a program.

It is good advice to start small and build on what is found to work; the methods and goals of individual programs are celebrated, and successes can be shared by professional school counselors across programs. This often leads to a cross-pollination effect that yields both diversity of approach and homogeneity of results. In other words, over time, professional school counselors will learn from each other what works and implement these strategies with their own populations after necessary refinements based on the needs of a differing school community. Different can still be effective!

Assessing Outcomes Through a Hierarchical Aggregated Process

As mentioned earlier, aggregation is the combining of results to provide a more global or generalized picture of group performance. Although such a practice may de-emphasize subgroup or individual performance, aggregation can also be a valuable tool when it comes to evaluating how well school counseling programs meet higher-level standards, such as the ASCA *National Standards* (Campbell & Dahir, 1997). Due to their more abstract or generalized wording, standards (sometimes called goals) are difficult, if not impossible, to directly measure. This is why curriculum development begins with a statement of standards (goals) that are then further described through a series of outcomes (sometimes called competencies). Although more specific and well defined, these outcomes are still ordinarily not amenable to direct measurement in the classic sense. Instead, educators rely on educational objectives (sometimes called behavioral objectives), such as those discussed in Chapter 10. Objectives are written in such specific, measurable terms that everyone (e.g., teacher, student, parent, professional school counselor) can tell when an objective has been met. The use of objectives, outcomes, and standards constitutes an aggregated hierarchical model and is an important way that professional school counselors can demonstrate the effectiveness of a school counseling program. Figure 5.6 provides an example of this aggregated hierarchical model.

In Figure 5.6, note the alignment of objectives to outcomes to standards. Objective 1 measures Outcome 1, which is aligned with Standard 1. Likewise, Objective 13 measures Outcome 6, which is aligned with Standard 2. Such a hierarchical structure allows the professional school counselor to conclude that meeting the lower-order objectives provides

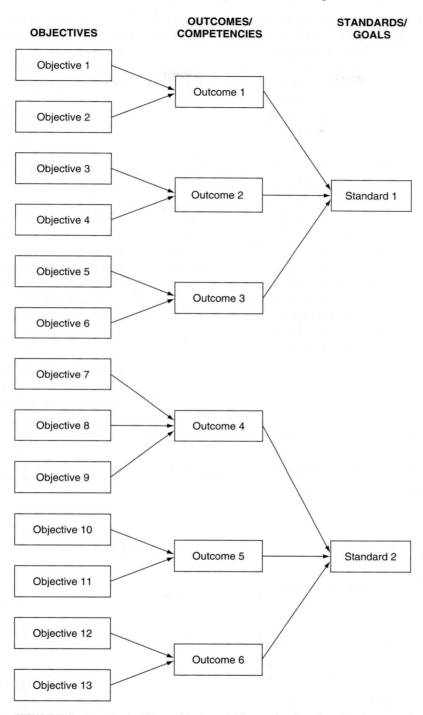

FIGURE 5.6   Aggregated hierarchical model for evaluating the effectiveness of a school counseling program.

evidence that higher-order outcomes and standards have been successfully met. For example, assume the professional school counselor provides evidence that Objectives 1 through 6 have been met. By extension, if Objectives 1 and 2 were met, then Outcome 1 was met. If Objectives 3 and 4 were met, then Outcome 2 was met. If Objectives 5 and 6 were met, then Outcome 3 was met. Because Outcomes 1 through 3 were met, the professional school counselor has provided evidence that Standard 1 was met. Success! In addition, areas of curricular strength have been identified.

Again referring to Figure 5.6, now consider a second example in which Objectives 7 through 10 were met, but Objectives 11 through 13 were not met. By extension, if Objectives 7 through 9 were met, then Outcome 4 was met. If Objective 10 was met, but Objective 11 was not met, then Outcome 5 either was not met or, more accurately, was only partially met. If Objectives 12 and 13 were not met, then Outcome 6 was not met. Now, because of some inconsistent results, interpretation is a bit cloudier. It is most appropriate to conclude that Standard 2 was only partially met because Outcome 4 was met, Outcome 5 was partially met, and Outcome 6 was not met. Given the inconsistency of the outcomes, it would be inappropriate to conclude that Standard 2 had been met; it would be equally inappropriate to conclude that Standard 2 had not been met. A conclusion of "partially met" identifies the hierarchical set of standards, outcomes, and objectives as a curricular area in need of improvement, additional attention to or revision of the criteria for successful performance, or both. From these examples, one can see that an aggregated hierarchical model can be a valuable curriculum evaluation method. It also underscores the importance of a measurable objective as the building block of an effective developmental curriculum (see Chapter 10).

Designing Outcome Studies

Although any data collected on counselor effectiveness can be helpful, in most instances, professional school counselors should measure outcomes or results by designing a research-type study. Importantly, a bit of forethought and planning can lead to much more meaningful conclusions. Research studies are typically empirical in nature and involve providing some control over how students are assigned to counseling interventions and the timing and circumstances under which data are collected. Campbell and Stanley (1963) explored helpful, easy-to-implement designs, and several of these designs that may be particularly useful to professional school counselors have been included in Table 5.4. Although a comprehensive treatise on this topic is beyond the scope of this text, the following are some of the relevant points professional school counselors should consider when designing outcome studies. Counselors generally receive an entire course in research and evaluation that can be useful in this context. The interested reader should consult Erford (2014) for a helpful source on research methodology and statistical analysis written specifically for counselors.

Answering several questions can help the professional counselor determine which research design to use.

1. ***Has the treatment already been implemented?*** So much for planning ahead! If the intervention has not already occurred, one has many possible options. If the intervention has already occurred, one is relegated to a nonexperimental design, probably a case study or static-group comparison design. It is critical to think about outcomes assessment in the early stages of

TABLE 5.4 Common Designs Used for Outcomes Research		
Nonexperimental Designs		
1. Pretest–posttest single group design		O I O
2. Case study		I O
3. Static-group comparison	group 1	O
	group 2	I O
Quasi-Experimental Designs		
4. Two-sample pretest–posttest design		R O
		R I O
5. Nonequivalent control group design		O I O
		O O
6. Time series design		O O O I O O O
True Experimental Designs		
7. Randomized pretest–posttest control group design		R O I O
		R O O
8. Randomized posttest only control group design		R I O
		R O

Note: R = participants are randomly assigned to groups; I = intervention (implemented treatment or program); O = observation or other data collection method.

planning for an intervention and certainly before the intervention has begun!

2. *Can I randomly assign participants to treatment conditions?* If the answer is yes, outstanding! Control over the random assignment of participants is critical to implementing true experimental designs. If one does not have control over assignment of participants, the professional school counselor must choose a quasi-experimental or nonexperimental design.

3. *Can I conduct (one or several) pretests, posttests, or both?* Usually, measuring the dependent variable both before (pretest) and after (posttest) is desirable, although certainly not essential.

The answers to these questions will help the professional school counselor choose the most useful and powerful design. For example, if the answers to the three questions are no, yes, and yes, respectively, the professional school counselor may opt for an experimental design (i.e., design 7 or 8 in Table 5.4). If the answers are yes, no, and posttest only, one is relegated to a nonexperimental design (e.g., design 2 or 3 in Table 5.4). As one can no doubt surmise, outcome studies require some level of planning early on in program development. Accountable professional school counselors plan ahead.

Most true experimental designs involve randomization of participants, which also randomizes various sources of error, allowing for the control of numerous threats to internal validity. True experimental designs allow causative conclusions to be reached. This is a big advantage when the professional school counselor wants to know conclusively if interventions caused significant improvements in students. For example, if a professional school counselor wants to know if a group intervention designed to improve study skills and academic performance was effective, he or she could use the randomized pretest–posttest control group design (design 7 in Table 5.4). The counselor would begin by randomly assigning students into two optimal-sized groups, designated control and treatment, and determining a data collection method (e.g., test, survey, observation) to measure an outcome of interest (e.g., academic achievement, study skills, social skills). The counselor would begin by administering the "test" (a dependent variable called the pretest) to all participants in both the control and the treatment conditions. Next, the counselor would implement the intervention (e.g., group counseling experience) with the treatment group, but not with the control group. (*Note:* The control group would either experience nothing or undergo a group counseling experience for some issue other than academic performance, study skills, social skills, etc.) On conclusion of the treatment (program, intervention), the professional school counselor would again administer the test (this time called the posttest) to participants in both groups. It would be expected that no change in the control group participants' scores would be observed (i.e., no statistically significant difference between pretest and posttest scores). However, if the group counseling experience was successful, it would be expected that a significant change would be observed in the treatment group (e.g., higher posttest scores than pretest scores, higher grades at the end of group than at the beginning). Of course, the other designs in Table 5.4 also could be used with this or other examples. However, quasi-experimental and nonexperimental designs do not allow the professional school counselor to conclude that the treatment was the "cause" of the changes noted in the participants. Thus, in many ways, results or outcomes from studies with experimental designs are more valuable and powerful.

A lot of thought must be given to the design of the outcome measure used. Often, nonsignificant results are due not to the intervention, but to the selection of an outcome measure not sensitive enough to demonstrate the effect of the treatment. Some outcome measures can be easily obtained because they are a matter of record (e.g., grade point average, percentage grade in math class, number of days absent, number of homework assignments completed) or already exist in published form (e.g., Conners-3, Achenbach System of Empirically Based Assessment [ASEBA], Beck Depression Inventory [BDI-II], Children's Depression Inventory [CDI]). Available outcome measures are plentiful. Still, sometimes professional school counselors need to design an outcome measure with sufficient sensitivity and direct applicability to the issue being studied (e.g., adjustment to a divorce, body image, social skills, math self-efficacy). When professional school counselors need to develop an outcome measure from scratch, the basics of scale development covered earlier in the discussion of needs assessments can be helpful. In addition, Weiss (1998) provided a dozen principles the assessor should consider:

1. Use simple language.
2. Ask only about things that the respondent can be expected to know.
3. Make the question specific.
4. Define terms that are in any way unclear.
5. Avoid yes–no questions.
6. Avoid double negatives.
7. Don't ask double-barreled questions [e.g., two questions in one].
8. Use wording that has been adopted in the field.
9. Include enough information to jog people's memories or to make them aware of features of a phenomenon they might otherwise overlook.
10. Look for secondhand opinions or ratings only when firsthand information is unavailable.

11. Be sensitive to cultural differences.
12. Learn how to deal with difficult respondent groups. (pp. 140–142)

These principles apply to most types of data collection procedures. Professional school counselors can use a wide range of procedures, each with advantages and disadvantages. Table 5.5 presents descriptions of several of the most common methods of data collection used by professional school counselors.

Action Research

Action research allows professional school counselors to focus on changing social, ecological, or client conditions in particular situations or settings by creating a study and intervention to explore and solve a particular problem, usually in the client's environment. Designed and conducted by practitioners or researchers, action research involves the analysis of data to improve practice and solve practical problems. Action research presents the professional school counselor with a number of advantages over traditional experimental research procedures because action research requires minimal training; helps develop effective, practice-based solutions for practical problems; and creates a collaborative atmosphere where professionals work together to address and improve conditions affecting students.

Erford (2014) proposed that action research follows a process of five steps. In step 1, professional school counselors

---

TABLE 5.5 Common Data-Collection Methods

1. *Interviews* of the professional school counselor, key personnel, or members of stakeholder groups can provide valuable data. Interviews can be structured, semistructured, or unstructured. Structured interviews present a formal sequence of questions to interviewees, with no variation in administration, thus generating clear evidence of strengths and weaknesses. Unstructured formats allow for follow-up for deeper exploration and are commonly used in qualitative studies. Usually, multiple respondents are required for patterns and conclusions to emerge. Face-to-face interviews are generally better than phone interviews, although usually more costly and inconvenient. Careful consideration must be given to question development, and interviewers must guard against introducing bias.

2. *Observations* can also be classified as informal or formal. Informal observations tend to yield anecdotal data through a "look-and-see" approach. Formal or structured observations usually involve a protocol and predetermined procedures for collecting specific types of data during a specified time period. Structured procedures tend to minimize bias. As an example of observation, professional school counselors can be observed implementing a developmental guidance lesson by a supervisor or peer.

3. *Written questionnaires, surveys, and rating scales* are usually paper-and-pencil instruments asking a broad range of questions (open ended, closed ended, or both). Questionnaires and rating scales typically ask for factual responses, whereas surveys generally solicit participant perceptions. By far the greatest weakness of this data collection method is that many participants do not complete or return the instrument (i.e., low return rate). It also requires a certain level of literacy. Few respondents take the time to write lengthy responses, so it is usually best to keep the questions simple and closed ended with the opportunity for participants to expand a response if needed. Multiscaled response formats (e.g., Likert scales) often provide more helpful results than yes–no questions. E-mailed or online versions of these instruments are becoming more commonly used.

4. *Program records and schedules* are a naturally occurring and helpful source of evaluation data. If stored on a computer in a database format, this kind of data is particularly accessible, and a professional school counselor is well advised to consider this ahead of time when determining how best to maintain electronic records and schedules. Archives should also be kept in good order to facilitate record searches. In particular, professional school counselors should keep previous program improvement documents and outcome study reports.

5. *Standardized and educator-made tests* provide objective sources of measurable student performance and progress in the academic, career, and personal–social domains. Individual, classroom, and schoolwide tests can be extremely helpful and powerful measures. Tests exist that measure academic achievement, depression, anxiety, substance use, distractibility, career indecision, and myriad other student behaviors. Likewise, professional school counselors can design and develop tests to measure student behaviors and characteristics, much like teachers design tests to measure academic achievement.

6. *Academic performance indicators* may include a student's grade point average or classroom grade but also includes daily work behaviors and habits (e.g., attendance, homework completion, disruptions) and attitudes (e.g., academic self-efficacy, attitude toward school).

7. *Products and portfolios* are real-life examples of performance. A product is anything created by a student (or the professional school counselor) that stemmed from a program standard (e.g., artwork, composition, poster). A portfolio is a collection of exemplar products that can be evaluated to determine the quality of an individual's performance.

refine the research question to be explored, which usually involves improving some practice or correcting a problem currently being experienced. Step 2 involves gathering data from the population under study. Notice the word *population* as opposed to *sample*. In action research that group experiencing the problem is the only group of importance; there is no interest in generalizing the results to other individuals. Triangulation is often attempted to answer the research question from several angles by using multiple data-gathering methods. In step 3, the professional school counselor analyzes the data stemming from the designed study (see Table 13.4). Step 4 involves creation of an action plan to create change and improve the situation in a way that stems from, validates, and supports the data that was gathered and analyzed. In other words, the professional school counselor's data analysis informs the needed changes to be undertaken. In this way, the change process is data driven. Finally, in step 5 the professional school counselor and research team evaluate the results observed as a result of the changes made to determine, " Did the changes resulting from the action plan produce the desired outcomes?"

Reporting the Results

Although professional school counselors, or perhaps an outside consultant, may write the majority of a report, the school counseling program advisory committee (SCPAC) should be involved at every step of the process. A comprehensive report may be helpful for SCPAC analysis purposes; however, a one- to two-page executive summary should also be prepared for release to building administrators, system administrators, and the school community. Erford (2014) suggested that dissemination of school counseling program results could occur through a written report, a verbal presentation, a multimedia presentation, journal articles, a website posting, a videotape, posters, social media, e-mail, or a newspaper article. For example, many schools now have websites, electronic newsletters, and social media accounts. The written executive summary could be added to these venues. Likewise, some schools send out e-mail blasts or text message bursts to parents electing to receive information through those electronic modes. A brief message could be posted directing parents to the written or electronic source for the full report. However, it is important to remember that not all parents may have these technologies and that those who do may not check these sources in a timely manner. Thus, some redundancy across sources or postings should occur to ensure everyone can obtain access to at least the executive summary, if desired.

Regardless of the vehicle for dissemination, results of the program outcomes should be released to relevant stakeholder groups at regular intervals after the results have been reviewed by the SCPAC, professional school counselors, and administration. As mentioned, the results

---

VOICES FROM THE FIELD 5.2

My high school counselor sat in her office most of the day. At least, that is what I assume because I rarely ever saw her elsewhere in the building. We were supposed to sign up for a time to speak with her about college during our senior year. I never did and so never actually spoke with her directly during my 4 years in high school. If I were asked how my school counselor influenced me or the rest of the school, I would have said that she did nothing. In today's economy full of layoffs and downsizing, it is so important to prove effectiveness. After all, it is much easier to cut a program that seems to do nothing than one that has data to show that it made a difference.

Accountability for professional school counselors can take a variety of forms. School counselors can make use of existing data to show effectiveness of their programs. Perhaps the school counselor is working with a group of students who struggle academically due to lack of organization or motivation. Or perhaps the school counselor is working with students who struggle to get along with others. The school counselor will want to monitor students' progress reports and discipline reports, communicate frequently with teachers and parents, and meet in teams with administration to report progress that has been made. The school counseling team in my school meets with teachers and administration once a week to discuss student concerns and to work together on ways to address these concerns. The school counseling team participates actively during these meetings sharing insights in a way that shows how involved we are in the students' lives.

Professional school counselors may also need to collect new data to show effectiveness of their program. Perhaps, the school counselor wishes to pilot a schoolwide program that has not been used before. After receiving administrative support for the program, the counselor will want to create a way to measure its effectiveness. I recently completed a program with my students aimed at improving school climate and student acceptance of one another. I created a survey to measure students' perception of the current school climate, which I administered before and after the intervention was complete. I compiled the data and was able to show that the program made a positive difference for many of the students.

Source: Julie Wentz, professional school counselor

As an elementary school counselor, I try to use data whenever possible to support my interventions. I believe that it is important to keep track not only of what I do as a counselor but also of how effectively I am meeting the needs of my students. Although I often feel like I don't have enough time to collect data for everything I do, I try to work it into my schedule as much as possible. There are often simple ways to collect data that do not take a whole lot of time.

I run a small guidance group entitled "Let's Pay Attention." The group targets second-grade students who have a hard time paying attention, completing work, listening to the teacher, or staying in their seat. A few months into the new school year, I ask teachers to refer students who fall into this category. My school uses a schoolwide discipline program that involves moving student "clips" (clothespins) on a colored chart: Green—Good job, Yellow—Warning, Blue—Lose recess, Orange—Call home, Red—Go to Principal. Teachers refer students who frequently move their clip. Last year I ran two second-grade "Let's Pay Attention" groups, each with four group members. Teachers reported how many times each student moved his or her clip in the month of November. There were 18 days of school in that month. Most students in a classroom moved their clips 1–2 times in the month; some moved their clips far more frequently than others, such as those listed in Table 5.6.

During the first group session of each small-group counseling experience, I read the book *Ethan Has Too Much Energy* by Lawrence Shapiro. After discussing the story, I asked the students to think about how they were like Ethan. Then each student came up with his or her own personal goal based on suggestions that the teacher had given me (e.g., completing center work, staying in seat, following directions). I took pictures of the students completing their goal. For instance, for completing work I took a picture of the student working at his desk. This picture was placed on the student's desk as a reminder of the goal. They also received a chart to track their progress toward their goal. Students received stickers on their chart to indicate when they had achieved the goal. I kept track of how many stickers the students earned each day.

In the subsequent six group sessions, the students learned about and practiced techniques for listening, following directions, improving visual/auditory memory, keeping the body still, and releasing tension and extra energy in their bodies. Each week when the students came to group, I would show them a graph of the amount of stickers they had earned. They were able to see whether or not they were making progress. Each week I talked with the students to set an individual goal for the following week.

At the end of the group, I used the sticker chart data to determine if the students had made progress and if my group was effective in helping students become more focused learners. Table 5.7 and Figure 5.7 show the students' progress toward their individual goals.

Based on these results, I saw that four students made progress, one student remained the same, and three students' behavior actually declined. I can see that the students who were working on completing their work improved the most during the course of the group. Aaron, who was working on staying in his seat, also improved somewhat. However, the students who were working on listening to the teacher and following directions either did not improve or seemed to get worse.

These results can tell me a number of things about the group. I know that the group was most effective for helping students stay in their seat and complete their work. However, it does not tell me which part of the group led to the improvement in behavior. The data also tell me that I need to adjust what I am doing in the group to focus more on listening and following directions to help those students better achieve their goals. But again, it's hard to tell what caused the decline in student behavior. It could just be that the teachers were more aware of when the students were not listening or following directions. Regardless, this year when I run the group again, I will try to fine-tune my groups to better help the students

TABLE 5.6 Results of a Schoolwide Monitoring Program

Student	Number of Times Clip was Moved in a Month
Garrett	10
Dan	11
James	8
Aaron	9
Sean	11
Thomas	9
Emma	7
Joshua	10

TABLE 5.7   **Monitoring Student Progress Toward Meeting Personal Goals**

Student	Personal Goal	Week 1	Week 2	Week 3	Week 4	Week 5	Week 6
Garrett	Completing Work	44	43	43	44	44	47
Dan	Completing Work	32	44	50	44	38	50
James	Listening to Teacher	42	38	38	34	38	35
Aaron	Staying in Seat	48	45	49	47	47	49
Sean	Listening to Teacher	50	50	47	44	50	50
Thomas	Following Directions	50	49	50	45	46	50
Emma	Completing Work	42	45	46	49	45	46
Joshua	Following Directions	43	46	44	47	46	39

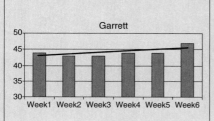
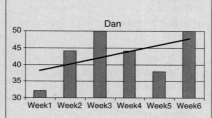
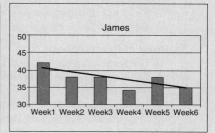
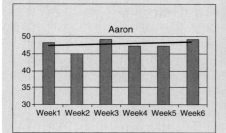
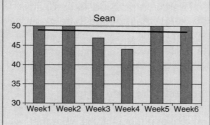
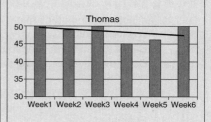
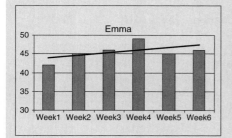
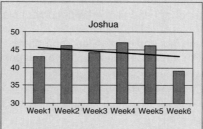

FIGURE 5.7   Monitoring individual student progress toward meeting personal goals.

who are working on listening and following directions, while at the same time continuing to help students who need to stay in their seats and complete their work.

Source: Emily M. Bryant, Professional Elementary School Coun-selor, Monocacy Elementary Center and Amity Primary Center, Daniel Boone Area School District, Pennsylvania

of the outcome studies are used to make substantive program improvements that then prompt more questions to be studied—and the process cycles again and again. This cycle is essential to the transformation and continuous quality improvement of any comprehensive developmental school counseling program.

PERFORMANCE APPRAISAL

The effectiveness of a school counseling program often relies on the competence and efficiency of its implementers. Although an entire book could be written on procedures for assessing the performance of professional school counselors, this section will provide but a few guiding

---

Observee: _____ Observer: _____ Date: _____

Directions: Circle the letters for each statement corresponding with your observation. Please write in any additional comments. *Key:* NA = not applicable; NI = needs improvement; S = satisfactory; VS = very satisfactory.

Presentation of Introductory Material

1. Indicated the purpose of the presentation.	NA	NI	S	VS
2. Provided preview/overview of presentation.	NA	NI	S	VS
3. Connected today's content to previous presentations or experiences.	NA	NI	S	VS

Body of Presentation

4. Content was arranged in a logical order.	NA	NI	S	VS
5. Assessed throughout presentation to determine if information was understood.	NA	NI	S	VS
6. Gave examples to help students understand ideas and/or to tie subject to prior knowledge that students possessed.	NA	NI	S	VS
7. Summarized important ideas throughout presentation.	NA	NI	S	VS

Conclusion of Presentation

8. Asked questions to see what students understood/learned, any misconceptions they might have, and what needed to be retaught/covered again.	NA	NI	S	VS
9. Summarized main concepts in presentation.	NA	NI	S	VS
10. Dealt effectively with any problems/questions that came up in the presentation.	NA	NI	S	VS
11. Previewed what will be covered next time, linking it to the current presentation.	NA	NI	S	VS
12. Evaluated what students learned to see if objectives were met.	NA	NI	S	VS

Overall Instructional Presentation

13. The material presented was important and aligned with content standards/competencies.	NA	NI	S	VS
14. Distinctions were made between fact and opinion, as appropriate.	NA	NI	S	VS
15. Statements were supported with reference to authoritative sources, as appropriate.	NA	NI	S	VS
16. Presented and encouraged divergent viewpoints.	NA	NI	S	VS
17. Included an appropriate amount of content for the available time period.	NA	NI	S	VS
18. All materials were ready.	NA	NI	S	VS
19. Presentation began on time.	NA	NI	S	VS
20. Presentation ended on time.	NA	NI	S	VS
21. Presentation time was used efficiently.	NA	NI	S	VS

Clarity of Presentation

22. Defined any new items, concepts, and/or principles.	NA	NI	S	VS
23. Explained why problems are solved using certain processes or techniques.	NA	NI	S	VS
24. Used clear and relevant examples to explain major ideas and connect them to students' prior knowledge.	NA	NI	S	VS

FIGURE 5.8 Instructional evaluation of a developmental guidance lesson.

Verbal Communication

25. Spoke clearly and could be easily heard.	NA	NI	S	VS
26. Raised and lowered voice to emphasize points and provide variety.	NA	NI	S	VS
27. Minimized use of speech distracters (e.g., ahh, OK).	NA	NI	S	VS
28. Speech rate was appropriate (neither too fast nor too slow).	NA	NI	S	VS
29. Invited participants to share.	NA	NI	S	VS
30. Answers and asks questions clearly.	NA	NI	S	VS
31. Gives students feedback when appropriate.	NA	NI	S	VS

Nonverbal Communication

32. Kept appropriate eye contact with students throughout presentation and when listening to student questions and responses.	NA	NI	S	VS
33. Mannerisms were comfortable and inviting, allowed students to participate (not too formal or casual).	NA	NI	S	VS
34. Facial and body movements matched speech and/or expressed intentions.	NA	NI	S	VS
35. Listened attentively to students' questions and comments.	NA	NI	S	VS

Classroom Management

36. Kept participants' attention.	NA	NI	S	VS
37. Encouraged everyone to participate.	NA	NI	S	VS
38. Was able to keep control of the group.	NA	NI	S	VS
39. Respected and valued all members of the group and differences between members.	NA	NI	S	VS

principles. It is not an exaggeration to say that the services provided by, and responsibilities of, the professional school counselor are among the most complex of any school employee. The advanced, specialized training certainly demands that individuals placed in a position to evaluate the counselor must also have equivalent training and advanced supervision skills. Thus, although the experiences and training of principals often provide a useful vantage point from which to evaluate teachers and secretarial staff, principals seldom have the training and counseling supervision experience to evaluate counselors effectively. That is not to say that principals lack the ability to provide helpful information regarding counselor performance. It is an infinitely better practice, however, to have counselor supervisors coordinate and participate in the appraisal of counselor performance. One facet of a professional school counselor's performance appraisal that a principal or other noncounselor administrator may be able to contribute to is evaluation of the professional school counselor's skill when providing a classroom-based developmental guidance lesson. The criteria for any evaluation always should be available well in advance. Figures 5.8 and 5.9 provide sample instructional evaluations adapted for the purpose of assessing a professional school counselor's skill in the classroom or less formal sessions.

Most professional school counselor performance appraisals are composed of a rating system that aggregates or averages responses across a variety of categories of work-related responsibilities. Generally, these rating schemes involve some indication of "Satisfactory" or "Unsatisfactory" performance in each of the targeted skill categories. Some performance appraisal forms allow greater differentiation in ratings—for example, "Unsatisfactory," "Inconsistently meets expectations," "Consistently meets expectations," and "Consistently exceeds expectations." This latter differentiation is particularly useful when incentives such as merit pay are in effect.

Numerous formats are used for professional school counselor performance appraisal. In fact, nearly all school systems tailor forms and criteria to their specifications and needs. Some are particularly comprehensive models, using a multipoint rating system. Figures 5.10 and 5.11 are actual performance appraisal documents from public school systems. Although briefly stated and somewhat open to interpretation, notice how the indicators and competencies serve as discussion points for an ongoing professional development dialogue between counselor and supervisor. Such discussions are meant to highlight a professional school counselor's strengths and weaknesses and guide him or her in the direction of needed improvement. This dialogue eventually results in a rating of "Satisfactory" or "Unsatisfactory" in each category under investigation; then an overall rating is determined, generally for retention purposes. Although performance appraisals do sometimes affect retention and dismissal of counselors, the truth is that the number dismissed for unsatisfactory performance is very small. Thus, the primary focus of the appraisal system should be, and in most instances is, to enhance the quality and competence of all those evaluated.

Many school systems have undertaken the task of revealing exemplary practices at the school level. Figure 5.12

Anne Arundel County Public Schools | Office of School Counseling

Professional School Counselor Observation

Name	School	Grade(s)
Date	Time in/out	Number of Students/ Participants

Objective:

To assist in determining the degree to which the professional school counselor is implementing a comprehensive, data-driven school counseling program that is preventive in design and developmental in nature toward achieving the school's identified goals.

Counseling Domain Observed:

☐ Academic Development ☐ Career Development ☐ Personal/Social Development

Delivery System Observed:

☐ **School Guidance Curriculum:** Classroom Instruction, Parent Workshop

☐ **Individual Student Planning:** Individual/Small Group Appraisal or Advisement

☐ **Responsive Services:** Individual/Small Group Counseling, Peer Facilitation, Crisis Response

☐ **System Support:** Professional Development, Teaming, Consultation, Collaboration

Pre-Observation Conference:

A pre-observation conference is highly recommended and should include the following questions for professional dialogue:

1 What is the intended outcome of the activity?

2 How was the target audience chosen?

3 How does this activity address the National Standards for School Counseling?

4 What, if any, specific concerns do you have with regard to the activity?

5 How will students be different as a result of their participation in the activity?

AACPS · Office of School Counseling · DPS/JH 2750/24 (New 10/08) page 1

FIGURE 5.9 Anne Arundel County Public Schools professional school counselor observation.

Professional School Counselor Observation cont.

6	How will you measure the impact/results of this activity?

7	What type of feedback will assist you in growing as a professional school counselor?

Observation and Feedback

Indicator	Evidenced	Not Evidenced	Comments
The activity has a clear focus aligned with the National Standards for School Counseling.			
The activity aligns with and supports the school's Improvement Plan and/or the AACPS School Counseling Program Essential Curriculum.			
The activity is designed to support the specific needs of the students/participants.			
The students/participants demonstrate an understanding of the content/focus as a result of participating in the activity.			
The school counselor informs students or participants of the goals, techniques, confidentiality and rules of the activity.			
The school counselor effectively manages behavior in order to facilitate a safe learning environment.			
The school counselor demonstrates effective interpersonal skills with students and/or participants.			
The school counselor utilizes perception, process, or results data to evaluate the effectiveness of the activity.			

Commendations/Recommendations:

Observer's Signature	Date	School Counselor's Signature	Date

AACPS · Office of School Counseling · DPS/JH 2750/24 (New 10/08) page 2

Source: Anne Arundel County Public Schools.

Anne Arundel County Public Schools | Division of Human Resources

Evaluation of Unit I—Professional School Counselors

Employee	Employee ID#
Title	School/Office
Completed by	

Goal-setting/Performance
Review Conference Dates

Required NLT	November 30	January 31	April 30	June 30

Actual (1)_____ (2)_____ (3)_____ (4)_____

The professional school counselor implements a comprehensive, data driven school counseling program that is preventive in design and developmental in nature to serve the academic, career and personal/social needs of students in addressing the school's identified goals. Toward that end, The American School Counseling Association recommends the majority of the school counselor's time be spent in direct service to all students so that every student receives maximum benefits from the program. The operational structure includes four elements that are interdependent and define a comprehensive school counseling program.

	A. Performance Standards	5 Outstanding Performance	4 Highly Effective	3 Standards Met/ Satisfactory	2 Needs Improvement/ Marginal	1 Standard Not Met/ Unsatisfactory	0 Not Assigned	Supporting Statement
	I. Foundation: This serves as the ground upon which the school counseling program is built and includes beliefs, philosophy, mission statement, and the ASCA standards for all three domains (academic, social/emotional, and career). A strong foundation is critical to ensuring the school counseling program is an essential and integrated component of the total educational program for student success.							
1	Exhibits values that support the achievement of all students							
2	Participates in continuous and relevant professional growth.							
3	Addresses all domains (academic, career, personal/ social) through the school counseling program.							
4	Participates in the development and implementation of a written mission statement aligned with the district and school mission that addresses advocacy for the equity, access, and success of every student.							

AACPS · DPS/JH 1330/160 (New 10/08) **1 of 3**

Distribution: Copies to   1—Human Resources   2—Employee   3—Principal or Supervisor

Employee Initials

FIGURE 5.10 Anne Arundel County Public Schools professional school counselor evaluation.

Evaluation of Unit I—Professional School Counselors

		5	4	3	2	1	0	
A. Performance Standards		Outstanding Performance	Highly Effective	Standards Met/ Satisfactory	Needs Improvement/ Marginal	Standard Not Met/ Unsatisfactory	Not Assigned	**Supporting Statement**

II. Delivery System:

Four components define the delivery system of a comprehensive school counseling program: Essential Curriculum, Individual Student Planning, Responsive Services, and System Support. The delivery is the how of the implementation process.

1	Delivers the Essential Curriculum to all students as outlined in the AACPS timeline.							
2	Works with individuals and/or small groups to analyze and evaluate students' interests, abilities, etc.							
3	Provides responsive counseling services through consultation, individual & small group counseling, crisis counseling, referrals, and peer facilitation.							
4	Develops, maintains, and updates (based on needs) a master calendar of school counseling events to ensure students, parents/guardians, school staff, and administrators know what, when, and where school counseling programs and activities are scheduled.							

III. Management System:

This system describes the processes needed to effectively manage the school counseling program, including use of data and action plans that maximize learning for all students. Attention to recommended time allocations is necessary, and carefully planned calendars serve as an indicator that the program is well managed. The management system identifies the "when, why, by whom and on what authority" of the comprehensive school counseling program.

1	Establishes a written management agreement that aligns with the time allocations suggested by the National Model, i.e. 80% of time is spent delivering services to students, staff, and parents.							
2	Implements a school counseling program that is built upon relevant data, assessing both short- and long-term needs.							
3	Implements targeted Intervention plans that are data-driven and include student outcomes that are aligned with the district strategic plan.							
4	Functions collaboratively as a team member by partnering with staff, parents, and community, e.g., participation on Advisory Councils, School Improvement Teams, IDT, Student Assistance, MSAP, Human Relations, and district level committees.							

AACPS · DPS/JH 1330/160 (New 10/08) 2 of 3

Employee Initials

(Continued)

A. Performance Standards	5 Outstanding Performance	4 Highly Effective	3 Standards Met/ Satisfactory	2 Needs Improvement/ Marginal	1 Standard Not Met/ Unsatisfactory	0 Not Assigned	Supporting Statement
IV. Accountability System: School counselors must collect and use data that support and link the school counseling program to students' academic success. An evaluation of the school counseling program must answer the question, "How are students different as a result of the school counseling program?" Further, a significant contribution to the system-level or School Improvement Plan must be evident. This means that results should be fully aligned with the district strategic plan and outcomes to support goals must be quantifiable and substantial regarding the number of students affected.							
1 Demonstrates significant program impact through perception and results data.							
2 Uses appropriate baseline data to set clear targets that are quantifiable and linked to the district strategic plan.							
3 Advocates for systemic change that supports optimal student achievement within schools.							
4 Regularly reviews results data to continually adjust and improve school counseling services.							

Total Score for HR Use   **0**   **Grand Total**

B. Additional Job-Related Information

C. Future Objectives for Consideration

D. Overall Evaluation

☐ *Outstanding*
☐ *Highly Effective*
☐ *Satisfactory*
☐ *Marginal*
☐ *Unsatisfactory*

Overall Comments

Signatures

Person Evaluated	Date	Evaluator	Date

Distribution: Copies to 1—Human Resources 2—Employee 3—Principal or Supervisor

Employee Initials

AACPS · DPS/JH 1330/1160 (New 10/08) **3 of 3**

Source: Anne Arundel County Public Schools.

Name

Professional Assignment

A complete description of the teacher evaluation process of the Howard County Public Schools is provided in the Guide to Teacher Evaluation and Professional Development.

Please place the appropriate letter
Symbol in the box next to the objective:

Circle either **Tenured** or **Nontenured**

S - Satisfactory
U - Unsatisfactory

School counselors and administrators must note that staff members selecting a differentiated supervision option as part of the professional development and evaluation process will receive a final overall evaluation rating of SATISFACTORY unless the staff member and administrator rewrite the Professional Development and Evaluation Objectives form prior to January 31.

1. INTERPERSONAL SKILLS
   Relates Effectively with Students
   Develops Collaborative Relationships with Administrative, Teaching,
   and Support Staff
   Fosters Positive Relationships with Families and Community Members
   Comments:

2. PLANNING AND PREPARATION/MANAGEMENT
   Demonstrates Knowledge of Guidance and Counseling Theory and Strategies
   Demonstrates Knowledge of Students
   Selects Appropriate Counseling/Instructional Goals
   Demonstrates Knowledge of Resources
   Designs Coherent Counseling/Instruction
   Assesses Students' Needs Effectively
   Comments:

3. THE CLASSROOM ENVIRONMENT/SCHOOL ENVIRONMENT
   Establishes a Culture for Learning
   Manages Counseling/Classroom Procedures Effectively
   Manages Student Behavior Effectively
   Organizes Physical Space Appropriately
   Comments:

(Continued)

FIGURE 5.11 Howard County Public School System school counselors evaluation form.

☐ 4. **DELIVERY OF INSTRUCTION/PROGRAM IMPLEMENTATION**
Communicates Clearly and Accurately
Uses Questioning and Discussion Techniques Effectively
Engages Students in Learning Activities Directed to Guidance Goals (Comar 13A05050)
and Student Needs
Provides Effective Feedback to Students
Demonstrates Flexibility and Responsiveness
Comments:

☐ 5. **PROFESSIONAL RESPONSIBILITIES**
Reflects on Guidance and Counseling
Supports and Maintains Accurate Records
Communicates with Families
Shows Professionalism
Grows and Develops Professionally
Comments:

☐ Overall Rating ☐ See attachments (Attachments are required for all overall ratings of unsatisfactory.)

_____
Counselor's Signature & Date

_____
Designated Evaluator's Signature & Date

_____
Principal's Signature & Date

Note: Must be given to counselor within five school days after it is signed by the principal and no later than the last duty day.

Distribution: Principal, Employee, Personnel File

HOWARD COUNTY PUBLIC SCHOOL SYSTEM
Framework for Excellence in Guidance and Counseling

DOMAIN 1   **INTERPERSONAL SKILLS**

INDICATOR 1A   RELATES EFFECTIVELY WITH STUDENTS
Knowledge of students
Interactions with students
Communication skills

INDICATOR 1B   DEVELOPS COLLABORATIVE RELATIONSHIPS WITH ADMINISTRATIVE, TEACHING, AND SUPPORT STAFF
Respect and rapport
Communication skills
Conflict resolution

INDICATOR 1C   FOSTERS POSITIVE RELATIONSHIPS WITH FAMILIES AND COMMUNITY MEMBERS
Respect and rapport
Communication skills
Conflict resolution

DOMAIN 2   **PLANNING AND PREPARATION/MANAGEMENT**

INDICATOR 2A   DEMONSTRATES KNOWLEDGE OF GUIDANCE AND COUNSELING THEORY AND STRATEGIES
Content
Application in a school setting

INDICATOR 2B   DEMONSTRATES KNOWLEDGE OF STUDENTS
Developmental needs of students and characteristics of age groups
Students' varied approaches to learning
Students' skills and knowledge
Students' interests and cultural heritage

INDICATOR 2C   SELECTS APPROPRIATE COUNSELING/INSTRUCTIONAL GOALS
Value
Clarity

Indicator 2D   DEMONSTRATES KNOWLEDGE OF RESOURCES
Resources for counseling
Resources for student support

INDICATOR 2E   DESIGNS COHERENT COUNSELING/INSTRUCTION
Long-/short-term planning
Integrated with individual school improvement planning
Learning/informational activities
Counseling/instructional groups
Counseling/instructional materials and resources

(Continued)

INDICATOR 2F	ASSESSES STUDENTS' NEEDS EFFECTIVELY
	Prevention and intervention appropriate to specific grade levels
	Use in designing or modifying guidance program appropriately

---

DOMAIN 3   **THE CLASSROOM ENVIRONMENT/SCHOOL ENVIRONMENT**

INDICATOR 3A	ESTABLISHES A CULTURE FOR LEARNING
	Development of life skills and career connections
	Expectations for learning and achievement

INDICATOR 3B	MANAGES COUNSELING/CLASSROOM PROCEDURES EFFECTIVELY
	Managing counseling/instructional groups
	Managing materials and supplies
	Performing non-instructional duties
	Supervising volunteers and paraprofessionals

INDICATOR 3C	MANAGES STUDENT BEHAVIOR EFFECTIVELY
	Expectations
	Monitoring student behavior
	Response to student misbehavior

INDICATOR 3D	ORGANIZES PHYSICAL SPACE APPROPRIATELY
	Safety and accessibility
	Respect for confidentiality
	Welcoming and inviting environment

DOMAIN 4   **DELIVERY OF INSTRUCTION/PROGRAM IMPLEMENTATION**

INDICATOR 4A	COMMUNICATES CLEARLY AND ACCURATELY
	Directions and procedures
	Oral and written language

INDICATOR 4B	USES QUESTIONING AND DISCUSSION TECHNIQUES EFFECTIVELY
	Quality of questions
	Discussion techniques
	Student participation

INDICATOR 4C	ENGAGES STUDENTS IN LEARNING ACTIVITIES DIRECTED TO GUIDANCE GOALS (Comar 13A05050) AND STUDENT NEEDS
	Variety of guidance interventions
	Materials, activities, technology, and assignments
	Relevant and thoughtful applications
	Counseling/instructional groups
	Lesson/unit structure and pacing
	Transitions across grades/schools/community

INDICATOR 4D	PROVIDES EFFECTIVE FEEDBACK TO STUDENTS Quality: accurate, substantive, constructive, and specific Equitability Timeliness
INDICATOR 4E	DEMONSTRATES FLEXIBILITY AND RESPONSIVENESS Adjustment of counseling strategies Response to students Persistence

DOMAIN 5	PROFESSIONAL RESPONSIBILITIES
INDICATOR 5A	REFLECTS ON GUIDANCE AND COUNSELING Accuracy Use in future guidance and counseling planning
INDICATOR 5B	SUPPORTS AND MAINTAINS ACCURATE RECORDS Record keeping Standards of confidentiality/security
INDICATOR 5C	COMMUNICATES WITH FAMILIES Information about the counseling/instructional program Information about individual students Opportunities for involvement in the counseling/instructional program School and community resources
INDICATOR 5D	SHOWS PROFESSIONALISM Student advocacy Collaborative problem solving Relationships with business and community Following federal, state, and local policies and procedures Adherence to the Code of Ethics of the American Counseling Association
INDICATOR 5E	GROWS AND DEVELOPS PROFESSIONALLY Enhancement of content knowledge and counseling skills Service to the school, district, and profession

Source: Howard County Public Schools.

Exemplary School Counseling Programs

Vision for School Counseling Programs

The school counseling program, in collaboration with faculty, parents, and community, will provide all students with the attitudes, knowledge, and skills for lifelong success. The comprehensive school counseling program integrates academic, career, and personal/social development and focuses on issues relevant to *all* students.

Students will participate in a planned, developmentally age-appropriate, and sequential school counseling program that is based on the National Standards for School Counseling. The program will prepare students to become effective learners, achieve success in school, and develop into contributing members of our society.

A. School-Level Factors Impacting Student Learning/Social Emotional/Healthy Development

The school counseling program is set up and run in a manner that supports student achievement.

Component I: Academic Support

ALWAYS EVIDENT	SOMEWHAT EVIDENT	NOT EVIDENT	FACTORS
O	O	O	1. The school counseling office requires the school counselors to learn about the strengths and interests of students and to use this information to identify appropriate strategies for accelerating student learning.
O	O	O	2. At the secondary level, the school administration includes a school counselor in facilitating and encouraging student movement to classes at the level of most appropriate challenge, including Honors, G/T, and AP classes.
O	O	O	3. The school administration ensures that students with special needs receive the appropriate support from school counselors to accelerate student learning.
O	O	O	4. At the high school level, the school administration, in collaboration with the school counselor, schedules all 10th and all 11th grade students to take the PSAT. Students use the results to identify areas in which they need additional preparation.
O	O	O	5. At the high school level, counselors ensure that all diploma-seeking students are strongly encouraged to take the SAT.

Component II: Program Development and Evaluation

ALWAYS EVIDENT	SOMEWHAT EVIDENT	NOT EVIDENT	FACTORS
O	O	O	1. The school counseling program is aligned with school improvement goals and is written on the School Counseling Program Plan. The School Counseling Plan should be approved by the principal.
O	O	O	2. The school counseling program uses a planning process to define needs, priorities, and program objectives.
O	O	O	3. The school counseling program educates the school staff, parents, and the community about the school counseling program through a public information program.
O	O	O	4. The school counseling program evaluates the effectiveness of individual activities and the overall program in meeting desired student outcomes.
O	O	O	5. The school counseling program continues to seek feedback from students, parents, and staff about the services provided by the counseling office.
O	O	O	6. The school counselor(s) meet on a regular basis within the department and with administration to assess the progress of the school counseling program.
O	O	O	7. School counselors provide differentiated services to help all students develop academic identities that foster achievement.

Component III: Staff Assignments

ALWAYS EVIDENT	SOMEWHAT EVIDENT	NOT EVIDENT	FACTORS
O	O	O	1. The Office of Student Services ensures that school counselors are certified by an accredited institution in the area of school counseling.
O	O	O	2. Administrators use the staffing parameters to develop a plan to keep the counselor's involvement in non-counseling duties to a minimum.

FIGURE 5.12 Howard County Public Schools exemplary school counseling programs.

Howard County Public Schools
School Counseling

ALWAYS EVIDENT	SOMEWHAT EVIDENT	NOT EVIDENT	FACTORS
O	O	O	3. Administrators ensure that the counselors are provided sufficient access to students so that time is available to implement effective school counseling program activities.
O	O	O	4. At the secondary level, counselor assignments in the department are made in such a way that counselor expertise and workload are taken into consideration.
O	O	O	5. At the high school level, administrators select highly competent counselors to serve as instructional team leaders.

Component IV: Materials and Resources

ALWAYS EVIDENT	SOMEWHAT EVIDENT	NOT EVIDENT	FACTORS
O	O	O	1. The Office of Student Services in conjunction with the school administration ensures that school counselors have multicultural instructional materials that reflect the ethnic and gender diversity of the school's students.
O	O	O	2. The Office of Student Services in conjunction with the school administration provides appropriate technology and ensures that school counselors use it to enhance student learning.
O	O	O	3. The Office of Student Services in conjunction with the school administration requires staff members to use professional development standards and resources and ensure that all professional development results in improving the learning of all students.
O	O	O	4. School Administrators, in collaboration with the school counseling office, ensure that all school counselors participate in ongoing leadership development.

Component V: Community Outreach/Involvement

ALWAYS EVIDENT	SOMEWHAT EVIDENT	NOT EVIDENT	FACTORS
O	O	O	1. The school leadership team collects data on the school climate and collaborates with the school counselor to make the climate welcoming and inviting for all visitors.
O	O	O	2. School counselors support the school-wide vision for parent/family involvement that supports student achievement in their children's education.
O	O	O	3. The school leadership team and the office of school counseling ensure that communication about the school counseling program for non-English speaking parents/families is available through written translations and oral interpreter services.
O	O	O	4. The school counselor has a process for identifying parents/families that are not partners in their children's education.
O	O	O	5. The school counselor has a process for analyzing the data and the reasons for the noninvolvement of identified parents/families.
O	O	O	6. Based upon the data analysis, the school counselor develops a plan for engaging families in their children's education.
O	O	O	7. The school counselor uses Central Office resources for additional support for parent/family involvement in their children's education.
O	O	O	8. The school counselor has a well-defined process for gathering and responding to feedback on practices for involving parent/families in their children's education.
O	O	O	9. The school counselor has a process to inform parents/families about the school counseling program and student progress. The process fosters two-way communication and ensures participation that is representative of the school community.

(Continued)

ALWAYS EVIDENT	SOMEWHAT EVIDENT	NOT EVIDENT	FACTORS
O	O	O	10. When necessary, the school counselor uses the services of ESOL Community Liaisons and the Office of International Student Services to facilitate family and community involvement in the education of students.
O	O	O	11. The school counselor develops and maintains educational partnerships that include support for improving achievement.

B. *Educator-Level Factors Impacting Student Learning/Social Emotional/Healthy Development*

Exemplary school counselors form a partnership with students and their families to promote the personal and social development of students in order to help students achieve high levels of cognitive development. They use research-based best practices to plan and implement lessons that effectively meet the needs of all learners.

Component I: Personal Development of Students

ALWAYS EVIDENT	SOMEWHAT EVIDENT	NOT EVIDENT	FACTORS
			All school counselors help students develop a positive academic identity. They…
O	O	O	1. Make it a daily habit to tell students, individually and collectively, that they are capable and competent learners. (Domain 3A)
O	O	O	2. Take explicit steps to know and understand students as individual learners. (Domain 3A)
O	O	O	3. Involve students in goal setting, self-assessment, and reflection. (Domain 2F-3)
O	O	O	4. Ensure that students know how they learn best and how to use that information to master their academic subjects. (Domain 2B-2)
O	O	O	5. Assist students with developing the character traits that will help them to be successful in school, as well as other settings. (Domain 3A-2, 3A-3, and 3C-1)
O	O	O	6. Use appropriate data about students' current level of personal development to plan future lessons. (Domain 2B-2)

Component II: Social Development of Students

ALWAYS EVIDENT	SOMEWHAT EVIDENT	NOT EVIDENT	FACTORS
			All school counselors help students become part of a community of learners. They…
O	O	O	1. Make all students feel welcome and that they are a part of a community of learners. (Domain 1A)
O	O	O	2. Give students a variety of purposes for being a part of a community of learners. (Domain 1A)
O	O	O	3. Create a physically, emotionally, and socially secure learning environment that encourages students to ask questions about what they are learning, especially when they are confused or not certain about what to do. (Domain 3D-1, 4B-3)
O	O	O	4. Create a learning environment that encourages high expectations, enables students to experience success, provides students with a sense of belonging, and promotes shared responsibility for the achievement of all. (Domain 2D-2)
O	O	O	5. Use appropriate indicators of the degree to which the student functions socially as a part of the community of learners to plan future school counseling programs. (Domain 2D-2)

Howard County Public Schools
School Counseling

Component III: Cognitive Development of Students

ALWAYS EVIDENT	SOMEWHAT EVIDENT	NOT EVIDENT	FACTORS
			All school counselors help students develop learning-to-learn skills. They ...
O	O	O	1. Use a variety of instructional strategies to keep students engaged in classroom guidance lessons. (Domain 2E)
O	O	O	2. Give students a variety of specific purposes for learning that connect to students' personal goals and interests. (Domain 2E)
O	O	O	3. Model and teach students how to use specific thinking skills. (Domain 2A-1)
O	O	O	4. Engage students in instructional activities that infuse and celebrate diverse cultural backgrounds. (Domain 2B-4, 4C-3)

Component IV: Prevention and Intervention

ALWAYS EVIDENT	SOMEWHAT EVIDENT	NOT EVIDENT	INDICATORS
			All school counselors provide a program which focuses primarily on prevention and intervention. They ...
O	O	O	1. Implement a comprehensive and balanced program. (Domain 2E)
O	O	O	2. Use the *Essential Curriculum for School Counseling* to develop thorough plans for units and individual lessons. (Domain 2C, 2E)
O	O	O	3. Involve students in personalized educational and career planning. (Domain 3A, 4C)
O	O	O	4. Provide individual counseling in a systematic and timely manner. (Domain 2B, 2E)
O	O	O	5. Provide small group counseling. (Domain 2E, 4C)
O	O	O	6. Provide classroom guidance to ALL students to address developmental needs. (Domain 4C)
O	O	O	7. Use effective techniques and strategies appropriate to counseling in the school setting. (Domain 2A)
O	O	O	8. Are aware of the needs of all sub-groups of the student population and seek to provide services to meet their needs. (Domain 2B)

Component V: Consultation

ALWAYS EVIDENT	SOMEWHAT EVIDENT	NOT EVIDENT	INDICATORS
			All school counselors use consultation skills to enhance the academic achievement of our students. They ...
O	O	O	1. Foster collaboration among school and community resources and service providers to enable students to learn as effectively as possible. (Domain 1C, 5D)
O	O	O	2. Collaborate with families to support learning and achievement in school by providing parent education and/or parent support groups. (Domain 1C, 5C)
O	O	O	3. Participate on school-based problem-solving teams. (Domain 5D)
O	O	O	4. Consult and collaborate with other staff members regarding academic development, career development, and personal/social development. (Domain 1B, 5C)
O	O	O	5. Provide parents and students with information about private and public medical, social, and mental health service providers. (Domain 5C)
O	O	O	6. Maintain a communication system that effectively collects and disseminates information about students to other professionals as appropriate. (Domain 1C, 5B)
O	O	O	7. Develop and maintain positive working relationships with representatives of community resources. (Domain 1C, 5D)

(Continued)

Howard County Public Schools
School Counseling

ALWAYS EVIDENT	SOMEWHAT EVIDENT	NOT EVIDENT	INDICATORS
O	O	O	8. Assess accurately students' and their families' need for referrals. (Domain 2F, 5C)
O	O	O	9. Facilitate an articulation between instructional levels which provides a smooth transition for students. (Domain 4C)

Component VI: Assessment

ALWAYS EVIDENT	SOMEWHAT EVIDENT	NOT EVIDENT	INDICATORS
			All school counselors use best practices for sharing assessment information. They ...
O	O	O	1. Interpret tests and other appraisal results to students, staff, and parents. (Domain 5C)
O	O	O	2. Use other sources of student data as assessment tools for the purpose of educational planning. (Domain 2D)

Component VII: Professionalism/Professional Development

ALWAYS EVIDENT	SOMEWHAT EVIDENT	NOT EVIDENT	FACTORS
			All school counselors practice professionalism in school counseling. They ...
O	O	O	1. Adhere to ethical and professional standards for school counseling. (Domain 5D)
O	O	O	2. Seek out opportunities for continuing professional development provided by the Office of School Counseling. (Domain 5E)
O	O	O	3. Comply with federal, state, and local policies and procedures. (Domain 5D)
O	O	O	4. Participate on the School Improvement Team, Instructional Intervention Team, and Student Assistance Team. (Domain 5E)

Source: Howard County Public Schools.

is such an attempt, as it provides both a vision for school counselors and expectations for other school personnel regarding the implementation of a comprehensive, developmental school counseling program. It is essential that professional school counselors held to performance standards such as these provide additional evidence and comments to give an appropriate context for those supervisors ultimately making evaluative decisions. Regardless of the evaluation system used, it is critical that the focus be on development of higher levels of counselor skills.

Summary/Conclusion

Accountability involves the demonstration of responsibility for professional actions. Professional school counselors demonstrate accountability by providing evidence that answers five primary questions. First, what are the needs of the school's student population when compared to these standards? A needs assessment can be implemented using one of two primary methods. A data-driven needs assessment evaluates needs demonstrated through derived information. Aggregated results are broken down (disaggregated) so they can be examined on the subgroup level. Such analysis is critical to demonstrate whether all students are given access to rigorous academic coursework and are benefiting from the curriculum. A perceptions-based needs assessment determines what primary stakeholder groups (e.g., teachers, parents, students) perceive as needs. These perceptions can be gathered through a variety of methods, but some form of quantifiable result is preferred so that various perceived needs can be compared and prioritized.

Second, is a comprehensive, standards-based program in place? A program assessment (e.g., audit, process evaluation) should be conducted annually near the end of the school year to determine whether a written school counseling program is being fully implemented.

Third, what services were implemented to address the identified needs and standards? A service assessment provides an accounting of who did what, how much, and for how long. This type of evidence is helpful in demonstrating that professional school counselors are using their time to provide valuable (or even not so valuable) services and is often requested by administrations and school boards. Unfortunately, service assessment is more of a process evaluation (i.e., how one spends one's time), rather than an outcomes evaluation (i.e., what valuable result has occurred by spending one's time that way). In other words, time is a process variable. Results stem from the actions one performs, given the precious commodity of time.

Fourth, what was the result of the implemented services? Some argue that results or outcomes studies are the most valuable facet of accountability. The assessment loop shows that the purpose of evaluation is continuous quality improvement. Data are collected to evaluate actions and interventions so that judgments can be made on the worth or value of services and programs. Often, traditional research designs can yield the most helpful and authoritative information about program or event quality. Because of the broad-ranging nature of standards and competencies, professional school counselors attempting to demonstrate the effectiveness of a developmental curriculum should use an aggregated hierarchical model in which evidence is collected at the objectives level to demonstrate whether higher-order competencies and standards have been met.

Fifth, how well is the professional school counselor performing? As a condition of employment, professional school counselors undergo periodic performance evaluation or performance appraisal. The purpose of this process is to determine the performance of the individual, rather than that of the program. Of course, if there is only one professional school counselor in the school, the individual appraisal often also reflects program quality. Professional school counselors should be aware of the evaluation criteria well in advance of any assessment, and such processes should be aimed at developing higher-level counseling skills and competencies.

Accountability applies to every facet of a school counseling program. The better prepared a professional school counselor is to engage in accountability activities, continuously collect evidence, and report on program performance, the more valuable he or she is to the school, school system, and profession. Being responsible for one's actions and the quality of services provided is an important ethical and professional responsibility.

Activities

1. Develop a preliminary needs assessment for a school in your community. What type of method did you use (questionnaire, classroom visits, etc.)? What types of needs were addressed in your assessment? How will this assessment influence the development of your program?
2. Interview a professional school counselor regarding the use of needs assessment. Ask to view a needs assessment recently given and what learning objectives were derived from student responses.
3. Conduct a role play with a partner in which you are the school counselor and your partner is an administrator. Using assessment and accountability, convince the administrator that your school counseling program is an important aspect of student academic success.

6

Outcomes Research on School Counseling Interventions and Programs

Susan C. Whiston, Rachel Feldwisch, and Barbara James

E ditor's Introduction: The science of school counseling involves empirical study of the methods, techniques, and procedures used by professional school counselors in their day-to-day work. The transformation of the profession must be guided by knowledge and understanding of what works, rather than by what or how much of something is done. Effective practices raise a profession to new heights, and it is with this focus that we explore what is known about the effectiveness of school counseling practices. As you will see, although some evidence exists regarding effective service provision, much more evidence is needed to document effectiveness and establish school counseling as an accountable profession. The transformed professional school counselor understands the vital nature of this mission and establishes collaborative partnerships to conduct field-based action research and outcomes evaluation to benefit students and the profession.

OUTCOMES RESEARCH IN SCHOOL COUNSELING

As we explore the practice of professional school counseling, it is important to examine whether the services professional school counselors provide are actually helpful to students. Although professional school counselors may believe certain approaches are effective, others—such as school board members, administrators, parents, and legislators—want documented evidence that reflects the effectiveness of school counseling. Furthermore, many of these individuals not only want confirmation that school counseling services are beneficial to students, but also evidence that these services are cost effective. In some school districts, professional school counseling positions may be eliminated unless there is empirical support documenting the effectiveness of professional school counselor activities. Whereas the previous two chapters have addressed the need for gathering data and using data for accountability, this chapter focuses on outcome research in school counseling.

One reason for being familiar with research related to the effectiveness of professional school counseling programs is the movement toward evidence-based practice. A few years ago the U.S. Department of Education (2005b) made it a goal to transform education into an evidence-based field. Evidence-based practices in education are those interventions or teaching methods used within a school that have empirical support. In determining whether a certain approach or intervention meets the criteria for evidence-based practices, individuals often look at the outcomes research conducted related to that approach or intervention. Outcomes researchers seek to understand the end results or effects on students of some practice or intervention. Outcomes research in the field of professional school counseling analyzes whether school counseling programs or components of such a program result in positive outcomes for students.

In addition to providing accountability information on the effects of school counseling interventions and services, outcomes research can provide pertinent clinical information that informs professional school counselors.

Counseling outcomes research can be a useful resource because it is designed to identify which approaches and activities produce positive changes for students. Outcomes research can aid professional school counselors in selecting counseling interventions and guidance activities that have been shown to be effective. Some have argued that without empirical information, practitioners are making uninformed decisions. Lambert (1991) contended that without a thorough knowledge of the counseling outcomes research, a practitioner cannot ethically counsel. He argued that counselors are ethically bound to provide the best services to their clients, and without a thorough knowledge of the research, they will not know what has been shown to be the "best." Given the significant responsibilities that professional school counselors have, it is important they choose interventions that are effective.

However, it is not always easy to be a good consumer of outcomes research. Outcomes research is published in a wide variety of journals, and it is often difficult for professional counselors to keep abreast of relevant findings. In addition, it is sometimes difficult to decipher results and identify valid and reliable findings that are pertinent to counseling practice. This chapter is designed to assist counselors by summarizing the outcomes research related to school counseling activities. Whiston (2002) argued that it is critical for professional school counselors to be informed about outcomes research and know which activities are supported or not supported by research. By summarizing the research in this area, this chapter is designed to give professional school counselors the empirical knowledge they need when making decisions about what works best with which students. The chapter also provides accountability information and outcomes research that can be communicated to other constituents (e.g., school boards and principals). In examining outcomes research, this chapter addresses the following set of questions: Is professional school counseling effective? Which students benefit from school counseling interventions? What are the effective methods for delivering school counseling programs? Does a fully implemented school counseling program make a difference?

IS PROFESSIONAL SCHOOL COUNSELING EFFECTIVE?

The question of whether professional school counseling is effective cannot be answered using the results of just one study. No single study can examine the multitude of duties performed by professional school counselors at all grade levels. Therefore, answering the question concerning the effectiveness of school counseling services requires an examination of the accumulation of school counseling research. One valuable resource is research reviews on professional school counseling. There are two types of research reviews: The first is the more common qualitative review, where researchers examine the studies and summarize the findings and trends; the second is based on meta-analytic techniques, where researchers seek to quantify the results by calculating an overall effect size (e.g., the mean of the control group subtracted from the mean of the experimental group and divided by the standard deviation of the control group). Cohen (1988) offered a helpful rule-of-thumb guideline for interpreting effect sizes derived from this formula: 0.20 is considered a small effect, 0.50 is considered a moderate effect, and 0.80 or higher is considered a large effect.

Results from qualitative reviews are generally supportive of the effectiveness of school counseling activities. Borders and Drury (1992) examined research studies and professional statements from counseling organizations published between 1960 and 1990. They concluded that school counseling interventions have a substantial impact on students' educational and personal development. Their review cited a number of studies that indicated students who received school counseling services showed improvements in terms of their academic performance, attitudes, and behaviors. In a systematic review of outcomes research in professional school counseling, Whiston and Sexton (1998) concluded that a broad range of activities professional school counselors perform results in positive changes in students. They found, however, that not all school counseling activities have been empirically investigated.

Meta-analytic reviews, as stated earlier, provide a quantitative measure of the degree to which school counseling interventions and programs are effective. A recent meta-analysis conducted by Whiston, Tai, Rahardja, and Eder (2011) provided some quantitative evidence concerning the degree to which school counseling interventions are effective. These researchers examined the school counseling literature since 1980 and found 117 school counseling studies, both published and unpublished (e.g., dissertations), that contained sufficient data to calculate an effect size (ES). In examining these 117 studies, Whiston et al. (2011) identified 153 school counseling interventions that involved 16,296 students. In terms of the effectiveness of all school counseling interventions, these researchers found an average unweighted ES of 0.46; however, when weighting the ES by the methods proposed by Hedges and Olkin (1985), they found a significant ES of 0.30. An ES of 0.30 is somewhat small, but it does indicate that on measures used in the studies, students who received a school counseling intervention were almost a third of a standard deviation above those who did not receive the intervention. Whiston et al. (2011) found that school counseling interventions were particularly effective in decreasing discipline problems (ES = 0.83) and in increasing students' problem-solving abilities (ES = 0.96). Whiston et al. (2001) also found that school counseling interventions were not homogeneous and that there was variation among the interventions, which reflects the fact that some interventions are more effective and that others have much smaller ESs.

Although school counselors do more than provide counseling and psychotherapy in schools, there are some recent meta-analyses that specifically support counseling in schools. Baskin et al. (2010) investigated counseling in schools and found a weighted effect size of 0.45. Sometimes meta-analyses are criticized for primarily relying on published articles, which may inflate effect sizes, as editors of journals are more likely to accept research studies with significant results. To test this possible bias, Reese, Prout, Zirkelback, and Anderson (2010) only used dissertations related to school-based counseling and psychotherapy. They found an overall effect size of 0.44, which is very consistent with the effect size found by Baskin et al. (2010).

If the results from these various reviews are combined, there appears to be support for the conclusion that school counseling interventions are moderately to highly effective. The qualitative reviews are also generally positive. As a caveat, however, these conclusions are based on a somewhat limited number of studies. Another concern noted by Whiston et al. (2011) was that many of the studies evaluating the effectiveness of school counseling have methodological limitations.

WHICH STUDENTS BENEFIT FROM SCHOOL COUNSELING INTERVENTIONS?

School counselors provide interventions to students at all grade levels and from a variety of racial and ethnic backgrounds, thus practitioners and policy makers may question if services are equally beneficial to this wide variety of students. Several meta-analytic reviews suggest that the effectiveness of school counseling services may differ according to student age. The first meta-analysis of school-based counseling and psychotherapy services was conducted by Prout and DeMartino in 1986, then replicated by Prout and Prout in 1998. Both studies concluded that elementary school students benefit more from school counseling services when compared to other school-age groups (Prout & DeMartino, 1986; Prout & Prout, 1998).

Although the latter study showed impressive effect sizes (1.31 for elementary school students compared to 0.73 for middle and high school students), a major shortcoming of this meta-analysis was the relatively small number of research studies included (i.e., only 17 studies). Recent meta-analyses of school-based therapeutic services have included greater numbers of studies (Baskin et al., 2010; Reese et al., 2010; Stice, Marti, Shaw, & Jaconis, 2009), but comparisons of effectiveness between age groups have yielded divergent results. The meta-analysis of 65 doctoral dissertations conducted by Reese et al. (2010) concurred with the original findings of Prout and colleagues, reporting an effect size that was greater for elementary school students compared to middle and high school students who received school-based counseling or psychotherapeutic services. However, in their meta-analysis of 107 school-based studies, Baskin et al. (2010) found that counseling interventions were less efficacious with children when compared to adolescents and hypothesized that this could be due to better developed cognitive skills and emotional intelligence among the older group. Yet another group of researchers (Whiston et al., 2011) found that "there were no significant differences between the effect sizes of guidance curriculum activities and responsive services interventions at the elementary, middle, or junior high, or high school levels" (p. 44). Whiston and colleagues (2011) called for more research in middle schools and high schools regarding the benefits of school counseling interventions, as more than half (50.4%) of the research studies utilized in their meta-analysis were conducted in elementary schools compared to 17.9% at the middle school level and 24.8% at the high school level.

Few researchers have examined differences in degrees of benefit from school counseling services between students of different ethnic backgrounds and genders. Therefore, meta-analyses regarding the efficacy of school-based counseling interventions seldom report data regarding gender and ethnicity (Baskin et al., 2010). Baskin and colleagues included information regarding gender and ethnicity in their meta-analysis of school-based counseling research, but these researchers did not find a significant difference between the effect sizes for these segments of the population.

Increasingly, professional school counselors are required to serve *all* students in a school. Questions related to which students benefit from school counseling activities are probably not as important as questions related to how professional school counselors can deliver a school counseling program effectively to all students. The next section of this chapter examines the research related to the methods of delivering school counseling programs and the effectiveness of the different modalities.

THE IMPORTANCE OF USING EMPIRICALLY BASED RESEARCH IN THE SCHOOLS

Empirically based and data-driven research related to the field of school counseling is a critical cornerstone for building a foundation of "efficacy" for our profession. School counselors impact the lives of students, parents, colleagues, and the community through academic, career and postsecondary, social and emotional, and developmental counseling and advising. As we are able to validate the level of that impact through outcomes that have empirically proven results, our profession will

benefit by having the leverage of accountability to argue for the placement of more counselors in more schools, lower student-to-counselor ratios, and more time to implement direct counselor-related services to our students and parents.

Source: Greg W. Chaffin, Counseling Department Chair, Bloomington High School North, Monroe County Community School Corporation, Bloomington, Indiana

WHAT ARE THE EFFECTIVE METHODS FOR DELIVERING SCHOOL COUNSELING PROGRAMS?

The field of school counseling increasingly is moving toward providing a systematic program. Professional school counselors do not solely focus on helping select students find scholarships and helping other students who are experiencing a crisis. The role of professional school counselors is to implement a comprehensive program for all students that is a key component of the larger school's purpose and mission.

For example, Sink and Stroh (2003) found that elementary students who attended schools with a comprehensive school counseling program for at least 5 years had slightly higher achievement scores than did students who attended schools with no systematic guidance program. In providing a school counseling program, counselors typically employ a variety of interventions and activities; hence, it is important to know which delivery methods result in the most positive benefits for students. As an example, professional school counselors may want to know whether it is more effective to counsel using groups or whether students benefit more from individual counseling. The American School Counselor Association (ASCA, 2012) has developed its *National Model*, which suggests three components of direct student services within a school counseling program (i.e., school counseling core curriculum, individual student planning, and responsive services). These three areas of program delivery will be used to organize our examination of the outcomes research on the effectiveness of these areas and on the particular types of activities that tend to be most effective.

School Counseling Core Curriculum

According to ASCA (2012), this core curriculum involves "structured lessons designed to help students attain the desired competencies and to provide all students with the

knowledge, attitudes, and skills appropriate for their developmental level" (p. xiv). In the past, school counseling core curriculum has been referred to as guidance curriculum. In recent years, there appear to be a number of curriculum materials developed for school counselors. As an example, Rowley, Stroh, and Sink (2005) surveyed 86 school counselors who listed 94 guidance curricular materials that they were using. In making decisions about how to invest their time, professional school counselors need to consider whether there is evidence that these guidance curriculum programs produce positive benefits for students.

Borders and Drury (1992) concluded that classroom guidance activities were effective; however, Whiston and Sexton (1998) did not find clear empirical support for classroom guidance activities. Whiston et al. (2011) identified 44 studies that evaluated guidance curriculum activities that had an overall weighted ES of 0.35. Hence, students who were in schools where guidance curriculum materials were implemented tended to score about a third of a standard deviation better than those students who did not receive these types of classroom and group activities. Of the guidance curriculum interventions evaluated, 40% were used with elementary school students, 26% with middle school students, 26% with high school students, and 7% with a mixture of students or with parents. Interestingly, although much of the research on guidance curriculum interventions is with elementary students, it seems that middle or junior high school students benefited the most (ES = 0.46) from guidance curriculum offerings. Whiston et al. (2011) also found that high school students seemed to benefit, with an average ES of 0.39, whereas the ES for elementary students was somewhat smaller (ES = 0.31).

The National Panel for Evidence-Based School Counseling (Carey, Dimmitt, Hatch, Lapan, & Whiston, 2008) used the outcome research coding protocol to evaluate the effectiveness of two widely used guidance programs (i.e., Student Success Skills and Second Step). The panel is an independent body that seeks to provide thorough and unbiased reviews of school counseling practices. Student Success Skills is a structured group and classroom guidance approach to teaching cognitive/metacognitive skills, social skills, and self-management skills to students in grades 5 through 9. The outcomes studies the panel used in evaluating Student Success Skills were Brigman and Campbell (2003), Campbell and Brigman (2005), and Webb, Brigman, and Campbell (2005). The coding protocol used required the panel to evaluate the programs' outcomes studies in seven domains. Concerning Student Success Skills, the panel found the program to have either "promising" or "strong" evidence in all domains except persistence of effect. The panel encouraged researchers to conduct additional research related to Student Success Skills and advised researchers to examine the long-term effects of the program on students' cognitive and social skills. It appears that the developers of the Student Success Skills program are continuing to evaluate its effectiveness. Brigman, Webb, and Campbell (2007) found that students who participated in the Student Success Skills program had higher mathematics achievement scores, as compared to students who did not participate, and their teacher found that their behavior improved after participating in the program.

Related to guidance curriculum activities at the elementary level, Rowley et al. (2005) found that elementary counselors were most likely to use guidance curriculum materials related to the personal/affective domain. Whiston et al. (2011) found that professional school counseling interventions designed to increase self-esteem had limited impact on students' self-esteem. In a well-designed study, Schlossberg, Morris, and Lieberman (2001) found that counselor-led developmental guidance units presented in ninth-grade classrooms have the potential to improve students' expressed behavior and general school attitudes, while also addressing their developmental needs. Sometimes school counseling curriculum programs are delivered by teachers in a school to more efficiently reach all students. Durlak, Weissberg, Dymnicki, Taylor, and Schellinger (2011) evaluated the effectiveness of social and emotional learning curriculums delivered specifically by teachers. These researchers found that these social and emotional learning curriculums delivered by teachers had an effect size of 0.34 on academic performance and an effect size of 0.62 on skills related to social and emotional learning. These results indicate that teachers can be effective in teaching curriculums related to social and emotional factors. Classroom guidance activities are a major emphasis of school counseling programs in some school districts; yet the research in this area could be more extensive. Rowley et al. (2005) found that with a few exceptions (e.g., the Missouri Comprehensive Guidance and Counseling Program), professional school counselors are predominately using curricular materials that have not been well researched. They recommended the development and evaluation of guidance curriculum materials that meet the needs of students and correspond to the ASCA's *National Standards for School Counseling Programs* (Campbell & Dahir, 1997). We concur with this recommendation and believe the development of empirically supported guidance curriculum materials is a crucial step in transforming school counseling.

THEORY INTO PRACTICE 6.1

CONDUCTING OUTCOME EVALUATION STUDIES OF SCHOOL COUNSELING INTERVENTIONS

I was a school counselor in P–12 schools for 9 years before entering a research-oriented doctoral training program. While serving as a school counselor, I was nervous about conducting research in my schools because I assumed that research methodology was way above my head and always involved complicated statistical knowledge that I did not possess. What I discovered is that I was involved in informal action research almost every week of my school counseling work and I did not realize it. Every time I gave a pre-/post-test before and after classroom lessons or groups, I was engaged in outcomes research.

So, what *are* the skills that school counselors need to perform outcomes evaluations in their schools? Professional school counselors already possess much of the knowledge and characteristics needed to perform outcomes research. For instance, two major requirements are curiosity and flexibility of thought, traits commonly associated with counselors. These attributes are a must when analyzing results that you did not expect. Asking yourself what these results might mean and what could have influenced them is crucial throughout the process, not just at the end. It is important to keep in mind that the process is "iterative," meaning that as you move along through the steps, you have to be prepared to make changes as a result of what you are finding. In other words, the steps of the research process are not necessarily linear but are often circular. For instance, you can expect small changes to your research question and your design as you are planning for implementation because the more you hone your question, the more you see potential obstacles and limitations. This is a normal and important part of the process; the better matched your design and methodology to your question, the more generalizable your results are likely to be. So, what *are* the steps in conducting an outcomes evaluation? Here is the basic breakdown:

1. **Know your resources.**
   Many great sources of information are out there to help you. Ask colleagues, local universities, and others for help. Resources can be found on the Center for School Counseling Outcome Research and Evaluation website (www.cscor.org). In addition, research textbooks can be very rich sources of guidance. Although many textbooks exist regarding methods for conducting research, limiting your perusal to those that are focused on implementation in schools can help narrow your focus. One good example of this type of research text is Gay, Mills, and Airasian (2011).

2. **State and refine your question.**
   Are you interested in the effects of a small-group intervention on student self-esteem, a large-group guidance lesson on student academic achievement, or a school counselor/parent consultation on student discipline referrals? Whatever your question, the intervention should be well defined, and the effect must be measurable.

3. **Choose an appropriate research design to match your question and your situation.**
   The National Panel for Evidence-based School Counseling discusses that experimental or quasi-experimental designs are the "gold standard" for outcome research when one is making causal claims about an intervention's effectiveness. They state, however, that at times less-rigorous designs can provide important information about whether an intervention "shows promise" and warrants further investigation (Carey et al., 2008). It is important to spend time evaluating whether your design is realistic and manageable as well as appropriate to your stage of investigation.

4. **Choose an appropriate outcome measure.**
   As stated earlier, your outcome must be measurable, and therefore, the instrument(s) that you use to measure it is very important. For instance, are you using student grades, number of discipline referrals, test scores, or self-report from students? Surveys, data from interviews, and other sources of information can be used to answer your question, but consider whether the measure is valid for the population you are sampling and whether it captures that construct about which you are seeking knowledge.

5. **Choose an appropriate data analysis method.**
   After you have gathered your data, you need to aggregate and analyze it appropriately. Statistical analysis can range from very simple t-tests (which you can do on your own with user-friendly statistical software) to very complex operations. If you are unfamiliar with statistical operations, seek consultation. Talking to a statistician can not only help with your data, but also help you to articulate your question and refine your methodology. Ask your district if they employ professional researchers and if they are available for consultation. Another option is to call your local university. More often than not universities are thrilled with the opportunity to partner with a field professional.

6. **Stay flexible when examining results.**
   THINK—If I discover through data analysis that a program I am using is not showing measurable effects, what are the questions that I should ask before drawing conclusions? How can I get answers to these questions? With whom should I consult about these results? What further investigation is warranted?

7. **Disseminate your results.**
   Be sure to share your results with other professional school counselors and other appropriate constituents. If the results are positive, then share those results with school board members, administrators, parents, and others. Even if the results show that an intervention does little to help students, other professional school counselors can benefit from that knowledge. The critical point is to share your outcome study through both formal and informal mechanisms.

Individual Student Planning

Individual student planning involves professional school counselors coordinating ongoing systemic activities designed to assist students in individually determining personal goals and developing plans for their future (ASCA, 2012). Whiston et al. (2011) found only 10 studies that addressed individual planning, and the majority of these were with high school students. The overall weighted ES was statistically significant (ES = 0.26).

According to Gysbers and Henderson (2012), professional school counselors often design individual planning around educational and career/vocational planning. In addition, one of the three areas in the ASCA's *National Standards for School Counseling Programs* (Campbell & Dahir, 1997) is career development. Also, Scruggs, Wasielewski, and Ash (1999) found that both students and parents would like professional school counselors to put more emphasis on career guidance and development activities. Therefore, it is important to examine the research related to effective career guidance and counseling activities.

There is support for the effectiveness of career counseling with clients at various developmental levels from both narrative reviews (Whiston & Oliver, 2005; Whiston & Rahardja, 2008) and meta-analyses (Oliver & Spokane, 1988; Whiston, Sexton, & Lasoff, 1998). The meta-analyses differ somewhat on the degree to which career interventions are effective. The first meta-analysis (Oliver & Spokane, 1988) indicated career interventions were highly effective, whereas the meta-analysis of more current research (Whiston et al., 1998) found career interventions to be moderately effective. These two meta-analyses were consistent in finding that individual career counseling and vocational classes were the most effective methods of delivering career counseling services.

Another meta-analysis related to career interventions found that counselor-free interventions are not effective and that interventions involving a counselor are significantly more efficacious (Whiston, Brecheisen, & Stephens, 2003). This finding is particularly important because many schools have purchased computerized career guidance programs or encourage students to use career resources on the Internet. Whiston et al.'s (2003) finding clearly indicated that students do not gain much when they use these resources alone; however, students do benefit from the use of computerized career guidance systems when they are integrated with other activities involving a counselor. In a recent survey of school counselors, the College Board Advocacy and Policy Center (2011) found that 75% of school counselors would like to spend more time on targeted activities such as career counseling and exploration. The outcome research in this area would indicate that these types of activities would be time well spent. Whiston et al. (1998) found that career interventions were more effective at the junior high/middle school level than at the high school level. A commonly used program for middle school students in various countries, the Real Game, was evaluated by Dimmitt (2007) with a large sample ($N = 617$) of middle school students from the United States. Dimmitt found that those students who participated in the Real Game scored higher in the domains of self-efficacy, school engagement, and prosocial behaviors, as compared to those who did not participate.

Within the area of individual planning, a major focus of many professional school counselors, particularly those at the high school level, involves encouraging and assisting students in entering college. A recent study (Bryan, Moore-Thomas, Day-Vines, & Holcomb-McCoy, 2011) found that student contact with a professional school counselor was a significant predictor of students applying for college. In particular, these researchers found that students who saw a school counselor for college information before the 10th grade had twice the odds of applying to one college as compared to not applying to any colleges and 3.5 times the odds of applying to two more colleges as compared to no colleges. They also found that student–counselor contact for college information after the 10th grade was a positive predictor of applying to college, although the odds were slightly lower. Furthermore, they found that student–counselor contact was particularly important with students from lower socioeconomic backgrounds, and those students who had no contact with a school counselor were significantly less likely to apply for any college than those who had contact with their professional school counselor. This study clearly indicates that professional school counselors can affect the college application process.

Responsive Services

Responsive services concern the role of the professional school counselor in assisting students with immediate issues that are usually affected by life events or situations in the students' lives (ASCA, 2012). Gysbers and Henderson (2012) suggested this component of a school counseling program concerns attending to students' issues or problems. Typical modalities employed in responsive services activities are individual counseling, group counseling, referral, and peer assistance programs.

In examining the school counseling research, Whiston et al. (2011) found 58 studies that examined 73 interventions that were classified as being responsive services. Once again, the weighted overall ES of 0.35 indicated that those who received the responsive services scored a little more than a third of a standard deviation above those who did not receive the interventions. It should be noted that elementary children seemed to particularly benefit from these services, with an ES of 0.40. Surprisingly, they found that only 10 studies evaluated different approaches to responsive services with middle or junior high school students, and these studies resulted in an ES of 0.22. It is perplexing that so few studies have been conducted with this early adolescent population when these students are often experiencing physiological changes, social pressures, and behavioral problems. Whiston et al. (2011) found the evaluation of 20 responsive services interventions with high school students, and these studies produced an ES of 0.35.

INDIVIDUAL AND GROUP COUNSELING Administrators, teachers, and parents sometimes question whether the time students spend in individual or group counseling is worth the time away from classrooms and other responsibilities. As mentioned earlier, Baskin et al. (2010) found a weighted effect size of 0.45 for counseling and psychotherapy provided in a school-based setting. Baskin et al. also found that counseling services were more effective when they were provided by a licensed clinician (e.g., a professional school counselor) as compared to a paraprofessional.

There are indications that individual counseling does not have to be lengthy to be effective. Littrell, Malia, and Vanderwood (1995) concluded that three approaches to brief individual counseling were effective with secondary students. Empirical support also exists for the use of brief counseling approaches with students who have learning disabilities (Thompson & Littrell, 1998). In terms of working with young children, Bratton, Ray, Rhine, and Jones (2005) found that play therapy can be quite effective, particularly when the treatment involves a humanistic approach.

Group counseling seems a prevalent approach among professional school counselors, as Steen, Bauman, and Smith (2007) found that 87% of the professional school counselors in their study reported facilitating groups in their schools. Whiston et al. (2011) found that group interventions were often evaluated (e.g., more than 45 studies) and produced a weighted ES of 0.36. Steen and Kaffenberger (2007) found that a small group for fourth and fifth graders resulted in language arts grades increasing by at least one letter grade for a majority of participants. In addition, there is research indicating that groups designed to assist students whose parents have divorced can have positive effects (Stathakow & Roehrle, 2003; Whiston & Sexton, 1998). In summarizing research on group counseling with students in schools, Gerrity and DeLucia-Waack (2007) and Riva and Haub (2004) concluded that these groups are generally helpful to students. In a meta-analysis of group interventions, Hoag and Burlingame (1997) found that groups conducted in schools were significantly less effective than those conducted in clinical settings. This may be due to the fact that school counselors have a plethora of responsibilities and often cannot devote the same time and energy to facilitating groups as clinicians in clinical settings can. This raises an important point about whether some principals and administrators understand the benefits of systematic group interventions and whether this lack of understanding may result in professional school counselors being directed toward other duties.

BULLYING AND VIOLENCE PREVENTION PROGRAMS
The issue of bullying is a pressing problem that has become prevalent in school settings (Espelage & Poteat, 2012).

Skiba and Fontanini (2000) reported that as many as 20% of students in the United States say they have been bullied. To respond to this issue, several researchers have developed and studied the effectiveness of bullying and violence prevention programs. Perhaps one of the most widely known antibullying programs is the Olweus Bullying Prevention Program. In studies of this program, Olweus (2005) found reductions in bullying behavior that approached around 50%. At implementation sites, he also noted a reduction in antisocial behavior and improvements in the social climate of the school. Smith, Schneider, Smith, and Ananiadou (2004) conducted a meta-analysis of 14 studies that evaluated programs that were consistent with the Olweus approach. They found the studies varied in their findings, but overall the effect sizes were small and not significant and generally were not consistent with the findings from Norway. They did find that programs that monitored the implementation and paid more attention to implementing all aspects of the Olweus model had slightly better results. On the other hand, in a more recent meta-analysis, Ttofi and Farrington (2011) found that programs inspired by the work of Olweus tended to work better than other bullying programs. They found the most important program elements associated with decreases in bullying included parent training/meetings, improved playground supervision, disciplinary methods, classroom management, teacher training, classroom rules, a whole-school antibullying policy, school conferences, information for parents, and cooperative group work.

Another popular antibullying program is Bullybusters. This psychoeducational program, targeting students in grades K–8, has been implemented in many schools across the United States (Newman-Carlson & Horne, 2004; Orpinas & Horne, 2006). Some of the initial studies of the implementations of Bullybusters found a 20% reduction in the number of bullying incidents reported in the first year (Beale & Scott, 2001). Another study of Bullybusters focused on the teachers implementing the program and noted several increases in their level of self-efficacy and ability to respond to incidences of bullying (Newman-Carlson & Horne, 2004). The study also found that the focused effort to increase these teachers' skills resulted in a reduction of bullying behaviors in the students whom the teachers taught.

The National Panel for Evidence-Based School Counseling (Carey et al., 2008) obtained positive results in its evaluation of Second Step: A Violence Prevention Curriculum (Committee for Children, 2002a, 2002b). Second Step is a social and emotional learning curriculum for students in kindergarten through eighth grade. The panel reviewed seven research studies related to Second Step and determined there was "strong" evidence in all the research domains. Furthermore, Second Step has been endorsed by the U.S. Department of Education as an exemplary program.

Still another program, PeaceBuilders, is a violence prevention program designed for grades K–5 (Flannery et al., 2003). In a study of the effectiveness of this program, Flannery et al. noted significantly higher ratings of social competence among K–2 students who received the intervention and moderately higher levels of social competence for students receiving the intervention in grades 3–5. Furthermore, in this study students in grades 3–5 who received the intervention were reported to be less aggressive, and all students who received the intervention had higher self-reported ratings concerning peace-building behaviors. Flannery et al. also found that many of these effects, particularly regarding improvements in social competence and reductions in aggressive behavior, persisted over time. Finally, Jenson and Dieterich (2007) studied the effects of the Youth Matters program on elementary school students in an urban school district. In this study, they found self-reported incidents of bully victimization decreased at higher rates for students at intervention sites versus students at controlled sites. Although a number of bullying and violence prevention programs currently exist, there remains significant room for the continued implementation and evaluation of such programs to address the rampant problem of bullying.

SCHOOL-BASED ALCOHOL AND DRUG PREVENTION PROGRAMS For many students, alcohol and drug use affects their performance in school. Therefore, professional school counselors may be interested in implementing substance abuse prevention programs. The Substance Abuse and Mental Health Services Administration (SAMHSA) created a database called the National Registry of Effective Prevention Programs (NREPP) to assist school counselors and other professionals with the selection of prevention programs (NREPP, 2012). At the time of this publication, the registry included 150 substance abuse prevention programs and featured "model" school-based drug and alcohol prevention programs that have been proven by rigorous outcomes research. Detailed analysis of each program is beyond the scope of this review, but the NREPP could serve as a resource for professional school counselors seeking to implement evidence-based substance abuse prevention programs.

Meta-analyses of school-based substance abuse prevention programs also provide helpful data for school counselors. Cuijpers (2002) conducted a review of drug and alcohol prevention literature that included three meta-analyses of school-based interventions. Cuijpers created the following list of important criteria regarding evidence-based practice in school prevention programs: models that include a social influence component are most effective, delivery methods should encourage student interaction, effect sizes are increased when a community component is added, peer leaders are preferable, incorporating life skills may strengthen effects, and programs should focus on intentions and commitment not to use. In a subsequent meta-analysis, Gottfredson and Wilson (2003) found that peer leaders were not only preferable, but also more effective when delivering prevention curriculum alone than when they shared instructional time with an adult. Effect sizes when teachers were involved were statistically insignificant (ES = 0.04 with teacher and peer, ES 0.05 with teacher only), compared to more significant effect sizes (ES = 0.20) when peers led the curriculum. School counselors making decisions regarding the implementation of substance abuse prevention programs should consider these findings as informed consumers of outcomes research.

SUICIDE PREVENTION PROGRAMS IN SCHOOLS Suicide has been ranked the third leading cause of death for young people in the United States (National Institute of Mental Health [NIMH], 2012) and is an ongoing concern among professional school counselors. The issue of suicidality may in fact be more pervasive, as statistics reflect only completed suicides and exclude other suicidal behaviors (Aseltine, James, Schilling, & Glanovsky, 2007). In a recent study, less than 20% of adolescents with a previous suicide attempt indicated that they would seek help from a counselor or other adult if they were to contemplate suicide in the future (Wyman et al., 2008). With these facts in mind, a variety of suicide prevention and intervention programs are available for use by professional school counselors, and several programs are supported by school-based outcome studies (Miller, Eckert, & Mazza, 2009).

The Signs of Suicide (SOS) program offers both universal prevention and indicated intervention, including a suicide education component for high school students and a screening tool that allows youth to identify their own risk of suicidality (Aseltine et al., 2007). SOS has been sponsored by several youth-serving entities, including ASCA, and was evaluated using randomized treatment and control groups containing a total of 4,133 students. Analysis of posttest data revealed significant differences between the treatment group and the control group; students who participated in the SOS program reported 40% fewer suicide attempts compared to the group that did not participate in SOS. Students in the SOS program group also had more adaptive attitudes regarding suicide and were more knowledgeable about suicide and depression (Aseltine et al., 2007).

Outcome data has also been collected for universal intervention programs that train "gatekeepers" in schools, which could include administrators, teachers, and support staff (Wyman et al., 2008). The expectation of these models is that trained helpers in the school would identify students at-risk for suicide and they would then refer them to professional school counselors or other school-based mental health professionals. Wyman et al. (2008) used a randomized controlled trial design to assess the impact of the Question, Persuade, Refer (QPR) suicide prevention program. The study included 249 school staff who were assigned to either the QPR trained or the non-QPR trained groups. Counselors were not participants in the study, but the trainings were co-led by counselors from each school building. Analyses of staff surveys revealed significant impact on self-evaluated knowledge (ES = 1.32), perceived preparedness (ES = 1.21), efficacy (ES = 1.22), and accessibility of services related to suicide prevention and intervention. Individuals who worked in roles where they frequently communicated with students regarding their well-being reported the most significant increase (14%) in questioning youth about suicide.

As agents of change in our school systems, counselors have the power to launch suicide prevention programs that will reduce our nation's youth suicide rate (Kalafat, 2003). In addition, professional school counselors are uniquely positioned to continue the collection and dissemination of outcome data regarding school-based suicide prevention that can shape future suicide-related programs in schools.

PEER MEDIATION In recent years, there has been an increased interest in peer mediation programs. Some of the earlier reviews of research in this area indicated that there was empirical support for peer counseling and peer mediation programs at both the elementary and the secondary levels (Borders & Drury, 1992; Whiston & Sexton, 1998). Whiston et al. (2011) found that peer mediation interventions were effective, with a weighted ES of 0.39; however, many of the outcome measures used involved assessing peer mediators' knowledge of the mediation process and did not involve measuring whether the peer mediation process had any effect on reducing conflict. This is consistent with McGannon, Carey, and Dimmitt's (2005) findings that students who provide the peer counseling often benefit to a larger degree from the service than do the students who are receiving the counseling. Wilson, Lipsey, and Derzon (2003) found that peer mediation programs had a small impact on aggressive behavior and that, as indicated previously, there are more-effective treatment approaches for aggressive behavior. Hence, professional school counselors should not assume there is conclusive

empirical support for peer mediation programs; more research is certainly needed in this area.

PARENT EDUCATION The benefits of parent training and family counseling are well established in the counseling and psychotherapy outcomes research (Kaminski, Valle, Filene, & Boyle, 2008; Kazdin, 2011; Lundahl, Nimer, & Parsons, 2006). Less is known, however, about the effectiveness of school-based parent training initiatives and programs. Hoard and Shepard (2005) conducted a meta-analysis of school-related outcomes of parent-centered prevention programs focused on school-related outcomes. They found that although parent education was used extensively during the 1970s and early 1980s, relatively little research was conducted that indicated this method of treatment was effective. In current research, they found that that very few studies targeted parent education as a single intervention or for a specific outcome. Rather, the vast majority of studies involved parent education as part of a multicomponent intervention package targeted for a range of problems. Effect sizes ranged from 0.02 to 1.03 for studies that tested separately the parent-education component, indicating that a wide disparity exists in the effectiveness of interventions. Of those studies that did not isolate the parent-education component, overall effect sizes ranged from 0.32 to 0.57, indicating that studies that included a parent-education piece yielded moderate effects. Results also indicated that parent education appeared to be more effective when targeting specific parent behaviors and when clear objectives were stated. A few "promising evidenced-based programs" emerged when compared to no-treatment control. The authors suggested that these programs warrant further study: the Reading Made Easy program, targeting parents helping children to read; and The Aware Parenting Model, targeting attentiveness, responsiveness, guidance, and parents' receptivity to their children's emotions.

In an age in which "engagement" of all stakeholders in school and community partnerships is the "watch word" and attention to building support for students is considered fundamental to achieving success, school counselors may need to examine their consultation and parent-training efforts to determine which parent-targeted interventions are effective in improving student outcomes. ASCA calls school counselors "the first line of contact for parents and students for assistance in academic, social or personal development." Because it is unlikely that school counselors will be able to meet individually with all parents and because ASCA recommends three contacts per child with caregivers per year, effective parent education programs that can be delivered in group environments may be an essential component when meeting this recommendation (ASCA, 2012).

In my school, we use Positive Behavior Supports as a way to teach behavior. One of my goals is to use this research-based intervention to help close the achievement gap that exists in student behaviors. In our school, the discipline data shows that even though African-American students only make up 35% of our student population, they account for over 80% of the students who receive office referrals for discipline. For the past 4 years, I've used research-based interventions to work with both students and teachers to make the process of sending students to the office more uniform and less ethnically biased.

The year I came into the guidance office was the year my district adopted Positive Behavior Supports (PBS), a concrete system of steps every teacher has to make before sending a student to the office. As a school committee, we developed an infraction rubric that lists student behaviors that teachers would address and student behaviors that administrators would address. Along with the list of responsibilities for each stakeholder, there was a list of possible interventions teachers could use when redirecting students in class. When we began to introduce our new methods to our staff, we did it collaboratively. Our principal gave us several faculty meetings to present our work and to receive feedback. One of the principles of PBS is that we get at least 80% approval from the staff. I learned that the easiest way to get teachers on board with my project was to allow them ample opportunity to give input and feedback.

One of the most difficult parts of PBS on which to gain teacher buy in was the idea that all students get to participate in the schoolwide reward. Some teachers were very firm in their belief that students with behavior issues should not be able to receive the reward. However, the research associated with PBS indicates otherwise. If a student has never participated in or experienced a positive event, how can that student really know what it feels like to be a part of it or really know that it is something they want to experience again? From a behavior perspective, students will only try to change their actions or to work toward a schoolwide goal if they have firsthand knowledge of how enjoyable the activity will be.

How has all of this affected the office referral gap? Overall, the number of office referrals decreased—significantly. We use the data to monitor outcomes monthly. For example, data from previous years have taught us that the number of office referrals increases in November, January, and April. Because of that, we have built in some reteaching lessons. During certain times of the year there are still disparities in the ethnic and gender makeup of the students receiving discipline records. Using Positive Behavior Supports, however, has definitely changed the overall atmosphere of our building.

Source: Samantha Franklin, Eastwood Middle School, MSD Washington Township, Indianapolis, IN

An example of a field-based outcome study comes from a collaboration between the Center for Urban and Multicultural Education, an educational research center affiliated with a large urban university, paired with a local school counselor to examine students' and parents' perceptions of the transition from middle school to high school (Smith, Feldwisch, & Abell, 2006). The Perception of Transition Survey, a 35-item Likert-type instrument that measured what participants were "worried about" and "looking forward to" in relation to high school, was developed from the earlier work of transition researchers Akos and Galassi (2004). The team of researchers administered this survey to groups of students at three different middle schools within the same school district. The researchers also had parents complete the survey. The results compared student and parent perceptions, finding that the school district was doing an exemplary job of supporting students during the transition but needed to expand its efforts to include more parent components.

What makes this research a true outcome measure of school counseling actually occurred outside the parameters

of the published work in subsequent data analysis by the school counselor and school administrators. The three middle schools that participated in the study were all within the same school district, but used different counseling and guidance techniques to prepare their students for high school. One middle school used a public video address system to provide large-group guidance regarding high school preparation and course selection, then pulled students from class into the hallway during advising time to finalize their schedules. The second middle school included classroom guidance regarding course selection and provided individual course selection advising by request of the students. The third middle school also included classroom guidance, but in addition sent home invitations to each student and their parents for a scheduled 30-minute counseling session to select high school courses and discuss 4-year high school plans. Following quantitative data analysis of the same surveys described earlier and qualitative analysis of student focus groups, researchers found that students in the third group (that included the 30-minute counseling session) had more accurate perceptions of the high school experience and performed better academically during the first semester of high school when compared to students in the other two groups. The outcome of this data analysis was used to support the continued inclusion of 30-minute conferences at the third middle school in this large metropolitan school district.

DOES A FULLY IMPLEMENTED SCHOOL COUNSELING PROGRAM MAKE A DIFFERENCE?

In the previous section of this chapter, the efficacy of components and activities of a school counseling program were reviewed. As the field moves toward comprehensive, developmental school counseling programs, it is important to examine the research related to school counseling programs, in particular the implementation of the *ASCA National Model* (ASCA, 2012). Walsh, Barrett, and DePaul (2007) found that newly hired elementary counselors' activities did correspond to the guidelines suggested in the *ASCA National Model*. On the other hand, Whiston and Wachter (2008) found that on the average, high school counselors reported spending 27% of their time in nonprogram activities.

To determine the effectiveness of professional school counseling programs, it is essential to examine the degree to which these programs make a difference in students' lives. Sink and Stroh (2003) found that the academic achievement scores of elementary students who consistently attended schools with a comprehensive school counseling program were significantly higher than those of students who were attending schools with no systematic guidance program. This positive finding regarding academic achievement is further substantiated because the researchers' sample was quite large—5,618 third and fourth graders. The importance of a well-designed school counseling program was also underscored by Fitch and Marshall (2004). These researchers used achievement test scores to determine high-achieving and low-achieving schools and found that professional school counselors in high-achieving schools spent more time in program management and coordination. Furthermore, high-achieving schools were more likely to have implemented a school counseling program that aligned with national and state standards as compared to low-achieving schools.

Lapan and his colleagues have conducted a number of studies related to whether more fully implemented school counseling programs are better for students. Lapan, Gysbers, and Petroski (2003) surveyed 22,601 seventh graders regarding their feelings of safety and other educationally related outcomes. Students attending middle schools with more fully implemented, comprehensive programs reported (a) feeling safer in school, (b) having better relationships with their teachers, (c) thinking their education was more relevant and important to their future, (d) being more satisfied with the quality of education at their school, and (e) earning higher grades. Lapan, Gysbers, and Sun (1997) compared schools with more fully implemented guidance programs to schools with a less programmatic approach. The students from schools with more fully implemented programs were more likely to report that (a) they had earned higher grades, (b) their education better prepared them for the future, (c) they had more career and college information available to them, and (d) their schools had a more positive environment. In another study, Gysbers, Lapan, and Blair (1999) found that school counselors from programs that were more fully implemented rated themselves as having higher levels of engagement with and more visibility in the community. In addition, although the results were somewhat mixed, those schools with more fully implemented guidance programs reported a reduction in the performance of nonguidance tasks, such as clerical or student supervision duties.

In the state of Utah, education personnel established the Utah Comprehensive Guidance Program in 1993. In a large study of schools in Utah, Nelson, Gardner, and Fox (1998) found that students in highly implemented, comprehensive guidance programs were more positive about their peers and felt their school had better prepared them for employment or further education, as compared to those students in schools designated as low in terms of implementing a guidance program. In addition, students in schools with highly implemented guidance programs tended to be more satisfied with the guidance they received, as compared to those in schools with a low implementation rating. In a more recent study, Nelson, Fox, Haslam, and Gardner (2007) examined student perceptions toward conceptual areas connected with comprehensive guidance programs. The authors measured percentages of positive responses from both middle school and high school students in regard to a number of domains (e.g., School Climate, Exposure to Career Information). Nelson et al. found that students viewed the areas of School Climate and Personal Student Academic Planning most favorably. In addition, they found generally positive responses on the measures of Student Involvement with Counseling and Quality of Help for Students from Counselors and Other Staff. Of the areas measured, the fewest positive responses were found in regard to Exposure to Career Information. In their review, Nelson et al. (2007) also compared performance by students at high-implementation schools versus performance by students at matched low-implementation schools on other outcome measures (e.g., ACT scores). The researchers found that students from high-implementation schools did better than did those in their matched low-implementation schools, with significant mean differences in performance. In addition, in comparing matched high- and low-implementation schools on the Iowa Tests of Basic Skills and Iowa Tests of Educational Development, Nelson et al. found that eighth graders from high-implementation middle schools showed performance superior to that of the comparison groups, albeit with small differentiation in mean differences between comparison groups.

One of the issues to be addressed in providing a comprehensive school counseling program is counselor-to-student ratios. The *ASCA National Model* (2012) recommended a counselor-to-student ratio of no more than 1:250. Carrell and Carrell (2006) sought to examine whether decreases in elementary counselor-to-student ratios influenced student outcomes. This study is important because the study design eliminated factors on which schools may differ (e.g., socioeconomic levels). Their results indicated that schools with higher counselor-to-student ratios were more likely to have higher numbers of students with recurring disciplinary problems. In another study of counselor to student ratios, Bryan et al. (2011) found that the number of school counselors had a significant influence on students applying to two or more colleges but had no effect on students applying to just one college. This is an important finding, as students are more likely to be accepted to college if they apply to multiple institutions. It may be that when the student-to-counselor ratio is smaller, counselors may have more time to help students apply to multiple colleges.

Summary/Conclusion

Reviews of outcomes research in professional school counseling generally indicate that school counseling activities have a positive effect on students. The reviewers, however, vary somewhat on the degree to which they believe there is empirical support for professional school counseling interventions. Meta-analytic reviews of school counseling interventions indicate that school counseling activities are moderately to highly effective. The conclusion that many school counseling interventions are effective may be heartening to professional school counselors, but we would suggest that it is an important time to communicate these findings to principals, parents, school board members, and legislators. Furthermore, these stakeholders should be informed that smaller counselor-to-student ratios are associated with better student outcomes.

This review of the school counseling outcomes research indicates that many school counseling interventions produce positive effects, but that not all interventions produce beneficial results for students. Therefore, professional school counselors need to be cautious in selecting activities. For example, at the elementary level, some guidance curriculum activities designed to increase self-esteem did not necessarily do so. On the other hand, a number of school counseling activities were supported by research. More fully implemented, comprehensive school counseling programs were found to result in better outcomes than were nonsystematic approaches to school counseling activities.

In conclusion, this analysis of the outcomes research on school counseling indicates that there is considerable need for more and better research in this area. Whiston et al. (2011) found that the majority of studies in their meta-analysis did not contain sufficient information about the treatment that would allow for replication of the study. They also found that many of the studies used outcomes measures that were author developed and often used only once. Whiston (2002) noted the lack of psychometrically sound outcomes measures suitable for school counseling research studies. Better and more research is needed because the lack of systematic and rigorous research may put the field in peril. Education is frequently the focus of public interest, and currently there is close scrutiny of educational practices. The public is no longer interested in funding educational programs without substantial evidence that these programs contribute to increased student learning. This is a critical time for professional school counselors and researchers to join together and provide more compelling documentation concerning the positive effects that school counseling programs have on children and adolescents. Without additional empirical support, some schools may eliminate professional school counseling programs. We would like to conclude this chapter by asking readers to consider ways that they might contribute to school counseling outcome research.

Activities

1. Begin the basic process of a research project on a topic related to school counseling. What topic would you like to gather data and information about? Would you use a qualitative or quantitative study? What would you hope or expect to find?

2. Choose an intervention you would like to implement in a school setting. Search the literature for empirically based outcomes studies pertaining to that intervention. What did you learn about this intervention from the literature? How will this affect your approach to implementing this intervention in a school setting?

3. Call a local school to find out if the counseling department offers counseling groups. Interview the professional school counselor who facilitates the groups. Has he or she noticed a difference in the student population since the program began? Ask what studies are conducted or what documentation is collected to demonstrate program outcomes and effectiveness. How might this intervention be effectively implemented in all schools?

Additional Resources

Center for School Counseling Outcome Research and Evaluation (University of Massachusetts Amherst):

http://www.csor.org

What Works Clearinghouse (U.S. Department of Education, Institute of Educational Sciences):

http://ies.ed.gov/ncee/wwc

SAMHSA's National Registry of Evidence-Based Programs and Practices:

http://www.nrepp.samhsa.gov

CHAPTER

7

Ethical, Legal, and Professional Issues in School Counseling

Lynn Linde

E ditor's Introduction: Before moving further into the "how-to" portion of this book, we must address some ethical, legal, and professional issues. Always remember that professional school counselors are first and foremost representatives of the school counseling profession. How you conduct yourself personally and professionally reflects on your colleagues. Knowledge and understanding of the issues reviewed in this chapter are but a starting point. Keep up to date with the laws, ethics, policies, and procedures that govern professional practice. The implementation of your professional responsibilities will require your undivided attention every day of your professional life.

PROFESSIONAL ASSOCIATIONS AND CREDENTIALING ORGANIZATIONS

One of the greatest challenges facing most professional school counselors daily is how to appropriately handle the many different ethical and legal situations they encounter. Due to the nature of school counseling, counselors must be prepared to help students who have a variety of problems. It is often difficult to know all that one needs to know. Fortunately, a number of resources and sources of information are available that can help guide counselors as they strive to assist students in an ethical and legal manner. The professional associations for counselors have created ethical standards for professional behavior and provide a wealth of current information, resources, and training. Federal and state governments continually enact laws and regulations that affect counselors, and the courts in the state and federal judicial branches hand down decisions that directly affect counselors' behavior. In addition, state boards of education and local school systems create policies, guidelines, and procedures that professional school counselors must follow. Each of these areas will be covered in detail in the sections that follow.

The American Counseling Association (ACA) is the professional association for all types of counselors. Its mission is to enhance the quality of life in society by promoting the development of professional counselors, advancing the counseling profession, and using the profession and practice of counseling to promote respect for human dignity and diversity. The ACA is a partnership of associations representing professional counselors who enhance human development. It comprises 19 divisions, which represent specific work settings or interest areas within the field of counseling; about 50 state or affiliate branches; and 4 regions, which represent major geographical areas. Thus, there is something for every counselor at both the state and national levels. The ACA influences all aspects of professional counseling through its programs, committees, and functions. This includes the credentialing of counselors and accreditation of counselor education programs, ethical standards, professional development, professional resources and services, and public policy and legislation.

The ACA has a number of standing committees, which address much of the professional business of the association. One of those is the Ethics Committee, which is responsible for updating the ethical standards for the association and investigating ethical complaints. When joining the ACA, one must sign a statement agreeing to abide by the *ACA Code of Ethics* (2005). The code is covered in more detail in the next section.

The ACA and its affiliates offer many training and professional development opportunities through state, regional, and national conferences, workshops, and learning institutes. ACA's *Journal of Counseling & Development* and the journals published by its divisions cover current research, professional practices, and other information valuable to the practicing counselor. Its monthly newsletter, *Counseling Today*, includes information about what is going on in the field, as well as covering special topics and providing notes about members and a governmental relations update. The ACA also publishes books about counseling and current trends and topics in the field, some of which are used as textbooks in counseling courses. ACA staff members are available for consultation on a variety of issues, represent the ACA before Congress and other organizations, and advocate for counselors and professional counseling. The ACA has recently developed e-mail newsletters targeted to counselors who practice in various settings, including one for school counselors; provides continuing education for members through the Web; and offers liability insurance as a member benefit for students. In summary, the ACA touches all counselors' lives, from the training they receive, to the requirements they must achieve to be credentialed, to the way in which they conduct themselves (regardless of the type of counseling practiced), to the professional development in which they engage.

The American School Counselor Association (ASCA) is a semiautonomous division of the ACA and addresses school counseling issues. The ASCA "supports school counselors' efforts to help students focus on academic, personal/social and career development so they achieve success in school and are prepared to lead fulfilling lives as responsible members of society" (ASCA, 2013). The ASCA also has local counseling association branches in nearly all 50 states. The ASCA targets its efforts toward professional development, publications and other resources, research, and advocacy specifically for professional school counselors. It publishes its journal, *Professional School Counseling*, six times a year and a bimonthly magazine, *The School Counselor*. The ASCA sends its members several e-mail newsletters and alerts on various topics pertaining to school counseling. It also offers its members liability insurance as part of membership. The ASCA has a number of committees that perform the work of the association. One of the main foci of the ASCA is *The ASCA National Model: A Framework for School Counseling Programs* (3rd ed.; ASCA, 2012). The *National Model* provides the framework for a comprehensive, data-driven school counseling program; more information about the model can be found in Chapter 2 and on the ASCA's webpage at www.ascanationalmodel.org.

The National Board for Certified Counselors (NBCC) began as a corporate partner of the ACA and is now an autonomous organization. Headquartered in Greensboro, North Carolina, the NBCC is the only national credentialing organization for professional counselors; all other licenses and certifications are granted through state and local entities. The NBCC has established the National Certified Counselor (NCC) credential and several specialty-area certifications. The National Counselor Exam (NCE) must be passed as part of the process for becoming nationally certified. The NCE is also frequently required by state counseling licensure boards for professional counselor licensure or certification.

The Counsel for Accreditation of Counseling and Related Educational Programs (CACREP) also began as a corporate partner of the ACA and is now an autonomous organization. CACREP is responsible for establishing state-of-the-art standards for counselor education programs. CACREP standards address program objectives and curricula, faculty and staff requirements, program evaluation, and other requirements for accreditation. Currently, more than 220 school counseling programs and more than 600 total counseling programs in all in the United States are CACREP accredited. Students who graduate from CACREP programs are usually in an advantageous position to be hired because their programs include 48 graduate credit hours and 700 hours of field placement. The CACREP standards are currently being revised; the target date for implementation of the new standards is 2016.

ETHICAL STANDARDS AND LAWS

Counselors are sometimes confused by the difference between ethical standards and laws and what one should do when these appear to be in conflict with each other. It may be helpful to take a look at the origin of both. Ethical standards are usually developed by professional associations to guide the behavior of a specific group of professionals. According to Herlihy and Corey (2006), ethical standards serve three purposes: to educate members about sound ethical conduct, to provide a mechanism for accountability, and to serve as a means for improving professional practice. Ethical standards change and are updated periodically to ensure their relevance and appropriateness.

Ethical standards are based on generally accepted norms, beliefs, customs, and values. The *ACA Code of Ethics* (2005) is based on Kitchener's five moral principles of autonomy, justice, beneficence, nonmaleficence, and fidelity (Linde, 2014). Autonomy refers to the concept of independence and the ability to make one's own decisions. Counselors need to respect the right of clients to make their own decisions based on their personal values and beliefs and must not impose their values on clients. Justice means treating each person fairly, but it does not mean treating each person the same way. Rather, counselors should treat clients according to client needs. Beneficence refers to doing good or what is in the best interests of the client. In counseling, it also incorporates the concept of removing conditions that might cause harm. Nonmaleficence means doing no harm to others. And fidelity involves the concepts of loyalty, faithfulness, and the honoring of commitments. This means that counselors must honor all obligations to the client, starting with the relationship.

Laws are also based on these same, generally accepted norms, beliefs, customs, and values. However, laws are more prescriptive, have been incorporated into a legal code, and carry greater sanctions or penalties for failure to comply. Both laws and ethical standards prescribe appropriate behavior for professionals within a particular context to ensure that the best interests of the client are met. When the two appear to be in conflict with each other, the professional must attempt to resolve the conflict in a responsible manner (Cottone & Tarvydas, 2007). Counselors must make their clients aware of the conflict and their ethical standards (see Activity 7.1). But because there are greater penalties associated with laws, counselors will often follow the legal course of action if there is no harm to their clients. Many ethical standards recognize that other mandates must be followed and suggest that counselors work to change mandates that are not in the best interests of their clients. In the absence of laws or other legal directives, courts may look to the established standards of behavior of a profession to determine liability (Wheeler & Bertram, 2012).

ACTIVITY 7.1

Consider a situation where the law and the ACA or ASCA code of ethics are in conflict with one another, such as:

a. When a minor child comes for confidential counseling, but the parent holds the confidence and privilege, or

b. When a minor child comes for substance use or reproductive counseling he or she is entitled to under the law, but is engaging in dangerous behaviors in these regards.

Role-play with a peer how you might approach your client in explaining the conflict and your ethical standards. What might you do to begin working toward changing legal mandates that are not in the best interest of your client?

Although the *ACA Code of Ethics* (2005) applies to all professional counselors, there are multiple codes of ethics produced by ACA divisions, state boards of counseling, and NBCC that apply to specific work settings or jurisdictions. Several divisions, including the ASCA, have their own codes of ethics; also, the Association for Specialists in Group Work (ASGW) has developed guidelines for best practices in group work. These codes of ethics and guidelines parallel the *ACA Code of Ethics*, but speak more directly to the specialty area. The ASCA's *Ethical Standards for School Counselors* (2010) discusses what ethical behavior consists of for those who work in a school setting and deal with issues specific to students; parents/guardians, colleagues and professional associates to the school, communities, and families; responsibilities to self; the profession; and maintenance of standards. Interestingly, however, only ACA, NBCC, and state counseling boards actually have mechanisms and hearing committees to enforce adherence to ethical codes; ACA divisions, such as ASCA, do not.

Many counselors belong to multiple organizations, each of which has its own code of ethics. They may also hold credentials from organizations or state credentialing boards that have a code of ethics as well. It is often hard to know which code takes precedence. Although each professional will have to make that determination individually, the answers to these two questions provide general guidelines. First, in what setting is the professional practicing, and is there a code that applies specifically to that setting? Second, in what capacity is the professional operating? In addition, all the codes are similar, and all concern behaving in an appropriate, professional manner; operating in the best interests of the client; and practicing within the scope of one's education, training, and experience. If a counselor is doing all that, then the existence of multiple codes of ethics should not be a significant issue.

ACA Code of Ethics

The ACA revises the *ACA Code of Ethics* at least every 10 years. The sixth and most recent revision became effective in August 2005, and the next version is due out in 2014. There are several significant changes from the *1995 ACA Code of Ethics and Standards of Practice*. The most obvious change is that the Standards of Practice, which described in behavioral terms the aspirational ethics set forth in the code, are no longer separate, but have been incorporated into the body of the code. Each section of the code now begins with an introduction, which sets the tone for that section and is a beginning point for discussion (ACA, 2005). Parts of the *ACA Code of Ethics* have been updated to reflect current thinking and practice in the field, and several new issues have been added. In addition, a glossary of terms has been added.

The issue of culture and diversity is critical in this iteration of the code. The preamble to the 2005 *ACA Code of Ethics* begins with the assertion that "members must recognize diversity and embrace a cross-cultural approach in support of the worth, dignity, potential, and uniqueness of people within their social and cultural contexts" (2005, p. 3). Multicultural and diversity issues were infused into this code, as opposed to being a separate section, and the section on diagnosis cautions counselors to view problems within a cultural context. These changes further support the need to view counseling in a cultural context. The concept of family must also be viewed from a cultural context; in many cultures, family includes many more people than those to whom one is biologically connected. This concept is reflected in the change from the term *family* to *support network* in the code, thus reflecting the reality of our clients' worlds.

The 2005 *ACA Code of Ethics* states that it serves five main purposes, as follows:

1. The *Code* enables the association to clarify to current and future members, and to those served by members, the nature of the ethical responsibilities held in common by its members.
2. The *Code* helps support the mission of the association.
3. The *Code* establishes the principles that define ethical behavior and best practices of association members.
4. The *Code* serves as an ethical guide designed to assist members in constructing a professional course of action that best serves those utilizing counseling services and best promotes the values of the counseling profession.
5. The *Code* serves as the basis for processing of ethical complaints and inquiries initiated against members of the association. (ACA, 2005, p. 3)

The *ACA Code of Ethics* is divided into eight areas: (A) The Counseling Relationship; (B) Confidentiality, Privileged Communication, and Privacy; (C) Professional Responsibility; (D) Relationships with Other Professionals; (E) Evaluation, Assessment, and Interpretation; (F) Supervision, Training, and Teaching; (G) Research and Publication; and (H) Resolving Ethical Issues. Each of these areas details specific counselor responsibilities and standards.

In general, the *ACA Code of Ethics* discusses respecting one's client and the background each client brings to the counseling setting; maintaining professional behavior with clients and other professionals; practicing with the best interests of the client in mind; and practicing within the limits of one's training, experience, and education. The last section provides direction for members resolving ethical dilemmas. Highlights from each of these areas are summarized later, but at this point, readers should locate the actual *ACA Code of Ethics* on the ACA website and peruse it in detail. The *ACA Code of Ethics* can be found at www.counseling.org/Resources/CodeOfEthics/TP/Home/CT2.aspx.

SECTION A: THE COUNSELING RELATIONSHIP A key issue addressed in this section is boundaries with clients and dual relationships. The period of time that a professional counselor and former client must wait to engage in romantic or sexual relationships was changed from 2 to 5 years, and the language was expanded to include not just clients, but also romantic partners or family members of former clients. This change highlighted the vulnerable nature of clients in a helping relationship. The previous *Code* emphasized the avoidance of nonprofessional relationships with clients outside the formal counseling relationship. The current ACA *Code* recognizes that this is not always possible and also recognizes that nonprofessional relationships with clients may even benefit clients (e.g., attending formal ceremonies, hospital visits, membership in community organizations, commerce), albeit when conducted with caution, consent, and good judgment.

Continued emphasis was placed on critical issues, including general client welfare and avoiding harm, appropriate termination of services, fees and bartering, and informed consent. The informed consent provision is particularly important because many state counseling boards now require written consent so that clients can choose a counseling relationship with a qualified provider from an informed consumer position. Section A.2.b specifies that informed consent includes, but is not limited to, purposes, goals, techniques, procedures, limitations, potential risks, and benefits of services; the counselor's qualifications, credentials, and relevant experience; the intended use of tests and reports, fees, and billing arrangements; the right to confidentiality and limitations; the continuation of services should the counselor become incapacitated; obtaining clear information about their records; participating in ongoing treatment planning; and right to refuse treatment at any time and the potential consequences for doing so. In addition, the ACA *Code* addresses the need to balance assent from minors and others incapable of giving consent without the assent of parents and family members who hold the legal rights of consent, protection, and decision making on their behalf. Section A also includes new standards for serving the terminally ill and facilitating end-of-life decisions, making the ACA one of the first national associations to address these issues. In doing so, the ACA directs counselors to receive adequate supervision and seek multiple professional collaborations and help clients exercise self-determination, establish high-quality end-of-life care, and participate maximally in decision making. Finally, the 1999 ACA *Ethical Standards for Internet Online Counseling* was integrated into A.12, broadening the *Code* to address issues of technology in providing counseling services, record keeping, and research applications.

SECTION B: CONFIDENTIALITY, PRIVILEGED COMMUNICATION, AND PRIVACY Several major changes were made to the confidentiality, privileged communication, and privacy section of the *ACA Code of Ethics*. Standard B.1.a was added to remind professional counselors to maintain sensitivity and awareness in regard to cultural meanings of privacy and confidentiality. Counselors should also be respectful of differing views and inform clients with whom, when, and how information will be shared. Another addition was Standard B.3.e, which took into consideration the transmission of confidential information and reflected the growing use of technology throughout the counseling process. This Standard advised counselors to take precautions to ensure confidentiality when using technologies such as computers, electronic mail, or voicemail.

A new and important addition was Standard B.3.f, which asserted that professional counselors should maintain the confidentiality of deceased clients as consistent with legal requirements and policies. Another significant change involved Standard B.4.b, which was renamed Couples and Family Counseling. The 2005 ACA *Code* stated that professional counselors must clearly recognize who is considered to be "the client," must discuss limitations and expectations of confidentiality during couples and family counseling, and should seek and document an agreement with all involved parties as to their individual rights to confidentiality or obligations to protect the confidentiality of the known information. This differed from the 1995 *Code,* which simply declared that permission was required when disclosing information about one family member to another.

Finally, Section B.5 was expounded on to address confidentiality and privacy when counseling clients who are minors or adults lacking the capacity to give informed consent. Professional counselors are directed to inform parents and legal guardians of the confidential nature of the counseling relationship as well as establish a working relationship with them to serve clients better. Counselors must also seek permission from the appropriate parties to disclose information. When working with this specific population, counselors are reminded to uphold written policies, federal and state laws, and ethical standards as applicable.

SECTION C: PROFESSIONAL RESPONSIBILITY Section C continued to place emphasis on issues such as professional competence, advertising and soliciting clients, professional qualifications, and public responsibility. One area that was significantly expanded on involved counselor impairment (Standard C.2.g). Professional counselors must be alert to signs of personal impairment and should refrain from providing or offering services if the impairment could potentially harm a client. If the problem reached the level of professional impairment, the counselor should seek assistance. Professional counselors are now also required to assist supervisors or colleagues in recognizing impairment and, if necessary, provide assistance, intervention, or consultation.

Standard C.2.h was added to address further the issue of counselor impairment or subsequent termination of practice. This new standard stated that counselors should follow a prepared plan for the transfer of files and clients when they leave a practice. In particular, counselors need to designate a specific colleague or "records custodian" and create a proper plan for file and client transfer in the case of their incapacitation, termination of practice, or death.

Another major change to this section included the addition of Standard C.6.e, which acknowledged that professional counselors must use techniques, modalities, or procedures that have a scientific or empirical foundation and are grounded in theory. If not, counselors should note their procedures or techniques to be "unproven" or "developing." The potential risks and ethical considerations of the procedures or techniques should be explained to the client, and counselors should take all necessary steps to protect the client from any potential harm. Counselors are still required to monitor their effectiveness and take any necessary actions to improve as professionals.

SECTION D: RELATIONSHIPS WITH OTHER PROFESSIONALS This section stressed the importance of interaction and relationships between counselors and other professionals. Professional counselors should become knowledgeable about their colleagues and develop positive working relationships and communication systems. Generally, the 2005 *ACA Code of Ethics* reorganized and renamed most of the standards in this section. It was also recognized that counselors may often be a part of an interdisciplinary team. Several new standards were created to reflect this development.

Professional counselors are reminded to be respectful of differing approaches to counseling services and the traditions and practices of other professional groups (Standard D.1.a). Inclusion of Standards D.1.b and D.1.c specifically addressed interdisciplinary relationships and teamwork, respectively. Professional counselors must work to develop and strengthen relationships with interdisciplinary colleagues. Professional counselors must also keep focused on how best to serve their clients when working in a team environment. To do so, counselors can contribute to and partake in any decisions that could potentially affect the well-being of clients by the use of the values, experiences, and perspectives of the counseling profession and other disciplines. Standard D.1.e reminded counselors that when working with an interdisciplinary team, it is their responsibility to clarify the ethical and professional obligations of individual members and the team as a whole. Professional counselors are encouraged to attempt to resolve ethical concerns initially within the team. If a resolution cannot be made within the team, counselors should pursue other means to address the concerns consistent with the well-being of the client.

SECTION E: EVALUATION, ASSESSMENT, AND INTERPRETATION

A noticeable change to this section involved the replacement of the word *tests* with *assessment*, which has a more integrative and broader connotation. In addition, *career assessment* was added to several standards, and further details were included. For example, Standard E.1.a now includes specific examples of measurements, including, but not limited to, personality, ability, interest, achievement, intelligence, and performance. It is still recognized that assessment is only one part of the overall counseling process, and that professional counselors must take into account cultural, social, and personal factors.

Historical and Social Prejudices in the Diagnosis of Pathology (Standard E.5.c) was a new addition to the 2005 ACA *Code* and stated that professional counselors should be aware of social and historical prejudices in the pathologizing and misdiagnosis of specific individuals and groups. In addition, counselors should be cognizant of the role of mental health professionals in the continuation of these problems. Not only does the revised *ACA Code of Ethics* take into consideration historical factors, but it was also changed to reflect the current trends in counseling.

The inclusion of Section E.13, Forensic Evaluation: Evaluation for Legal Proceedings, denoted the increased presence of professional counselors in legal proceedings and subsequent legal matters. This new section outlined the primary obligations for counselors, the consent for evaluation, and the necessity to avoid potentially harmful relationships in regard to forensic evaluations. The primary obligation of professional counselors conducting forensic evaluations is to generate objective findings that are supported by appropriate techniques and information. Counselors are entitled to form their own professional opinions, but must define any limitations in their testimonies or reports. Counselors also are not permitted to give "expert testimony" for one of their clients.

SECTION F: SUPERVISION, TRAINING, AND TEACHING

This section was heavily revised and expanded in certain sections, such as supervisory relationships and student welfare and responsibilities. The focus still remained on fostering professional relationships and creating appropriate boundaries between supervisors and their students. The ethical obligations of both parties are clearly set forth, and counselors should be accurate, honest, and fair during the training and assessment of students.

Areas that were focused on include counselor supervision and client welfare, counselor supervision competence, supervisory relationships, supervisor responsibilities, counseling evaluation and remediation, responsibilities of counselor educators, student welfare and responsibilities, evaluation and remediation of students, roles and relationships between educators and students, and multicultural/diversity competence in counselor education and training programs. As with Section A, Standards F.3.e and F.10.e were included to address the change from dual relationships to potentially beneficial relationships between counselor educators or supervisors and students. Because the revisions to this section are too numerous and beyond the scope of this chapter, individuals are encouraged to go to the ACA website and consult in-depth the 2005 ACA *Code of Ethics*.

SECTION G: RESEARCH AND PUBLICATION

An important change to note was the replacement of the term "human subjects" with "research participants." The revised *ACA Code* also recognized that independent researchers who may lack access to an Institutional Review Board might design and conduct research programs as well. These independent researchers are advised to seek out and consult with researchers who are acquainted with Institutional Review Board procedures to make appropriate safeguards available to research participants.

Further additions or clarifications included the disposal of research documents and records of relationships with research participants when there are intensive or extended interactions. Professional counselors are obligated to take the appropriate steps to destroy any documents or records that contain confidential data or may identify research participants within a reasonable period after the completion of a research study or project. Section G.3 outlined the restrictions on relationships with research participants that included nonprofessional relationships, sexual or romantic interactions, and sexual harassment, as well as potentially beneficial interactions.

Finally, the publication section of the 2005 *ACA Code of Ethics* was expanded. Standard G.5.b was added, which specifically stated that professional counselors do not plagiarize or present another person's work as their own. In addition, the standard concerning professional review of documents presented for publication was expanded to include making valid publication decisions, reviewing materials in a timely manner, avoiding biases, and evaluating only those documents that fall within one's field of competency.

SECTION H: RESOLVING ETHICAL ISSUES   This final section provided information and suggestions pertaining to the resolution of ethical issues. Three main changes were made in regard to legal conflicts, unfair discrimination, and reporting ethical violations. Standard H.1.b stated that if there was a conflict between ethical responsibilities and laws, professional counselors should make known their commitment to the *ACA Code of Ethics* and work to alleviate the conflict. Counselors may follow legal requirements or regulations if the ethical conflict cannot be resolved in this manner.

The second change included an increase in procedural details for professional counselors reporting a suspected ethical violation (Standard H.2.c). When informal resolution is inappropriate for an ethical violation, or the issue is not correctly resolved, professional counselors are directed to seek further action, such as referring to voluntary national certification bodies, state or national ethics committees, state licensing boards, or any suitable institutional authorities. It is further stated that this standard is not applicable if a professional counselor has been retained to review the work of the counselor who is in question, or if it would violate any confidentiality rights.

The addition of Standard H.2.g was the final major change to Section H. It was stated that professional counselors absolutely should not deny a person's advancement, admission to academic programs, employment, promotion, or tenure based only on their having made an ethics complaint or their being the subject of an ethics complaint. This standard provided some protection against unfair discrimination for counselors who have made an ethics complaint or been the subject of one.

The *ACA Code of Ethics* is currently undergoing revision; it is expected that the new standards will be adopted in 2014. Feedback gathered in preparation for the revision process indicated that changes are needed particularly in the use of social media, counseling via technology, and electronic record keeping and transmittal.

THEORY INTO PRACTICE 7.1

CONFIDENTIALITY

Virtually every professional counselor can attest to the fact that ethics are easy to conceptualize, yet incredibly difficult to put into practice. Even the most seasoned counselors find it taxing to determine the most ethically sound course of action, given that in some circumstances, the policies are "clear as mud." Confidentiality is a concept that we learn on day one, and for good reason. Easy to grasp and vital for the success of the profession, confidentiality becomes almost second nature. However, counselors may find themselves more cognizant of confidentiality when placed in certain challenging situations. In these cases, the question is not, "When do I breach confidentiality?" but rather, "How do I share confidential information with parents or colleagues in an ethical manner?"

There are a few pitfalls surrounding confidentiality counselors-in-training may fall into that can be easily avoided if time is taken to consider the context of the situation and the parties involved. For many of my colleagues in my master's program, the challenge of switching from the role of teacher to school counselor was exacerbated by the different codes of ethics that guide each occupation. For teachers, information and concerns about students are shared freely with little to no censorship. Collaboration and the sharing of such information are crucial for teachers, so they can tailor educational strategies and approaches based on the information gathered from other staff members. Counselors, on the other hand, are ethically bound to protect the information gained behind closed doors with the exception of suspected incidents of harm to self or others. A friend of mine training to become a school counselor after 10 years of teaching laughed as she recalled her first parent–teacher conference during her internship. A teacher asked why the usually high-achieving student was having trouble in his class, and my friend was ready to divulge the student's troubles at home when she (luckily) remembered which role she was expected to fulfill that day. As a teacher, she had free reign of what she chose to share at these meetings. As a counselor, she needed to choose her words more wisely, careful to not breach confidentiality in front of such a large audience. In these situations, counselors must always remember the role they are expected to fulfill and carefully monitor how they collaborate with staff members.

Should I find it necessary for a teacher to know that a child is suffering, I use broad, generalized language to convey my message and advocate on behalf of a student while still maintaining confidentiality. For example, if a child is dealing with a drug-addicted parent, and it is affecting their academic performance, I may say, "Susie is dealing with a lot in her personal and family life and may need some additional support. Please do not hesitate to contact me if you notice any behaviors that are out of the ordinary for her or if you have any concerns." If teachers press me for more information, I just kindly remind them that as much as I would love to share with them, I need to maintain that level of trust with the students so I cannot disclose such information.

Another situation that challenged my understanding of confidentiality occurred when I taped a counseling session for my school counseling internship. Per the requirements of my program, I was to record a session with an individual for evaluation of my clinical skills by my school supervisor. After receiving parental permission to do so, I was surprised when a week after taping I received a voicemail from the child's father. The father requested to have a copy of the videotape so that he could see everything that was discussed in our session. He stated that he was the parent and that he felt he had the right to know what was going on with his son. A multicultural component confounded this situation because the father was Pakistani, and his belief was that problems were resolved within the family. Although the father was

absolutely correct that he has the right as a parent to know what occurs in counseling with his minor child, I was hesitant to turn over the tape for fear that I would diminish the sense of trust and safety his son felt within our counseling sessions. Unfortunately, much of what the child shared pertained to his animosity toward his father. As a counselor, we must make decisions in the best interest of our clients (in this case the elementary-aged child), but we must also respect parental rights. Faced with an ethical dilemma, I consulted with my supervisor on the best course of action and returned the father's call the next day.

In my discussion with the father, I acknowledged that as the parent, he had a right to know the content of our session; however, to successfully perform my job, I needed to maintain a sense of trust with the child. If I were to give him the videotape, I would eliminate all sense of security for the child and strip him of his ability to speak freely during our sessions out of fear that he would be punished for his thoughts. In addition, I explained that I was uncomfortable that I could not ensure the copy did not accidentally end up in the wrong hands. After emphasizing this notion of trust, I asked the father if he was willing to compromise with me. I told him I would meet with his son and ask the son's permission if it was okay to share some of the content of our sessions. More specifically, I would only share what the child specified I could. This way, the child's opinion was taken into consideration, and the father received what he wanted to know. I followed up with the father after every session, and at the time of termination, the father and child were both happy and reported better communication.

Although confidentiality is a concept put into practice on a daily basis, instances still arise where an ethical decision-making model must be followed. If counselors find that they struggle with maintaining confidentiality, they may want to reflect on the following things: their role within the school, who they can consult with if faced with a dilemma, what purpose their information sharing serves, and how they can reframe the information to protect the client yet still convey their message.

Source: Caitlin J. Eckert, Professional School Counselor, Maryland

ASCA *Ethical Standards for School Counselors*

In addition to the ACA, other counseling organizations have established codes of ethics. The ASCA (2010) has developed a parallel set of ethical standards that specifically addresses counseling practice in the schools. As in the ACA's standards, these standards discuss putting the counselee's best interests first, treating each student as an

individual and with respect, involving parents as appropriate, maintaining one's expertise through ongoing professional development and learning, and behaving professionally and ethically. There are seven sections of the ASCA (2010) *Ethical Standards for School Counselors*, which are meant to guide the ethical practice of school counselors, provide self-appraisal and evaluation information by peers, and inform stakeholders of responsible counselor behaviors. Although many of the provisions overlap with the *ACA Code of Ethics* explained earlier, what follows is a discussion of additions, extensions, and clarifications provided in the ASCA code.

A. RESPONSIBILITIES TO STUDENTS   School counselors are concerned with, and make available to students, comprehensive, developmental, data-driven programs that address the academic, career, and personal-social needs of all students. They respect and accept the diverse cultural and individual values and beliefs of students and do not impose their own values on the students or students' families.

Professional school counselors disclose the limits of confidentiality and gain informed consent as appropriate. Confidentiality and informed consent are challenging issues when dealing with minor children, and school counselors involve important persons and support networks and consider laws, regulations, and policies as appropriate to ensure that parents/guardians are active partners in their minor child's school experiences. School counselors acknowledge and support the parent's legal and inherent rights. When students participate in small-group counseling experiences, school counselors notify parents/guardians. As with adult clients, a student's right to confidentiality is surrendered when the student presents serious and foreseeable harm to self or others.

School counselors use brief, solution-focused approaches when possible and strive to maintain an appropriate professional distance from students so as not to engage in a dual relationship that would jeopardize the effectiveness of the primary counseling relationship. School counselors especially avoid online social networking relationships with students through various communication mediums. School counselors also take steps to ensure that students understand the nature of, and how to report the occurrence of, cyberbullying.

School counselors separately store sole-possession notes used as memory aids and destroy these notes when the student transfers to another school or school level or graduates. If the notes may possibly be needed in a future court proceeding, the school counselor uses best judgment in the maintenance of these sole-possession records. This issue of sole-possession notes is covered in more detail later in this chapter.

B. RESPONSIBILITIES TO PARENTS/GUARDIANS   School counselors establish appropriate collaborative relationships with parents and respect parental rights and responsibilities. Unless prevented by court order, school counselors honor parental requests for student records and periodic reports. This especially applies to noncustodial parents who may ask for periodic performance reports that the custodial parent may chose not to provide. Legally, a noncustodial parent is allowed access to the student's information, unless a judge has ordered otherwise.

C. RESPONSIBILITIES TO COLLEAGUES AND PROFESSIONAL ASSOCIATES   School counselors understand the school's "release of information" process and that parents of minor children must provide written permission for this release. School counselors work with their supervisor/director and counselor educators, as appropriate, to implement a data-driven, competencies-based comprehensive school counseling program.

D. RESPONSIBILITIES TO SCHOOL, COMMUNITIES, AND FAMILIES   As an advocate for all students within the school community, professional school counselors notify appropriate officials of conditions that systematically limit the effectiveness of the school counseling program or other curricular components. School counselors also engage in community partnerships to obtain resources that support their comprehensive program and promote student success. Professional school counselors advocate for the hiring of only qualified and appropriately trained school counselors and only accept employment for a position for which they are qualified.

E. RESPONSIBILITIES TO SELF   As do all counselors, school counselors function within the boundaries of their training and experience. They are responsible for maintaining physical and mental self-care and wellness and engage in continuous personal and professional growth throughout their careers. This presumes that school counselors will remain current with research and practice innovations in broad areas that influence school counseling practice (e.g., advocacy, cultural competence, technology, leadership, assessment data). Recall that as counselors become more experienced, the standard of care expectations increase. Thus, as professional school counselors become more experienced, the expectations for their ethical and legal performance also increase. School counselors use culturally inclusive language, create equity-based programs that promote the performance and achievement of all students, and maintain current membership in professional associations.

F. RESPONSIBILITIES TO THE PROFESSION   Professional school counselors follow legal and policy dictates regarding conducting research and program evaluation. They clearly articulate that what they say or write as a private individual is just that, and not as a representative of a school or profession. School counselors also do not use their school counselor position to recruit clients for private practice.

Professional school counselors do provide mentoring and support to school counselors in training, make sure those candidates have professional liability insurance, and ensure that university counselor supervisors conduct at least one on-site visit for each practicum or internship student so they can observe and evaluate the candidate face to face.

G. MAINTENANCE OF STANDARDS This final section provides school counselors with specific guidance on how to handle ethical dilemmas in the field and by colleagues. It is important that school counselors work through the appropriate channels and steps to remedy ethical challenges. Whereas a colleague who behaves in an unethical manner is problematic and needs to be addressed when evident, ethical codes and hearing committees often serve an educative function to promote high standards and good practice. These procedures are relatively common across ethical codes of conduct and will be addressed more comprehensively in the next section.

Decision Making Using Ethical Standards

ACA, ASCA, and other counseling professional organizations have developed guides to ethical decision making that can be used when a professional counselor is concerned about a particular situation and needs to determine if an ethical dilemma exists. The ACA's model involves seven steps: (a) identify the problem, (b) apply the *ACA Code of Ethics*, (c) determine the nature and dimensions of the dilemma, (d) generate potential courses of action, (e) consider the potential consequences of all options and choose a course of action, (f) evaluate the selected course of action, and (g) implement the course of action (Forester-Miller & Davis, 1996).

Stone (2009) has taken the ACA model and applied it to the school setting. As Stone and others caution, professional counselors using either of these models or any other ethical decision-making model would not necessarily come to the same conclusion. There is seldom one correct way of handling any given situation, and each counselor brings a different background, values, and belief system to each dilemma. However, if one reflects on the moral principles and continues to practice with these in mind, it is likely that the dilemma can be resolved in the client's best interests.

Remley and Herlihy (2010) suggested four self-tests to consider when a decision has been made. First, in thinking about justice, would you treat others this same way if they were in a similar situation? Second, would you suggest to other counselors this same course of action? Third, would you be willing to have others know how

you acted? Fourth, do you have any lingering feelings of doubt or uncertainty about what you did? If you cannot answer in the affirmative to the first three tests and in the negative to the fourth test, perhaps the decision was not ethically sound. It is always appropriate and ethically sound to consult with a colleague when working through a dilemma to ensure that all aspects of the issue have been examined and that all possible problems have been discussed. Activity 7.2 will help you integrate the information on ethical and legal issues in counseling and apply ethical decision-making principles to numerous scenarios.

ACTIVITY 7.2

Ethical Decision Making

For each numbered situation, indicate whether the behavior is ethical (E) or unethical (U), and cite the standard or standards from the *ACA Code of Ethics* or the *ASCA Ethical Standards for School Counselors* that apply. The person in question in each scenario is underlined.

Situation #1: John, a counselor at a middle school, is developing his own practice. He knows that he cannot see the students on his school caseload in his practice, but is actively recruiting from the families of his counselees and the other students not on his caseload in the school.

E_____   U_____   Standard(s)_____

Situation #2: Emily, a high school counselor, is working on her dissertation for her doctorate. She is using information about students in the school in her data collection. She asks the parent who volunteers in the counseling office to help her pull the data and input it into her analysis.

E_____   U_____   Standard(s) _____

Situation #3: There are two counselors in a medium-sized middle school. George eats lunch in the teacher's lounge every day with the other faculty members; Maria does not. One lunchtime Maria goes into the lounge to buy a soda and overhears George sharing detailed information with the staff about a student with whom he is working. Maria talks to George, questioning whether his behavior is ethical.

E_____   U_____   Standard(s)_____

(Continued)

Situation #4: Celeste is an elementary counselor. She has a master's degree in school counseling and a doctorate in Administration and Supervision. Her business cards indicate that she is **Dr. Celeste Forrester;** she corrects anyone who does not address her by her title.

E_____   U_____   Standard(s)_____

Situation #5: Mark is a high school counselor. He lives in the community where he works, and his children attend the feeder middle school. Mark coaches his son's basketball team, and some of the players have older siblings on Mark's caseload.

E_____   U_____   Standard(s)_____

Situation #6: A ninth-grade student comes to see Jasmine, who is one of the counselors at her school but not the one to whom she is assigned. The student thinks she might be pregnant and has heard that her counselor always calls the parents whenever a student tells him that she might be pregnant, and she doesn't want her parents to know. Jasmine agrees to meet with the student and after a lengthy counseling session sends her to a center in the community that handles pregnancy issues. Jasmine agrees not to call the student's parents or to tell the other counselor about their session.

E_____   U_____   Standard(s)_____

CULTURAL REFLECTION 7.1

How might professional school counselors across diverse cultural backgrounds view the "gray areas" often encountered when applying ethical standards? How might students, parents, and educators from diverse cultural backgrounds view the ACA or ASCA ethical codes?

OTHER SOURCES OF INFORMATION AND GUIDANCE

Although ethical standards provide an important foundation for guiding counselor behavior, counselors must become familiar with a number of other sources of information if they are to maintain the highest standards of ethical and legal behavior. Each of these other sources is described next.

The Court System

Counselors are affected by three main types of laws: statutory law, which is created by legislatures and interpreted by courts; constitutional law, which results from court decisions concerning constitutional issues; and common law, which results from court decisions on issues not governed by statutes. There are 51 U.S. court systems—the court systems for the 50 states and the federal system. Both state and federal courts can issue decisions affecting counselors, and both are usually composed of tiers. The structure of state courts varies, but generally consists of trial courts—which include courts of special jurisdiction such as juvenile court and small claims court—and courts of appeal. All states have a court that is the final authority to which cases may be appealed. The name of this court varies across states. In Maryland and New York, it is called the court of appeals; in West Virginia, it is called the supreme court of appeals; in other states, it is called the superior court. One must be careful in reading state court decisions to note which court rendered the decision, as the names are not consistent across states. Certain cases from the highest court in each state may be appealed to the U.S. Supreme Court. Decisions from state courts are binding only on persons living within that state, but may serve as persuasive precedent for a similar case in another state.

The federal court system is a three-tiered system. The approximately 100 U.S. district courts form the first tier of the federal system. They are general trial courts that hear cases involving federal law, disputes between citizens that involve over $75,000, and disputes where the United States is a party. There are 13 circuit courts of appeals. Decisions issued by a circuit court of appeals are binding only on those states within that court's jurisdiction. However, decisions issued by one circuit court may influence the decision rendered by a court in another circuit when the same issue arises. Parties may request the U.S. Supreme Court, the highest court in the country, to review rulings by circuit courts of appeals.

Statutory Law

Statutory law is the body of legislation passed by the U.S. Congress and state legislatures. Much of the structure of education and health services and many of the policies that govern their implementation are found within these statutory mandates. The U.S. Congress has authority to pass legislation related only to those powers specified in the Constitution, and it has enacted a number of laws that affect counselors who work both in schools and in other settings under its power to provide for the general welfare. The majority of legislation influencing schools and counselors is passed by state legislatures and is of two types: legislation passed to implement federal legislation and new, state-specific legislation. State laws may be more restrictive than federal legislation, but may never be less restrictive.

State and Local Agencies

Most state departments of education have the ability to enact regulations that are binding on the school districts within the state. The state's board of education passes regulations that encompass areas not addressed through state legislation or that add detail to state legislation such as implementation plans and more specific definitions. State agencies, including education departments, also develop policies, which are often detailed explanations of how to implement specific laws. Last, state agencies may issue guidelines, which are actually suggestions about how to address a specific issue. Unlike regulations and policies, guidelines are not mandates and do not have to be followed. However, because they do represent an agency's current thinking regarding a particular issue, local policies generally do not deviate too far from them.

Although it is not a regulation, the state attorney general may issue an opinion or advice of counsel. This guidance is frequently issued in response to a new court case or law or to the request of a state agency. The advice or opinion is the attorney general's legal interpretation of what that law or case means for the agency or agencies affected and usually suggests what the agency needs to do to comply. The advice or ruling is often incorporated into policy or guidelines by the agency.

Local school systems and agencies may also develop their own policies, procedures, and guidelines. School systems, in particular, often take state regulations and policies and rewrite them to reflect their specific local situation; these are often then adopted by the local board of education. Local mental health departments or agencies may also further define state policies and procedures to reflect their jurisdiction-specific needs. Finally, individual schools or centers may have additional policies or guidelines in place for certain issues that further direct the manner in which a professional school counselor must act.

VOICES FROM THE FIELD 7.1 ETHICAL CONSIDERATIONS IN THE SCHOOLS

The professional school counselor is faced with a number of ethical situations on a daily basis. Although ethical standards and practices are clearly established by the professional organizations that guide us (i.e., the ACA and ASCA), I have found that the situations I am often presented with as a school counselor fall into a gray area. This point was illustrated by a recent school counseling intern; as we handled a tricky abuse case, she asked, "At what point will I just know what to do?" Although I believe you never just know, it is my opinion that counselors must rely on their training and stay abreast of policies, regulations, and current practices. This being noted, it is with time and many experiences with challenging situations, as well as having established a network of professional counselors and/or supervisors with whom to consult, that I believe one becomes effective in dealing with the ethical, legal, and professional aspects of this profession.

To be effective, it is imperative to know when you "don't know" what to do. Not knowing does not imply or suggest ineptitude; however, acting when you really "don't know" can be risky and even unethical. Certainly, experience can breed confidence, but it remains important for each counselor to continually stay up to date and also to take time to reflect on his or her actions. As a new counselor, each action I took was slow and deliberate. I reviewed policy and consulted with supervisors and other colleagues on each and every case. Decisions today come more quickly, but I continue to be deliberate in my judgment and consult frequently with colleagues to ensure I am acting in the best "ethical" interest of the student.

Understanding your role in any given situation is also an important consideration. Professional school counselors have a unique position within the school building and are bound often by a different standard of ethics. This can be further complicated as, by instinct, many school counselors see themselves as "helpers." The professional school counselor functions and "helps" within certain legal and ethical standards set forth by professional organizations, as well as by the school systems in which we are employed. Being effective is often different from "helping." One must continually examine attempts to be "helpful" for the sake of helping. For example, counselors sometimes find themselves in ethical dilemmas with staff members by sharing perhaps too much information in an effort to help or by functioning outside their role as a school counselor and inadvertently "counseling" fellow staff members who seek advice. Balancing the desire to help with the ethics of the job can be tricky, but it is necessary.

It is important to remember that we serve students first, yet are responsible for having relationships with many stakeholders in that student's life such as teachers, administrators, staff, parents, and the community. It can be complicated to juggle the demands of running an effective program, while balancing the unique needs of the people whom we ultimately serve. It is important to educate all stakeholders about the role of the professional school counselor, including ethical and professional responsibilities. This should be done frequently, informally during collaboration with staff and formally during in-service opportunities.

Recently, at a system counseling department chair meeting, I was asked to facilitate a discussion about ethics and the school counselor. The engagement level of the participants was high, as this topic lends itself easily to great discussion. The biggest piece of advice that resulted after reviewing many articles and ethical standards is to consult your colleagues when in doubt. Many counselors admitted that they are sometimes hesitant for fear a colleague might see them as ineffective. The ASCA and ACA highly recommend peer consultation in times of confusion, and consultation actually can serve to protect you legally. If your actions are found to be questionable, courts or review boards often ask, "Would another counselor have acted the same way?" Although middle and secondary counselors often use their team or department as a sounding board, elementary counselors are frequently the sole counselor in the school and must branch out. Many school systems allow networking opportunities via planned professional development or meetings. The system where I am employed establishes counseling cluster groups to meet monthly for this purpose.

The job of a professional school counselor is multifaceted because it is results based. It is not about how much a school counselor does in a given day, but rather how effective the actions of the school counselor have been. Counselors need to hold themselves to a high standard of accountability with regard to each action and remain attuned to the ethical, legal, and professional implications in their day-to-day interactions.

Source: Jennifer Elsis, Professional School Counselor, Bodkin Elementary School, Anne Arundel County Public School System, Maryland

MAKING DECISIONS

Failure to understand the law—and by extension, policies, procedures, and guidelines—is not an acceptable legal defense. It is incumbent on the professional school counselor to become familiar with all the various sources of information and guidance that are available to carry out his or her responsibilities in an ethical and legal manner. Fortunately, there are many ways of staying abreast of current information.

In most work settings, with the exception perhaps of private practice, counselors have a supervisor or other person in authority who can help them become familiar with the regulations, policies, and guidelines relevant to that setting. Most schools and many community agencies have administrative manuals that incorporate all these sources of information into continually updated binders. The ACA news magazine, *Counseling Today*, highlights issues and hot topics in counseling, as do other professional journals and newsletters. There are also a number of commercially available newsletters that cover recent court rulings and their impact in different work settings. The Internet has become an invaluable tool for finding current information and resources. Guillot-Miller and Partin (2003) identified over 40 sites that include information relevant to ethical and legal practices for counselors. Professional associations for counselors and other mental health professionals, institutions of higher education, state and federal government agencies, government-funded organizations, and professional and legal publishers all continuously update their websites and are good sources of current information.

There may be times when mandates appear to be in conflict with each other. In such cases, common sense should prevail. There may be a therapeutically logical reason to follow one particular mandate, rather than another one. Counselors should follow the logical course of action and document what they did and why. For example, if a counselor is working with a suicidal student, but believes that telling the parents will result in an abusive situation, the counselor should handle the situation as an abuse case and tell Child Protective Services about the suicidal behavior. In addition, if following a particular policy, guideline, or regulation is not in the best interest of the students in the counselor's work setting, as per the ethical standards, the counselor should work to change the mandate.

Two other issues are sometimes confusing for counselors. The first concerns the different ways in which counselors in different settings operate. Some mandates—and particularly those that are the result of federal or state legislation or court cases—cover all counselors. For example, child abuse and neglect laws apply to all counselors, regardless of the setting in which they work. But the implementation of some mandates, particularly as they become policy and guidelines, may look very different in different settings. Schools have perhaps the greatest number of mandates under which staff must operate, yet professional school counselors seldom need permission to see students (Remley & Herlihy, 2010), particularly if there is an approved, comprehensive, developmental counseling program. A mental health counselor employed by an outside center or agency, but working either in a school or in a school-based health center, needs signed, informed consent to see those same students. In some cases, local school systems have mandated an opt-in program, which is a program that requires signed, informed consent for students to participate in different aspects of the comprehensive guidance program. In such cases, professional school counselors working in nearby systems or even schools may operate very differently.

The second issue concerns counselors who hold multiple credentials. A counselor may work as a professional school counselor, but hold state certification or licensure and work as a mental health counselor outside school. The counselor may need permission to do something as a professional school counselor, but not need permission to do the same thing as a mental health counselor, or vice versa. Under which set of mandates should the counselor operate?

The solution to both of these issues is the same: Employees must follow the mandates that apply to their work setting. Counselors are required to operate under the mandates of the system that employs them or, in the case of volunteers, the mandates of the entity under whose auspices they are working. If a counselor is employed by a school system as a counselor, then he or she must follow the mandates of the local school system. Teachers who have a degree in counseling or another related mental health degree, but who continue to be employed as teachers, do not have the same protections as counselors because they are not employed in a mental health capacity. They need to check their system's policies carefully to see if they are covered by any protections such as confidentiality.

VOICES FROM THE FIELD 7.2   DECISIONS ARE NOT ALWAYS BLACK AND WHITE

Many school counseling programs require school counselors to take an ethics course or receive training regarding ethical decision making. In this training, various scenarios are discussed and standards of conduct are reviewed. I left my ethics course feeling relieved that I had a specific set of guidelines to adhere to when faced with difficult situations. In addition to making sure I understood the ethical guidelines established by the American School Counseling Association, I became familiar with state and local laws and policies that affected school counselors. As I set up my first office, I made sure to have these current guidelines and laws at my fingertips. However, I soon learned that every ethical situation did not have a specific black-and-white answer. For example, the parent of one of the students on my caseload did not believe in school counseling and specifically asked me to not ever meet with his son. After learning from a teacher that this student was having suicidal thoughts, I was faced with the ethical dilemma of meeting with this student and going against the parent's consent or not following my county's mandated protocol for suicide threats. According to the ASCA, there are guidelines about obtaining parent consent, and there are guidelines about taking appropriate actions to prevent student harm. Trying to decide which guideline to follow was difficult. I consulted with my colleagues and principal, and together we came up with a plan. I learned the value of consulting with my colleagues.

When working with adolescent students, topics such as sexual experiences, sexually transmitted diseases, and pregnancy come up during individual counseling sessions, and school counselors find themselves facing ethical dilemmas surrounding issues of confidentiality. It is important to stay informed about local laws, policies, and procedures within your own state, as these laws and policies surrounding confidentiality can vary. I have had students share with me that they are questioning their sexual orientation. There are no specific guidelines, laws, or policies that speak specifically to counseling gay, lesbian, or questioning students in a school setting, other than to be nonjudgmental. These situations call for school counselors to apply ethical guidelines to individual situations based on interpretation. Sometimes these ethical dilemmas are the result of directives given to school counselors by administrators and principals that may be in conflict with specific guidelines school counselors have to follow according to policies and procedures set by their county or their professional organization. In these situations, having established resources such as the county's Office of School Counseling to consult with and get support from is key in making the right decision. It is vital that school counselors enter the field with an established plan for making ethical decisions that should include examining local and state guidelines, laws, policies, and procedures, as well as consulting with colleagues and outside resources if necessary, as no two situations are the same.

Another aspect of acting ethically responsible when working with students is examining your own core values and beliefs. I work in a community where going to a 2- or 4-year college after high school is not the top priority for many of the families. Many of these families run successful small businesses and want their children to work for their business right out of high school. Although my own belief is that obtaining a college degree should be a goal for every student, I need to be respectful of the hopes and dreams of the families I serve and of each individual student's postsecondary career goals. Being consciously aware of the differences between your own core values and beliefs and the values and beliefs of a particular family you are serving can ensure you are taking extra precaution to remain objective so that you can guide students into making choices that are right for them.

Source: Tracy MacDonald, Professional School Counselor, Chesapeake Bay Middle School, Anne Arundel County Public School System, Maryland

ADDITIONAL LEGAL CONSIDERATIONS

In developing an ethical stance, professional school counselors must take all the aforementioned sources of information into account. However, several other influences must be considered (Herlihy & Corey, 2006; Stone, 2009; Wheeler & Bertram, 2012). Each counselor brings to every counseling relationship the sum of his or her experiences, education, and training. Each also brings to the setting that which makes him or her unique: that is, values, morals, and spiritual influences. Who a counselor is strongly influences the stance he or she takes on issues. Professional school counselors must continually be aware of how their own beliefs and values impact the way they think about issues, the students and their needs, and the options that they perceive to be available. Counselors must also continually examine their behavior in light of cultural bias and multicultural understanding. When deciding on a course of action for their clients, counselors must always try to do what is in the best interests of the clients. At this point in your training, identify three sources of information that can help you make ethical and legal decisions. Now identify three colleagues or other persons with whom you can consult about professional issues or cases.

Professional Competence

In addition to being knowledgeable about mandates, as was previously discussed, there are a number of further steps counselors should take to ensure ethical and legal behavior. Several of these are mentioned in the ethical standards, but it is important to reemphasize them. As reported by Cottone and Tarvydas (2007) and Wheeler and Bertram (2012), counselors should

- Maintain professional growth through continuing education. Although counselors must attend continuing education opportunities to renew national credentials, state credentials, or both, it is important to stay current with theories, trends, and information about clients and different populations.
- Maintain accurate knowledge and expertise in areas of responsibility. Information changes so quickly that counselors must ensure they are providing quality and effective services to their clients. One way of achieving this goal is through professional development, but counselors may also gain information through reading, consultation with colleagues, supervision, and other means.
- Accurately represent credentials. As stated in the ethical standards, counselors should claim only those credentials they have earned and only the highest degree in counseling or a closely related mental health field. Counselors who hold doctorates in non–mental health fields should not use the title "doctor" in their work as a counselor. This is a particular problem in school settings, where counselors earn doctorates in administration and supervision, or related fields, but continue to work as counselors and use the title "doctor" in their job. Furthermore, counselors should not imply in any way that their credentials allow them to work in areas in which they are not trained.

- Provide only those services for which they are qualified and trained. The easiest way for counselors to get into trouble professionally is to provide services for which they are not qualified, either by training or by education. This is particularly true when using counseling techniques. Counselors should have training in using a particular technique before using it. Reading about a technique is not equivalent to implementing it under supervision. Professional school counselors should also not try to work with students whose problems go beyond their expertise. If a professional school counselor is put in a situation where there are no other counselors to whom to refer the student, the counselor should consult with colleagues and ask for supervision to ensure the effectiveness of the counseling.

"Can I Be Sued?" and "What Is Malpractice?"

The answer to "Can I be sued?" is, of course, yes. Anyone can be sued for almost anything, particularly in our litigious society. But the more important question is "Will I be found guilty?" The answer to this question is much more complex.

If professional school counselors fail to exercise *due care* in fulfilling their professional responsibilities, they can be found legally liable for harm caused to an individual by such failure. A court may find negligence if the duty owed to the client was breached in some way, resulting in injury or damages. In counseling, it is more common for counselors to be sued for malpractice. Malpractice, the area of tort law that concerns professional conduct, has been defined as "negligence in carrying out professional responsibilities or duties" (Wheeler & Bertram, 2012, p. 34). Generally, for a counselor to be held liable in tort for malpractice, four conditions have to be met (Stone, 2009): A duty was owed to the client (now the plaintiff) by the counselor (now the defendant); the counselor breached the duty; there is a causal link between the breach and the client's injury; and the client suffered some damage or injury.

An example of negligence would be a counselor who failed to report an abuse case. The counselor had a duty to the client and failed to fulfill that duty. With malpractice, the client suffers due to lack of skill or appropriate behavior on the part of the counselor. An example of malpractice would be a counselor who used hypnosis to treat a client with an eating disorder when the counselor was not trained to use the technique of hypnosis. The situation would be further complicated if this technique was not recognized as being particularly effective for treating eating disorders.

The standard of practice will be used in any liability proceeding to determine if the counselor's performance was within accepted practice. The standard of practice question is "In the performance of professional services, did the counselor provide the level of care and treatment that is consistent with the degree of learning, skill and ethics ordinarily possessed and expected by reputable counselors practicing under similar circumstances?" (ACA, 1997, p. 9).

The standard of practice will be established through the testimony of peers. These peers are called as expert witnesses because they are considered to be experts in the field under question. For professional school counselors, the expert witnesses will be other school counselors (Stone, 2009). The standard of practice is an ever-evolving level of expectation and is influenced by two major factors: education and experience. The standard is not an absolute one, but rather a variable one. It will be much higher for a counselor who has practiced for a number of years and pursued advanced graduate training or professional development than it will be for a counselor in the first year of practice immediately following graduate school. The more training and experience a counselor possesses, the higher the standard to which the counselor will be held accountable. The assumption is that a counselor should know more each year he or she practices through experience and training and should therefore be held to a higher standard with each additional year. Using this standard of practice, a counselor will usually be found guilty of malpractice if one or more of the following situations occur (Wheeler & Bertram, 2012):

- The practice was not within the realm of acceptable professional practice.
- The counselor was not trained in the technique used.
- The counselor failed to follow a procedure that would have been more helpful.
- The counselor failed to warn and/or protect others from a violent client.
- The counselor failed to obtain informed consent from the client.
- The counselor failed to explain to the client the possible consequences of treatment.

Several professional publications (Wheeler & Bertram, 2012) have reported that sexual misconduct is the primary reason that liability actions are initiated against counselors. School staff, counselors, and other mental health professionals have been accused of committing sexual abuse or misconduct. It may be that other problems, such as failure to

use a more appropriate technique, are actually more common, but most clients lack the ability to recognize therapeutic problems and may just have a general sense that "it isn't working or helping" and choose to terminate.

Although the number of professional school counselors who are sued is increasing, the number still remains very small. Parents are more likely to request their child not be included in certain guidance program activities or to complain to the principal or central administration about a program or behavior. In rare cases, parents may sue, but the vast majority of cases against school counselors have been rejected by the courts. In school settings, violating or failing to follow school system mandates will get a professional school counselor in trouble faster than almost any other behavior. Depending on the counselor's action, the system may choose to reprimand the professional school counselor. In extreme cases, the counselor's employment may be terminated. Professional school counselors must also be knowledgeable about their communities. They may have a legal right to implement certain programs or conduct certain activities, but if the community is not supportive of those activities, they are going to face opposition.

When a professional school counselor is faced with any legal action, the first thing the counselor should do is call a lawyer and then inform the counselor supervisor, if there is one. Most agencies, clinics, practices, and schools are accustomed to dealing with such legal issues and may even have a procedure for what to do. Professional school counselors should never attempt to reason with the student or contact the student's lawyer without advice of counsel. It is important to not provide any information to, or discuss the case with, anyone except the counselor's lawyer or the person designated to help the counselor. Just as professional school counselors advise clients to get professional mental health help when they have personal problems, counselors must get legal help when they have legal problems.

Subpoenas

Many counselors will receive a subpoena at some point in their professional career. Counselors, and particularly professional school counselors, probably receive subpoenas most often in cases involving custody disputes, child abuse or neglect allegations, and special education disputes, and these subpoenas can be brought forward on behalf of, or against, the counselor's client/student. In most cases, one of the parties in such a dispute believes that the counselor may have some information that will be helpful to his or her case. Professional school counselors need to pay attention to subpoenas because they are legal documents. At the same time, they need to consider whether the information being requested is confidential because professional school counselors may be limited in what they can share. Under no circumstances should the counselor automatically comply with the subpoena without discussing it first with the client (or the student's parents in the case of a minor child), the client's attorney, or both or without consulting the agency's or school system's attorney. According to the ACA (1997), a counselor should take the following steps when receiving a subpoena:

1. Contact the client or the client's attorney, and ask for guidance. If you work for a school system, contact the school system's attorney to seek guidance.
2. If the aforementioned parties advise you to comply with the subpoena, discuss with the student, family, or attorney the implications of releasing the requested information.
3. Obtain a signed informed-consent form to release the records. That form should specify all conditions of release: what, to whom, and so forth.
4. If the decision is made to not release the records, cooperate with the client's attorney in filing a motion to quash (or in some areas, asking for a protective order). This will allow you to not comply with the subpoena.
5. Maintain a record of everything you and the client's attorney did; keep notes regarding all conversations and copies of any documents pertaining to the subpoena.

An attorney who wants information may also ask a judge to issue a court order. A court order permits the release of confidential information, but does not mandate its release (ACA, 1997). If both a subpoena and a court order are received, the counselor must release the information with or without the client's consent. Failure to do so may result in the counselor being held in contempt of court.

There are two important things to remember about subpoenas: do not panic, and do consult an attorney. Subpoenas are legal documents, but you have enough time to consider the implications of releasing the information and to seek legal advice.

CONFIDENTIALITY

For clients to feel free to share sometimes sensitive and personal information during a counseling session, they must feel that they can trust the counselor not to share what is disclosed during sessions with anyone else without their permission. This sense of trust and privacy, called confidentiality, is essential for counseling to be successful. Confidentiality is the cornerstone of counseling and is

what separates the counseling relationship from other relationships where information is shared. Confidentiality belongs to the client, not to the counselor. The client always has the right to waive confidentiality and allow the counselor to share information with a third party.

Counseling minors presents particular challenges with respect to the issue of confidentiality. Every state sets the age of majority; for most states, it is 18 years of age. Most students are minors and therefore not legally able to make their own decisions. Thus, these students have an ethical right to confidentiality, but the legal right belongs to their parents or guardian (Remley & Herlihy, 2010). Approximately 20 states protect professional school counselor–client confidentiality through statutes (Cottone & Tarvydas, 2007), but many include significant restrictions.

Professional school counselors often ask what to do if parents want to know what is discussed during counseling sessions with their children. Legally, parents, and only parents, have the right to know what is being discussed. However, the child might not want the information shared with the parent. Section B.5.b, Responsibility to Parents and Legal Guardians, of the *ACA Code of Ethics* states

Counselors inform parents and legal guardians about the role of counselors and the confidential nature of the counseling relationship. Counselors are sensitive to the cultural diversity of families and respect the inherent rights and responsibilities of parents/gaurdians over the welfare of the children/charges according to law. Counselors work to establish, as appropriate, collaborative relationships with parents/guardians to best serve clients. (ACA, 2005, p. 8)

Section B.2 of the ASCA *Ethical Standards for School Counselors* states

a. Inform parents/guardians of the school counselor's role to include the confidential nature of the counseling relationship between the counselor and student.
b. Recognize that working with minors in a school setting requires school counselors to collaborate with students' parents/guardians to the extent possible.
c. Provide parents/guardians with accurate, comprehensive and relevant information in an objective and caring manner, as is appropriate and consistent with ethical responsibilities to the student. (ASCA, 2010, p. 4)

These statements leave professional school counselors with a dilemma. To resolve this dilemma, Remley and Herlihy (2010) suggested that the counselor first discuss the issue with the student to determine if he or she is willing to disclose the information to the parent/guardian. If the child will not disclose, then the counselor should try to help the parent understand that the best interests of the child are not served by disclosure. If this does not work, then the professional school counselor should schedule a joint meeting with the parent/guardian and student to discuss the issue. If the parent/guardian still is not satisfied, then the professional school counselor may have to disclose the information without the child's consent. Some counselors would suggest that this type of situation may be reflective of some deeper family issue. Although the parent or guardian has a legal right to the information, there may be an underlying "family secret" that the parent/guardian does not want known, and the school counselor should be sensitive to any difficulties the child may be demonstrating. Or this situation may be the result of cultural differences, and the professional school counselor needs to be more aware of and sensitive to the family's traditions and beliefs.

Many professional school counselors suggest that at the beginning of the first session of each new counseling relationship, the professional school counselor should discuss confidentiality with the student, explain what it means, and point out the limits of confidentiality. Some professional school counselors choose to hang a sign on the wall of their office that outlines this information as reinforcement of what is discussed in the first session. Although this issue appears to be simple on the surface, in reality it is a very complex issue that has generated a significant amount of research and professional discourse. As the use of technology increases in counseling settings, the discussions will continue and expand. There are significant challenges to keeping electronic information confidential.

Limits to Confidentiality

These provisions are included in the *ACA Code of Ethics* (2005, p. 2):

- Section B.1.a: "Counselors respect client rights to privacy. . . ."
- Section B.1.c: "Counselors do not share confidential information without client consent or without sound legal or ethical justification."
- Section B.1.d: "At initiation and throughout the counseling process, counselors inform clients of the limitations of confidentiality and seek to identify foreseeable situations in which confidentiality must be breached."

There are several instances in which counselors must break confidentiality. These are delineated within Section B.2.a of the *ACA Code of Ethics* and Section A.7 of the ASCA *Ethical Standards for School Counselors*. The most important of these is the "duty to warn." When a professional school counselor becomes aware that students are in danger of being harmed, as in instances of abuse, or that clients are likely to harm themselves or someone else, like in instances of potential suicidal or homicidal actions, the professional school counselor can break confidentiality and tell an appropriate person.

The duty-to-warn standard was first set out in the 1976 court decision in *Tarasoff v. Regents of the University of California*. In this case, the client, a graduate student, told his psychologist about his intent to kill a girl (named Tarasoff) who had rejected his advances. The psychologist told the campus police and his supervisor, but did not warn the intended victim or her family. The majority of the California Supreme Court ruled that the psychologist had a duty to warn a known, intended victim. This case established the legal duty to warn and protect an identifiable victim from a client's potential or intended violence and has been the basis for many other court decisions across the country. In the ensuing decades, some cases have extended the duty-to-warn standard to include types of harm other than violence and foreseeable victims in addition to identifiable victims. Section B.2.a of the *ACA Code of Ethics* now reads: "The general requirement that counselors keep information confidential does not apply when disclosure is required to protect clients or identified others from serious and foreseeable harm . . ." (ACA, 2005, p. 2).

Several other situations constrain the limits of confidentiality, as delineated in the *ACA Code of Ethics* (2005):

- *Subordinates.* Confidentiality is not absolute when subordinates, including employees, supervisees, students, clerical assistants, and volunteers, handle records or confidential information. Every effort should be made to limit access to this information, and the assistants should be reminded of the confidential nature of the information they are handling.
- *Treatment teams.* The client should be informed of the treatment team and the information being shared.
- *Consultation.* The professional school counselor always has the right to consult with a colleague or supervisor on any case. In such instances, the counselor should provide enough information to obtain the needed assistance, but should limit any information that might identify the client.
- *Groups and families.* In group or family counseling settings, confidentiality is not guaranteed. The counselor may state that what goes on in the sessions is

confidential, and the members may agree. However, because there is more than one client in the group, it is impossible to guarantee confidentiality.

- *Third-party payers.*   Information will sometimes have to be sent to a mental health provider, insurance company, or other agency that has some legitimate need for the information. The counselor will disclose this information only with the client's permission.
- *Minors.*   There are special considerations regarding confidentiality and minors that will be discussed in detail in the next section.
- *Contagious, life-threatening diseases.*   Unlike the duty-to-warn standard, the ACA ethical standards state that the counselor is justified in disclosing information about a client to an identifiable third party if that party's relationship with the client is such that there is a possibility of contracting a contagious, life-threatening disease and the client does not plan on telling the third party. It should be noted that the word used is *justified*, not *should* or *must*. This wording leaves it up to the counselor to decide if the third party is at risk and must be warned.
- *Court-ordered disclosure.*   Subpoenas were previously discussed. Even if ordered to reveal confidential information by a judge, counselors should limit what they reveal to what is absolutely necessary.

In summary, confidentiality is a very complex issue, but essential to the effectiveness of counseling. Clients have an ethical right to confidentiality, and counselors must make every effort to ensure this right. However, there are specific cases where it is not only permissible, but also essential to break confidentiality to protect the client or to protect others from the client.

Confidentiality and Privileged Communication

The term *confidentiality* is used in discussions about counseling, whereas the term *privileged communication* is the legal term to describe the privacy of the counselor–client communication. Privileged communication exists by statute and applies only to testifying in a court of law. The privilege belongs to the client, who always has the right to waive the privilege and allow the counselor to testify. Clients have an ethical right to confidentiality, and the ethical standards for the mental health professions detail the boundaries of confidentiality. Privileged communication is more limited, and federal, state, and local mandates determine its parameters. Whether a client–counselor relationship is considered privileged communication varies widely across jurisdictions. Even within a jurisdiction, a counselor in private practice may be covered by privileged communication provisions, but the school counselors who

work in that same jurisdiction may not be. It is essential that counselors become familiar with their local mandates and policies to determine the extent to which privileged communication applies to their situation.

MINOR CONSENT LAWS

All states have a minor consent law that allows certain minors to seek treatment for certain conditions, usually involving substance abuse, mental health, and some reproductive health areas. These laws are based on federal law, 42 U.S.C. § 290dd-2, and federal regulation, 42 C.F.R. Part 2, which reference the confidentiality of patient records for drug and alcohol abuse assessment, referral, diagnosis, and treatment. These federal mandates further prohibit the release of these records to anyone without the client's informed consent and include clients under the age of 18 years, even if they are in school and living with parents or guardians.

Over the past 10 years, there has been a movement to increase the number of student assistance teams and student assistance programs (SAPs) in schools. These teams usually consist of an administrator, one or more student services professionals (e.g., professional school counselor, school social worker, pupil personnel worker, school psychologist, or school nurse), and teachers and may include a substance abuse assessor from a local agency or similar professional. School staff members refer students who are suspected of having a substance abuse problem to this team. The team members are trained to deal with substance abuse issues and, if they believe the student has a substance abuse problem, will have the student assessed and referred for appropriate assistance.

The controversy surrounding this program concerns the role of parents or guardians in this process. Under the federal law, the student can go from referral through completion of treatment without the parents' or guardians' knowledge. Substance abuse professionals are divided regarding whether it is possible to successfully treat students who abuse substances without the family's involvement. Other professionals have concerns about the ability of young adolescents to seek treatment without any family knowledge or involvement.

As the federal law has been incorporated into state statutes, states have taken different approaches to deciding to whom this law applies and for what. In general, the patient must be old enough to understand the problem, the treatment options available, and the possible consequences of each option. Some states have no age limits and maintain that a minor has the same capacity as an adult to consent to certain services. On the other hand, some states have decided on a specific age, usually 12 years and older, at which the minor may consent to mental health treatment, reproductive or substance abuse services, and treatment for sexually transmitted infections (STIs) and human immunodeficiency virus/acquired immune deficiency syndrome (HIV/AIDS). According to the Guttmacher Institute's *State Policies in Brief: An Overview of Minors' Consent Law* (2005, 2009, 2013), 26 states and the District of Columbia allow all minors to consent to all contraceptive services, 21 states allow minors to consent to contraceptive services in one or more circumstances, and 4 states have no law covering contraceptive services for minors. Thirty-two states and the District of Columbia allow minors to consent to prenatal treatment when pregnant, whereas 13 states have no law. All 50 states and the District of Columbia allow minors to consent to treatment for STIs and HIV/AIDS. Eighteen states and the District of Columbia allow, but do not require, the doctor to inform the parent about mental health services, and 29 states do not, whereas the other four states allow contact under some circumstances. Twenty-one states and the District of Columbia allow general medical care, and 29 states do not. Three states and the District of Columbia allow abortion services, 40 states require parental consent and/or notification, and seven states have no law. More information can be found on the Guttmacher Institute webpage at http://www.guttmacher.org/statecenter/spibs/spib_OMCL.pdf.

As you can see, there is tremendous variation across the 50 states in what is permissible and required under the law. There is also some question about the applicability of these laws to school settings. The laws clearly cover medical personnel and certain conditions. A school nurse is covered, but a professional school counselor or school psychologist may not be covered. It is critical that counselors and other student services personnel become familiar with the minor consent law in the state in which they work to ensure compliance. Staff must also investigate local policies. A state law may allow a professional school counselor to address reproductive issues and substance abuse without parental consent or notification, but a local policy may prohibit such counseling. The laws cover minors seeking advice and/or treatment. If a minor is not seeking help, then the law may not apply, and the counselor would follow other policies or procedures in dealing with these issues.

The legal issues aside, this is the law that raises a tremendous number of ethical issues for counselors. A number of professionals question the ability of young adolescents, in particular, to access these services without the family's involvement. Should a professional school counselor help a 13-year-old who abuses substances seek treatment without the family's knowledge? How successful will the adolescent's recovery be? What about a 15-year-old who is abusing drugs and engaging in risky sexual behaviors? What is the counselor's ethical responsibility? The problem this law presents for many counselors is that it allows them to assist adolescent clients legally, but it may conflict with their personal beliefs. Some professionals believe behaviors such as these can cause harm to the client and therefore they have a duty to warn that supersedes all other responsibilities. Other counselors work with the adolescent to help him or her involve the family, whereas still others believe that telling the family will work against the adolescent's obtaining help.

Another issue is that many parents do not understand that their children can seek treatment in these areas without parental consent. Parents will be understandably angry and distrustful when they discover their child has a sexually transmitted infection (STI) or abuses substances, and the counselor knew and did not tell them about it. Counselors need to be prepared to deal with the aftermath of such discoveries. They need to think through their positions on these issues very carefully and be honest with clients about their beliefs. Professional school counselors should not wait until they are faced with a situation to figure out where they stand on an issue. How might you address parents who are understandably angry over a minor consent issue and are now distrustful of you as their child's professional school counselor? What precautions might you take to avoid this situation?

RECORDS AND PERSONAL NOTES

Educational Records

Educational records are all the records of a student's achievement, attendance, behavior, testing and assessment, and school activities, as well as any other such information that the school collects and maintains on a student. Schools frequently divide student records into cumulative records, health records, special education records, and confidential records, including psychological evaluations. In reality, this is done for the convenience of the school; all these records are considered to be part of the educational record. The only exceptions are personal notes, reports to Child Protective Services for abuse or neglect, and, in some states, reports from law enforcement agencies regarding students' arrests for reportable offenses.

The inspection of, dissemination of, and access to student educational records must be handled in accordance with the Family Educational Rights and Privacy Act (FERPA) of 1974 (20 U.S.C. § 1232g). This law, which is often referred to as the Buckley Amendment, applies to all school districts, pre-K–12 schools, and postsecondary institutions that receive federal funding through the U.S. Department of Education. Nonpublic schools that do not accept federal funding are exempt from this law. New regulations for FERPA were enacted in January 2009. The new regulations provide clarity for those who need to understand and administer FERPA and make important changes to improve school safety, access to data for research and accountability purposes, and the safeguarding of educational records (Family Educational Rights and Privacy Act [FERPA], 2013).

FERPA requires that schools or systems annually send a notice to parents or guardians regarding their right to review their children's records and to file a complaint if they disagree with anything in the record. The system has 45 days in which to comply with the parents' request to review the records. There are penalties, including loss of federal funding, for any school or system that fails to comply. The law also limits who may access records and specifies what personally identifiable information can be disclosed without informed consent—that is, what constitutes directory information or pubic information. Under FERPA, only those persons "with a legitimate educational interest" can access a student's record. This includes the new school when a student transfers. The sending school may send the records without the parents' consent, but should make every attempt to inform the parent that it has done so. The major exception to this limitation relates to law enforcement; the school must comply with a judicial order or lawfully executed subpoena. The school must also make whatever information is needed available to the school's law enforcement unit. In emergencies, information relevant to the emergency can be shared (see www.ed.gov/print/policy/gen/guid/fpco/ferpa/index.html). All states and jurisdictions have incorporated FERPA into state statutes and local policies, with some degree of variance among them on such aspects as what constitutes directory information.

The right of consent transfers to the student at 18 years of age or when the student attends a postsecondary institution. The law does not specifically limit the rights of parents of students over 18 years of age who are still in secondary school. The new regulations clarify that information about a student in a postsecondary institution can be shared with his or her parents under any circumstance if the student is claimed on the parents' income tax forms or in a health or safety emergency, regardless of the student's tax or dependency status.

The Protection of Pupil Rights Amendment (PPRA) of 1978, often called the Hatch Amendment, gives parents additional rights. It established certain requirements when surveys are given to students in pre-K–12 schools; it does not apply to postsecondary schools, as students can consent on their own. If the survey is funded with federal money, informed parental consent must be obtained for all participating students in elementary or secondary schools if they are required to take the survey and questions about certain personal areas are asked. PPRA also requires informed parental consent before a student undergoes any psychological, psychiatric, or medical examination, testing, or treatment or any school program designed to affect the personal values or behavior of the student. Further, PPRA gives parents the right to review instructional materials in experimental programs.

The No Child Left Behind Act of 2001 (NCLB) included several changes to FERPA and PPRA and continued to increase parents' rights. The changes apply to surveys funded either in part or entirely by any program administered by the U.S. Department of Education. NCLB made minor changes to the seven existing survey categories and added an additional category. PPRA now requires that

- Schools and contractors make instructional materials available for review by parents of participating students if those materials will be used in any U.S. Department of Education–funded survey, analysis, or evaluation.
- Schools and contractors obtain written, informed parental consent prior to students' participation in any U.S. Department of Education–funded survey, analysis, or evaluation if information in any of the following listed areas would be revealed:
  - Political affiliations or beliefs of the parent or student;
  - Mental and psychological problems of the family or student;
  - Sex behavior or attitudes;
  - Illegal, antisocial, self-incriminating, or demeaning behavior;
  - Critical appraisals of other individuals with whom the student has close family relationships;
  - Legally recognized privileged or analogous relationships such as those of lawyers, ministers, and physicians;
  - Religious practices, affiliations, or beliefs of the parent or student (added by NCLB); and
  - Income other than such information as is required to determine eligibility or participation in a program. (20 U.S.C. § 1232h)

The new provisions of PPRA also apply to surveys not funded through U.S. Department of Education programs. These provisions give parents the right to inspect, on request, any survey or instructional materials used as part of the curriculum if created by a third party and involve one or more of the eight aforementioned areas. Parents also have the right to inspect any instrument used to collect personal information that will be used in selling or marketing. Parents always have the right to not grant permission or to opt their child out of participating in any activity involving the eight previously delineated areas. PPRA does not apply to any survey that is administered as part of the Individuals with Disabilities Education Improvement Act (IDEA).

As can be seen from the previous discussion, there are many constraints in schools to assessing, testing, and surveying students. Because individual school systems or districts may have further defined this legislation, it is essential that professional school counselors become familiar with the requirements of the policies and procedures for their specific school system.

The word *parents* has been used in the preceding discussion about student records. The law does recognize the right of students over 18 years of age to access their own records and accords them the same rights as parents of students under 18 years of age. However, the law does not specifically limit the right of parents whose child is over 18 years of age to also access that child's records, particularly in cases where the child is still living at home and is financially dependent on the parents. The law also gives noncustodial parents the same rights as custodial parents. Unless there is a court order in the child's file that limits or terminates the rights of one or both parents, both parents have the same access to the child's records. School personnel must also provide copies of records such as report cards to both parents if requested.

The word *parent* is used to reference the legal guardian of the child, who may not be the biological or adoptive parent of the child, but rather some other legally recognized caregiver. Stepparents and other family members have no legal right to the student's records without court-appointed authority, such as adoption or guardianship. This is particularly problematic in situations where a relative provides kinship care; that is, the relative has physical custody 24 hours a day, 7 days a week, but no legal custody of the child. Legally, this person providing kinship care has no educational decision-making rights for the child and cannot access that child's records or give consent. The crack epidemic and HIV/AIDS have created a situation where millions of children under 18 years of age are involved in informal kinship care situations. The American Bar Association (2009) estimates that over 6 million children, or approximately 1 in 12, are currently living in a household headed by grandparents or other relatives. Only 21 states have enacted legislation enabling the caregiver to enroll a child in school and/or extracurricular activities without formal guardianship. Kinship care may be the best situation for children, but these situations present significant legal implications for schools.

Outside agencies may not access the records of any student without the signed consent of the parent. Some states have worked out interagency agreements wherein a parent signs one form that designates which records may be shared with which agencies, making individual forms unnecessary. Local policies dictate whether signed informed consent is needed to share information at school team meetings such as student assistance programs, individualized education programs, or student services meetings when personnel from outside agencies are regular members of the team.

Personal Notes

Most professional school counselors keep two types of notes: counseling notes and personal notes. Counseling notes record their interactions with their students and may include such information as when the student was seen, the reason for the session, the outcome, and the expected follow-up. Counselors probably do not keep counseling notes on all their students, given counseling caseloads, but may keep counseling notes for those students they see individually or in group. These notes are covered under FERPA and may be considered part of the educational record.

Personal notes, or sole-possession notes, are written by professional school counselors to serve as an extension of their memories and to record impressions of the client or the counseling session. As such, they are not considered part of the educational record. These notes must remain "in the sole possession of the maker" and cannot be shared with anyone except "a substitute maker." A substitute maker is someone who takes over for the counselor in the counselor's position, in the same way a substitute teacher takes over for the regular teacher. A substitute maker is not the counselor who becomes responsible for the child the next year or in the next school.

The important point to remember about personal notes is that such notes must remain separate from the educational record. Once any information in the personal notes is shared, it is no longer confidential. If professional school counselors keep their personal notes in their offices, they should keep them separate from all other records and secured, such as in a locked file cabinet. Some counselors go so far as to keep them in their car or house, but this is not necessary unless there are problems with security in their office. As technology is more commonly used in counseling offices, professionals may prefer to keep their personal notes on the computer. However, that is not a good idea unless the counselor can absolutely guarantee that no one can access the program or break through firewalls. Even keeping the personal notes on disk is questionable. Stories of computer hackers breaking codes and paralyzing websites for hours are frequently reported in the news. It is preferable to keep personal notes separate and to not tell anyone they exist, even if there is nothing of particular interest in them. The information is confidential, and the professional school counselor needs to ensure its security. Information from the personal notes would be shared only in those cases when there is a clear duty to warn or when a judge requires that confidentiality be broken and the information shared.

ACTIVITY 7.3

How might you store your personal notes as a professional counselor? What precautions will you take to keep them secure? If subordinates are involved, what precautions will you take to ensure confidentiality?

THE HEALTH INSURANCE PORTABILITY AND ACCOUNTABILITY ACT OF 1996

The Health Insurance Portability and Accountability Act of 1996 (HIPAA) required that the U.S. Department of Health and Human Services (HHS) adopt national standards for the privacy of individually identifiable health information, outlined patients' rights, and established criteria for access to health records. The requirement that HHS adopt national standards for electronic healthcare transactions was also included in this law. The resulting Privacy Rule was adopted in 2000 and became effective in 2001. The Privacy Rule sets national standards for the privacy and security of protected health information. It specifically excludes any individually identifiable health information that is covered by FERPA. Thus, health records in schools that fall under FERPA are specifically excluded from HIPAA. However, in reality, the situation is not quite that simple, particularly in the area of special education. Many schools receive mental, physical, and emotional health assessments of students that have been conducted by outside providers whose practices are covered by HIPAA regulations. In previous years, such assessments and reports automatically became part of the educational record. This may no longer be the case, particularly if the provider requests that the report not be redisclosed. As HIPAA continues to impact health information, school systems must develop policies and procedures to address any potential conflicts between FERPA and HIPAA. Professional school counselors must be aware of these issues and any school policies.

CHILD ABUSE

Another issue professional school counselors must deal with that has clear legal mandates is child abuse and neglect. Efforts to recognize and intervene in child abuse cases began in the late 1800s and were modeled on the laws prohibiting cruelty to animals. In 1961, *battered child syndrome* was legally recognized, and by 1968, all 50 states had laws requiring the reporting of child maltreatment. In 1974, the National Child Abuse Prevention and Treatment Act became federal law. The act was later reauthorized with changes and renamed the Keeping Children and Families Safe Act of 2003. The law defined child abuse as physical or mental injury, sexual abuse or exploitation, negligent treatment, or maltreatment of a child under the age of 18 years or the age specified by the child protection law of the state in question, by a person who is responsible for the child's welfare, under circumstances that indicate that the child's health or welfare is harmed or threatened (42 U.S.C. § 5101).

The law is very clear regarding who must report child abuse and neglect cases. Every health practitioner, educator, human services worker, and law enforcement officer must report suspected abuse or neglect, generally within 24 to 72 hours of first "having reason to suspect." It is incumbent on the person who first suspects the abuse or neglect to call Child Protective Services to report it. The oral report must be followed up by a written report in most cases. Each state may have slightly different procedures for reporting; some states allow up to 7 days for submission of the written report and identify different agencies to which the report must be made. What does not change is the legal mandate to report.

There is no liability for reporting child abuse, even if a subsequent investigation determines no evidence that abuse or neglect occurred, unless the report is made with malice. However, most states do have serious penalties for failure to report. These penalties may include loss of certification or license, disciplinary action, or termination of employment.

Parents or guardians have no rights to information during this process. The school or other entity making the report should not inform the parents that a report is being made. It is the responsibility of the department of social services and the law enforcement agency to contact the parent and conduct the investigation. It is critical that professional school counselors and other professionals understand the laws regarding child abuse and neglect cases and follow the procedures exactly. It should be emphasized that the person submitting the report does not have to prove that abuse has occurred; it is enough to have reason to suspect it.

Professional school counselors are sometimes put in an awkward position when another staff member is the first person to suspect abuse, but he or she is not willing to make the report and asks the counselor to do it. In such

ACTIVITY 7.4

Handling Abuse and Neglect

Become familiar with local or state processes of reporting suspicions of abuse and neglect to Child Protective Services. What might you do if another professional or staff person in your building or agency approaches you about their suspicion of child abuse or neglect?

a case, if the staff member will not make the report, the professional school counselor should do it, but should apprise the administrator of the circumstances surrounding the report. Regardless of who submits the report, the student will need support and assistance throughout the process.

SUICIDE

For many years, the standard that was used in the profession for dealing with potential suicide cases was that set out in the *Tarasoff* decision, which was previously discussed. As a result of the *Tarasoff* ruling, counselors had a duty to warn if there was a foreseeable victim. According to Remley and Herlihy (2010), subsequent court decisions interpreted the case differently; some judges ruled that the duty exists even when there is no foreseeable victim, or if the client unintentionally injures the victim, a class of persons to which the victim belongs, bystanders, and other individuals. In general, when dealing with a potentially suicidal client, the professional school counselor would conduct a lethality assessment, determine the seriousness of the threat, and then, based on the seriousness of the threat, decide whether the duty to warn was applicable.

The *Eisel* case in Maryland changed the standard for many school counselors. In that case, two middle school students became involved in Satanism and, as a result, became obsessed with death and self-destruction. Friends of Nicole Eisel went to their school counselor and told her that Nicole was thinking about killing herself. This counselor consulted with Nicole's school counselor. Both professional school counselors spoke with Nicole, who denied thinking about killing herself. Shortly thereafter, on a school holiday, Nicole's friend, who attended another school, shot Nicole and killed herself in the park behind the school. Mr. Eisel sued the school, the school system, and the professional school counselors. After the circuit court dismissed

the case, Mr. Eisel appealed to the court of appeals, which in its decision of October 29, 1991, stated: "Considering the growth of this tragic social problem in the light of the factors discussed above, we hold that school counselors have a duty to use reasonable means to attempt to prevent a suicide when they are on notice of a child or adolescent student's suicidal intent" (*Eisel v. Board of Education,* 1991).

On the facts of this case as developed to date, a trier of fact could conclude that the duty included warning Mr. Eisel of the danger. The case was remanded back to the circuit court to decide the issue of liability for both the school system and the professional school counselors. The case finally concluded eight years after it began with a finding that the school system and the professional school counselors had acted appropriately, given the circumstances, their training, and the policies in place at the time.

However, the court's decision had a major impact on professional school counselors in the state of Maryland. This decision removed the counselor's ability to determine whether the duty to warn is applicable. As a consequence, professional school counselors in Maryland must always tell the parent whenever there is any indication from a child or someone else that the child is thinking about suicide, regardless of the seriousness of the threat. Further, they must inform the principal or the principal's designee. Many of Maryland's school systems now apply this procedure to all student services personnel employed by the school system.

Although this case is legally binding only on professional school counselors in Maryland, it has become the standard used in subsequent cases elsewhere. For example, a federal circuit court in Florida made a similar ruling in 1997 in *Wyke v. Polk County School Board*, and several other courts are following suit. But courts in some other states have rejected the *Eisel* decision and have found in favor of the school systems. Professional school counselors must be aware of the policies within their system. Some courts clearly are ruling in favor of the duty to warn, as opposed to counselor discretion.

CULTURAL REFLECTION 7.2

How might professional school counselors, students, parents, and educators from diverse cultural backgrounds view the duty to warn responsibility of the professional school counselors? Discuss times when the duty to warn may not be in the student's best interest.

Prior to beginning my internship as a school counselor, I was required to take a course on ethics. I learned the ACA and ASCA codes of ethics and how I would need to apply my knowledge when I started working with students. I also learned about the laws that would influence my work with kids. When I first started interning, I put certain things into place to ensure that I fulfilled all the ethical policies that I had learned in graduate school. Before I was able to work with kids, I was required to obtain liability insurance. I did so by joining the American Counseling Association. In addition to providing liability insurance as part of my student membership, they also provided me with issues of *Counseling Today*, which are full of practical information I have used to inform my practice. I know that I am protected in the event that a problem occurs because of my choice to be professionally affiliated with the ACA. I also have picked up a lot of useful tips by reading the articles in *Counseling Today*. I regularly turn to my ethical training when situations become tricky.

One of the first components of every code of ethics applying to my profession is informed consent and how to handle confidentiality. Because the clients I work with are minors, confidentiality must be handled in a way that is quite different from working with adults. Every counseling office I've interned in has had a poster explaining confidentiality, which also states the limitations to confidentiality. Whenever I work with a new student, I go over what confidentiality means and explain that I keep the things kids tell me confidential unless they say that they are going to harm themselves or someone else. I also explain to students that I am a student myself learning to be a counselor and that I am at the school to practice all the things that I have learned in graduate school. Typically, I keep in contact with parents of students that I see regularly. Whenever a child has told me something that I think the parent would be curious about, I ask the student if they are comfortable with me sharing what we talked about with the family. Many of the students I have worked with have openly encouraged me to talk with their parents or teachers about the things we've discussed. However, there have been a few times that students had reasons that they did not want me to share information with the family. These situations can become tricky, and I have benefitted greatly during these times from having my supervisor to consult with. Consulting with other professionals in the field has been particularly helpful to me as I learn the art of my craft and gives me greater confidence in the decisions that I make.

As a new counselor, I constantly seek advice from my supervisors, from my peers during my internship seminar class, and also from the literature. As the *ACA Code of Ethics* states, I must not work outside the realm of my professional competence. When I first started working with clients, I asked questions frequently to receive feedback from my supervisors. When I felt that I had become "stuck" during the therapeutic journey with a student, I asked for advice and read through the research relevant to the student's challenges. My supervisors have shelves full of books that they refer to when working with students, and I have made use of these resources during my time spent in the office. At times, a student presents a challenge that is outside of my scope of expertise. In addition, the school system I intern with has specific policies for how to handle things like suicide intervention and disciplinary issues. Knowing the policies of your school system is a must. When policies dictated how I was to handle a situation, I always consulted with my supervisor and often worked in conjunction with my supervisor in handling these situations.

Working in a school setting often means working in teams. As an intern, I have worked with teachers, administrators, families, and other staff members. I regularly spend time in meetings consulting with other stakeholders, discussing the challenges and strengths of the students, and brainstorming solutions. Each member of the team sees the student from a different perspective, and taking the time to share those perspectives helps each person on the team to gain a more complete picture of the student as a holistic being. I have learned so much about the student by being able to communicate with teachers and other staff members who have known the student longer than I. Opening the lines of communication with the family also provided me with additional information and new ideas for how to support the student. Communication with other members of the educational team has helped me to see the needs of the school as a whole in addition to gaining a better picture of the needs of individual students.

School counselors are in a position to gain an understanding of the school as a system. Our positions as counselors are unique because we are able to influence the system as well as the individual. ASCA suggests that school counselors should implement a data-driven, comprehensive program. The ASCA code of ethics delineates responsibilities for the counselor when using data to protect the confidentiality of the students and report accurate findings. During my internship, I was required to complete a data project in which I collected student responses anonymously and compiled the before and after data to show how my interventions influenced the student body as a whole. I created a survey designed to determine the

Ethical, Legal, and Professional Issues in School Counseling **171**

students' perception of school climate and clearly explained the purpose of the survey. Students were informed that filling out the survey was voluntary, anonymous, and that their responses would not be used in any way against them. When compiling the results, I dedicated extra time to re-checking my score counts to ensure the greatest possible accuracy in reporting the data.

The ASCA code of ethics delineates how to obtain informed consent from students and families. During one of my internships, I conducted small-group guidance lessons during class time. My supervisor helped me to access the available data to identify students who might benefit from the groups I was running. Prior to beginning group sessions, I met with each student individually. I spent some time getting to know each student, explaining the purpose of the group, how often and how many times we would meet, that we would meet during class time, but that we were going to rotate the scheduling so that they would not miss one class more than once, and that participation in the group was voluntary. I had a student tell me that he did not want to participate, so I respected the student's decision and let him know that he was still welcome should he change his mind. I sent students home with an informed consent document for the family to look over and sign. As my supervisor noted, students would be missing class for group, and parents needed to be made aware of that. During the first session of each of the groups, I went over and explained confidentiality and encouraged students to keep things that are said in group for the group setting. We spent the majority of the session discussing the topic of trust and trustworthiness. Students understood that trust would need to be earned and that confidentiality could not be guaranteed.

In conclusion, ethical practice in counseling can seem quite complex. However, reflecting on Kitchener's five principles: autonomy, nonmaleficence, beneficence, justice, and fidelity, makes ethical practice seem much less complicated. I ask myself these questions when I think about my work with students. Am I acting in good will to help the client help himself or herself? Am I doing everything I can to avoid harm to the client? Am I promoting independence and sending the client the message that I believe in his or her power to make things better? And, am I behaving in a trustworthy manner to help and/ or protect the client to the best of my ability? At the end of the day, my goal is to answer "yes" to all these questions and to go above and beyond what is legally and ethically mandated.

Source: Julie C. Wentz, professional school counselor

Summary/Conclusion

If one were to survey practicing school counselors regarding the "hot issues" in counseling, the list would likely include eating disorders, HIV/AIDS, self-mutilation, autism and Asperger's syndrome, bullying, harassment, changing family structures, mobility, cultural diversity, sexual orientation, depression, loss and grief, students with special needs, emotional disturbance, gangs, and a host of other topics. So how does a counselor help the 13-year-old who believes he is gay? Or the 16-year-old who is starving herself to death? Or the incarcerated parent who wants the professional school counselor to read his letters to his children in school because the mother will not let him have any contact with his children? Here are some final words of wisdom to help guide you as a professional school counselor:

- Always document in writing what you did and why you did it.
- If you did not follow a policy, document why you did not (e.g., you did not call the parent in a suicide case because it was handled as an abuse case).

- Know federal, state, and local laws, regulations, policies, and guidelines.
- Consult with a colleague or supervisor when you have questions or doubts.
- Read and use resources.
- Consult with a lawyer when appropriate.

Professional school counselors must be prepared to deal with these issues and more every day of their professional lives. Many of these areas do not have clear laws, regulations, court cases, or policies to guide counselors toward legal and ethical behavior. Professional school counselors need to try to do what is in the best interest of their clients and to help their clients see what that is. They must advocate for their students because frequently they will be the only support that these students have. Professional school counselors must never stop believing and having faith that what they do makes a difference in the lives of children.

Activities

1. In small groups, discuss the ethical and legal considerations that would have to be taken into account in this case: Susan is a 17-year-old high school senior in your school. She has come to you describing her plan to commit suicide. She tells you, the professional school counselor, but explains that you cannot tell anybody because if her parents find out she will be abused. She wants to commit suicide because she recently found out that she is pregnant by her 25-year-old boyfriend.

2. Interview a professional school counselor who has received a subpoena and have him/her tell you the steps he/she followed.

3. After reviewing the ACA and ASCA ethical codes, break into small groups and list ethical "hot topics." Discuss the real-life implications of these issues in a school setting.

4. Provide a scenario to the class involving a suicidal student. In small groups, decide what to do given the situation. Give particular emphasis to ethical and legal procedures.

5. As a small group, create a realistic counseling scenario that involves a touchy ethical issue and decide how to handle the scenario incorporating the legal and ethical standards that professional school counselors must adhere to.

8

Culturally Competent School Counselors: Affirming Diversity by Challenging Oppression

Cheryl Holcomb-McCoy and Stuart F. Chen-Hayes

Editor's Introduction: The transformed professional school counselor is culturally competent, respectful of human diversity, and a school leader in ensuring that oppressive systemic barriers to academic, career, college readiness, and personal/social development are removed. To achieve this goal, professional school counselors must explore and know their own culture and biases and then open themselves to, and seek to understand, the cultures of the diverse populations they serve. This chapter includes a Professional School Counselor Multicultural Competence Checklist and multiple case studies to help your journey toward cultural competence and challenging multiple oppressions.

CASE STUDY 8.1

Janice is a middle-class, Jewish professional elementary school counselor in a wealthy suburban school district. In recent years, there has been a large influx of multilingual working-class Taiwanese students of indigenous ethnicity and Buddhist faith into her school. Because these students never self-refer for counseling and because she has never attended the local Buddhist temple or consulted with spiritual leaders of the local Taiwanese Buddhist community, Janice erroneously assumes they have no school or family concerns. In speaking with a Taiwanese teaching colleague, Fang-Ting, Janice realized she needs to take a different approach. Fang-Ting invited her to attend the Buddhist temple and meet members of the community. She offered to translate for Janice and Janice asked what she could do to better support the students, many of whom have parents working 14-hour shifts in local restaurants and factories. Janice has a subsequent meeting with members of the Buddhist temple, who agree to set up a series of career and college access workshops for parents and guardians on weekend mornings, and Janice volunteers to facilitate them with a translator. Although Janice originally thought they would want to focus on personal/social issues with parents working such long hours, the community was clear that they wanted to focus on career and college access in the United States, their primary reason for immigrating—ensuring a better life for the next generation.

CASE STUDY 8.2

John, a White, middle-class professional urban high school counselor, is puzzled as to why there is an achievement gap at his school with Native American, African-American, and Latino/a students, 90% of whom qualify for free and reduced lunch, who are overrepresented in special education classes, and who are accepted to college and universities at a significantly lower rate than White and Asian students are. He wonders what can be done to change the attainment gap that is evident because few of the school's poor and working-class Latino/a, African-American, and Native American students who are accepted into college subsequently graduate from college with diplomas. John creates an action plan using the *ASCA National Model* (2012) and decides to offer multiple school counseling core curriculum lessons on college aspirations, access, and readiness during the day and multiple parent/guardian workshops for parents and guardians of first-generation students of color. He also pushes to ensure much higher rates of participation in Advanced Placement (AP) and International Baccalaureate (IB) classes at his school by students of color who had been barred from classes due to low GPAs until his advocacy stopped that gate-keeping practice. At the end of the year, he was able to show his effectiveness through his results report and the increased percentages of first-generation college-going students of color applying to and being accepted by both 2- and 4-year colleges. He repeated his interventions over the next 6 years and was able to show a significant improvement in the number of students of color who graduated from college since he began his interventions.

CASE STUDY 8.3

Kay, an African-American professional middle school counselor in a rural school district, feels uncomfortable providing school counseling core curriculum lessons on personal–social and academic skills transitions to a class of students recently immigrated from Central America, all of whom qualify for free and reduced lunch. Kay cannot speak Spanish, and the only Spanish-speaking staff member is a custodian. Kay found Silvia, a bilingual middle school alumna of Guatemalan descent who needed a community service project in her high school and asked her to co-teach and translate for a series of academic and personal–social competencies school counseling core curriculum lessons at a Saturday school academy. The students were thrilled to have a role model who had "made it" in their eyes and pre- and posttest data indicated significant improvement in attendance and grades by students attending the Saturday academy lessons provided by Silvia. Qualitative data indicated the middle school students felt at ease with lessons translated in Spanish by Silvia, who motivated them to be successful due to her cultural familiarity with their immigration, language, family, and cultural situations.

CASE STUDY 8.4

Ricardo, an upper-class, Latino professional urban middle school counselor, avoids personal/social counseling with students whom he perceives as being lesbian, bisexual, gay, or transgendered because he fears they will "out him" as a gay Latino. One day, however, a star student athlete is found to have committed suicide at the school due to being teased about being gay by other students. Ricardo realizes that he has the skills to intervene and make sure that students have an out role model at school. Shaking with fear, he decided to come out at the memorial for the student. Rather than being ostracized, Ricardo found staff, students, and especially the family of the student who died embracing him and his courage. He worked with other school leaders to adopt the Family Acceptance Project's evidence-based model for suicide prevention with LGBT and questioning youth and families (www.familyproject.sfsu.edu) and developed a gay-straight alliance at school as key prevention tools.

The dilemmas faced by the professional school counselors in Case Studies 8.1–8.4 have become commonplace. This is due, in part, to the fact that never before has the U.S. population been as multiethnic, multicultural, and multilingual as it is today (Banks & Banks, 2010). For instance, in 2009 Latino/a students accounted for 22.1% of all public school students, up from 15.6% in 1999. During this same period, African-American student enrollment decreased slightly, from 17.2% to 16.8%, whereas White student enrollment fell sharply, from 62.1% to 54.1% (U.S. Department of Education, National Center for Educational Statistics., 2012). These figures are expected to change as the number of students of color enrolling in school increases each year, with the largest increases in student population among

Latino/as and Asian/Pacific Islanders. Although currently one of every eight residents of the United States is Latino, it is projected that Latinos could account for one of every five residents by 2035, one of every four by 2055, and one of every three by 2100 (Saenz, 2009).

Based on these rapidly changing demographic projections, the skills of affirming diversity and challenging oppression are key components of the professional school counselor's transformed role. In fact, knowledge and skill about multiculturalism as a key component of the school counseling profession is no longer viewed as desirable, but is mandatory. Professional school counselors, like other school professionals, are becoming more aware of the need to be knowledgeable about the manner in which students' diverse characteristics affect the learning process and, more important, how students are differentially affected in their schools based on ethnicity, race, language, disability status, social class, and other cultural identities.

In many school districts, professional school counselors are preparing themselves for their diverse clientele by taking courses in foreign languages, enrolling in extensive multicultural counseling training, and consulting with leaders from diverse communities. Professional school counselors are also beginning to play a major role in school reform initiatives and efforts to improve the academic achievement of historically oppressed students (e.g., The Education Trust). At the same time, it is unclear whether professional school counselors are effective in their work with students from diverse and/or oppressed backgrounds. Some research has even suggested that professional school counselors maintain the status quo in terms of educational outcomes for ethnic/racial minority students (Perna et al., 2008).

In response to the increasingly diverse caseloads of professional school counselors, the American School Counselor Association (ASCA, 2009) adopted the following position on cultural diversity: "Professional school counselors promote academic, career, and personal/social success for all students. Professional school counselors collaborate with stakeholders to create a school and community climate that embraces cultural diversity and helps to remove barriers that impede student success." In addition, in the 2010 revision of the ASCA's *Ethical Standards for School Counselors*, multicultural, diversity, and anti-oppression competencies were addressed in Section E.2, Multicultural and Social Justice Advocacy and Leadership:

Professional school counselors:

a. Monitor and expand personal multicultural and social justice advocacy awareness, knowledge, and skills. School counselors strive for exemplary cultural competence by ensuring personal beliefs or values are not imposed on students or other stakeholders.

b. Develop competencies in how prejudice, power and various forms of oppression, such as ableism, ageism, classism, familyism, genderism, heterosexism, immigrationism, linguicism, racism, religionism, and sexism, affect self, students and all stakeholders.

c. Acquire educational, consultation and training experiences to improve awareness, knowledge, skills, and effectiveness in working with diverse populations: ethnic/racial status, age, economic status, special needs, ESL or ELL, immigration status, sexual orientation, gender, gender identity/expression, family type, religious/spiritual identity, and appearance.

d. Affirm the multiple cultural and linguistic identities of every student and all stakeholders. Advocate for equitable school and school counseling program policies and practices for every student and all stakeholders, including use of translators and bilingual/multilingual school counseling program materials that represent all languages used by families in the school community, and advocate for appropriate accommodations and accessibility for students with disabilities.

e. Use inclusive and culturally responsible language in all forms of communication.

f. Provide regular workshops and written/digital information to families to increase understanding, collaborative two-way communication, and a welcoming school climate between families and the school to promote increased student achievement.

g. Work as advocates and leaders in the school to create equity-based school counseling programs that help close any achievement, opportunity, and attainment gaps that deny all students the chance to pursue their educational goals.

Considering the ethical and professional obligations of professional school counselors to be culturally competent, this chapter's main objectives are to (a) clarify the language and terminology used when discussing multicultural competence, affirming diversity, and challenging oppression; (b) discuss the need for culturally competent professional school counselors; (c) offer ways in which professional school counselors can integrate multiculturalism in their school counseling programs; (d) offer a checklist that can be used to assess professional school counselors' perceived multicultural competence; (e) provide case studies of actual professional school counselors challenging multiple oppressions through closing achievement and opportunity gaps; and (f) offer case studies that can be used to facilitate one's development of competence when working with students' multiple cultural identities and challenging oppression.

For clarification, the term *culturally diverse* is used throughout this chapter to denote distinctions in "the lived experiences and the related perceptions of and reactions to those experiences, that serve to differentiate collective populations from one another" (Marshall, 2002, p. 7). These distinctions are affected directly by the complex interactions of racial/ethnic classification, social status, historical and contemporary circumstances, and worldview. Racial/ethnic designations are used throughout the chapter when discussing cultural diversity, and other factors such as social class, gender, religion, sexual orientation, language, disability, and immigration status have been incorporated into various discussions. Racial/ethnic and social class identities have been highlighted throughout the chapter because of their historical correlations with the achievement, opportunity, and attainment gaps that persist among cultural groups in U.S. schools (Barton & Coley, 2009).

MULTICULTURAL AND ANTI-OPPRESSION TERMINOLOGY

Much of the frustration in understanding multiculturalism and anti-oppression theory is due to misuse of and confusion about the terminology. In a classic article, Johnson (1990) suggested that more time be devoted to clarifying multicultural terminology in counselor education graduate programs. In his study of counselor trainees' ability to make distinctions between the concepts of race and culture, he found that trainees offered definitions that were "badly confounded, containing vague and simplistic notions of culture and race" (p. 49). Culture, race, ethnicity, and various types of oppression are contrasted in this section.

The term *culture* has been defined in a variety of ways. Decades ago, Goodenough (1981) described culture as consisting of the following components: (a) the ways in which people perceive their experiences of the world so as to give it structure; (b) the beliefs by which people explain events; (c) a set of principles for dealing with people, as well as for accomplishing particular ends; and (d) people's value systems for establishing purposes and for keeping themselves purposefully oriented. More recently, and drawing from a more traditional perspective, Wehrly (1995, p. 4) described culture as "a dynamic construct that includes the values, beliefs, and behaviors of a people who have lived together in a particular geographic area for at least three or four generations." Culture has also been described narrowly, to include only an individual's ethnicity or nationality, and broadly, to include an individual's economic status, gender, religion, and other demographic variables. Banks and Banks (2010) defined culture as the way in which people interpret, use, and perceive artifacts, tools, or other tangible cultural elements. And Geertz (1983) suggested that members of a specific culture do not experience their culture as a humanly constructed system.

Instead, they experience culture as the way things are and the way things should be. This phenomenon is generally referred to as *ethnocentrism*. In other words, individuals within a cultural group tend to believe that their ideas about the world are simply "common sense."

Similar to *culture*, *race* is a term that has been defined in various ways. For many years, behavioral scientists used *race* to denote genotypically homogeneous human groupings (Kluckhohn, 1985). However, according to Baba and Darga (1981), the practice of racial classification by biological characteristics is practically impossible. Within psychology and counseling, researchers across subfields have studied race and ethnicity, generating a variety of distinct literatures that were well integrated. Empirical literature now demonstrates that race shapes individuals' psychological experiences. We now know from this research that racial identity can be an important predictor of attitudes, beliefs, motivation, and performance (Scottham & Smalls, 2009; Steele, 2007; Yip, Seaton, & Sellers, 2006). *Merriam-Webster's Collegiate Dictionary* (2012, p. 1024) defines *race* (or racial group) as a "family, tribe, people, or nation belonging to the same stock." Frankenberg (1999), in her book, *White Women, Race Matters: The Social Construction of Whiteness*, suggests that race is an indicator of difference but of what kind of difference is unknown. She goes on to argue that race does not identify differences in culture and that we cannot say conclusively that on the basis of skin color (i.e., race) that someone participates in particular cultural practices. Nevertheless, race remains a political and psychological concept that can shape the everyday life of individuals and more important, the power structures in the society in which one lives. Markus (2008) captured the construct of race as

> a dynamic set of historically derived and institutionalized ideas and practices that (1) sorts people into ethnic groups according to perceived physical and behavioral human characteristics; (2) associates differential value, power, and privilege with these characteristics and establishes a social status ranking among the different groups; and (3) emerges (a) when groups are perceived to each other's world view or way of life; and/or (b) to justify the denigration and exploitation (past, current or future) of, and prejudice toward, other groups. (p. 654)

It is critical for professional school counselors to remember that race has been and continues to be used in schools to carry out such practices as the stereotyping of groups by students' academic achievement; tracking; the identification of students for special education; and low teacher expectations for students of color, particularly students of color who are also poor, have disabilities, or are English language learners.

In contrast to race, *ethnicity* was defined by Terry and Irving (2010, p. 111) as group membership "based on genealogy, national origin, and ancestry. Ethnicity does not change, even though characteristics of a specific ethnic group's culture may change." It is within this ethnic identity that an individual is socialized to take on the group's values, beliefs, and behaviors.

Oppression, in contrast to other terms in this chapter, can be defined in an equation: **Oppression = prejudice × power**. Here, prejudice means maintaining incorrect conscious or unconscious attitudes, feelings, and beliefs to the effect that members of a cultural group are inferior or that a group's cultural differences are unacceptable (Arnold, Chen-Hayes, & Lewis, 2002). Power is the ability to control access to resources and includes control of, or over, the images of what is culturally appropriate. Power and power over are maintained and used on individual, cultural, and systemic levels (Israel, 2006).

Young (2011) further expanded the definition of oppression by delineating five conditions of an oppressed group: exploitation, marginalization, powerlessness, cultural imperialism, and violence. *Exploitation* refers to the steady transfer of the results of the labor of one social group to the benefit of another. *Marginalization* refers to the process by which individuals or groups of people are permanently confined to lives of social marginality because they are not attractive or not perceived as "acceptable" to people in the dominant culture. Young emphasizes that marginalization is particularly harmful because it means people are both expelled from participation in social life and subjected to material deprivation. *Powerlessness* is defined as having to take orders without having the right to give them. *Cultural imperialism* refers to the dominance of one group's experiences and culture and its establishment as the norm. Young claimed that cultural imperialism occurs when the experiences and perspectives of oppressed groups seem "invisible" to the dominant group. Paradoxically, the oppressed group is stereotyped and marked out as the "other." *Violence* is a manifestation of oppression because of the social context, which makes violence possible and, in some cases, acceptable. Violence is systemic because it is often directed at members of oppressed groups simply because they are members of that group.

Other forms of oppression include individual, cultural, systemic, internalized, and externalized oppression. *Individual oppression* is behavior based on conscious or unconscious negative assumptions about people who are culturally or racially different. Examples are telling jokes, staring at someone "different," and targeting a person for a crime solely because of his or her skin color. *Cultural oppression* occurs when the standards of appropriate actions, thought, and expression of a particular group are seen as negative (overtly or covertly). As a result, a member of the oppressed group must change his or her behavior to be accepted by the dominant group. An example of cultural oppression is the recognition of heterosexuality as the only sexual orientation in a school's curriculum. *Systemic/institutional oppression* includes unequal power relationships in institutions that result in the inequitable distribution of resources. It can include inflexible policies and procedures unresponsive to cultural differences. Systemic oppression can involve the use of power to limit others based on their race, cultural background, or both. Examples include women and ethnic minorities being paid less for work comparable to that of White men (Feagin, 2006). *Internalized oppression* is characterized by an individual believing the stereotypes about his or her group and then acting accordingly (Chen-Hayes, 2009). *Externalized oppression*, on the other hand, occurs when an individual targets members of nondominant groups for oppression, violence, coercion, and control based on a belief (conscious or not) that members of the nondominant group are inferior or otherwise deserving of control, coercion, or violence. Table 8.1 defines eleven oppressions named in the *ASCA Ethical Standards for School Counselors* (ASCA, 2010).

School counselors can find evidence of oppression in K–12 school data. School data (e.g., achievement scores, grades) can illustrate groups of students that are achieving and those that are not. Likewise, data can indicate inequities among groups of students regarding college application rates, graduation rates, dropout rates, suspension rates, attendance rates, percentages of students in special education, and percentages of students identified as gifted/talented. These are examples of achievement, opportunity, and attainment gaps. *Achievement gaps* are the differences in academic performance among groups of K–12 students based on ethnicity/race, gender, social class, disability status, language status, and other variables. *Opportunity gaps* are the differences in resources given to K–12 students in terms of quality of instruction, college preparatory curriculum, quality of teachers, access to a school counseling program with specific indicators of skill development, access to career and college development skills and counseling, and other opportunities that differentiate who is able to graduate from college and obtain a satisfying, well-paying career. *Attainment gaps* are the differences among groups who attain a college diploma based on data disaggregated by ethnicity/race, gender, social class, disability, and language identities, among others. As school counselors monitor data (Chen-Hayes, 2009; Dimmit,

---

TABLE 8.1 Eleven Forms of Oppression in K–12 Schools

Ableism: Prejudice multiplied by power used by persons without disabilities toward persons with disabilities (developmental, emotional, intellectual, physical) that limits access to individual, cultural, and systemic resources

Ageism: Prejudice multiplied by power used by persons aged 18–49 years that limits children, adolescents, and adults 50+ access to individual, cultural, and systemic resources

Beautyism: Prejudice multiplied by power used by persons with dominant appearances that limits persons who are obese or with other nondominant appearances access to individual, cultural, and systemic resources

Classism: Prejudice multiplied by power used by wealthy and upper-middle-class persons that limits poor, working, and lower-middle-class persons access to individual, cultural, and systemic resources

Familyism: Prejudice multiplied by power used by persons in traditional families that limits single persons, single parents, same-gender parents, same-gender couples, divorced persons, cohabiting couples, homeless families, and adoptive/foster families access to individual, cultural, and systemic resources

Genderism: Prejudice multiplied by power used by traditionally gendered persons that limits transgender and gender-variant persons access to individual, cultural, and systemic resources

Heterosexism: Prejudice multiplied by power used by heterosexuals that limits lesbian, bisexual, and gay persons access to individual, cultural, and systemic resources

Linguicism: Prejudice multiplied by power used by dominant language speakers that limits nondominant language speakers or those who speak with an accent or dialect access to individual, cultural, and systemic resources

Racism: Prejudice multiplied by power used by dominant racial group members (Whites in the United States) that limits nondominant racial group members (people of color and mixed-race persons in the United States) access to individual, cultural, and systemic resources

Religionism: Prejudice multiplied by power used by dominant religious group members (Christians in the United States) that limits nondominant religious, spiritual, or nonreligious group members (Jews, Muslims, Hindus, Jains, Buddhists, Pagans, atheists, agnostics) access to individual, cultural, and systemic resources

Sexism: Prejudice multiplied by power used by men and boys that limits access by women and girls to individual, cultural, and systemic resources

Source: Adapted from Chen-Hayes, 2009

Carey, & Hatch, 2007; Holcomb-McCoy, 2007a), they can formulate action plans, create interventions, and gather results of their effectiveness in challenging the oppression manifested in achievement, opportunity, and attainment gaps.

Multicultural and Social Justice Counseling

The multicultural counseling movement has maintained its significance and momentum in the field of counseling (Ponterotto, Casas, Suzuki, & Alexander, 2010). And more recently, there have been more references to the notion of a multicultural–social justice counseling movement in the literature (Hook & Davis, 2012). Even with the energy around multicultural counseling and social justice, there is still no consistent definition of multicultural counseling. Over 20 years ago, Locke (1990) referred to multicultural counseling as a counseling relationship in which the counselor and client differ as a result of socialization in unique cultural or racial or ethnic environments. However, Vontress (1988) noted, "[I]f the counselor and client perceive mutual cultural similarity, even though in reality they are culturally different, the interaction should not be labeled cross-cultural counseling" (p. 75). It has also been debated whether or not to narrowly define multicultural counseling as a relationship

between two or more ethnically or racially diverse individuals. According to Arredondo and D'Andrea (1995), the definition of multicultural counseling provided by the Association for Multicultural Counseling and Development (AMCD) relates to "five major cultural groups in the United States and its territories: African/Black, Asian, Caucasian/European, Hispanic/Latino, and Native American or indigenous groups which have historically resided in the continental United States and its territories" (p. 28).

Other counseling professionals and professional organizations, including the Council for Accreditation of Counseling and Related Educational Programs (CACREP, 2009), view multicultural counseling from a universal perspective and include characteristics of not only race and ethnicity, but also gender, lifestyle, religion, sexual orientation, and so on. CACREP's definition further emphasizes the implication of a pluralistic philosophy. The term *pluralistic* in the accreditation procedures manual and application is used to "describe a condition of society in which numerous distinct ethnic, racial, religious, and social groups coexist and cooperatively work toward interdependence needed for the enhancement of each group" (CACREP, 2009, p. 61).

More recently, the terms *social justice counseling* and *social justice perspective* have been used in the literature instead of multicultural counseling (D'Andrea & Heckman, 2008). Social justice counseling, according to Crethar, Rivera, and Nash (2008), addresses issues related to both individual and distributive justice. They also suggested that social justice counseling involves the promotion of equity, access, participation, and harmony. Holcomb-McCoy (2007a) argued that professional school counselors should shift to more of a social justice perspective to challenge the achievement inequities found in many schools. She suggested that professional school counselors are in the perfect position to advocate for social justice and challenge systemic social injustices (e.g., overrepresentation of African-American students in special education, underrepresentation of Latino and African-American students in gifted and honors courses). Her social justice framework for school counselors includes six components: (a) counseling and planning interventions (e.g., empowerment-based counseling), (b) consulting (e.g., parent and teacher consultation), (c) connecting schools, families, and communities, (d) collecting and using data to identify inequities, (e) challenging bias, and (f) coordinating student services to support and emphasize rigor and academic success for all students. According to Holcomb-McCoy, a school counselor is able to work from a social justice perspective if each of these six areas is emphasized in a counseling program.

Multicultural Competence

Perhaps one of the greatest challenges confronting the multicultural counseling movement is determining how to operationalize multicultural counseling competence. Since the 1970s, a growing body of literature has addressed the need for multicultural competence in counseling and in the training of future counselors (Ancis & Rasheed, 2005; Collins & Pieterse, 2007). Multicultural theorists have defined cultural competence as a specific area of competence that includes (a) cultural awareness and beliefs, (b) cultural knowledge, and (c) cultural skills. Cultural competence is achieved when a counselor possesses the necessary skills to work effectively with clients from various cultural backgrounds. Hence, a counselor with a high level of multicultural counseling competence acknowledges client–counselor cultural differences and similarities as significant to the counseling process. On the other hand, a counselor with a low level of multicultural competence provides counseling services with little or no regard for the counselor's or client's ethnicity or race.

Over the past four decades, the literature related to the impact of cultural/racial/ethnic factors on the counseling process has grown (Ivey, D'Andrea, Ivey, & Simek-Morgan, 2007). And research has provided evidence that multicultural counseling training is associated with greater self-perceived multicultural competence (Castillo, Brossart,

Reyes, Conoley, & Phoummarath, 2007), including greater cultural self-awareness and increased cultural knowledge and skills (Manese, Wu, & Nepomuceno, 2001). Nevertheless, most of these studies are limited by their lack of a comparison group, which is important for controlling for potential extraneous variables that may influence growth in multicultural competence.

To highlight the importance of becoming a culturally competent professional counselor, the American Counseling Association (ACA) formally endorsed the Multicultural Counseling Competencies (Sue, Arredondo, & McDavis, 1992), and the 2009 CACREP accreditation standards refer specifically to social justice and multiculturalism in counseling. The standards require programs to include studies that address "theories of multicultural counseling, identity development, and social justice" (p. 11). Similarly, the American Psychological Association Accreditation Guidelines mandate that students "acquire and demonstrate substantial understanding and competence with regard to issues of cultural and individual diversity" (p. 11). Social justice is not referred to in the APA guidelines for accreditation. Also, the 2005 *ACA Code of Ethics* refers to multicultural counseling competence concepts (Pack-Brown, Thomas, & Seymour, 2008).

In addition to the three-dimensional framework of self-perceived multicultural competence (i.e., attitudes, skills, and knowledge), other perspectives regarding self-perceived multicultural competence have been offered. Holcomb-McCoy and Myers (1999) suggested that there could be more than three dimensions to multicultural counseling competence. They proposed that one must know multicultural terminology and racial identity–development theories. More recently, Whaley and Davis (2007) defined multicultural competence as "a set of problem solving skills" (p. 565). Sue and Torino (2005) suggested that counselors demonstrate multicultural competence by striving for adherence to the Multicultural Counseling Competencies endorsed by the American Counseling Association.

Because there has been debate in the literature suggesting that many studies reflect counselors' perceived multicultural competence rather than actual multicultural competence demonstrated in counseling sessions, some scholars have used different methods of measuring multicultural competence. Several studies have used counselor responses to multicultural cases, and others have utilized observer ratings of counselors. In one study, Constantine (2001) found that previous multicultural training predicted higher client ratings of counselors' multicultural counseling competence. And more recently, Spanierman, Poteat, Wang, and Oh (2008) found that affective responses to racism, specifically White counselors' affective and emotional responses to racism, greatly influenced demonstrated and perceived multicultural counseling competence.

Sue (1998) offered a more scientific approach to cultural competence. He suggested that cultural competence consists of three characteristics: being scientifically minded, having skills in dynamic sizing, and being proficient with a particular cultural group. *Being scientifically minded* stresses the counselor's ability to form hypotheses, rather than reaching premature conclusions about the status of culturally different clients. The second characteristic, *having skills in dynamic sizing*, reinforces the importance of the counselor's skill in knowing "when to generalize, when to individualize, and finally when to be exclusive" (p. 446). The counselor's ability to use dynamic sizing decreases his or her tendency to use stereotypes, while still embracing the client's culture. In other words, the use of dynamic sizing is one's ability to appropriately categorize experiences and behaviors. Third, the characteristics of *being proficient with a particular cultural group* include the counselor's expertise or knowledge of the cultural groups with which he or she works, sociopolitical influences, and specific skills needed to work with culturally different clients.

THE NEED FOR CULTURALLY COMPETENT SCHOOL COUNSELORS

As stated previously, professional school counselors are faced with the challenge of providing services that enhance the academic, career, and personal/social development of all students, regardless of their cultural background. One of their major challenges, however, is the need to create developmental school counseling programs that help to close attainment, achievement, opportunity, and funding gaps among groups of students in K–12 schools. These gaps exist not only in terms of standardized test scores, but also in areas such as Advanced Placement (AP) and International Baccalaureate (IB) course participation and test taking, high school graduation rates, college entrance and graduation rates, and earned income. For instance, scores on the 2009 version of the National Assessment of Educational Progress (NAEP; U.S. Department of Education, 2012) revealed the continued achievement gaps between African-American and Latino/a students and their White peers. Scores on the reading portion of the test at the fourth-grade level showed that 75% of White students scored at the basic level or above, whereas only 44% of Latino/a students and only 40% of African-American students did so.

The achievement, attainment, funding, and opportunity gaps are demonstrated in other ways as well. For instance, the Education Trust (2013) reported that African-American and Latino/a students were underrepresented on several different measures of academic and career/college achievement. For instance, the College Board (2012a) reported that underserved students of color and

low-income students remain underrepresented in AP classrooms. And, there are gaps in the percentages of students who receive a score of "3" or better. Sixty-three percent of White test takers scored 3.0 or better compared with 47% of Latino/a test takers. And, only 29% of Black test takers scored "3" or better on AP exams. And, high school graduation and dropout rates continue to be a significant national problem. Although more high school students are graduating on time, dropout rates continue to increase for some groups. The national graduation rate increased to 75.5% in 2009, up from 72% in 2001. And the number of "drop-out" factories—high schools where at least 60 percent of students do not graduate on time—fell from 2,007 in 2002 to 1,550 in 2010. Graduation rates, however, vary by race, with 91.8% of Asian students, 82% of Whites, 65.9% of Latinos, and 63.5% of Blacks graduating on time (Balfanz, Bridgeland, Bruce, & Fox, 2012). Discussions regarding professional school counselors' role in addressing these inequities and disparities in equitable access to rigorous courses, student achievement, and graduation rates are relatively new in the school counseling literature. The Education Trust's Transforming School Counseling Initiative (TSCI) sparked a dialogue among school counseling professionals regarding how professional school counselors can assist in closing the gaps between student groups (Education Trust, 2013).

INTEGRATING MULTICULTURAL AND ANTI-OPPRESSION TOPICS IN SCHOOL COUNSELING PROGRAMS

Professional school counselors can play a pivotal role in combating oppression and assisting culturally diverse students in achieving success in academics; in career and college attainment; and in personal, social, and cultural skills. To begin, however, professional school counselors must recognize that traditional school counseling is embedded in White or European culture and that this limits its cross-cultural utility. Professional school counselors typically lack the specific training necessary to address the problems and effects of oppression and multiple cultural identities because most counselor education programs do not offer consistent training (e.g., coursework, field experiences) in anti-oppression work and cultural history and in the related awareness, knowledge, and skills needed to work effectively with multiple cultural groups and identities.

To effectively assist students of historically oppressed backgrounds, professional school counselors must engage in interventions that create social environments for students that support social justice. The concept of social justice is central to the practice of multicultural school counseling. Social justice refers to equity, equality, and fairness in the

THE CRITICAL NEED FOR MULTICULTURALLY COMPETENT SCHOOL COUNSELORS

There is a real need for culturally competent counselors because, regardless of the school setting, a counselor will have a student population that is diverse. At the same time, there tends to be more White, middle-income, and female counselors. If these counselors are not culturally competent, then they tend to "check out" on students because they don't know what to do or how to work with students. As a result, counselors are frustrated and rely on biases and faulty assumptions about students. Their biases and worldviews get in the way of meeting the needs of all students. And students "check out" on counselors because they realize that counselors do not understand them, and then students don't see counselors as a viable resource.

Source: Dr. Julia Bryan, Counselor Educator, Pennsylvania State University

distribution of societal resources (Holcomb-McCoy, 2007a). Social justice includes a focus on the structures and outcomes of social processes and how they contribute to equality. The professional school counselor's role is to develop practices that contribute to social justice. For instance, professional school counselors might reach out to community members and organizations to develop school counseling services that are closely aligned with the community's goals for its students and families. More important, professional school counselors should be involved in community organizing that mobilizes people to combat common community problems and increases community members' voices in schools. For example, a professional school counselor, as an advocate for improved housing for low-income parents in her school, might attend city council meetings with local community members and lobby for a new housing policy.

There is a limited amount of literature on strategies and interventions specifically designed for culturally diverse students. However, this section will include an overview of how multicultural topics and/or diversity topics can be integrated into existing school counseling programs. To begin, empowerment-focused interventions will be described. These have been suggested in the literature as a means of promoting the well-being of culturally diverse persons. Next, discussions of how multicultural topics may be integrated into typical professional school counselor delivery modes and functions (e.g., individual counseling, group counseling, assessment, consultation, and data collection and sharing) will be offered.

Empowerment-Focused Interventions

Empowerment is a construct shared by many disciplines (e.g., community development, psychology, economics). How empowerment is understood or defined varies among these perspectives. Rappaport (1987) noted that it is easy to define empowerment by its absence, but difficult to define in action, as it takes on different forms in different people and contexts. As a general definition, empowerment is a process of increasing personal, interpersonal, or political power so that individuals, families, and communities can take action to improve their situations. It is a process that fosters power (i.e., the capacity to implement) in disenfranchised and powerless groups of people, for use in their own lives, their communities, and their society, by acting on issues that they define as important. Interestingly, the word *empowerment* can be disempowering when it is understood to mean the giving of power by the powerful to the powerless. Therefore, the appropriate role of the professional school counselor is to help students and parents build their own power base.

Empowerment is multidimensional, social, and a process. It is multidimensional in that it occurs within sociological, psychological, and economic dimensions. Empowerment also occurs at various levels, such as individual, group, and community. Empowerment, by definition, is a social process, as it occurs in relationship to others. It is a process that is similar to a path or journey, one that develops as we work through it. One important implication of this definition of empowerment is that the individual and community are fundamentally connected.

Although the literature on empowerment theory describes empowerment as a method that can incorporate multiple levels of intervention, most of the current work has focused on individual or interpersonal empowerment. The literature has discussed methods and strategies for moving individuals to a point where they feel a sense of personal power. One such strategy is the development of critical consciousness (Zimmerman, 2000). *Critical consciousness* has been described as involving three psychological processes: (a) *group identification*, which includes identifying areas of common experiences and concern with a particular group;

(b) *group consciousness*, which involves understanding the differential status of power of groups in society; and (c) *self- and collective efficacy*, which is described as perceiving one's self as a subject (rather than an object) of social processes and as capable of working to change the social order. For individuals to understand that their problems stem from a lack of power, they must first comprehend their group's status in society, as well as the overall structure of power in society. At the individual level, professional school counselors can help students feel empowered by facilitating discussions about their group identifications and helping them to understand how their group membership has affected their life circumstances. Students can empower themselves by taking responsibility for their own learning, by increasing their understanding of the communities in which they live, and by understanding how they as individuals are affected by current and potential policies and structures. Equipped with this greater understanding and with new confidence in themselves, students can develop new behavior patterns and perspectives.

An empowerment approach to working with students requires that professional school counselors provide students with the knowledge and skills needed to think critically about their problems and to develop strategies to act on and solve problems (Lee, 2001). Professional school counselors and students must work collaboratively to help students take charge of their lives. For instance, professional school counselors might help facilitate the problem solving and decision making of students by building on their strengths. Rather than counselor-assumed student problems, the focus should be on problems identified by the students. The problem-solving process can include problem identification, the selection of one problem, the choosing of a goal to solve or minimize the problem, the identification of available resources to assist in goal attainment, and the generation of activities to achieve the goal.

Individual Counseling

Individual counseling theories and techniques tend to be based on traditional, Eurocentric theories that are often inappropriate for students of diverse cultural backgrounds. According to D'Andrea and Daniels (1995), one of the most serious problems in school counseling is that "most counseling theories and interventions, which are commonly used in school settings, have not been tested among students from diverse student populations" (p. 143). Very few counseling approaches have been specifically designed and validated for use with specific cultural groups. For this reason, professional school counselors should seek and develop individual counseling strategies that are effective with culturally diverse students.

Professional school counselors should also be aware of the pervasive influence that culture has on the counseling process (Holcomb-McCoy, 2007a). In the school setting, counselors should be aware of the impact of culture on students' ways of thinking, belief systems, definitions of self, decision making, verbal and nonverbal behavior, and time orientation. For instance, some non-Westernized cultures place more emphasis on "being" than on "doing." In the Native American and Asian cultures, self is not seen as an entity separate from the group or from nature. In addition, African Americans and other nonmainstream Western cultures see family as an extended unit that does not necessarily limit itself to "blood" relatives. These varied cultural beliefs and practices can be significant in the individual counseling process and have profound effects on the behavior of children and adolescents. Perusse and Goodnough (2004) contributed an edited text full of individual counseling suggestions using a transformative approach across multiple domains (academic, career, and personal/social) and cultural groups.

Group Counseling

When implementing groups in schools, multiculturally competent school counselors must facilitate the cultural development of group members. This can be done by understanding and acknowledging the reality that students are socialized within a society in which some groups have a history of suffering stereotypes, prejudice, oppression, and discrimination. When forming groups, professional school counselors should consider how students from differing cultural backgrounds will relate to each other and to the group leader. Professional school counselors should be familiar with the literature on selecting and planning for culturally diverse groups (e.g., Anderson, 2007; Asner-Self & Feyissa, 2002). For instance, when reviewing the strengths of same-gender and same-race groups, Brown and Mistry (1994) noted that these groups have advantages when the group task is associated with issues of personal identity, social oppression, and empowerment.

Professional school counselors who lead groups must remember that students bring diverse patterns of behavior, values, and language to groups. Students might bring experiences of oppression and particular feelings about themselves, their group identity, and the larger society to the group. When problems of dissatisfaction or conflict among group members occur, the professional school counselor should remember that the issues may be caused by cultural differences, not by an individual member's personal characteristics or flaws in the group process. Perusse and Goodnough's (2004) edited text on leadership

VOICES FROM THE FIELD 8.2	KEEP FOCUSED ON THE GOAL

When it comes to working with parents in schools, culture plays a major role, and a counselor cannot assume that strategies that work with one set of parents will work for another. The important idea to keep in mind is that all families, regardless of race, culture, or socioeconomic status, want their children to succeed.

Source: Ileana Gonzalez, Professional School Counselor, Broward County, Florida

and advocacy in school counseling contains multiple ideas for group counseling, including culturally competent small- and large-group outlines in academic, career, and personal/social development.

Consultation

Despite the attention focused on multicultural counseling, less emphasis has been placed on the significance of culture in the consultation process. Consulting is a significant responsibility for professional school counselors (Ramirez & Smith, 2007). Given the vast amount of time professional school counselors spend consulting with parents, teachers, and administrators of diverse backgrounds, a discussion of the multicultural competence of school-based consultants is warranted. Professional school counselors acting in the role of consultant should be sensitive to the cultural differences among the three parties in the consultation process: consultant, consultee, and client. Professional school counselors who consult with culturally different teachers and parents should ensure that such teachers or parents understand that their input is welcomed and in many cases is necessary for the success of the intervention. It is just as important, however, to consider the cultural differences of the client. Although the consultation process involves indirect contact with the client, the consultant should not forget that the client is the focus of the consultee's problem; therefore, the culture of the client will have an impact on the change process.

School-based consultants should also focus on conceptualizing the problem or concern of the consultee (e.g., parent, teacher) within a cultural context. Assessing the influence of culture on the consultee's and client's perception of the problem and interpersonal interactions is critical to the consultation process. For instance, a Taiwanese student who is overly concerned about involving her parents in her college choice should not be considered immature by a teacher because of his or her own cultural beliefs. Because the Taiwanese culture emphasizes parental respect, the consultant must ensure that the student is not penalized for behaving in a culturally appropriate manner.

School-based consultants should be able to identify and challenge a consultee's stereotypical beliefs and biases because, ultimately, these faulty perceptions can affect the consultation outcomes. Prejudicial attitudes within the consultation process may be manifested in outright rejection or the provision of inadequate interventions. Clearly, school-based consultants need to be vigilant to detect and deal with negative racial attitudes, negative cultural attitudes, or both (Rogers, 2000). By identifying the consultee's biased and prejudicial statements or assumptions, the school-based consultant is more apt to be able to eliminate negative cultural attitudes that might possibly affect the consultee's or client's problem. Oftentimes, for example, teachers will consult with a professional school counselor but fail to recognize their own biased beliefs that are directly or indirectly creating a problem for a student.

Assessment

Given the prevalence of standardized achievement and aptitude tests in today's schools, it is imperative that professional school counselors understand the cultural appropriateness of assessment instruments used frequently in schools (Rhodes, Ochoa, & Ortiz, 2005). The assessment of students from diverse backgrounds is complex and needs to be performed with professional care and consideration. Professional school counselors should be able to evaluate instruments for cultural bias and identify other methods for assessing culturally diverse students. In addition, professional school counselors should be competent in relaying assessment results to culturally diverse students and parents. It is important to remember, however, that there is not one instrument that is totally unbiased. Therefore, professional school counselors should know that their judgments in assessing the cultural appropriateness of an instrument and providing unbiased interpretations are key in the process of culturally sensitive assessment. Biased interpretations, for instance, of a student's test results can lead to inappropriate decisions regarding a student's needs. Professional school counselors must always be cognizant of the presence of unjust assessment practices, which lead to tracking students of color and poor students in low-performing classes, excluding racially or culturally diverse students from gifted and talented programs, and disproportionately identifying students of color for special education services.

Finally, professional school counselors should be aware of the testing options for English language learners. Generally, the options for these students are to have a test translated, use an interpreter for the test, use a test that is norm referenced in their first language, or use a bilingual test administrator. Professional school counselors must challenge linguicism (Chen-Hayes, Chen, & Athar, 2000) and ensure that bilingual students receive a fair and appropriate testing environment, as well as an opportunity to present a fair representation of their skills, abilities, and aptitudes.

School Counseling Core Curriculum Lessons

School counseling core curriculum lessons (ASCA, 2012) are used to relay information or to instruct a large group of students in the classroom. These lessons are an effective way for professional school counselors to address cultural sensitivity and issues pertaining to race, gender, sexual orientation, disabilities, or any diversity-related issue. Perusse and Goodnough (2004) included multiple school counseling curriculum lessons on culturally diverse aspects of academic, career, and personal/social development, looking at multiple oppressions including ableism (Coker, 2004), racism (Bailey & Bradbury-Bailey, 2004), sexism (Stone, 2004), heterosexism (Smith & Chen-Hayes, 2004), and multiple oppressions (Jackson & Grant, 2004) as they affect K–12 students.

Professional school counselors can help students become more culturally sensitive by implementing school counseling core curriculum lessons focused on affirming differences, using accurate multicultural terminology, exploring one's biases, learning about ethnic/racial identity–development models, understanding diverse worldviews, and challenging the various oppressions. In addition to the aforementioned resources, sample classroom school counseling core curriculum lessons might include the following activities related to multicultural issues:

1. Students are given case studies of students dealing with racism, classism, heterosexism, ableism, linguicism, sexism, multiple oppressions, and so forth. They are then asked to discuss the feelings of the students featured in the case studies and ways to solve problems dealing with oppressive behavior—and particularly solutions for challenging systemic barriers that keep certain groups of students from achieving access and success.
2. Students are asked to define *stereotype* and then brainstorm stereotypes that students have or have heard about different groups of people. They then discuss the dangers of stereotypes and where students can go to find accurate information about persons of diverse cultural identities.
3. Students are asked to interview a classmate or classmate's family members about their experiences with prejudice, power, and various forms of oppression. This activity is followed by a large-group discussion of themes that have emerged and the similarities and differences with various oppressions.
4. Students invite diverse persons from the community to discuss their personal ethnic/racial/cultural histories. This activity can be done in a large auditorium with 60 to 65 students. Students should have prepared questions for the panelists about how they have dealt with prejudiced people, racism, and oppression.
5. Students read *A People's History of the United States* (Zinn, 2003), or excerpts from it, and then do a family history explaining how their ancestors, as well as current members, have been subject to, or have subjected others to, oppression based on ethnicity, race, gender, social class, language, immigration status, disability, and other identities.

School Counseling Program Coordination

Professional school counselors provide a variety of services directly and indirectly to students, parents, and teachers. At the same time, professional school counselors are responsible for coordinating school counseling program activities and services that involve individuals and programs outside the school. Professional school counselors' coordinating activities may range from coordinating a peer-mediation program to coordinating family counseling services. Multicultural aspects of coordination include being sensitive to the diverse needs of those persons inside the school and in the community. Professional school counselors should coordinate schoolwide programs relevant to the needs of all students, particularly those from culturally diverse backgrounds. Schoolwide programs that develop the skills needed to affirm all cultures and to handle conflict resolution promote respect for various worldviews.

Also, professional school counselors should take the time to meet and develop relationships with referral sources that are representative of their school's communities. Professional school counselors should be familiar with services offered both in ethnic/racial communities and in the larger community. For instance, a professional school counselor in a community with a large percentage of Muslim students should contact and begin a working relationship with local mosques. Or a professional school counselor seeing out lesbian, bisexual, gay, transgendered, and questioning students should contact and assess the services and/or curricula provided by national organizations with local chapters that specialize in working affirmatively with gay and lesbian youth and their families (Ryan & Chen-Hayes, in press), such as Parents and Friends of Lesbians and Gays (PFLAG; www.pflag.org), the Gay, Lesbian, Straight Education Network (GLSEN; www.glsen.org), the Family Acceptance Project (www.familyproject.sfsu.edu), TransFamilyAllies (www.transfamily.org), or the Welcoming Schools Project (www.welcomingschools.org) from the Human Rights Campaign.

Data Collection and Sharing

Collecting and analyzing meaningful data about the characteristics and academic performance of students and about school organization and management helps highly diverse schools "identify achievement gaps, address equity issues, determine the effectiveness of specific programs and courses of study, and target instructional improvement" (Lachat, 2002, p. 3). Data are collected, analyzed, and interpreted to make school counseling program improvements, as well as total school improvements. The use of data to effect change within the school system is integral to ensuring that every student receives the benefits of the school counseling program. To create a data-driven school counseling program, professional school counselors must work with administrators, faculty, and advisory council members to analyze data to create a current picture of students and the school environment. This picture focuses discussion and planning around students' needs and the professional school counselor's role in addressing those needs. Professional school counselors should be proficient in the collection, analysis, and interpretation of student achievement and related data. Professional school counselors monitor student progress through four types of data: (a) achievement data, (b) attainment data, (c) school culture data, and (d) standards- and competency-related data. The ASCA Code of Ethics (2010) and the *ASCA National Model* (2012) also recommend that school counselors focus on opportunity gap data.

Student achievement data measure students' academic progress and include grade point averages, standardized test scores, academic standards–based test scores, and SAT/ACT scores. Attainment data measure those factors that the literature has shown to be correlated to academic achievement and include these data fields: gifted and talented patterns, transition patterns, special education identification, promotion and retention rates, course enrollment patterns, and graduation rates. School culture data include data regarding attendance, suspensions and expulsions, faculty-to-student relationships, school climate, student attitudes, and dropout rates. Standards- and competency-related data measure student mastery of the academic, career, and personal/social competencies delineated in the *ASCA National Model* (2012) and can include the percentage of students who have a 4-year plan on file, the percentage of students who have participated in job shadowing, the percentage of students who have set and attained academic goals, and the percentage of students who have applied conflict resolution skills.

Professional school counselors who strive to be culturally competent disaggregate data by variables to see if there are any groups of students who may not be doing as well as others. These data often shed light on issues of equity and focus the discussion on the needs of specific groups of students. Although there are many variables by which data may be separated, the common fields include gender, ethnicity/race, socioeconomic status, home language, disability, attendance, grade level, and teacher(s). To determine whether specific programs are not working for certain students—underachieving students, students with excessive absenteeism, and dropouts—data can be disaggregated by the courses taken or even by the teachers who taught them to identify and consider relevant school influences. The performance of students with similar personal characteristics can be disaggregated to determine which courses and instructional strategies are most effective with them. Differences between student grades and scores on standardized tests can be reviewed to determine whether there are lags in course content or poor preparation for some types of tests (Lachat, 2002; see Theory into Practice 8.1).

THEORY INTO PRACTICE 8.1

SOCIAL JUSTICE: USING DATA TO ADDRESS REFERRAL INEQUITIES

A professional middle school counselor in a rural district in Arizona becomes increasingly disturbed by the number of teacher referrals she has received regarding the behavior and/or social/personal concerns of Native American students. She decides to collect and analyze her counseling referrals by the race of the student. The data confirm her suspicion that more Native American than White students have been referred to her. Next, she decides to analyze the

(Continued)

data by the referring teacher. Her results indicate that there are four teachers that repeatedly refer Native American students for counseling. After discussing the data with her administrator, they decide to review and analyze school achievement and attainment data by race. They find that Native American students have lower achievement scores in all academic areas. The school counselor and administrator decide to present the data to the school. The administrator meets individually with the four teachers who disproportionately refer Native American students for counseling. The administrator shares the data with each of the four teachers, and they discuss ways that these teachers can take a more proactive and strengths-based approach with Native American students.

VOICES FROM THE FIELD 8.3	PROFESSIONAL SCHOOL COUNSELORS CHALLENGING OPPRESSION IN K–12 SCHOOLS

In this section, case studies of professional school counselors who have used the previously discussed strategies for becoming culturally competent are highlighted.

CASE STUDY 8.5

Having learned about the Transforming School Counseling Initiative and the importance of professional school counselors focusing on academic success for all students, James Martinez, a bilingual, Puerto Rican professional middle school counselor, asked his assistant principal for data measuring the results of academic services for students who were failing three or more classes. James was overwhelmed with the response. The assistant principal not only gave him the data on students' failing grades, but also wanted to give him more data on other issues. Based on the data, James developed a program to monitor the performance progress of students who were failing and advocated for equitable academic services to support the diverse learning needs of boys of color. When the superintendent and the school board asked school counselors what their role was in the schools he sent his newly created brochure on school counseling programs and services offered at Peekskill, New York, Middle School to the administrators, along with handouts on transformative school counseling programs and a summary of his data collection used to challenge academic inequities. James Martinez is now principal at Fox Run Elementary School, Norwalk, Connecticut.

CASE STUDY 8.6

Winnie Crespo-Batu, a Puerto Rican, bilingual/bicultural professional school counselor in the Bronx, was concerned about the academic success of the Puerto Rican and Dominican students at the school where she performed her internship and worked as a bilingual teacher. She realized that systemic linguicism was occurring. Winnie found that Puerto Rican students were often transferred into English as a second language (ESL) classrooms simply because they possessed Latino/a surnames and without any screening of their language abilities. After months of advocating for a change in the policy of ESL inclusion, Winnie convinced the principal to place students on the basis of their language skills, rather than simply sorting them by surnames. Students, parents, administrators, and staff all benefited from her challenging linguicism.

CASE STUDY 8.7

When Caribbean-American Theresa Wyre was a Bronx high school counselor, she tired of the focus on "at-risk" students who were failing, as opposed to her preferred focus on "at-promise" students and building on their strengths and potential for academic, career, and college success. As she collected data on academic success at her school, she challenged her students and her teaching colleagues to strive for high expectations and high achievement. She created a series of workshops to directly challenge the internalized and externalized racism, classism, and heterosexism adversely affecting students and teachers. Through her school advocacy efforts, she created dissatisfaction with the status quo and instead created an environment in which *all* students learned to challenge oppressive myths. Ms. Wyre is now an assistant principal at the High School for Writing and Communication in the Bronx.

CASE STUDY 8.8

Inez Ramos, a professional school counselor at Health Opportunities High School in the Bronx, is Latina, bilingual, and a strong student advocate. At a public meeting, she openly questioned the New York City Board of Education chancellor on why he was not providing more financial and administrative support for the academic and emotional needs of K–12 students, particularly poor children of color, and increased school counselor hiring. Her question was replayed on several New York City television stations and resulted in her being asked to discuss her concerns with the chancellor.

CASE STUDY 8.9

When Puerto-Rican American Kimmerly Nieves was a middle school counselor at New Rochelle's Albert Leonard Middle School, roughly 50% of the school's student body was poor and working-class students of color, including African-American and Latino/Chicano students, and the other 50% was White and Jewish students of middle- and upper-middle-class backgrounds. The staff was primarily White. Kimmerly developed multicultural school counseling lessons and implemented them. She found support from administrators, staff, and a diverse range of parents. She found that many of the White teachers embraced her efforts to increase academic success for all students. Her unwavering work in support of the concept that the cultural identities of all learners must be affirmed by all members of the school for greater academic success has modeled multicultural and anti-oppression competencies for the community. Her outreach to students and parents of color in particular was critical in demonstrating trust and credibility on the part of professional school counselors—and all educators—in ensuring academic success for all students. Kimmerly is now principal at Jefferson Elementary School in New Rochelle, New York.

INCREASING PROFESSIONAL SCHOOL COUNSELORS' MULTICULTURAL COMPETENCE

As DeLucia-Waack, DiCarlo, Parker-Sloat, and Rice (1996) stated, "[M]ulticulturalism is best viewed as a process or a journey rather than a fixed end point" (p. 237). Because this is a process, it is important for counselors to have a variety of learning experiences that enhance multicultural competence. This section offers five ways in which professional school counselors can increase their level of multicultural competence: investigate one's own cultural or ethnic heritage; attend workshops, seminars, and conferences on multicultural and diversity issues; join counseling organizations focused on cultural and social justice equity competency; read literature written by culturally diverse authors; and become familiar with multicultural education literature.

Investigate Personal Cultural, Racial, and Ethnic Heritage

Researchers have documented the importance of self-awareness as a requirement for effective counseling with clients (Corey, Corey, & Callanan, 2006). Self-awareness is essential to becoming multiculturally competent. Speight, Myers, Cox, and Highlen (1991) suggested that the acceptance of others' cultures and differences increases as one's self-knowledge increases. For this reason, many multicultural counseling courses and training seminars focus on increasing school counselor candidates' self-awareness.

Professional school counselors should explore their ethnic, racial, and other cultural identities. For many White counselors, this is a difficult process because they often don't see themselves having an ethnicity or an affiliation with a racial identity. However, almost everyone can trace his or her family history, values, and experiences, with the exception of some persons who have been adopted or have no access to family members. For some, this can mean exploring the values of their family of origin or examining written histories of their families' "roots." In addition to exploring one's family history, White counselors should spend time exploring the concept of White privilege and the issues that result from such privilege. For instance, White counselors should have an opportunity to explore what it means to be White, the benefits of White privilege, and the guilt associated with being a member of the dominant racial culture in terms of power and privilege in the United States.

Attend Workshops, Seminars, and Conferences on Multicultural and Diversity Issues

For many professional school counselors, one course in multicultural counseling is not the answer to their lack of multicultural competence. In addition to the content learned in the course, most counselors need additional training when they are employed. Given the importance of multiculturalism in counseling, most counseling organizations have developed special workshops, weekend seminars, and annual conference presentations that cover issues related to multiculturalism, various oppressions, and creative approaches for working with diverse clientele.

Join Counseling Organizations Focused on Cultural and Social Justice Equity Competencies

It is important that professional school counselors not only attend workshops and seminars related to multiculturalism and diversity, but also join organizations that are focused primarily on increasing multicultural and social justice equity competencies. Such counseling organizations as AMCD, Counselors for Social Justice (CSJ), and the Association for Lesbian, Gay, Bisexual, and Transgendered Issues in Counseling (ALGBTIC) are dedicated to combating oppression and increasing cultural sensitivity in the counseling profession.

Read Literature Written by Culturally Diverse Authors

Literature can be a useful tool in learning about other cultures. Through reading about other cultures, the professional school counselor's worldview is broadened, and he or she is introduced to the present and past realities of people of those cultural groups. Cornett and Cornett (1980) indicated that the reading experience encourages readers to engage in critical thinking when they begin to realize how selectively some U.S. historical and sociopolitical events have been and still are reported. One of the authors uses Zinn's (2003) *A People's History of the United States* to teach multicultural counseling because it uses a narrative format to present the personal and systemic stories that illustrate how ethnic, racial, social class, and gender oppressions have been intertwined for centuries in the United States and how members of oppressed groups and their allies have resisted and continue to resist oppression in the forms of racism, classism, and sexism in the United States and the rest of the Americas. It gives a powerful understanding to how affirming diversity is not enough; culturally competent professional school counselors must also be advocates for social justice and equity.

Become Familiar with Multicultural Education Literature

It is imperative that professional school counselors stay abreast of the literature and research pertaining to multicultural education. The teacher education profession has a long history of exploring teachers' lack of multicultural competence and their biased behavior in the classroom. For professional school counselors to play a pivotal role in changing some of the institutional barriers for ethnic minority students, they must be aware of the most current research related to multicultural pedagogy and curriculum.

PROFESSIONAL SCHOOL COUNSELOR MULTICULTURAL COMPETENCE CHECKLIST

Perhaps one of the first steps to becoming a multiculturally competent professional school counselor is determining areas of personal improvement needed. At the end of this chapter is a checklist that can be used by professional school counselors to determine areas for additional multicultural counseling training and exploration. Based on the AMCD's Multicultural Counseling Competencies (Arredondo et al., 1996) and multicultural education literature, the checklist encompasses those behaviors, knowledge, and awareness that have been noted as important for culturally competent work in school settings. The checklist can be completed by professional school counselors and school counselor candidates annually to monitor progress and needs for further exploration. In addition, professional school counselors in training benefit from the use of case studies of actual professional school counselors who have created culturally competent schools through challenging oppression and from the use of practice cases.

Practice Cases

Another step in the process of developing multicultural counseling competence is for professional school counselors to openly question their thoughts and behaviors when working with students of color and other nondominant cultural identities: "What additional knowledge, awareness, or skills do I need to effectively work with this student?" "Am I effective when working with students of this particular ethnic, racial, linguistic, or cultural background?" "How are my beliefs, values, and biases affecting the counseling process with this student?" Professional school counselors who answer these questions are better able to understand their level of multicultural competence and need for further multicultural counseling training.

In addition to questioning their thoughts and behaviors, professional school counselors can use case studies to begin discussions with colleagues. Following are three cases that involve sensitive cultural issues arising in a school. The task of the reader is to think about how to work with the student(s), parents, and teachers involved and to determine his or her own level of multicultural competence. These vignettes can be used for large- and small-group discussions with other school counselors who are seeking to improve their multicultural competence.

CASE STUDY 8.10

Brandon is a 15-year-old student at a high school in a predominately upper-middle-class White suburb. Brandon has lived most of his life in this community, but has recently begun hanging out in the African-American section of the suburb and has announced that he has converted to Islam from Christianity. Brandon is biracial: his mother is White and his father is African American. His parents are concerned about Brandon because he has become very angry at his parents' supposedly "White lifestyle" and has asked to live with his father's parents. His parents want you, the professional school counselor, to talk to Brandon about their concerns.

CASE STUDY 8.11

You are a professional school counselor at a diverse elementary school. The ethnic/racial composition of the student population is 41% White, 25% African American, 25% Asian, 5% Latino/a, and 2% Native American; 33% of the students are on free or reduced lunch; 29% of the students are English language learners; and 22% of the students have one or more learning, physical, developmental, or emotional disabilities. The ethnic/racial makeup of the teaching staff is 95% White and 5% "other," and all are at least working class or middle class. There are no teachers who speak English as a second language, and some teachers have physical and emotional disabilities. Since the student population has become increasingly diverse, you have become more cognizant of teachers making racist, classist, linguicist, and ableist jokes and stereotypical comments about students of color, poor and working-class students, English language learners, and students with disabilities in the teachers' lounge. You have become very uncomfortable with the comments.

CASE STUDY 8.12

Maria is a bilingual, Mexican 11th grader with severe asthma and obesity and is eligible for free and reduced lunch at the high school in which you are a professional school counselor. Maria has just received her SAT scores, which were a 1250 total on Critical Reading and Mathematics. She has also received several letters from competitive colleges and universities. Nevertheless, Maria tells you that she doesn't want to go to college. Instead, she would like to find a job so that she can help her family financially.

Summary/Conclusion

With the increasingly diverse student population of today's schools, there is a critical need for professional school counselors who are able to provide effective school counseling programs that offer both culturally competent and anti-oppressive programs to all students to help close achievement, opportunity, and attainment gaps in K–12 schools. As professional school counselors work with larger numbers of students of color and students of other multiple cultural identities, they need to adjust their perceptions and school counseling programs to address these students' diverse needs. This chapter has focused on several ways in which professional school counselors can integrate cultural competence; anti-oppression work; and multiple cultural identity awareness, knowledge, and skills into school counseling programs to increase student success and demonstrate school counselor cultural competence. This chapter is only an introduction; the goal for professional school counselors is to continue the journey of developing greater cultural competence. Engagement in the process of developing cultural competence and affirming diversity through challenging oppression provides professional school counselors an unparalleled opportunity to achieve personal and professional growth and demonstrable skills to better the lives of all students through data-driven school counseling programs.

This chapter began with an introduction to important multicultural and anti-oppression terminology because it is imperative that professional school counselors first know how to define and conceptualize cultural and oppressive incidents that occur in schools. In addition, a brief discussion of how cultural and anti-oppression practice might be integrated into components of developmental school counseling programs was provided. Considering that a major goal for professional school counselors is learning how to discuss oppression and cultural topics freely and openly in school settings, this chapter included case studies to stimulate dialogue among counselors on how they might react to or resolve issues related to oppressive school practices, students' cultural differences, or both. Continuous dialogue and skill building regarding issues of oppression in schools should be initiated by professional school counselors.

Professional school counselors who want to assess their multicultural competence can complete the Professional School Counselor Multicultural Competence Checklist included in the activities for this chapter. This checklist is unique in that it includes 11 dimensions of professional school counselor multicultural competence: multicultural counseling, multicultural consultation, understanding racism and student resistance, understanding racial and/or ethnic identity development, multicultural assessment, multicultural family interventions, social advocacy, developing school–family–community partnerships, understanding cross-cultural interpersonal interactions, multicultural career assessment, and multicultural sensitivity.

Overall, this chapter has provided an introduction to multicultural counseling in schools and the ways in which oppressive beliefs and practices impact student success. It is important to note, however, that it is impossible to prepare in advance for all the different experiences one might encounter in schools. Instead, professional school counselors need to acquire the knowledge and skills that will allow them to critically assess and intelligently address the various challenges encountered by students and their families.

Activities

1. Collaborate in a small group to outline a developmental school counseling lesson plan with specific activities and content on the awareness, knowledge, and skills needed by students and staff to combat at least two of the oppressions discussed in this chapter. Link this activity to the *ASCA National Model* (ASCA, 2012) or your state's school counseling model and specific state learning standards/outcomes for a specific grade and building level (e.g., 5th-grade elementary students, 8th-grade middle school students, 10th-grade high school students).

2. Discuss the multicultural demographics (ethnicity/race, gender, sexual orientation, disability status, social class, language status, religious/spiritual identity, and other variables), as well as the multicultural competence levels of the teaching and school counseling staff, of the K–12 schools that you attended. How will you be similar or different when you are working as a professional school counselor?

3. Go to The Education Trust's website (www.edtrust.org), and find a piece of local or national data that best illustrates the racism and classism involved in a current achievement, access, or attainment gap facing poor and working-class students or students of African American, Latino/a, or Native American ethnic/racial identity, including bilingual students, students with disabilities, or both. Once you have located the piece of data, what would you do as a culturally competent professional school counselor to challenge systemic barriers in a school that has that type of gap?

4. On the Professional School Counselor Multicultural Competence Checklist that follows, check whether you are COMPETENT or NOT COMPETENT on each of the items.

Directions: **Check whether you are COMPETENT or NOT COMPETENT on each of the following items.**

	Competent	Not Competent

Multicultural Counseling

1. I can recognize when my beliefs and values are interfering with providing the best services to my students.
2. I can identify the cultural bases of my communication style.
3. I can discuss how culture affects the help-seeking behaviors of students.
4. I know when a counseling approach is culturally appropriate for a specific student.
5. I know when a counseling approach is culturally inappropriate for a specific student.
6. I am able to identify culturally appropriate interventions and counseling approaches (e.g., indigenous practices) with students.
7. I can list barriers that prevent ethnic minority students from using counseling services.
8. I know when my helping style is inappropriate for a culturally different student.
9. I know when my helping style is appropriate for a culturally different student.
10. I can give examples of how stereotypical beliefs about culturally different persons impact the counseling relationship.
11. I know when my biases influence my services to students.
12. I know when specific cultural beliefs influence students' responses to counseling.
13. I know when my helping style is inappropriate for a culturally different student.

Multicultural Consultation

14. I know when my culture is influencing the process of consultation.
15. I know when the culture of the consultee (e.g., parent, teacher) is influencing the process of consultation.
16. I know when the race and/or culture of a student is a problem for a teacher.
17. I can initiate discussions related to race/ethnicity/culture when consulting with teachers.
18. I can initiate discussions related to race/ethnicity/culture when consulting with parents.

Understanding Racism and Student Resistance

19. I can define and discuss White privilege.
20. I can discuss how I (if European/American/White) am privileged based on my race.
21. I can identify racist aspects of educational instruction.
22. I can define and discuss prejudice.
23. I can identify discrimination and discriminatory practices in schools.
24. I am able to challenge my colleagues when they discriminate against students.
25. I can define and discuss racism.
26. I can discuss the influence of racism on the counseling process.
27. I can discuss the influence of racism on the educational system in the United States.
28. I can help students determine whether a problem stems from racism or biases in others.
29. I understand the relationship between student resistance and racism.
30. I am able to discuss the relationship between student resistance and racism.
31. I include topics related to race and racism in my classroom guidance units.
32. I am able to challenge others' racist beliefs and behaviors.
33. I am able to identify racist and unjust policies in schools.

(Continued)

Directions: **Check whether you are COMPETENT or NOT COMPETENT on each of the following items.**

	Competent	Not Competent

Understanding Racial and/or Ethnic Identity Development

34. I am able to discuss at least two theories of racial and/or ethnic identity development.

35. I can use racial/ethnic identity development theories to understand my students' problems and concerns.

36. I can assess my own racial/ethnic identity development in order to enhance my counseling.

37. I can assist students who are exploring their own racial/ethnic identity development.

38. I can develop activities that enhance students' racial/ethnic identity.

39. I am able to discuss how racial/ethnic identity may affect the relationships between students and educators.

Multicultural Assessment

40. I can discuss the potential bias of two assessment instruments frequently used in the schools.

41. I can evaluate instruments that may be biased against certain groups of students.

42. I am able to use test information appropriately with culturally diverse parents.

43. I can advocate for fair testing and the appropriate use of testing of children from diverse backgrounds.

44. I can identify whether or not the assessment process is culturally sensitive.

45. I can discuss how the identification stage of the assessment process might be biased against minority populations.

46. I can use culturally appropriate instruments when I assess students.

47. I am able to discuss how assessment can lead to inequitable opportunities for students.

Multicultural Family Interventions

48. I can discuss family counseling from a cultural/ethnic perspective.

49. I can discuss at least two ethnic groups' traditional gender-role expectations and rituals.

50. I can anticipate when my helping style is inappropriate for a culturally different parent or guardian.

51. I can discuss culturally diverse methods of parenting and discipline.

52. I can discuss how class and economic level affect family functioning and development.

53. I can discuss how race and ethnicity influence family behavior.

54. I can identify when a school policy is biased against culturally diverse families.

Social Advocacy

55. I know of societal issues that affect the development of ethnic minority students.

56. When counseling, I am able to address societal issues that affect the development of ethnic minority students.

57. I can work with families and community members in order to reintegrate them into the school.

58. I can define "social change agent."

59. I am able to be a "social change agent."

60. I can discuss what it means to take an "activist counseling approach."

61. I can intervene with students at the individual and systemic levels.

62. I can discuss how factors such as poverty and powerlessness have influenced the current conditions of at least two ethnic groups.

63. I am able to advocate for students who are being subjected to unfair practices.

64. I know how to use data as an advocacy tool.

Directions: Check whether you are COMPETENT or NOT COMPETENT on each of the following items.

	Competent	Not Competent

Developing School–Family–Community Partnerships

65. I can discuss how school–family–community partnerships are linked to student achievement.
66. I am able to develop partnerships with families that are culturally different than me.
67. I am able to develop partnerships with agencies within my school's community.
68. I can define a school–family–community partnership.
69. I am able to discuss more than three types of parent involvement.
70. I am able to encourage the participation of ethnic minority parents in school activities.
71. I am able to work with community leaders and other resources in the community to assist with student (and family) concerns.

Understanding Cross-Cultural Interpersonal Interactions

72. I am able to discuss interaction patterns that might influence ethnic minority students' perception of inclusion in the school community.
73. I can solicit feedback from students regarding my interactions with them.
74. I can verbally communicate my acceptance of culturally diverse students.
75. I can nonverbally communicate my acceptance of culturally diverse students.
76. I am able to assess the manner in which I speak and the emotional tone of my interactions with culturally diverse students.
77. I am able to greet students and parents in a culturally acceptable manner.
78. I know of culturally insensitive topics or gestures.

Multicultural Career Assessment

79. I can develop and implement culturally sensitive career development activities where materials are representative of all groups in a wide range of careers.
80. I can arrange opportunities for students to have interactions with ethnic minority professionals.
81. I am able to assess the strengths of multiple aspects of students' self-concepts.
82. I can discuss differences in the decision-making styles of students.
83. I can integrate my knowledge of varying decision-making styles when implementing career counseling.
84. I can integrate family and religious issues in the career counseling process.
85. I can utilize career assessment instruments that are sensitive to cultural differences of students.
86. I can discuss how "work" and "career" are viewed similarly and differently across cultures.
87. I can discuss how many career assessment instruments are inappropriate for culturally diverse students.

Multicultural Sensitivity

88. I am able to develop a close personal relationship with someone of another race.
89. I am able to live comfortably with culturally diverse people.
90. I am able to be comfortable with people who speak another language.
91. I can make friends with people from other ethnic groups.

Source: "Assessing the Multicultural Competence of School Counselors: A Checklist," by C. Holcomb-McCoy, 2004, *Professional School Counseling, 7,* pp. 178–186. Copyright 2004 by ASCA. Reprinted with permission.

Leadership and Advocacy for Every Student's Achievement and Opportunity

Stuart F. Chen-Hayes and Yvette Q. Getch*

Editor's Introduction: Key to transforming the school counseling profession is the transformed school counselor's use of leadership and advocacy skills as change agents for equity and social justice to ensure academic, career, college readiness, and personal/social competencies for every student and in publicizing program interventions and outcomes for all stakeholders. Transformative school counseling programs deliver achievement and opportunity competencies to all students via annual academic, career, college readiness, and personal/social planning for every student, school counseling core curriculum for every student, and group and individual counseling for some students based on the American School Counselor Association (ASCA) Code of Ethics, the *ASCA National Model*, and the National Office for School Counselor Advocacy (NOSCA) career and college readiness components (ASCA, 2010, 2012; Mason, Ockerman, & Chen-Hayes, 2013; NOSCA, 2010).

PROFESSIONAL SCHOOL COUNSELORS: LEADING AND ADVOCATING

The school counseling profession has put leadership and advocacy in a central place for all professional school counselors as part of the National Center for Transforming School Counseling's (NCTSC) new vision for school counseling (NCTSC, 2013) in the ASCA *National Model* school counseling program framework (ASCA, 2012), in the National Office for School Counselor Advocacy (NOSCA) *Eight Components of College and Career Readiness Counseling* (NOSCA, 2010), and in the 2009 Council for Accreditation of Counseling and Related Educational Programs (CACREP) standards (CACREP, 2009). School counselor educators have written on the critical roles of advocacy and leadership by transformed school counselors in school counseling programs to increase student achievement and college and career readiness opportunities and equity for every student (Bryan, Holcomb-McCoy, Moore-Thomas, & Day-Vines, 2009; Carey & Dimmitt, 2012; Chen-Hayes, 2007; Chen-Hayes, Ockerman, & Mason, 2013; Janson, 2009; Lapan, 2012; Mason & McMahon, 2009; McMahon, Mason, & Paisley, 2009; Ratts, DeKruyf, & Chen-Hayes, 2007).

Whereas some educators use a deficit model referring to "at-risk" students, transformed school counselors instead focus on student strengths and refer to students facing achievement and opportunity gaps as "at promise." This change in language helps school counselors lead and advocate to challenge stakeholder beliefs that not all students can achieve high levels of academic success in rigorous coursework or graduate from college. Students of color, poor and working-class students, students with disabilities, and bilingual students are among the nontraditional groups of students who have not received equitable academic, career, and college access and personal/social

---

*The authors would like to thank Deryl F. Bailey, Bradley T. Erford, and Emily M. Miller for the contributions to this chapter from the prior editions.

opportunities and resources from schools and school counseling programs (ASCA, 2010, 2012; Bryan et al., 2009; Education Trust, 2005; Lapan, Gysbers, Bragg, & Pierce, 2012; Lapan, Whitcomb, & Aleman, 2012; see also Chapters 3 and 4). Professional school counselors advocate and lead to ensure every student's success by providing equitable achievement and opportunity outcomes (ASCA, 2010, 2012; Chen-Hayes et al., 2013; Hatch & Chen-Hayes, 2008; McMahon et al., 2009).

Professional school counselors implement transformative school counseling programs based on the *ASCA National Model* (ASCA, 2012) advocating for students from historically oppressed populations based on ethnicity, race, social class, language, disability, sexual orientation, gender, gender identity/expression, appearance, immigration status, family type, spirituality/religion, and so forth, as outlined in the *ASCA Ethical Standards for School Counselors* (ASCA, 2010). An outcomes-based, transformative school counseling program staff uses advocacy and leadership for equity and systemic change that benefits every student (ASCA, 2012; Hatch & Chen-Hayes, 2008; McMahon et al., 2009).

When professional school counselors develop and maintain a school counseling program based on advocacy and leadership with specific competencies and outcomes that demonstrate how professional school counselors help students to succeed in academic, career/college access, and personal/social domains, they empower all stakeholders to challenge unjust institutional and systemic practices that deny the best career and college readiness opportunities to all students such as tracking students academically; barriers to taking honors, Advanced Placement, and International Baccalaureate courses; little or no college or career counseling until the end of high school; and failure to monitor student completion of college and career assessments, college applications, and FAFSA forms (ASCA, 2012; NOSCA, 2010). The transformed professional school counselor leads and advocates to remove barriers to student performance and overcome social injustice through modeling advocacy and leadership strategies and implementing a transformative school counseling program that includes an advisory council and a strong school counseling public awareness and support program, including dissemination of a vision, mission, goals, and annual program outcomes to all stakeholders (ASCA, 2012). Creating public awareness of and support for the school counseling program, including the dissemination of outcomes in closing achievement and opportunity gaps (ASCA, 2010, 2012), demonstrates transformative outcomes (see Chapters 3 and 4).

Achievement gaps are disparities in academic performance found among different groups of students based on ethnicity/race, gender, ability/disability, social class, and language status (monolingual, bilingual, ELL; see Chapter 8). Opportunity gaps are the disparities between students of diverse cultural identities receiving school counseling program services; rigorous coursework including honors, Advanced Placement, and International Baccalaureate courses (International Baccalaureate, 2013); college and career readiness counseling; the best teachers; and changing this by disaggregating data on ethnicity/race, gender, ability/disability, social class (free and reduced lunch), and language identities to find inequitable policy and practice patterns in need of change (ASCA, 2010, 2012; Bryan et al., 2009; Chen-Hayes, 2007; Vela-Gude et al., 2009). Achievement, opportunity, attainment (e.g., who graduates from college with a diploma and who does not, based on cultural and economic group), and funding gaps (e.g., who gets the most money for schools based on tax levies and who gets the least) exist between students of color and White students and between students from low-income families (often students of color) and students from middle- and upper-income families (Bryan et al., 2009; Chen-Hayes, 2007; Vela-Gude et al., 2009).

Why are these gaps prominent if all students can learn? In some cases, students of color, poor and working-class students, recent immigrants, bilingual students, and students with disabilities have little or no access to school counseling program services, school counselor-to-student ratios are too high especially in high-poverty rural and urban areas (Lapan, 2012; Lapan, Whitcomb, & Aleman, 2012), and some school counselors dismiss students' academic, career, and college access potential (Bryan et al., 2009; Vela-Gude et al., 2009). Many school systems, however, have taken bold steps to reform and have demonstrated that students of color and students from low-income households can excel academically in K–12 classrooms and in college. The Education Trust annually honors school districts and individual schools that have closed significant achievement and opportunity gaps throughout the United States (Education Trust, 2013), and the National Office for School Counselor Advocacy (NOSCA) offers annual Inspiration Awards for individual high schools with demonstrable increases in college access and attendance rates (College Board, 2008b). According to a report released by the Education Trust (1999), *Dispelling the Myth: High Poverty Schools Exceeding Expectations*, successful high-poverty schools demonstrated these characteristics:

1. Extensive use of state/local standards to design curriculum and instruction, assess student work, and evaluate teachers
2. Increased instructional time for reading and mathematics

3. Substantial investment in professional development for teachers focused on instructional practices to help students meet academic standards

4. Comprehensive systems to monitor individual student performance and to provide help to struggling students before they fall behind

5. Parental involvement in efforts to get students to meet standards

6. Accountability systems with real consequences for adults in the school

Therefore, in high-poverty schools, professional school counselors must use advocacy, leadership, systemic change, and collaboration skills (ASCA, 2010, 2012) and services to help close achievement and opportunity gaps for every student. For example, equity-focused school counseling programs use ASCA Student Standards (ASCA, 2012), NOSCA's eight college and career readiness components (NOSCA, 2010), and Common Core standards to design curriculum and instruction and assess student learning in collaboration with teachers. School counseling programs contribute to student academic success by integrating student learning styles and multiple intelligences in school counseling core curriculum lessons (see Chapter 10). Professional school counselors work with academic intervention teams and other educators collaboratively in school leadership, data, and inquiry teams to monitor student progress weekly and determine what policies and practices in school need to change to ensure equity is achieved by every student. Professional school counselors collaboratively design and implement not only professional development workshops for teachers and administrators but also parent and guardian workshops to increase awareness of achievement, opportunity, attainment, and funding gaps and devise specific advocacy and leadership strategies, skills, and outcomes for systemic change in schools, including closing achievement gap action plans and results reports (Chen-Hayes et al., 2013; Hartline & Cobia, 2012).

Professional school counselors play a pivotal role in monitoring student performance. Professional school counselors assist students with career and college curriculum offerings and decision making and with personal and social concerns. For example, some middle and high school counselors resent being forced to construct student schedules. Although professional school counselors should not be high-paid clerks, professional school counselors must be engaged as educational leaders and advocates, ensuring that all students receive outstanding teaching and that no students are marginalized or tracked with teachers who lack credentials or who do not believe all students can learn at high levels. Thus, during master schedule creation,

professional school counselors need to ensure that all students receive rigorous courses, including college and career preparatory curriculum with high levels of mathematics, science, and literacy courses ensuring career and college readiness (Trusty & Niles, 2003). Professional school counselors encourage parent and guardian involvement by educating them about the importance of rigor in academics and career and college access and readiness starting in elementary school (NOSCA, 2010) and ensure they are notified immediately for collaboration when students begin to experience academic concerns in school using a strengths-based approach (Ratts et al., 2007).

This chapter focuses on professional school counselors as achievement and opportunity advocates and leaders promoting systemic changes in schools and communities through transformative school counseling programs providing measurable outcomes based on the *ASCA National Model* (ASCA, 2012), the National Center for Transforming School Counseling's new vision of school counseling (2013), and the National Office for School Counselor Advocacy's *Eight Components of College and Career Readiness* (NOSCA, 2010). Professional school counselors as leaders and advocates help eliminate barriers that impede the growth and performance of all students, particularly students of African, Latino/a, and Native American Indian ethnic and racial identities; poor and working-class students; bilingual students; and students with developmental, emotional, intellectual, learning, and physical disabilities (ASCA, 2010).

PROFESSIONAL SCHOOL COUNSELORS AS LEADERS

Leadership is one of four skills necessary to successfully implement the *ASCA National Model* (ASCA, 2012; Janson, 2009; McMahon et al., 2009) and is inextricably tied to advocacy. Being an advocate requires strong leadership skills, especially when advocating for systemic change in K–12 school policies and practices. A leader has a "vision" for change, communicates that vision effectively to others, helps supporters create desired changes, and promotes considerable planning and dedication (Dollarhide, Gibson, & Saginak, 2008).

Although professional school counselors are encouraged by the *ASCA National Model* (ASCA, 2012) to lead by ensuring that all students benefit from challenging academic coursework that prepares them for career and college readiness (NOSCA, 2010), schools provide school counselors with additional opportunities for leadership. Whether closing an achievement gap, increasing awareness about ending cyberbullying, or creating a college-going culture in every school, teaching students how to be leaders, modeling responsible and healthy behavior, or creating a safe and welcoming school culture, school counselors lead the way in improving school environments so all students can learn successfully (Dollarhide, 2003).

School counselors demonstrate Bolman and Deal's (1997) four kinds of leadership: structural leadership, human resources leadership, political leadership, and symbolic leadership. All four domains are integral to effective leadership in schools (Dollarhide, 2003; Mason & McMahon, 2009). These leadership styles can be used one at a time, or when appropriate, a few may be combined to achieve the desired result. *Structural leadership* comprises the nuts and bolts of an effective leadership campaign. It involves creating an organized plan for change, as well as determining how to best put that plan into action, such as by implementing results reports and action reports for small-group work, school counseling core curriculum lessons, and closing achievement and opportunity gaps (ASCA, 2012).

Human resources leadership may come most naturally to school counselors, as it necessitates implementing the beliefs around equity that most school counselors possess. This kind of leadership requires school counselors to empower and motivate every K–12 student for academic, career, and college success. At the heart of human resources leadership is the capacity to form positive working relationships and demonstrate trust and support of others' abilities to help enact change.

Political leadership may be the most difficult kind of leadership for some school counselors, as it has the potential for dissension (Dollarhide, 2003). Political leadership requires the integration of advocacy, an understanding of how systems work, and the ability to make a strong and convincing argument, establish compromises, and connect with people in power. Political leadership is most likely to lead to conflict because it directly involves changing unfair organizational or systemic structures that are in place, a task that may unsettle those in power who are content with the status quo. Yet this is the key leadership skill needed to close achievement and opportunity gaps in schools successfully.

Finally, *symbolic leadership* is the public relations component. Symbolic leadership involves creating and communicating a vision of change to others to gain supporters and allies. Professional school counselors as change agents for equity (Mason et al., 2013) must communicate their belief to others in a persuasive, inspiring, sincere, and relevant way to effectively close gaps and ensure equity and access for every K–12 student. Professional school counselors need to be competent in each type of leadership to create equitable change in schools and school counseling programs.

In conjunction with these four types of leadership, a successful leader must master other leadership skills. One

essential aspect of leadership and advocacy is being proactive (ASCA, 2010, 2012). For example, professional school counselors continually monitor the school climate and use data to identify and address achievement and opportunity gaps and unfair school policies or practices in areas such as attendance, disciplinary issues, referrals to the school counseling department, grades, test scores, college-going rates, college entrance exam scores (PSAT, PLAN, ACT, SAT), and college graduation rates (ASCA, 2012; NOSCA, 2010). School counselors as leaders constantly monitor school climate with data and in regular interactions with all stakeholders so that inequity issues can be addressed proactively, using specific data points and key school counseling program interventions: planning for every student, school counseling core curriculum lessons for every student, and group and individual counseling strategies for some students (ASCA, 2012). In addition to being proactive, successful school counseling leaders build strong alliances and collaborate with all stakeholders, including students, building leaders, teachers, parents and guardians, and community members. It is easier for professional school counselor leaders to be effective change agents for equity and exert political leadership when they have good rapport with influential stakeholders who assist and support them in closing gaps (Chen-Hayes et al., 2013; Hartline & Cobia, 2012; Mason et al., 2013).

CULTURAL REFLECTION 9.1

How might professional school counselors from diverse backgrounds view the leadership role of the professional school counselor? How might students, parents, and educators from diverse backgrounds view the leadership role of the professional school counselor?

Research in School Counseling Leadership Practices

Dollarhide et al. (2008) conducted a qualitative study observing the leadership successes and failures of new school counselors. School counselors successful in leadership had specific commonalities: They held themselves accountable for achieving their goals, conveyed their vision and garnered support and validation for their work, reframed resistance as a learning experience, persevered through resistance, and found ways to improve their leadership abilities throughout the process. School counselor participants who did not achieve leadership goals had similarities. They did not seek the support of others or were unable to gain support, did not hold themselves accountable for leadership efforts, set goals that required resources and access beyond what they could procure, did not improve deficits in their leadership abilities, and allowed others to define their role as a school counselor.

Based on their results, Dollarhide et al. (2008) recommended these leadership strategies for new school counselors: Start with reasonable and realistic leadership goals, approach the work with determination, resolve to work through resistance, build a strong support system, seek supervision and support from supervisors and colleagues, and be clear about the role of a school counselor.

Janson (2009) studied the perceptions of leadership practices by 40 high school counselors using a Q sort methodology based on 40 school counselor leadership behavior statements. Results suggested four types of school counselor leadership among the participants: (a) Self-Focused and Reflective Exemplar, (b) Ancillary School Counseling Program Manager, (c) Engaging Systems Change Agent, and (d) Empathetic Resource Broker.

Self-Focused and Reflective Exemplars were driven by inner beliefs, values, experiences, and reflection about leadership. Ancillary School Counseling Program Managers were focused most on administrative details, providing excellent counseling services, and interacting in caring and

meaningful ways with other stakeholders, but unlikely to advocate for social justice or challenge the status quo (Janson, 2009). Engaging Systems Change Agents were most similar to transformed school counseling, as they valued the impact of politically assertive leadership behaviors on systems (e.g., school, community) more than on individual students, including challenging the status quo and advocating for social justice. Last, Empathic Resource Brokers conceptualized leadership as providing resources to staff and students with a caring demeanor, but were least likely to use data or focus on systemic change of the four types that emerged from the study.

Mason and McMahon (2009) identified key components of school counselor leadership in a statewide study done in a southeastern U.S. state with 305 school counselors. Their study indicated that school counselor leadership is a function of the school counselor's age, experience, and size of the school. Ultimately, all professional school counselors must reflect on and evaluate their leadership strengths and areas to improve. Because leadership and advocacy are intertwined, school counselors must develop leadership skills to effectively advocate for equity and systemic change (ASCA, 2012; Chen-Hayes et al., 2013; Hartline & Cobia, 2012; Janson, 2009; Mason et al., 2013).

THEORY INTO PRACTICE 9.1

GRADUATE STUDENTS LEADING, CRITIQUING, IMPLEMENTING, AND EVALUATING TRANSFORMED K–12 SCHOOL COUNSELING PROGRAMS AT LEHMAN COLLEGE OF THE CITY UNIVERSITY OF NEW YORK

Since 1999, Lehman College has been one of over 20 transformed Counselor Education/School Counseling program "companion institutions" with the NCTSC. In the first semester of the Lehman graduate program, school counselor candidates get to practice a leadership role in schools as they experience a 10-hour prepracticum in a K–12 school. Their assignment is to critique the site's school counseling program strengths and areas to improve in terms of school counselor professional identity; use of the *ASCA National Model* and success in closing achievement gaps; career/college readiness interventions including success with closing opportunity gaps; and multicultural and social justice issues, including multiple oppressions and how the school counseling program intervenes. School counselor candidates usually share written materials with stakeholders ahead of time, such as a copy of the NCTSC's new vision definition of school counseling, an ASCA Model Executive Summary, the NOSCA eight career and college counseling components, and the ASCA Code of Ethics.

School counselor candidates then set up meetings to interview five stakeholders: a school counselor, a building

leader, a teacher, a parent or guardian, and a student. They ask stakeholders questions from four areas of The ACCESS Questionnaire (Chen-Hayes, 2007). School counselor candidates can be nervous at first when "asked to swim in the deep end of the pool" in their first semester, but the results of the assignment are profound. Students compose a research paper comparing and contrasting what they found in the research literature and learned in class versus what they have found at their school counseling program site. In the last class, the students are asked what they think the greatest changes are that have occurred in transforming school counseling practice at their school site based on their interviews and sharing of information.

The results are intriguing for both school counselor candidates and the school counseling program sites since 2002. In some cases, stakeholders get defensive and fearful that the transformed school counselor candidate is going to make them look bad. In other cases, stakeholders had no idea that the transformed school counselor was a leader and advocate to close gaps. Students in schools often have never heard of the school counseling program model before or think that the school counselor is only there if they get in trouble. Many parents and guardians and teachers also are shocked to hear about the changes in school counseling and school counseling programs when compared to their experiences in schools.

Perhaps the most profound changes are with school counselor site supervisors and building leaders. Many school counselors and building leaders have been inspired by these first-semester school counselor candidates to adopt the *ASCA National Model* and a stronger focus on NOSCA's eight career and college readiness components

after having completed the interviews. For school counselor candidates, they have now seen the power of living the transformed role as graduate students. And if they can make this kind of change in their first semester, it leads to even more powerful changes in practicum and internship classes, where they work collaboratively at their sites to improve school counseling programs in various ways including use of data to find one achievement gap and one opportunity gap, create action plans, implement interventions, and then evaluate their outcomes and share them with all stakeholders.

Leadership in Professional School Counseling Organizations at Local, State, and National Levels

There are many ways for professional school counselors to become involved in leadership positions locally, at the state level, and in national membership and advocacy organizations. The profession needs graduate students and full-time school counselors who will help shape the future of the school counseling profession focused on closing achievement and opportunity gaps for all students K–12 (ASCA, 2010, 2012; NCTSC, 2013; NOSCA, 2010). Mason et al. (2013) developed the CAFÉ Model, Change Agents Advocating for Equity, as a leadership tool focused on the school counselor's need to lead in all aspects of student development and gap closing in schools and school counseling programs.

At the local level, the easiest place to take a leadership role is in the school building or at the district and school board levels. School counselors need to be on the front lines focused on equity for all students with data and research in hand showing the power of reducing school counselor ratios and how that impacts students, particularly poor and working-class students, who often have little or no access to school counselors and school counseling programs due to funding gaps compared to better-resourced public and independent schools (Carey & Dimmitt, 2012; Chen-Hayes et al., 2013; Lapan, 2012).

At the state and regional levels, it's important to join the state branch of ASCA (www.schoolcounselor.org) and ACA (www.counseling.org) to get involved on a committee, as an elected leader, attend or present at a state conference, write in a state school counseling journal, or advocate for school counseling programs by lobbying local and state legislators to create a state-level office for school counseling programs (McMahon et al., 2009) and fund more school counselors, and share evidence- and research-based school counseling programs that close achievement and

opportunity gaps to demonstrate our effectiveness (Carey & Dimmitt, 2012). ASCA members can participate in leadership by becoming members of the social media network ASCA SCENE.

In addition, graduate students, school counselors, and site supervisors can become members of the Association for Counselor Education & Supervision (ACES; www .acesonline.net) and join a regional branch of ACES (North Atlantic, NARACES; North Central, NCACES; Rocky Mountain, RMACES; Southern, SACES; Western, WACES) and participate in national and regional conferences by developing presentations on school counseling and writing in an ACES or regional journal on school counseling topics for graduate students, counselor educators, and supervisors.

At the national level, join ACES, ACA, and NACAC; sign up for the OWN THE TURF CAMPAIGN; and take advantage of free resources from NOSCA, CESCAL, and the Center for School Counseling Outcome Research and Evaluation (CSCORE). In 2011, Drs. Stuart Chen-Hayes and Melissa Ockerman were appointed co-chairs of the ASCA Transforming School Counseling and College Access Interest Network (TSCCAIN) and grew the membership to over 150 graduate students, site supervisors, and school counselor educators focused on advocacy and leadership in transforming school counseling, college access counseling within the profession, external public relations working on issues including accurate use of the current terms school counselor, school counseling program, and school counseling department in K–12 schools (McMahon et al., 2009), giving feedback on ASCA model and CACREP Standards revisions, and collaborating with NCTSC, NOSCA, CSCORE, ASCA, ACA, and various professional stakeholder groups in schools to promote transformed school counseling and college access K–20. The group meets monthly via teleconference on Sunday evenings and posts agendas and minutes on CESNET, the ACES member LISTSERV.

PROFESSIONAL SCHOOL COUNSELORS AS ADVOCATES

Similar to leadership, advocacy is the intentional effort to change existing or proposed policies, practices, and learning environments on behalf of all students and families (Ezell, 2001). Osborne et al. (1998) presented a model of advocacy encouraging counselors to take individual or collective actions on behalf of all students to promote justice and improve academic and environmental conditions.

For professional school counselors, advocacy is defined as ensuring high levels of academic, career, and college readiness and personal/social competencies fostered in every K–12 student. All K–12 students need a school counseling program to advocate on their behalf. But are all professional school counselors ready, willing, and able to implement school counseling programs focused on advocacy for all students' achievement and opportunities? How professional school counselors transform the perceptions and roles of school counselors and school counseling programs to create positive achievement and opportunity outcomes for every K–12 student is essential. School counselors advocate as change agents for equity by speaking out against policies and practices that have been "business as usual" that contribute to achievement, opportunity, attainment, and funding gaps.

Too often, professional school counselors become overwhelmed with administrative concerns (e.g., bus and hall duties, discipline, attendance, testing, lunch monitoring, relentless paperwork, schedule changes, constant crises) and become entrenched in the system. The school counselor is the "go-to" person at the school. If problems arise, a job needs to be done, or new responsibilities arise, then administrators, teachers, staff, and parents often turn to the school counselor (College Board National Office for School Counselor Advocacy [NOSCA], 2011). As a result, professional school counselors who should be advocating for all students and encouraging changes in the system end up "gatekeepers of the status quo," supporting and maintaining an inequitable system that harms entire groups of students because they cannot figure a way out from under the inappropriate roles and job responsibilities that take them away from counseling—delivering lesson plans, workshops, activities, and educational planning—for all students (College Board, 2012b).

House and Martin (1998) suggested that professional school counselors not support and maintain such ineffective systems, but instead become "catalysts and leaders focused on removing the institutional barriers that continue to result in an achievement gap between poor and minority youth and their more advantaged peers" (p. 284). House and Martin also encouraged professional school counselors to be "dream-makers" rather than "dream-breakers." Advocacy for every student's academic achievement and career and college readiness opportunities must be infused throughout the counselor education curriculum if new professional school counselors are to be properly prepared for their roles as educational change agents (CACREP, 2009; NOSCA, 2010).

Challenging Barriers to Achievement and Opportunity

Student populations in public and private schools across the United States continue to change dramatically by ethnicity/race, immigration status, language background, and social class. The percentage of students of color has increased substantially along with that of bilingual and multilingual students, with many lacking fluency in English (U.S. Department of Education, 2012). In addition, the percentage of students identified as low income or poor has increased (Education Trust, 2004). By the year 2020, children and adolescents of color will comprise over 50% of public school students, and they are the dominant group in most major U.S. cities, in older suburbs, and increasingly in rural areas.

Professional school counselors advocate for all students and families, especially students for whom achievement, opportunity, attainment, and funding gaps remain a challenge. Young men of color, particularly African-American, Latino/a, Native American and some Asian men from low-income households who are bilingual and/or who have disabilities, are especially in need of targeted interventions to close achievement and opportunity gaps. You can see evidence of what happens with achievement and opportunity gaps in terms of who is admitted to college and how those gaps also affect attainment gaps at www.CollegeResults.org. Created and updated by the Education Trust, College Results Online (2013) is an interactive database of who is graduating from public and independent 4-year colleges in the United States and who is not, based on gender, ethnicity/race, social class (Pell Grant and other financial aid eligibility), and 4-, 5-, and 6-year graduation rates. Professional school counselors can share this data with all K–12 stakeholders and work collectively to close gaps that assist more students to reach successful completion of their college and career dreams.

To be outstanding advocates for all students, professional school counselors and their colleagues must understand their own biases, recognize potential harm when dealing with culturally diverse students and parents, and be open to change in personal worldviews (see Chapter 8). When professional school counselors and other educators have developed multicultural competencies, they can understand the social and political forces operating around and within the school community. When professional school counselors and other educators recognize their own inappropriate beliefs, attitudes, actions, and inactions, they see how these beliefs become policies and practices that work against equity for all students. They change their attitudes and behaviors to advocate for all students and challenge inappropriate barriers that disproportionately harm students of color, poor and working-class students, students with disabilities, and bilingual students. If this recognition does not occur, professional school counselors and colleagues may never be a proactive force for equity and closing achievement and opportunity gaps.

With these changes come new challenges for professional school counselors who believe all students can learn. Becoming sensitive to multicultural issues and multiple oppressions (see Chapter 8) is an important step for a professional school counselor advocating for every student. Instead of blaming a student's family for academic concerns, transformed school counselors recognize oppressive forces built into the social, economic, and political forces shaping policies and practices of the school as sources of academic concerns. The student's issue may be a response to ableism, classism, heterosexism, linguicism, racism, or sexism, in schools, communities, or society (ASCA, 2010; Chen-Hayes, 2009). This redirects the professional school counselor's response to empowering the student and school counseling program policies and practices to formalize an action plan for equity and success within the system (ASCA, 2012; Chen-Hayes et al., 2013; Mason et al., 2013). However, recognition and knowledge does not produce action alone. A national survey of several thousand school counselors and administrators showed 88% of school counselors said equity was important and that they strongly believed that students from underrepresented backgrounds, including low-income or immigrant families, should get extra support needed to succeed. However, only 67% of school counselors responding felt they were successful in providing the support needed to create an equitable environment for students from underrepresented backgrounds (College Board, 2012b).

The professional school counselor needs to advocate for and encourage equitable change within the school community so that all students feel safe and receive the academic, career, and college readiness and personal/social competencies they need for a good life (ASCA, 2010, 2012; Chen-Hayes et al., 2013; Mason et al., 2013; NOSCA, 2010). This means school counselors must become change agents. We can no longer sit on the sidelines and cheer students on. We must become involved at all levels to facilitate equitable changes that will lead to the success of all students (Mason et al., 2013). All students, parents, and guardians must have full access to career and college readiness information and curricula throughout their K–12 experience (ASCA, 2010; NOSCA, 2010). This approach, part of a transformative school counseling program, helps the professional school counselor move beyond treating problems or issues as single incidents (ASCA, 2012).

ADVOCACY IN TRANSFORMED SCHOOL COUNSELING PROGRAMS

Professional school counselors advocate for and with clients on both the microlevel and the macrolevel (Gibson, 2014; Ratts et al., 2007). On the microlevel, school counselors advocate on behalf of students and teach self-advocacy skills. However, because not all issues can be addressed on the microlevel, school counselors also intervene on the macrolevel for students in larger district and community contexts for more broad-based change.

An example of this was when school counselor educators, including Drs. Stuart Chen-Hayes, Jamie Cheek, Trish Hatch, Toni Tollerud, and Joy Whitman, met at a Summer Transforming School Counseling Academy sponsored by the National Center for Transforming School Counseling in 2009 in Houston, Texas, and developed the idea of a national conference for school counselors and other K–12 educators on lesbian, bisexual, gay, transgender, queer, and questioning students' issues. Dr. Trish Hatch and the Center for Excellence in School Counseling and Leadership (CESCAL) implemented the idea into "Supporting Students Saving Lives," an annual conference held right after National School Counseling Week each President's Day weekend in San Diego, California (CESCAL, 2013).

Effective school counselors assess their school and community climate so that change can be enacted at appropriate levels (Bemak & Chung, 2005; Mason et al., 2013). For instance, if a problem exists within a school due to large numbers of bilingual students and families but no staff who speak languages other than English in the larger community, schoolwide change results in limited improvement for students. Under these circumstances, the transformed school counselor finds translators, develops a bilingual school counseling program website, and takes classes to develop basic fluency in a second language to mobilize efforts to close achievement and attainment gaps for bilingual students.

ACA ADVOCACY COMPETENCIES IN SCHOOLS

To assist school counselors advocating for and with clients on both the microlevel and the macrolevel, four members of the American Counseling Association (ACA) and Counselors

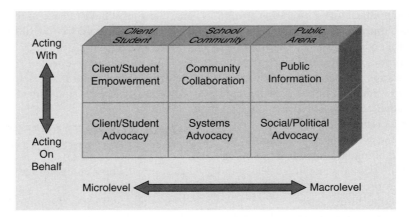

FIGURE 9.1 The American Counseling Association Advocacy Competencies.
Source: Lewis, J., Arnold, M. S., House, R., & Toporek, R. (2003).
Advocacy competencies [Electronic version]. Retrieved from
http://www.counseling.org/Publications

for Social Justice (CSJ)—Dr. Judy Lewis, Dr. Mary Smith Arnold, Dr. Reese House, and Dr. Rebecca Toporek—developed the *ACA Advocacy Competencies* describing the skills counselors need to possess to advocate for clients and students (see Figure 9.1 and Table 9.1). According to the *ACA Advocacy Competencies*, there are three domains where counselors advocate for change: client/student advocacy, school/community advocacy, and public arena advocacy (Gibson, 2014; Ratts et al., 2007). There are two levels within each domain; one level involves advocating with a stakeholder or system, and another level involves advocating on behalf of a person or system.

The two levels within the client/student advocacy domain are client/student empowerment and client/student advocacy (Gibson, 2014; Ratts et al., 2007). Client/student empowerment involves teaching clients self-advocacy skills, helping clients develop a strategy or plan for self-advocacy, and assisting clients in becoming knowledgeable and aware of their situations and identifying the skills and assets that they can use in the advocacy process. Although the primary goal is for the client or student to advocate on his or her own behalf, the school counselor serves as a mentor and assistant throughout the process. Professional school counselors might use this level to help students become more assertive, address a bullying situation, improve their communication skills, ensure college and career access materials are available in multiple languages, and work through conflicts. Parents and guardians are empowered by providing resources and information to help them through confusing school paperwork, policies, and practices to adequately advocate

for their children. The second level in this domain, client/student advocacy, involves direct school counselor endeavors to enact change or secure certain resources *for* students. To be an effective student advocate, school counselors must create action plans for initiating change, which often involves communicating their plan to important stakeholders and gaining supporters and allies to assist them in achieving their goal, such as ensuring that the dropout rate in a high school is cut by 75% through school counseling program interventions and then results reports share outcomes with all stakeholders (ASCA, 2012). This process requires all four leadership domains discussed earlier in this chapter.

The two levels within the school/community advocacy domain are community collaboration and systems advocacy (Gibson, 2014; Ratts et al., 2007). A professional school counselor involved in community collaboration works with community organizations to aid their advocacy efforts. For example, if a professional school counselor observes an increase in crime in his or her community negatively affecting students' ability to learn and feel safe, that school counselor may (a) create a bridge by meeting with local law enforcement officers to collaboratively tackle issues in the school and (b) collect data on how to decrease crime through positive school interventions.

Another example is partnering with school counseling programs at local universities and in prosecutors' offices to develop programs to reduce truancy. Graduate school counseling students can work to connect parents and guardians to needed resources, including support and referrals to appropriate services and agencies. In addition,

TABLE 9.1 The American Counseling Association Advocacy Competencies

Client/Student Empowerment

- An advocacy orientation involves not only systems change interventions but also the implementation of empowerment strategies in direct counseling.
- Advocacy-oriented counselors recognize the impact of social, political, economic, and cultural factors on human development.
- They also help their clients and students understand their own lives in context. This lays the groundwork for self-advocacy.

Empowerment Counselor Competencies

In direct interventions, the counselor is able to:

1. Identify strengths and resources of clients and students.
2. Identify the social, political, economic, and cultural factors that affect the client/student.
3. Recognize the signs indicating that an individual's behaviors and concerns reflect responses to systemic or internalized oppression.
4. At an appropriate development level, help the individual identify the external barriers that affect his or her development.
5. Train students and clients in self-advocacy skills.
6. Help students and clients develop self-advocacy action plans.
7. Assist students and clients in carrying out action plans.

Client/Student Advocacy

- When counselors become aware of external factors that act as barriers to an individual's development, they may choose to respond through advocacy.
- The client/student advocate role is especially significant when individuals or vulnerable groups lack access to needed services.

Client/Student Advocacy Counselor Competencies

In environmental interventions on behalf of clients and students, the counselor is able to:

8. Negotiate relevant services and education systems on behalf of clients and students.
9. Help clients and students gain access to needed resources.
10. Identify barriers to the well-being of individuals and vulnerable groups.
11. Develop an initial plan of action for confronting these barriers.
12. Identify potential allies for confronting the barriers.
13. Carry out the plan of action.

Community Collaboration

- Their ongoing work with people gives counselors a unique awareness of recurring themes. Counselors are often among the first to become aware of specific difficulties in the environment.
- Advocacy-oriented counselors often choose to respond to such challenges by alerting existing organizations that are already working for change and that might have an interest in the issue at hand.
- In these situations, the counselor's primary role is as an ally. Counselors can also be helpful to organizations by making available to them our particular skills: interpersonal relations, communications, training, and research.

Community Collaboration Counselor Competencies

14. Identify environmental factors that impinge upon students' and clients' development.
15. Alert community or school groups with common concerns related to the issue.
16. Develop alliances with groups working for change.
17. Use effective listening skills to gain understanding of the group's goals.
18. Identify the strengths and resources that the group members bring to the process of systemic change.
19. Communicate recognition of and respect for these strengths and resources.
20. Identify and offer the skills that the counselor can bring to the collaboration.
21. Assess the effect of counselor's interaction with the community.

(Continued)

TABLE 9.1   The American Counseling Association Advocacy Competencies (*Continued*)

Systems Advocacy

- When counselors identify systemic factors that act as barriers to their students' or clients' development, they often wish that they could change the environment and prevent some of the problems that they see every day.
- Regardless of the specific target of change, the processes for altering the status quo have common qualities. Change is a process that requires vision, persistence, leadership, collaboration, systems analysis, and strong data. In many situations, a counselor is the right person to take leadership.

Systems Advocacy Counselor Competencies

In exerting systems-change leadership at the school or community level, the advocacy-oriented counselor is able to:

22. Identify environmental factors impinging on students' or clients' development.
23. Provide and interpret data to show the urgency for change.
24. In collaboration with other stakeholders, develop a vision to guide change.
25. Analyze the sources of political power and social influence within the system.
26. Develop a step-by-step plan for implementing the change process.
27. Develop a plan for dealing with probable responses to change.
28. Recognize and deal with resistance.
29. Assess the effect of counselor's advocacy efforts on the system and constituents.

Public Information

- Across settings, specialties, and theoretical perspectives, professional counselors share knowledge of human development and expertise in communication.
- These qualities make it possible for advocacy-oriented counselors to awaken the general public to macro-systemic issues regarding human dignity.

Public Information Counselor Competencies

In informing the public about the role of environmental factors in human development, the advocacy-oriented counselor is able to:

30. Recognize the impact of oppression and other barriers to healthy development.
31. Identify environmental factors that are protective of healthy development.
32. Prepare written and multi-media materials that provide clear explanations of the role of specific environmental factors in human development.
33. Communicate information in ways that are ethical and appropriate for the target population.
34. Disseminate information through a variety of media.
35. Identify and collaborate with other professionals who are involved in disseminating public information.
36. Assess the influence of public information efforts undertaken by the counselor.

Social/Political Advocacy

- Counselors regularly act as change agents in the systems that affect their own students and clients most directly. This experience often leads toward the recognition that some of the concerns they have addressed affected people in a much larger arena.
- When this happens, counselors use their skills to carry out social/political advocacy.

Social/Political Advocacy Counselor Competencies

In influencing public policy in a large, public arena, the advocacy-oriented counselor is able to:

37. Distinguish those problems that can best be resolved through social/political action.
38. Identify the appropriate mechanisms and avenues for addressing these problems.
39. Seek out and join with potential allies.
40. Support existing alliances for change.
41. With allies, prepare convincing data and rationales for change.
42. With allies, lobby legislators and other policy makers.
43. Maintain open dialogue with communities and clients to ensure that the social/political advocacy is consistent with the initial goals.

Source: Lewis, J., Arnold, M. S., House, R., & Toporek, R. (2003). *Advocacy competencies* [Electronic version]. Retrieved from http://www.counseling.org/Publications

school counselors and school counseling candidates demonstrate advocacy through community, school, and university partnerships (Oliver, 2012).

Systems advocacy involves a more direct effort by school counselors to change a system. Instead of allying themselves with existing organizations to help address a problem, they will spearhead the effort themselves. To be systems advocates, school counselors must understand how systems work, use data to make a compelling case for change, design a plan for change, communicate their vision of change to others, work through fears, and continually evaluate the success of their advocacy efforts. Engaging systems advocacy requires school counselors to develop skills in leadership and community organization. Unfortunately, few professional school counselors (31%) currently collaborate with businesses, organizations, or government agencies to create interventions or facilitate change in community systems (College Board, 2012b).

The two levels within the public arena advocacy domain are public information and social/political advocacy (Gibson, 2014; Ratts et al., 2007). The public information level involves creating and distributing materials about important topics to the community. Professional school counselors working from this level create school counseling program websites, blogs, and wikis; write school counseling newsletters; send e-blasts; and design school counseling program brochures with helpful information for all stakeholders, including parents and guardians, about their children's development and how to address various issues (e.g., accessing community mental health resources, navigating the special education system, helping their children achieve academically, and helping with the eight components of career and college readiness counseling; NOSCA, 2010). The social/political advocacy level involves contacting local and state representatives and policy makers to raise awareness about issues and working to create change on a much broader level. Professional school counselors will challenge the oppressions that are behind the achievement and opportunity gaps that result in unfair practices facing students of color (racism), poor and working-class students (classism), bilingual students (linguicism), and students with disabilities (ableism; ASCA, 2010; Chen-Hayes, 2009). To become an effective social/political advocate, school counselors must collaborate with other stakeholders, develop strong working relationships with influential community members, gain supporters, and join forces with local organizations addressing the same issue. Once again, developing competence in the four leadership domains is vital for successful social/political advocacy.

In addition to the ACA Advocacy Competencies, Trusty and Brown (2005) developed advocacy competencies

for professional school counselors: dispositions, knowledge, and skills necessary for professional school counselors to effectively operate as advocates for their students, schools, and communities. Four essential school counselor dispositions are highlighted: the advocacy, family support/empowerment, social advocacy, and ethical dispositions. School counselors with an advocacy disposition will welcome the opportunity to be an advocate and, as such, work through resistance and ruffle some feathers to achieve academic, career, and college equity for all K–12 students. School counselors with a family support/empowerment disposition will recognize the family as a key stakeholder and work to teach families how to advocate for their children and adolescents. Professional school counselors with a social advocacy disposition advocate on behalf of others when they recognize unfair situations, as when they empower lesbian, bisexual, gay, and transgendered students, who are often stigmatized and subjected to harassment in schools. Finally, school counselors with an ethical disposition behave in accordance with applicable school counselor codes of ethics (ACA, 2005; ASCA, 2010) at all times.

Beyond possessing the necessary advocacy dispositions, professional school counselors must have the appropriate knowledge and skills to advocate (Trusty & Brown, 2005). School counselors should have knowledge of how systems work, knowledge of how to resolve conflicts, and an awareness of advocacy models they can use to structure advocacy efforts. In addition, school counselor advocates should have or gain skills in effective communication, collaboration and teaming, problem solving, organization, and coping mechanisms, including having strong allies both at work and outside work who can be counted on for a listening ear when the going gets tough.

Unfortunately, a recent survey of professional school counselors indicates that many school counselors do not receive the education and training needed to carry out advocacy strategies, particularly when counselors are working with marginalized student populations. For example, data from the College Board (2012b) indicated only 49% of school counselors surveyed had specific training regarding closing the achievement gap. So although advocacy competencies exist, these data indicate many school counselors still lack the requisite skills and training necessary and may not have the knowledge to identify when and what skills to use to close gaps.

Advocacy may be an arduous process and particularly draining for professional school counselors who want to be liked by everyone. Bemak and Chung (2008) referred to this desire to be universally beloved and esteemed as the *nice counselor syndrome*, which, they theorized, resulted in school counselors supporting the current system's status quo, even when inequities such as achievement and opportunity gaps are evident. Advocacy often requires disrupting a system, a process that can result in discontent for those comfortable with the existing system. As a result, professional school counselors may receive adverse responses to their actions and be viewed as nuisances. Nonetheless, school counselors must find ways to ensure that all students have access to quality education and opportunities for career and college access. Bemak and Chung (2008) suggested multiple strategies to help school counselors become more comfortable with advocacy: Use data to make a case, connect change efforts to the school's mission, do not take resistance personally, find supporters, develop a realistic plan based on data and research, remember to act ethically at all times, and above all, trust the process. With the proper competencies, knowledge, and self-care strategies, professional school counselors can make vital changes at multiple levels that improve the lives of every K–12 student and society as a whole.

CULTURAL REFLECTION 9.2

How might professional school counselors in training from diverse backgrounds view the advocacy role of the professional school counselor? How might students, parents, and educators from diverse backgrounds view the advocacy role of the professional school counselor? Do perceptions of the importance of advocacy vary across cultures?

Empowering Students with Achievement and Opportunity Competencies

Professional school counselors and school counseling programs play an important role by advocating on behalf of all students and teaching them how to advocate for themselves and others in academic, career, college access, and personal/social domains. What kind of advocates do students need? Students need advocates who use data to recognize when student needs are not being met and when students are being squashed emotionally and intellectually by policies and procedures that should enhance their academic and personal/social well-being. There is no more effective way to do this than to model advocacy behaviors and teach self-advocacy skills to students and families. Advocacy should not end

with students. Professional school counselors advocate on behalf of all students, parents and guardians, teachers, and communities.

To be an effective advocate, school counselors need conviction, knowledge, and skills (Ezell, 2001). The entire community and individual members (including professional school counselors) must believe all students can achieve at high levels and deserve career and college readiness opportunities (ASCA, 2010; NOSCA, 2010), Professional school counselors convey this belief and expectation to all students in recognizing inequities using data from school report cards and by acting to change inequitable policies and practices. For example, if a student is placed in a lower-level academic class but has the potential to succeed in a more advanced class, the professional school counselor can step in and advocate on the student's behalf or advocate alongside the student. Even more important, students, families, and all education stakeholders can be empowered with data to end all tracking and insist that all students receive rigorous coursework and a high-level college and career preparatory curriculum in all classes, especially mathematics (Trusty & Niles, 2003). Advocating with the student means that the professional school counselor demonstrates the condition; ensures the student has the necessary information to express the discrepancy; helps the student meet with the necessary parties (parents, teachers, administrators); and provides support and direction to the student before, during, and after meetings.

Professional school counselors recognize when it is necessary for them to take the lead in advocating on behalf of students and when it is more beneficial to play a supportive role. There are occasions when the professional school counselor will attempt to advocate on behalf of a student, but the student and even parents or guardians may fear help. Being an advocate for a student does not mean doing what is easy; it means doing what is right for that student and his or her academic, career, and college access goals. Too often, in the case of students of color, immigrant students, poor and working-class students, and students with disabilities, low academic expectations dictate the decisions made by professional school counselors, administrators, parents and guardians, and even students who have bought into the adults' mistaken beliefs about their skills. Professional school counselors acting as advocates for students must explain the reason for their decisions and stand firm. Theory into Practice 9.2 discusses student fears of achievement and opportunity advocacy.

Professional school counselors can help students recognize external barriers that affect their well-being and academic achievement and then assist them in formulating

THEORY INTO PRACTICE 9.2

STUDENT FEARS OF ACHIEVEMENT AND OPPORTUNITY ADVOCACY

As a professional school counselor, educational leader, and student advocate, I advocate for students and find them fearful about my advocacy. On one occasion, an African-American male student requested a schedule change that would have removed him from an honors-level class, placing him in an average-level class. After reviewing the student's academic records, speaking with teachers regarding his academic performance and potential, and reviewing the student's goal to attend college, I denied the student's request. I explained to the student that, when I compared his previous academic performance to his present performance (e.g., lack of effort evidenced by missed assignments and poor attendance), it was evident that his poor performance was not because he could not do the work, but because he chose not to do the work.

The student and his parents were not happy with my decision and went to the principal to appeal my decision. I was immediately summoned to the principal's office. After explaining how and why I made the decision I did (sharing with the principal the information from teachers, student records, and the student's desire to attend college), the principal informed me, "As a counselor you are oftentimes the student's last hope. Therefore, you should be advocating for the student." I was stunned that the principal could not see that I was being an advocate for the student. I was very confident that the student could handle the work in the upper-level course, and this course would strengthen the student's chances of being admitted into college. It was for this reason that I did not honor the student's request. In the end, the principal honored the student's request.

Think: Based on your knowledge of school counseling and advocacy, how would you have handled this situation? How do the professional school counselor and the principal differ in how they perceive and use advocacy? What advocacy strategies could the school counseling program develop if this situation arises in the future?

plans to confront these barriers (Toporek, 1999). It may be necessary for professional school counselors to accompany students when they initially approach the identified barriers and then gradually encourage students to take the lead in advocating for themselves. Remember, involving students in the process gives students ownership and empowers them.

Professional school counselors must remove barriers to student learning. This includes identifying cultural attitudes, stereotypes, and misunderstandings that lead to students being placed in environments counterproductive to learning and achieving at high levels. Examples include students tracked into lower-level classes, students taught by underqualified teachers or teachers teaching out of subject area, and groups of students placed disproportionately in special education. Overwhelmingly, this includes young men with African-American, Latino, and Native American ethnic and racial identities. However, it is not enough for counselors to assist students and their families in seeing these inequities. Professional school counselors must resolve the inequities. When advocating for removing barriers, professional school counselors work not at the systemic level modeling social advocacy behaviors and conveying support to students and their parents and guardians. Closing achievement and opportunity gaps are a primary function of school counselors (NCTSC, 2013). Bruce, Getch, and Daigle (2009) reported that small-group

interventions can be successful in closing the achievement gap for African-American students on high-stakes tests. Pass rates on math examinations increased from 38.7% to 63.2%, and pass rates on English language arts examinations increased from 74.2% to 84.2% after the implementation of a small-group intervention by school counselors. Taking action by developing and implementing interventions to reduce or ameliorate inequities models social advocacy by removing barriers, promoting high expectations, and supporting student achievement.

Professional school counselors teach students how to advocate on their own behalf and on behalf of peers. They do so on a group level by teaching students how to use conflict resolution skills and peer mediation and by assisting students with organizational skills, study skills, and test-taking skills (ASCA, 2012). Students also need to learn how to advocate for career development and college development skills in elementary, middle, and high school to ensure they are well prepared for their future. Students need to learn self-advocacy skills for two important reasons. First, it is essential that students become more active in the decisions that affect their academic careers. Professional school counselors also educate students and families about managing school system bureaucracy. Far too often, students, parents, and guardians lack these skills. Parents and guardians often defer to school personnel as the authority. When schools make decisions, parents and guardians may assume the professionals making these decisions act in the best interests of their children. Professional school counselors can demonstrate the inequities and assist students and their families as partners through the bureaucratic labyrinth to ensure students receive opportunities to succeed (Epstein & Associates, 2009).

Professional school counselors assist students and their families by informing them of what resources are available in the school and community and how to access them (ASCA, 2010). Connecting parents or guardians and children to these resources is vital. Although this can be done in a traditional group fashion, professional school counselors must recognize that some students and families may need systemic assistance in accessing resources. Professional school counseling programs lead by ensuring all materials in the school are provided in languages spoken by parents and guardians and that students and families receive specific information on accessibility issues and accommodations that can be provided for various disabilities (e.g., developmental, emotional, intellectual, physical, learning). Financial and transportation resources and child care during parent–teacher nights and meetings are essential services to advocate for ensuring increased family involvement in schools.

Finally, students need to be empowered as leaders for life in their elementary, middle, and high school communities. Professional school counselors develop leadership academies, peer tutoring, and peer counseling programs and encourage and expect all students to participate in extracurricular activities such as student government, athletics, the arts, and academic-related subjects to increase their leadership skills, which, in turn, can provide students with a basis to learn advocacy skills (College Board, 2009). Students need to be encouraged to evaluate the success of the school and the school counseling program through anonymous surveys and needs assessments, and student representation on the school counseling program Advisory Council should be ensured (ASCA, 2012).

Empowering Parents and Guardians with Achievement and Opportunity Advocacy Skills

Parents and guardians often approach schools and school personnel as the "authority." When parents and guardians present issues and receive answers from school staff, parents and guardians often take that information as fact or accept it as "just the way it is." Parents and guardians, especially recent immigrants, may not understand the political or bureaucratic nature of schools. Professional school counselors inform families about how the school operates and provide parents with information and resources about how their child's school is performing compared to other schools (Education Trust, 2011). However, it is not good enough for school counselors to merely tell families where they can find this information; the information needs to be provided so that parents and guardians can understand it. In a recent publication, "Parents Want to Know About America's Schools," the Education Trust spells out what public schools are required to report. Public schools are required by law to produce school-level report cards, but their content is limited, varies by state, and may not provide parents and guardians with sufficient information to make informed educational decisions for their children. For example, school-level report cards may not provide parents with specific information about how funds are allocated to individual schools, how students progress from one year to the next, individual school climate including encouragement of student learning, and the quality of teachers at individual schools (Education Trust, 2011). Although parents and guardians are often strong advocates for their children, collaboration between parents and guardians and all stakeholders, including professional school counselors, increases the effectiveness of advocacy (Epstein & Associates, 2009).

Professional school counselors help parents and guardians to maneuver through unfamiliar territories to access services. They also help parents and guardians understand and interpret information from the school through websites, brochures on the school and the school counseling program, bulletin boards, letters, and handouts to understand their rights as parents and guardians. Collaborating with students and families by assisting them with college applications and information can increase the number of students who actually complete the college application process. In one research study, intentional interventions for Latino/a students increased the college application completion rate from 5% to 16% (Marisco & Getch, 2009). Once parents and guardians have the information they need in an understandable form, they may then need assistance in determining how and when to use that information. Intentional counseling programs can provide parents and students with information on how to use the information they access.

Parents and guardians are often faced with many barriers, including lack of respite care or appropriate child care, repeated crises that place a strain on the family, isolation, lack of transportation, financial difficulties, work schedule conflicts, time constraints, guilt, and sometimes stigma related to disability issues (Friesen & Huff, 1990). These barriers make it difficult for parents and guardians to become involved in support groups and advocacy activities. Professional school counselors assist parents and guardians in identifying resources that will allow them to access the services they need, thereby reducing barriers for participating in activities important to their children's success.

Parents and guardians may need assistance in effectively communicating their needs, desires, and concerns to school personnel. Such assistance may involve teaching parents and guardians the mechanics of communication, including compromise, persuasion, and negotiation (Epstein & Associates, 2009). Parents and guardians also may need help identifying whom they need to include in communication and what they need to communicate. Assisting parents and guardians, especially those from underrepresented cultural backgrounds and languages in recognizing the best or most appropriate time to address issues or take calculated risks is an important school counseling program objective.

Professional school counselors recognize when it is necessary to advocate on behalf of parents and guardians because parents and guardians may be reluctant to disagree with professionals perceived as having expertise or power (Friesen & Huff, 1990). In these instances, professional school counselors collaborate with parents and guardians and educators to remove barriers to achievement and opportunity. Professional school counselors often recognize when educators distort information or lack sensitivity to family concerns. Professional school counselors explain the content of jargon-laden written reports for parent and guardian review, such as standardized test score reports, college admissions examination processes, fee waivers, and accommodations, and college affordability applications like the FAFSA (ASCA, 2010; NOSCA, 2010). They ensure family concerns are heard and that written reports and applications accurately reflect the reality of complicated situations. Some parents and guardians may not possess the literacy skills or financial resources to advocate on their child's behalf for the full range of academic and career and college access opportunities. The professional school counselor's advocacy is vital in these instances.

Oftentimes, families become frustrated when they know their rights. Parents and guardians may advocate on behalf of their children and run into a brick wall. When this occurs, professional school counselors may bear the brunt of family frustrations. Professional school counselors should be candid with parents and guardians and share knowledge about the system, possible roadblocks, and possible delays or red tape that may be encountered. This precaution allows professional school counselors to maintain open communication with parents and guardians and often reduces parent and guardian frustration. Parents and guardians who demonstrate strong advocacy skills are valuable members of school leadership teams and school counseling program advisory councils (ASCA, 2012).

Finally, many schools have hired a family coordinator. Professional school counselors can easily collaborate with family coordinators to empower parents and guardians as collaborative achievement and opportunity advocates for all students in schools.

Empowering Educators with Achievement and Opportunity Advocacy Skills

Professional school counselors assist teachers and other educators in recognizing inequities that exist in the school system and use data to correct them (ASCA, 2012). These inequities include differential treatment of students from low-income families and students from middle- or high-income families, students of color and White students, students who are intellectually gifted and those who are average, students with and without disabilities, and students who speak only English and students who are learning English and speak a different native language. Professional school counselors encourage and challenge teachers to examine their own biases and practices. Challenging teachers to do this has a risk, but it is imperative to do so if school counseling programs and schools in general are to change so that all students can achieve. In many ways, teachers are the school environment, and professional school counselors must encourage teachers to create an environment that supports all students, with data and evidence showing that all students learn at high levels in every classroom.

When professional school counselors witness stereotyping and self-fulfilling prophecies in action based on ignorance and misinformation about certain groups of students, it is their duty to challenge the misinformation as systematic advocates. What should professional school counselors do when overhearing teachers making defeatist statements like "Kids from homes like that are doomed," "What do they expect us to do with 'those' children?" and "Why should I have to have a child with a disability in my class?" These statements indicate biases from teachers who do not believe all students can learn and achieve at high levels. Professional school counselors can provide annual in-service training (Hartline & Cobia, 2012) and frequent informal activities to increase teacher knowledge and effectiveness. Informal activities include sharing success stories, empirical career and college readiness research, utilizing technology (e.g., webpages, blogs, wikis), discussing the professional school counselor's role, consulting with teachers, and using evidence-based practices collected by the Education Trust's National Center for Transforming School Counseling and the Center for School Counseling Outcome Research and Evaluation (CSCORE; Carey & Dimmitt, 2012; Education Trust, 2013).

It is important for professional school counselors to consistently model advocacy systemically and individually. Not all teachers have the requisite skills to effectively work with students, parents and guardians, or administrators. Professional school counselors have training in communication, interpersonal relationships, problem solving, conflict resolution, collaboration, and team building, which enable collaboration among school personnel and promote high levels of achievement and opportunity for all students (Clark & Stone, 2000). Teachers may look to professional school counselors for assistance in solving classroom-management concerns, family concerns, learning issues with students, career and college readiness, and staff support.

Professional school counselors provide in-service training on effective classroom-management skills and assist teachers in learning techniques to create a safe, equitable, and learner-friendly environment for all students. Professional school counselors also work with teachers to help communicate with parents and administrators. This training should include multicultural information so counselors can help teachers communicate and collaborate with persons from various economic, linguistic, ethnic/racial, and other cultural backgrounds and persons with disabilities. Unfortunately, teachers are not typically taught advocacy skills, and some may not feel advocacy is a teacher's responsibility. To be a true advocate, one must speak out about injustice and abolish barriers to student success, well-being, and academic achievement.

Professional school counselors encourage teachers to be leaders in the school and community. Strong leaders who believe in the potential of all students can change the school environment and influence others to make changes that facilitate the inclusion, achievement, and opportunities for all students. It may involve organizing a community service project for the year where teachers participate in a project facilitating interaction with students' families who work second and third shift whom they might not otherwise meet. Professional school counselors encourage teachers to participate in school events and as extracurricular advisors for sporting events, club activities, recitals, art exhibitions, contests, and so forth. When teachers become actively involved in the school and the larger community, they are more likely to recognize the achievement and opportunity needs and inequities that exist. They can see which groups of students are involved in activities and which students head right home after school instead. In turn, students notice and appreciate teachers who attend events and internalize these efforts as evidence that teachers believe in them.

Most important, school counseling programs ensure that specific academic, career, college readiness, and personal/social competencies are defined and taught each year to all students (ASCA, 2012; NOSCA, 2010). Working collaboratively with teachers as advocates to deliver school counseling core curriculum lessons in each of these areas is a key part of achievement and opportunity advocacy. The *ASCA National Model* (2012) delineates delivery of the school counseling core counseling curriculum as a shared task with teachers each year for each grade level. Successful school counseling programs have strong teacher input and collaboration and ensure teachers are a vital component of the school counseling program advisory council.

THEORY INTO PRACTICE 9.3

ABSENCES DUE TO A CHRONIC MEDICAL CONDITION/HEALTH DISABILITY

When my son was in the ninth grade, I received a letter indicating that we had exceeded the number of parent notes/excuses allowed for the semester. Confused, I contacted the school counselor who said she would get with the case manager about the issue. Later, I received a call from the case manager indicating that my son's paperwork to substantiate his health disability was outdated. I was enraged. We had a transitional IEP meeting the spring before to make sure everything was in place before he transitioned to high school. No mention was made of additional paperwork needed, and we signed his IEP with accommodations, including allowing for excessive absences in the IEP. We scheduled another meeting, and I was told I needed another letter from his physician, and then after documentation was provided, the case manager informed me that the decision was made that my son would be allowed eight excused absences with a parent note for his health disability, and if he exceeded these, another meeting would be called. As a parent, I was infuriated. My child is protected under both IDEA and Section 504 of the Rehabilitation Act. The school cannot impose a limit on his excused absences based on his disability. My son exceeded the 8 days, and another meeting was called. I work full time as a school counselor educator,

I know his rights, and I'm still hitting the brick wall of bureaucracy. What would happen if I didn't know my child's rights under the law?

   Think: How can a school counseling program help parents, guardians, and teachers understand the procedures for ensuring that children with special needs are well cared for and supported in terms of individual and systemic advocacy policies and practices? How can a school counseling program ensure that parents, teachers, and administrators understand the rights and protections afforded to children with health or other disabilities?

Empowering School Systems for Achievement and Opportunity Advocacy

Professional school counselors work with students, parents, guardians, teachers, administrators, and all other school personnel. Working as a team is important; the most important requirement for ensuring the success of the school counseling program is to have administrators "on board" and supporting these efforts. Some principals fail to support professional school counseling programs because of previous experiences with ineffective school counselors (Keys, Bemak, Carpenter, & King-Sears, 1998). Educating principals and other building and district leaders on the changing roles of professional school counselors and the key function of systemic achievement advocacy is important. Establishing effective relationships with building and district leaders is essential if counselors are to take advocacy-related risks as change agents in school counseling programs. Several strategies that enhance relationships between counselors and building and district leaders include maintaining a respectful demeanor, communicating effectively and often, and asking for overt signs of support for the school counseling program.

   Professional school counselors can improve communication and be more effective in team building if they involve building and district leaders in school counseling activities. Professional school counselors can invite building and district leaders to attend education, career, or college information sessions; school counseling curriculum lesson planning sessions; conferences with parents and guardians; and other activities that do not breach confidentiality (ASCA, 2012). Formal and informal meetings can also enhance communication among counselors and building leaders because they provide an opportunity not only to share information, but also to build rapport. They also offer a mechanism whereby professional school counselors can bring forward ideas and issues that affect students, teachers, and schools. Ideally, this occurs through school leadership, inquiry, and data team meetings, where the professional school counselor is an essential figure in advocating for academic achievement for all students, using data, and demonstrating school counseling program results.

Professional school counselors need to work collaboratively with all school personnel (ASCA, 2010, 2012). To do this, counselors use skills in interpersonal communication, group process, human development, multiculturalism, assessment, leadership, advocacy, and counseling. Working collaboratively also means that all stakeholders understand the professional school counselor's role (Chen-Hayes, 2007).

   Professional school counselors provide staff development training and research data to promote system change. Staff development training should emphasize the promotion of high standards and expectations for all students. Counselors can share success stories of schools that have emphasized high achievement for all students as telling examples of how important expectations are in achieving academic success. Counselors can also use these opportunities to "challenge the existence of low-level and unchallenging courses" (House & Martin, 1998, p. 289). As long as low-level courses exist, schools perpetuate old ideas that some students can achieve and others cannot. Many schools continue to disproportionately place students of color, students from low-income families, students with disabilities, and students who are bilingual in low-level courses. Thus, the students who need the most receive the least, and their academic, career, college readiness, and personal/social opportunities are diminished by the actions, policies, and practices of educators and administrators.

   Professional school counselors need to be visible in the school and the community in delivering the school counseling program. To do this, they must be out of their offices and in classrooms delivering school counseling core curriculum lessons and in public areas of the school daily. They are proactive and implement outreach programs to inform students about academic, career, college readiness, and personal/social opportunities; motivate students to achieve at high levels; dispel myths harmful to students; and provide opportunities for students to develop their talents (Chen-Hayes, 2007; NOSCA, 2010). It is difficult to predict problems that may occur if the professional school counselor is not out and about in the school, communicating with students and school personnel. Visibility and accessibility are the keys, and administrators may be more apt to provide support when they view professional school counselors and school counseling programs as active, integral players in the achievement and success of students and schools.

Professional school counselors and school counseling programs assist administrators in creating student- and family-friendly schools. These schools communicate that students, parents, and guardians are valued members of the community, and their input and presence are welcome. One important value to convey is that all children and adolescents are expected to excel. Creating an environment that empowers students and families, and enhances communication and collaboration among students, parents, guardians, and educators. When a safe,

welcoming environment is established, it is more likely that parents, guardians, and students will communicate their concerns and needs to school personnel. This open communication creates an opportunity to recognize the needs and disparities that exist in schools and provides an avenue for productive, cooperative change. Finally, administrators are welcomed as a key part of the school counseling program advisory council (ASCA, 2012; see Chapter 4) and help create and evaluate goals, objectives, and outcomes for the year for each grade level and benchmarks used to assess school counseling program outcomes for student achievement, opportunity, and college access results each year.

CASE STUDY 9.1

Derrick's Dream of Going to College

"Mr. Shell, I want to go to college." This was the announcement Derrick made as he entered his school counselor's office. Derrick was an African-American student currently in his junior year. During the intake meeting with his school counselor, Derrick described his future plans, which included attending college. Unfortunately, his school counselor had to tell him that his diploma choice (a transitional diploma) would prevent him from attending college unless (a) we changed the diploma choice and started him in ninth-grade classes again or (b) he earned a GED after completing high school. Both the student and his guardian told the school counselor that they were unaware that his current diploma choice would make his diploma "useless." They did not recall anyone explaining the repercussions of this choice of diploma during any of his meetings.

The school counselor investigated what had happened and found the following. Derrick had left his assigned school to attend another school within the same school district because the assigned school did not make AYP. Derrick had initially received placement in a general education classroom with an additional special education teacher for support. However, at his new school, the IEP team placed the student in small classes (self-contained) and changed his diploma type to a transitional diploma. Apparently Derrick's guardian had signed the IEP without fully understanding that this change meant Derrick would not earn Carnegie units and would not be able to apply to colleges/universities or jobs without first earning a GED. After Derrick's assigned school met the requirements for AYP, the new school strongly encouraged him to return to his assigned school. Derrick and his guardian accepted this recommendation.

Unfortunately, time had passed, and Derrick was now a senior. How had the very system that was to support him and advocate for him, failed so miserably? Fortunately, Derrick's school counselor is committed to advocacy for and the success of all students. The professional school counselor collaborated with the director of exceptional education to modify Derrick's schedule. Although Derrick remained on a transitional diploma, core classes were added to his schedule so that he would be exposed to more rigor and information. The school counselor provided all the information necessary for Derrick to prepare for college applications, including fee waivers for the SAT and ACT and accommodations (such as extended time). The professional school counselor and IEP team also assisted Derrick in registering and studying for his tests. Derrick did well on both tests, and the school counselor helped to develop a script for use with college admissions representatives detailing the student's situation. In addition, the school counselor wrote letters of recommendation detailing the challenges that the student overcame and his strategies for success. As a member of the team, the special education coordinator ordered testing so that the student's records would be current (up to date) for submission to a college office of disability services.

Fortunately, all the advocacy efforts paid off. Derrick was accepted to a small, private, liberal arts college after sharing his story with the administration and after they received supporting documentation from the high school. He has successfully completed 1 year with passing grades in all his classes. He used accommodations through the office of disability services to receive extended time and took advantage of free tutorials.

1. Based on your knowledge regarding school counseling, in what way(s) did the professional school counselor and special education coordinator demonstrate advocacy for Derrick?
2. What additional steps would you have taken to ensure that Derrick was successful in pursuing his college plans?
3. What specific policies and procedures should be put into place to handle appropriate diploma selection and class selection for students with disabilities?
4. Should the advocacy stop at the school level? If not, how can the school counselor approach systemic advocacy?
5. What systemic advocacy approaches should you take if you discover that students with disabilities are being encouraged to choose diplomas that will limit their opportunities to pursue postsecondary educational opportunities?

Empowering Community Stakeholders for Achievement and Opportunity Advocacy

Outside the school environment, professional school counselors are presented with unique opportunities to work with the community as a whole. School counseling programs should have networks to connect parents, guardians, and students with resources that will help all students succeed (ASCA, 2010, 2012). Professional school counselors also can assist parents, guardians, and school personnel in organizing community efforts to assist schools in instituting a higher standard for all children and adolescents. To do this, professional school counselors must be involved in the community and be aware of available organizations and resources. Professional school counselors should enlist the support of various community organizations, including civic organizations, places of worship, businesses, colleges, social service agencies, and individual volunteers. Unfortunately, important parties are often left out of the collaborative efforts of professional school counseling programs. These untapped resources include physicians, local mental health resources, politicians, lawyers, support groups, and other leaders in the community.

Connecting parents and guardians with organizations creates a network of support that can be used to change schools at a systems level. Professional school counselors encourage community involvement in education and facilitate activities that promote and provide support for students' academic achievement (ASCA, 2012; NCTSC, 2013). Networking within the community facilitates the creation of quality services and opportunities for students and encourages the development of a community culture that supports and values all students and expects all students to succeed. In doing so, the professional school counseling program can play an important role in integrating the community into the schools, thereby supporting and promoting system changes that will enhance the educational opportunities for all students. Community members also play a critical role as a part of the school counseling program advisory committee and are encouraged to take an active role in shaping the implementation and evaluation of the school counseling program each year (ASCA, 2012).

THEORY INTO PRACTICE 9.4

EXCLUSIONARY PRACTICES BASED ON DISABILITY

Brittany is a sixth-grade student in regular education classrooms with support and pulled out for language arts. She began struggling in math even with supports in the classroom. The special education teacher called for an IEP meeting to discuss Brittany's current placements and supports. During the meeting, the suggestion was made that Brittany attend community-based instruction on Friday mornings, which meant she would not be in her regular math class and would miss her language arts class. When her mom objected, the special educator said, "Now Ms. Jones, there is nothing wrong with community-based instruction. We teach kids how to go to the store and buy their own groceries, etc." Ms. Jones stated that she knew what community-based instruction was and that Brittany did not need it. Ms. Jones explained that she taught Brittany those skills at home but she could not teach Brittany math as it was taught at school. The special educator then asked, "Well, does Brittany know her own shoe size and clothing size? Can she pay for these things and know the correct change she should get?" Ms. Jones became angry and said, "She knows those things and she shops with me regularly, I don't need your help in daily living or independent living

(Continued)

skills, I need you to teach my daughter her math and other academic skills." The special educator then said, "Well, if she doesn't go to community-based instruction on Friday, we have no one to support her in math or language arts because her support teacher and I are away at community-based instruction on Fridays." Ms. Jones quickly responded, "Then the real issue is you don't have supports for my daughter; it is not that this is the best plan for her. I do not want her pulled out for community-based instruction. She needs math, language arts, and keyboarding. Surely you can find a way to provide that to her on Fridays." The response from the IEP team indicated they had nowhere to place her on Fridays, and Ms. Jones said, "My daughter has an Individualized Education Plan, not a program based on school schedules and what is convenient for staff. Keyboarding is a skill she needs. Surely there is a keyboarding

class on Friday mornings she could attend?" The assistant principal agreed that there was but said eighth graders were in that class. Ms. Jones then said, "Well, is there something going on with the eighth grade where she would be put at risk in some way?" The team assured Ms. Jones that wasn't the case but still pushed for the community-based instruction. The meeting ended without a firm resolution but with the IEP team stating that they would look into a solution and investigate the keyboarding option.

What are ways a school counselor could intervene and advocate on behalf of this student? What are the responsibilities of school counselors in regard to the academic achievement and placement of students with disabilities? What are the systemic issues involved with this situation and family, and what can be done to change oppressive school policies and practices?

PUBLICIZING SCHOOL COUNSELING PROGRAM ACHIEVEMENT AND OPPORTUNITY ADVOCACY OUTCOMES

Both internal and external publics are important in the ongoing dialogue about the role and function of professional school counselors and school counseling programs. Internal publics include students, parents, guardians, educators, and other school system employees. External publics include those outside the school system who have a stake in student success, including politicians, businesses, agencies, and the general community. Part of the professional school counselor's essential role in schools is to ensure that school counseling programs are defined and affirmed as supporting the academic, career, college, emotional, personal, and social success of all learners in a school and to use data to back up achievement and opportunity outcomes (ASCA, 2012). If school counseling programs do not function in the role of achievement and opportunity advocates for all students with demonstrated outcomes, in an era of tight school budgets, professional school counselors are expendable. The media, however, often covered professional school counselors only during times of crisis on school grounds. Rare is the news story discussing the proactive role professional school counselors play daily in schools through transformed school counseling programs. Professional school counselors need to create school counseling program advisory councils (ASCA, 2012; see Chapter 5) that assist in spreading the word inside and outside the school about the school counseling program's achievement and opportunity gap outcomes.

Many superintendents, principals, teachers, and other school staff know little about what professional

school counselors or school counseling programs do for student success. Therefore, professional school counselors must undertake specific internal and external public relations strategies to inform all stakeholders about the professional school counseling program's role and mission in the school as achievement and opportunity advocates for all students. The more all members of the school and community know about the professional school counselor's role in the school counseling program, the better the support from all stakeholders.

A strong internal and external public relations effort is essential to ensure that school counseling programs delivered by state-certified professional school counselors are seen by others as central to the school's mission of educating all students effectively. First, professional school counselors, school counseling programs, and their allies need to target external publics—such as legislators, local politicians, community-based organization workers, clergy and members of places of worship, and workers in businesses—to explain the specific benefits provided by professional school counselors through school counseling programs. Second, internal publics—such as students, teachers, administrators, parents and guardians, school social workers and psychologists, school counseling and teaching practicum and internship students, school secretaries, janitors, lunchroom personnel, and bus drivers—must be informed of the professional school counselor's role and the school counseling program's mission, services, activities, competencies, and achievement and opportunity outcomes (ASCA, 2012) to ensure that professional school counselors are not relegated only to pushing paper, responding to crises, or providing discipline. As professional school counselors' job descriptions and roles as achievement and opportunity advocates are developed and clarified, professional school counseling programs must publicize to internal and external publics in six specific equity-focused roles advocated by the national center for transforming school counseling's new vision of school counseling (ASCA, 2010, 2012; NCTSC, 2013). Chen-Hayes (2007) summarized these roles with the acronym TACKLE: Teaming and collaboration, Advocacy, Culturally competent counseling and program coordination, Knowledge and use of technology, Leadership, and Equity assessment using data. As professional school counselors put achievement and opportunity advocacy for all students at the center of their work, they become invaluable to the mission of all schools. When they lead and challenge systemic and institutional barriers to learning with data, school counselors ensure all students have the resources and high expectations to succeed in school. Proactive professional school counselors publicize their work in academic, career, college readiness, and personal/social success for all students (ASCA, 2012). School counselors who do so are social justice advocates educating themselves about the needs, issues, career, college, and personal goals, and barriers faced by all students, (Getch & Johnson, 2012), and especially students struggling to achieve at high levels.

From Status Quo Gatekeepers to Systemic Change Advocates and Leaders

In the past, many professional school counselors and school counseling programs helped to maintain the status quo in schools (Hart & Jacobi, 1992). Specifically, they have been criticized for neglecting or unfairly judging students, particularly if they were (a) students of color, particularly African, African-American, Caribbean, Latino/a, or Native American students; (b) tracked in low- or middle-ability groups; (c) uninterested in or perceived as unable to handle college preparatory class material; (d) bilingual or spoke Black English or English with an accent or lacked fluency in English as a second language; (e) students with one or more developmental, emotional, physical, or learning disabilities; (f) girls seen as not needing college or careers; (g) boys seen as having too many discipline problems to be good students; (h) perceived as less than worthy of success due to being lesbian, bisexual, gay, transgendered, or gender variant; (i) from a nontraditional family; (j) immigrants; (k) seen as having a nontraditional appearance, including being overweight; or (l) from a nondominant religious or spiritual belief system. In other words, professional school counselors used various forms of oppression to unfairly sort students based on biases toward children and youth with nondominant race, class, gender, sexual orientation, gender identity or expression,

disability, language, family type, religion/spirituality, and other cultural identities (ASCA, 2010, 2012; Chen-Hayes, 2009; Nieto, 2004).

It is after incidents such as these that public awareness and support for professional school counselors and school counseling programs takes on such urgency—challenging past practices and demonstrating how professional school counselors and school counseling programs have changed to include academic success for all students and achievement and opportunity advocacy as the top priority (ASCA, 2010, 2012). So not only do professional school counselors and school counseling programs need to publicize their changing roles and the data-based results of their successes, but also they must recognize that there is just as much work to be done with adults in schools and communities who had poor experiences with professional school counselors.

One way to overcome past difficulties is for professional school counselors and school counseling programs to advocate for academic, career, and college readiness for all students (NOSCA, 2010). Lewis and Bradley (2000) defined the counselor's role as that of a social change agent and an advocate in schools and communities. Information about counselor advocacy efforts to foster academic success, high standards, and high aspirations for all students is welcome news to most parents, guardians, teachers, and principals. However, many stakeholders remain unclear regarding the professional school counselor's role as achievement and opportunity advocates for all students in a school counseling program (ASCA, 2012; Chen-Hayes, 2007). To clarify the school counselor's role in academic achievement, data must be provided and school counselors must be held accountable for demonstrating how they communicate with parents and stakeholders, disseminate information, engage the community, and facilitate workshops, meetings, and forums that foster the academic success of all students (Epstein & Voorhis, 2010).

Nieto (2004) shared outstanding school reform efforts promoting equity for all students through access to learning. According to Nieto, positive school reform (a) is antiracist and antibias, (b) reflects the belief that all students have talents and strengths that can enhance their education, (c) is based on the notion that those most intimately connected with students need to be meaningfully involved in their education, (d) is based on high expectations and rigorous standards for all learners, and (e) is empowering and just. This framework for equitable educational reform meshes with the school counseling program's advocacy role for all students' academic success and career and college readiness (ASCA, 2012; Bryan et al., 2009; Chen-Hayes, 2007; Ratts et al., 2007).

Savvy School Counselors Publicize Achievement and Opportunity Gap Outcomes

Professional school counseling programs have a multitude of ways in which they can promote public support and awareness. The *ASCA National Model* (ASCA, 2012) discussed the importance of all schools having a mission, a vision/beliefs statement, and specific annual goals focused on academic success and opportunities for all students. The mission, vision, and goals statements guide the school counseling program in terms of the outcomes all students will achieve in a school counseling program. Schmidt (2008) listed important ways to market and publicize the professional school counselor's role and function as part of a school counseling program, including (a) print and Web-based brochures, (b) a professional school counselor's column in the school or local newspaper, (c) the use of websites and a school counseling program page, (d) speaking engagements at local events, and (e) classroom presentations. In addition, Schmidt advocated attention to (a) outreach in print formats, such as newsletters, handouts, bulletin boards, and disclosure statements; (b) uses of technology, including websites, interactive communications with parents and teachers via e-mail, and computer training for parents; (c) school counseling program advisory boards; and (d) partnerships formed with other community members interested in the academic, career, and interpersonal success of children, youth, and families. Each of these ideas is an effective way of spreading the word about the professional school counselor's essential role as an academic success advocate.

Similarly, the ACA's Public Awareness and Support Committee developed guidelines for promoting professional counselors. Attention to internal and external public relations, according to activities in the ACA public awareness and support packet (see www.counseling.org/Counselors), includes the need for professional school counselors to deliver talks and presentations and to work with the media explaining what counseling programs do in schools and communities. Specific suggestions for professional school counselors include (a) call or write television and radio stations and newspapers to promote the latest activities of or awards for the school counseling program and students; (b) interview current and former students, parents, administrators, and teachers about how professional school counseling programs have made a difference in their lives; (c) create a school counseling program webpage; (d) create a school counseling program Listserv and encourage local media to access it for story ideas and questions related to referrals; (e) sponsor specific community or school events and ask local media to cover them to publicize the school counseling program's role in prevention efforts; (f) request that professional school counselor license plates be offered by your state to promote the profession's visibility externally; and (g) advocate with local and state legislators to better fund and support school counseling programs (ACA, 2014).

School counseling programs are a vital resource in the school for all persons, but not all students have equitable access to them (Lapan, 2012). Using a framework of advocacy for academic achievement and career and college readiness opportunities for all learners, coupled with the importance of addressing personal/social issues, professional school counselors and school counseling programs assist students, their families, and educators in a successful learning process in schools. Using recent models of school counseling focused on ensuring academic success and high expectations for all students, professional school counselors convey the importance and power of school counseling programs to internal and external publics by sharing outcomes of effectiveness in closing achievement and opportunity gaps (ASCA, 2010, 2012). Using print and digital resources and public speaking opportunities both inside the classroom and in community meetings, it is easy and important to effectively publicize and support the transformed new vision of professional school counselors as achievement and opportunity advocates for all students.

CASE STUDY 9.2

Tyler and the Bully

Tyler is a 7-year-old first grader who has a growth disorder that makes him much smaller than even the smallest kindergartners. One night Tyler told his mom that his privates hurt, and on investigation, his mom found a bruise on his penis. When she asked what happened, Tyler explained that a fourth grader had kicked him while he was waiting to get on the bus after school. His mom asked if this was the only time he had been kicked, and Tyler sadly said, "No, Mom, this kid punches me in the stomach or kicks me every day." His mom asked how long this had been going on, and Tyler replied, "I don't know, a long time—it's so long I can't remember when it started." When his mom asked if he had told a teacher,

Tyler replied, "Momma, that would be tattling. I'm not a tattletale!" His mom asked if there were other kids around, and Tyler said there were, but they just watched. Tyler's mom was upset and called Tyler's teacher, who said she'd talk with the professional school counselor. Tyler's grades had been sinking for some time now, and his mom was very worried about his safety and his academics. When Tyler returned home from school the next day, his mom asked him if the kid had kicked or punched him. Tyler said, "No, he had to apologize to me, and he spent, like, the whole day in the principal's office."

1. How did the professional school counselor and administrator advocate for Tyler?
2. What additional steps would you take to ensure Tyler's safety and academic success?
3. What specific laws and school policies and procedures address bullying and school violence in your state, and where can you advocate for stronger protections?
4. In addition to the "principal's office" what other school counseling program interventions are needed for the bully and bystanders?
5. What systemic advocacy approaches should you take if you discover that multiple students are bullied and/or bystanders?

Summary/Conclusion

Quality achievement and opportunity are not allocated equitably to all children and adolescents in public, public charter, and independent schools and school counseling programs (Carey & Dimmitt, 2012; Lapan, 2012). Research substantiates that particular groups of children and adolescents in the United States are consistently provided fewer resources based on inequitable funding of schools, inconsistent access to college and career counseling (NOSCA, 2010), teachers teaching out of subject area, lack of access to rigorous coursework, and a host of other academic policies and practices resulting in achievement, opportunity, attainment, and funding gaps (ASCA, 2010, 2012; Education Trust, 2013; NOSCA, 2009).

Professional school counselors and school counseling programs are in a critical position to advocate and lead for positive changes in school policies and practices that promote high levels of achievement and opportunity for every student (ASCA, 2010, 2012; College Board, 2008b). Professional school counselors and the data-driven transformative school counseling program must be a link between schools and communities showing specific effectiveness in advocating and leading to close achievement, opportunity, and attainment gaps (ASCA, 2010, 2012; College Board, 2008b). They must be visible in schools and communities as achievement and opportunity advocates for every student giving away academic, career, college access, and personal/social competencies to all students with intensive planning and via school counseling core curriculum lessons (ASCA, 2012). To be achievement and opportunity advocates, professional school counselors must have the requisite TACKLE (Chen-Hayes, 2007) skills from the NCTSC's transformed new vision of school counseling:

Teaming and collaboration, Advocacy, Culturally competent counseling and program coordination, Knowledge and use of technology, Leadership, and Equity assessment using data to work with students, parents, guardians, teachers, administrators, civic organizations, agencies, and the community, as well as the ability to demonstrate these skills in closing achievement and opportunity gaps with specific outcomes. To make a difference, professional school counselors ensure their school counseling programs are data driven, are action oriented, and demonstrate their belief that all students deserve the academic, career and college readiness, and personal/social resources to access the very best academic, career/college, and personal/social opportunities during and after K–12 schooling.

Professional school counselors and school counseling programs recognize that nondominant ethnic/racial identity, social class, ability/disability identity, and language status are used unfairly by some educators to create barriers to learning and achievement success by all K–12 students (Nieto, 2004). Professional school counselors and school counseling programs advocate for the elimination of barriers faced by students from all nondominant cultural identity groups (ASCA, 2010, 2012; NCTSC, 2013).

Professional school counselors position themselves and their school counseling programs as leaders and achievement and opportunity advocates for every K–12 student as an integral part of the school and the community. We challenge you to become facilitators of change, embracing the challenge as a risk taker to create, develop, implement, and evaluate data-driven outcomes of your school counseling program to ensure successful achievement and opportunity for every student.

Activities

1. Imagine the following scenario: You, as a professional school counselor, speak to the principal because an African-American student, your advisee, was suspended from school for fighting. The other student, who was White, was not suspended. How would you proceed to advocate for your advisee with the principal?

2. Write a letter to an elected representative advocating for or against upcoming legislation that will affect your students.

3. Imagine a parent faced with barriers such as lack of appropriate child care and transportation, financial difficulties, and work schedule conflicts. Develop strategies to minimize the barriers.

4. Interview local professional school counselors and ask them to what extent they serve as leaders in their school and community. What leadership efforts have they made? Have they been successful? What have they learned from their experiences?

5. Visit a school in your area that helps economically disadvantaged youth succeed academically. Interview the principal, professional school counselor and at least one teacher. Determine what is being done to help their students achieve.

10 Developmental Classroom Guidance

Gary E. Goodnough, Rachelle Pérusse, and Bradley T. Erford

Editor's Introduction: Whether conducted by the professional school counselor or the classroom teacher, developmental classroom guidance is a common and efficient method for implementing the comprehensive, developmental school counseling curriculum. Unfortunately, professional school counselors have not consistently focused on designing academically rigorous lesson plans, activities sensitive to diverse learners' needs, and assessment and follow-up procedures to determine the effectiveness and continuity of classroom guidance activities. The school reform movement, with its emphasis on academic performance, requires this of classroom teachers. The same is expected of the transformed professional school counselor.

In the past, professional school counselors were hired almost exclusively from the ranks of classroom teachers. It was implicitly assumed that these counselors, as former teachers, understood the role of teacher and could assume such a role. Beginning in the 1970s, states began to drop their requirements that professional school counselors be certified, experienced teachers (Randolph & Masker, 1997). It became clear to counselor educators and state officials that restricting entry into one profession (counseling) by requiring experience in a related profession (teaching) not only was a historical bias, but also served to lower the number of eligible and willing candidates for professional school counselor positions. Currently, only seven states require professional school counselors to have experience as teachers (American School Counselor Association [ASCA], 2012). Most counselor educators suggest that this movement toward opening the ranks to nonteachers has benefited the profession (Bringman & Lee, 2008).

With the advent of comprehensive, developmental school counseling programs, professional school counselors at all levels are in the classroom. Most have responsibility for delivering their program directly, as well as indirectly, to students. Direct delivery of a school counseling curriculum means that professional school counselors have a significant role in teaching students in classrooms. Thus, professional school counselors, although increasingly not rooted in the teaching profession, nevertheless need to become knowledgeable of effective teaching methods. Clearly, this is a tall order. To become a teacher, one must receive an undergraduate degree—in some cases, a graduate degree—and then complete a teaching internship. In 43 states, many new school counselors do not have this background, but will assume significant teaching responsibilities.

In this chapter, it is our intention to outline and discuss some pedagogically sound ways in which professional school counselors can provide for students' academic, career, and personal/social development. In so doing, it is our hope that professional school counselors will be able to better implement the classroom component of their comprehensive school counseling programs.

THE SCOPE AND RESPONSIBILITY OF THE DEVELOPMENTAL GUIDANCE SPECIALIST

The *ASCA National Model* (2012) charges professional school counselors with the responsibility of implementing programs to assist all students in their academic, career, and personal/social development. As discussed in the previous chapter, professional school counselors intervene at multiple levels, including the classroom. The *ASCA National Model* suggests that as programs are increasingly data driven, local districts inevitably determine the precise percentage of time spent in delivering classroom guidance. Still, for general guidelines the work of Gysbers and Henderson (2012) is helpful. They suggest that at the elementary school level, approximately 35% to 45% of the counseling

"Megan, would you like to run the classroom guidance lesson next week?" my supervisor inquired after I had spent several weeks observing. *By myself? Am I ready for this? What if I mess up? What if the students become out of control?*

"Of course, sounds great!" I replied, trying to sound confident.

During the lesson, part of a curriculum series, sixth graders are to write a letter to a mentor they can look to for guidance during their teenage years. Attempting to be as prepared as possible, I studied the lesson plan over and over, trying to commit it to memory. Not much, however, could prepare me for my largest concern: the students' reactions. Even though my supervisor would be there, I wanted to show her, and prove to myself, that I could manage 25 sixth graders. *But how will I keep so many students under control?*

On the day of the lesson, I quickly ran it through my head one last time as I arrived at the classroom. *Twenty-five sixth graders staring at me. Do not mess up.* I introduced myself to the class and outlined the lesson. *Okay, going well so far.* I asked the students to explain what they

had covered in the previous lesson. Silence. I reworded the question. Silence. *They can tell I am nervous. I don't know if I can do this.* I was so worried about the students being out of control, I had not considered that they might say nothing at all. Through a combination of nerves and desperation, I began to increase my energy. I walked around the room, trying to engage the students. Hands started rising into the air and the lesson gained momentum. *Phew!* After a productive discussion, I explained the letter activity and let the students work. *Were my directions clear? Do the students understand why they are doing this?*

As they finished, a few students shouted out, "Miss Krell! Come here! Read my letter!" I was shocked by the amount of pride they took in their letters and how excited they were to mail them out. At the end of the lesson, my supervisor was smiling. "That was awesome," she mouthed to me, while I let out a huge sigh of relief and let the students pass to their next class.

Source: Megan Krell, School Counseling Intern, University of Connecticut

program be devoted to implementing the curriculum. At the middle school level, an appropriate amount of counselor time devoted to curriculum is 25% to 35%, and at the high school level, the recommendation is that 15% to 25% of the program time be dedicated to the guidance curriculum.

Although counselors are not the only professionals delivering the school counseling curriculum, professional school counselors clearly commit significant resources to teaching. The ASCA (2013), in its position statement on comprehensive school counseling programs, supports the teaching role in stating that professional school counselors "teach skill development in academic, career and personal/social areas." With the decline in the number of counselors having backgrounds as teachers, professional school counselors must develop their teaching skills if they are to fulfill their roles within comprehensive, standards-based programs. Although many learn these important skills during their internship experiences (Peterson, Goodman, Thomas, & McCauley, 2004), there is an undeniable need to address this potentially important skill during preservice trainings.

THE EFFECT OF CLASSROOM GUIDANCE ON STUDENT DEVELOPMENT

Lending credence to the discussion of the effect of classroom guidance on student achievement is a statewide study conducted in Missouri high schools (Sink, 2005),

which found that students who were in schools with a fully implemented model guidance program including classroom guidance reported higher grades, better preparation and information for future goals, and a more positive school climate. According to Holcomb-McCoy (2007b), studies exist that demonstrate the positive effects of classroom guidance on specific outcome measures. In their classic review of the literature, Borders and Drury (1992) found studies that showed classroom guidance activities had positive effects on a variety of student behaviors, including classroom behaviors and attitudes, exam preparation, school attendance, career goals, college attendance, career planning skills, and coping skills.

With the advent of the accountability issues raised in the *ASCA National Model*, the Transforming the School Counseling Initiative, the No Child Left Behind Act of 2001 (NCLB), and the Race to the Top Program (U. S. Department of Education, 2012), there is a necessity for professional school counselors to demonstrate that their interventions are effective. Such is also the case with classroom guidance interventions. There is a move away from simply counting how many times an intervention is used and toward describing how effective an intervention is. One way to show effectiveness is to collect data both prior to and after the intervention, known as a pretest–posttest design. It is not enough to say that one has conducted a certain number of classroom guidance activities. Professional school counselors must demonstrate that these activities are effective in accomplishing an instructional objective and that students are different as a result (Dimmitt, Carey, & Hatch, 2007). Many data points can be used in a pretest–posttest design. A professional school counselor might access school files to find out about grades, standardized test scores, and graduation rates, or, once data are already collected, disaggregate the data by gender, ethnicity, and socioeconomic status. For example, if one were conducting a classroom guidance unit on bullying behavior, one might count the number of bullying incidents on the playground or the number of discipline referrals to the assistant principal before and after the unit.

Besides collecting pretest and posttest data, professional school counselors might collect content evaluation data and process evaluation data from the students and teachers in the classroom. When conducting an evaluation based on the content of the classroom guidance activity, professional school counselors might use pretest and

posttest measures resembling a quiz. For younger children, professional school counselors might use a Smiley–Frowny Form or a Feelometer (LaFountain & Garner, 1998). For older children, they might use multiple-choice and open-ended questions based on the unit. For example, Young (2005) conducted a classroom guidance activity based on the portrayal of Theodore Roosevelt. His content evaluation contained 10 multiple-choice questions asking students to identify facts presented during the activity.

A process evaluation is aimed at identifying which parts of the classroom guidance activity went well and which parts can be improved on. Especially when a classroom intervention is new, it is important to get feedback from students and teachers about ways to improve the lesson the next time it is taught. A process evaluation might contain questions such as those in Figure 10.1. Some classroom guidance curriculum materials have

---

Classroom Guidance Lesson: _____

Counselor: _____

1. I found this lesson to be: (Check one)

_____

Very   Somewhat   Not At All
Helpful   Helpful   Helpful

2. I especially enjoyed:

_____

_____

3. I think the following could be done differently:

_____

_____

4. I found the counselor to be: (Check one)

_____

Very   Somewhat   Not At All
Helpful   Helpful   Helpful

5. Overall, I would rate this lesson: (Circle one)

    1   2   3   4   5   6   7   8   9   10
    AWFUL   EXCELLENT

6. COMMENTS: _____

_____

_____

FIGURE 10.1 Process evaluation.

already been evaluated for effectiveness. The website for the Center for School Counseling Outcome Research (www.umass.edu/schoolcounseling), located at the University of Massachusetts, Amherst, contains research briefs and monographs based on published works that show the effectiveness of school counseling interventions. Among those evidence-based programs are Cybersmart (http://www.commonsensemedia.org/educators/curriculum/cyberbullying/NASP/), Second Step (www.cfchildren.org/ssf/ssindex), Student Success Skills (www.studentsuccessskills.com), and Peacebuilders (www.peacebuilders.com).

DEVELOPMENTAL THEORY

It is relevant to stress the importance of a comprehensive, developmental approach to classroom guidance. Within this framework, it has been argued that to be successful in implementing a classroom guidance curriculum, the professional school counselor must adhere to an overall theory of counseling. To this end, human development

theories are most appropriate for professional school counselors to consider. Borders and Drury (1992) emphasized that developmental stages are the basis for effective counseling programs. They identified several human development theories, including those of Piaget, Erikson, Loevinger, Kohlberg, Gilligan, and Selman. Havighurst and Super are also important developmental theorists. The challenge for professional school counselors is how to translate developmental theory into practical ideas for classroom guidance. Table 10.1 contains examples of what professional school counselors might do in relation to the domains of cognitive, career, and personal/social development theory when presenting classroom guidance lessons.

Consistent among each of these theories is the concept that developmental changes occur over the life span of the individual and that achievement of each developmental task is dependent on the successful accomplishment of earlier tasks (Erford, 2015). Thus, professional school counselors must ensure that relevant developmental changes are addressed in a sequential, orderly manner

TABLE 10.1 Classroom Applications for Cognitive, Career, and Personal/Social Development Theory

	Developmental Theorist	Key Concepts	How It Translates to Classroom Guidance
Cognitive	Piaget	Preoperational	Use props and visual aids.
			Use actions and words to give instructions.
			Use hands-on activities.
		Concrete operational	Use actions, props, and hands-on activities.
			Use brain teasers, mind twisters, and riddles.
		Formal operational	Set up hypothetical questions.
			Have students justify two opposite points of view.
			Use song lyrics to reflect on topics.
			Teach broad concepts that are open to discussion.
	Vygotsky	Sociocultural theory, co-constructed process, cultural tools, private speech, scaffolding	Provide examples, use prompts, and give feedback.
			Encourage students to challenge themselves.
			Teach students to use tools such as homework planners and technology.
			Use peer tutoring.
	Neo-Piagetian theories of Demetriou & Case	Executive functioning	Use acronyms to encourage memorizing of any "step-based" learning or strategies.
		Working memory	Encourage cognitive flexibility by asking questions that seek connections between learning and experiences.

	Developmental Theorist	Key Concepts	How It Translates to Classroom Guidance
Career Development	Super	Curiosity, exploration, career maturity	Plenty of materials with career-related information should be available.
			Career information should be integrated into all disciplines.
	Gottfredsen	Orientation to sex roles	Take care not to use gender-stereotyped materials.
		Orientation to social valuation	Help expand career areas outside those typical of students' socioeconomic status.
	Holland	Role of personality and environment	Differentiate the learning environment to reflect personality styles, i.e., social learning groups for social types, hands-on learning for realistic types.
	Bandura	Self-efficacy	Use activities that foster goal attainment and positive self-attributions.
Personal/Social	Erikson	Initiative versus guilt	Allow students to choose an activity.
			Teach in small steps.
			Use costumes and props.
		Industry versus inferiority	Have students set and work toward goals.
			Delegate tasks to students to encourage responsibility.
			Use charts to keep track of progress.
		Identity versus role confusion	Invite guest speakers for career day.
			Include examples of women and people of color in your discussions.
	Kohlberg	Moral reasoning based on the ethic of justice	Conduct lessons on bullying, cheating, and peer relationships.
	Gilligan	Moral reasoning based on the ethic of care	Use themes of care as a basis to organize the curriculum: caring for self, caring for family and friends, caring for strangers and the world.

VOICES FROM THE FIELD 10.2   **USING DEVELOPMENTAL GUIDANCE AND DATA TO BUILD SCHOOL COUNSELING PROGRAMS**

School counseling must truly be comprehensive, addressing the domains of academic, personal/social, and career development. For many years, particularly in public high schools, the primary focus of school counselors was scheduling. In years past, private/independent schools had no school counseling services. The assumption was that all students in private schools were going to college, and it was the mind-set of many educators to just teach the students. Today, many more students in public and private schools have serious issues and are bringing those issues inside the school building. As a result, schools have recognized that

professional school counselors are integral to the school mission and that their work must be comprehensive to address the needs of the whole student.

Classroom guidance is an important piece of the developmental, comprehensive guidance program because it helps professional school counselors connect with every student, while meeting students' academic, career, and personal/social needs. With the large caseloads of professional school counselors, classroom guidance is an important vehicle for making these connections with students. Through classroom guidance, school counselors become

(Continued)

visible throughout the school and are able to build rapport with students, letting students know counselors are available to provide important services that will benefit them.

As a school counselor, the use of data has become critically important to me in terms of measuring the success of a comprehensive, developmental school counseling program. Since its inception, NCLB has caused educators to use data to assess educational programs. Insofar as professional school counselors are concerned, we embrace data/accountability to measure and assess our school counseling programs. We need adequate training to effectively measure what is working, what is not working, and where adjustment is needed in this area of data/accountability. Through accountability, we demonstrate that professional school counselors provide useful services to students, evidence to back our mission and belief that all students can benefit from comprehensive, developmental school counseling programs that meet the academic, personal/social, and career development needs of all students.

Source: Kenneth Barrett, Professional School Counselor, Old Mill High School, Anne Arundel County Public Schools, Maryland

within a pre-K–12 curriculum. Using this comprehensive, developmental model, professional school counselors avoid delivering their services in isolated units. Instead, they build on previous efforts and successes toward a meaningful outcome. As an example of this hierarchical learning, Nicoll (1994) suggested a five-stage framework, based in Adlerian psychology, for the implementation of classroom guidance programs. These five stages are (a) understanding of self and others, (b) empathy skill development, (c) communication skills development, (d) cooperation skills development, and (e) responsibility skills development. Nicoll noted that each of the five stages could be repeated throughout each grade and adapted to appropriate developmental levels. Thus, the framework would be applied in such a way that each year builds on previous years.

CULTURAL REFLECTION 10.1

How might students of diverse cultural characteristics (e.g., gender, race/ethnicity, affectional orientation, religious traditions, ability/disability) respond to the traditional developmental approaches infused into our modern educational systems (and as summarized in Table 10.1)? In what ways do these approaches embed or remove oppression and marginalization experienced by diverse students in modern society attempting to access, attain, and achieve a quality education based on rigorous standards?

THE ROLE OF THE PROFESSIONAL SCHOOL COUNSELOR IN DELIVERING THE CURRICULUM

Professional school counselors implement their curricular role in three ways—through consultation, collaboration, and direct teaching. Although the most visible modality is that of providing instruction directly to students and parents, professional school counselors also implement their curricular role in indirect ways (Clark & Breman, 2009). For instance, a professional school counselor might consult with a middle school team of teachers as they plan a unit on ecosystems. In working with the teachers, the professional school counselor can become a resource to help integrate guidance curriculum components into the unit. In this case, classroom teachers are teaching the school counseling curriculum and are helping to promote the career maturity of students by providing world-of-work information as one of several important parts of the unit. By becoming involved with teachers as they plan, counselors educate the educators and are able to reach a wider audience more consistently.

A second way in which professional school counselors implement their curricular role is by working collaboratively not only in the planning phase, as in the previous example, but also in the implementation phase. In this case, a high school counselor might meet regularly with the physical education (PE) teachers to plan adventure-based education. The teachers and professional school counselor could then implement the program as a team, with each professional responsible for an area of expertise. For example, the PE teacher might attend primarily to the physical fitness components of a ropes course, and the professional school counselor could attend more directly to the team-building and positive social interaction aspects of the program.

Although it is true that all members of a school community share responsibility for implementing a counseling curriculum, professional school counselors may still directly deliver a significant portion of it themselves. For instance, in this third service delivery method, counselors in an elementary school program might teach developmentally appropriate units on conflict resolution to multiple grade levels. At the high school level, they might administer interest inventories to sophomores and then follow up with interpretation and a series of carefully designed lessons to facilitate students' career growth.

Counselors, by virtue of their professional preparation, are the individuals best suited to teach the content, skills, and processes of conflict resolution. They understand the role of interests in career development and know how to foster the career maturity of high school students. For these reasons, it is not uncommon for professional school counselors to be directly involved in teaching students every day. Although it is vital to the ultimate success of the school counselors' curriculum to engage teachers and staff in supporting and reinforcing the program components, many counselors, particularly in elementary and middle schools, nevertheless spend a significant amount of time teaching.

SETTING UP AND MANAGING A CLASSROOM ENVIRONMENT

Arranging the Classroom

Classroom arrangement not only creates an atmosphere or climate for learning, but also communicates the teaching philosophy and interaction expectations of the instructor. In a practical sense, how a professional school counselor chooses to physically set up a learning environment depends on the desired interaction strategies to be used during implementation of the lesson. For example, if the goal is to get students to explore an interpersonal issue in a deep and personally meaningful way, the professional school counselor might break the students into groups of two to four and have them cluster in small

circles in several areas around the room or around small tables. On the other hand, if the goal is simply to impart information on how to fill out a college application, a typical classroom-style setup may suffice. The important point is that teaching style, learning style, instructional strategies, and participant seating should combine to form an effective learning atmosphere.

Figure 10.2 contains drawings of several typical seating arrangements used by professional school counselors. A lecture hall or classroom-style setup creates a formal, businesslike, and often cold and sterile atmosphere that leaves no question of who is in charge. It sets the expectation that students are there to be taught and emphasizes one-way communication, with periodic pauses for questions. When discussion does occur, it is typically funneled through the instructor. The classroom-style setup lends itself to an authoritarian-instructor style, relegating student participation to secondary status. Many students take a passive role or are minimally active and engaged.

The U-shaped or V-shaped arrangement with the instructor at the open end still creates a formal or instructor-centered atmosphere indicating the instructor is in command, but it also indicates that there will be opportunities for interaction. The philosophy conveyed by the U shape is that interaction can occur between participants, even though the instructor will still function as the primary source of information.

The small-tables arrangement presents a more relaxed, informal, student-centered atmosphere where all

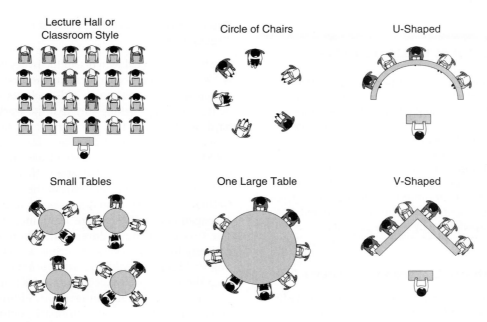

FIGURE 10.2 Classroom arrangements.

will have the opportunity to discuss, share, explore, and problem solve. In this arrangement, the instructor is more of a facilitator and serves as a catalyst and resource to all of the small groups. The small-tables environment sets an expectation of active participation on the part of all students and is used primarily for small-group work and learning. Putting student desks into a circle or block is a modification of this arrangement.

The one-table (round or square) arrangement conveys the expectation of participation and free exchange of information. Generally, this arrangement is viewed as less formal, although the presence of a table often inhibits maximum expressiveness. Most important, the instructor's authority and status can be de-emphasized, and he or she can be viewed as a participant in the group. This arrangement has a high potential for learning because a small-group environment can be a positive force in learning, and all students have the opportunity for significant involvement.

The circle-of-chairs arrangement presents a friendly, relaxed, warm atmosphere in which all participants are expected to be fully engaged. In many ways, interpersonal–social learning is dependent on the extent of participation, depth of cohesion, and quality of peer relationships. The instructor role must be conveyed as that of a group facilitator and participant who is also expected to learn from the group.

The arrangement of chairs, tables, desks, or even participants themselves will convey a learning atmosphere and instructor philosophy to all participants. The instructional objectives, strategies, and activities should lead the professional school counselor to choose an appropriate classroom arrangement.

CULTURAL REFLECTION 10.2

School environments are systems, and students of diverse cultural characteristics (e.g., gender, race/ethnicity, affectional orientation, religious traditions, ability/disability) are embedded within these systems. How might the structural setup of a classroom and instructional style of the teacher enhance and inhibit a student's ability to access, attain, and achieve a quality education based on rigorous standards? How might the classroom environment (structure and style) become vehicles for reducing the oppression and marginalization experienced by diverse students?

Working with the Classroom Teacher's Rules

It is rare for the professional school counselor to have his or her own classroom. More typically, counselors are in an itinerant role wherein they teach in different classrooms.

As a result, professional school counselors usually present lessons to intact classroom groups. In the elementary school, these classroom groups often are taught by one teacher for the entire day. Certain norms are already established by the teacher and students relative to behavior and discipline. As a professional who "comes and goes," it is important for the professional school counselor to have an understanding of these norms so that students have some consistency and know what to expect. Typically, teachers appreciate it as well when professional school counselors follow the basic rules in the classroom. This is not to suggest that professional school counselors must rely solely on the teachers' rules for classroom management and discipline. In fact, professional school counselors usually augment and adapt some rules to meet their personal style and professional role. Nevertheless, it is best not to contravene basic classroom rules, as this may serve to confuse students and annoy teachers.

One of the typical roles of professional school counselors is that of a consultant to classroom teachers. Counselors sometimes provide help with implementing classroom-management strategies and working effectively with children who present teachers with significant challenges. It is important that professional school counselors themselves be able to deal effectively with the wide range of students present in classrooms and to prevent discipline problems from arising. When problems do arise, it is imperative that professional school counselors attend to the issues in effective ways that are respectful to the student and his or her classmates.

Preventing Discipline Issues in the Classroom

The best way to deal with discipline issues in the classroom is by preventing occurrences in the first place. A well-designed lesson is essential. This includes several components, including making sure that the work is neither too hard nor too easy, that the work is not boring, and that expectations and instructions are clear (Geltner & Clark, 2005). Further information about presenting clear, effective lessons will be provided later in this chapter.

A good lesson is only part of the equation, however. Geltner and Clark (2005) suggested several classroom-management skills that are fundamentally important. The first is getting children's attention and keeping it properly focused. Several strategies are effective for getting and keeping children's attention. One is working to keep the whole group alert and on task through positive strategies such as encouragement, enthusiasm, praise, nonsarcastic humor, and dramatic delivery. Another strategy is enlisting student involvement in the lesson.

Teachers and professional school counselors do this by using an interesting variety of voice tones, piquing students' curiosity, using suspense, and connecting with students' interests and fantasies.

A second general management component that prevents discipline issues from occurring is having a smooth flow to one's lessons, a quality referred to as *momentum*. Momentum is composed of several parts, two of which will be described. One facet involves the ready availability of sufficient quantities of materials that students will need during the lesson. Few occurrences are as distracting to the flow of a lesson as having too many students sharing a finite resource material. Second, professional school counselors need to be aware of several things going on simultaneously—what teachers refer to as having "eyes in the back of your head." Classroom educators know what most groups and individuals are doing at any given time; further, they know what comes next in the lesson and what potential stumbling blocks might exist for off-task behavior during transitions. Being aware and knowledgeable, they seek proactively to prevent problems from occurring.

Managing Disruptive Behaviors as a Counselor in the Classroom

Despite educators' best efforts at prevention, children sometimes behave in ways that educators find disruptive. Professional school counselors know that students often bring with them concerns from home or from peer relationships that have little to do with being in class. These matters can make it difficult for students to benefit from regular instruction. A discipline plan needs to take into account that there are sometimes quite understandable reasons for children's misbehavior. Counselors, as consultants, help teachers see this and provide advice on dealing with it. Professional school counselors working in classrooms need to have strategies to handle problems directly.

When discipline problems arise, professional school counselors must first decide if there is a need to deal with the problem. They need to know what behaviors require intervention. It is important that teachers' rules be respected; still, professional school counselors need to have a sense of their comfort level with different types of student behavior. Professional school counselors need to behave in a way that helps students understand that the responsibility for the classroom's environment belongs to students and that professional school counselors are not police officers present to enforce oppressive rules. This being said, it is important to have strategies available to deal with difficult behaviors in respectful and effective ways. Having such

strategies is particularly important for professional school counselors who, by virtue of being in the classroom, set up potentially conflicting dual relationships with students whom they may later counsel.

There are several approaches that professional school counselors can take in addressing discipline problems that arise in the classroom setting. Effective approaches are based on the notion that the professional school counselor does not act in an authoritarian manner, but rather embodies democratic principles. As a result of their professional preparation and personal demeanor, most professional school counselors do not tend toward authoritarianism. A mistake often made, however, is to move toward the polar opposite of authoritarianism—that of passivity, where the professional school counselor becomes a nondisciplining "nice guy." Although all professional school counselors wish to be liked by students, being passive relative to student classroom misbehavior can both undermine the respect students have toward professional school counselors and render lessons ineffective. Of the several approaches to discipline and classroom management available to counselors, a classic approach developed by Driekurs and Cassell will be discussed here. For an in-depth discussion on classroom management and discipline, see Lemov (2010) or Charles and Senter (2005).

Driekurs and Cassell (1974) classified student misbehavior according to the goals toward which students strive. Their system is reflective of Driekurs's conceptions of misbehavior derived from his work with Alfred Adler. Driekurs noted that classroom misbehavior stems from one of four student goals: seeking attention, having power, getting revenge, and showing inadequacy. Students who seek power or revenge often feel powerless or oppressed. It is particularly important to develop a healthy nonauthoritarian relationship with these students. As a result of their work in providing responsive services in the school, professional school counselors often know these students quite well and, indeed, have developed strong, healthy relationships with them. When professional school counselors have strong alliances with these students and the counselor's presence in the classroom is not authoritarian, then it is unlikely that misbehaviors stemming from the goals of power and revenge will be apparent in class. According to Driekurs, students who withdraw or show inadequacy are discouraged and need encouragement. Obviously, professional school counselors should provide such support. Dinkmeyer and McKay (1980) operationalized these principles in their classic book *Systematic Training for Effective Teaching*.

Attention-seeking behavior is the most common form of classroom misbehavior and the one that is most amenable to the application of logical consequences. Logical consequences are based on the belief that social reality requires certain behaviors. It is not the power of the professional school counselor or the teacher that requires students to behave in certain ways, but the requirements of a just social order. Punishment is not meted out by the authority; rather, the professional school counselor, in conjunction with the class, makes it known that certain behaviors have certain consequences. Professional school counselors using this discipline strategy do not get in power struggles with students. They refrain from judging students or thinking of them as bad, and in a caring manner they help students realize that certain behaviors result in certain consequences. The consequences need to be logically related to the student misbehavior. It is important as well that the consequences reflect the social order, not the authority of the professional school counselor or the teacher. As such, professional school counselors do not imply any moral judgment toward the student and use a kind, but firm voice. Anger has no part in discipline (Geltner & Clark, 2005).

Professional school counselors seek to prevent discipline issues from arising by having well-designed lessons. They are aware of potential times during their lessons when children might tend toward off-task behavior, and they seek to mitigate such behavior proactively. Professional school counselors act in a way that is clearly perceived as being nonauthoritarian, yet neither are they passive. By embodying democratic, authoritative principles of classroom management and discipline, professional school counselors are able to enact their role as educator in a positive manner. Armed with such knowledge about the interpersonal role of the professional school counselor as educator, it is now necessary to know how to go about creating and designing a curriculum to implement.

CRAFTING A CURRICULUM

The process of developing a school counseling curriculum, although unique in some ways, is similar to that used to develop curriculum in other subject areas. Whereas in some states subject-area curriculum decisions are made at the state level, educators in other states create the entire curriculum at the local level. Locally, curricula are often developed via committees having representatives from stakeholder groups such as parents, community members, administrators, and central office staff. Whether at the state or local level, social studies experts play a large role in the development of a social studies curriculum. In mathematics curriculum development, the contributions of mathematicians and their professional organizations are central. Likewise, in the development of a school counseling curriculum, the professional school counselor and the extant professional literature play primary roles.

The school counseling leadership team (Kaffenberger, Murphy, & Bemak, 2006) or the school counseling program advisory committee (see Chapter 2) develops a curriculum that supports the counseling program's vision and overall goals. Regardless of the name of the group that provides leadership to the curriculum-writing process, curriculum development is a schoolwide responsibility requiring the active commitment and involvement of administrators and teachers. Because of professional school counselors' knowledge of the subject matter, however, leadership for developing a comprehensive curriculum is often provided by, or at least shared with, the professional school counselor or guidance director. Questions such as "How do professional school counselors decide what will be taught in each grade level?" and "What factors determine the curriculum goals and priorities?" will be addressed in the next section.

The *ASCA National Model* (2012) should be considered when crafting a curriculum. In addition to considering national standards, professional school counselors in many states incorporate standards from their state guidance and counseling models, as well as the state curriculum standards. Forty-two states now have their own comprehensive programs (ASCA, 2013). Regardless of whether a local counseling program is guided by national standards or by a state program, a central component of the program is a theoretical foundation that fosters the academic, career, and personal/social development of students.

Within a state or national program foundation, professional school counselors, working together with a steering committee or advisory group, assess students' guidance and counseling needs as perceived by important constituencies in the school and community. Comprehensive program professionals (Gysbers & Henderson, 2012; see Chapter 5) recommend that a formal needs assessment be administered at the outset of a move to a comprehensive program and then readministered about every 3 years. In this way, the program consistently represents the perceived needs of the supporting community. During this formal needs assessment, students, parents, teachers, administrators, and the wider community are asked about their perceptions of student needs. In states where comprehensive programs exist, these formal needs assessments reflect the state's curricular priorities and also incorporate local stakeholders' perceptions into the program.

Needs are also assessed on a regular basis in a less formal way. An example of informal needs assessment involves professional school counselors speaking regularly with teachers, students, and staff and responding to changing needs in a timely way. For instance, recently there has been an increased focus on bullying prevention and intervention. Some states (e.g., New Hampshire) have enacted legislation designed to foster systemwide prevention and intervention. Many professional school counselors assess student and staff concerns regarding bullying and assist the system and the students in creating bully-free and safe environments. On a more local scale, professional school counselors respond to myriad specific classroom and grade-level requests by teachers and administrators. These requests range from teaching social skills in a particularly difficult second-grade class to addressing sexual harassment with seventh graders. After conducting the formal needs assessment, and in conjunction with national standards and state standards, the school counseling leadership team or advisory council decides on the student outcomes appropriate for the locality (Kaffenberger et al., 2006). These student outcomes reflect what students need to know or be able to do on graduating from high school. Many school systems use the ASCA *National Standards for School Counseling Programs* (Campbell & Dahir, 1997) as their outcomes. In this case, the nine standards, three each from the domains of academic, career, and personal/social development, are the outcomes. These outcomes are further broken down into a series of competencies that, when accomplished, will lead to the outcome or standard. Finally, methods of assessment are detailed. (See Figure 10.3 for a flowchart of this process.) It is important to have agreed-on methods by which to judge the attainment of competencies. This process of generating an integrated curriculum is often done in conjunction with a district's comprehensive strategic plan.

This focus on aligning curriculum with standards is just one method of generating the school counseling curriculum. The second way is when classroom curriculum competencies emerge from the goals of the school counseling program as identified by data (American School Counselor Association, 2012). In these instances, the curriculum is generally not tied to any preexisting set of standards.

Regardless of genesis, the next phase in curriculum development involves deciding how to help students meet the competencies. Professional school counselors and teachers sometimes create their own curriculum materials and sometimes use commercially available curricula. As a result of the NCLB legislation, there has been a recent emphasis in schools on using commercial curricula for which research evidence of effectiveness exists. Using these *evidence-based*

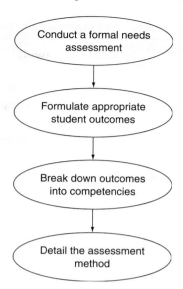

FIGURE 10.3 Steps involved in crafting a curriculum.

curricular materials supports the efficacy of professional school counselors' classroom interventions. When schools carefully adopt a commercial curriculum that matches their outcomes and implement it in a pedagogically sound manner, students are then in a position to achieve the desired competencies. In their study of the national trends related to professional school counselors and curriculum materials, Rowley, Stroh, and Sink (2005) surveyed school districts in 12 states about the type of curricular materials they used in implementing their guidance curriculum. Although the authors do not suggest which are the best or most effective published curricular resources, they do provide a table that lists over 20 curricular materials currently being used by those school counselors surveyed. For a description of several commonly used commercially available curricula, see Table 10.2. Classroom guidance lesson plans can also be found in journal articles, in books, and on the Internet. Curriculum design and the creation of units and lessons will be discussed in the next section.

TABLE 10.2   Examples of Commercially Available Curricula

Program Name/Grade Level	Topic	Websites for More Information
4Rs (K–6)	Social/Emotional Integrated with Language Arts	www.morningsidecenter.org
Bullyproof (4–5)	Bully Prevention	www.wcwonline.org/title42.html
Caring School Community (K–6)	Social/Emotional	www.devstu.org
Educators for Social Responsibility Programs (K–12)	Conflict Resolution	www.esrnational.org/

(Continued)

TABLE 10.2 **Examples of Commercially Available Curricula** (*Continued*)

Program Name/Grade Level	Topic	Websites for More Information
Flirting or Hurting? (6–12)	Sexual Harassment	www.wcwonline.org/title229.html
Kelly Bear C.A.R.E.S. Program (K–4)	Character and Resiliency Skills	www.kellybear.com/index.html
I Can Problem Solve: Raising a Thinking Child (pre-K–6)	Problem Solving	www.researchpress.com/product /item/4628
Michigan Model for Health (K–12)	Social/Emotional Health	www.emc.cmich.edu/mm/default.htm
MindUP (K–8)	Social/Emotional	www.thehawnfoundation.org/mindup
Olweus Bully Prevention Program (K–9)	Bully Prevention	www.violencepreventionworks.org /public/index.page
PASSPORT program (1–5)	Social Skills, Problem Solving, & Decision-Making Skills	www.researchpress.com/books/815 /passport-program
Peacebuilders (K–12)	Conflict Resolution/Bullying & Violence Prevention	www.peacebuilders.com
Positive Action (K–12)	Social/Emotional	www.positiveaction.net
Project ACHIEVE (pre-K–8)	Academic, Social/Emotional	www.projectachieve.info
Project ALERT (7–8)	Substance Abuse Prevention	www.projectalert.com
Promoting Alternative Thinking Strategies–PATHS (pre-K–6)	Social/Emotional	www.channing-bete.com/paths
Ready to Learn (K–1)	Learning & Social Skills	www.studentsuccessskills.com/index .html
Ready for Success (2–3)	Academic, Social, and Self-Management Skills	www.studentsuccessskills.com/index .html
Responsive Classroom (K–6)	Social Responsibility	www.responsiveclassroom.org
RULER Approach (K–12)	Social/Emotional	www.therulerapproach.org
Second Step (pre-K–8)	Violence Prevention	www.secondstep.org
SOS–Signs of Suicide (6–12)	Suicide Prevention	www.mentalhealthscreening.org /programs/youth-prevention -programs/sos
Lions Quest Programs: Skills for Action (9–12)	Character Education, Life Skills, Service Learning, Social/Emotional Learning	www.lions-quest.org/progoverview .php#
Skills for Adolescence (6–8); Skills for Growing (K–5); Skillstreaming (pre-K–8)	Social Skills	www.skillstreaming.com/
Social Decision Making/Problem Solving Program (K–8)	Bully Prevention	www.ubhcisweb.org/sdm
Stop, Walk & Talk (K–5)	Bully Prevention	www.pbis.org/common/pbisresources /publications/bullyprevention_ES.pdf
Student Success Skills (4–9)	Academic, Social, and Self-Management Skills	www.studentsuccessskills.com/index .html
Talking About Touching (pre-K–3)	Personal Safety	www.cfchildren.org/talking-about -touching.aspx
The Real Game (K–12)	Career Exploration	www.realgame.com/usa.html
Too Good for Drugs (K–12)	Alcohol and Drug Abuse Prevention	www.mendezfoundation.org/toogood
Too Good for Violence (K–12)	Violence Prevention	www.mendezfoundation.org/toogood

CREATING UNITS AND LESSONS

Scope and Sequence

To help students achieve the academic, career, and personal/social outcomes determined by leadership and advisory teams, professional school counselors must develop a comprehensive curriculum within their school or district. The breadth or content of the program provides its scope. Ideally, this is a pre-K–12 effort; however, in districts, it is done by building level. In these cases, elementary counselors develop the elementary curriculum, middle school counselors develop their curriculum, and high school counselors put together the secondary curriculum.

In curriculum design, it is important to ensure that grade-level learning is neither isolated from other grade levels nor redundant. Providing a school- or districtwide curriculum that builds skills and competencies sequentially is essential (Roberts, Kellough, & Moore, 2010). It is also important to establish the connection between the content of the counseling curriculum and the content in other subject areas. For instance, social studies in the seventh grade might contain a unit on the medieval period, including the conflicts and battles of the time. Thus professional school counselors might choose to weave their conflict resolution curriculum in with the social studies curriculum (and perhaps English and other curricula) for a more integrated learning experience for students.

Conceptualizing a Unit

How professional school counselors conceptualize a curriculum unit depends on the model of curriculum implementation. As suggested, professional school counselors implement their curriculum either by teaching directly or by working collaboratively with teachers to present units and lessons together. A third model of implementation involves professional school counselors consulting with teachers and having teachers teach the lessons and units.

Professional school counselors who directly teach conflict resolution might choose to adopt a schoolwide approach to implementing this competency by using commercially available, evidence-based curriculum materials. Professional school counselors using a locally developed curriculum need to understand how to create and teach high-quality units and lessons. Many elementary counselors spend a set amount of time in different grade levels; it is not uncommon for professional school counselors to devise a curriculum unit that includes one lesson per week spanning 8 weeks. In this case, the professional school counselor devises eight lessons in one general competency area, with one or more student outcomes being the anticipated result. The process of creating and teaching units and lessons is an important part of the role of the professional school counselor as educator.

In many schools, particularly at the elementary level, the professional school counselor's role in developmental classroom guidance includes itinerant, classroom-to-classroom teaching. It is important for professional school counselors to organize and present their units and lessons in classrooms in a manner that is coherent, clear, and effective. To achieve this, professional school counselors engage in a level of instructional planning equivalent to that which teachers use.

LEARNING CONSIDERATIONS FOR PLANNING UNITS AND LESSONS

Professional school counselors see students as learners in a holistic sense. According to Gardner's (1999) theory of multiple intelligences, there are eight intelligences: linguistic, logical-mathematical, spatial, bodily-kinesthetic, naturalist, musical, intelligence about other people (interpersonal), and intelligence about ourselves (intrapersonal). Students may display significant cognitive strengths and weaknesses in one or more of these intelligences (see Table 10.3). Understanding that students enter the learning environment with multiple cognitive strengths and weaknesses implies that instruction as well as assessment should be varied. At a minimum, this suggests that instruction should seek to help students develop in cognitive, affective, and psychomotor–kinesthetic–behavioral domains. Although these domains have much overlap and are not entirely discrete, the following discussion highlights their focus.

In the cognitive domain, there are six levels or categories of cognitive understanding (Roberts et al., 2010): knowledge, comprehension, application, analysis, synthesis, and evaluation. Within a lesson plan or unit, it is important to teach to and evaluate within several of the categories of the cognitive domain. In teaching conflict resolution, it might be helpful for students to have knowledge of the terms and words that describe the process of resolving conflict peaceably. Further, professional school counselors need to be sure that students show they understand the material. The domain of comprehension attends to this and is ascertained by having students explain or describe what they have learned. As an example of these first two levels, professional school counselors might devise a game-show activity to help students learn and show their understanding of terms such as *de-escalation* and *negotiation*. Applying the knowledge (application) can be taught by devising scenarios and having students be able to choose which particular conflict resolution strategy might best be applied in a given situation.

TABLE 10.3 Gardner's Multiple Intelligences Summarized

Linguistic intelligence involves the ability to use language (native or otherwise) to express ideas and understand the ideas of others. Poets, writers, orators, speakers, and lawyers rely on linguistic intelligence.

Logical-mathematical intelligence requires an understanding of the underlying principles of some kind of causal system or the manipulation of numbers, quantities, and operations. Scientists, logicians, engineers, and mathematicians rely on logical-mathematical intelligence.

Spatial intelligence involves the ability to represent the spatial world internally in your mind. It is important in the arts and sciences. For example, if you possess spatial intelligence and are artistic, you may gravitate toward painting, sculpture, or architecture. Surgeons, topologists, navigators, and chess players rely on spatial intelligence.

Musical intelligence involves the capacity to think musically—so much so that the music is omnipresent and free flowing. The musically intelligent are able to hear patterns, recognize them, remember them, and perhaps manipulate them.

Bodily-kinesthetic intelligence involves the ability to use your whole body or parts of your body (e.g., hands, fingers, arms) to solve complex motor problems. Such activities may involve making something or performing some action or production. Athletes, carpenters, dancers, and actors rely on bodily-kinesthetic intelligence.

Interpersonal intelligence involves understanding how to get along with other people and how to solve problems of an interpersonal nature. Teachers, clinicians, salespersons, and politicians rely on interpersonal intelligence.

Intrapersonal intelligence involves having an understanding of oneself. If you possess intrapersonal intelligence, you know what you can and cannot do and when to ask for help. You can control impulses and are self-motivated.

Naturalist intelligence involves the human ability to discriminate among and classify living things (e.g., plants, animals) and features of the natural world (e.g., clouds, rock configurations). Hunters, farmers, botanists, and chefs rely on naturalist intelligence. Children also frequently display these capabilities in classification hobbies.

In other lessons in the unit, a professional school counselor might want students to analyze the relationships among violence, bullying, and conflict by discussing and hypothesizing how to manage real conflicts that arise on the playground. A synthesis-level objective of a conflict resolution unit might have students combine knowledge learned about a specific conflict in social studies class—for example, the Revolutionary War—and have them act out a mediation session between the British and Americans. The final level of cognitive skill, evaluation, might be addressed by having a "courtroom" in which students sit on panels as "judges" and evaluate the effectiveness of the mediation sessions using the knowledge they have gained. All these cognitive levels of understanding might be included as a professional school counselor plans a unit on conflict resolution.

Cognitive learning is important, but it is not the sole means through which a holistic understanding of curricular areas occurs. The affective domain is also an important aspect of instruction. It focuses on using and developing intra- and interpersonal intelligences. Although some consider teaching for affective understanding more difficult to conceptualize and assess, Krathwohl, Bloom, and Masia (1964) developed a system of affective understanding that is modeled after Bloom's cognitive levels. In this system, understanding is organized on a continuum that ranges from surface-level learning to those types of affective understanding that reflect the personal internalization of values.

The five levels of affective learning are receiving, responding, valuing, organizing, and internalizing (Krathwohl et al., 1964). At the receiving level, students might simply be aware of the affective aspect of a lesson. For instance, some students who were observing the courtroom scene might listen attentively to the proceedings; they are receiving affective instruction. At the responding level, we may ask the observing group to discuss how they believe the "actors" felt during their role play. The valuing domain is critical in affective learning. Again, using the example of conflict resolution, professional school counselors might focus on valuing by asking students how they feel when they are called belittling names by their peers. As such, this group brainstorming activity would be addressing students' values regarding respect. After several lessons, professional school counselors might ask students to monitor their own and others' behaviors regarding conflict, thus providing a gauge for ascertaining the depth to which affective learning (and ultimately behavioral change) has occurred.

The fourth and fifth levels in the affective domain are typically longer-term goals and may, in fact, be ultimate standards or outcomes within a comprehensive program. Nevertheless, lessons often address these levels. For instance, in the organizing domain, teaching typically refers to conceptualizing and arranging values. In our example of the Revolutionary War and conflict resolution, professional school counselors and teachers can engage students in understanding and organizing their values relative to peaceful conflict resolution and notions of liberty and fairness. Finally, we want lessons to help students internalize their beliefs and develop consistency between their beliefs and their actions. This can be done by teachers and professional school counselors during regular class meetings when students discuss and process the events of the day. For an in-depth discussion of a classroom and schoolwide approach to developing interpersonal values and respect, see Charney (2002).

The final broad area of learning is the psychomotor–kinesthetic–behavioral domain. Harrow (1972) discussed four areas within this hierarchy: moving, manipulating, communicating, and creating. Because they concern skill development in areas of gross- and fine-motor coordination, moving and manipulating focus on areas of learning that are typically less relevant to the professional school counselor's curriculum. Communicating and creating are the domains that are the most salient. For instance, in a lesson on conflict resolution, students might improve their communication skills and be able to create solutions to problems that have led to conflict in the past.

In a well-designed unit, professional school counselors attend to learning and development in the cognitive, affective, and psychomotor–kinesthetic–behavioral domains. To ensure adequate attention to the levels of learning and development, professional school counselors create learning objectives for each of the instructional activities.

Learning Objectives

When the counseling curriculum is competency-based, it is necessary that the lessons result in measurable outcomes. One way to ensure attainment of outcomes is to write learning objectives for each lesson. Learning objectives focus the professional school counselor on the desired outcomes of students' participation in the lesson. To address the holistic needs relative to student development, it is helpful for professional school counselors to write objectives that are reflective of the cognitive, affective, and psychomotor-kinesthetic-behavioral domains of instruction. With this focus in mind, consider the components of thoroughly conceived and written learning objectives.

There are four parts that make up measurable learning objectives, referred to as the ABCDs of learning objectives (Erford, 2010). First, the audience (A) for whom the objective is intended needs to be stated. In most cases, this is the student, although it could be the learning group or the whole class. It is not uncommon for many learning objectives to include the phrase "The student will be able to. . . ."

Second, the expected behavior (B) needs to be stated clearly. These behaviors are typically stated using descriptive verbs that address the cognitive, affective, or psychomotor–kinesthetic–behavioral outcome around which the lesson is structured. Using the example of conflict resolution again, one cognitive domain outcome might read, in part, "The student will be able to identify behaviors that lead to conflict." A learning objective that addresses affective learning at the valuing level, yet is still written in behavioral terms, might state, "Students will voice their beliefs regarding. . . ." Finally, a learning objective might be more oriented toward psychomotor–kinesthetic–behavioral outcomes. An example of this might be "The class will create a process allowing students to solve conflicts without teacher intervention."

In addition to denoting the audience and the expected measurable outcomes, learning objectives typically include the conditions (C) under which the learning will occur and be observed. This third component specifies when or how the intended behavior will be measured. One of the examples with the inclusion of this third component might read, "After observing role plays, the student will be able to identify behaviors that lead to conflict."

The fourth and final component of a well-written learning objective is the degree (D) of the expected performance, or how frequently students will need to exhibit the behavior for the objective to be considered met. If there were three role plays and students successfully identified the behaviors in two of the three, the professional school counselor needs to know whether that level of performance is considered successful. With the inclusion of the level of expected performance, the complete learning objective would read, "After observing three role plays, the student will be able to identify behaviors that lead to conflict in at least two of the three scenarios."

If students do not achieve the competency or do not achieve it at the specified rate, then the professional school counselor may decide to design a new learning activity to reach the desired outcome. See Table 10.4 for a summary of the ABCDs of learning objectives with examples from the cognitive, affective, and psychomotor–kinesthetic–behavioral domains.

TABLE 10.4 Components of Measurable Learning Objectives by Learning Domain

	Cognitive Domain	Affective Domain	Psychomotor–Kinesthetic–Behavioral Domain
Component A **Audience:** Specify the audience for whom the objective is intended.	The student will . . .	Students will . . .	The class will . . .
Component B **Behavior:** Specify the expected behaviors.	The student will be able to identify behaviors that lead to conflict.	Students will voice their beliefs regarding respectful behavior.	The class will create a process allowing students to solve conflicts without teacher intervention.
Component C **Conditions:** Specify the conditions under which learning will occur and be observed. How will the intended behavior be measured?	After observing role plays, the student will be able to identify behaviors that lead to conflict.	After discussing the components of respect, students will voice their beliefs regarding respectful behavior.	At the end of four meetings on playground behavior, the class will create a process allowing students to solve conflicts without teacher intervention.
Component D **Degree:** Specify the expected degree of performance. Specify what is acceptable performance.	After observing three role plays, the student will be able to identify behaviors that lead to conflict in at least two of the three scenarios.	After discussing the components of respect, at least two thirds of the students in the class will voice their beliefs regarding respectful behavior, including both significant personal experience and considerable content from the discussion.	At the end of four meetings on playground behavior, the class will create a process allowing students to solve conflicts without teacher intervention. If it reduces the need for teacher intervention by 25%, it will be considered successful.

CONSTRUCTING DIFFERENTIATED DEVELOPMENTAL LESSONS AND ACTIVITIES

Students in school today come with a variety of academic, cultural, and emotional backgrounds. As such, the "one size fits all" model of instruction is not an effective method, nor one that will ensure that they are learning the skills being taught. Differentiated instruction in the classroom is defined by Tomlinson and Allan (2000, p. 4), as "a teacher's reacting responsively to a learner's needs." School counselors employ strategies to differentiate by designing classroom guidance lessons that incorporate differences in individual learning styles. When the evaluative data shows students need more time with a concept or skill, professional school counselors follow up in small-group or individual settings. The information gleaned from process and content data should drive the instruction. The curriculum should be grounded in increasing student knowledge, attitudes, and beliefs about their academic, personal/social, and career development; however, it is incumbent on the school counselor to assess what students already know, what they need to know, and what have they learned. It is because of these assessment pieces that classroom guidance lessons must be flexible enough to adjust to the students' needs.

Lessons can be conceptualized as having three distinct parts: an introduction, the developmental activities of the lesson, and the conclusion. A well-designed lesson increases the likelihood that students will invest their energies in learning the material and that they will learn what is being taught. Further, a pedagogically sound lesson captures students' interest and allows them to extend their knowledge and competency.

Introducing Lessons

There are two important aspects to introducing a lesson to students. One is to communicate to students an overview and the overall objective of the lesson. When professional school counselors do this clearly, students develop an itinerary of their learning and know what the expected learning objectives will be. The second important aspect of lesson introduction is to help students to understand that they already know something about the topic at hand and that, during the lesson, they will be working to extend their knowledge or skills (Saphier, King, & D'Auria, 2006).

Typically, students already know some information about the areas being taught. For instance, a school counseling program may be working toward the outcome that "Students will acquire skills to investigate the world of work in relation to knowledge of self and to make informed career choices" (Campbell & Dahir, 1997, p. 25). Because this is a program outcome or standard, learning will have been developed at various checkpoints throughout previous grades. Therefore, it is likely that students will already have some knowledge of the required skills, as well as how to go about making informed choices. In fact, if we have vertically articulated the curriculum properly, the counseling curriculum builds in a sequential and logical manner. Let us posit that the specific eighth-grade benchmark is that students will understand their interests, motivations, skills, and abilities. Prior to the eighth grade, students likely will have had some curricular and personal experiences supportive of the benchmark. Activating this previous knowledge helps provide the groundwork for a productive educational session.

Activating previous knowledge helps students orient themselves to the lesson. It shows them that they already know some important information and that the topic at hand is not entirely new. Done well, it also motivates students and provides a continued rationale for their efforts. There are several ways school counselors can activate students' previous knowledge and, in so doing, effectively introduce a lesson.

One method frequently used is semantic mapping (Hedrick, Harmon, & Wood, 2008). In a semantic mapping exercise for the career development example, the professional school counselor might ask the class, "What motivates people to receive good grades or work hard?" The professional school counselor might list the students' responses in logical categories suggesting internal motivators (wanting to learn the material, being interested in it) and external motivators (making the honor roll, being rewarded by parents). The professional school counselor can show students what they already know on the topic and get them actively involved in the lesson.

Developmental Activities

Once students' previous knowledge has been activated and they have been oriented to the topic, they are ready to engage in the learning activity. Learning activities are student experiences that facilitate mastery of the lesson's objectives. It is essential to clearly delineate learning objectives because understanding what students are to learn not only helps professional school counselors design lessons that are most likely to accomplish that end, but also allows them to conduct meaningful assessment. There are two broad areas of understanding that can help guide professional school counselors as they design learning activities: multiple intelligences and level of activity.

As discussed earlier, students can be considered to have multiple intelligences. Given this theory, professional school counselors make efforts to structure and implement their lessons to draw on the variety of cognitive strengths and weaknesses that students may have. Schools have traditionally focused on fostering linguistic or verbal learning. For instance, both traditional, teacher-led discussions and most writing assignments draw heavily on linguistic intelligence. Although professional school counselors will want to teach to and assess students' language and verbal skills, they have a broad understanding of intelligence and design lessons likely to draw on a variety of student strengths. For instance, learning can both occur and be expressed through music. Tapping into students' musical intelligence might involve having students create a song, rap, or chant that describes the steps involved in problem solving or conflict resolution (Hoffman, 2002). Other activities can involve drawing on knowledge of self (intrapersonal intelligence). In a lesson on feelings, this intrapersonal approach might ask students to reflect on times they were sad. Interpersonal intelligence is activated when professional school counselors ask groups to work together to come up with a solution to a problem. Other avenues for learning include artistic, spatial, naturalist, logical-mathematical, and kinesthetic modalities. To access these avenues, professional school counselors often use role plays and art during lessons. Professional school counselors design a variety of activities that draw on the multiple intelligences students may possess to teach and assess the learning objectives.

In a similar vein, there are many types of teaching strategies relative to student activity level. These range from the teacher or expert at the front of the class to those strategies that keep all students actively involved in their learning. Generally, it is better pedagogically for the professional school counselor to keep students active as opposed to passive. This is not to suggest that professional school counselors never stand before a group of students and explain information. In fact, this may be an important aspect of some lessons. Still, this type of learning experience limits student participation to only one sense—auditory learning. Professional school counselors can increase the students' experience to two senses by adding visual activities (e.g., pictures, videos, and overheads) to their presentations (Roberts et al., 2010). Although the addition of visual cues does not amount to what is considered active learning, it involves the student in more than merely listening to the teacher or counselor. The more active levels of student involvement have students simulating or engaging in direct experiences.

Using an example of teaching conflict resolution, professional school counselors might have students role-play conflict deescalation strategies to provide a simulated experience. In a lesson on connecting interests to career clusters, all students might take a computerized interest assessment individually and then work with a partner or in small groups to investigate several career clusters. Many teachers and professional school counselors use cooperative learning groups (CLGs) to foster students' active learning. In CLGs, students work together, each having a specific role within the group (Roberts et al., 2010). Finally, when teachers and professional school counselors use peer mediators to help resolve conflict, the type of learning students experience is direct and reflects real life. Professional school counselors are aware of the various levels of learning and strive to help students be as active as possible during lessons and units.

Conclusion, Assessment, and Follow-Up

On completing the planned developmental activities, it is important to reinforce and conclude the session's learning by summarizing the essential points of the lesson. An experienced classroom educator will usually plan for at least 2 to 5 minutes to successfully summarize and end the lesson. Many professional school counselors also prefer to have the students contribute to the summary as a way of promoting an additional learning experience and testing students' comprehension of and knowledge gained from the day's lesson. It is generally most efficient to begin the summary by restating the lesson's objective(s) and briefly reviewing how the lesson built on previously developed skills and knowledge. Next, the professional school counselor should strive to encapsulate the content of the developmental activities, highlighting the important content and experiences. Finally, experienced professional school counselors should help students to generalize the classroom experience to real-world experiences by asking students how the lessons learned can apply to life outside the classroom or to their short- or long-term academic, career, or personal/social goals.

Skilled classroom educators know that this generalization process, accompanied by real-life homework assignments, is the best way to get students to remember the classroom-based learning and transfer it to daily life.

Perhaps the most essential and overlooked part of guidance instruction is the assessment of learning objectives. For some reason, many professional school counselors develop the self-defeating perception or attitude that "What we do can't be measured or evaluated." Nothing could be farther from the truth. In fact, it is this errant attitude that has put the profession in jeopardy in this age of educational accountability and reform. Can you imagine a math, science, reading, or social studies teacher explaining that he or she can't measure what children have learned or can do as a result of his or her instruction? It sounds equally ridiculous when principals or other stakeholders hear this from professional school counselors! Of course effective school counselors produce measurable gains in students' learning. The key, however, is to plan for assessment when the learning objectives are written, rather than after the lesson is taught.

Well-written learning objectives are the key to effective instruction and outcomes. If a learning objective is written in accordance with the model in Table 10.4, assessment is made simple because the audience, expected behavior, measurement parameters, and expected level of performance have already been specified. At this point, all the professional school counselor needs to do is collect the data as specified in the learning objective and apply the specified criterion. For example, consider the cognitive domain learning objective shown in Table 10.4: "After observing three role plays, the student will be able to identify behaviors that lead to conflict in at least two of the three scenarios." To document that the learning objective has been met, the professional school counselor must design three role plays and write out a list of behaviors leading to conflict that the student may observe. Then the scenarios are presented one at a time, and the student is asked to write at least one observable behavior for each scenario that led to the conflict. If the student is able to discern behaviors that were on the list compiled by the professional school counselor for two of the three scenarios, the learning objective has been met.

Of course, one of the real values of assessment is that it helps to inform our practice, and another is that it helps to demonstrate accountability. If assessment of learning objectives indicates student nonmastery, then it follows that the instructional process must be analyzed and improved. Were the objectives clearly stated? Were the expectations too high? Were the activities ineffective?

Were the assessment criteria and strategies inappropriate? Each of these steps in the process must be visited, analyzed, and, if necessary, refined or redesigned before the lesson is repeated. Too often in education—and school counseling—professionals continue to implement ineffective curricula and even blame the unsuccessful students. Professional school counselors, as educators, must look to the processes and strategies implemented and further tailor them to the needs of the students.

Chapter 5 discussed outcome assessment procedures and program evaluation in detail, stating that those types of programmatic assessments should be conducted systematically. The assessment of learning objectives at the classroom level is just as important. Logically, if a professional school counselor successfully implements a guidance curriculum as documented by assessments of learning objectives at the classroom level and if these objectives directly relate to the school counseling program's outcomes, then the evaluation of the program will also result in success.

Finally, follow-up is an essential part of the learning process frequently disregarded by professional school counselors. Why should busy professional school counselors "waste time" on follow-up? After all, when someone has been "fixed," that's the end of the story, isn't it? Not at all! Many children require booster sessions to review, apply, and extend what they have learned. Regarding personal/social and mental health interventions, recidivism, or slipping back into old habits and behaviors, is a huge problem. If nothing else, simply checking back with students within a few days or weeks after a lesson or intervention can bolster their learning and behavioral change. Another part of follow-up may involve follow-up assessment procedures to ensure that changes in learning and behavior are continuing. Such valuable information helps the professional school counselor and classroom teacher to be responsive to potential recidivism and act accordingly.

Follow-up is a way of checking progress and shoring up support for students. It is arguably the most important, most cost-effective step in the process because it prevents all previous instructional or intervention time and effort from being wasted! In other words, choosing not to spend a few minutes on follow-up could lead to hours of wasted instructional or intervention effort. Figure 10.4 presents a flowchart of the process for constructing developmental lessons and activities.

Professional school counselors, as educators, are knowledgeable about how students learn. They are aware of students' multiple intelligences and design learning activities that attend to the development of the whole

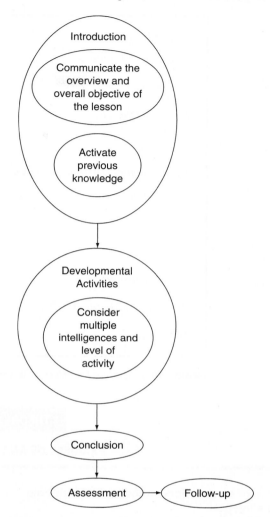

FIGURE 10.4 Constructing developmental lessons and activities.

student. Lessons featuring cognitive learning are commonly taught alongside lessons that address both affective and psychomotor–kinesthetic–behavioral domains of learning. Professional school counselors design units and lessons for students at all grade levels—they carefully plan what the objectives are for the lesson and how they will both teach the lesson and evaluate learning. Figure 10.5 shows a planning outline for professional school counselors to use as they prepare their lessons. Theory into Practice 10.1, 10.2, and 10.3 show lessons and examples of counseling curriculum at the elementary, middle, and high school levels, respectively, as examples of how to apply the content of this chapter to developmental curricular planning.

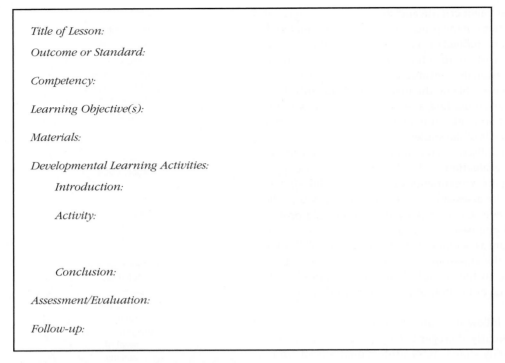

Title of Lesson:

Outcome or Standard:

Competency:

Learning Objective(s):

Materials:

Developmental Learning Activities:

　Introduction:

　Activity:

　Conclusion:

Assessment/Evaluation:

Follow-up:

FIGURE 10.5　Outline for effective lesson plans.

THEORY INTO PRACTICE 10.1

EXAMPLE OF AN ELEMENTARY SCHOOL LESSON

Title of Lesson: **Understanding your multiple intelligences**

> **Outcome or Standard:** Students will acquire the attitudes, knowledge, and skills that contribute to effective learning in school and across the life span (Campbell & Dahir, 1997).
>
> **Competency:** (a) Identify attitudes and behaviors that lead to successful learning; (b) Apply knowledge of learning styles to positively influence school performance.
>
> **Learning Objective:** After completing the Teele Multiple Intelligences Inventory (Teele, 2000), 90% of fifth-grade students will be able to identify their top three intelligence strengths as determined by personal ratings.
>
> **Materials:** One copy of the Teele Multiple Intelligences Inventory and a pencil for each student.

Developmental Learning Activities:

Introduction: Begin with a discussion of how every student has different learning strengths and weaknesses. For example, some students would rather work in groups, others

alone. Some like to think out loud, others in silence. Some like to draw a picture of how something works, others would rather act it out. Then solicit several examples of learning strengths from students (thereby connecting the current objective to previous knowledge).

Activity: Pass out one copy of the Teele Multiple Intelligences Inventory to each student, and read the directions for completing the inventory aloud. Because the inventory is pictorial, no reading or language skills are required. After the directions are completed, allow 15 minutes for students to complete the inventory. When time is up, explain how to transfer student responses to the scoring form and "score" the inventory. After students have scored their own inventories, have them write the titles of their top three categories (intelligences) on a sheet of paper. Use Table 8.3 of this text (Gardner's multiple intelligences) to explain to students the skills associated with their top three intelligences.

Conclusion: Next, lead students in a discussion of their interests and skills related to each intelligence on their list and challenge students to think about what they have done to develop these abilities, and what they could do to develop these abilities to even higher levels.

Assessment/Evaluation: At the end of the session, collect student papers containing their top three intelligences and determine the percentage of fifth-grade students who have determined their top three choices. If 90% of the students complied, the objective has been met.

Follow-up: In a future session, review Gardner's eight intelligences and ask students to share events when they were using these abilities to master academic content.

THEORY INTO PRACTICE 10.2

EXAMPLE OF A MIDDLE SCHOOL LESSON

Title of Lesson: **Understanding Sexual Harassment**

Outcome or Standard: Students will understand safety and survival skills (ASCA National Standard C within "Personal/Social Development"; Campbell & Dahir, 1997).

Competency: Students will learn about the relation between rules, laws, safety, and the protection of individual rights.

Learning Objective(s):

1. After group discussion and counselor-led instruction, all students will be able to identify the correct definition of sexual harassment. (This is basic *knowledge* within the cognitive domain of understanding.)
2. Subsequent to group discussions, all students will describe incidences of sexual harassment they have seen or experienced and how these incidences made them feel. (This objective supports the development of the *responding* level of affective learning.)

Materials: Large-sized paper, markers.

Developmental Learning Activities:

Introduction: The professional school counselor begins by initiating a discussion with students about respectful behavior. (This serves as groundwork to connect the current learning objectives to previous knowledge.) The professional school counselor then asks the students to brainstorm in pairs about how respectful behavior is sometimes codified in rules and laws. Pairs then share ideas with the larger group, and the counselor writes the ideas on the board. (Make a connection to previous knowledge, this time regarding social studies. The activity of having students work in pairs increases the level of student involvement and is called Think, Pair, Share [Saphier & Gower, 1997].)

Activity:

1. The counselor asks students to get into groups by gender, i.e., all male and all female groups. Their task is to brainstorm examples of disrespectful behavior they have seen or heard that is directed toward one gender or the other.
2. Groups write their experiences on large sheets of paper. Then representatives from the groups tape the sheets of paper on the walls.
3. The counselor discusses the students' experiences, paying particular attention to how it feels or might feel to be the recipient of such behavior.
4. Finally, using the concepts generated, the counselor shares with the students the definition of sexual harassment (unwanted behavior directed at a person based on his or her gender). The counselor can provide examples of sexual harassment that the students have not generated (for example, see Strauss, 1994, for a thorough listing of commonly reported types of student-to-student sexual harassment).

Conclusion: The professional school counselor asks students to share ideas about how the knowledge they have generated can be used to better their environment. (This is also a lead into the follow-up activity below.)

Assessment/Evalution:

1. At the beginning of the next session when the professional school counselor meets with the group, he or she reads the students the three possible definitions of sexual harassment. Students vote by a show of hands which definition is correct. (This attends to the first learning objective and provides a time lapse so that the counselor can ascertain whether students retained the information.)
2. Accomplishment of the second learning objective is completed by the lesson itself. By observing the group's process and outcome (as demonstrated by students' verbal and written responses), the professional school counselor determines the degree to which the objective is met.

Follow-up:
In a subsequent session, the counselor has students work in mixed-gender groups to create a system of classroom and school norms regarding sexual harassment.

THEORY INTO PRACTICE 10.3

EXAMPLE OF A HIGH SCHOOL LESSON

Title of Lesson: **Career Exploration and Postsecondary Planning**

Outcome or Standard: Students will acquire the skills to investigate the world of work in relation to knowledge of self and to make informed career decisions (ASCA National Standard A within "Career Development"; Campbell & Dahir, 1997).

Competencies:

1. Students will develop skills to locate, evaluate, and interpret career information.
2. Students will learn about the variety of traditional and nontraditional occupations.
3. Students will develop an awareness of personal abilities, skills, interests, and motivations.

Learning Objective(s):

Using the Internet, students will be able to locate self-assessments, career assessment materials, career information, and postsecondary options in sufficient quantity and quality so that they are able to write a paper about their postsecondary choices (knowledge, application, analysis, and synthesis).

Materials: Computer lab with access to the Internet, a list of Websites.

Developmental Learning Activities:

Introduction: The counselor introduces the topic of postsecondary planning and the importance of self-assessment in career decision making. The counselor gives an overview of the use of assessment materials and their strengths and limitations in helping select appropriate postsecondary options.

Activity:

1. Students meet in groups of four to discuss the types of postsecondary options and career choices in which they may already be interested. Each student generates at least three postsecondary options.
2. In a computer lab at a computer, students begin by taking an interest inventory online. The counselor should provide students with some website addresses where they can access a career quiz.
3. Students identify 10–12 careers that seem interesting and look for other relevant websites to explore these occupations (such as Occupational Outlook Handbook: http://stats.bls.gov/oco/).

Conclusion: Students share their experience and relate what they found to be surprising, or what reinforced earlier beliefs about themselves.

Assessment/Evalution: In collaboration with the English teacher, students are asked to prepare a paper about their postsecondary choices and the developmental steps they could take to reach their goals. (This analysis-synthesis-level assessment is in the cognitive domain. If students accomplish this higher level task, they will have shown that they also mastered the knowledge and application-level objectives.)

Follow-up: The professional school counselor meets with the English teacher to discuss future classroom guidance units to bolster student learning and decision making in the career domain. In addition, the professional school counselor offers groups based on postsecondary options (such as a 4-year college group, a 2-year college group, a job-entry group, a military group) that will meet on a regular basis and address barriers and other issues relevant to postsecondary and career options.

VOICES FROM THE FIELD 10.3   TAKING IT TO THE NEXT LEVEL

As I enthusiastically entered my first year as a middle school counselor determined to deliver an effective program, I quickly realized the many different perceptions the education community holds regarding the role of a professional school counselor. Surprisingly, few were related to school counselors delivering a meaningful program to support student development and achievement. School counselors in my area historically provided responsive services focused on helping students individually. Over the years, school counselors have been working hard to change these perceptions and have developed programs that reach many students and are preventive in nature.

Some contemporary programs focus on targeted interventions for various student groups within a school. However, many of these programs are not data driven and lack methods to measure the program's success. More important, what about all the students who are not in targeted student groups and therefore do not benefit from the school counseling services? It is now time to take these programs to the next level and begin implementing comprehensive, developmental school counseling programs that reach every student.

As part of a five-person dynamic school counseling team, I have had the experience of delivering a comprehensive, developmental school counseling middle school program to approximately 1,400 students per year. The program was designated a Recognized ASCA Model Program (RAMP) in 2008 by the American School Counselor Association. There are many benefits to running a program that is aligned with a nationally recognized model. The program clearly identifies and targets all stakeholders, which include students, their families, and teachers. The program goals are aligned with the overall mission of the school and address the academic, social/emotional, and career needs of all our students. The program provides direct services to students, including individual counseling, group counseling, and classroom guidance activities. Equally important, the program provides indirect services, which include regular parent communication via conferences, phone calls, and e-mail, as well as support to all teachers when counselors attend interdisciplinary meetings and attendance meetings and respond to teachers' concerns about individual students in a timely manner. The program is data driven and is formally evaluated each year. When specific interventions or parts of the program are determined to no longer be effective, new interventions are properly researched and implemented. In addition, the program has a Guidance Advisory Council made up of counselors and teachers who meet on a monthly basis to collaboratively identify areas that need improvement and work together toward making the program better.

One of the challenges of running a comprehensive, developmental school counseling program is making sure that the program continues to run effectively every day regardless of expectations to participate in any noncounseling duties, mandatory meetings, or statewide testing. As a professional school counselor, I know that these challenges can be overcome because the school community can vividly see how students are different as a result of this program. As a relatively new school counselor, delivering a sound program has helped me to increase my skills and knowledge of school counseling and has allowed me to take part in the overall school community effort to link professional school counselors with running programs that support and enhance learning.

Source: Tracy MacDonald, Professional School Counselor, Chesapeake Bay Middle School, Anne Arundel County Public Schools, Maryland

Summary/Conclusion

Professional school counselors provide direct services to students through a number of roles, including that of classroom educator. Professional school counselors spend time in classrooms teaching developmental lessons to students. Through these lessons, counselors seek to implement a comprehensive, developmental curriculum made up of standards from the academic, career, and personal/social domains. The ultimate goal of the professional school counselor in this role is for all students to achieve the developmental outcomes that the local school counseling leadership team deems essential.

To reach this important goal, professional school counselors work with teachers to integrate the counseling curriculum with other components in the school's curriculum. Professional school counselors ensure that all students receive instruction in the counseling curriculum by teachers, by teacher–counselor teams, or by professional school counselors themselves. When professional school counselors deliver the curriculum themselves, they strive to maintain the high standards of the teaching profession. This means that they manage the classroom well and create positive learning environments for students. Most important, professional school counselors know how to design effective, interesting lessons for diverse groups of students. At times, this means starting from scratch and creating one's own unit or plan. Other times counselors incorporate lesson elements from well-researched, commercially available curricula. Whether they use their own or commercially available curricula, professional school counselors help students attain important cognitive, affective, and behavioral outcomes.

Activities

1. Think back to when you were in elementary, middle, or high school. Who was your favorite teacher? Why was he or she your favorite? How can you honor the memory of that teacher in your work as a developmental guidance classroom specialist?
2. Go to a local school and ask to observe a master teacher for a half day. Note the following:
   a. How does the teacher introduce lessons?
   b. What rules seem to be implicit in the classroom? What rules are explicit?
   c. How do students treat each other? What is your sense of the teacher's role in this?
   d. How active are students? How does the teacher help them to learn?
3. Brainstorm five classroom guidance lessons that you could develop that would be appropriate for the education level you are interested in pursuing. For one of the five lessons, create a full lesson plan. Make sure to include appropriate headings and activities for the age group with which you are working.

CHAPTER

11

Academic Development and Planning for College and Career Readiness K–12

Stuart F. Chen-Hayes and Melissa S. Ockerman

ditor's Introduction: This chapter focuses on how transformed school counselors are critical players in the academic development and planning for career and college success of all students, particularly those who have been underserved historically, and partner with key national organizations that assist school counselors in delivering academic development competencies resulting in career and college access, readiness, and success for every student.

ACADEMIC AND CAREER PLANNING IN THE MODERN ERA

Transformed school counselors assist every student to reach their academic, career, and college dreams beginning in kindergarten. Professional school counselors create, implement, and evaluate developmental school counseling programs focused on K–12 academic development skills, experiences, and rigorous coursework that lead to career and college opportunity, access, and readiness for every student. In this chapter we address ensuring rigorous academics with appropriate supports for all students and why this educational reform is the most important policy and practice change that school counselors in every school can implement to ensure equity. Definitions, key advocacy and leadership strategies for academic equity, the National Office for School Counselor Advocacy's (NOSCA) eight components of college and career readiness counseling (NOSCA, 2010), and a specific focus on the second NOSCA component, academic planning for career and college readiness, are all addressed. The chapter asks essential questions that help professional school counselors reach these goals. To begin, it's important to look at the data for cultural groups most underserved in K–12 public education in the United States.

Who Are the Underserved in U.S. K–12 Education?

The American School Counselor Association (ASCA) *Ethical Standards for School Counselors* (ASCA, 2010) expects professional school counselors to be academic advocates for all students, particularly those for whom schools have traditionally been least successful, including poor and working-class students of all races, with young men of color performing at the lowest levels on average (College Board, 2013a; Duncan & Murnane, 2011; Education Trust, 2013; Lee & Ransom, 2011); students with emotional, physical, developmental, and learning disabilities (Baumberger & Harper, 2007; Marshak, Dandeneau, Prezant, & L'Amoreaux, 2009; Milsom & Dietz, 2009; Trolley, Haas, & Patti, 2009); LBGT students (Gay Lesbian and Straight Education Network [GLSEN], 2008, 2009a, 2009b, 2009c, 2012; Ryan & Chen-Hayes, in press); first-generation, immigrant, and undocumented students (Chen-Hayes, 2013); boys; and students from nondominant family types (e.g., single parent, mixed-race, divorced, adoptive, foster, homeless, LBGT-headed; Chen-Hayes, 2013). These groups of individuals are not all achieving consistent academic success that leads to well-paying careers and college access.

Another major concern for professional school counselors is high school and college graduation and dropout rates. For example, The Young Men of Color Initiative data from the College Board Advocacy and Policy

Center (Lee & Ransom, 2011) show stark futures for a majority of young men of color (e.g., Asian, African American, Latino, Native American Indian). Unemployment, underemployment, incarceration, and lack of postsecondary education are all concerns, with a wider number of most young men of color neither attending college nor engaged in full-time employment. Transformed school counselors create school counseling programs that recognize this data and begin working in kindergarten to turn around achievement and opportunity gaps facing students for whom school has been the least successful, including young men of color (ASCA, 2010, 2012; Holcomb-McCoy, 2007a, 2007b).

With professional school counselor-to-student ratios averaging over 459:1 (ASCA, 2014b), school counselors must work differently and more effectively to help all students reach their career and college dreams, particularly students for whom school has been the least successful. Planning, school counseling core curriculum

(SCCC) lessons, and academic development activities become center-stage interventions to help school counseling programs reach as many students as possible during the school day (ASCA, 2012). It is critical that school counselors reach out and engage all students using multiple methods and no longer rely on serving only those who drop by the school counseling office for career and college access information and competencies (Bryan, Holcomb-McCoy, Moore-Thomas, & Day-Vines, 2009). Professional school counselors who regularly deliver competencies in career and college access can substantially raise college application rates and build social capital, especially for students who have been least likely to receive it from schools or elsewhere (Bryan, Moore-Thomas, Day-Vines, & Holcomb-McCoy, 2011). To do this effectively, professional school counselors need to develop academic planning and career and college readiness skills with the knowledge of key organizations and frameworks available to assist in the process (Chen-Hayes, 2013; Chen-Hayes, Ockerman, & Mason, 2013).

CULTURAL REFLECTION 11.1

The Center for Civil Rights Remedies at The Civil Rights Project released a report detailing the disparate out-of-school suspension rates. Among their troubling results were the following:

- National suspension rates show that 17%, or 1 out of every 6 Black schoolchildren enrolled in K–12, were suspended at least once. That is much higher than the 1 in 13 (8%) rate for Native Americans; 1 in 14 (7%) for Latinos; 1 in 20 (5%) for Whites; or the 1 in 50 (2%) for Asian Americans.
- For all racial groups combined, more than 13% of students with disabilities were suspended. This is approximately twice the rate of their non-disabled peers.
- One out of every four (25%) Black children with disabilities enrolled in grades K–12 was suspended at least once in 2009–2010. (p. 2)

These students are not only missing valuable class time. Researchers noted that out-of-school suspension leads to increases in dropout rates and a greater likelihood of future incarceration.

1. What is the connection between discipline and suspension policies and future academic success?
2. What are underlying reasons for the disparate suspension rates among Black and Latino students and students with disabilities as compared to their peers?
3. What is the school counselor's role when it comes to disparate discipline policies?

What Are the Key Organizations and Frameworks in Career and College Readiness Helping Professional School Counselors as Systemic Change Agents?

Campbell and Dahir (1997) authored the ASCA *National Standards* as the first school counseling standards for K–12 students in three domains: academic, career, and personal/social. The intent behind the ASCA *National Standards*, renamed the ASCA Student Standards (ASCA, 2012), was to join other standards-based disciplines in education. Professional school counselors deliver specific skills from the nine ASCA standards and related competencies and indicators, including goal-setting and decision-making skills providing academic success and preparation for postsecondary education options through comprehensive school counseling programs. Ideally, school counselors provide one third of their direct services time delivering specific competencies in each of the following three domains (Campbell & Dahir, 1997):

Academic Domain:

A. Students will acquire the attitudes, knowledge, and skills that contribute to effective learning in school and across the life span.
B. Students will complete school with the academic preparation essential to choose from a wide range of substantial postsecondary options including college.
C. Students will understand the relationship of academics to the world of work and to life at home and in the community.

Career Domain:

A. Students will acquire the skills to investigate the world of work in relation to knowledge of self and to make informed career decisions.

B. Students will employ strategies to achieve future career goals with success and satisfaction.

C. Students will understand the relationship between personal qualities, education, training, and the world of work.

Personal/Social Domain:

A. Students will acquire the knowledge, attitudes, and interpersonal skills to help them understand and respect self and others.

B. Students will make decisions, set goals, and take necessary action to achieve goals.

C. Students will understand safety and survival skills.

At the same time, in the late 1990s, a nonprofit educational advocacy organization called the Education Trust hired Pat Martin, a former math teacher, school counselor, building leader, and district administrator, and Reese House, a counselor education professor emeritus, to develop and implement the Transforming School Counseling (TSC) Initiative (see Chapter 3). The TSC has two components: (a) revisioning both how districts develop school counselors in service, and (b) reevaluting how counselor education programs admit, teach, and supervise future school counselors to focus on closing achievement and opportunity gaps using strategies Chen-Hayes (2007) summarized with the acronym TACKLE: **T**eamwork and collaboration, **A**dvocacy, **C**ulturally competent counseling and coordination, **K**nowledge and use of technology, **L**eadership, and **E**quity assessment using data.

When ASCA published the first edition of the *ASCA National Model* (2003), it incorporated the ASCA national standards (Campbell & Dahir, 1997); comprehensive developmental school counseling programs effective in academic, career, and college success for students (Gysbers & Henderson, 2012); Johnson & Johnson's (2001) results-based school counseling methods; and some key transformed school counseling (TSC) skills: advocacy, leadership, use of data for equity, teaming and collaboration, and systemic change (Martin & House, 2002). The focus on the model included closing achievement and opportunity gaps as a key intervention for school counselors using process, perception, and results data (renamed outcome data in ASCA, 2012). Soon after, Dr. Trish Hatch founded the Center for Excellence in School Counseling and Leadership (CESCAL) to encourage greater school counselor skills in using the ASCA model and a focus on evidence-based practice supporting schools' academic mission in K–12 schools.

Pat Martin and Dr. Reese House created the National Center for Transforming School Counseling (NCTSC) in 2003 focused on working with school counselors and school counselor educators continuing the work of TSC to close achievement and opportunity gaps. Soon afterward, Drs. Jay Carey and Carey Dimmitt founded the Center for School Counseling Outcome Research and Evaluation (CSCORE) to promote increased research for evidence-based practice and assessment in school counseling, including academic development skills along with career and college readiness and personal/social interventions and disseminating the research and evaluation results (Carey, Dimmitt, Hatch, Lapan, & Whiston, 2008).

Pat Martin moved to the College Board soon after CSCORE was launched and created the National Office for School Counselor Advocacy (NOSCA) with Counselor Educator Dr. Vivian Lee and school counselor April Martin as leading voices in helping current and future school counselors focus on career and college readiness counseling. They developed a strategic planning tool and the "Own the Turf" campaign encouraging all K–12 school counselors to focus their work on the eight components of college and career readiness counseling (Table 11.1; NOSCA, 2010).

In the 2010 revision of the ASCA ethical code for school counselors, clear language about the school counselors' role in academic development and college and career readiness was added, including closing achievement and opportunity gaps through a school counseling program and annual academic/career/college readiness and personal/social planning (ASCA, 2010). Also in 2010, Public Agenda released a study that had major methodological shortcomings yet demonstrated school counselors in their sample had a poor reputation and were spending less than 38 minutes per student annually in college readiness skills with students, which resulted in a large degree of student and public dissatisfaction with school counselors.

TABLE 11.1   NOSCA's 8 Components of College and Career Readiness Counseling

- College aspirations
- Academic planning for college and career readiness
- Enrichment and extracurricular engagement
- College and career exploration and selection processes
- College and career assessments
- College affordability planning
- College and career admission processes
- Transition from high school graduation to college enrollment

The Public Agenda report created controversy both inside and outside the school counseling profession. It was followed in 2011 by the largest national study of school counselors from the College Board's Office of Advocacy and Public Policy and NOSCA. Their 2011 study showed over 5,000 middle and high school counselors in all 50 states were committed to the NOSCA eight components but didn't necessarily have the training or resources to implement them (NOSCA, 2011).

At the same time, Association for Counselor Education and Supervision (ACES) members rallied to create a new focus for the School Counseling Interest Network, which became the Transforming School Counseling College Access Interest Network (TSCCAIN) in 2011, co-led by Drs. Stuart Chen-Hayes and Melissa Ockerman. The network meets monthly via teleconference with over 180 members focused on transforming school counseling, closing achievement and opportunity gaps, and college access, readiness, and admission counseling. At the end of 2011, the National Center for Transforming School Counseling released *Poised to Lead,* a brief on the essential role of school counselors in career and college readiness counseling (Hines, Lemons, & Crews, 2011).

The College Board's Office of Advocacy and Public Policy and NOSCA released a second annual national school counselor study that also included building leaders agreeing that school counselors should implement the NOSCA eight, but also revealing a disparity between what administrators thought school counselors should do and the resources/time school counselors had available to implement the NOSCA eight components (NOSCA, 2012). Both annual NOSCA school counselor studies demonstrated a shared commitment between most school counselors and administrators toward school counselor involvement in college and career readiness responsibilities with academic development a key component. The challenge, however, was that not all professional school counselors had demonstrated skills in implementing the NOSCA eight components. Furthermore, many building and district leaders have not cleared the pathway of other non-counseling-related tasks so that professional school counselors can focus more time on college and career readiness (College Board, 2012b).

Achieve (2012), a national organization focused on conceptualizing and implementing the Common Core State Standards, published a brief on school counselors' role in implementing Common Core (see Chapter 2). This was a first mention of school counselors in Common Core materials as key participants in helping increase academic rigor in schools. Although Common Core has its detractors concerned about a narrowing of the curriculum, others applaud its conceptual and hands-on focus of greater depth and breadth in teaching K–12 students to higher academic levels. The challenge for everyone is effectiveness in implementing Common Core and how it will lead to better student learning and teaching. The Achieve brief discussed the importance of school counselors focusing on our role in academic success, greater depth in student learning using higher-order cognitive skills, and how school counselors can collaborate with teachers and building leaders for raising student achievement.

Greater collaboration also has begun between the National Association for College Admission Counseling (NACAC) and counselor educators. In 2013, NACAC released a third edition of *Fundamentals of College Admission Counseling,* with multiple chapters written by school counselors and counselor educators specializing in school counseling, including a focus on academic planning, equity, and college and career access for all students. NACAC traditionally has had membership from some high school counselors and many college admission officers in colleges and universities. The first edition of *Fundamentals* was conceived by Director of School Counseling at Monson, Massachusetts, High School, Bob Bardwell, who recognized school counselors and counselor educators needed a text focused on college admission counseling. The third edition focused for the first time on equity and college readiness (NACAC, 2013).

What Are Key Assessment and Learning Tools That School Counselors Use in Collaboration with Other Educators to Strengthen Academic Preparation in Schools?

Advanced Placement (AP) courses are offered to students in some high schools across the country to study college-level material that is taught using a similar curriculum nationwide. If students pass an exam with a qualifying score, they may receive college credit and/or advanced placement into higher-level college courses. However, too many students have access to no AP classes in their high schools, let alone the full range of AP courses, so access is not equitable for all U.S. high school students. Transformed school counselors committed to equity (ASCA, 2010, 2012; NOSCA, 2010) work to increase access for the quantity and quality of AP courses so that all students have access to them in high school. For example, Ohrt, Lambie, and Ieva (2009) studied one high school's success at increasing Latino and African-American high school student access to AP courses.

Many U.S. high schools have added AP classes now available in 34 subjects: Art History, Biology, Calculus AB, Calculus BC, Chemistry, Chinese Language and Culture, Comparative Government and Politics, Computer Science A, English Language and Composition, English Literature and Composition, Environmental Science, European

The dropout rate in Chicago Public Schools hovers around 50%, and the college-going rate is climbing but is not as high as we would like it to be. Keeping these statistics in mind, I wanted to know how much the students in my middle school knew about life after high school. To do this, I distributed a schoolwide needs assessment to our seventh- and eighth-grade students. Unfortunately, our students did not know much about postsecondary options. I worked in a school where 91.7% of our student population was Latino/a and 98.6% of our students low income. Many of these students would be first-generation high school graduates. I could only imagine the possibilities for these students if they were to attend college.

It became a priority of mine to collaborate with our teachers to develop a schoolwide initiative to create awareness about college and careers. One of our first activities was to have groups of students research a college and give a short presentation about that college. It was an eye-opening experience for our students! They learned about community colleges, 4-year universities, what a major was, what a bachelor's degree was, and what you needed to do in high school to achieve these goals. We then had speakers from local universities discuss the college admissions process and presented the students with course catalogs. Our students were excited about this, and there was a buzz in our school about the opportunities that would await our students after high school. These activities correlated with the selective enrollment process in Chicago Public Schools. This process is considered to be as competitive as some Ivy League schools. By discussing university entry, our students gained insight into how important grades and test scores actually were.

In addition to college awareness, we discussed what obtaining a college degree could do for our students. I learned from the interest inventories that most students did not know what a college degree could do. I discussed with the students the monetary value of an education and how their salaries will reflect the education they receive. Obtaining a bachelor's degree versus just graduating from high school could result in over one million dollars of additional income by the time they retire.

To expand on this gained knowledge, we held a career fair featuring neighborhood residents who attended our school and went on to college. These alumni shared their experiences and discussed their various careers with our students. These activities made it seem more possible that our students have options after high school. We then went on to do a career match assessment so our students could match their interests with future careers. This was a simple assessment where students chose activities they are interested in. Our teachers gave the assessments to the students in English classes, and I went into the classrooms to discuss the results with the students. We discussed what the careers were, how many years in college they would need for the career, and a possible salary for that career. These conversations did not stop after the activities, as many of the teachers incorporated college/career awareness into their lesson plans.

Source: Michelle Dluzak, middle school counselor, Chicago Public Schools

History, French Language and Culture, German Language and Culture, Human Geography, Italian Language and Culture, Japanese Language and Culture, Latin, Macroeconomics, Microeconomics, Music Theory, Physics B, Physics C Electricity and Magnetism, Physics C Mechanics, Psychology, Spanish Language, Spanish Literature and Culture, Statistics, Studio Art 2-D Design, Studio Art 3-D Design, Studio Art: Drawing, U.S. Government and Politics, U.S. History, and World History (College Board, 2013b).

ACT, ASPIRE, EXPLORE, AND PLAN ASSESSMENTS ACT provides a series of college and career readiness and admission assessments. The ACT test is used as one of two major college admission exams, and the test scores provide specific feedback to teachers and students about academic strengths and areas to improve before college. Plan is ACT's precollege admissions exam given to high school sophomores to assess potential success on the ACT exam and how teachers and students can refocus academic energies on certain subjects prior to taking the ACT for successful learning and stronger college admission. Explore is ACT's career exploration program for eighth and ninth graders, and Aspire is ACT's early college and career readiness assessment for elementary through high school grades focused on assisting teachers and learners with the specific content strengths and areas to improve for career and college readiness (ACT, 2013). All high school students deserve the option to take both the ACT and Plan as part of their college preparation, but historically the ACT has been administered more in the Midwest and Southern regions of the United States, and cost is a factor in many rural and urban underfunded public school districts.

CAREER TECHNICAL EDUCATION (CTE) CTE Career Clusters and Pathways (see Table 11.2) were redesigned to focus on the shifting career environments facing the

TABLE 11.2   CTE Career Clusters & Pathways Linked with Plans of Study (CTE, 2013b)

1. Agriculture, Food, and Natural Resources Pathways:
   - Food Products and Processing Systems
   - Plant Systems
   - Animal Systems
   - Power, Structural, and Technical Systems
   - Natural Resources Systems
   - Environmental Service Systems
   - Agribusiness Systems
2. Architecture and Construction Pathways:
   - Design/Preconstruction
   - Construction
   - Maintenance/Operations
3. Arts, A/V Technology, and Communications Pathways:
   - A/V Technology and Film
   - Printing Technology
   - Visual Arts
   - Performing Arts
   - Journalism and Broadcasting
   - Telecommunications
4. Business Management and Administration Pathways:
   - General Management
   - Business Information Management
   - Human Resources Management
   - Operations Management
   - Administrative Support
5. Education and Training Pathways:
   - Administration and Administrative Support
   - Professional Support Services
   - Teaching/Training
6. Finance Pathways:
   - Securities and Investments
   - Business Finance
   - Accounting
   - Insurance
   - Banking Services
7. Government and Public Administration Pathways:
   - Governance
   - National Security
   - Foreign Service
   - Planning
   - Revenue and Taxation
   - Regulation
   - Public Management and Administration
8. Health Science Pathways:
   - Therapeutic Services
   - Diagnostic Services
   - Health Informatics
   - Support Services
   - Biotechnology Research and Development
9. Hospitality and Tourism Pathways:
   - Restaurants and Food/Beverage Services
   - Lodging
   - Travel and Tourism
   - Recreation, Amusements, and Attractions
10. Human Services Pathways:
    - Early Childhood Development and Services
    - Counseling and Mental Health Services
    - Family and Community Services
    - Personal Care Services
    - Consumer Services
11. Information Technology Pathways:
    - Network Systems
    - Information Support and Services
    - Web and Digital Communications
    - Programming and Software Development
12. Law, Public Safety, Corrections, and Security Pathways:
    - Correction Services
    - Emergency and Fire Management Services
    - Security and Protective Services
    - Law Enforcement Services
    - Legal Services
13. Manufacturing Pathways:
    - Production
    - Manufacturing Production Process Development
    - Maintenance, Installation, and Repair
    - Quality Assurance
    - Logistics and Inventory Control
    - Health, Safety, and Environmental Assurance

(Continued)

TABLE 11.2 CTE Career Clusters & Pathways Linked with Plans of Study (CTE, 2013b) (*Continued*)

14. Marketing Pathways:
- Marketing Management
- Professional Sales
- Merchandising
- Marketing Communications
- Marketing Research

15. Science, Technology, Engineering, and Mathematics Pathways:
- Engineering and Technology
- Science and Math

16. Transportation, Distribution, and Logistics Pathways:
- Transportation Operations
- Logistics, Planning, and Management Services
- Warehousing and Distribution Center Operations
- Facility and Mobile Equipment Maintenance
- Transportation Systems/Infrastructure Planning, Management, and Regulation
- Health, Safety, and Environmental Management
- Sales and Service

United States and global hiring in current and future decades (CTE, 2013a). CTE state standards focus on every student being career- and college-ready by recognizing that similar skill sets are needed for both success in college and most careers. What is unique about the newest CTE state standards is updated career clusters with specific pathways for how students can reach those careers, including clear academic plans demonstrating the specific courses necessary to move along the pathway successfully to reach the career goal (CTE, 2013b). CTE recognized that not all students were receiving the appropriate coursework needed for success in high school, which prevented success in both career and college access and readiness (CTE, 2013a, 2013b).

Common Core State Standards have been adopted by 45 U.S. states as a unifying set of learning goals for K–12 public schools. The first standards are in mathematics and literacy with other subjects to follow. The standards have been developed jointly by the National Governors Association and the Council of Chief State School Officers with feedback from varied K–12 stakeholders. They are designed to increase academic depth and breadth and to ensure more students graduate from high school career- and college-ready in terms of academic preparation (Common Core State Standards Initiative, 2013).

FAIRTEST   Fairtest is a nonprofit organization focused on challenging inappropriate biases and use of high-stakes testing including college admissions exams. Fairtest maintains a database of 850+ colleges that do not use high-stakes admissions exams or that are test optional, including many highly selective U.S. colleges and universities. The list can be accessed at www.fairtest.org.

INTERNATIONAL BACCALAUREATE   International Baccalaureate (IB) programs include elementary, middle school, and high school curricular frameworks with the final 2 years of high school leading to the IB diploma. The focus is on challenging educational experiences for students that include an international perspective, use of inquiry-based methods, and thematic education that is delivered to students using cross-disciplinary methods. The goal is to better understand self and others in a diverse world, and the focus is on affirming diverse perspectives. The IB offers a 2-year high school diploma program that is often seen as college-level in scope and depth, and many colleges reward credit for IB diploma exams (International Baccalaureate, 2013). Professional school counselors are encouraged to develop IB programs with stakeholders to bring this unique and powerful way of learning into schools to help more students partake in challenging curricular experiences that provide career and college readiness through intensive academics.

COLLEGE BOARD   PSAT, SAT-I, and SAT Subject Exams have been developed by the College Board to assist students with college admission and college credit and/or advanced standing in college courses with SAT Subject Exams. Like ACT, SAT is administered usually in the junior year of high school, and PSAT is administered in the sophomore year of high school. PSAT can be used as a diagnostic by students and teachers to address areas of concern in terms of student learning prior to taking the SAT (College Board, 2013b).

STUDENT SUCCESS SKILLS   Student Success Skills, developed by Brigman and Campbell (2003) and refined by Brigman, Webb, and Campbell (2007), is an evidence-based curriculum to assist elementary and middle school students increase academic achievement and social skills competencies for school success. It has been peer-reviewed by the Center for School Counseling Outcome Research and Evaluation (CSCORE) and helps students improve academic achievement and school success behavior. It is available for school counselors, teachers, and parents and guardians at www.studentsuccessskills.com.

What Is College and Career Readiness?

Savitz-Romer and Bouffard (2012, p. 16) asserted that "there is mounting evidence that there is less distinction today than there used to be between the skills that support college and career readiness." They noted that given the increased number of jobs that require advanced skills and knowledge, all young people should at least have the opportunity of having college as a viable option. They defined *college access* as skills for college enrollment and matriculation that lead to successful graduation with a degree. The Southern Region Educational Board (SREB, 2013) defined *college-ready* as a high school graduate having the reading, writing, and math knowledge and skills to qualify for and succeed in entry-level, credit-bearing, college-degree courses without needing remedial classes. Similarly, being *career-ready,* or ready to enter and advance in a job or succeed in training for a good job, means that high school graduates can read, comprehend, interpret, and analyze complex technical materials, can use mathematics to solve problems in the workplace, and can pass a state-approved industry certification or licensure exam in their field. Moreover,

> a career-ready person effectively navigates pathways that connect education and employment to achieve a fulfilling, financially-secure and successful career. A career is more than just a job. Career readiness has no defined endpoint. To be career ready in our ever-changing global economy requires adaptability and a commitment to lifelong learning, along with mastery of key academic, technical and workplace knowledge, skills and dispositions that vary from one career to another and change over time as a person progresses along a developmental continuum. Knowledge, skills and dispositions that are inter-dependent and mutually reinforcing. (Career Readiness Partner Council, 2012)

One of the myths is that all students should and will go to a 4-year college. A 4-year college degree is not the goal for all students. But in the current economy, everyone needs some sort of postsecondary education, be it a 2-year or 4-year college degree or a specialized career/tech preparation program (CTE, 2013a). For example, CTE revised the 16 career clusters and pathways with specific plans of student achievement that link careers to specific academic curricular frameworks, including specific courses that students can choose to be successful in specific career and technological education pursuits after high school (CTE, 2013b; see Table 11.2).

Every student successfully educated for college and career readiness is academically prepared for both college and career postsecondary options. In the old "sort and select days," a process that is still in place in some schools in the United States, one set of students goes to college, and another goes directly into jobs with little career-related training. Now most fields have converged so that the skills needed for college are the same skills needed in career and technological education fields (CTE, 2013a). Therefore, professional school counselors must develop interventions that expose every student to all types of postsecondary options. The resources that assist in college/career access and readiness competencies must be provided to all students starting in the early elementary grades leading to the introduction of more advanced competencies throughout the high school years (Chen-Hayes, 2013; Chen-Hayes et al., 2013). NOSCA has published elementary, middle, and high school guides specific for professional school counselors seeking to implement NOSCA's eight components, including academic planning for career and college with multiple stakeholders such as parents/guardians, teachers, students, families, and community members (see Table 11.3 for curriculum resources).

What Are the Data?

STUDENT OUTCOME DATA   First and foremost, all data needs to be disaggregated. We must gain a clear understanding of how all subgroups of students are achieving (e.g., race/ethnicity, socioeconomic status, language, sexual orientation, gender identity/expression, ability/disability). Data then gives us the ability to notice trends in relation to achievement and attainment of students. For example, professional school counselors need to know grade point averages, state proficiency test scores, ACT/SAT average scores, attendance rates, and discipline referral data delineated by subgroups. With an eye toward groups of students that historically have been underserved, professional school counselors must monitor and track graduation rates, dropout rates, college entrance and completion rates, AP/IB/honors course access and completion patterns, scholarships completed and rewarded, and FAFSA application completions.

TABLE 11.3 Resources and Websites

College and Career Readiness Curricula and Guides for Academic Development:

- AVID (Advancement Via Individual Determination) evidence-based college access/readiness curriculum system: www.avid.org
- College Ed: The College Board's grade 7–12 career and college planning curricula and workbooks: http://professionals .collegeboard.com/k-12/planning/collegeed
- College Workshops for Students Curriculum (Grades 7–12; NACAC): www.nacacnet.org
- Elementary School Counselor's Guide to Implementing NOSCA's 8 Components of Career and College Readiness Counseling: http://media.collegeboard.com/digitalServices/pdf/advocacy/nosca/11b-4383_ES_Counselor_Guide_WEB_120213.pdf
- Fitzpatrick, C., & Constantini, K. (2011). *Counseling 21st century students for optimal college and career readiness: A 9th–12th grade curriculum.* New York, NY: Routledge.
- High School Counselor's Guide to Implementing NOSCA's 8 Components of Career and College Readiness Counseling: http://media.collegeboard.com/digitalServices/pdf/nosca/11b-4151_HS_Counselor_Guide_web.pdf
- Middle School Counselor's Guide to Implementing NOSCA's 8 Components of Career and College Readiness Counseling: http://media.collegeboard.com/digitalServices/pdf/advocacy/nosca/11b-4382_MS_Counselor_Guide_WEB_120213.pdf
- The Real Game series: Research-based curriculum helping students and adults imagine, as clearly as possible, through role-playing, experiential future-based scenarios, the future they would love to be living, so they can become intentional and purposeful in achieving their dreams (Grade 3–adult): http://www.realgame.org/ or http://www.schoolspring.com
- Schellenberg, R. (2008). *The new school counselor: Strategies for universal academic achievement.* Lanham, MD: Rowman Littlefield Education.
- Schellenberg, R., & Grothaus, T. (2009). Promoting cultural responsiveness and closing the achievement gap with standards blending. *Professional School Counseling, 12,* 440–449.
- Schellenberg, R., & Grothaus, T. (2011). Using culturally competent responsive services to improve student achievement and behavior. *Professional School Counseling, 14,* 222–230.

DVD/Streaming Video:

- Chen-Hayes, S. F., Saud Maxwell, K., & Bailey, D. F. (2009). *Equity-based school counseling: Ensuring career and college readiness for every student.* DVD. Alexandria, VA: Alexander Street Press/Microtraining Associates.

Internet Resources:

- **ACT:** Information on Aspire, Explore, Plan, and ACT tests, test preparation, college search, career world of work map, financial aid, and test registration: www.actstudent.org
- **Advising Undocumented Students for College Admission:** http://professionals.collegeboard.com/guidance/ financial-aid/undocumented-students
- **The Algebra Project:** Using mathematics as an organizing tool to ensure a quality public school education for every child in the United States: www.algebra.org
- **American Association of Community Colleges:** Promoting community college recognition and advocacy; student access, learning, and success; leadership development; economic and workforce development; and global and intercultural education: www.aacc.nche.edu/
- **American Indian College Fund/Tribal Colleges: Empowering Native American Indian College Education:** www.collegefund.org/content/tribal_colleges
- **Association for Career and Technical Education:** www.acteonline.org
- **Big Future:** Career and college exploration and planning tools (free): http://collegeboard.org
- **Braintrack:** 10,000 higher education institutions in 194 countries: www.braintrack.com
- **Bright Outlook:** Occupations expected to grow rapidly in the near future with large numbers of job openings and/or new/emerging fields: http://www.onetonline.org/find/bright?b=0&g=Go
- **Bureau of Labor Statistics** (BLS): www.bls.gov

- **Campus Pride:** LBGT student leaders: http://www.campuspride.org/
- **Career Cluster Search:** Discover occupations of interest to then focus education plans on obtaining necessary knowledge, competencies, and training for success in a particular career pathway: http://www.onetonline.org/find/career?c=0&g=Go
- **Career Cruising:** Engaging and inspiring people of all ages to achieve their full potential in schools, career, and life (products include digital career and college planning tools): http://public.careercruising.com/us/en/products/
- **Career Decision-Making Tool:** http://acrn.ovae.org/decision.htm
- **Career Guide to Industries:** www.bls.gov/ooh/about/career-guide-to-industries.htm
- **Career Key:** Research-based career and college major information and assessments: www.careerkey.org
- **Career Key Map of Career Clusters and Pathways:** www.careerkey.org/asp/education_options/ck_map_career_clusters.html
- **Career OneStop:** Pathways to career success: www.careeronestop.org
- **Career Planning Internet Sites** (at National Career Development Association): http://www.ncda.org/aws/NCDA/pt/sp/resources
- **Career Readiness Partner Council:** Coalition of organizations in education, policy, business, and philanthropy disseminating a comprehensive vision and definition of career readiness: www.careerreadynow.org
- **Career Resource Library:** Careers, labor market information, workforce development, and job trends: www.acinet.org
- **Center for the Study of Race and Equity in Education:** The Center aims to publish cutting-edge implications for education policy and practice, with an explicit focus on improving equity in P–12 schools, colleges and universities, and social contexts that influence educational outcomes: www.gse.upenn.edu/equity/
- **College Advising Guide for Undocumented Students (NACAC):** http://www.nacacnet.org/research /KnowledgeCenter/Pages/View-by-Subject.aspx?MetaTopic=Undocumented%20Students
- **The College Board:** Connecting students to college success and opportunity (English/Español): www.collegeboard.com
- **College Board International:** Study college abroad information for students around the world: international. collegeboard.org or http://www.collegemajors101.com
- **College Major Environments:** Choosing the best fit (using Holland Codes/RIASEC/personality/environment fit): http:// www.careerkey.org/asp/education_options/holland_college_major_environments.html
- **College Major-Personality Match Importance:** http://www.careerkey.org/asp/education_options/personality_college _major_match_why_important.html
- **College Majors 101:** www.collegemajors101.com or http://www.careerkey.org/asp/match_up_personality_to_college_ majors.htm#personality or http://www.christiancollegeguide.net
- **CollegeMeasures.org:** Informing and improving the decision-making process for students, parents, and policy makers. Making available key data through 2-year and 4-year college data tools enabling users to make smarter decisions and a more efficient, productive, and effective higher education system: www.collegemeasures.org
- **College Navigator** (at National Center for Educational Statistics): http://nces.ed.gov
- **College Partnerships and Articulation Agreements:** Key to successful transfer-student transitions between two-year community colleges and four-year colleges and universities (all 50 states): http://www.finaid.org/otheraid/partnerships .phtml
- **College Planning for Students with Disabilities:** http://www.educationquest.org/11th-12th-grade-students /information-for-students-with-disabilities/
- **College Prep Calendar: Grades 9–12 (NACAC):** www.nacacnet.org
- **College Results Online:** Graduation rate database for 4-year U.S. colleges/universities allowing disaggregated data comparisons across divergent school types and cultural identities from the Education Trust: www.collegeresults.org or http:// www.collegeweeklive.com
- **Colleges That Change Lives:** Advancing a student-centered college search process: www.ctcl.org
- **Common Core State Standards Initiative:** Preparing U.S. students for college and career: www.corestandards.org or http://www.ctcl.org/
- **Common Data Set Initiative:** Collaborative effort among higher education data providers to improve the quality and accuracy of data for students making college decisions: www.commondataset.org

(continued)

Table 11.3 Resources and Websites (*Continued*)

- **Community College Research Center:** Conducting research on the major issues affecting U.S. community colleges and developing practice and policy that expands access to higher education and promotes success for all students: ccrc.tc .columbia.edu/

- **The Completion Arch:** Measuring community college student success with a Web-based tool providing quick and easy access to national, state, and initiative-level data that describe the progress and success of community college students: http://www.corestandards.org

- **CTE:** Career Technical Education preparing U.S. students of all ages to succeed in education and careers in a global economy: www.careertech.org/

- **Early College High School Initiative:** 240 public high schools in 28 states and DC combining academic rigor and the opportunity to save time and money to motivate students to compress high school diploma completion time with the first 2 years of college and a targeted focus on low-income youth, first-generation college goers, English language learners, students of color, and other young people underrepresented in higher education: www.earlycolleges.org

- **Economic Value of College Majors Study,** "What's it Worth?" (Georgetown University Center on Careers and Education in the Workforce): http://cew.georgetown.edu/whatsitworth/

- **Employment Guide/Worker Rights for Young Workers:** http://labor-studies.org/work-related/your-rights-on-the-job /your-rights-on-the-job/

- **Fairtest.org:** Lists over 800 colleges and universities that involve no admissions tests or are test-optional: www.fairtest.org

- **Fast Web:** http://www.fastweb.com/

- **FinAid:** Guide to financial aid and scholarships: http://www.finaid.org/

- **Future Job Projections** (USA): www.bls.gov/oco/oco2003.htm

- **Going to College:** Selecting a college and living college life for persons with a disability: http://www.going-to-college .org/overview/index.html

- **High-Quality Decision Making** (research-based ACIP model: alternatives, consequences, information, plans): http:// www.careerkey.org/asp/your_decision/high_quality_decisions.html or http://www.indeed.com/

- **Information Interviewing: 8 Steps of Career Exploration:** http://www.careerkey.org/asp/career_development /information_interviewing.html

- **International Association for Educational and Vocational Guidance: Educational and Career Development:** www.iaevg.org

- **International Baccalaureate** (English, Español, Français): www.ibo.org

- **Job Corps**: Free education/training for youth, career, and GED/high school diploma education: www.jobcorps.gov

- **Job-Hunt:** www.job-hunt.org

- **Job Shadow:** Shadow real people's jobs online: www.jobshadow.com

- **Jobs for the Future:** Education for economic opportunity: www.jff.org

- **LGBT-Friendly Campus Climate Index:** National listing of LGBT-friendly campuses: www.campusprideindex.org

- **My Child's Future:** Parent involvement = future success (career development and educational/college planning suggestions for parents and guardians of elementary, middle, and high school students): http://www.mychildsfuture.org/parents /item.htm?id=0

- **My Future, My Way: First Steps Toward College: Student Aid on the Web's Middle School College Planning Site** (includes downloadable workbook; English, Español): http://studentaid.ed.gov/PORTALSWebApp/students/english /introducing.jsp?backURL=/gotocollege/collegefinder/advanced_find.asp&Language=en&returnurl=/students/english /introducing.jsp

- **My Road:** College Board's career and college planning website (free access for PSAT users): https://myroad.collegeboard .com/myroad/navigator.jsp

- **National Association of Intercollegiate Athletics (NAIA) Eligibility Center:** www.playnaia.org

- **National Career Development Association** (NCDA): Internet-based career planning resources: www.associationdatabase.com
- **National Career Development Guidelines Activities for High School Students** (digital educational games): http://acrn.ovae.org/ncdg/ncdg_activities.htm
- **Naviance:** http://www.naviance.com/ or http://www.naviance.com/about
- **O*NET Online:** Career exploration and job analysis: online.onetcenter.org
- **Occupational Employment Statistics and Wage Estimates:** www.bls.gov
- **Occupational Outlook Handbook** (English/Español): www.bls.gov
- **Occupational Outlook Quarterly:** online: www.bls.gov/opub/ooq/home.htm
- **Parents' Role in Career Development for Children and Youth:** http://www.careerkey.org/asp/career_development/parents_role.html
- **Plans of Study:** 16 CTE career clusters and career pathways for advising high school students' academic course selection and beyond (school counselors and parents/guardians): www.careertech.org/career-clusters/resources/
- **Project on Student Debt:** http://projectonstudentdebt.org/ or http://www.payscale.com
- **Science Buddies:** Science fair project ideas and STEM career descriptions: www.sciencebuddies.org
- **Self-Directed Search:** Research-based electronic assessment to discover careers and college major(s) that match your interests and abilities: www.self-directed-search.com/
- **UNCF:** http://www.uncf.org/sections/ForStudents/ForStudents.asp or http://www.teachers-teachers.com/
- **Vocational Schools Database** (RWM): www.rwm.org
- **Women's College Coalition:** Transforming the world through the education and success of women and girls: www.womenscolleges.org or http://www.workcolleges.org
- **World-of-Work Map:** How occupations relate to each other based on work tasks—working with data, data and things, working with things, ideas and things, working with ideas, people and ideas, working with people, people and data: www.act.org/world/plan_world.html
- **Young Men of Color Initiative:** Improving educational participation and college completion for young men of color: http://advocacy.collegeboard.org/college-preparation-access/young-men-color-initiative and http://youngmenofcolor.collegeboard.org/

SCHOOL COUNSELING PROGRAM DATA Professional school counselors must also have systems to track and monitor their work in all domains of the ASCA model: foundation, management, delivery, and accountability (ASCA, 2012). In addition, school counselors need to carefully plan and monitor how to address the National Student Standards. In relation to academic preparation, school counselors must collect school-specific data from stakeholders (e.g., students, staff members, parents, community members) through needs assessments and outcome evaluations. Professional school counselors also look to student data (e.g., graduation rates, dropout rates, college-going rates) to determine needed interventions. Using data garnered from these sources, professional school counselors design and create interventions and measure them using pretest and posttest scores. Data from these tests determine academic, personal/social, and college/career interventions that are most effective and interventions that need to be modified.

What Is Equity in College and Career Readiness Academic Outcomes?

Equity and equality are distinct terms. *Equality* means treating all students the same, and equal treatment is certainly not enough to ensure all students are career and college ready. *Equity* means that some students may need much more in terms of resources to level an uneven playing field that continues to reward the students who are the best resourced with college graduation and deny this accomplishment to students with fewer resources. Getting into college is far easier than graduating from college with a completed diploma. How to promote equity in school counseling programs for career and college readiness includes (at least) the following actions:

1. Ensure every student has access to rigorous courses in middle and high school. Instead of a focus on only scheduling students into courses, scheduling must become equity-focused to ensure all students get strong

teachers, that all students are challenged in their course selections, and perform to the best of their abilities.

2. Ensure every student has an annual academic, career, college access, and personal/social plan with the school counselor that includes feedback from family and teachers (ASCA, 2010).

3. Ensure every student has access to academic, college access, career, and personal social competencies through school counseling core curriculum lessons taught or cotaught by a professional school counselor.

4. Focus 80% of professional school counselor time on direct services for students (e.g., planning, school counseling core curriculum lessons, group and individual counseling) with two thirds of the time spent on academic, career, and college success skills (ASCA, 2012).

5. Disaggregate data for students of color, students with disabilities, poor and working-class students, bilingual students, and other cultural groups to ensure that all groups receive equitable academic skills, including challenging honors, AP, and IB courses, and reduce barriers to access such as minimum GPA or grade requirements for advanced classes, by teacher recommendation only, or only if no suspensions or disciplinary referrals have occurred.

6. Data should be collected showing who is admitted to college by districts and who graduates on time as well as in 5- or 6-year college graduation rates disaggregated by cultural identities and career information in terms of types of jobs and starting salaries.

7. Data should be collected on the college costs incurred by students and disaggregated by cultural identities. This should include the information regarding the amount of debt after college graduation incurred by students and their families.

8. Ensure that students have access to career/technology education options, including the 16 core career clusters, pathways, plans of study, and linkages to the common career technical core (CCTC) standards (CTE, 2013a, 2013b).

How Can School Counselors Lead and Advocate Systemic Change for College and Career Readiness in School Counseling Programs?

Professional school counselors, through data-driven school counseling programs, are critical players in ensuring all students are college- and career-ready through two primary interventions: delivering school counseling core curriculum lessons (ASCA, 2012) and annual planning for every student. This means that school counselors do not simply schedule courses but become advocates for academic rigor and college admission to ensure that the best teachers are teaching all levels of students in the school. Professional school counselors must also ensure that barriers to Advanced Placement (AP), International Baccalaureate (IB), and other rigorous courses are eliminated so all students have the chance to study the most rigorous courses with adequate supports to succeed and pass the exams (AP Exams, SAT Subject Exams, IB Diploma Exams) that will allow for future college success. School counselors must also be seen as academic leaders championing the cause that all students not only have the right to take AP, IB, and honors coursework, but also the resources to be successful. International Baccalaureate (IB) programs can start in elementary schools, unlike, AP courses, which are offered only in high schools. When professional school counselors advocate with teachers, administrators, and parents and guardians to create rigorous IB programs at the elementary and middle school levels, more students receive the chance for earlier advanced academic success that leads to stronger outcomes in high school academics and beyond.

NOSCA EIGHT COMPONENTS OF COLLEGE AND CAREER READINESS COUNSELING

As referenced in Table 11.1, the eight NOSCA components provide a road map for K–12 school counselors to help students gain the knowledge, skills, and academic preparation needed to become college and career ready. At each academic level (i.e., elementary, middle, and high school), NOSCA provides practical and innovative ideas for how to implement knowledge, skills, and academic preparation in school counseling programs. According to NOSCA's 2012 annual survey of school counselors, "more than two-thirds of school administrators support school counselors in incorporating the Eight Components as part of their counseling practice" (p. 6). Let's take a look at the second NOSCA component to provide a key blueprint for school counselors to help children and adolescents chart their academic success after high school in terms of college and career readiness. The second NOSCA component, *Academic Planning for College and Career Readiness*, addresses the intrinsic link between rigorous academic preparation and college/career goals and outcomes for K–12 students. At all educational levels, this includes ensuring students are mastering reading, writing, math, science, history, and world languages skills, including enrollment in rigorous coursework.

What Is Academic Planning and Development?

As discussed previously, professional school counselors must be diligent in creating annual academic plans for all students to ensure rigorous course planning (ASCA, 2012). Chen-Hayes created ACCESS/ACCOMPLISHMENTS Plans (Chen-Hayes, 2013; Chen-Hayes et al., 2013) as a K–12 academic planning tool that also includes career, college access, and personal-social competency questions for goal setting to be updated annually with a professional school counselor. The ACCESS/ACCOMPLISHMENTS plan can become part of the student's annual academic record if desired as a way to systematize annual planning and review for every student and school counselor. Many states now require some form of annual academic planning for students, and others require career plans, but no state has yet created a mandate for academic, career, college access, and personal/social plans that follow both the nine ASCA student standards and the NOSCA eight competencies. Professional school counselors must inform students and parents/guardians about the connection between rigorous coursework and college completion (Adelman, 2006). For example, researchers found that adding just one Carnegie unit in intensive math (i.e., 3 hours of work per week for 16 weeks) more than doubles the likelihood of college completion (Trusty & Niles, 2003, 2004). Thus, school counselors must act in proactive and intentional ways to ensure that all students have access to rigorous courses and are provided with the necessary academic support to successfully complete the courses.

Given that the number one reason students give for dropping out of school is boredom (MetLife Survey of the American Teacher, 2002), professional school counselors must directly link academics with real-world relevancy to keep students engaged. ASCA makes this connection explicit in the Academic domain of the ASCA National Student Standards (ASCA, 2012):

- Standard 1: Students will acquire the attitudes, knowledge, and skills that contribute to effective learning in school and across the life span.
- Standard 2: Students will complete school with the academic preparation essential to choose from a wide range of substantial postsecondary options, including college.
- Standard 3: Students will understand the relationship of academics to the world of work and to life at home and in the community.

As addressed in the next section, professional school counselors must create evidence-based academic interventions in each of these three standards to develop K–12

students' competencies as lifelong learners with specific academic skills to be productive world citizens in career and college pursuits.

What Is K–12 Academic Development?

The ASCA academic student standards must be developmentally appropriate and executed systemically and sequentially beginning in kindergarten. Waiting to make clear connections between academics and college/career until students' junior year in high school (a year when many schools commence this focus) is 10 years too late. As purported by Chall (1996), students must master "learning to read" by third grade so that they are then able to make the transition to "reading to learn." The inability to do so results in students' inability to independently access the general curriculum (e.g., students must be able to read a social studies text to learn key concepts), thereby setting them up for academic failure. Moreover, students who enter middle school with limited reading and math abilities will then be placed in remedial courses. This downward academic trajectory is evidenced when entering ninth-grade students are underprepared to take advanced-level courses in high school. Given that a rigorous high school curriculum greatly increases bachelor's degree completion for all students (Adelman, 2006), students who are academically ill-prepared beginning in elementary school are placed at a grave disadvantage for college and career advancement.

Thus, professional school counselors at all levels must make the commitment to ensure students are given equal access to an academically rigorous curriculum and that these efforts intentionally build on one another from grades K–12 to produce college- and career-ready students on graduation. At the elementary level, professional school counselors must help ensure that students are reading and writing at grade level and successful in passing state-mandated tests. Beginning in middle school, professional school counselors must help students develop a rigorous course plan that includes successful completion of Algebra I by the eighth grade. This is imperative for setting students toward successful completion of advanced college preparatory geometry, algebra II/trigonometry, and precalculus or calculus mathematics courses in high school. In high school, rigorous courses should align with university admission requirements (NOSCA, 2011), and school counselors must be vigilant about ensuring access to such courses for all students, including those historically underserved and underrepresented in STEM (Science, Technology, Engineering, and Math) careers, particularly students of color, poor and working-class students, students with disabilities, girls, and bilingual students.

What Are the School Counselor's Roles and Responsibilities in Academic Planning and Development?

Interestingly, the 2012 NOSCA National Survey of School Counselors (College Board Advocacy and Policy Center, 2012) revealed that counselors and administrators share similar ideas regarding school counselors' leadership role in their schools. In fact, 98% of administrators agreed with the statement, "It is important for school counselors to exercise leadership in advocating for students' access to rigorous academic preparation, as well as other college and career readiness counseling" (p. 5).

Contrary to some administrators' perspectives, this does not mean that school counselors are test coordinators or programmers in their schools. In fact, professional school counselors are trained to offer much more in the area of academic achievement. Rather than counting test booklets for mandated state testing, school counselors are trained to prepare students for these high-stakes tests through study skill and executive functioning development. Following a tiered-development model, professional school counselors offer these services via schoolwide interventions (e.g., creating peer tutoring programs), large-group interventions (e.g., school counseling core curriculum lessons focused on evidence-based study strategies), small-group interventions (e.g., targeted for groups of students who experience test anxiety), and individual counseling with students in need of intensive assistance with self-regulation and healthy study habits. Moreover, professional school counselors at every level can interpret test data to students and parents/caregivers to help them to better understand areas of strength and growth. From this data, targeted and relevant academic interventions can be put into place in consultation and collaboration with teachers and administrators.

Although professional school counselors should not be "programmers" or the architects of the master schedule, they can and should use their time with students as equity-focused advocates for curricular rigor helping all students select the most challenging college and career-readiness academic courses congruent with the student's career/college goals. These annual academic planning sessions should also include a discussion of the importance of academic rigor and a commitment to high expectations for all students.

Research indicates that social capital (i.e., connections within and between family, community, and school networks) and human capital (i.e., abilities and knowledge gained through education) are salient predictors of college enrollment (McKillip, Rawls, & Barry, 2012). Because not all students have parents/caregivers with the social or human capital to advocate for them, school counselors are professionally obligated to do so on their behalf. Thus, a professional school counselor becomes responsible to "provide regular workshops and written/digital information to families to increase understanding, collaborative two-way communication, and a welcoming school climate between families and the school to promote increased student achievement" (ASCA, 2010, p. 6). As such, the professional school counselor becomes a vital liaison between home and school and a central figure in ensuring academic expectations are consistently communicated throughout the student's K–12 career. Moreover, school counselors should be diligent in providing individualized college preparatory information to students who may lack it at home and help them to formulate personal academic and career goals (McKillip et al., 2012).

How Does the School Counselor Collaborate Effectively with Teachers, Administrators, and Parents and Guardians in Academic Development for Students?

It is essential that professional school counselors collaborate with teachers regarding school counseling core curriculum that connects academic standards to necessary career/college competencies. For example, school counselors can work with the English department to plan lessons around resume writing and writing college essays. Parent workshops need to be created and implemented on topics such as homework help, career and college assessments, college preparatory curriculum, the college application process, and financial aid and scholarships. In doing so, professional school counselors must be vigilant about connecting their work back to the mission and goals of the school. They can do this by using data to show the effectiveness of their interventions and by consistently advocating for a rigorous curriculum for all students. Demonstrating efficacy through the use of data helps administrators view school counselors as integral partners in the career and college preparatory process.

What Are the Critical Interventions?

According to Roderick, Nagaoka, and Coca (2009):

> . . . [the] central strategy to improve college access and performance must be to ensure that students leave high school with the academic skills, coursework, and qualifications they

need. Simply, high school students who graduate with higher test scores, better grades, and more rigorous coursework are more likely to enroll in and graduate from four-year colleges. (p. 188)

Conley (2011) and Roderick et al. (2009) asserted there are four key areas to focus on in skill development and college readiness competencies: (a) content knowledge of specific subject areas; (b) "core academic skills" such as critical thinking, analysis, and writing; (c) executive functioning skills such as self-regulation, time management, and problem-solving; and (d) "college knowledge" comprised of an understanding of how to complete all facets of the college application process, including financial aid and admissions. In fact, according to a study from the Consortium on Chicago School Research, students who had been accepted to a 4-year institution and completed the FAFSA were 50% more likely to actually enroll into the institution than students who had been accepted but never completed the FAFSA (Roderick et al., 2009).

Professional school counselors can leverage their expertise by collaborating with teachers in the first two critical areas. Specifically, they can ensure that all students have access to advanced coursework and are provided the necessary tutoring and academic resources to be successful. To build executive functioning skills and increase "college knowledge," professional school counselors can facilitate classroom instruction, organize college visits and information sessions, and sponsor parent/guardian workshops on these topics. Furthermore, school counselors can broker services from local universities to discuss admissions processes, affordability, and financial aid options and host FAFSA completion workshops.

Yet even if students master these four skill sets and are accepted into the college of their choice, a professional school counselor's work is not yet completed. According to research from the Harvard Graduate School of Education and Center for Educational Policy Research (2012), between 10% and 20% of high school seniors who intend to go to college never enroll in a college course. And even more alarming, the illuminating *From High School to the Future: Potholes on the Road to College* report found that only 41% of Chicago seniors who stated that they aspired to attend college actually did so (Roderick, Nagaoka, Coca, & Moeller, 2008). NOSCA (2012) noted that the summer of transition between high school graduation and college enrollment is a critical time for students. They recommend that professional school counselors broker community resources that provide the necessary scaffolding during the summer months to help seniors successfully transition into college.

Summary/Conclusion

Your journey as a K–12 professional school counselor involves ensuring every student is career- and college-ready with regular and systematic academic planning. Key frameworks such as the ASCA *National Model*, ASCA Student Standards, the Transforming School Counseling Initiative (TSCI), and the NOSCA Eight Components for College and Career Readiness helped lay the foundation for school counselors to engage in meaningful academic and career/college counseling interventions. To be successful in this endeavor, professional school counselors must collect and analyze disaggregated data. Doing so gives school counselors a clearer understanding of achievement and attainment patterns of all students and is used to build school counseling programs that dismantle achievement, opportunity, and attainment gaps within their schools.

To this end, professional school counselors can strengthen academic and career/college preparation by advocating for access into rigorous courses, conducting annual planning for every student using ACCESS/ACCOMPLISHMENTS plans, delivering school counseling core curriculum lessons for all students, and intensive group and individual counseling for some students. Importantly, these efforts must begin in kindergarten and be executed in a developmentally appropriate and systemic fashion. Thus, professional school counselors at all levels must be committed to K–12 interventions that build on each other so that students graduate from high school ready for college and careers.

However, professional school counselors cannot do this work alone. They must leverage the expertise of teachers, building leaders, parents/guardians, and community members. Leading collaborative data-driven interventions that focus on key subject content knowledge, core academic skills, executive functioning and college knowledge, professional school counselors can assist all students in reaching their college and career dreams.

Activities

1. What academic planning is done by school counselors in your district? Is there a written plan that is completed with every student updated annually? If not, how might you initiate this process as a graduate student or new professional?

2. What percentage of students in your district has access to and completes AP, IB, or honors courses? What can you do to increase the number of students who have access to AP, IB, and honors courses in your district?

3. Many adults in schools believe elementary school is too young to focus on career and college readiness. How would you counteract this argument? Where would you find data to challenge this belief?

4. What are the strengths of Common Core standards and what are concerns about their limitations? Interview a building leader, a teacher, and a school counselor in your district to learn about their feedback on the Common Core standards conceptually and the implementation of the standards in your district.

5. Talk to K–12 math and science teachers and building leaders in your district and ask what professional school counselors can do in small-group work and large-group school counseling core curriculum lessons to support student success, including critical thinking skills and other higher-order cognitive skills in learning math and science based on disaggregated data.

CHAPTER 12

Promoting Career Planning in Schools

Hyoyeon In, Patrick Akos, and Spencer G. Niles

E ditor's Introduction: When professional school counselors provide career and educational guidance to students, they influence the future by helping clarify developmental decisions that often last a lifetime. Although educational and career planning have been responsibilities of professional school counselors for decades, the school reform movement has placed renewed emphasis on challenging students to pursue rigorous academic coursework, oftentimes regardless of future aspirations. In the future, professional school counselors must continue to challenge students academically, while building support systems and contingencies for exploring diverse vocational and avocational opportunities. In other words, professional school counselors must help students pursue a rigorous academic path, while supporting important developmental life-role decisions that will affect students long after high school.

THE TRADITION OF CAREER-PLANNING INTERVENTIONS IN SCHOOLS

Providing career assistance to students has always been an integral part of the work performed by professional school counselors. During most of the 20th century, professional school counselors fostered their students' career decision making by administering and interpreting interest inventories and aptitude tests. In the 1950s, however, Donald Super (1957) proposed a developmental perspective emphasizing career development as a lifelong process. Super's theory created a paradigm shift within the career development field. Specifically, the focus of career interventions shifted from a single-point-in-time event of making a career decision to the manifestation of career behaviors over time. Super outlined career development stages and tasks, proposing that development through the life stages could be guided "partly by facilitating the maturing of abilities and interests and partly by aiding in reality testing and in the development of self-concepts" (Super, 1990, p. 207).

In addition to Super's contributions to the field, changes in population, economics, and technology in the past few decades have enhanced the need for professional school counselors to emphasize educational planning and career development. Accelerating globalization and advancing technology has altered job titles, roles, and structure within the workplace (Amundson, 2005, 2006; Danziger & Ratner, 2010; Savickas, 2011; Young, Marshall, & Valach, 2007). Job markets have increasingly called for skilled workers over unskilled workers, and income gaps between these two groups are growing (Danziger & Ratner, 2010). Employment has become less stable with decreasing full-time and long-term job opportunities and more prevalent temporary and part-time employment (Amundson, 2005, 2006; Savickas, 2011). These trends make it more critical to assist students in developing educational and career plans that are adaptive to the evolving world of work and to promote a sense of agency in the construction of a career (Savickas, 2005).

CAREER PLANNING TODAY

Career development for youth is a prominent component of the current standards for developmental school counseling programs established by the American School Counselor Association (ASCA; Campbell & Dahir, 1997). The ASCA *National Standards for School Counseling Programs* identify as goals of comprehensive, developmental school counseling programs these three core areas of development: academic, career, and personal/social. All three areas are interrelated and occur together in multiple systems. The *National Standards* specify three important areas of student career development:

- *Standard A.* Students will acquire the skills to investigate the world of work in relationship to knowledge of self and to make informed career decisions.
- *Standard B.* Students will employ strategies to achieve future career success and satisfaction.
- *Standard C.* Students will understand the relationship among personal qualities, education and training, and the world of work. (p. 16)

The competencies include the development of career awareness and employment readiness; the acquisition of career information; and the identification of, and development of skills to achieve, career goals.

Among the academic competencies in the *ASCA National Model* (2012) are several statements on educational planning that are interconnected with those for career development. Educational planning is the means through which linkages are forged, for students as well as stakeholders, between academic achievement and postsecondary options (Hobson & Phillips, 2010). Although the interdependence of school and work is often overlooked by students, the educational-planning process, when started early enough (i.e., middle school at the latest), can help students become aware of how their school performance relates to post–high school goal achievement and how to access, attain, and achieve rigorous standards, thereby increasing motivation to work hard in school. For example, Trusty and Niles (2004) demonstrated the long-term effects (e.g., completion of a bachelor's degree) of course taking in middle and high school. According to Hobson and Phillips, an effective educational-planning process eliminates making a career choice by chance because it creates a foundation for a student's career development and prosperity as a citizen. Rigorous academic coursework completed during middle school builds this foundation. Whereas Chapter 11 provided a more specific and detailed overview of educational planning and postsecondary access, achievement, and attainment, we mention educational planning as

appropriate throughout this chapter due to its essential relationship to the career development process.

Educational and career planning can and should be infused into the school counseling curriculum in all grade levels. In elementary school, students should first become acquainted with the concept of educational and career planning (Trusty, Niles, & Carney, 2005) through learning about the salient relationship between school performance and the world of work and postsecondary education. When students reach middle school, where it is hoped that they are introduced to careers at a more complex level and obtain self-knowledge about their skills, interests, and values through inventories and other career activities, the stage will be set for them to start thinking in more concrete terms about their educational, career, and life goals. These goals will then form the basis for making choices about the courses they take while in middle school, as well as helping them to create a tentative blueprint for their high school course taking.

It is through this kind of sequential educational-planning process that students are continually reminded about the school–work connection. More important, however, this process provides students with many and varied opportunities to learn about themselves and engage in mindful planning and preparation that will help to ensure that their decisions about life after high school are made thoughtfully, in advance, and with their personal life goals in mind (Hobson & Phillips, 2010).

Along with the importance and integration of educational planning, emergent career theory continues to affect practice. Lapan (2004) created *The Integrative Contextual Model of Career Development* based on decades of career development research. This model highlights six primary career development constructs, including positive expectations, identity development, person–environment fit, vocational interests, academic achievement, and, last, social/prosocial skills and work readiness behaviors. Gysbers and Lapan (2009) argued that the development and internalization of these six constructs is the key to maximizing the career development of students.

Similarly, drawing on three existing theories (i.e., hope theory [Snyder, 2002], human agency theory [Bandura, 2001], and career meta-competencies [Hall, 1996]), Niles, Amundson, and Neault (2010) developed *The Hope-Centered Model of Career Development* (HCMCD) that emphasizes the central role of hope in career development. Specifically, the HCMCD identifies the essential steps and competencies of career planning, which include self-reflection, self-clarity, visioning, goal setting and planning, implementing, and adapting. According to Niles et al., hope enables students to engage in these career-planning steps even in the face of challenges, and thus, fostering hope in students is an integral part of career development interventions. These two models each recognize interaction between individuals and environment, emphasize adaptability, and constitute strength-based models.

Finally, Savickas (2012) proposed a new paradigm of life design career interventions by abstracting several constructivist and narrative career counseling approaches. This paradigm highlights the process to "(a) construct career through small stories, (b) deconstruct these stories and reconstruct them into an identity narrative or life portrait, and (c) coconstruct intentions that lead to the next action episode in the real world" (Savickas, p. 15). The life design approach has great potential for student career intervention by empowering students to become authors of their lives. Specifically, students can make meaning out of their life stories, examine cultural biases embedded in these stories, and actively construct self, identity, and career paths. Although a full description of these three models is beyond the scope of this chapter, these constructs are integrated into the programs and interventions later.

Life-span, life-space theorists define *career* as the total constellation of life roles that people engage in over the course of a lifetime (Super, 1980). Career development tasks include developing the skills necessary not only for selecting and implementing an occupational choice, but also for selecting, adjusting to, and transitioning through a variety of life roles, with an emphasis on helping students develop life-role readiness (Niles & Harris-Bowlsbey, 2013). Empirical research also shows that adolescents' career needs and concerns encompass work roles and non-work roles (Code, Bernes, Gunn, & Bardick, 2006), supporting the need for school counselors to address various life roles beyond work. Counselors using this multisystemic approach to career development ask questions such as: "What skills are necessary for successful performance as a student, worker, citizen, and so forth?" "What types of awareness do students need to acquire to make effective personal, educational, and career decisions?" "What knowledge is essential for students to make informed choices about life-role participation?" and "What skills do I need to accomplish my desired life roles?" The ASCA *National Model* (2012) supports this idea of life-role readiness by focusing on the holistic development of each student in the three core areas of academic, career, and personal/social development. These foci (i.e., ASCA *National Standards*, educational planning, career development strengths, and life-role readiness) encompass the content for a K–12 educational- and career-planning program.

IMPLEMENTING SYSTEMATIC AND WELL-COORDINATED CAREER-PLANNING PROGRAMS

To help students acquire the knowledge, skills, and awareness necessary for effectively managing their career development, counselors implement systematic and well-coordinated educational- and career-planning programs (Herr, Cramer, & Niles, 2004). Professional school counselors recognize that the piecemeal implementation of such programs limits the degree to which they can positively influence students. Moreover, an unsystematic and poorly coordinated intervention program often creates confusion about the meaning and purpose of career programs among those not directly involved in their creation and implementation. The *ASCA National Model* (2012) is one example of a comprehensive and systematic program that can be implemented.

Specific to career development and similar to the *ASCA National Model*, a five-stage planning model for implementing systematic educational and career intervention programs was recommended by Herr et al. (2004):

Stage 1. Develop a program rationale and philosophy.

Stage 2. State program goals and behavioral objectives.

Stage 3. Select program processes.

Stage 4. Develop an evaluation design.

Stage 5. Identify program milestones. (p. 310)

An important component of stage 1 is the needs assessment, used to determine appropriate program rationales, goals, and interventions (Herr et al., 2004). The needs assessment provides benchmarks against which program outcomes can be assessed. Herr et al. emphasized the importance of incorporating teachers, students, parents, and community participants in the needs assessment to increase their understanding of, and involvement in, career development programs. Clearly, a properly conducted needs assessment provides a firm foundation on which effective educational and career intervention programs can be constructed.

An implicit theme in these recommendations is that program planners need to be sensitive to the political climate in which they operate. In some locations, not clearly connecting career development interventions to the academic curriculum or student academic achievement (e.g., educational planning) will significantly decrease the chances of program success. Also, not adequately communicating successful program outcomes will result in the program resources being vulnerable to funding cuts. If school personnel view the program as an additional burden to their already heavy workloads, then there is little chance that the program will succeed. Thus, the "marketing" of the program to all stakeholders and its coordination and integration into current goals are important aspects of program development and implementation. Clearly defined behavioral objectives that address the specific needs of program participants will be useful in marketing the program and providing outcome data demonstrating program benefits.

Another theme implicit in these recommendations for implementing systematic educational- and career-planning programs is the importance of taking a team approach to service delivery. The *ASCA National Model* (2012) emphasizes this team approach to service delivery in the stress it places on collaboration. Working with administrators, professional and support staff, parents, and community members, the professional school counselor can add depth and variety of experience to the school's career development program. For example, in some districts, professional school counselors need to coordinate and connect with others in the school working toward career development outcomes (e.g., career development coordinators, career and technical education staff, career decisions elective instructors). Counselors may, at times, provide classroom instruction, and teachers may, at times, perform more counseling-related functions. Although there is no one prescription for how the roles and responsibilities should be defined, it is logical that counselors take the lead role in developing and implementing the programs. For example, bringing together parents and professionals within the community for a career fair would provide a much wider base of knowledge and firsthand experience about various careers than would merely using the information that the counselor could locate.

To address career development within the traditional academic curriculum, professional school counselors integrate career development interventions into the classroom. For example, students in an English class can conduct research projects to explore a potential career path. In this format, academic development (by engaging in research) and career development (by gathering occupational information) are connected with a writing assignment. Students learning about government can be introduced to presidents and legislators not only as historical figures, but also as real people who have job descriptions and earn salaries and who possess specific job qualifications. This type of integration or infusion of career- and educational-planning concepts into the curriculum enhances the academic and career development of students.

Professional school counselors are often the only professionals in the school system with specific training in career development; therefore, professional school counselors possess the knowledge of career development theory and practice necessary for formulating appropriate program interventions. Moreover, the processes typically used in program delivery relate to counselors' primary areas of expertise. These processes are counseling, assessment, career information services, placement services, consultation procedures, and referrals.

In addition, the professional school counselor is usually the primary figure within the school that helps students with educational planning. Throughout the middle and high school years, educational planning and career development are inextricably tied to one another because decisions that are made about class choices and high school pathways often correlate with the postsecondary options that are available. Hobson and Phillips (2010) suggested that the professional school counselor discuss the following three areas with students and parents: the amount of postsecondary training the student is willing to attain, the career in which the student is currently interested, and the type of training or education that is required to attain that career. At the same time, professional school counselors can help students understand the connection between current academic activities and future careers. Counselors can also play an important role in program delivery by helping teachers communicate to parents the ways in which systematic career development programs can enhance student achievement.

Career Assessment

Assessment is another indispensable component of career planning and development. It is through the use of formal assessments (i.e., inventories, aptitude tests) and informal assessments (i.e., checklists, card sorts, interviews) that students begin to learn about themselves and their interests, skills, and values related to the world of work. Results from assessments also provide professional school counselors with a starting point for guiding students in the career-planning process. Therefore, it is vital that professional school counselors remain current in their knowledge about which career assessments are suitable for use with school-aged youth, as well as possessing a general understanding of assessment so that they can make informed decisions about which assessments to use with their student population.

There are numerous career assessments on the market, and a full listing of them is beyond the scope of this chapter. Nonetheless, a variety of formal assessments appropriate for use with students will be briefly discussed to give readers a sense of the types of assessments available to professional school counselors. Kuder has a career- and educational-planning system that allows students in middle school and high school to create an online career portfolio that includes their educational plan, as well as their results from three assessments: the *Kuder Career Search with Person Match*, which helps students to identify their interests and then links them to the most fitting career cluster; the *Kuder Skills Assessment*, which helps students to identify their skills and then links them to the most fitting career cluster; and *Super's Work Values Inventory*, which helps students to identify which values are most important to them in their work. Additional information about the Kuder Career Planning System can be found online at www.kuder.com/solutions/kuder-career-planning-system.html.

The *Self-Directed Search* (SDS), created by John Holland, is an assessment that is suitable for high school students. The SDS uses the test-taker's information about his or her interests to determine personality type, which is presented in the form of a three-letter Holland code. In the results report, the individual is also given information about occupations and college majors compatible with his or her code. Information about the SDS can be accessed at www.self-directed-search.com. The *Strong Interest Inventory* (SII) is another assessment based on Holland's typology, which can be used with high school students to help them find their Holland code and learn about occupations that correspond to their code. The SII can be purchased online at www.cpp.com/products/strong/index.asp.

The *Hope-Centered Career Inventory* (HCCI), developed by Niles, Yoon, Balin, and Amundson (2010), is an assessment corresponding with the hope-centered model of career development. The HCCI helps students in eighth grade and above to identify their strengths and weaknesses among the following essential career competencies: hope, self-reflection, self-clarity, visioning, goal setting and planning, implementing, and adapting. The results report provides students with strategies for bolstering these competencies. These results also inform school counselors about students' hope-centered career competency patterns, thereby enabling counselors to provide effective career interventions. For instance, if the result of the HCCI shows that a student is low in self-reflection and self-clarity, but high in goal setting and planning, a counselor may revisit the student's self-understanding and examine if the student's career goals reflect the student's self-awareness. The counselor might focus on engaging the student to intentionally examine his/her interests, values, and/or abilities before prematurely committing the student to specific career goals. Information about the HCCI can be accessed at http://mycareerflow.com/login.php.

The career style interview (CSI) assessment, developed by Savickas (1989, 2005), is the informal narrative assessment that helps students discover their life themes and construct their life stories. The CSI comprises open-ended questions about role models; earliest life recollections; favorite saying or motto; favorite books, magazines, or movies; leisure; and favorite subjects in school. Professional school counselors ask these questions to draw out students' narratives. Counselors and students collaborate to find life themes that underlie these stories, a process that enables students to write the next chapter of their careers congruent with these themes.

O*NET, a career resource center, offers career assessments related to interests, abilities, and values: The *O*NET Interest Profiler* measures users' interests based on Holland's six types, the *O*NET Ability Profiler* measures users' skills in nine areas important to many occupations, and the *O*NET Work Importance Profiler* measures users' work values in six different categories. O*NET also compiles information about a multitude of occupations. For each occupation, a summary is provided describing the tasks, skills, knowledge, abilities, activities, interests, values, salaries, and trends associated with that career. Students can visit online.onetcenter.org/find to explore and learn about occupations of interest. For more information on O*NET's career resources and products, visit www.onetcenter.org.

Finally, the professional school counselor must use emerging technology to sustain an educational- and career-planning program. In the past, technology was used primarily for computer-assisted career guidance systems (CACGSs), but more recently the Internet has emerged as the primary way to use technology in career development programs. Just as Internet tools have blossomed for use with educational planning (e.g., College Board), career assessment, career exploration, and job information websites have been created that are easy to access and inexpensive. A handful of these websites will be briefly introduced in this chapter.

The *Occupational Outlook Handbook* (OOH), a well-known reference developed by the U.S. Department of Labor, provides individuals with considerable information about labor market trends for hundreds of occupations. High school students can use the OOH to research occupations of interest to them and glean information regarding the training and educational requirements needed to enter the field, as well as typical worker salaries and future job prospects. The OOH is available online at www.bls.gov/OCO. There is also a companion website for students in grades 4 through 8 (www.bls.gov/k12), which provides visitors with similar information in age-appropriate language. To search for occupations, students can click on a school subject that they enjoy, which then links them to a sampling of careers associated with that subject.

Students interested in beginning their job search can use the following websites as a jumping-off point: Quint Careers (www.quintcareers.com/job-seeker.html), the Riley Guide (www.rileyguide.com), JobHuntersBible (www.jobhuntersbible.com), CareerBuilder (www.careerbuilder.com), Monster (www.monster.com), Simply Hired (www.simplyhired.com), Indeed (www.indeed.com), and Going Global (http://www.goinglobal.com). The first three websites provide visitors with guidance and tips on how to find a job on the Internet, including information about interviewing and about writing resumes and cover letters. The last five websites are job search engines. Going Global especially offers worldwide career and job information including cultural advice about various countries.

There are a variety of ways that professional school counselors can integrate technology into their career development programs. For example, a classroom guidance lesson that focuses on career exploration could center on the use of technology. Students can use the Internet to take an inventory of their own career interests and then search for specific information on jobs that align with those interests. The Internet also can be used to gather information on creating cover letters and resumes when teaching students about employability skills and to coach students on the job-search process. In addition, students can create electronic portfolios using Web-based software to manage their educational and career plans

Developing a systematic and coordinated educational- and career-planning program across grades K–12 requires understanding the developmental tasks confronting students as they progress through school. Understanding these tasks prepares school personnel to work collaboratively in program development and implementation. A comprehensive understanding of the career development process also sets the stage for developing program interventions that are sequential and cohesive.

ELEMENTARY SCHOOL

During the elementary school years, children begin formulating a sense of competence and interests through greater interaction with the world beyond their immediate families. Interactions with peers, teachers, parents, and community members shape children's self-perceptions. Through exposure to adult life patterns via observations in schools, community activities, home, and the media, children draw conclusions about their lives. The conclusions they draw include assumptions about their current and future place in the world.

Obviously, there is tremendous variability in the quality-of-life patterns to which children are exposed. Television, for example, often provides children with examples of men and women in gender-stereotyped roles and occupations (e.g., only women working as nurses, only men working as auto mechanics, women taking primary responsibility for homemaking and parenting). It also may provide very limited perceptions of careers for people of color. Children use this information to draw conclusions about the life patterns that are appropriate for them. As children are increasingly exposed to stereotypical behaviors and expectations of majority groups, they begin to eliminate nontraditional life patterns and narrow occupations for further consideration. The *ASCA National Model* (2012) addresses the discussion of traditional and nontraditional career choices in several of the career development competencies.

Gottfredson (1996) contended that a gender-based elimination process begins as early as the age of 6 years. She also suggested that between the ages of 9 and 13 years, children begin to eliminate those occupations from further consideration that they perceive to be less prestigious for their social class. Variables such as race or gender stereotyping and prestige rankings interact with self-perceptions of abilities and interests, as well as family and community expectations. These influences shape the decisions young people make about potential occupational options. An additional variable that influences students' perceptions of certain careers is geography. Students who have resided in more rural locations may have been exposed to entirely different jobs than those who have grown up in urban areas. At the elementary school level, students develop a basic sense of self (e.g., the activities in which they enjoy participating, the things they like and do not like) that provides the foundation for career exploration activities. Developing a sense of personal competence and positive self-worth is an important goal for elementary school children to achieve. Erikson (1963) noted that children who do not achieve this goal will struggle as they attempt to move forward in educational and career planning. Students also learn how to interact effectively with others. They learn that as they grow, they will take on additional responsibilities. By learning school rules, students develop a basic understanding of the importance of cooperative behavior within institutions. Erikson noted that developing a sense of initiative and industry during the elementary school experience provides children with a solid foundation from which they clarify their identities during secondary school.

The primary focus of career development interventions in the elementary school is awareness of important self-characteristics (e.g., values, interests, capacities).

According to the *ASCA National Model* (2012), professional school counselors need to promote self-knowledge; academic self-concept; and awareness of skills, interests, and motivations in relation to careers. Along with the ASCA *National Standards* covering career development, the U.S. Department of Labor, National Occupational Information Coordinating Committee (USDOL/NOICC, 1992) developed National Career Development Guidelines (see http://acrn.ovae.org/ncdg.htm) to help counselors identify developmentally appropriate goals and interventions across the life span. The specific career development competencies identified as appropriate for elementary school children fall within three categories: (a) self-knowledge, (b) educational and occupational exploration, and (c) career planning. Encouraging students to participate in activities relating to their interests nurtures a sense of autonomy, the anticipation of future opportunities for exploring, and the beginning of planful behaviors (Super, 1990). When interests connect with skills and capacities, a positive self-concept emerges, which in turn provides the foundation for coping with the career development tasks of adolescence. As children move toward adolescence, they must accomplish four major career development tasks: (a) become concerned about the future, (b) increase personal control over their lives, (c) convince themselves to achieve in school and at work, and (d) develop competent work habits and attitudes (Super, Savickas, & Super, 1996). School counselors need to be mindful of these major tasks and help students successfully achieve them and further develop positive self-concepts.

Another focus of career development interventions with elementary school children is to provide an environment in which each student's natural sense of curiosity can flourish (Super, 1990). Curiosity provides the foundation for exploring; children naturally express curiosity through fantasy and play. Children often engage intensely in fantasy-based play related to occupations such as physician, firefighter, teacher, and nurse. Curiosity can be guided to help students learn accurate information about themselves and their environments. For example, field trips to occupational environments related to a child's fantasy-based interests reinforce the child's sense of curiosity and stimulate further exploration and the gradual crystallization of interests (Super, 1957). Also, children need to receive accurate information about a variety of educational and career options and engage in educational and occupational exploration. School personnel must work to challenge the gender and racial occupational stereotypes that confront children. The use of nontraditional models (e.g., male nurses and female engineers) and exposure to a broad range of occupational environments is encouraged during the elementary school years. Because gender stereotyping is prevalent in society, students in elementary school should be encouraged to examine beliefs about female and male roles in society and how the various life roles interact to shape the overall life experience. Teaching children about the importance of diversity helps them learn how to interact more effectively with others in the school and community.

Educational and career planning is essential in elementary school. A study by Blackhurst, Auger, and Wahl (2003) found that fifth-grade students had a limited understanding of specific job skills and educational requirements for commonly known occupations, believing inaccurately that many widely known jobs require a college degree. These findings point to the possible need for professional school counselors and teachers to spend time introducing students to the training and educational requirements for a variety of popular occupations to ensure that students do not needlessly rule out potential careers early in their lives based on faulty beliefs, as well as to make sure students are aware of the full range of postsecondary options that exist beyond 4-year colleges, such as vocational and technical colleges. Raising student awareness about the training and educational requirements for occupations that interest them may also serve to heighten their motivation to do well in school. To help students develop the skills necessary for effective career planning, they are also taught decision-making strategies.

Although important decisions about postsecondary plans will not be made until later in their education, students in elementary school should begin exploring possible career pathways and become aware of how the skills they are learning in school are used in various careers. Teachers and professional school counselors can play a key role by helping students connect the dots between the learning that occurs in school and the skills necessary for the world of work. For example, professional school counselors could collaborate with teachers to present classroom guidance lessons showing students how math skills are needed by doctors and nurses to ensure that patients receive the appropriate amount of medicine, how newspaper and magazine writers need excellent writing skills to convey important and interesting stories to the public, how skills learned in art are useful for architects and graphic designers, or how almost all jobs require workers to have strong interpersonal and problem-solving skills. Making these connections can provide students with increased understanding of the importance of school and a solid foundation for future educational and career goal-setting. Collectively, these interventions provide the basis for effective educational and career planning during secondary school.

CAREER DEVELOPMENT ACTIVITIES FOR ELEMENTARY SCHOOL STUDENTS

The possibilities for career development activities in elementary school are endless. This is the time to use creative and engaging activities to introduce students to possible occupations and raise their awareness about the diverse careers that exist. Thus, developmental classroom guidance lessons and schoolwide initiatives are the most efficient and appropriate ways to deliver this information. Because students at this level have shorter attention spans than older students, it may be helpful to limit lessons to 20–30 minutes.

Practical Ideas for Career Development Activities

- Ask students to identify and discuss the jobs that they have observed in their communities and then add to their knowledge base by introducing a few new ones.
- Encourage students to identify the "jobs" they currently have as students and sons or daughters. They can use this self-knowledge to create a "Me and My Job" booklet that highlights their interests, as well as their "job" responsibilities at school and home.
- Classroom teachers can have students brainstorm jobs in the classroom (e.g., messenger, equipment manager) and apply and be paid (school rewards) for work done within the school.
- Fill paper grocery bags with two to five items that are associated with a specific career. Take the items out of each bag one by one, and have students guess the type of worker that uses those items. For example, one bag could contain a stethoscope and blood pressure cuff to represent a doctor.
- Ask students to draw a picture of a job they might want to have when they are older.
- Give each student a letter of the alphabet, and ask the students to select a job that begins with that letter, draw a picture of the job, and write three tasks or activities that are related to that occupation. Bind the students' work together to create an "Alphabet Career Book" for the school's library.
- Read a developmentally appropriate story (e.g., *Worm Gets a Job* by Kathy Caple for students in second grade and below) to a class, and then have the students identify the various jobs that were discussed in the book.
- Expose students to women who work in traditionally "male" occupations and men who work in traditionally "female" occupations.
- For students in grades 3 to 5, require each student to complete an interview with an adult about his or her career. Questions should focus on what the adult does and the schooling needed to prepare for that career. After interviews have been conducted, students can share their findings with the class.
- For fifth-grade classrooms with access to computers and the Internet, have students visit the children's *Occupational Outlook Handbook* website (www.bls.gov/k12), select an occupation that interests them, and fill out a worksheet describing the job's training requirements, typical salary, and future outlook. Students can then take turns sharing their information with the rest of the class and commenting on whether the information they found made them more or less interested in the job and why.
- Engage students in a discussion about the connection between education and career planning. Ask students: "How does school help you in career planning?" After this discussion, instruct each student to choose a career and research the career online at the children's *Occupational Outlook Handbook* website (www.bls.gov/k12) to determine the skills taught in school that are needed for success in that occupation.
- Challenge students to look into the future and think about how the jobs they are currently interested in might be different in 15 to 20 years. Using a computer lab, provide students with time to research the education, training, and skills they will need to be successful in these "future careers."
- Host a career day or career week during which students' parents and members of the community visit the school to talk about their occupations. Before visitors come to speak, it is important to meet with students and develop a list of questions that they can ask speakers. These questions can then be typed up and distributed to students prior to each presentation. Following the career day, the professional school counselor can conduct a booster session during which students are asked to reflect on and process their thoughts about the careers they learned about.
- Arrange field trips to nearby businesses to help students get a sense of the types of occupations that exist in those fields (e.g., hospital, grocery store, library, bank). Like with a career day, students should develop questions to ask their tour guide before the trip, and professional school counselors should ensure that there is time for processing afterward.
- On a more global level, carve out a small amount of time during every classroom guidance lesson, whether it is career related or not, to have students

identify how the skill being taught in the lesson is integral to success in the workplace and engage them in a brainstorming session to come up with the types of occupations that are most likely to need that skill to be effective.

- Provide parents with links to any websites used in the career development program so that they have the chance to explore these sites with their children at home and reinforce the learning that occurred in school.

VOICES FROM THE FIELD 12.1 **CAREER DEVELOPMENT IN THE ELEMENTARY SCHOOL**

I use career development classroom guidance lessons as well as schoolwide events to address career competencies with my elementary students. The classroom guidance lessons vary among grade levels. In kindergarten, we focus on career awareness and explore the multitude of jobs available by looking at different tools that jobs use. I link this activity to a kindergartener's job as a student and the tools used every day in class such as pencils, erasers, glue, and crayons. We also focus on nontraditional jobs by matching girls and boys to jobs such as mechanic, nurse, doctor, and teacher. I intentionally match the genders to nontraditional jobs and then present images of real people working in the nontraditional jobs.

As students get older, I link career planning to academic goal setting. Third-grade students focus on exploring their interests, abilities, and favorite subjects and then link them to future careers. Fourth- and fifth-grade students delve deeper into career development theory by completing interest inventories and learning about John Holland's personality theory. We incorporate technology into career planning and use the Bureau of Labor Statistics website to research jobs that match with their personality type. Students research the education required for a career, the job outlook, and subjects used. Video clips of nontraditional jobs are shared through media center resources. Within each career lesson, community members and parents are incorporated as students share interviews they have conducted with family members about what they like and dislike about their jobs, the subjects they use, and the education they received.

The career development lessons culminate in a schoolwide Career Week, which ignites excitement among all students about future careers. Video bios of community members are shared with the entire school population on the "Morning Show." Students are able to dress up as a favorite future career. Kindergarteners and fourth- and fifth-grade students participate in a Career Day. Approximately 20 community members are scheduled to present to these students and bring visual props or interactive materials to engage the students. The activity is then linked to academic learning through writing lessons that result in thank-you notes and summary reports of what students learned. The impact on students is tremendous as they learn how subjects in school eventually are used in careers, thereby increasing motivation to learn those skills. They also see the multitude of opportunities that are available in the world of work, which is especially valuable for students who have not been exposed to a diverse number of occupations within their family environments. Furthermore, they begin to see realistically how grades, school attendance, and good homework habits relate to getting a good job with sufficient pay. For younger students, Career Day plants the seeds for future questioning and learning in the school environment. Finally, the events connect the school community to the community at large and involve key community stakeholders in the educational process.

Source: Angela Poovey, Professional School Counselor, Dillard Drive Elementary, Wake County Public Schools, Raleigh, North Carolina

MIDDLE OR JUNIOR HIGH SCHOOL

Students at the middle or junior high school level are confronted with a more sophisticated set of developmental tasks than they experienced during their elementary school years. The developmental change of transitioning from childhood to adolescence presents a challenge to the young person. Physiological and social development leads the early adolescent to take strides toward independence; these strides, however, are often accompanied by feelings of insecurity, conflict, fear, and anxiety. As a result of their advancing development, middle or junior high school students are preoccupied with belonging and are influenced significantly by same-gender peers. Moreover, adolescence is a "time of seeking identity" (Hess, Magnuson, & Beeler, 2012, p. 59), wherein middle or junior high school students explore the self and the world of work. These personal and social developmental tasks experienced by middle or junior high school students highlight that career development interventions should focus on helping these students crystallize their identities and shape positive self-concepts. Counselors need to challenge students to become involved in the career development process, while offering supportive assistance as students acquire additional information about self and career.

Middle or junior high school students demonstrate a growing understanding of the world of work. Often, this progress is the result of students' participation in school activities, hobbies, and part-time work. Research findings show that, compared to younger children, middle or junior high school students tend to engage in more conscious and focused career explorations (Hartung, Porfeli, & Vondracek, 2005) and demonstrate a more advanced understanding of the career decision-making process (Howard & Walsh, 2010). For instance, Howard and Walsh found that sixth graders considered personal interests and abilities as important factors in choosing and attaining a career, and 15% to 20% of them were able to explain the dynamic interplay between personal, environmental, and interpersonal factors related to career choice and attainment. Research also has demonstrated the benefits of intentional career preperation during middle or junior high school years. For instance, Hirschi, Niles, and Akos's (2011) study of Swiss eighth graders found that students' career explorations and planning contributed to increased career decisiveness and congruence

As these students transition between Super's (1980) growth and exploration stages, they encounter the task of crystallizing occupational preferences. Super et al. (1996) stated the following about the crystallization process:

> When habits of industriousness, achievement, and foresight coalesce, individuals turn to daydreaming about possible selves they may construct. Eventually, these occupational daydreams crystallize into a publicly recognized vocational identity with corresponding preferences for a group of occupations at a particular ability level. (p. 132)

To establish an appropriate course of action for high school and beyond, educational- and career-planning interventions during middle or junior high school must be directed toward helping students cope successfully with the tasks of crystallizing and specifying occupational preferences (Super et al., 1996).

Further, middle or junior high school students are required to translate self and career awareness into an educational plan for the remainder of their secondary school education. Through educational planning, students make important choices about their future careers. For example,

during the eighth grade, a student is expected to identify a specific pathway of academic classes that will lead to certain possibilities on graduation. Without sufficient coursework or achievement, he or she may find that the postsecondary option that was desired is no longer available because requirements were not met early in the educational-planning process, as explored in depth in Chapter 11.

Variability in career development among middle or junior high school students certainly exists. For students who do wish to attend college, it is essential that they begin talking about these plans with their parents and the appropriate school staff while in middle or junior high school so that they can take classes that will adequately prepare them for the rigorous courses (i.e., college prep) they will need to take once they reach high school (Hobson & Phillips, 2010). Equally relevant are the students who do not have any postsecondary plans or goals. These students will be at a distinct disadvantage later in their academic career if they find that they have not achieved high enough grades or taken the necessary classes to prepare themselves for the occupation or continuing education they desire (Trusty et al., 2005). This is why a focus on educational planning is necessary during the seventh and eighth grades. Hobson and Phillips (2010) addressed the notion of balancing the high career aspirations of students with the influence of others. They suggest that the professional school counselor can play a role in coaching students as they make course selections, while attempting to attend to both the dominance of their parents and the influence of their peers.

Exploration can take place in numerous ways. Through classroom guidance on self-exploration (e.g., using Holland's [1992] theory), students can use computers to take the Career Key (Jones, 2004) and learn more about their own personality types. On discovering their types, students may look through a list of correlating career options and begin to explore these options through activities such as career days, job shadowing, and Internet searches. Teaching students how to locate, understand, and use career information fosters independent activity in educational and career planning. To this end, students can be taught the Holland (1992) occupational codes as a means for developing self-understanding and organizing occupational information. In addition, by participating in community volunteer work, students can learn about themselves and the concept of work. Students can also be encouraged to learn more about themselves not only as that knowledge pertains to important characteristics (e.g., interests, skills, values), but also in terms of considering the life roles that are important now and that are likely to be important in the future The link between school activities and future opportunities first developed during elementary school must continue to be strengthened. Guest speakers representing a variety of occupations can discuss the relationship between learning and work. Specific subject areas can be linked to occupational success, and the importance of lifelong learning for occupational success can be stressed. In addition, guest speakers can share the academic struggles they have faced and how they have overcome those challenges to achieve their career goals (Rivera & Schaefer, 2008). This will foster hope in students who may have struggled with academic challenges. To reinforce the importance of academic access, achievement, and attainment, professional school counselors can inform students about the positive correlation between the level of academic attainment and the amount of income workers earn.

During the middle or junior high school years, an educational and career portfolio is started for every student. Included in this portfolio are interest inventories, career exploration information and activities, educational-planning materials, results from Internet searches, resources acquired at career fairs or job shadowing, and any other information that will add to the student's career development process. Using this portfolio, the student and professional school counselor can meet throughout the year and discuss the career development process using easy-to-access information that is specific to the student. Although this portfolio is started during middle or junior high school, it should be passed on to the high school counselor and maintained throughout the high school years. It is during the high school years that items in the portfolio will reflect more specific career choices.

THEORY INTO PRACTICE 12.2

CAREER DEVELOPMENT ACTIVITIES FOR MIDDLE OR JUNIOR HIGH SCHOOL STUDENTS

Professional school counselors working at the middle or junior high school level need to help students determine their career interests, skills, and values so that they have enough self-awareness when they reach high school to create suitable educational plans. Middle or junior high school is the ideal time to engage students in educational planning, career exploration, awareness, information gathering, and future goal-setting.

Practical Ideas for Career Development Activities

- Administer a career interest inventory, skills assessment, and values inventory (see the section on assessment at the beginning of this chapter for specific instruments that may be helpful in this process) to students. These inventories can be found online, in paper form, or through computer-assisted career programs and software (e.g., Career Futures or Choices Explorer [www.bridges.com], Kuder Career Planning System [www.kuder.com/solutions/kuder-career-planning-system.html], Career Cruising [www.careercruising.com], and Coin Educational Products [www.coinedu.com/products/middle.cfm]). Using the results from these inventories, help students pinpoint one or two career clusters that are of interest to them to begin exploring in more detail.
- Present a classroom guidance lesson to students in the computer lab introducing them to the host of available online resources to help them learn about careers. Ask students to research one occupation on each website and write down their findings.
- Ask students to make a list of the occupations they think women most commonly work in and the occupations they think men most commonly work in and have them share their lists with the class. Teach students about nontraditional career opportunities and how certain jobs have been stereotyped and discriminated against as "male jobs" or "female jobs." Present common myths related to nontraditional jobs, as well as information about the realities of these jobs. End with a discussion about the implications of such stereotyping.
- Ask students to make a list of the occupations that they see in schools, communities, families, and/or media and to rank those occupations according to their perceived prestige. Discuss what criteria they used when ranking occupations (e.g., required education, pay, work environment, social reputation). End with a discussion as to how their personal and social values and cultural/familial contexts might affect their perceived occupational prestige.
- Inform students about the importance of educational and career goal setting. Create a goal-setting worksheet that asks students to list two educational goals and two career goals that they have for themselves. For each goal they set, provide space for them to list the specific steps they will need to take to achieve each of their goals. Allow sufficient time for students

(Continued)

to share some of their goals with the class, and ask them what they can begin doing in the next few days or weeks to start working toward their goals.

- Deliver a classroom guidance lesson on the connection between school and work and then assign students the task of conducting one informational interview with a professional in the community to learn about the professional's work environment and the skills learned in school that lead to success in that occupation.
- Prepare a presentation introducing students to the wide range of postsecondary possibilities (e.g., 4-year college, community college, vocational school, job training) and provide a sampling of occupations corresponding to each pathway. Engage students in a discussion about how their performance in middle or junior high school and high school has a significant influence on the possibilities that will be available to them on graduation from high school.
- Introduce students to the concepts of lifestyle and life roles and have them write down how they currently spend their time and what their current life roles are, as well as what they would like their lifestyle to be like and what life roles they think will be important to them when they are adults. Make sure to explain the variety of factors that make up a lifestyle, how different people prefer different lifestyles, and how money is only one part of the equation. Provide students with examples of the kinds of lifestyles associated with well-known careers (e.g., a doctor's lifestyle, a teacher's lifestyle, a banker's lifestyle). Once students have completed this task, ask them to research careers of interest to them and see how many they can find that would allow them to support their desired lifestyle and fulfill the life roles that are important to them.

- Collaborate with teachers to find ways to integrate career development activities into students' core classes. For example, professional school counselors could team up with science teachers to present information about science-related careers and the education necessary to pursue those careers.
- Host a career day or career fair where students have the opportunity to meet and hear from professionals who work in a diverse range of occupations.
- Work with students to begin creating a career portfolio, to house the results from their assessments, as well as any other important documents, activities, projects, or research that they accumulate throughout middle or junior high school that will aid them in the career and educational decision-making process once they reach high school. Consider diverse formats of portfolios (Williams & Wehrman, 2008). Electronic portfolios are easy to access and update and can contain various formats of information (e.g., video clips of students' performance). However, electronic portfolios may require specific software, hardware, and technological skills, whereas anyone can easily create and review paper-based portfolios. As an alternative, the combination of paper-based portfolio and electronic portfolio can be used.

VOICES FROM THE FIELD 12.2   CAREER PLANNING AT THE MIDDLE SCHOOL

As a first-year counselor in the only middle school in a small school district, I've faced many challenges. Our school counseling program is making progress toward reflecting the ideals of the *ASCA National Model*, which means we often spend time advocating for our role and have to find time to dedicate to our students when we have many other responsibilities that take up a great deal of our time. One issue we have struggled with is determining how to devote sufficient time to career development outside the standard high school program planning. In today's society, middle school counselors must advocate for time with students dedicated to career development and exploration because of the challenging job market our students will face.

In the first few months of the year, I had limited opportunities to conduct classroom guidance lessons and small-group counseling sessions on academic or personal/social topics with my seventh graders. However, when I requested time to discuss career exploration with the students, no one questioned the meaningfulness of this type of lesson, especially because I included a career interest inventory that would help students determine the careers in which they might be successful. In addition, there was full administrative and staff support for attending a career fair hosted at the state university across town.

These career exploration activities may have been the first meaningful exposures our students had in understanding the importance of discussing careers because of the immediacy of decisions they will make regarding high school program planning. Although middle school students may developmentally be able to make the connection between school and future work, we struggled to get all students to understand the value of these experiences. Middle school students are too often negatively influenced by their peers, and unfortunately the overall composition of the class dictates how successful many activities can be. These facts are important to keep in mind when planning and executing career development activities, and it was a hard lesson I had to learn during my first year. However, by collecting data, both before and after conducting the career development activities, it was possible for me to determine how to improve the lessons and make them even more meaningful for all students. This will make it easier to advocate for time with students when the amount of time allotted for counselors to work with students is becoming increasingly more limited with the high academic standards placed on schools today.

Source: Megan A. Kingsley, Professional School Counselor, Buford Middle School, Charlottesville City Schools, Virginia

HIGH SCHOOL

As students transition from middle or junior high school to high school, they focus more directly on the task of identifying occupational preferences and clarifying career and lifestyle choices. According to Super (1957), the tasks of crystallizing, specifying, and implementing tentative career choices occur during early (ages 12–15 years), middle (ages 16–18 years), and late (ages 18–24 years) adolescence.

When adolescents complete the relevant training and preparatory experiences, they then implement their occupational choices by acquiring positions in their specified occupations. Thus, the key elements of a successful school-to-work and school-to-postsecondary education transition involve being able to implement and adjust to career choice(s). Through a developing *career maturity,* adolescents develop their career decision-making readiness. To reflect adults' heterogeneous and nonlinear career development process, Super and Knasel (1981) proposed the term *career adaptability.* Savickas (1997) defined career adaptability as "readiness to cope with the predictable tasks of preparing for and participating in the work role and with the unpredictable adjustments prompted by changes in work and working conditions" (Savickas, 1997, p. 254). The concept of career adaptability can be expanded to children and adolescents in light of diverse contextual factors (e.g., race, SES, gender) that render their career development processes heterogeneous and complex (Niles & Harris-Bowlsbey, 2013; Savickas, 1997). Further, in line with career adaptability, today's dynamic world of work makes it more crucial for high school students to develop their abilities to be vigilant about the changing work environment and adjust their career goals and plans accordingly.

Because the majority of secondary school students in the United States enter work immediately on leaving high school or do not attend or finish college, developing workforce readiness is an important focus of career development intervention in high school. The definition of *workforce readiness* changes with the times. Until recently, this term may have focused solely on helping adolescents acquire training for a specific job. However, as today's work world is rapidly changing and workers are making multiple job transitions throughout their lives, employers are now more concerned with transferrable skills including basic numeracy and literacy, teamwork, flexibility, problem-solving, and interpersonal skills (Organisation for Economic Cooperation and Development, 2010; Savickas, 2011; Stone & Lewis, 2012). Therefore, cultivating these transferrable skills is essential for high school students to become successful workers.

Likewise, school-to-work career development intervention calls for comprehensive career development services beyond a sole emphasis on traditional workforce development. Gysbers and Lapan (2009) argued that students' successful postsecondary transitions should be facilitated within a comprehensive guidance and counseling program framework focused on key career constructs outlined in Lapan's (2004) model (i.e., positive expectations, identity development, person–environment fit, vocational interests, academic achievement, and social skills and work readiness behaviors). The enhancement of these core career constructs during the high school years is linked to adaptive transitions into adulthood across various life domains. In Lapan, Aoyagi, and Kayson's (2007) longitudinal study, high school seniors who developed these career constructs were more satisfied with their personal and work lives and accomplished higher levels of education 3 years after completing high school. The *ASCA National Model* (2012) reinforces these ideas through its career development competencies. In particular, several of the competencies emphasize the transition from school to work and the relationship between learning and work (e.g., each student should demonstrate an understanding of the value of lifelong learning and have the skills necessary to adjust to career transitions).

Baker and Gerler (2008) emphasized the importance of providing "transition enhancement" assistance to secondary school students as they progress toward further education, training, or employment. They recommended that, because such transitions are a regular part of high school students' development, counselors view transitions as a process, rather than as events or a sequence of events. The basic needs of students coping with the transition process can be classified into the categories of support, awareness, and skills. Because most adolescents have lived their lives primarily in the arenas of home and K–12 schools, postsecondary work, training, and education present new challenges and experiences. Professional school counselors can aid in normalizing the transition process by providing reassurance to students that, although somewhat frightening, these new opportunities will present them with normal challenges and that many of the competencies they have developed thus far will be useful to them as they move forward.

When conceptualized as a process, the school-to-work and school-to-school transition skills build on career development competencies students have developed throughout their educational experiences, including the self-awareness, occupational awareness, and decision-making skills. Transition skills also build on the basic educational competencies related to reading, writing, and arithmetic (Baker & Gerler, 2008). For example, composing a resume and cover letter requires self-awareness, occupational awareness, and writing skills. Performing effectively in a job or college interview requires skill in oral communication and interpersonal communication. Acquiring information about jobs, colleges, and training programs requires research, technology, and reading skills. Transition skills can also be expanded to include skills related to stress and anxiety management. The ASCA (2012) takes the position that counselors in the school must assume the primary (but not sole) responsibility for fostering these skills in students. Thus, school counselors must provide a systematic set of interventions to foster student career development competencies throughout K–12 education to proactively bolster students' readiness to cope with the career development tasks they are likely to encounter. The counselors also must be competent in developing and delivering strategies to help students who face difficulty in coping with career development tasks.

High school students continue the momentum gained in self-knowledge during the middle or junior high school years. Stone and Lewis (2012) stressed that high school career development programs must help students "test their evolving identities against the reality of occupations" (p. 51). Work-based learning activities and technical training can provide students with the opportunity to evaluate their self-characteristics within an occupational context and to understand how academic knowledge is applied to workplace settings.

High school students grow increasingly aware of the relationship between educational achievement and career planning as the need to choose postsecondary options becomes more immediate. Work and extracurricular experiences help high school students increase their understanding of the need for positive attitudes toward work and learning and develop more sophisticated interpersonal skills. Professional school counselors must facilitate students to advance their skills in locating, evaluating, and interpreting career information and to refine their job search skills. High school students often do not recognize the transferable skills they have developed through their education, extracurricular, and/or work experiences (Alexander & Hirsch, 2012). Therefore, professional school counselors need to help them identify their skill sets they possess and market their skills through the resume and interview process.

Adolescents in high school also must continue to develop and refine their decision-making skills. Clarifying students' values is integral in the career decision-making process, and examining life-role salience provides opportunities to explore students' values attached to each life role (Niles & Harris-Bowlsbey, 2013). The approaching inevitability of participation in multiple life roles motivates students for additional clarification of life-role salience. Using a group guidance format, students can examine their life-role salience by responding to such questions as these: "How do you spend your time during a typical week?" "How important are the different roles of life (e.g., student, worker, citizen) to you?" "What do you like about participating in each of the life roles?" "What life roles do you think will be important to you in the future?" "What do you hope to accomplish in each of the life roles that will be important to you in the future?" "In which life roles do members of your family participate?" and "What do your family members expect you to accomplish in each of the life roles?" Always have students consider a full range of possible career paths so that students are not locked into one option and also so that students have an alternative in case one of their plans does not work out (Rosenbaum, Stephan, & Rosenbaum, 2010).

Community resources are useful to expose students to a variety of career options. For example, high school counselors can invite local employment administrators to address local employment trends and opportunities. Local university admission officers can be invited to explain the admissions process to students. Moreover, community members and recent graduates can share their career paths with students. Students can also gain occupational information by engaging in job shadowing, summer enrichment programs, and/or informational interviews. Parent and guardian involvement in students' career planning and choice is critical for helping high school students with their career development tasks. Evening informational sessions and newsletters can be effective tools to inform parents and guardians about the career development tasks that their children may encounter (Niles & Harris-Bowlsbey, 2013).

Savickas (1999) reinforced the importance of orienting students to the tasks they will face and the decisions they will make during their secondary school years. Discussing the items on career development inventories such as the *Career Maturity Inventory* (Crites, 1978) or the *Adult Career Concerns Inventory* (Super, Thompson, & Lindeman, 1988) is one technique that Savickas suggested for helping secondary school students consider the career development tasks they will encounter as they move through high school. In addition, Savickas suggested that a positive attitude toward making educational and career plans, a willingness to become actively involved in the career development process, the motivation to acquire information about the world of work, and decision-making

abilities are some of the competencies high school students need to manage their career development effectively.

In essence, high school provides the opportunity for adolescents to build on the career development competencies they acquired during middle or junior high school. As life after high school moves from being remote to more immediate, adolescents must learn to assume greater responsibility for their career planning. Participation in multiple life roles becomes a serious component of the career-planning process. High school students' degrees of career adaptability/maturity and preparedness for the life roles are varied. Thus, school counselors must consider students' different needs and provide each student with appropriate assistance to prepare for life after secondary school.

THEORY INTO PRACTICE 12.3

CAREER DEVELOPMENT ACTIVITIES FOR HIGH SCHOOL STUDENTS

It is crucial that high school students begin the process of tentatively crystallizing their career and educational goals so that they can begin serious consideration of possible postsecondary paths. Professional school counselors can play a valuable role in this process by providing students with opportunities to learn about their options, as well as about the skills and academic performance necessary to pursue those options.

Practical Ideas for Career Development Activities

- Administer interest inventories to students that provide them with information about careers and college majors potentially suitable for them (e.g., Holland's assessment, the *Self-Directed Search*). Have students research two or three careers and college majors that sound interesting to them.
- Help all students create a 4-year educational plan (this is a requirement of many public schools). Use students' postsecondary goals and results from career assessments to help guide course selection.
- Inform students that different occupations require different levels of education. In a computer lab, show students a few helpful career websites and ask them to locate occupations that require certain degrees. For example, encourage students to find two occupations requiring a high school diploma, two occupations requiring vocational/technical school experience, two occupations requiring a

bachelor's degree, two occupations requiring a master's degree, and two occupations requiring a doctoral degree. Engage students in a discussion about how knowing specific educational requirements for various occupations might guide their choice of courses in high school.

- Present a lesson on decision making to students, and teach them a specific decision-making model. Inform students that sound decision-making skills will enable them to make educated choices about their postsecondary plans. Break students into small groups, provide each group with a decision-making scenario, and encourage each group to resolve the situation in the scenario using the decision-making model. Once students have shared their work with the rest of the class, initiate a discussion about how the decision-making model could be used to help them choose a college or a career.
- Run counseling groups for students on topics related to career development and educational planning (e.g., choosing a college, succeeding in college, finding a job, choosing a career).
- Connect with local companies and professionals to provide students with job shadowing opportunities.
- Collaborate with English teachers to present lessons to 11th and 12th graders on how to write a resume and cover letter.
- Host a mock interview day for 11th and 12th graders. Bring in members of the community to conduct

(Continued)

brief mock interviews with students, as well as providing them with feedback. Prior to this event, make sure to collaborate with teachers to disseminate information to all 11th and 12th graders about interview preparation, tips, and best practices.
- Advertise local job and college fairs, or host your own.
- Invite college representatives to visit campus and hold information sessions for interested students.

- Hold information sessions about financial aid and scholarship opportunities for students interested in attending college.
- Offer job workshops to assist students in finding and applying for jobs.
- If the high school you work at has a career resource center, create a scavenger hunt to orient students to the career and educational information and resources available to them.

| VOICES FROM THE FIELD 12.3 | CAREER DEVELOPMENT AND EDUCATIONAL PLANNING IN THE HIGH SCHOOL |

In working with high school students, I have discovered that they are aware that long-term academic and career development is necessary; however, they often lack knowledge of how to start this process and what career exploration resources are available. As a high school counselor, my focus is usually twofold: help the student to better understand his/her personal attributes, interests, and aptitudes, while also introducing the specifics of career exploration (e.g., career searching, job readiness, career development resources). I think one of the biggest challenges school counselors face is helping students gain an accurate knowledge of the "basics" surrounding a particular career (e.g., starting salary, education needs, typical workday). For example, I want my students to understand that, if becoming a doctor or a lawyer is a career aspiration for them, then they must be willing to attain a significant amount of postsecondary training. I also find that a large percentage of students' career exploration tends to be shaped by parental/environmental influences and salary aspirations. Encouraging students to see beyond salary numbers in career investigation is a major task for school counselors because I see that students often limit their career exploration to careers that have been historically known for their higher-end salaries (e.g., doctors, lawyers, professional athletes), and environmental influences usually promote this type of focus. Thus, using available career exploration tools to expand students' perspectives, as well as introducing them to the plethora of occupational fields, is one of my primary jobs as a professional school counselor.

In reality, career development sometimes gets overshadowed by other counselor responsibilities such as academic planning and/or responsive services; thus, it is important that school counselors be creative in the ways in which they introduce career development strategies to students. Using resources that are easily accessible through technology gives students an opportunity to do some level of self-directed career exploration, which I have found to be critical, given the time constraints school counselors sometimes face. Collaboration between the school counselor and the school's career development coordinator (CDC) can be another valuable tool for school counselors when implementing a comprehensive career development program. At my school, I tend to facilitate the self-awareness piece and introduce students to career exploration resources, and the CDC coordinates more of the practical components of career exploration by organizing career fairs, bringing in guest speakers, and collaborating with the local business alliance. Time restraints and other responsibilities are a reality in the day-to-day work of school counselors; thus, it is critical, when establishing a comprehensive career development program, that we expand on what has been historically done in regard to career development with our students and utilize emerging resources.

Source: Brooke Comer, Ninth-Grade Counselor, Athens Drive High School, Wake County Public Schools, Raleigh, North Carolina

---

MULTICULTURAL IMPLICATIONS OF CAREER PLANNING

Culture is a key consideration when designing a K–12 educational- and career-planning program. As one example, the impact of gender on career circumscription in elementary school was highlighted earlier. Another example is the concept of decision making as an independent process.

This may be typical of European Americans, but is often not true of many other cultures (e.g., Hispanic, Asian), who tend to make decisions in a more collective or linear manner. Thus, the professional school counselor must be aware of how culture intersects with and influences all aspects of career and educational planning in elementary, middle or junior high, and high school and provide career development interventions in a culturally responsive manner.

Having an understanding of the client's time orientation, problem-solving strategies, and view on social relationships becomes a vital factor when discussing careers. For example, in collectivistic cultures, social relationships tend to be interdependent, and decision making is likely group oriented (Coleman & Yeh, 2008). Thus, for a student from collectivistic cultures, career choice may not be a sole matter of his/her personal career interests; rather, family or community needs, interests, and values may be importantly taken into account. In some traditional collectivistic cultures, elder family members often have a greater influence on familial decision making than in other cultures, and parents' wishes may be highly respected in student's career planning and choices. Gysbers, Heppner, and Johnston (2009) point out that it may be Western culture-centric to view this collectivistic decision making as overdependent and immature.

Summarizing two literature reviews (Hartung et al., 2005; Watson & McMahon, 2005), Porfeli, Hartung, and Vondracek (2008) concluded that "economically impoverished and African American and Hispanic children tend to maintain less prestigious career aspirations" (p. 28). Similarly, Gysbers Heppner, and Johnston (2009) stated that marginalization, oppression, and discrimination against racial/ethnic minority and low SES populations might undermine development of work role salience, and this may lead them to low-income, unskilled jobs. Consistent with this, racial and ethnic minority students tend to perceive more constrained career opportunities and greater career barriers than do Whites (Fouad & Byars-Winston, 2005). In addition, adolescents in disenfranchised communities often lack resources to build the informal networks that might lead them to work-based learning and job opportunites (Halpern, 2012). Thus, professional school counselors need to put their efforts into identifying career resources that these students can access and into reducing stereotypes and biases. Moreover, counselors must help students think through how their contextual factors might facilitate or hinder their adaptive vocational development and make informed career decisions based on accurate information and resouces.

The career development theories' traditional assumption of "the centrality of work in people's lives" (p. 55) may not be universal across cultures (Gysbers et al., 2009) because cultural values influence the relative centrality of life roles such as a worker, student, religious believer, and/or family member. Professional school counselors should be mindful that students seek to express their values within their salient life roles, and their values and value expressions are influenced by cultural and socioeconomic factors (Niles & Harris-Bowlsbey, 2013). In this regard, the next section addresses life-role readiness and salience in detail to promote multicultural career interventions.

Developing Life-Role Readiness and Salience

An essential approach to addressing academic, career, and personal/social development emphasizes the importance of developing students' life-role readiness. The life-role readiness concept is based on developmental approaches to school counseling (Myrick, 2003a). According to Myrick, developmental approaches contain objectives and activities directed to the following eight content areas:

1. Understanding the school environment
2. Understanding self and others
3. Understanding attitudes and behavior
4. Making decisions and solving problems
5. Developing interpersonal and communication skills
6. Developing school success skills
7. Achieving career awareness and engaging in educational planning
8. Developing community pride and involvement

Each of these content areas focuses on specific life roles. For example, *understanding the school environment* focuses on the life role of student, *developing community pride and involvement* focuses on the life role of citizen, and *achieving career awareness and engaging in educational planning* focuses on the life role of worker. Counseling activities within each content area are essentially intended to help students cope with the task of identity formation within the context of developing life-role readiness. *Life-role readiness* can be defined as the possession of the knowledge, attitudes, and skills necessary for effective life-role participation in a multicultural society. For example, among other things, effective parenting requires basic knowledge about child development, a positive attitude toward parenting as a life role, and the skills necessary for providing basic child care. Likewise, life-role readiness related to the leisure role requires basic knowledge about specific leisure activities, a positive attitude toward leisure as a life role, and the basic skills necessary for participating in specific leisure activities.

Developmental school counseling interventions should include learning opportunities that foster the development of the knowledge, attitudes, and skills necessary for effective life-role participation (i.e., life-role readiness). By providing these learning opportunities within a context that is sensitive to cultural diversity, professional school counselors help students avoid adherence to the cultural uniformity myth and cultural ethnocentrism. That is, students learn to appreciate and value cultural differences in life-role behavior.

CULTURAL REFLECTION 12.1

A student's ethnicity and family traditions may call for duties and responsibilities that are unique. How might the life role of "sibling" be different for a White adolescent than for a Hispanic adolescent; a female rather than a male adolescent; or other cultural characteristics?

Encouraging students to discuss life-role salience is useful because life-role salience provides the motivating force behind the development of life-role readiness (Super et al., 1996). If a life role is important to someone, then it is likely that the individual will engage in the behaviors necessary to prepare to take on that life role. Likewise, when salience is low, there is often little motivation to develop the requisite behaviors for effective participation in that role.

Addressing the issue of life-role salience, Super (1980) noted that work is only one role among many that individuals play. He identified the primary roles of life (e.g., student, worker, citizen, homemaker) and noted that some roles are more important than others at particular points in time. For example, some adolescents attend high school, work in part-time jobs, and are also parents. For a majority of adolescents, the life role of peer is paramount in middle or junior high and high school. Others devote a majority of their time to leisure, student, and family-of-origin activities. Developing life-role readiness requires secondary school students to identify their salient life roles and to examine the relationship between their goals and their current life-role activities.

Obviously, patterns of life-role salience among secondary students are significantly influenced by contextual factors, including immediate contextual factors (e.g., family, cultural heritage, level of acculturation) and distal contextual factors (e.g., economics, environmental opportunities for life-role participation). Hence, it is important for students to be aware of the ways in which contextual factors interact with identity development to shape life-role salience. In support of this argument, Diemer and Blustein (2006) found that urban adolescents' critical understanding of contextual barriers (e.g., sociopolitical inequity) to their career paths was positively associated with commitment to their future careers, clear vocational identity, and the salience of work role in their lives.

Often, students simply "inherit" patterns of life-role salience that are passed on from the dominant culture. Such inheritances can be problematic when they are embedded with beliefs based on gender and racial stereotypes. For instance, researchers have found gender differences that coincide with traditional gender-role expectations in life-role salience, such that female adolescents and young adults, compared to male counterparts, are more oriented to taking care of home and children (Cinamon, 2010; Yaremko & Lawson, 2007). Other studies have found that women possess more balanced-gender roles at work and family, whereas men hold more traditional gender roles that regard men as bread earners (Gere & Helwig, 2012; Judge & Livingston, 2008).

CULTURAL REFLECTION 12.2

How are women with high worker role salience placed at a disadvantage in the workforce by traditional gender role expectations? How might men limit their opportunities for participating in the home and family when they adhere to traditional expectations for life-role salience? By raising their awareness of the influence of the dominant culture on life-role salience, students will be less likely to allow beliefs reflecting racist and sexist attitudes to influence their beliefs about life-role salience.

INTERVENTION To foster life-role readiness and salience, professional school counselors can encourage students to address several topics. First, counselors at the elementary school level can introduce students to the primary roles of life (e.g., student, worker, family member, citizen). After developing life-role awareness in the elementary school, middle or junior high school students can be encouraged to identify the life roles that are important to them (i.e., their life-role salience). Second, students can identify the contextual factors (e.g., family, culture, economics, new occupational options) influencing their life-role salience. Third, middle or junior high and high school students can be encouraged to participate in specific activities that foster the development of life-role readiness. Together, these topics provide a conceptual framework around which counseling interventions that facilitate life-role readiness in a multicultural society can be constructed.

Professional school counselors can use a group guidance format to help students identify the life roles they are currently spending most of their time emotionally committed to and expect to be important to them in the future. With regard to the latter, professional school counselors can help students construct strategies for preparing for their salient life roles. For example, if the life role of parent is expected to be salient in the future, students can discuss ways to plan and prepare for that role. Counselors can also encourage students to examine areas of potential role conflict and discuss strategies for coping with excessive demands from multiple life roles. Through group guidance and classroom discussions, students can explore how different cultures often influence the values individuals seek to express in life roles (e.g., seeking to express self-actualization in work for the student from a Eurocentric cultural background or seeking to express cultural identity in work for the student from an Asian background). In these discussions, professional school counselors can encourage students to identify how they perceive and interpret the role expectations emanating from their cultures of origin and how these expectations influence their life-role salience and decisions of whether a particular life role is important. Particular attention can be paid to exploring how these expectations influence students' understandings of the behaviors required for effective role performance.

To effectively address life-role salience in sociocultural and familial contexts, Gibson (2008) suggested professional school counselors use career family trees and career genograms for elementary and secondary school students. Students can explore the interactions among family background, cultural prescriptions, and career planning through creating and processing the career family trees and career genograms. The genogram provides a tool for tracking career decisions across generations and identifying sources of important career beliefs and life themes that students have acquired. Gibson also recommends that the family tree and genogram techniques should be implemented with the respect of and sensitivity to diverse family structures, including blended family, single-parent family, and/or same sex parents. This technique can be expanded to address the same topics for other life roles. By using the genogram, professional school counselors can encourage students to identify the beliefs and life themes pertaining to specific life roles (e.g., parent and citizen) that they have acquired from members of their immediate and extended families. Counselors can also use the information provided by the students to contrast the influences on life-role salience emanating from group-oriented cultures with influences from more individualistic cultures. Terms such as *cultural assimilation* and *cultural accommodation* can be introduced in these discussions. The effects of gender-role stereotyping on life-role salience can also be examined here and challenged in these discussions. The goal of these interventions is to increase student awareness of the factors influencing their beliefs about the primary roles of life.

Knowing which life roles are salient and how contextual factors influence one's life-role salience is a starting point for developing life-role readiness. Professional school counselors must also encourage students to participate in activities that foster further development of life-role readiness. Super's (1957, 1977) theory is also useful in this regard. Super suggested that by actively planning for career decisions, exploring occupational options, gathering occupational information, learning how to make occupational decisions, and reality-testing tentative occupational choices, individuals develop their readiness for participating in the life role of worker.

An educational- and career-planning portfolio is an effective tool for helping students engage in purposeful planning, exploring, information gathering, decision making, and reality testing related to the life roles of student and worker. This can be expanded to a "life-role portfolio" by addressing students' readiness for life roles beyond those of student and worker. Students can be encouraged to plan, explore, and gather information for each of the major life roles.

For example, students who anticipate one day being a parent can plan for this role by considering how parenting interacts with other roles. Students can explore different styles of parenting by interviewing parents about their parenting practices and philosophies. Students can also gather information about the skills required for effective parenting (e.g., perhaps by taking a parenting class). Through these activities, students can learn about the factors that are important to consider in making decisions about parenting. Finally, students can reality-test their interest in parenting through participating in child care activities. Thus, the life-role portfolio stimulates counselor and student meetings focused on planning, exploring, information gathering, decision making, and reality testing vis-à-vis the major life roles. When the portfolio is used over successive years, it also provides developmental documentation of activities and decisions related to major life roles. This expanded use of the portfolio is an example of a counseling activity that is intended to help students cope with the task of identity formation within the context of developing life-role readiness. It also provides additional opportunities for discussing contextual influences on life-role salience.

Summary/Conclusion

According to the *ASCA National Model* (2012), one of the primary roles of any professional school counselor is to facilitate a career development program. A major goal of professional school counseling programs is to facilitate student development toward effective life-role participation. Professional school counselors must initiate appropriate developmental guidance activities in elementary school (e.g., self-awareness, curiosity) and facilitate culmination of this process with assistance in the transition to school, work, and a variety of life roles. Professional school counselors can enhance students' life-role readiness by helping students develop life-role awareness and by encouraging students to examine their life-role salience and the contextual factors that influence it. To foster the continued development of life-role readiness, professional school counselors can encourage students to engage in planning, exploring, information gathering, decision making, and reality testing vis-à-vis the major roles of life. In addition, the program should anticipate adaptations to various cultural backgrounds and the utilization of technology. By systematically addressing these topics throughout grades K–12, professional school counselors facilitate the development of life-role readiness in their students and increase the probability that students will cope successfully with life-role tasks in school and beyond.

Activities

1. Develop a career exploration activity for the grade level of your choice using technology.
2. Plan a classroom guidance session for elementary students that discusses traditional and nontraditional occupations.
3. Plan a career development group for high school students that focuses on employability skills.

13

Counseling Individuals and Groups in School

Bradley T. Erford*

Editor's Introduction: The responsive services of individual counseling and group counseling have long been effective tools in the professional school counselor's toolbox and continue to be so in the transformed role. It is essential that professional school counselors have a strong background in developmental counseling theory, as well as more specialized approaches to individual counseling and group work—especially brief, solution-focused models. Such breadth of training reflects belief in both the developmental nature of many childhood struggles and the value of time-limited counseling interventions.

INDIVIDUAL COUNSELING IN SCHOOLS

Meagan, age 6, is in Mrs. Hendrick's first-grade classroom. Recently, Meagan has been crying in class and withdrawing from activities. On talking with Meagan's mother, Mrs. Hendrick learns that Meagan's mother and father separated last month. Mrs. Hendrick wonders if it would be helpful for Meagan to talk with you, the professional school counselor.

Since starting 10th grade, 16-year-old Eric has been skipping classes. Consequently, his grades have dropped from Bs and Cs to Ds and Fs. One of Eric's friends stops by your office and tells you that he thinks Eric has become involved with a gang and is thinking about dropping out of school.

The start of this academic year has been especially difficult for several students on the sixth-grade team. Two students experienced the death of a parent. One student had a sister killed in an automobile accident. Another sixth grader recently lost his grandmother, with whom he had a very close relationship. Mr. Tobias, the school principal, approaches you to see if there is anything you can do to help.

Andrea, age 10 years, is new to the school. She is Romanian and was adopted in July by an American family. She speaks limited English and has made very few friends. Andrea has heard that you are available to talk with students who are having difficulties, but she is embarrassed to approach you.

Stephen, a 15-year-old boy, is questioning his sexual orientation. Last week, somebody defaced his locker by writing "gay" and "fag" on it. He comes to you distressed, angry, and hurt, stating, "Sometimes I think I'd be better off dead."

Mrs. Macon, the physical education teacher, has noticed that Abby, one of her eighth-grade students, has lost weight over the course of the past quarter and is extremely thin. She tires easily in gym class, refuses to shower afterward, and is wearing sweaters even though it is warm outside. "I'm worried that Abby has an eating disorder," Mrs. Macon tells you. "What can we do?"

Professional school counselors in elementary, middle, and high school settings are likely to face issues similar to these situations during the course of their work. When faced with such situations, it is important to know how to respond. Comprehensive, developmental school counseling programs provide the means for addressing students'

*Special thanks to Sam Gladding, Debbie W. Newsome, and Elisabeth S. Harper for contributions to earlier editions of this chapter.

immediate needs and concerns through the component called responsive services. *Responsive services* provide special help to students who are facing problems that interfere with their personal, social, career, or educational development. Specific interventions may be preventive, remedial, or crisis oriented. Individual counseling and small-group counseling are two activities that are classified as responsive services (American School Counselor Association [ASCA], 2012; Gysbers & Henderson, 2012). Other activities that are considered part of the responsive services component include crisis counseling, referrals, consultation and collaboration, and peer facilitation.

Although the amount of time allocated for responsive services differs from school to school, general guidelines specified in the *ASCA National Model* (2012) have been set for different grade levels. Suggested allocations include 20% to 30% in elementary schools, 30% to 40% in middle schools, and 25% to 35% in high schools (ASCA, 2012; Gysbers & Henderson, 2012). In this chapter, the focus is squarely on the counseling component of responsive services by describing strategies for working with individuals and groups in schools, as well as providing an overview of crisis counseling and crisis intervention in schools. Greater detail regarding crisis intervention, suicide, and threat assessment is provided in Chapter 15.

Family changes, violence, poverty, chronic illness, and interpersonal difficulties, as well as typical developmental transitions, are just a few of the myriad issues that can interfere with students' personal, social, career, and academic growth. When these or other concerns negatively affect a student's development and progress, individual counseling may be warranted. Professional school counselors make decisions about how to administer individual counseling services, keeping in mind that these services need to closely align with the educational mission and philosophy of educating all students to high levels of academic, career, and personal/social success (ASCA, 2012). In the following sections, a definition of counseling in school settings is provided, followed by a discussion of developmental factors that affect the counseling process, a general model for individual counseling in schools, and two theoretical approaches to counseling that have been used effectively in schools: solution-focused brief counseling and counseling using choice theory.

"Counseling is a professional relationship that empowers diverse individuals, families, and groups to accomplish mental health, wellness, education, and career goals" (ACA, 2010). The ultimate goal of implementing counseling interventions is to promote students' personal and social growth and to foster their career and academic process. Some of the concerns that may be addressed in school counseling include academic problems, relationship issues, grief and loss, family concerns, anger control, sexual issues, and stress management. Referrals for individual counseling may come from students, parents, teachers, or others who are involved with students. Although individual counseling cannot meet the needs of all students in K–12 schools (Eschenauer & Chen-Hayes, 2005), it represents a vital component of a comprehensive, developmental school counseling program.

Individual counseling involves a confidential relationship between a student and the professional school counselor that can last from a single session to several sessions. Not all one-on-one meetings with students are considered individual counseling (Brown & Trusty, 2005b; Schmidt, 2008). What distinguishes individual counseling from other forms of interaction is the close emotional contact between the student and the professional school counselor. Also, with individual counseling, the focus is on the student's problem or concern, and the goal is to help the student make positive changes in coping, in adapting, or in specific behaviors that are problematic (Brown & Trusty, 2005b).

Because professional school counselors are responsible for a wide range of services and because they typically serve a large number of students, teachers, and parents, it is critical for counselors to assess who will benefit from individual counseling relationships within the school setting. The *ASCA National Model* (2012) clearly states that professional school counselors do not provide long-term psychotherapy. Instead, they work within a developmental framework on issues that have direct relevance to educational success. If more expanded counseling services are needed, it is appropriate to engage in referral and consultation practices with outside agencies and community resources (see Case Study 13.1).

Identifying which students will benefit the most from individual counseling services can pose a tremendous challenge for professional school counselors. Additional challenges include how to integrate these services into the school day, how to conduct the counseling process, and how to evaluate the effectiveness of the interventions. Professional school counselors need to be proactive in making decisions about how to conduct individual counseling, with whom, at what time, and under what circumstances. As they make those decisions and deliver individual counseling services, professional school counselors will want to take into account the various developmental changes and challenges that influence the students with whom they work.

DEVELOPMENTAL CONSIDERATIONS

Counseling with children and adolescents differs in multiple ways from working with adults. Indeed, interventions that are appropriate for adult populations may be ineffective

CASE STUDY 13.1

The Case of Carlos

Carlos, an 8-year-old third grader, was referred to the professional school counselor by his teacher for being disruptive in class. The teacher feared that Carlos was having problems in the home that might be distracting him from his schoolwork. Assisted by a Spanish translator, the professional school counselor met with Carlos and his mother and discovered that Carlos had been in the United States for only 6 months and that getting to the United States had been a very traumatic experience.

Six months earlier, Carlos was sitting in his school classroom in Mexico when his mother, who had abandoned the family 3 years earlier to move to the United States, showed up at his school and told him that they were leaving. That same day they began their journey to the United States.

Because of the language barrier between the professional school counselor and the student's mother (the mother did not speak or understand any English), the professional school counselor decided to refer the family to an agency in the community that offered bilingual counseling. Through counseling, Carlos was able to express his anxiety and stress over leaving his home for a foreign land where people spoke a foreign language and looked very different from him. Family counseling at the agency also helped build family trust and cohesion among Carlos, his mother, and his two siblings.

As Carlos's language skills increased and his anxiety decreased, he began making friends at school. His behavior improved, as did his academic progress. Throughout the process, the professional school counselor served as a link among the school, the home, and the community counseling agency, which helped ensure that all systems were working together to facilitate Carlos's developmental and educational success.

and even detrimental if applied to children. Knowledge of developmental theory can help professional school counselors make decisions about what approaches to use with students at different levels. Moreover, such knowledge helps professional school counselors make informed decisions about whether a particular behavior is developmentally appropriate or is out of the range of "normal" (Vernon & Erford, 2014).

Development is multidimensional and complex and is marked by qualitative changes that occur in many different domains (Erford, 2015). In this section, an overview of some general developmental characteristics associated with students in elementary, middle, and high school is provided. Readers also may wish to refer to texts that provide in-depth descriptions of child and adolescent development (e.g., Berk, 2010; Erford, 2015).

Early Childhood

Counselors working in elementary schools may work with children in kindergarten or even preschool. Children between the ages of 2 and 6 are in the *early childhood* stage. During this period, children refine their motor skills, they begin to build ties with peers, and their thought and language skills expand rapidly. To understand the way young children think and use language, it is helpful to refer to Jean Piaget's stage-constructed theory of cognitive development. Although current research indicates that the stages of cognitive development are not as discrete and clear-cut as Piaget hypothesized, his description of cognitive development provides a relatively accurate picture of how children think and reason at different ages (Erford, 2015).

According to Piaget (1963), children between 2 and 7 years of age are *preoperational*, which means they are developing the ability to represent objects and events through imitation, symbolic play, drawing, and spoken language. They are most likely egocentric, implying that they cannot see the viewpoint of another. Preoperational children may attribute lifelike qualities to inanimate objects and have difficulty with abstract nouns and concepts such as time and space (Vernon & Erford, 2014). They are likely to engage in magical thinking and may offer imaginative explanations for things they do not understand. As children progress through early childhood, they become better able to represent and recall their feelings. As they near the end of the preoperational stage, their emotional self-regulation improves.

Erik Erikson's psychosocial theory (1963, 1968) provides another way to understand children's development. Erikson described development as a series of psychological crises that occur at various stages. The manner in which each crisis is resolved, along a continuum from positive to negative, influences healthy or maladaptive outcomes at each stage. Young children are in the process of resolving the developmental crisis of *initiative versus guilt*. *Initiative* refers to being enterprising, energetic, and purposeful.

Children in this stage are discovering what kinds of people they are, particularly in regard to gender. Because of their increased language and motor skills, they are capable of imagining and trying out many new things. To navigate this period successfully, children need to be given a variety of opportunities to explore, experiment, and ask questions. Understanding adults can be instrumental in helping young children to develop self-confidence, self-direction, and emotional self-regulation.

Play is an extremely important activity for children in this age group. Through play, children find out about themselves and their world. Professional school counselors will want to use some form of play when working with young children. Play provides a way for children to express feelings, describe experiences, and disclose wishes. Although young children may not be able to articulate feelings, toys and other play media serve as the words they use to express emotions (Landreth, 2002). Materials used to facilitate play include puppets, art supplies, dolls and dollhouses, tools, and toy figures or animals.

Play therapy has become an accepted and research-based approach to intervening with school-aged children, and although an expanded treatise is beyond the scope of this chapter and text, an increasing number of elementary school counselors are finding play therapy an adaptable approach to help young and less verbal students process and communicate emotional content.

Middle Childhood

Children between the ages of 7 and 11 years are in *middle childhood.* During this time period, children develop literacy skills and logical thinking. Cognitively, they are in Piaget's *concrete operational* stage, meaning that they are capable of reasoning logically about concrete, tangible information. Concrete operational children are capable of mentally reversing actions, although they still can only generalize from concrete experiences. They grasp logical concepts more readily than before, but they typically have difficulty reasoning about abstract ideas. Children in this stage learn best through questioning, exploring, manipulating, and doing. As a rule, their increased reasoning skills enable them to understand the concept of intentionality and to be more cooperative.

From a psychosocial perspective, children in middle childhood are in the process of resolving the crisis of *industry versus inferiority.* To maximize healthy development, they need opportunities to build up a sense of competence and capability. When adults provide manageable tasks, along with sufficient time and encouragement to complete the tasks, children are more likely to develop a strong sense of industry and efficacy (Erford, 2015). Alternatively, children

who do not experience feelings of competence and mastery may develop a sense of inadequacy and pessimism about their capabilities. Experiences with family, teachers, and peers all contribute to children's perceptions of efficacy and industry.

Negotiating relationships with peers is an important part of middle childhood. Being accepted in a peer group and having a "best friend" help children develop competence, self-esteem, and an understanding of others (Vernon & Erford, 2014). Some of the interpersonal skills children acquire during middle childhood include learning to get along with age-mates, learning the skills of tolerance and patience, and developing positive attitudes toward social groups and institutions. Professional school counselors can help children develop their interpersonal skills through developmental guidance activities and group counseling, as well as through individual counseling.

Adolescence

Adolescence is the period when young people transition from childhood to adulthood. During adolescence, youth mature physically, develop an increased understanding of roles and relationships, and acquire and refine skills needed for performing successfully as adults. Puberty marks the beginning of adolescence, with girls typically reaching puberty earlier than boys. For most students, *early adolescence* (ages 11–14 years) begins in middle school, *midadolescence* (ages 15–18 years) begins in high school, and *late adolescence* (18 years through young adulthood) occurs at the end of high school and continues throughout the early twenties.

As young people enter adolescence, they begin to make the shift from concrete to formal operational thinking. The transition takes time and usually is not completed until at least age 15 years (Erford, 2015). Adolescents moving into the formal operational stage are able to deal with abstractions, form hypotheses, engage in mental manipulation, and predict consequences. As formal operational skills develop, adolescents become capable of reflective abstraction, which refers to the ability to reflect on knowledge, rearrange thoughts, and discover alternative routes to solving problems. Consequently, counseling approaches that provide opportunities to generate alternative solutions are more likely to be effective with adolescents than with younger children.

A new form of egocentrism often emerges during adolescence, characterized by a belief in one's uniqueness and invulnerability. Egocentrism may be reflected in reckless behavior and grandiose ideas. Related to this heightened sense of uniqueness is the adolescent phenomenon of feeling constantly "on stage." It is not uncommon for adolescents to feel that everyone is looking at them, leading to increased anxiety and self-consciousness. These feelings tend to peak in early adolescence and then decline as formal operational skills improve.

The onset of puberty often triggers the psychosocial crisis Erikson (1968) called *identity versus role confusion*. A key challenge during adolescence is the formation of an identity, including self-definition and a commitment to goals, values, beliefs, and life purpose. To master this challenge, adolescents need opportunities to explore options, try on various roles and responsibilities, and speculate about possibilities. Sometimes adolescents enter a period of role confusion, characterized in part by overidentification with heroes or cliques, before they develop a true sense of individuality and recognize that they are acceptable human beings (Thomas, 2005).

Spending time with peers continues to be important throughout adolescence. As adolescents develop self-confidence and sensitivity, they base their friendships on compatibility and shared experiences. Intimate friendships increase, as do dating and sexual experimentation. Counseling may involve helping these young people deal with issues of complex relationships and decision making about the future.

It is important to keep in mind that developmental generalizations may not be applicable to all ethnic or cultural groups. For example, the search for self-identity may be delayed, compounded by a search for ethnic identity, or even nonexistent among certain groups of adolescents (Erford, 2015). Also, research on Piagetian tasks suggests that some forms of logic do not emerge spontaneously according to stages, but are socially generated, based on cultural experiences. Developmental theories provide useful guides for understanding children and adolescents; however, no theory provides a complete explanation of development, nor does any theory take into account all cultural perspectives.

Developmental knowledge helps professional school counselors build relationships, assess concerns, and design effective interventions for students at all grade levels. By understanding developmental levels and their implications, professional school counselors are better prepared to meet the needs of the children and adolescents whom they counsel and the parents and teachers with whom they consult.

A COUNSELING MODEL FOR CHILDREN AND ADOLESCENTS

Models of individual counseling can range anywhere from three to a multitude of stages. The model presented in this section is adapted from Orton (1997) and consists of the following phases: *building a counseling relationship*,

assessing specific counseling needs, *designing and implementing interventions*, and *conducting evaluation and closure*. Generic and nonlinear in nature, the model can be applied to different theoretical orientations and situations, and certain phases can occur throughout the counseling process.

Building a Counseling Relationship

Key to any successful counseling experience is the development of an effective working relationship built on mutual trust and acceptance. Developing a counseling relationship sometimes takes longer with children than with adults because children may need more time to believe that an adult can help them. Essential factors involved in building a counseling relationship include establishing rapport, clarifying the counseling role, and explaining confidentiality.

ESTABLISHING RAPPORT To build relationships successfully, professional school counselors need to tailor their responses and interactions to fit the specific needs of each student, taking into account developmental experiences, sociocultural background, and reasons for referral. Perhaps the most important first step is being willing to enter completely into that student's world, with no preconceptions, expectations, or agenda. It is important to be fully "with" student clients, accepting them for who they are at that moment. All judgment needs to be suspended so that the counselor can remain open to what the student is sharing, either verbally or nonverbally. As the relationship is being established, listening skills are just as important as questioning skills. Professional school counselors can create bridges of trust and understanding by listening carefully to what young people have to say; giving them undivided attention; and responding sensitively to feelings, reactions, and cultural cues.

It helps to be knowledgeable about a variety of rapport-building approaches. For example, play and art media can help professional school counselors establish relationships with young children who have difficulty verbalizing. With older children, games like Jenga and "in-house" basketball can provide a nonthreatening introduction to the counseling process. Use a dry-erase whiteboard and markers with children, inviting them to draw pictures or symbols that illustrate things they would like you to know about them. As a variation, ask students to create an *About Me* collage by decoratively writing their names in the center of a piece of art paper. Then ask students to select magazine pictures that illustrate things about them, including strengths, interests, relationships, or other characteristics they want to reveal at that point, and paste them on the

REFLECTIONS OF A FIRST-YEAR MASTER'S STUDENT ON CONDUCTING INDIVIDUAL COUNSELING AT AN ALTERNATIVE SCHOOL DURING PRACTICUM

I completed my practicum experience at the New School, which hosts students who have been referred from their home schools because of behavior problems. Problematic behaviors range from minor classroom disruptions and peer conflicts to aggressive and sometimes violent displays of anger. During the first 3 weeks of my practicum, I was regularly questioned by the school's administrators, teachers, and staff: "Do you know what you're getting yourself into with *these* students?" I spent the first month at the site building relationships with administrators, teachers, and staff—and, most important, with the students.

I found it surprisingly easy to build rapport and empathize with the students. I expected to have to work extremely hard to tear down barriers to trust and communication to establish a counseling relationship. Interestingly enough, a smiling face and an attentive ear were more than enough to gain the students' respect. Many of the students with whom I worked had rarely had an adult willing to spend time with them and listen to their opinions, fears, anger, and experiences. Teachers and administrators were shocked when students returned to classrooms or the office talking with me calmly after walking out of a classroom, yelling profanities at the teacher, and banging lockers. This was the turning point: I'd won the teachers over.

One of the factors that makes building a relationship with children different from building a relationship with adults is that children may have no idea what counseling is all about. They may be confused about the counseling process

or reluctant to participate. In schools, students frequently are referred by teachers or parents, and it is these adults, not the students, who want change to occur. Consequently, the students may not be motivated to make changes.

When children are "sent" to counseling, rather than self-referred, they may be resistant to the counseling process. One professional middle school counselor in a local public school shared her strategy for working with students who have been referred by parents or teachers:

> If a child is ready to talk, I sit back, relax, and hear her story. If she is not, I'll generally do something temporarily diverting, such as say, "You know, I realize we're supposed to talk about whatever it is you've been sent here for, but do you mind if we do something else for a while? Do you see anything here that you'd like to do?" I keep lots of games and toys, art supplies, clay, etc. out and about, and almost always something will catch a child's interest. (Niedringhaus, 2000, p. 1)

When students are self-referred, resistance may not be an issue. However, in such situations the need to obtain parental consent for counseling services can become a concern. Some counselors will not counsel students without parental consent. Professional school counselors need to be aware of state regulations, school policies, professional ethical codes, and limits of confidentiality as they make decisions about counseling individual students.

---

paper. Their choices serve as a springboard for further discussion and provide a lens for glimpsing their subjective worlds. Other children may be eager to talk, and the professional school counselor can respond accordingly by listening reflectively, summarizing, probing, and clarifying.

CLARIFYING THE COUNSELING ROLE Professional school counselors are responsible for explaining to students the purpose and nature of the counseling relationship (ASCA, 2010). Providing an age-appropriate explanation of the counseling role can help establish structure and initiate the development of a collaborative relationship. With younger students, the professional school counselor might say something like "My job is to help children with lots of different things. Sometimes people have unpleasant feelings they want to talk about. Other people might want help figuring out a problem. I wonder what I might be able to help you with?" With older students, it might be helpful to

ask students to describe what they think individual counseling entails, after which the professional school counselor can provide clarification as needed.

EXPLAINING CONFIDENTIALITY During the initial phase of counseling, it is necessary to clarify confidentiality and its limits. The ASCA's (2010) ethical standards state that professional school counselors have a responsibility to protect information received through confidential counseling relationships with students. Confidentiality should not be abridged unless there is a clear and present danger to the student, other individuals, or both. Also, professional school counselors have the responsibility of explaining the limits of confidentiality to their students and of notifying students regarding the possible necessity of consulting with others. Moreover, professional school counselors recognize that, although their primary obligation for confidentiality is to the student, that obligation must be balanced with an understanding of parent/guardian "legal and inherent rights to be the guiding voice in their children's lives, especially in value-laden issues" (ASCA, 2010, p. 2).

The way a professional school counselor approaches the issue of confidentiality with students depends on the students' age. With young children, the counselor will want to use words that they can understand. As noted earlier, in some cases professional school counselors will not counsel with students, especially young children, before obtaining parental permission. Also, it often is in the child's best interest to consult with parents or teachers during the process. Therefore, the counselor might say to the student, "Most of the things you and I talk about in here are between you and me, unless you tell me that you are planning to hurt yourself or someone else. If you tell me something that I think your mother (father, guardian, other caregiver, teacher) needs to know, you and I will talk about it before I tell anything."

Adolescents often have a heightened concern about privacy and confidentiality in the counseling relationship (Remley & Herlihy, 2010). Professional school counselors who work with adolescents can help students understand confidentiality and its limits from the outset. Keeping this in mind, it is important for adolescents to feel free to disclose their concerns in an atmosphere of trust. Balancing issues related to trust and minor consent laws can often be challenging.

In addition to the ethical issue of confidentiality, a number of state and federal statutes affect the counselor–client relationship in school settings. Each state has its own laws that directly influence the practice of counseling in schools. For example, many states mandate privileged communication, which is a client's right to have prior confidences maintained during legal proceedings. If clients are under the age of 18 years, their parents maintain the right to privileged communication. Privilege is not absolute, and several exceptions to privilege exist, including child abuse, with those exceptions varying from state to state (see Chapter 7). It is the professional school counselor's responsibility to stay abreast of state statutes and exceptions to privilege.

Professional school counselors also need to be aware of federal statutes that affect their work with students and limits to confidentiality. In particular, the Family Educational Rights and Privacy Act (FERPA), enacted in 1974, ensures that parents' rights to information about their children's education are honored. Part I of FERPA specifies that parents have the right to access school records about their children. Because this stipulation refers to the school's educational records, professional school counselors are advised to keep their counseling records separate from the official educational records (Wheeler & Bertram, 2012).

As noted by Linde in Chapter 7, counseling notes are confidential, and the professional school counselor needs to ensure their security.

Part II of FERPA requires parental consent for medical, psychiatric, or psychological evaluations of children under 18 years, as well as for participation in school programs designed to affect a student's personal behavior or values. Thus, parental or legal guardian consent is needed when administering formal assessment instruments to students that are not administered to all students as an aspect of the school's regular curriculum. Ordinarily, this includes individualized psychological or educational testing (e.g., to determine special education or Section 504 eligibility) and specialized individual screening processes (e.g., testing for the gifted program).

It is not unusual for professional school counselors to face dilemmas regarding the requirements of confidentiality; minor students' requests for information; and counselor responsibilities to parents, teachers, and colleagues. By keeping the lines of communication open and taking responsibility for knowing state and federal law, it may be possible to prevent potential problems from arising.

Assessing Specific Counseling Needs

Assessment is an integral part of the counseling process that can, in and of itself, be therapeutic. The purposes of assessment are to gain a better understanding of the child's needs and to establish goals for meeting those needs. Assessment methods, which can be informal or formal, help the professional school counselor understand the student's current problems within the context of his or her unique developmental and contextual history. Consider the case of Gabriella (13.2).

EXPLORING STUDENT CONCERNS Whereas counselors in mental health settings conduct intake interviews to collect information about client concerns, counselors in school settings typically do not conduct formal intake interviews. Nonetheless, some form of early and ongoing assessment is warranted for accurate case conceptualization and effective intervention planning. Often, professional school counselors begin this process with an informal interview through which students' concerns are explored. It is important for professional school counselors to effectively collect information without turning the session into a fact-finding question-and-answer period. When exploring students' concerns, it is important to use active listening skills, be sensitive to nonverbal expressions, and probe gently and sensitively.

The type of information collected during early stages of assessment varies according to developmental levels and

CASE STUDY 13.2

The Case of Gabriella

Gabriella, a second-generation Latina student in the ninth grade, has been referred to you, the professional school counselor, because she has been falling asleep in class for the past 2 weeks. You know Gabriella, but have not conducted individual counseling with her until now. During your initial meeting with Gabriella, she tells you that she is just tired because she has to stay up late to take care of her younger brother while her mother and stepfather are working. In a subsequent session, Gabriella reveals that the real reason she is so tired is because she is afraid to go to sleep at night. On further questioning, she reveals that her stepfather has been touching her in ways that make her uncomfortable and that during the past month he has been coming into her room at night. She insists that he has not done anything except touch her in "an embarrassing way." She now keeps her door locked at night and stays awake as long as she can, until she is sure that her stepfather has gone to bed.

- What are your responsibilities to Gabriella?
- What are your legal and ethical responsibilities in this situation?
- What would you do in this situation? What considerations should you keep in mind?
- What factors make this situation challenging?

student concerns. If professional school counselors will be working with the student for more than just a few sessions, Orton (1997) suggested that information be gathered in the following areas:

- *The student's specific concerns.* The manifestation, intensity, frequency, and duration of concerns should be explored. In what settings and around what individuals are the concerns evidenced? To what extent are the concerns developmentally appropriate?

- *The student's physical, cognitive, emotional, and social development.* Depending on the situation, it may be beneficial to consult with parents and teachers to get more information about the student's medical history, cognitive functioning, and ability to express and regulate emotions. It also is helpful to gather information about socioeconomic and sociocultural factors that have influenced the student's development.

- *Relationships between the student and his or her parents, siblings, classmates, and teachers.* Understanding the nature and quality of relationships the student has with family members and peers is a key component of assessment. The degree to which these areas are explored depends on the nature of the problem. For example, if a student is not turning in homework, the professional school counselor will want to gather information about what is going on at home and in the school that may be contributing to the problem.

- *The student's school experiences, including academics, attendance, and attitude.* Academic and social

successes or failures play important roles in a student's overall development. Students who experience repeated failures often have poor self-esteem and may engage in disruptive behaviors to compensate. Also, school failure may signify a learning disorder that typically requires formal testing for diagnosis.

- *The student's strengths, talents, and support system.* Implementing a strengths-based approach to assessment can help take the focus off the problem so that it is possible to begin moving more toward solutions. Solution-focused brief counseling (SFBC), which is addressed later in the chapter, places particular emphasis on assessing students' strengths. Creative activities, checklists, and various qualitative assessment methods are useful tools for evaluating strengths and supports.

INFORMAL AND FORMAL ASSESSMENT Informal assessment includes observation and qualitative assessment activities. Observation can occur in counseling sessions or in the classroom. Qualitative assessment emphasizes a holistic study of students using methods that typically are not standardized and do not produce quantitative raw scores (Erford, 2014). A variety of qualitative assessment methods can be used with children and adolescents, including informal checklists, sentence completion activities, writing activities, decision-making dilemmas, games, art activities, storytelling, self-monitoring techniques, role-play activities, and play therapy strategies (e.g., Erford, 2014; Vernon & Erford, 2014). Informal assessment procedures of this nature can reveal patterns of thoughts and behaviors relevant to concerns and issues. They can be especially helpful with young children, who may not know exactly what is bothering them or who lack the words to express their concerns verbally.

In some situations, professional school counselors may wish to obtain information through the use of formal assessment instruments, which require students to respond to standardized measurements. Formal instruments that have sound psychometric properties provide a way for professional school counselors to gain a somewhat more objective view of children's behaviors and attributes than do informal methods of assessment. Examples of formal assessment include standardized behavioral checklists, values scales, interest and skill inventories, self-concept measures, and personality inventories. Professional school counselors have been trained in appraisal procedures and have the ability to use these instruments effectively with students.

By evaluating counseling needs though interviews, informal assessment, and formal assessment, the professional school counselor can gain a better understanding of the student's concerns within his or her developmental and environmental context. This understanding can then be used to set goals, design and implement interventions, and conduct evaluation and closure of the counseling process.

Designing and Implementing Interventions

After a relationship has been established and initial assessment conducted with a child, what is the next step? Interventions should be developed and selected after carefully considering the student's developmental level, cultural background, personality characteristics, and particular circumstances. Other considerations that need to be taken into account are time constraints, teacher and parental support, and the counselor's level of expertise. In addition, it is important to select interventions that are evidence informed and evidence based (Galassi, Griffin, & Akos, 2008). If, during the course of counseling, it becomes apparent that the student's problems are more serious and chronic, requiring long-term psychotherapy, then the professional school counselor will want to refer him or her to mental health counselors or other helping professionals within the school or community (ASCA, 2012). When it is necessary to refer, the professional school counselor can continue to play a significant role by working collaboratively with clinical mental health counselors and other referral sources.

INTENTIONALITY AND FLEXIBILITY Being intentional implies taking steps to set goals for counseling with the student. Being flexible refers to recognizing that no single counseling approach is best for all students or all problems.

By designing interventions in ways that are both intentional and flexible, professional school counselors can personalize the intervention for the student within the context of a collaborative relationship.

One way professional school counselors can intentionally plan interventions is by asking specific questions related to the following areas (Vernon, 2004):

1. *Vision.* What could be different? How could things be better? What would be ideal?
2. *Goal setting.* What is going well? What needs to be worked on?
3. *Analysis.* What is enabling or interfering with achieving these goals? What is getting in the way of resolving the problem?
4. *Objective.* What specifically does the student want to change?
5. *Exploration of interventions.* What has already been tried and how did it work? How does the student learn best? Who will be involved in the helping process? What has research shown to be the most effective intervention for this type of concern?

In many ways, these guiding questions are similar to those that guide SFBC, an approach that we describe in further detail later in the chapter.

SELECTING INTERVENTIONS In making decisions about which interventions to use, professional school counselors can select from a wide range of theoretical approaches. Although no single theoretical approach to counseling children and adolescents has been found to be more effective than another (e.g., see Chapter 5; Carmichael & Erford, 2014; Erford, 2014), some approaches are more suited to school settings than others. Brown and Trusty (2005b) outlined six aspects of counseling theory for professional school counselors to consider as they make decisions about interventions:

1. The degree to which the theory (or model) focuses on the *counseling relationship*, including the relationship between the counselor and students as a whole.
2. The degree to which the theory enhances *student empowerment*.
3. The amount of attention devoted to students' *overt behavior*.
4. The usefulness of the theory at students' various levels of *development*.
5. The *flexibility* of the theory to fit various student characteristics, student problems, and school counseling delivery formats.
6. The *time span* of counseling associated with the theory. (p. 292)

An additional consideration is the degree to which the theory or model takes into account issues related to diversity and cultural strengths.

Theoretical approaches that seem to be particularly effective in school settings include Adlerian counseling, reality therapy/choice theory, cognitive-behavioral counseling, and SFBC (Brown & Trusty, 2005b; Schmidt, 2008). Other models and structures that are effective with school-aged children include multimodal counseling, Gestalt techniques, and family counseling approaches (Brown & Trusty, 2005b). A variety of expressive arts techniques—including art, music, clay, puppetry, storytelling, drama, bibliotherapy, sand play, and other forms of directive and nondirective play therapy—can guide the counseling process and promote healing and growth (e.g., Gladding, 2011; Newsome & Gladding, 2014). Sklare (2005) and Galassi and Akos (2007) emphasized the use of strengths-based school counseling (SBSC) approaches with students, which build on students' strengths and assets. "In SBSC, the focus is on strengths promotion rather than problem reduction, although the two latter functions do remain important in the school counselor's role. Strengths promotion often simultaneously accomplishes the twin goals of problem prevention and problem reduction" (Galassi et al., 2008, p. 177).

Professional school counselors need to select counseling approaches systematically (Schmidt, 2008), matching the approach and intervention with the presenting issue and taking developmental, cultural, and other contextual factors into account. For example, a professional school counselor working with a student with attention-deficit/hyperactivity disorder may find cognitive-behavioral approaches useful, with an emphasis on specific tasks related to organization, self-monitoring, and impulse control. For students who have difficulty completing assignments, reality therapy (Glasser, 2000), which focuses on the present and future rather than the past, may be the treatment of choice. Professional school counselors using this approach ask students to evaluate their actions and determine whether they want to change. Together, the student and the counselor design a plan for change that emphasizes personal control. For adolescents struggling with depression, cognitive theory, which focuses on recognizing automatic thoughts and their effects on emotions, may be the preferred approach.

IMPLEMENTING INTERVENTIONS After the professional school counselor and the student have collaboratively selected interventions, it is time to implement the plan. Professional school counselors can empower students by affirming their resilience, offering affirmation and encouragement, and providing acceptance and stability (Peterson, 2004). Depending on the situation, counselors should consult with other people in the school or family invested in the success of the intervention. It may be important to inform teachers and parents that the situation may get worse before it gets better. In some cases, it may be helpful to work with teachers on designing a behavior contract, recognizing that teachers are more likely to implement a plan they have collaborated on to create.

Conducting Evaluation and Closure

Implementation of interventions also includes working with the student to evaluate progress. Evaluation of the counseling relationship, interventions, and outcomes is an ongoing process. As with assessment, evaluation methods can be informal or formal. Informal evaluation involves observing changes in the student's thoughts, feelings, and behaviors. It also includes monitoring interactions during counseling sessions and being aware of personal responses to the child. Formal evaluation of counseling outcomes may include checklists completed by teachers and parents, grades in academic areas and in conduct, and self-reports completed by students.

Measuring progress in counseling can be challenging because evaluation tends to be subjective, and not all counseling goals are stated in measurable terms. Finding ways to demonstrate the effectiveness of counseling is important, however, and professional school counselors are encouraged to incorporate formal and informal methods of outcome evaluation into their work with students, teachers, and parents. Single-case study experimental designs (single subject research designs) provide one effective way to conduct outcomes research evaluating the effectiveness of professional school counselors' interventions (Eschenauer & Chen-Hayes, 2005; Erford, 2014).

Closure, sometimes called termination, refers to the ending of the counseling relationship, either naturally or circumstantially (Schmidt, 2008). Newsome and Gladding (2014) indicated that it is the least researched and most neglected aspect of counseling. In school counseling, the process of ending the helping relationship deserves particular attention. Closure is facilitated when professional school counselors reinforce the progress students have made, encourage them to express their feelings about ending the helping relationship, and determine resources for continued support.

Solution-Focused Brief Counseling

Brief counseling approaches, including solution-focused brief counseling (SFBC; e.g., Metcalf, 2008; Murphy, 2008; Sklare, 2005), are advocated in the school counseling literature and are particularly valuable in schools where time constraints are crucial. Brief counseling models parallel the generic model for individual counseling presented in this chapter by encouraging students to (a) assess the problem in concrete terms; (b) examine previously attempted solutions; (c) establish a specific, short-term goal; and (d) implement the intervention. Because of its utility in school settings, a particular form of brief counseling, SFBC (Sklare, 2005), is discussed next.

OVERVIEW OF SFBC   SFBC is an approach that "has shown great promise and that allows counselors to provide effective counseling to students in less time" (Charlesworth & Jackson, 2010, p. 139). It emphasizes strengths, resources, successes, and hope and is a model that can be used with students from diverse backgrounds. Sklare (2005) attributed the SFBC model primarily to de Shazer (1985), though many other innovative practitioners have contributed to its evolution (e.g., Berg & Miller, 1992; Berg & Steiner, 2003; O'Hanlon & Weiner-Davis, 1989; Selekman, 1997; Walter & Peller, 1992). Charlesworth and Jackson (2010) cited numerous studies supporting the efficacy of SFBC in school settings. Sklare (2005) referred to research providing support for the use of SFBC with students from culturally diverse backgrounds.

CORE BELIEFS, ASSUMPTIONS, AND CONCEPTS   The core beliefs on which SFBC is based were originally proposed by de Shazer (1985) and Berg and Miller (1992) and are summarized by Sklare (2005) as follows:

- "If it ain't broke, don't fix it." Do not make an issue out of something that is not an issue for the student.
- "Once you know what works, do more of it." Once successes are identified, professional school counselors have students replicate them.
- "If it doesn't work, don't do it again." Repeating ineffective strategies does not make sense; it is more productive to try out new strategies. (pp. 9–10)

In addition to these core beliefs, Sklare (2005) presented five assumptions and four concepts that guide the SFBC model:

- *Assumption 1.*   Counselors should focus on solutions, rather than problems, for change to occur.
- *Assumption 2.*   Every problem has identifiable exceptions that can be discovered and transformed into solutions.
- *Assumption 3.*   Small changes have a ripple effect that leads to bigger changes.
- *Assumption 4.*   Student clients have the necessary resources to solve their problems.
- *Assumption 5.*   Constructing goals in positive terms (what clients want to happen) is more effective than stating them in negative terms (an absence of something). For example, "I want to get to class on time"

represents a positive goal; "I don't want to get in trouble" represents a negative goal.

- *Concept 1.*   Avoid problem analysis. SFBC addresses what is working for students, rather than exploring the etiology of their problems.
- *Concept 2.*   Be efficient with interventions. Because counseling in schools is time limited, professional school counselors want to get the most accomplished in the minimum amount of time.
- *Concept 3.*   Focus on the present and the future, not the past. Past events are only highlighted in the process of finding exceptions to problems.
- *Concept 4.*   Focus on actions, rather than insights. Insight requires a level of cognitive development that young students may not have. Also, insight is not necessary for change to occur.

IMPLEMENTING THE SFBC MODEL   Sklare (2005) suggested that professional school counselors begin the first session with students by explaining the SFBC approach. He provides the following as an example of what professional school counselors might say to students:

> I want to let you know how this is going to work. I am going to ask you a lot of questions, and some of them are going to sound kind of crazy and will be tough to answer [for some students, informing them that the questions will be hard to answer is intriguing and challenging]. Some of the answers you give I'm going to write down on my notepad, and I'm going to use these notes to write you a message. When I finish, I will tell you what I was thinking about and read the message to you. I will make a copy of the message so you can take one with you and I can keep one. What do you think about this? (p. 20)

After the process has been explained, the next step is to help the student formulate clear goals. As assumption 5 indicates, goals need to be stated in positive rather than negative terms. Sklare (2005) classified goals as (a) positive, (b) negative, (c) harmful, and (d) "I don't know" goals. Skillful questioning on the part of the professional school counselor can help the student state positive goals that are observable, behaviorally specific, measurable, and attainable.

Professional school counselors can use a wide range of techniques to help students develop positive goals and envision solutions. Following are examples of those techniques:

- *The miracle question.*   With young children, the professional school counselor might ask, "Suppose I had a magic wand and waved it over your head and the problem was solved, what would be different? What would you see yourself doing differently?" (Sklare, 2005, p. 31). If students state wishes that are impossible (e.g., "I would not live here anymore"), the professional school counselor can ask questions like "How would things be different for you if your miracle happened?" and "What would other people notice?"

- *Identifying instances and exceptions.* Following assumption 2, professional school counselors can ask students to think of a time when the miracle has already happened to some extent. For example, the professional school counselor might say, "Tell me about a time when you were getting along with your teacher. What was going on then?"
- *Mindmapping.* Mindmapping refers to identifying specific behaviors that led to success in the past. Identifying concrete steps that were beneficial in the past can help students create a mental road map to guide them in the future.
- *Cheerleading.* Supporting and encouraging students, acknowledging their accomplishments, and expressing excitement when a new behavior is successfully implemented is called cheerleading. Sklare (2005) pointed out that it is important to be genuine in cheerleading and to avoid patronizing.
- *Scaling.* Scaling can be used to establish baselines, set goals, and measure progress. For example, the

professional school counselor might ask the student, "On a scale of 0 to 10, with 10 being the day after the miracle has happened and the problem is solved, where are you right now?" Subsequent questions might be "What would it take for you to move to a _____ on the scale?" and "How would you know when you were at a _____? What would be happening?"

- *Flagging the minefield.* Helping students anticipate obstacles that might impede their progress gives them an opportunity to consider ways to overcome those obstacles before they are encountered. Reviewing strategies in advance can help keep students from being caught off guard and can empower them to make positive choices.

SFBC is an example of one of several forms of brief counseling. Although this and other brief approaches may not be appropriate for every student in every situation, professional school counselors can incorporate models like SFBC as one way to effectively deliver individual counseling services. For a more in-depth description of the model, readers are encouraged to refer to Sklare's (2005) text, *Brief Counseling That Works: A Solution-Focused Approach for School Counselors and Administrators.* The case in Theory into Practice 13.1 illustrates ways an elementary school counselor uses SFBC in her work with students.

THEORY INTO PRACTICE 13.1

USING SOLUTION-FOCUSED BRIEF COUNSELING IN THE SCHOOLS

I find solution-focused brief counseling to be extremely helpful and effective in individual counseling sessions. I begin each meeting by asking the student to describe his or her feelings using a number. I have a poster hanging in my office that displays a number line and appropriate feelings for each number. For example, a "one" means extremely sad, depressed, or angry and a "ten" means that everything feels perfect! When the student pinpoints his or her feelings, I have a starting point for my session. Whether the issue is grief and loss, divorce, anxiety, self-esteem, or friendships, by using this measure, I am able to determine how they are feeling at the moment. From that point, we can work to improve this number during the session and then set goals for the week ahead.

Recently, I've been working individually with a 9-year-old female with severe anxiety. Prior to tests, she finds herself shaking and nauseous. She also experiences headaches and will often break into hives following the stressful event. At our first meeting, I asked her to point to how she was feeling on my number line. She directed me to the 2–3 range and

claimed that she has difficulty controlling herself when there is an upcoming test. Together, in our first session, we compared worries and anxiety to planting seeds. I explained to her that, when we focus on our worries and pay special attention to them, they grow—just like a seed that is given water and sunlight. Following our discussion, we talked about ways that we could spend less time focusing on anxious thoughts and more time on ways to enjoy being at school. When asked to point to the number line at the end of the session, she had improved to a 5! She was still preoccupied with her anxiety, but began to see that focusing on it was not the answer.

In subsequent sessions with the same child, I began to focus on relaxation techniques. Together, we came up with a set of four techniques that work for her. We continue to meet and work on her ability to relax. She rates herself prior to every session and following every session, allowing both of us to evaluate the effectiveness of each activity and conversation.

Source: Melissa Snapp, Elementary School Counselor at Lewisville Elementary School, Winston-Salem/Forsyth County Schools

Reality Therapy/Choice Theory

Reality therapy, like SFBC, was designed to be brief and has been shown to be particularly effective in school settings (Brown & Trusty, 2005b; Henderson & Thompson, 2011). William Glasser, founder of reality therapy (2000), began working with school systems in the 1960s to apply reality therapy to education. Over the course of his career, Glasser wrote several books on the topic, including *Schools Without Failure*, *The Quality School: Managing Students Without Coercion*, *The Quality School Teacher*, and *Every Student Can Succeed*. Reality therapy provides school counselors with a systematic way to address students' needs and wants, in both their personal and their educational lives. It works well in individual and small-group counseling, as well as in guidance (Brown & Trusty, 2005b). RT fits well with the *ASCA National Model*'s (2012) goal of reaching as many students as possible because it provides a brief framework to accomplish concrete improvements in areas self-identified by students and empowers them to take responsibility for their behaviors.

CORE BELIEFS, ASSUMPTIONS, AND CONCEPTS Choice theory, also created by Glasser (1998), serves as a theoretical basis for reality therapy. Henderson and Thompson (2011, p. 115) summarized choice theory with the following statements:

- "The only person whose behavior we can control is our own." People are responsible for themselves and their actions.
- "All long-lasting psychological problems are relationship problems that result from attempts of people to control other people." We get into trouble when we try to control others.
- "Past events have everything to do with what we are today, but we can satisfy our basic needs only in the present and make plans for the future." Reality therapy focuses on the present and future, rather than on the past.
- "Satisfying the needs represented by the pictures in our quality world is the way we meet our needs for survival, freedom, power, fun, and love and belonging." If we can identify and attain our quality worlds—what we want our lives to be like—we will accomplish the five basic needs common to all people.
- "Total behavior is all that we do, including acting, thinking, feeling, and physiology." Regarding total behavior, we have the most control over our actions and thoughts.

QUALITY WORLD Glasser believed that everyone has a quality world that includes images that make up the life we'd like to have, including people, things, experiences, and values (Seligman & Reichenberg, 2011). People are motivated by what is in their quality worlds, so they are more likely to find satisfaction in life if they are aware of what is in their quality worlds and if those things are attainable and meet their basic needs.

FIVE BASIC NEEDS According to Glasser (1998), people have five basic needs:

- *Belonging*—the need to give and receive love;
- *Power*—the need to feel in control of one's self, to feel competent;
- *Fun*—the need to experience pleasure and enjoy life;
- *Freedom*—the need to be without limitations, to make one's own choices; and
- *Survival*—the need to eat, breathe, and have shelter, safety, and physical comfort.

Glasser believed that by intentionally including each of these needs in their quality worlds, people are more likely to get their basic needs met.

TOTAL BEHAVIOR According to Glasser (1998), all our behaviors are directed at satisfying our needs. He defined *total behavior* as the four parts of our overall functioning: action, thinking, feeling, and physiology. We have the most control over our actions and thoughts, which means that they are easiest to change. Therefore, to better satisfy our needs, we can *choose* to change our actions and thoughts. By making better choices, we end up having more control over attaining our quality worlds and meeting our five basic needs.

IMPLEMENTING THE RT MODEL Essentially, treatment in reality therapy involves helping students make better choices to meet their needs. Henderson and Thompson (2011, pp. 117–118) described eight steps for practicing RT with students:

Step 1. Build the relationship. Because reality therapy often involves some confrontation, it is important to build trust between counselor and student first.

Step 2. The student identifies and describes the present behavior.

Step 3. The student evaluates the present behavior and is likely to change this behavior only if the student believes that it is not working. To help the student, the counselor can ask questions such as these: "How does this behavior help you?" "How does it hurt you?" "Does it help you get along with your teacher?"

Step 4. The student is encouraged to identify alternative behaviors he or she could try to better meet personal needs. The counselor can assist if the student is stuck, but ultimately the student is responsible for coming up with ways to replace the problem behavior with a healthier behavior.

Step 5. The student chooses one new behavior and commits to trying it.

Step 6. In a second session, the counselor and the student review the outcome of the student's attempt at a new behavior. If the student reports being unsuccessful, the counselor does not concentrate on why or allow the student to give excuses.

Step 7. The student is allowed to face logical consequences, such as a lower grade on an assignment turned in late. The student is not punished.

Step 8. Don't give up on students who have a hard time changing their behaviors. Give these students extra sessions, working with them longer than they expect you to.

Because treatment can often involve adjusting what a student includes in the quality world, it is helpful for the counselor and the student to first identify what the student's quality world includes. Questions to help understand a student's quality world include these:

- Who are the most important people in your life?
- If you become the person you want to be, what will you be like (ask for specific traits and characteristics)?
- What is something you've done that you are really proud of?
- What does it mean to be a friend?
- What are your most deeply held values?

Once these things have been identified, the school counselor can help the student evaluate whether these things are realistic and responsible—in essence, do these images match the student's five basic needs? One way professional school counselors can use RT effectively with students is by asking five questions (Henderson & Thompson, 2011):

1. What have you tried so far to help your problem?
2. How has that been working? (Are you getting what you want?)
3. What else could you try?
4. Which of these are you ready to commit to trying?
5. When can we meet again to see if your idea has helped?

Henderson and Thompson (2011) summarized reality therapy this way: "Counselors are in the business of teaching people better ways to meet their needs. From the reality therapy point of view, counseling is a matter of learning how to solve problems, teaching people, in effect,

to become their own counselors" (p. 116). Although reality therapy may not be appropriate for all individuals, it can be effectively used to help many students with issues ranging from minor concerns to more serious problems (Glasser, 2000b).

Individual counseling represents an essential responsive service in comprehensive, developmental school counseling programs. Another powerful and effective means of helping students with situational and developmental concerns is group counseling. In school settings, group work, including group counseling, is often viewed as the intervention of choice.

CULTURAL REFLECTION 13.1

How might professional school counselors-in-training from diverse cultural backgrounds view the importance of working with students one-on-one? How might students, parents, and educators from diverse cultural backgrounds view the role of the professional school counselor providing individualized responsive services?

GROUP COUNSELING IN SCHOOLS

Group counseling, in addition to individual counseling, represents a mode of delivering direct services to students and is an integral part of a comprehensive, developmental school counseling program (ASCA, 2012). From a developmental and a pedagogical perspective, students often learn best from each other (Goodnough & Lee, 2010); therefore, group settings are ideal places to conduct both preventive psychoeducational work and remedial counseling. Groups provide a social environment in which members can learn and practice new behaviors, exchange feedback, and experience support. They allow students to develop insights into themselves and others and provide an effective, efficient way of helping students deal with developmental and situational issues.

Group work is one of the professional school counselor's most specialized skills (Goodnough & Lee, 2010). It represents a central means of delivering services in a comprehensive, developmental school counseling program. In this section, ways to set up and conduct group work in school settings are described. Before examining those activities, however, the types of groups that are most prevalent in school settings are discussed.

Types of Groups

Group work in schools can be classified in several different ways (e.g., Cobia & Henderson, 2007; Goodnough & Lee, 2010). The Association for Specialists in Group Work

(ASGW, 2000) defined four types of group work: task group facilitation, group psychoeducation, group counseling, and group psychotherapy. Task groups, also called work groups, are made up of members working together on a particular assignment or task. Examples in a school setting include student assistance teams, crisis response planning groups, and peer-helper orientation groups (Jacobs & Schimmel, 2005). Group psychotherapy, which is used with people who may be experiencing severe maladjustment, chronic maladjustment, or both, is usually conducted in community mental health settings, not schools.

Our focus in this section is on the two types of groups involving students led most frequently by professional school counselors: *psychoeducational groups* and *counseling groups*. In educational settings, psychoeducational groups include guidance groups, which typically are conducted in classrooms and are described in Chapter 10, and smaller (usually fewer than 10 members), growth-oriented groups that help students learn new skills and develop an awareness of their values, priorities, and communities. Counseling groups, although also growth oriented, are designed to help individuals who are experiencing some form of stress in their lives, such as loss of a family member, family changes, or issues related to sexual identity.

Although psychoeducational and counseling groups are conceptualized here and elsewhere as two distinct entities, it is more accurate to consider them along a continuum, with psychoeducational groups tending to be more structured and content oriented and counseling groups tending to be less structured and more process oriented. In reality, any number of topics (e.g., grief and loss, stress management, school success) can be the focus of either a psychoeducational group or a counseling group. Goodnough and Lee (2010), who classify groups in schools as *developmental, remedial,* and *school climate* groups, point out that psychoeducation has a place in all types of group work, as does group processing, which refers to interpersonal interactions among members within the group (Gladding, 2012). The professional school counselor's role is to design groups intentionally and balance content and process appropriately.

PSYCHOEDUCATIONAL GROUPS Psychoeducational groups use educational methods to help students gain knowledge and skills in several domains, such as personal identity, interpersonal interaction, developmental transitions, social maturity, academic achievement, and career planning (Bergin, 2004). When young people in psychoeducational groups face natural age and stage developmental tasks together, they frequently master more than the specifically targeted skills. Interaction within the group can promote an improved sense of well-being, leading to the prevention of future problems as group members develop new resources and coping skills.

Psychoeducational groups tend to focus on central themes that correspond with students' developmental levels. For example, young children may benefit from friendship groups or problem-solving groups. Older children and adolescents may respond well to groups that focus on stress management, assertiveness training, or boy–girl relationships. Topics for psychoeducational groups come from several sources. In part, professional school counselors select topics based on the academic, career, and personal/social domains outlined in the planned scope and sequence of a comprehensive, developmental school counseling program. In addition, professional school counselors can select topics based on the results of needs assessment surveys distributed to students, parents, teachers, and related school personnel. Furthermore, professional school counselors can use student outcome data to make decisions about specific psychoeducational groups that will benefit their students. For example, if academic achievement has declined or if behavior referrals have increased, professional school counselors can create and implement psychoeducational groups that focus on study skills, work habits, or anger management (Paisley & Milsom, 2007).

Psychoeducational groups vary in format according to the topic and the age of the students in the group. Regardless of the specific format selected, professional school counselors will want to take a number of factors into account as they prepare to lead psychoeducational groups, including students' developmental levels, multicultural issues, school climate, and the overall purpose of the school's counseling program (Akos, Goodnough, & Milsom, 2004). Furr (2000) outlined a six-step model for psychoeducational groups that moves from a statement of purpose to a session-by-session design that includes didactic, experiential, and processing components. The model includes the following sequential steps:

1. *Stating the purpose.* Psychoeducational groups should be guided by a clear statement of the reason for the group's existence that answers the following questions: (a) What is the primary content focus of the group? (b) What population is expected to benefit from participating in this group? (c) What is the purpose of the intervention (i.e., remediation, prevention, development)? (d) What is the expected outcome of participating in the group (e.g., change in thoughts, affect, behavior, or values)?
2. *Establishing goals.* Clearly defined goals describe how a student may change as a result of the group experience. Goals need to be achievable, measurable, short term, and clearly articulated. For example, a

goal for a psychoeducational group designed to help students build self-esteem might be "To develop an understanding of the relationship between self-talk and self-esteem and to learn to modify inappropriate self-talk" (Furr, 2000, p. 45).

3. *Setting objectives.* Objectives specify the steps needed to reach the group goals. To build on the previous example, an objective for reaching the goal of understanding the relationship between self-talk and self-esteem might read, "Participants will learn the definition of self-talk and be able to differentiate between positive, negative, and coping self-talk" (Furr, 2000, p. 45).

4. *Selecting content.* Group content includes didactic, experiential, and process components. *Didactic content* refers to the information that will be taught directly to group members, such as information about types of self-talk. *Experiential activities* help group members learn by doing, rather than just by listening or discussing. To help students connect the experiential and didactic components, professional school counselors use the *process component*. It is important to plan processing questions in advance, first focusing on what happened during the activity and then moving to group members' reactions to and reflections on the experience. Please see Chapter 10 for an excellent discussion of learning objectives and lesson development that applies nicely to the content selection and process components of group work.

5. *Designing exercises.* There are multiple resources professional school counselors can access that describe group exercises that can be adapted to meet the needs of a particular group. Group exercises can generate discussion and participation, help the group focus, promote experiential learning, provide the group leader with useful information, increase group comfort, and facilitate fun and relaxation (Jacobs, Masson, Harvill, & Schimmel, 2011). It is important to select theoretically grounded, developmentally appropriate exercises so as to enhance the group experience, not just fill time or provide entertainment. Role playing, imagery, and creative arts are just a few examples of the types of exercises that can be used effectively in psychoeducational groups. Furr (2000, p. 41) stated, "Without exercises, the psychoeducational group would become a vehicle that only conveys information rather than changes perceptions and behavior." As stated earlier, effective group leaders take steps to fully process the exercises with the participants.

6. *Evaluating the group.* Evaluation is an important component of any group activity. *Process evaluation* refers to ongoing, session-to-session evaluation of how the group members perceive their experiences, whereas *outcome evaluation* measures the overall effectiveness of the group experience, particularly in regard to individual change. Additional attention to evaluation is given later in this chapter.

COUNSELING GROUPS In addition to psychoeducational groups, professional school counselors offer counseling groups that are primarily remedial in nature. Group counseling is remedial "when it addresses topics or issues that impair the learning and development of specific groups of students" (Goodnough & Lee, 2010, p. 174). It is often employed with children who have special life-event concerns, such as the death of a family member, family changes, teenage parenting, or school failure. Group counseling is also appropriate for children who have disruptive or acting-out behavioral problems (e.g., violent outbursts, defiance, poor peer relationships). A large body of research supports the efficacy of group counseling in schools (e.g., Erford, 2014; Goodnough & Lee, 2010; see Chapter 4). Group counseling can help reduce social isolation and negative emotions, as well as increase positive peer relations and a sense of belonging.

In group counseling, the affective as well as the cognitive and behavioral domains of students are emphasized. The group creates a climate of trust, caring, understanding, and support that enables students to share their concerns with their peers and the counselor. Through group experiences, members maximize the opportunity to help themselves and others. Group counseling frequently takes one of three approaches to dealing with persons and problems: crisis centered, problem centered, and growth centered (Myrick, 2003a).

Crisis-centered groups are formed due to some emergency, such as conflict between student groups. These groups usually meet until the situation that caused them to form is resolved. Crisis-centered groups may also form as a result of crisis intervention for large-scale trauma that affects the school's population. For example, in the aftermath of the tragedy of a school shooting incident, crisis-centered groups can help students process their feelings and develop ways of coping. Sometimes groups that were formed because of a crisis continue to meet after the crisis has passed and develop into either problem- or growth-centered groups. For example, after a fight between fourth and fifth graders, students in one school formed a "peace group," whose initial purpose was to resolve problems among the children who had been in open conflict. As the group continued to develop, however, its purpose expanded to finding ways to identify problems in the school and to correct them in a productive way.

Crisis counseling for groups, as well as schoolwide crisis counseling, is described more completely in Chapter 15. Professional school counselors do not have a choice whether to include crisis counseling in their comprehensive school counseling program. Controlled simulations of potential crises and interventions can help prepare professional school counselors to cope more effectively when crises arise. The American Counseling Association (ACA) has created a Responding to Tragedy resource link on its website (www .counseling.org) that provides helpful information for such situations.

Problem-centered groups are small groups that are established to focus on one particular concern that is interfering with educational progress. Problem-centered groups, which can also be considered issue-based groups, are beneficial to students who have demands placed on them that are beyond their current ability to handle. Examples of issue-based group topics include coping with stress, resolving conflicts, making career choices, getting better grades, dealing with family changes, and ending substance abuse. Like members of crisis-centered groups, students in problem-centered groups are often highly motivated and committed to working on their situations and themselves.

Growth-centered groups focus on the personal and social development of students. Their purpose is to enable children to explore their feelings, concerns, values, and behaviors about a number of everyday subjects such as developing social competence and making transitions. Often, growth-centered groups are formed after classroom guidance lessons have been presented on a particular topic, such as managing anger or making friends. Students are identified who would benefit from additional focus on the topic through growth-centered counseling groups.

Setting Up Groups in Schools

Several factors need to be considered in planning for group work in schools. In particular, professional school counselors will want to give attention to each of the following areas:

- Collaborating with school staff and parents,
- Determining group topics,
- Planning the logistics (e.g., group size, length of sessions, scheduling, group composition),
- Recruiting and screening group members, and
- Establishing group guidelines and confidentiality.

In this section, an overview of each of these important topics is provided. Readers are encouraged to refer to the sources cited for more in-depth information on each topic.

COLLABORATING WITH SCHOOL STAFF AND PARENTS

For group work in schools to be effective, professional school counselors need to have the support of the school administration, teachers, and parents. To gain this support, professional school counselors work collaboratively with school faculty and parents to develop awareness of the centrality and importance of group counseling services in their schools (Steen, Bauman, & Smith, 2007). Among the barriers to successful group work is the justifiable concern about the possibility of students missing class to participate in group sessions. Schools are held accountable for students' academic performance; consequently, it is important to demonstrate ways group counseling can enhance, rather than diminish, student performance.

Open, clear communication about the nature and purpose of a comprehensive, developmental school counseling program is the key to successful group work in schools. Professional school counselors can lead in-school workshops early in the academic year. At this time, they can explain the overall comprehensive school counseling program, which includes group counseling, an example of responsive services. Similarly, professional school counselors can introduce the program to parents through an orientation at the first Parent Teacher Association or Parent–Teacher–Student Association meeting. Other suggestions for communicating with faculty and parents include the following (Greenberg, 2003; Ripley & Goodnough, 2001):

- Distribute needs assessment surveys to obtain suggested topics for group counseling, suggestions for a schoolwide counseling focus, and specific parent or teacher concerns.
- Consult with teachers frequently, and encourage them to let you know about particular student needs.
- Meet regularly with the principal to discuss program concerns and goals. Inform the principal of activities taking place within the program, including group work.
- Send notes to faculty announcing such things as the topics for groups that are being formed, dates of standardized testing, and general activities of the program.
- Visit classrooms to introduce yourself to students and inform them about all the services offered by the school counseling program, as well as guidelines for participation.
- Share information about group goals and objectives and, when appropriate, written materials about group topics.
- Provide outcome data to faculty and parents regarding the effectiveness of the groups that you coordinate.
- Encourage faculty and parents to give you feedback about what they have observed.
- Have a clear process for establishing groups, selecting students, scheduling sessions, and obtaining parental or guardian permission.

DETERMINING GROUP TOPICS There are several ways to make decisions about which groups to offer. As discussed earlier, administering a needs assessment survey to students, parents, and teachers is an effective way to select group topics. One approach to the survey can ask respondents to develop a list of topics they think would be helpful to discuss in small groups. Another option is for the professional school counselor to list group topics and have the respondents indicate whether they are interested (Jacobs & Schimmel, 2005). A third option is to use a confidential "counselor suggestion box" in which students place their ideas for group topics and other concerns (Stroh & Sink, 2002). Yet another way to make decisions about what groups to offer is to examine existing data. School databases about attendance, test scores, retention, and other information can provide additional sources of information about schoolwide needs (Jacobs & Schimmel, 2005; Paisley & Milsom, 2007).

Group topics are directly connected to the academic, career, and personal/social development of students. Whereas many topics (e.g., building self-esteem, establishing peer relationships) are applicable across grade levels, others (e.g., transitioning to high school, teenage pregnancy) are more developmentally specific. Also, although general topics may be applicable across grade levels, the specific manner in which they are addressed differs according to developmental level. An example of sample group topics that might be offered at various grade levels is presented in Table 13.1.

PLANNING THE LOGISTICS (GROUP SIZE, LENGTH OF SESSIONS, SCHEDULING, GROUP COMPOSITION) Early in the planning process, professional school counselors will want to consider several factors related to the logistics of group formation. Generally speaking, the younger the child, the smaller the number of group members and the shorter the session (Gladding, 2012). Children have shorter attention spans and tend to be easily distracted in a large group. With young elementary school children, it is advisable to limit the group to no more than five students (Gazda, Ginter, & Horne, 2008). When working with children as young as 5 or 6, groups may be limited to three or four members, with sessions lasting only 20 minutes (Henderson & Thompson, 2011). With older elementary school children and preadolescents (ages 9–12 years), groups may consist of five to seven students and meet from 30 to 45 minutes (Gazda et al., 2008). Adolescents (ages 12–19) typically meet for one class period, which lasts between 40 and 50 minutes. Group size should be limited to no more than eight members, with six being ideal (Jacobs et al., 2011). When groups get too large, it is difficult for all members to participate, and groups are more likely to lose focus. These are "rule of thumb" guidelines; group size and session length should be based on a number of factors, including students' developmental levels, the purpose of the group, and the nature of the problems with which students are dealing (Brown & Trusty, 2005b).

Scheduling groups can be a challenging task, especially in middle and high schools. With the increased call for raising achievement on standardized testing, many teachers are understandably reluctant to release students from classes. Consequently, it is imperative to work collaboratively with teachers in designing group schedules. In some educational settings, group sessions are rotated so that students do not have to miss the same class more than once. Another option is for professional school counselors to consult with teachers to determine whether there is a time during the day when attending a group counseling session would have the least impact on student learning.

Another logistical consideration relates to the group's composition. Should the group be homogeneous or heterogeneous in regard to such factors as gender, age,

TABLE 13.1 Sample Group Topics for Elementary, Middle, and High School Students

Elementary School	Middle School	High School
Dealing with feelings	Peer pressure	Assertiveness training
Friendship	Interpersonal relationships	Dating/relationships
Academic achievement	Organizational/study skills	Test-taking anxiety
Family changes	Body image	Teen parenting
Self-esteem	Transitioning to high school	Personal identity
Career awareness	Understanding interests and skills	Career exploration and planning
Social skills	Conflict management	Managing stress
Problem solving	Being new to the school	Transitioning to college or work
Valuing diversity	Multicultural issues/sensitivity training	Gay, lesbian, bisexual issues

Note: These topics represent just a few of the many topics that professional school counselors may use in their settings.

and ethnicity? Decision making about group composition is complex, and there are few definitive answers. Although there is considerable disagreement regarding whether to separate groups by gender, Henderson and Thompson (2007) stated that most counselors prefer a balance of both sexes in a group unless the problem to be discussed (e.g., some sex education topics) is such that the presence of the opposite sex would hinder discussion. In regard to age, it is generally agreed that groups should be composed of members who are relatively close in age, both developmentally and chronologically (Gladding, 2012). Ethnic and cultural diversity in groups is desirable unless the topic is specific to a particular group.

Some groups lend themselves to homogeneity with regard to the issues that are addressed. In such cases, the groups are homogeneous in that the students are experiencing similar concerns, and being together can contribute to a sense of universality (Yalom & Leszcz, 2005). Examples of homogeneous groups include groups for children whose parents are divorced and groups for adolescents questioning their sexual orientation. However, there also are benefits to heterogeneity in membership. Group members can learn from each other about different ways of addressing problems (Goodnough & Lee, 2010). Also, heterogeneity may be desired in a group for social skills development or anger management so as to have role models in the group. In general, groups should possess some in-group heterogeneity, but not so much that group members have little in common.

RECRUITING AND SCREENING GROUP MEMBERS Professional school counselors recruit potential group members in several ways. One way to recruit members is to provide parents, teachers, and students with an information notice that describes what the group is about and what is expected of its members. Flyers, bulletin boards, newsletters, and word of mouth also can be used to promote group participation. Professional school counselors often have special knowledge about students, gained through long-term relationships and through communication with teachers and parents. This special information may allow school counselors to identify potential group members. Also, particularly when groups are topic specific, students may volunteer to participate.

Not all students who volunteer or are referred, however, are suitable for a group. Therefore, professional school counselors will want to conduct screening interviews to determine whether the student is a candidate for group participation and whether the student wants to participate. Screening potential group members is a practice endorsed by the ACA (2014) and by the ASGW (2000). Screenings may be conducted individually or in small groups.

During screening interviews, the professional school counselor talks with students about the group, its purpose, and expectations of its members. Students are encouraged to ask questions about the group so that they can make informed decisions about joining (Corey, Corey, & Corey, 2010). Through this interactive process, the professional school counselor can assess students' motivation and level of commitment. Issues to be taken into account in making decisions about whether a student is suitable for a group include emotional readiness, willingness and ability to participate interactively, willingness to accept the rules of the group (e.g., confidentiality), and desire to be helpful to other group members (Erford, 2011). If a student has been referred to the group (whether self-referred or other-referred) and it appears that he or she is not ready to be in a group, Erford suggested that the professional school counselor consider initiating individual counseling, with one of the goals being to get the student ready to become a member of a group.

If the professional school counselor and the particular student decide that the student is ready to participate, a letter requesting permission for participation should be sent to his or her parents or guardians, assuming that notification is appropriate. The letter should include information about the type of group, the length and number of sessions, and the activities that will take place in the group, as well as the professional school counselor's contact information. Some school systems or states may have a policy mandating or recommending notification of and approval for students to participate in groups. The most recent ASCA ethical code (2010) also states that parents and guardians should be notified if the counselor considers it appropriate and consistent with school board policy or practice. Professional school counselors will want to follow their school policy or state law in regard to parent notification. In addition to obtaining permission from parents, professional school counselors should ask students to sign consent and assent forms so that everyone is in agreement about the purpose of the group and the procedures involved before the group begins (Gladding, 2012).

ESTABLISHING GROUP GUIDELINES AND CONFIDENTIALITY Early in the process, professional school counselors will want to discuss group procedures and expectations with all group members. Corey et al. (2010) recommended having a pregroup meeting designed to help members get acquainted and to prepare them for the group experience. During this time, students can be asked to sign informed consent forms. Group rules can be discussed and confidentiality clarified.

Group guidelines are needed to create the foundation for cooperative group relationships. In most cases, it is advisable to get students' input in establishing the ground rules to foster a sense of ownership and investment. Examples of ground rules, which can be adapted to match the developmental level of group members and the purpose of the group, include being a good listener, participating in the group, sharing experiences and feelings, not interrupting, showing respect for group members, and maintaining confidentiality. The concept of confidentiality is especially important, as professional school counselors are bound by their professional code of ethics to protect the confidentiality of group members (ACA, 2005; ASCA, 2010). Some professional school counselors ask students to sign contracts in which they agree to not discuss outside the group what happens in the group.

Professional school counselors also need to let students know that confidentiality in a group setting cannot be guaranteed. As sensitive matters are brought up during group discussion, professional school counselors can remind members about confidentiality and its limits.

Conducting Group Work

The reader may have already taken or will soon take a course in group counseling. In that course, one develops knowledge and skills related to group dynamics, effective group leadership, group stages, ways to work with different populations, and legal and ethical aspects of group work, among other topics. It would be beyond the scope of this chapter to discuss each of those areas or to provide suggestions for group sessions on various topics, although many excellent sources address the scope and practice of group work. Instead, in this section, the role and functions of group leaders in schools are outlined, and suggestions for planning, implementing, and evaluating groups in schools are provided.

ROLE AND FUNCTIONS OF GROUP LEADERS To be effective, group leaders must be able to function in a variety of ways at different times. Bergin (2004) described the professional school counselor's role during the group process in this way:

> During the group process, the counselor concentrates on promoting the development of group interaction, establishing rapport among group members, leading the group progressively through all four stages, and encouraging individual members' self-exploration and personal decision making. The counselor guides the group as it discusses individual and joint concerns, models appropriate attending and responding behaviors, and reinforces members for supporting one another during their individual

self-exploration. In addition, the counselor confronts resistance sensitively, redirects negative behavior, and encourages the group's efforts to become self-regulatory. The counselor safeguards the group's integrity by enforcing the rules the group establishes for itself. (p. 360)

Professional school counselors who lead groups need to develop knowledge and skills in several areas. Following are five noteworthy areas:

1. **Be clear about the purpose of the group.** Is the group primarily a psychoeducational group or a counseling group? What goals and outcomes are desired for students who participate in the group? Group leaders need to clarify the group's purpose and help members move in that direction.

2. **Know how to relate developmental theory and counseling theory to group work.** As stated earlier in this chapter, a strong grounding in developmental theory is essential for any type of counseling work with children. It also is important for professional school counselors to apply counseling theory to the group process so that they can feel confident about the strategies they are using (Goodnough & Lee, 2010). Cognitive therapy, reality therapy, Adlerian therapy, and SFBC represent four theoretical approaches that have been shown to be effective in group work with students. A professional school counseling intern describes her experiences using reality therapy with a group of fifth graders in Voices from the Field 13.2.

3. **Be knowledgeable about the topic or content being covered in the group.** Professional school counselors will want to acquire knowledge and information about a wide range of topics, including such things as stress management, grief and loss, sexual identity development, study skills, bullying, teenage parenting, divorce, stepfamilies, acculturation, and racial identity development. There are many resources available that contain a wealth of information about topics and about ways to present them at different developmental levels. It may be helpful for professional school counselors to create a portfolio that includes information about various topics, suggestions for group exercises related to those topics, and specific developmental and cultural considerations.

4. **Be creative and multisensory.** Children and adolescents respond well to activities that engage their minds and their senses. Professional school counselors can use art, drama, music, movies, and props to generate discussion and participation, help the group focus, and promote experiential learning (Jacobs et al., 2011). Moreover, employing a variety of creative methods

I have found reality therapy to be a useful model of counseling to use with students, both individually and in groups. Most recently, I was asked by a fifth-grade teacher to talk with her female students about gossiping and spreading rumors. The teacher had been approached by several parents and students about what she described as a widespread problem. I decided to talk with approximately 10 girls and ask what they thought about gossiping to determine whether they viewed it as a problem and something they wanted to stop doing. They all indicated that they wanted to change their behaviors. Using the five questions of reality therapy, we worked together to define the problem and examined whether the behaviors were helping them get what they wanted. After determining that gossiping and spreading rumors were not getting them what they wanted, the girls came up with ideas for behaviors that would help them get what they wanted. They selected one behavior to "try out."

I checked back with the girls individually to see how things were progressing and to see if they needed any other ideas to try. I charted the process on the board in their classroom and showed them how they could follow that same outline when trying to solve other problems they experienced. I suggested that they revisit that process

together if they got stuck and let them know that they could contact me for more help if needed.

I also led an anger management group for sixth-grade students who self-referred. They all thought that their ways of handling anger were interfering with their lives and wanted help learning ways to manage it differently. Using reality therapy, we explored the students' behavior and determined whether it was getting them what they wanted. Because the behaviors were not working, we came up with lists of at least five alternative behaviors. Each student decided on an idea to try. The group was six sessions long, and we spent four sessions discussing new behaviors selected to replace old behaviors. By the final group session, each student had new ideas about ways to handle anger more effectively.

Working as a professional school counselor can be challenging because of the number of students who need assistance. Working with students in groups provides a way to reach several students simultaneously. Using reality therapy with students gives them an opportunity to change behaviors and also teaches them a process that they can employ when other concerns arise.

Source: Cassie Cox Evans, Professional School Counseling Intern, Wake Forest University, North Carolina

provides a way to address students' different learning styles, thereby enhancing the overall group experience. Examples of creative, multisensory group activities are described in Table 13.2. For other examples, readers are referred to Gladding (2011) and Jacobs et al. (2011).

5. *Possess multicultural understanding.* For group leaders to work effectively with all populations, they need to be culturally competent (Hays & Erford, 2014). Multiculturally competent counselors have the self-awareness, knowledge, and skills needed to interact successfully with people from different cultural backgrounds. They recognize their own values, biases, and assumptions and are open to diverse value orientations and assumptions about human behavior (Corey et al., 2010). Multiculturally competent group leaders understand the different cultures of their group members, and they also recognize how different cultural backgrounds might affect members' participation in the group (Jacobs & Schimmel, 2005). Professional school counselors can refer to the *ASGW Principles for Diversity-Competent Group Workers* (ASGW, 2012) for guidance in addressing issues of diversity with sensitivity and skill.

PLANNING, IMPLEMENTING, AND EVALUATING GROUPS To maximize the group experience, it is important for leaders to plan for sessions ahead of time (Erford, 2011; Jacobs & Schimmel, 2005). An example of a six-step model for psychoeducational groups was presented earlier in the chapter. As with individual counseling, group leaders will want to balance *intentionality* (planning) with *flexibility* (being responsive to the needs of the group at a given time). When groups are focused on specific topics such as stress management, study skills, or anger management, leaders can plan the content and activities for each session in advance. Planning a series of sessions in this way is a "big picture" reminder that helps the leader keep the group focused and goal oriented.

Some general suggestions for beginning, middle, and ending sessions include the following:

- During beginning sessions, group leaders strive to create a safe environment in which members feel free to share their experiences. The creation of cohesion and trust, which begins during the initial session, contributes to the overall success of the group. Some

---

TABLE 13.2 Introductory Group Activities

Elementary School: *Coat of Arms*

Create a coat of arms by drawing a shield and dividing it into four equal sections. Explain to children that a coat of arms tells different things about a person. Ask group members to create a shield that illustrates things they would like other people to know about them. The group leader might give specific suggestions such as "In the first section, draw or write something about your family. In the second section, draw or write something that you are really good at. In the third section, draw or write about a good book or something that you have read recently. In the last section, draw or write what you have a lot of fun doing."

Middle School: *Decorating My Bag*

Ask group members to cut out pictures representing themselves from magazines or newspapers. Tape or paste these pictures, along with other symbols, on the outside of their paper bags. Also, as part of the exercise, students can put loose pictures and symbols that they are not yet ready to share inside their bags. The students can use the bags to introduce themselves to one another in relation to the pictures and symbols on the outside of the bags. During subsequent sessions, as trust develops, provide students with opportunities to share the material inside the bags, as they see fit.

High School: *Empty Chair Introductions*

Ask group members to think of someone whom they trust and value. This person can be a friend or family member. Ask members to stand behind their chairs, one at a time, and pretend to be that friend or family member. Then ask the student how that person would introduce the student. Next, the student, speaking as the trusted individual, introduces the "empty chair" as though the student were sitting in it. After introductions have been made, encourage group members to share what they learned about each other.

---

of the activities that take place during the initial group session (unless there has already been a pre-group meeting) include introducing members, discussing the group's purpose, establishing ground rules, explaining confidentiality, and discussing expectations. Suggestions for activities to include in an initial session are presented in Table 13.2. Also, during the beginning sessions, leaders will want to take note of how group members relate to each other and how they relate to the purpose or content of the group (Jacobs & Schimmel, 2005).

- The format of subsequent sessions will vary according to the age of the group members and the purpose of the group. In general, it is helpful to establish a routine that is used in all group sessions (Gilbert, 2003). Following are suggested elements to include in this routine:
  1. Welcoming members individually,
  2. Reviewing group rules,
  3. Summarizing what occurred during the previous session,
  4. Focusing on the current topic or issue,
  5. Leading an experiential exercise related to the topic,
  6. Processing the exercise, and
  7. Leading a closing activity in which members describe what they have learned or how they experienced the session.

- During these "middle" sessions, general goals include moving to a deeper level where feelings are identified and shared and group cohesion, support, and awareness are increased.
- The final group session is a time of summary and termination. Goals for the final session include helping group members to focus on the future, instilling hope, and helping members to translate insights into behaviors (Corey et al., 2010). Termination of the group should be planned in advance, with leaders announcing two to three meetings before the final session that the group experience will be ending. Like the initial session, the final group session tends to be structured. Students discuss their feelings about the group ending and identify what they have learned from the group experience. There are a number of ways to conclude groups, many of which include a time of group celebration. Some of the tasks that may occur during the group's closing stage include the following:
  1. Reviewing and summarizing the group experience,
  2. Assessing members' growth and change,
  3. Finishing business,
  4. Applying change to everyday life,
  5. Providing feedback,
  6. Handling good-byes, and
  7. Planning for continued problem resolution. (Jacobs et al., 2011, p. 362)

Giving group members an opportunity to evaluate the group experience takes place either during the final session or during a follow-up meeting. Evaluation is needed to determine the usefulness of the group and its effect on the members (Erford, 2011; Steen et al., 2007). Group evaluation can take several forms. Brief questionnaires and surveys with incomplete statements are two ways to evaluate students' perceptions and learning. Examples of incomplete statements include the following:

The group helped me at school by _____.

One thing I learned in this group was _____.

The most helpful part about being in this group was _____.

One thing I wish we had done differently was ____, and to improve the group, I suggest _____.

In addition to asking group members to evaluate the group, professional school counselors can design pretest and posttest surveys to evaluate outcomes (Akos & Martin, 2003). Professional school counselors may also want to ask teachers, parents, or both to evaluate the group based on their observations of students after the group sessions have ended. Such evaluations are particularly helpful when the group focus was improved behavior (e.g., anger management, study skills, social skills). Finally, following up with students approximately 6 to 8 weeks after the group has ended can provide professional school counselors with additional information about the group's impact and effectiveness.

CULTURAL REFLECTION 13.2

How might professional school counselors-in-training across diverse cultural backgrounds view the importance of working with students in small groups? How might students, parents, and educators from diverse cultural backgrounds view the role of the professional school counselor providing small-group responsive services? What barriers and access points exist for using small-group interventions with culturally diverse students?

Summary/Conclusion

Individual counseling and group counseling are important components of a comprehensive, developmental school counseling program. They represent responsive services and provide ways to address students' needs and concerns. In particular, individual counseling and group counseling are ways to help students who are facing problems that interfere with their personal, social, career, or academic development.

The manner in which professional school counselors carry out individual counseling and group work is affected by a number of factors, including the developmental characteristics of the students, personal philosophical orientations, and specific school demands. In this chapter, counseling in school settings was defined. Certain developmental characteristics of children and adolescents, particularly as they relate to the counseling process, were described. A model of individual counseling was presented, which included building a counseling relationship, assessing specific counseling needs, designing and implementing interventions, and conducting evaluation and closure. Also, because of their utility in school settings, two theoretical models of counseling, SFBC and RT, were presented. These approaches allow professional school counselors to provide effective counseling to students in a brief amount of time.

Whereas some students have needs that warrant individual counseling, a larger number of students can be reached when they participate in psychoeducational or counseling groups in schools. Psychoeducational groups use educational methods to help students gain knowledge and skills in several domains. They help group members to develop new resources and coping skills, which may prevent problems in the future. Counseling groups tend to be more remedial than psychoeducational groups and may be crisis centered, problem centered, or growth oriented.

Regardless of the type of group offered, several issues need to be considered by professional school counselors as they plan for group work. Important factors associated with setting up groups include collaborating with school staff and parents, determining group topics, making decisions about group composition and scheduling, screening students, and establishing group guidelines. Factors related to conducting groups effectively include demonstrating effective group leadership skills; planning for initial, middle, and final group sessions; and conducting group evaluation. Professional school counselors can effectively use group work, as well as individual counseling, with students to enhance development and remediate problems.

As a final note, group work in schools represents an integral domain in the *ASCA National Model* (2012) and the Transforming School Counseling Initiative (TSCI). We encourage you to read about some of the new directions school counseling groups are taking (e.g., wellness, self-advocacy, academic achievement with African-American males), which are described in depth in the 2007 edition of *The Journal for Specialists in Group Work*. This special edition, produced by ASGW, focuses on group counseling in schools and has a plethora of information that professional school counselors will find useful.

Activities

1. Role-play an individual counseling session with an adolescent who is considering dropping out of school. Use the premises from solution-focused brief counseling or reality therapy to guide your session.
2. Develop an interview for screening members for a group topic of your choice (e.g., children from changing families, social skills, study skills).
3. Develop a psychoeducational group for young children in a school setting using Furr's six-step model for psychoeducational groups.

Helping Lab Videos

To help further your understanding of some of the topics in this chapter, go to MyHelpingLab at www.myhelpinglab.com and view the following video clips:

Counseling Individuals and Groups in Schools: Child Counseling and Psychotherapy,
Module 4 (Narrative Therapy with Children, "Using Client's Stories to Define the Problem"),
Module 9 (Play Therapy, "Using Role Plays and Projection in Play Therapy"),

Module 11 (Multimodal Therapy, "Addressing Emotions from a Structural Profile" and "Listing Coping Skills for Dealing With Emotions"), and
Module 13 (Reality Therapy, "Exploring a Client's Need for Power" and "Helping Clients Develop 'Their' Goals and Plans").

14

Consultation, Collaboration, and Encouraging Parent Involvement

Bradley T. Erford*

Editor's Introduction: Consultation and collaboration are efficient interventions that not only allow professional school counselors to address the issue at hand, but also provide models for consultees and collaboratees to take responsibility for solving their own problems in the future. The collaborative model encompasses the establishment of partnerships with parents and community organizations to solve systemic problems and remove barriers to student performance. The practices of collaboration and partnering hold tremendous potential for the transformation of the school counseling profession. Professional school counselors are in a wonderful position to build bridges between students who are in need and necessary community resources, be they human or material. Students whose parents are involved in and supportive of their educational journey achieve higher levels of performance and are better adjusted socially and emotionally. Collaboration, outreach, and school–community partnering are processes meant to get parents and the community involved in the educational enterprise. Although these processes may diverge from a traditional role, the transformed role of the professional school counselor makes such initiatives crucial. The discerning professional school counselor will also note that many of the suggestions may require only an initial impetus followed by delegation of responsibilities to colleagues and volunteers, thus preventing professional school counselors from perpetually investing valuable time and resources over the long term.

THE COUNSELOR AS CONSULTANT: CASE EXAMPLES

Samantha is a kindergarten student in Mrs. Miller's class at River Falls Elementary School. Samantha has few friends and limited social skills. She is often bossy and frequently demands to have things her own way. Mrs. Miller has met with little success in helping Samantha respond more appropriately. Running short of ideas for how to intervene, she refers Samantha to the professional school counselor.

Alberto is a ninth-grade student who is having difficulty with math class and is in danger of failing the course. Although his other courses are challenging, he is managing passing grades. Mr. Long, Alberto's math teacher, feels Alberto's behavior contributes to his problem with math. According to Mr. Long, Alberto interrupts him and his classmates frequently. Alberto is rude in class, generally making sarcastic comments to Mr. Long and the other students. Most of his classmates consider Alberto to be a big annoyance. Alberto has started to cut class. On the surface, Alberto exhibits an "I don't care" attitude. Mr. Long recently referred Alberto to the school's Student Support Team. Alberto's professional school counselor is a team member.

---

*In the first edition of this text, portions of this chapter were written by Susan G. Keys, Alan Green, Estes Lockhart, Peter F. Luongo, Gayle Cicero, and Pat Barton.

Westwood Middle School is located in a culturally diverse urban area. A recent increase in discipline referrals for aggressive behavior has prompted Westwood's School Improvement Team to make the promotion of school safety an important goal for the year. Westwood's principal, Ms. Johnson, has charged the school's four professional school counselors with taking the lead in developing a comprehensive school violence prevention program.

These three cases represent typical referrals that a professional school counselor at the elementary, middle, or high school level might receive in the normal course of his or her work. The professional school counselor represents an important resource for teachers who are confronted by students for whom the usual methods of instruction and discipline are often less than successful. Parents and family members also seek support from the professional school counselor when confused or uncertain about what is normal development or expected behavior and how to help their child when personal, interpersonal, or academic difficulties arise. Administrators also use the professional school counselor's expertise when looking to solve problems involving individual students, as well as problems that affect larger groups of students, family members, and staff. In each of these cases, the professional school counselor may respond using a number of different roles—counselor, consultant, program developer and coordinator, or classroom educator—and in all likelihood will use a combination of roles to provide assistance to teachers, staff, families, and students.

This chapter looks in detail at one of these roles: the counselor's consultant or collaborative role. The *ASCA National Model* (American School Counselor Association [ASCA], 2012) points to the importance of consultation and collaboration services in a comprehensive, developmental school counseling program. Collaboration and consultation are effective methods for intervening in developmental student issues by working with essential people in the student's life (e.g., parents, teachers). Furthermore, consultation and collaboration have been important services provided by counselors for decades, across many settings. In schools, the collaborative approach to consultation currently predominates because it allows the professional school counselor to become an active agent of change even after a course of action has been agreed to by all parties. How might professional school counselors, as collaborators and consultants, approach the problem-solving process in each of the preceding cases? What models of consultation might professional school counselors draw on? How do professional school counselors integrate their expertise with the skills and knowledge of other problem solvers? This chapter

explores these and other questions as a way of discovering more about the professional school counselor's very important consultant role.

CULTURAL REFLECTION 14.1

How might professional school counselors across diverse cultural backgrounds view the importance of the consultation and collaboration role of the professional school counselor? How might students, parents, and educators from diverse cultural backgrounds view the consultant/collaborator role of the professional school counselor?

CONSULTATION MODELS

Models of consultation can be distinguished by the type of interaction that occurs between the consultant and the person or persons seeking the consultant's help. Three types of interaction are triadic-dependent, collaborative-dependent, and collaborative-interdependent.

The Triadic-Dependent Model: Traditional Expert-Directed Consultation

Traditionally, consultation is thought of as a problem-solving process that involves a helpseeker, referred to as a consultee (e.g., teacher, administrator, family member); a helpgiver (i.e., consultant); and a third person that is the focus of concern (i.e., client or student). This three-party relationship is referred to as triadic. In this type of relationship, the consultant provides services indirectly to the client through the consultant's work with the consultee (see Figure 14.1).

Counseling, in contrast, is considered a direct student service because the professional school counselor works in direct contact with the student. In some situations, the professional school counselor may combine different types of services; in effect, the counselor may consult with teachers or family members of a student (indirect service to the student) and provide the same student with one-on-one or group counseling services (direct service to the student).

In the triadic-dependent model, the consultant is viewed as the expert from whom the consultee seeks assistance to remediate a problem with the client (see Figure 14.2). In effect, the consultee is dependent on the consultant's advice and recommendations. The consultant works through the consultee to bring about change for the client. Although the expectation is that the consultation ultimately ends in improved achievement, affect, attitude, or behavior for the student, the immediate recipient of this service is the administrator, teacher, or family

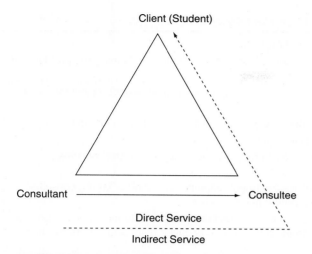

FIGURE 14.1 Consultation as indirect service to the client.

member, not the student. The immediate goal of the consultation might be increasing the skills, knowledge, and objectivity of the consultee so that the consultee is better able to implement an intervention plan designed to achieve change for the student.

Many consultations that professional school counselors conduct with teachers and family members fall under the triadic-dependent relationship category. Using this model, the professional school counselor would meet with a teacher or family member (or both) to assess their perspectives on the student's problem. The professional school counselor might collect additional data through observations, consultations with other teachers or professionals, and meetings with the student. As a consultant, the professional school counselor makes recommendations to the consultee, with the consultee being

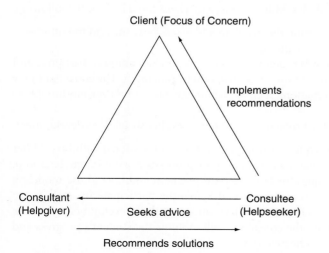

FIGURE 14.2 Consultation as a triadic-dependent relationship.

the one responsible for implementing the prescribed plan. The consultant's recommendations may include interventions that focus on change for the client, the consultee, and the system.

Bergan and Kratochwill's (1990) behavioral consultation is an example of a triadic-dependent consultation model. Within this model, the consultant, as a behavioral expert, draws on principles of behaviorism to help define the problem, identify environmental conditions that maintain the problem, generate solutions that result in changes in behavior for the client or the consultee, and change the social context within which the client or consultee functions. Professional school counselors who help teachers and family members acquire the skills and knowledge necessary to implement a behavior management plan draw on this particular consultation model. Watson, Watson, and Weaver (2010) proposed a four-step behavioral consultation model that is similar to other models of collaboration and consultation: (a) problem identification, (b) problem analysis, (c) plan implementation, and (d) plan evaluation. During plan implementation, behavioral contracting, positive reinforcement, and response cost are strategies that might be implemented. Each of these strategies would result in client-focused change. However, if the consultant needed to spend time educating the teacher or family member about how to implement these procedures, then the consultation would include both client-focused and consultee-focused interventions. Kahn (2000) suggested using a solution-focused consultation model (SWOT model) using the following steps: (a) presession and initial structuring, (b) establishing consultation goals, (c) examining exceptions, (d) helping consultee decide on a solution, and (e) summarizing and complimenting (p. 250). Table 14.1 includes helpful suggestions for conducting effective triadic-dependent consultations with parents and teachers.

The Collaborative-Dependent Model: Partnership and Problem Solving

In a collaborative-dependent relationship, the helping process departs from a view of the consultant as a solitary expert. The consultee continues to depend on the consultant's (a) problem-solving expertise, (b) knowledge of normal and abnormal development, and (c) skills for effecting client and systemic change. In a collaborative-dependent relationship, the consultant also recognizes and engages the knowledge and expertise of the consultee regarding both the student's and the system's strengths and weaknesses, the contextual factors that influence the student, and the student's reaction to previously attempted interventions (see Figure 14.3).

TABLE 14.1 Suggestions for Conducting Effective Triadic-Dependent Consultation

- Make sure the environment for the consultation is comfortable and professional.
- Quickly establish the purpose of the consultation, identifying the client (usually the student) and defining the problems or issues of concern.
- Try to minimize anxiety and maximize cooperation quickly. Maintain a friendly, professional demeanor, even in the face of angry or emotional consultees. Do not become defensive.
- Give the consultee the opportunity to tell his or her story. Be supportive, help as necessary, and listen actively.
- Get to the point efficiently, and avoid educational or psychological jargon.
- Establish clear boundaries for the consultee (usually the parent or teacher) so that the student, not the consultee, becomes the focus of problem identification and intervention.
- Probe for any factors or conditions that may be relevant to effective treatment planning, including what the consultee has tried previously and any condition that may contraindicate a potential intervention.
- Focus on the student's behavior, not the student. Reframe the presenting behaviors in terms of student needs to provide alternative perspectives to consider in treatment. Often, understanding the goal of behavior helps adults to better help the student meet those needs.
- Classroom observation can be a helpful way of collecting additional information about the context surrounding student behavior and performance.
- Be sure to develop a working relationship with the consultee as an equal partner in the endeavor. Try to have the consultee suggest potential interventions and evaluation plans.
- Provide resources (e.g., books, handouts, websites) that can help the consultee better understand the issues and interventions.
- Be sure to schedule follow-up procedures during the initial consultation. All interventions must be tracked and evaluated. When consultees fail to achieve the desired results, they may assume that either they are incompetent or the consultant is incompetent. Follow-up and evaluation ensure an atmosphere of cooperation and continued addressing of issues until a successful resolution is reached. Most counseling interventions require adjustments or even a completely different approach.
- Document in writing contacts with consultees or others involved with the issue.

CASE STUDY 14.1

Samantha

How might a professional school counselor who functions as a consultant within the triadic-dependent model respond to Mrs. Miller in the case of Samantha? After receiving Mrs. Miller's initial referral, the counselor–consultant will take several steps to develop a more thorough understanding of Samantha and Mrs. Miller's concerns. These could include the following:

- An initial consultation session with Mrs. Miller to better define the problem and assess how she and the other students typically respond when Samantha is disruptive and demanding.
- Observation of Samantha in Mrs. Miller's classroom to further identify occasions when Samantha is disruptive and demanding and to see firsthand any patterns that may exist in how others respond to Samantha. The consultant may also spend time observing Samantha in less-structured situations such as the lunchroom and playground to determine if the same behaviors exist in these contexts.
- A meeting with Samantha to determine her perception of the problem and further assess her social skills development.

The consultant will integrate all information and in a subsequent consultation session (or sessions) with Mrs. Miller will recommend strategies Mrs. Miller might use to encourage Samantha to exhibit more positive behavior in the classroom. These strategies could include teaching Mrs. Miller new techniques for positive reinforcement and how to use modeling to teach Samantha new social skills. The consultant might also recommend that Samantha participate in small-group counseling sessions (with the consultant then functioning as counselor) focused on social skill development. Because follow-up and accountability are essential to successful outcomes, the consultant will monitor the student's progress and maintain contact with Mrs. Miller to determine the intervention's effectiveness.

THEORY INTO PRACTICE 14.1

IMPLEMENTING THE TRIADIC-DEPENDENT MODEL

As a professional school counselor serving the needs of four nonpublic schools, my caseload far exceeds the numbers suggested by the ASCA. This being the case, consultation makes up a significant portion of my daily work. One of the most common types of consultation that I engage in is behavioral consultation.

Will is a sixth-grade student whose teacher, Mrs. Jones, approached me because of Will's trouble with organization. To begin the consultation process, I set up a meeting with Mrs. Jones and a second one with her and Will's parents, Mr. and Mrs. Brown. In my meeting with Mrs. Jones, I discovered that she was most concerned about the lack of follow-through that appears to be going on at home. She shared that once things go home, she never sees them again. Homework, tests, and even field trip permission forms rarely come back to school with Will. In fact, Will almost missed the sixth grade's first field trip because of this. Along with this concern, she shared that Will typically leaves her class with the wrong books when they switch classes. Will also becomes easily distracted and appears off task frequently when he is in her classroom. Mrs. Jones shared that the other teachers who see Will throughout the day share her concerns.

In between the meeting with Will's teacher and the meeting with Will's teacher and parents, I observed Will in the classroom setting to get a better understanding of the issues at hand. Before Will's parents came to school for the meeting, Mr. Brown contacted me to voice some concerns. He wanted me to be aware of the fact that he and his wife were concerned that Mrs. Jones wasn't very organized. They believed that Mrs. Jones's relaxed methods of organization were not helping their son to be an effective student. He said that they had not been notified about Will's difficulties prior to when we set up our meeting. Mr. Brown also shared that he thought it would be a good idea for his son to work on anger management skills in weekly counseling sessions with me.

I began the meeting with Will's parents and teacher by thanking everyone for coming and agreeing to find a way to all work together to help Will meet his potential. After giving Mrs. Jones and Mr. and Mrs. Brown a chance to voice their concerns, I shared what I had observed during my classroom observation. We discussed what Mrs. Jones and Mr. and Mrs. Brown had tried in the past to help Will. With the input I received from Will's parents and

teacher, along with my observation, we shared the following suggestions:

- Seat Will in a place where he will be close to the teacher.
- Create a nonverbal signal for the teacher to give to Will to refocus him.
- Provide an extra desk to help Will learn how to organize (keep supplies in one, books in the other).
- Give Will time during homeroom, lunch, or recess to organize his desk.
- Provide redirection for Will instead of issuing demerits on the first offense.
- Get Will color-coded folders and book covers so that he can quickly grab what he needs when it's time to switch classes.
- Keep lines of communication open between school and home. Parents and teacher can e-mail each other to provide updates and evaluate how well the plan is working.
- Write homework on the board and give time for students to copy it down at the beginning of class.
- Have teachers initial the homework book after Will copies homework down; have parent initial it when homework is complete.
- Give Will a folder specifically for papers that he needs to show his parents.
- When possible, give Will a choice of when to complete his homework (e.g., after school, after dinner, before basketball practice).
- Provide counseling sessions focusing on anger management and organizational skills.

At the end of the meeting, we planned to meet again in 2 weeks to evaluate how well the plan was working once it was implemented. At our follow-up meeting, Mrs. Jones shared that she had noticed significant changes in Will's organizational skills and off-task behaviors. She was happy with his progress and saw no need to revise the plan, but would continue to implement my suggestions. Mr. and Mrs. Brown wanted more consistent feedback from Mrs. Jones, but aside from that, they were pleased with Will's progress and saw no need to meet again unless things changed for the worse. I closed the meeting by asking both Mrs. Jones and Mr. and Mrs. Brown to contact me in the future with updates or further concerns.

Source: Katie Young, Professional School Counselor, Pennsylvania

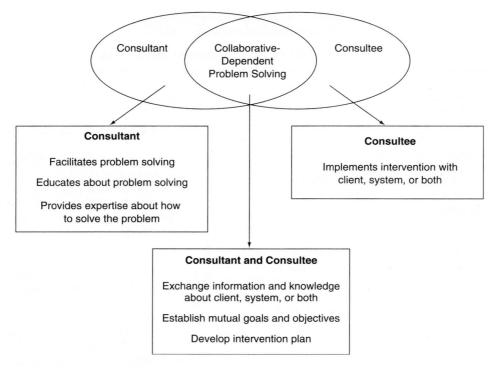

FIGURE 14.3 Consultation as a collaborative-dependent relationship.

Creating a partnership relationship is important to this process. Consultants who work within a collaborative-dependent relationship may educate consultees about the problem-solving process itself, as well as facilitating how the actual problem-solving process unfolds. Importantly, and in some ways in contrast to a triadic-dependent model, the collaborative professional school counselor is seen not as an expert, but as a partner in defining the problem, implementing interventions, and providing evaluation and follow-up services. Together, the consultant and the consultee establish mutual goals and objectives for the student and develop an intervention plan. The consultee is responsible for implementing the intervention plan with either the student and the classroom system (if the consultee is a teacher) or the student and the family system (if the consultee is a family member). The consultant and the consultee depend on the knowledge and skills each person brings to the problem-solving process.

A collaborative-dependent consultation relationship may focus on help for a specific client (student-focused consultation), on help for the consultee (consultee-focused consultation), or more broadly on change within the organizational context or system (system-focused consultation). Schein's classic process model illustrates system-focused consultation. As a process consultant, the professional school counselor, using Schein's (1969) model, approaches problem solving by examining six different variables critical to the organizational system: (a) communication patterns, (b) group members' roles and functions, (c) processes and procedures for group problem solving and decision making, (d) group norms and group growth, (e) leadership and authority, and (f) intergroup cooperation and competition. Within a process consultation model, the focus of change is the organizational system, with the consultant contributing expertise on assessment and interventions related to system change. These variables are also relevant for the consultant who wants to bring about change in a family system.

CASE STUDY 14.2

Alberto

As a member of the school's Student Support Team, the professional school counselor participates in the initial review meeting for Alberto's case. Other participants include the referring teacher, Mr. Long; the school's assistant principal; a special education resource teacher; the school psychologist; the school nurse; and the school social worker. Alberto's academic record indicates that math has been a consistent area of weakness for Alberto; however, he has always managed passing grades. No special education services have been provided in the past, and the team does not feel a referral for such services is warranted. After reviewing case information, the team makes two recommendations: (a) that Alberto be invited to participate in an after-school math tutoring session and (b) that Mr. Long and the professional school counselor work on helping Alberto develop a more positive classroom demeanor.

After meeting with Mr. Long and visiting his class during math time, the professional school counselor, functioning as a consultant, meets with Mr. Long again to establish mutual goals and to develop an intervention plan. Mr. Long is well recognized in the school for his expertise as a math teacher. The consultant is careful to convey respect for Mr. Long's expertise and to support his interest in helping Alberto to be successful in his classroom. The consultant stresses the need for the two of them to agree on a mutual goal and plan for helping Alberto.

When visiting in Mr. Long's classroom, the consultant observes that Mr. Long has the students compete as teams in weekly math quizzes. The team that scores the most points earns a homework pass for one night. This competition seems to make Alberto uncomfortable, with a noticeably higher rate of disruptive behavior occurring at these times. During the consultation session, the consultant shares this observation about Alberto with Mr. Long. Together, they devise a plan for how students can practice their math skills (the reason for the competition) in a way that supports cooperative learning and minimizes stress for Alberto, as well as for the other students. This system-focused intervention will be implemented by Mr. Long, the consultee. The consultant will remain in contact with Mr. Long in an assessment or accountability role to ascertain if the solution is bringing about a change in Alberto's behavior.

The Collaborative-Interdependent Model: Addressing Issues with Multiple Causes Across Multiple Contexts

Triadic-dependent and collaborative-dependent consultation models are helpful when seeking change for an individual client or family or for a single organizational system related to normal developmental problems. But when problems are more complex—as is particularly the case with the multicausal and multicontextual problems of youth who are at risk—these more traditional models are too limited in scope to provide comprehensive solutions. A collaborative-interdependent relationship is a useful alternative.

A collaborative-independent model emphasizes an interdependent problem-solving process in which family members, educators, counselors, youth, and members of the broader community contribute as equal participants (see Figure 14.4). Unlike previously discussed models that rely heavily on the counselor–consultant as an expert, a collaborative-interdependent model does not presume that any one person has sufficient knowledge or information to understand the problem and develop and implement solutions. Ultimately, it is the sharing and transferring of knowledge and information among all problem solvers that enables the group to determine and implement a more comprehensive plan. The plan may include change for an individual student, new knowledge and skills for team members (including the consultant), and change for the organizational system. Each person in the group is interdependent on the expertise of the other group members in formulating and executing the problem-solving plan.

Consultation is a process, and collaboration is a style of interaction within the process. Collaboration refers to how people interact during the problem-solving process.

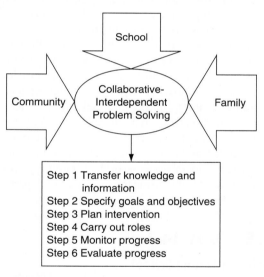

FIGURE 14.4 Consultation as a collaborative, interdependent relationship.

Professional school counselors who use collaboration work within a team framework. To have convened a team, however, does not necessarily mean that the team functions collaboratively. Although family members, teachers, and other professionals and community members may share information about a problem and may have knowledge of what each is doing to solve the problem, they are not necessarily functioning collaboratively unless they actively involve each other in carrying out their functions. The interdependence of a collaborative style extends to all phases of the problem-solving process—problem identification, goal-setting, strategy development and implementation, and evaluation.

There are several distinguishing features of a collaborative style of interaction:

- Collaboration is *voluntary*. People who come together to solve complex problems must want to collaborate for a collaborative style of interaction to occur. Collaboration cannot occur merely because it has been mandated by an administrator.
- Collaboration requires *parity* among all participants. Parity suggests that each participant has an equal voice in decision making and that all team members value equally each member's input. This characteristic is often the most difficult to support in the school setting. Administrative oversight in some schools precludes parity. In some schools, the school-based professionals often decide outcomes before the team even assembles, with the team more of a rubber stamp of what the "school experts" feel should be done, rather than an interactive body that values the expertise of family and community members. Attitudes and assumptions by some school professionals about those who are economically disadvantaged or culturally diverse may also prohibit parity. Professional school counselors–consultants need to pay particular attention to issues of parity and seek to provide balance in the crucial discussions among teachers, administrators, and students and their families.
- Collaboration depends on *shared responsibility* for decision making. In a school context, shared responsibility suggests that it is not the school (e.g., teachers) alone or the family members alone or the community alone that is responsible for "fixing the problem." Each participant has a role in identifying the problem, setting objectives, implementing solutions, and evaluating outcome. Not all team members necessarily contribute equally to the implemented solution, nor is the division of labor necessarily equal across all members. The degree to which any team member contributes is directly dependent on the need for that individual's skills and expertise.
- Collaboration is based on *mutual goals* and a *shared accountability* for outcomes. All participants must agree on what the team is to accomplish. Commitment from each member is critical. Each member may contribute a different expertise to achieve the desired outcome, but the desired end result must be supported by all partners. Responsibility for outcomes—successes as well as disappointments—is shared by all members.
- Individuals who collaborate *share their resources* without dictating how these resources are to be used. How to best use resources becomes a part of the collaborative decision-making process.

What is the consultant's role in helping professionals and family members function collaboratively? First, the consultant can model a collaborative style when interacting with teachers and family members. Engaging others as equals in the problem-solving process sends a clear message that the consultant does not perceive himself or herself as "the expert." In addition, the consultant encourages a collaborative process by (a) seeking others' perspectives, (b) being open to new ways of conceptualizing problems, (c) integrating others' suggestions in intervention plans, (d) reinforcing others' ideas, (e) being flexible in how he or she defines and executes his or her own role, and (f) assisting a team in establishing group norms that reflect collaboration.

CASE STUDY 14.3

Westwood Middle School

To address the needs of Westwood Middle School, the four professional school counselors develop a violence prevention work group consisting of local higher education institution partners, relevant community resource agencies, family members, and school staff—including administrators, teachers, and student support personnel. The purpose of the group is to develop a useful and comprehensive solution to the violence and aggressive behavior problems at Westwood Middle School.

Because the discipline referral problem at Westwood Middle is an ongoing issue, the work group develops a violence prevention initiative that includes primary and secondary prevention strategies. After reviewing data and collaboratively brainstorming, the group finds that the students need to develop positive social, problem-solving, and anger management skills. Skill development will occur through (a) classroom guidance lessons, jointly planned and delivered by the professional school counselors and teachers; (b) activities integrated within the broader educational curriculum, delivered by classroom teachers; (c) small-group counseling sessions, led by the professional school counselors and other student services personnel, including the school psychologist, school social worker, and school-based mental health clinicians; and (d) educational classes for students and family members provided at the local community center, with community center staff co-leading evening training sessions with the school counseling staff.

The work group also recommends staff development on school safety, including the integration of skill training into the broader curriculum, strategies for responding to volatile students, and skills for classroom management. Staff development sessions will be jointly planned and implemented by a professional school counselor, teacher, student support staff, and community representatives from the work group. A school newsletter for family members will highlight all prevention efforts. Family members who participate in the work group will advise about how best to disseminate program information to families and how to engage family members in training and workshop opportunities. The work group invites community leaders to join them in developing employment opportunities for youth.

The work group consults with the school's administrative staff on redesigning the school's discipline referral process so that a student referred for a discipline problem is automatically involved in identifying more productive ways of behaving. This process also ensures that a student referred for a discipline problem is referred to the Student Support Team for further evaluation and that an intervention plan is designed specifically for that student. Intensive counseling sessions with the professional school counselor or a school-based mental health clinician may be part of the intervention plan.

Each member of the work group is involved in all phases of the problem-solving process—from problem and need identification through evaluation. Each member assumes multiple roles based on his or her particular area of expertise. Communication among work group members, role sharing, and shared accountability for outcomes underscore the group's interdependence and collaborative nature. For example:

- In addition to the previously mentioned skills training and counseling services, *professional school counselors* provide leadership within the work group by coordinating the group's work, establishing norms for a collaborative group process, modeling collaborative behavior, and recommending program evaluation procedures.
- The *school-based mental health clinicians* and other *community mental health practitioners* help the group identify contributing mental health problems and facilitate the referral of students and family members who are in need of more intensive services to community-based services. These clinicians also participate with professional school counselors and student support staff members in providing training for school staff about risk factors and warning signs for mental health problems.
- *Faculty members* in the departments of counseling, social work, and school psychology at a nearby university provide the work group with information about theoretical models and "best practices" for primary and secondary intervention. These professionals also provide leadership for the work group in exploring grant funding to support prevention initiatives and in ensuring linkage of this smaller program with broader partnership initiatives between the school system and their respective departments.
- *Teacher* representatives team with professional school counselors and mental health clinicians to implement staff development workshops. The teacher work group representatives also provide leadership to the group on how best to integrate school violence prevention skill training within the broader curriculum.
- *Family members* in the group serve as liaisons between the work group and other parents to communicate the goals and strategies of this initiative to the broader community. Family members also help to identify neighborhood leaders who can provide the work group with information about community needs.

Through this team process, the professional school counselor functions as one of many *collaborative consultants*. Each member of the team joins his or her expertise with the expertise of other members to develop and implement a comprehensive prevention plan. Work group members function interdependently, both during the team process itself and when enacting their roles during the implementation of the comprehensive prevention plan.

THEORY INTO PRACTICE 14.2

IMPLEMENTING THE COLLABORATIVE-INTERDEPENDENT MODEL

During my school counseling internship at a public elementary school, I recall when a collaborative-interdependent relationship was both a practical and a beneficial approach. As a new counselor, I did not presume that I yet had sufficient knowledge and experience with a particular student to execute the most comprehensive and beneficial problem-solving plan. Furthermore, those interacting with this student on a daily basis would need to be privy to any information available and possibly work as a team after a plan was in place to later support the student.

(Continued)

The collaboration process began when a fourth-grade teacher explained to me that her student was acting in a bizarre and confused manner. The teacher also observed that the student appeared disheveled and dirty. Her student relocated from a neighboring school to this school about 5 months earlier when the student's home burned down and she lost everything. At this juncture, I collaborated with the rest of the fourth-grade team who interacted with the student on a regular basis, and there was consensus among the fourth-grade teachers about the student's condition—and no viable ideas about how to help the student.

I continued the process by observing the student within the classroom setting during different intervals of the day on two different occasions. I saw a young lady who was, indeed, disheveled and who quite possibly hadn't bathed in some time. She appeared very tired and maintained a glazed-over expression, possibly from something more extreme than fatigue and boredom. I later approached the student, inviting her to speak with me. The student didn't ask why or about what I wished to speak with her, and she welcomed the invitation.

It was during this meeting that she told me about seeing ghosts and how the ghosts visit her at home, speak to her, and are angry with her. She presented as emotionally disconnected and depressed. As part of the interview, I asked her if she had thoughts about hurting herself. She said she had thoughts of cutting her hair off and then cutting her head off. After some gentle prodding, she revealed she would use her mom's large kitchen knife.

I stayed with this young lady until my supervising school counselor arrived, after asking the student if we could invite the professional school counselor to be with us. At this point, because of comments the student made, I was concerned about possible sexual abuse and suicidal ideation. My supervisor and I agreed strongly that this student needed an immediate suicide assessment and needed to be supervised by a guardian, parent, or responsible adult until the assessment was completed and a plan was in place to ensure the safety and well-being of this child. The principal and teachers were notified, the parents were contacted, and the student was transported to an appointment with a local youth service bureau staffed by clinical mental health professionals (e.g., psychologists, counselors, social workers) who were briefed on the situation.

From that moment on, the expertise of all of these professionals was used to help and support this student. This collaborative-interdependent process—involving teachers, myself, my school counselor supervisor, the principal, the student's parents, and clinical mental health professionals from the local off-site youth services agency—proved beneficial as we met to develop a comprehensive treatment plan to best serve the complex needs of this at-risk student.

Source: Brigitte Scheerer, School Counselor, Loyola University Maryland

CONSULTATION PROCESS

As indicated in the previous discussion of consultation models, effective consultation in a school setting requires skill in problem solving and an ability to form collaborative relationships with other experts, including family members. A consultant who works within a school setting must also be astute about the systemic issues that affect the consultant's ability to fully implement his or her role and function. This section describes these issues through a six-step system-based process model for school consultation (see Table 14.2). Although each step is presented sequentially, the process is not linear and may involve repeated patterns and cycles.

Step 1: Enter the System

In addition to having physically entered the school building, the professional school counselor as consultant needs to be psychologically ready to enter the organizational system that exists within the building. Both the professional school counselor who is new to the building and the seasoned professional school counselor need to enter the school's system with a mind-set that is (a) flexible in its approach to problem

solving, (b) committed to establishing collaborative relationships, and (c) motivated to encourage the types of systemic changes that may be needed to promote student learning.

Many professional school counselors enter the building ready to provide direct counseling services to students most in need. Counseling is an important role for the professional school counselor. In fact, many professional school counselors would probably view counseling as their most important role. The problems confronting many student–clients, however, may require a more comprehensive plan that engages the multiple systems (school, classroom, peer, family, neighborhood–community) that are a part of the student's life. Consultation provides a means through which the professional school counselor can access the range of systems necessary for long-term change. Hence, it is important for professional school counselors to perceive their role broadly—a role that includes both direct counseling services and the indirect services of consultation. Being ready to enter the school system and encouraging system-focused changes presupposes an indirect service orientation.

As the consultant enters the school's system, it is important to understand the goals of the system and how

TABLE 14.2 System-Based Process Model for School Consultation

Step	Components
Enter the system	Enter the system physically and psychologically
	Clarify role perceptions
	Perceive self as a direct and an indirect service provider
	Understand the goals of the system
Joining the system	Learn system rules and metarules
	Observe positions of power
	Build alliances
	Establish communication with subsystems
	Maintain objectivity
Initiate problem solving	Create group norms based on parity, mutual goals, shared decision making, shared resources, and shared expertise
Frame change	Identify goals
	Determine outcome measures
	Empower participants as change agents
	Think multisystemically
	Encourage flexible roles and permeable boundaries
	Protect change
Evaluate change	Monitor progress
	Assess outcomes
	If no progress occurs or if change is in an undesired direction, assess reasons
	Protect change
Facilitate closure	Debrief
	Terminate consultation services for identified student
	Maintain relationships with other professionals
	Reinitiate consultation process for new students and problems

these goals relate to the consultant's role. Schools exist to support the academic achievement of students. Test scores and other measures of academic success drive what happens in schools. The consultant who can directly link his or her program to the school's mission will have an easier time gaining support from faculty and administrators. It is also important for the consultant to have a clear understanding of the school's perception of his or her role. A misperception of that role by the consultant, school administrator, faculty, or family member can create expectations for different types of services. Failure to meet these unrecognized expectations can place the consultant at a disadvantage. Clarifying these expectations, therefore, is an important step in the entry process.

Step 2: Join the System

Leaving at the school door all expectations that faculty and administrators "should" recognize how much the consultant has to offer is an important part of joining the school system. Schools are very busy places. Teachers are under enormous pressure to produce "educated" students. Earning the respect of teachers, administrators, and family members is an important part of joining the system. Consultants can begin to acquire this respect—can, in effect, "join with the school system"—by attending to the six points that follow.

LEARN THE SYSTEM RULES AND METARULES Knowing the policies and procedures that govern professional behavior within the system is essential. The consultant will need to know (a) the larger school system's policies and procedures related to a number of issues, including confidentiality, reporting of abuse, and parental notification about service delivery, as well as (b) the specific school's interpretation of how these policies and procedures are implemented at the school level. For example, it might be school board policy that parents are to be notified of a change to the student's educational plan, including the addition of counseling services, before instituting the changes. How that policy is carried out at the school level could differ from school to school. One school might ask the student to deliver a written message to the parents, another school might notify the parents in writing by mail, and still another school might allow a brief grace period before notifying parents.

It would be easy for the consultant if all the school rules were written in a manual that the consultant could read. Many are, but as is apparent from the previous discussion, having a written policy or rule does not mean it is interpreted and executed similarly across all schools. Many unwritten and unspoken rules, or *metarules*, also exist that can be learned only through interaction with the system. Metarules exist in how teachers manage their classrooms, and these rules can differ from teacher to teacher. Some teachers resent interruptions, preferring not to have students leave the classroom for counseling services or not to have other professionals enter the room during class time. Other teachers may be more open to the ebb and flow of students' movement, more willing to excuse students from their classes, and quite comfortable with other professionals entering the room to speak with them or observe a student.

OBSERVE EXPLICIT AND IMPLICIT POSITIONS OF POWER Nothing, be it an academic program or a counseling and consultation service, works well in a school without the principal's support. It is important for the consultant to join with, and maintain sufficient contact with, the school principal. Demonstrating how the consultant's work directly relates to the principal's agenda is an important avenue for gaining acceptance and support from the principal. Allotting ample consultation time with the principal allows the consultant to maintain lines of communication and act as a support to the principal. This will often involve learning the principal's schedule and putting in extra time to be able to catch up with the principal when he or she is available. Valuing the principal's contributions and recognizing the principal as an essential collaborator constitute an important part of joining the school system.

Not all people in a school who occupy a position of power have an accompanying title that suggests such status. All experienced school professionals know that most school secretaries occupy an implicit power position within the school. Some control who has access to the principal, and others are an important communication link between teachers and parents—and possibly between the consultant and parents. In some schools, other professionals in the building may hold a certain teacher or teachers in high esteem. Such teachers can enhance or jeopardize change, depending on whether or not they support the initiative. The consultant who is not accepted by these power figures may find it difficult to accomplish his or her mission.

BUILD ALLIANCES THROUGH SHARED AGENDAS, RECOGNITION OF INDIVIDUAL STRENGTHS, AND SUPPORTIVE ACTIONS Having the principal's support does not necessarily mean the consultant will have the support of others in the building. As suggested earlier, the need for others to perceive a common agenda between themselves and the consultant is critical to the consultant's acceptance. Forming an alliance with those who hold explicit and implicit positions of power is an important strategy. Taking the time to get to know others, to offer assistance that may make others' jobs easier or help them to be more successful, and to explicitly recognize others' strengths are helpful ways of offering support and building alliances. Such actions must be conveyed and perceived as sincere and genuine.

Some alignments can be a serious hidden danger for consultants. For example, certain teachers might be in conflict with the school principal over any number of issues. If the principal sees the consultant aligning with these individuals, then the consultant unknowingly can experience resistance from the principal and those aligned with the principal. Being aware of staff alignments around issues affecting counseling and consultation services is an important part of the joining process.

In general, the consultant must be sensitive to giving the impression of aligning with any one group against another. In some instances, the school could perceive the consultant and family to be aligned against the school. If the consultant and family meet and make school-related decisions that are then conveyed to the teacher or administrator, the rest of the school understandably could feel left out. It is important for the consultant to be cautious about forming alignments with families that position the consultant and family against the school. It is important for the consultant to work toward collaboration with staff and families, rather than fragmentation.

ESTABLISH COMMUNICATION WITH MEMBERS OF ALL RELEVANT SUBSYSTEMS The school as a system is made up of several subsystems—administrative, staff, faculty, parental, student–peer, and community. Each of these subsystems may also be composed of smaller subsystems. For example, special education faculty and regular education faculty could be subunits within the larger faculty subsystem. When working with students with complex needs, interventions may need to involve several, or even many, layers of subsystems. Getting to know and be known by members of these different subsystems can be an important first step in establishing a working relationship. Face-to-face contact through consultation services; attendance at staff, parent–teacher, and community meetings; participation in classroom activities; and announcements about services provided by the consultant in the school newsletter can provide avenues for connecting with subsystems. Developing an awareness of the types of issues that might create friction between subsystems is also important. Special education and regular education teachers will need to work together when implementing inclusive procedures for students. Collaboration may be hindered, however, by territorial issues and role rigidity. The consultant can provide a neutral perspective as subsystems strive to overcome the barriers that prohibit problem solving.

MAINTAIN OBJECTIVITY Joining with a system can take time. Acceptance by a few may precede acceptance by many. The consultant may do everything right, and still some members of the system may resist accepting the consultant as a team member and may impede full implementation of the consultant's services at the school. This can be frustrating and discouraging. The consultant may begin to resent the challenges presented by the school. Reframing challenges as opportunities and seeing resistance as a systemic reaction to change, rather than a personal affront, are important if the consultant is to maintain objectivity. A loss of objectivity as the consultant is in the process of joining with the system could threaten the consultant's ability to eventually effect client, consultee, and systemic change.

STAY "ONE DOWN" Teachers, administrators, and the consultant all act as helpers in the school setting. Many schools have a number of individuals in addition to the professional school counselor who deliver some type of mental health services. These might include social workers, school health nurses, crisis intervention counselors, and school psychologists. To work effectively, the consultant needs to work in a way that is not threatening to anyone's territory. Also, the consultant who is trying to acquire acceptance by a system has a harder time gaining acceptance if other professionals perceive his or her interactions as intimidating. Consultants who seek acceptance by the faculty or family subsystem need to minimize status differences between themselves and teachers and family members. Acknowledging the expertise of the other person, seeking advice, asking for assistance, and being open to trying new approaches are all ways the consultant can

overtly recognize another person's skills and knowledge and covertly maintain a "one-down" position.

Step 3: Initiate Problem Solving

After entering and joining the school system, the consultant is in a position to initiate problem solving. This begins the working stage of the process model. The stages of problem solving remain the same regardless of whether the consultant is implementing a triadic-dependent, collaborative-dependent, or collaborative-interdependent type of relationship. As indicated, problem complexity often determines which consultation model the consultant uses.

The consultant begins the problem-solving phase of the consultation process by collecting information to assist in identifying the problem. This could mean working directly with the student, meeting with teachers and family members, and participating as part of a problem-solving team. Collecting and integrating available data about the student and the broader system occur at this stage of the process. The focus of problem solving could be an individual student, such as Samantha from our earlier example; or the consultee, such as Mrs. Miller, who needed to learn new skills; or a classroom system, as in Mr. Long's math class; or the broader systemic issue of increased violence and aggression at Westwood Middle School. Regardless of the focus, a thorough understanding of the student's, consultee's, or system's needs, including strengths and weaknesses, is an important part of a comprehensive assessment of the problem.

The opportunity to function as a consultant within a team context occurs frequently in today's schools. In addition to specific content knowledge about a particular problem, the consultant brings to the team knowledge of group dynamics and an ability to facilitate the group process. Most school teams are task oriented; group process issues, so central to the ability of a team to function collaboratively, are often unnoticed or ignored. Without an attention to process, it will be difficult for a collaborative dynamic to emerge. Without strong process skills, it will be difficult for the consultant to become an integrated part of the school system and difficult for the consultant to establish a collaborative identity.

The consultant can use his or her expertise to facilitate a team's movement through the developmental stages of group process. The consultant can work to (a) establish collaborative group norms, (b) encourage cooperative rather than competitive behavior, (c) explicitly recognize the expertise of all participants, and (d) create communication patterns that allow all to participate equally in the problem-solving process. Establishing a collaborative team process might also require educating the school administrator about collaboration and acquiring the administrator's support prior to initiating this type of team process.

Step 4: Frame Change

During this fourth step of the process, the consultant works with others to set goals and shape an action plan for accomplishing goals that is realistic and that can be executed reasonably by those involved. A collaborative style of interaction continues as team members (if the consultant is working in a group context) or individuals (if the consultant is working with an individual teacher or family member) ascertain their roles in supporting client change. When framing change, the consultant may find the following points helpful.

1. *Identify goals.* After a thorough assessment of the problem in the initial problem-solving phase, appropriate goals are identified. These could include outcomes for the student, the consultee, and the system. Establishing concrete objectives further refines and defines each goal statement. Goals and objectives for students will need to be connected to academic achievement to be consistent with the school's larger mission.

2. *Determine outcome measures.* The measures and methods to be used in the evaluation process need to be considered prior to conducting the actual evaluation. Clarifying how outcomes will be measured at this point in the process also helps ensure that goals have been appropriately operationalized.

3. *Empower participants as change agents.* Some teachers and family members may feel less able to be or less committed to being part of a solution. Family members may blame the school for the problem, whereas some teachers may feel that the student's problems are a result of poor parenting. The consultant needs to reframe problems so that the emphasis is on common goals and how each person can help, rather than who is at fault. Affirm teacher and family strengths, and use these strengths as part of the change process. Create hope that change can be accomplished. When the consultation is student focused, it is important for the consultant to remember that, although client change may be the explicit outcome, change in the consultee or system might be a first step toward change for the student.

4. *Think multisystemically.* Many of the students with whom the consultant will work have very complex problems, with no single easy solution. Change for the individual is often predicated on change in the systems within which the individual is embedded. This would suggest that to be comprehensive, an action plan would need to include more than interventions targeting the individual. A word of caution is important here: A school that is open to viewing the student as the identified problem may not be open to examining staff or family actions that affect the student. Such a change in focus could result in a great deal of resistance. The consultant will need to proceed prudently, being careful to offer suggestions tentatively. Earlier work in forming alliances and building a collaborative ethic will help support such efforts. In some cases, the consultant may work separately with a particular teacher or parent to help shape a change in the classroom and family subsystems.

5. *Encourage flexible roles and permeable boundaries.* When people assemble to solve problems, quite often they bring with them a particular notion of how change should occur and what their role is or is not in that process. Creative solutions often reside in being able to step outside such preconceived notions. Initially, the professional counselor may have viewed his or her role primarily as one of direct service. To redefine that role to include consultation—using a variety of models—suggests flexibility. In another instance, a teacher may see himself or herself primarily as someone who conveys academic material within a specific discipline. Asking the teacher to conduct or co-lead classroom activities focused on social-emotional issues would encourage role flexibility. As people begin to collaborate, the boundaries that often separate and restrict professionals and families can become more permeable and less rigid.

6. *Plan to protect change.* Creating expectations about what might happen once participants enact the plan for change is a way to protect the change effort from failure. The wise consultant lets participants know ahead of time what they might expect; for instance, things might get worse before they improve. Strategize about what to do if the unexpected happens. Protect change by creating a system of shared accountability; make sure the action plan identifies who is responsible for what and describes benchmarks for evaluating progress. Recognize persistence, and remember the importance of linking student change to academic achievement. Creating mechanisms for ongoing communication and sources of support is also important.

Step 5: Evaluate Change

Monitoring progress and determining whether goals have been accomplished are tasks that are part of the evaluation process. Consistent with the shared accountability ethic of collaboration, those involved in the intervention are potential participants in the evaluation. Collecting data, summarizing and recording information, and developing mechanisms for sharing data are all tasks that can be shared.

The evaluation should assess if change has occurred, and if so, the degree to which it has occurred. If no change is noted or if undesired change has occurred, the consultant can help assess the reason for a lack of progress and make recommendations for revising the intervention. Decisions about continuing the intervention are also made at this time.

Step 6: Facilitate Closure

Bringing the consultation relationship to closure can be a very different process for the school-based consultant who remains in the school than for a consultant who physically leaves the building at the end of the consultation. In the former case, although the intervention for a particular client may have ended, the consultant remains in relationships with the professionals in the building. Debriefing with consultees allows an opportunity to reflect on not only achieved outcomes, but also the process of working together. Debriefing provides an opportunity for the consultant and other team members to assess how well they collaborated as a group.

SCHOOL CONSULTATION AND COLLABORATION WITH DIVERSE POPULATIONS

Although substantial attention has been given to issues of multicultural diversity in the counseling profession in general, infusion of multicultural research and practices into the area of collaboration and consultation has been slow in coming. Despite a lack of research and even a lack of emphasis on cross-cultural consultation in training programs, most educational professionals perceived that they had the necessary skills and training to work effectively with culturally and linguistically diverse students (Roache, Shore, Gouleta, & de Obaldia Butkevich, 2003). But within the literature, some approaches and modified consultation strategies have emerged that may help professional school counselors to even more effectively address the needs of culturally diverse youth, as well as their families and teachers.

Although the basic processes of multicultural collaboration or consultation are virtually identical to the processes discussed earlier, the framework or lens of the professional school counselor must account for cross-cultural issues that may impede the effectiveness of interventions. Even though the professional school counselor and parent may speak the same language and be of the same ethnicity, socioeconomic differences may indicate that cross-cultural modifications may be necessary for effective consultation to occur. Ingraham (2000) proposed a multicultural school consultation framework to

focus school professionals on the important facets of effective cross-cultural consultation. Her model consists of five components:

1. *Domains of consultant learning and development* involve knowledge and skill requirements in eight competence domains, including

   Understanding one's own culture . . . Understanding the impact of one's own culture on others . . . Respecting and valuing other cultures . . . Understanding individual differences within cultural groups and multiple cultural identities . . . Cross-cultural communication/ multicultural consultation approaches for rapport development & maintenance . . . Understanding cultural saliency and how to build bridges across salient differences . . . Understanding the cultural context for consultation . . . Multicultural consultation and interventions appropriate for the consultee(s) and client(s). (p. 327)

2. *Domains of consultee learning and development* involve the knowledge, skills, confidence, and objectivity to deal with diverse circumstances.
3. *Cultural variations in the consultation constellation* involve cultural similarity between and among the consultant, consultee, and client.
4. *Contextual and power influences* involve societal influences, balance of power issues, and "cultural similarity within a differing cultural system" (p. 327).
5. *Hypothesized methods for supporting consultee and client success* involve knowledge, skills, and strategies of various supportive interventions in areas such as how to frame problems. This component also encompasses the professional school counselor's commitment to professional development.

Competence in the area of multicultural consultation is essential to the effective functioning of the professional school counselor in a diverse society. From time to time, professional school counselors may need to work with interpreters, and schools need to be proactive in locating, collaborating with, and training interpreters to better meet the needs of linguistically diverse students and their families.

In general, the effectiveness of collaboration and consultation approaches relies on the consultant and consultee participating as equal partners. But one should not expect the approaches discussed in this chapter to be equally effective with consultees from all cultures. More directive styles of consultation, as opposed to more indirect collaboration styles, may be more effective with consultees from some cultures, such as Asian Americans. As great diversity exists in society and in the school population, great diversity must exist in the professional school counselor's intervention approaches to collaboration and consultation.

COLLABORATIVE CONSULTATION: REACHING OUT TO THE BROADER COMMUNITY

Students with complex problems are typically involved in the broader community of core social institutions. Core social institutions are those enduring structures whose mission is to provide the basic level, the core, of public services. These services for children include child welfare services, to protect children, and the juvenile justice system, to protect the public from children's misdeeds.

The collaborative consultation model has to engage and be responsive to this context and advocate for the integration of basic services. When children simultaneously appear in multiple systems, simply connecting the different professionals in the system is insufficient. Collaborative consultation supports an integrative approach that demands a shared responsibility for defining, planning, and moving with good intent for the student. This is an outcomes focus and places a premium on collaboration across systems of care. Helping professionals, no matter what core social institution they represent (public education, by definition, is a core social institution), need to be unburdened of the routine administrative responses to children's needs so that they can concentrate on creative and joint responses to complex needs. Through collaborative consultation, the definition of *helping* moves away from the narrow confines of any one core social institution to the focus of what these institutions can do together for children in question.

To create an effective, integrated network of community–school professionals, professional school counselors (as collaborative consultants) need to be familiar with other core social institutions—how they function and who in these systems represent potential partners. Bringing these potential partners together to create positive outcomes for students expands the consultant's role to include a community liaison function. Although partnering with community resources is essential to effective school counseling programs, it is perhaps even more vital that educators partner with parents and involve them deeply in their children's education. It is this essential topic that becomes the focus of the remainder of this chapter.

VOICES FROM THE FIELD 14.1 **STAYING CONNECTED THROUGH COLLABORATION AND PARTNERING**

As a relatively new professional school counselor who has worked at the high school, middle school, and elementary school levels, I have found collaboration to be a particularly vital part of the job. This past year I was working at four schools and with many students of different grade levels. I would have missed a lot of pertinent information about those students had I not proactively communicated with their teachers and families, with administrators and other staff members, and with staff from community resources and agencies. The information included things that sometimes did not come up during my individual counseling sessions with the students, including information about academics, social and emotional issues, and events going on in the students' lives. In the limited time allotted for counselor–student sessions, the students sometimes neglected to talk about certain things that were going on in their lives, or they might simply not have been thinking about them (and, therefore, did not express them) at that particular time, or sometimes they did not see the information as important. Communicating with professionals and family members who were important in these students' lives added invaluable perspectives on these students' "worlds."

Teachers see students almost every day and, therefore, are excellent judges and sources of information on how students are doing. In my experience, teachers saw more than just the academic side of things. They also were privy to information about, and observed, a student's relationships with friends and other significant people in the student's life. Teachers were able to notice when something was different with a student and when that student might need help.

School administrators often saw yet a different side of students. Administrators had information about difficulties a student may have experienced. Some administrators had frequent contact with parents via school functions, meetings, or phone calls or by living in the same community and, therefore, had a good sense of what the students' home lives were like.

I found that families frequently had still a whole different perspective on how their children were faring. They saw their children outside school, had known them for the longest time, and knew them well. Families also were usually keenly aware of changes in children's behavior, especially at home or in social settings outside the school.

Other school personnel working in areas or programs such as Healthy Start or probation services and people staffing community resource programs also proved to be vital resources for me. They were a great help in finding out what resources were available to students and what steps needed to be taken to get those services to the students. For example, this past year I worked closely with a woman from a Healthy Start program whom I went to often when I needed to match specific resources available in the community to the needs of a particular student. She was able to provide detailed information about resources in the community and had the firsthand experience to anticipate which community resource would, in fact, be a good fit with a particular type of problem.

Without collaborating with teachers, administrators, families, other school staff members, and professionals in the community, I would not have been able to work as effectively with the students. With collaboration, I was able to piece together a more complete picture of the student and develop a truer sense of the problems that student was experiencing. We mutually drew from each other's expertise, and collectively we were able to generate a number of possible approaches to working with a student. By staying in constant communication, we were able to better select those approaches that worked, monitor the student, and better evaluate how that approach was succeeding. Working together helped the students more than any one of us working alone. I found that helping students to the best of *my* ability meant working as a team.

Source: Megan Kidron, Professional School Counselor, Lake County Office of Education, Safe Schools Healthy Students, Middletown, California

ENCOURAGING PARENT/GUARDIAN COLLABORATION IN THEIR CHILDREN'S EDUCATIONAL EXPERIENCES

Today, schools harbor a population of students with academic, personal, and social problems that create barriers to academic success. Complex and multifaceted issues are forcing professional school counselors to assess and redefine their current roles. Although schools have traditionally stood alone in their mission to educate children, children are arriving in the classroom with needs that far exceed traditional educational methods. As health care organizations continue to limit services offered, including mental health services, it has become increasingly critical for professional school counselors to work with other human service professionals to meet their students' wide-ranging needs.

Professional school counselors are well positioned to act as proactive change agents in the school setting. Training in group processes and an understanding of the cycle of change are necessary skills acquired in counselor training. School reform has redefined the roles of many school professionals, including professional school counselors. All must become actively engaged in strengthening relationships among schools, families, and communities.

True collaboration includes jointly agreeing to identify and address specific problems and areas of service. This description goes far beyond talking about problems, learning about resources, and coordinating service delivery. When true collaboration exists, all parties equally share the outcomes. This process requires consensus building and may not be imposed hierarchically. Collaborators must learn about each other's roles and explain their own. Expertise in the process of goal setting is critical. Through collaboration, professional school counselors will gain a clearer understanding of what other agencies can contribute and how they function (resources and procedures).

By developing personal relationships, people will become more willing to respond and work together for all children. They must remind themselves that their leadership efforts will improve the academic achievement of students.

Schools are in the business of education, and this generation of professional school counselors must be trained to work effectively with others to meet the needs of students and their families. It is critical to understand the system in which one works. Professional school counselors need to collect and analyze data when identifying needs and creating partnerships.

Schools have many gatekeepers, rules, regulations, and structures that make collaboration difficult, and staff members can feel threatened by the appearance of other professionals. Professional school counselors need to help staff members to recognize the benefits of developing relationships with other agencies and service providers. Families and outside agencies must learn the school's rules and regulations with a special sensitivity to hierarchy and the structure of the system. Professional school counselors can facilitate these collaborative efforts.

A number of studies have underscored the challenges to school–agency collaboration, as well as curative factors. For example, Ponec, Poggi, and Dickel (1998) conducted a study to explore, understand, and describe the therapeutic relationship shared among professional school and community counselors engaged in collaborative relationships. Although mutual concerns focused on confidentiality and the responsibility of financial obligations, community counselors expressed the value of personal interaction and identified time (specifically, a 9-month cyclical school calendar) as an impediment to those interactions. Ponec et al. concluded that it is only through the enhancement of communication that the ability to be effective helping professionals can be advanced. Personal knowledge, interaction, a perception of professionalism, and teamwork will develop and enhance the collaborative effort.

SCHOOL OUTREACH AND CHANGING FAMILY NEEDS

Schools have traditionally engaged in outreach strategies such as the fall open house and parent–teacher conferences. Other strategies such as parent resource centers, home visits, and positive phone calls are less common. Doing a better job of making schools more family-friendly is within the reach of all educators. In particular, professional school counselors are in a key position to increase opportunities for parents to be involved in and supportive of their child's education. Today's parents seem to fall into one of three categories:

1. Parents who are able to, and do, prepare their children for success in school on their own. They initiate contact with the school and take the steps to maintain a continuous line of communication with the school. Working with such parents requires little effort on the part of the professional school counselor and school officials.

2. Parents who want to help their children be successful in the school setting, yet do not take the steps necessary to do so. Sometimes the reticence may be due to a lack of knowledge of what to do; sometimes it may be due to a lack of resources. These are the parents to reach out to and continuously encourage. Often, professional school counselors encounter parents with no health insurance or no transportation or with rigid work schedules and demands. Counselors must use their listening skills to hear and respond to these parents' needs.

3. Parents (a small percentage) who do not have the skills or interest necessary for involvement in their child's school success. These are the truly challenging families who are often living at the subsistence level and who may be involved with multiple agencies and organizations, all attempting to intervene to assist the family toward independence. Counselors' consultation, coordination, and collaborative skills are put to the test with these families.

The great majority of parents care about their children's education. They understand that an education is their child's ticket to success in the job market and the avenue to a better lifestyle than, perhaps, they were able to provide. Job and family demands, however, engage much of parents' time, often to the exclusion of school involvement. Parents in low socioeconomic groups and those who speak English as a second language also tend to shy away from school involvement. Professional school counselors should view such families as a welcome challenge to their communication skills and creative thought processes and invite these parents to become involved in the school. Table 14.3 suggests some ways in which parent involvement in school and community activities can be accomplished.

Parent involvement initiatives around the world have been effective in improving achievement and a wide variety of childhood adjustment difficulties (Center for Public Education, 2011). Parent involvement in the home makes an even greater difference in achievement than parent involvement at school. Thus, the challenge and impetus for professional school counselors and educators in general must be to actively engage parents and guardians in the academic lives of their children.

Correlative studies have indicated that parental involvement predicts student achievement (Center for Public Education, 2011), student attendance, and dropouts (Wright & Stegelin, 2003). As a more specific example,

TABLE 14.3   Possible Types of Parental Involvement

Type of Involvement	Sample Activities
1. Parenting	Parent education workshops
	Home visits at transition points
2. Communicating	Yearly conference with every parent
	Weekly folder of student work sent home
3. Volunteering	Parent room or family center
	Class parent
4. Learning at home	Information on homework policies
	Summer learning packets or activities
5. Making decisions	Active PTA or PTO
	District-level councils and committees
6. Collaborating with community	Service to community
	Service integration through partnerships

when parents are trained to help increase their children's achievement at home, significant improvements have been documented. Darling and Westberg (2004) reported that parents who were trained to teach their children how to read using guided exercises and questioning produced significantly better results than did parents who simply listened to their children read—which most do.

The research on parental involvement indicates that most involved parents are White, married mothers with higher levels of education and socioeconomic status (Berthelson & Walker, 2008). Parent involvement is far more common in elementary schools than in high schools, with the transition from elementary to middle school resulting in an average decline in parent participation by half. However, some research indicates that when educators deliberately seek out, encourage, and invite parent involvement, factors such as educational and socioeconomic levels are eliminated as differentiating factors. Studies have explored what motivates parents to become involved in schools and student achievement (e.g., Benson, 2004). Table 14.4 provides some suggestions for increasing parent involvement in student achievement and the schools. Of course, a major benefit of parent involvement is frequently greater parental satisfaction with the quality of education their children are receiving.

Henderson's (1987) classic study is often cited as conclusive evidence of the effectiveness of parent involvement in student achievement, but Mattingley, Prislin, McKenzie, Rodriquez, and Kayzar (2002) correctly pointed out that less than half of the studies Henderson reviewed explored the effect of interventions and that only one out of every five of the reviewed studies was published in a refereed journal. Likewise, White, Taylor, and Moss (1992),

reviewing 172 research studies, found the evidence of effectiveness of parent involvement unconvincing. Much better research is needed in this area before conclusive results can be stated with confidence. Better research is likely to occur soon, given that parent involvement was one of six targeted and funded areas in the No Child Left Behind Act.

Opportunities for parent involvement in the school (and school counseling program) include serving on an advisory committee; staffing registration or special events tables; presenting at career fairs or career programs; providing character education or social skills training (after brief training by the professional school counselor); grandparents days; coffee or tea gatherings with teachers, counselors, or administrators; computer training days; parent visitation days; special events days (e.g., field day, cookout, talent show); awards assemblies; ice cream socials; community fund-raising dinners; parent workshops; field trips; and parent–child events (e.g., father–son, mother–daughter, father–daughter, mother–son, grandparent)—among many others. The limits to parent involvement are primarily the limits of creativity and time.

CULTURAL REFLECTION 14.2

How might professional school counselors from diverse cultural backgrounds view the role of the professional school counselor when encouraging parental/guardian involvement in their children's educational achievement and opportunity? How might students, parents, and educators from diverse backgrounds view the leadership role of the professional school counselor when encouraging parental/guardian involvement? What cultural barriers and access points might exist?

TABLE 14.4 A Dozen Strategies for Increasing Parent Involvement

1. Focus on student achievement (academic and otherwise) as a school and extended community.
2. Acknowledge parent contributions at school or community events, as well as through print and personalized expressions of gratitude.
3. Be specific in giving directions so that parents understand exactly what you expect them to do.
4. Use varied and repeated types of communications to solicit volunteers. These may include personal, phone, or written contacts by educators, other parent volunteers, and even students. Recruitment must be a continuous process.
5. Include parents in the planning and decision-making stages of programs to enhance feelings of ownership.
6. Find out what parents are interested and skilled in doing so that volunteer activities will match parent needs, interests, and skills.
7. Develop a school climate that is positive, inviting, and interactive. Make the school a place that parents want to be.
8. Provide (at least) monthly opportunities for parents to visit the school and interact with the educators and parent volunteers.
9. Provide parents with resources and information that help them to help their children learn at home.
10. Encourage the rest of the family (e.g., grandparents, aunts, uncles, siblings), neighbors, employers, and community leaders to get involved.
11. Select a coordinator of volunteer activities to keep everyone moving in sync. This can be a parent volunteer.
12. Provide niceties (e.g., refreshments, name tags) and remove barriers to participation (e.g., provide transportation and/or babysitting).

COMMUNICATING EFFECTIVELY WITH PARENTS AND GUARDIANS

Although parents and school personnel often seem to have similar goals, both can set up roadblocks to effective communication. Berger (2000) identified six parental roles that inhibit their ability to communicate with schools, albeit often unintentionally: Protector, Inadequate-me, Avoidance, Indifferent parent, Don't make waves, and Club-waving advocate. These roles can potentially become roadblocks to successful communication. Likewise, schools often unintentionally install roadblocks to successful communication. Berger also identified five roles that educators might assume to hamper communication between home and school: Authority figure, Sympathizing-counselor, Pass-the-buck, Protect-the-empire, and Busy teacher. School staff must treat parents and guardians as partners in education, involving each to maximize the potential of all students. Professional school counselors need to connect to and develop authentic relationships with educators and parents who adopt these counterproductive roles to help both groups get what they most desire, a quality education for their students and children. The bottom line is that educators and parents must be helped to adopt what Blue-Banning, Summers, Frankland, Nelson, and Beegle (2004) called the six themes of collaborative family–professional partnerships: communication, commitment, equality, skills, trust, and respect.

Although job and family demands, as well as cultural and socioeconomic backgrounds, pose a temporary roadblock to school involvement, most parents want guidance from schools on ways to support their children's learning. Contact by the professional school counselor is often the first step toward making parents feel welcome in the school during student registration, back-to-school nights, new-families gatherings, and so on. In addition, contact with parents can often be made by letter, website, e-mail, phone call, text message, blog pages or home visit. For example, text messaging or e-mailing a parent/guardian to notify him or her of a child's missing assignment or the need to prepare for an important examination is a fast and efficient way of communicating. Likewise, teachers can post study guides or assignments on websites that students or parents/guardians can access. Technology can make learning and communication more efficient, but parents/guardians, students, and educators must work together to make it so.

Most schools today are concerned about communicating with parents. Many schools provide newsletters and flyers to distribute information to families. This one-way communication is quite common. Ideally, schools will consider some methods of two-way communication, allowing parents an opportunity to express ideas and concerns, give feedback, and interact with school personnel. Some examples of two-way communication are phone calls; e-mail; home visits; text messages; conferences; breakfast with a grade-level team, professional school counselor, or administrator; and community meetings to discuss a particular topic or concern. Educators cannot wait for parents to make the first contact, but must communicate with all families about school programs and procedures, individual student progress, and ways parents can help their children at home.

Although teachers remain the first line of defense in the communication effort, professional school counselors continue to be critical in maintaining ongoing dialogue with families. They may inform parents of special concerns regarding their child, provide updates on their child's progress with modifications and interventions, coordinate workshops to increase parents' skills, or assist in connecting families to needed community-based services.

Through parent workshops, parents learn the importance of two-way communication. If families are to be truly involved as partners in their children's education, they must learn the skills of listening to their children and expressing their concerns regarding their children's learning success. Teachers, as well, need to develop good listening and communicating skills to effectively convey their students' progress. Together, teachers, parents, and professional school counselors make an effective team to support children's learning success.

Many of the following strategies for communicating with families are outlined in the U.S. Department of Education publication *Reaching All Families* (2008). They may be used by professional counselors to open lines of communication with parents and clarify the counselor's role in the school setting:

- *Welcome letter.* Generally sent home by teachers at the beginning of the school year, this letter provides a good opportunity to include the counselor's introduction, as well as to underscore the partnership of parent, teacher, and counselor in meeting the needs of the whole child.
- *Home–school handbook.* Most schools publish a handbook of general school policies and procedures. This is another forum for defining the professional school counselor's role and function.
- *Information packets.* These packets provide more-detailed information about the role of the counselor in the school setting. The packets may include information on school policy and procedures, as well as on services offered by the school. By adding pertinent telephone numbers, this packet becomes an easy reference for parents to access needed people, programs, and services.
- *Calendars.* Weekly, monthly, or annual calendars highlight counselor-planned or -coordinated meetings

and events for parents. They may also include encouraging and informative parenting tips, upcoming community events, family resources, and appropriate television shows and movies. They should be simply designed, only one page in length, and posted on the refrigerator door or family bulletin board for easy reference.

- *School newsletter.* Counselors often maintain a regular column in the school newsletter. This is another opportunity to connect with parents by providing parenting and child development tips from a variety of resources. It is important to use clear, simple language that avoids educational or counseling jargon in these articles and to address the needs of the audience.
- *Open house.* Publicity, planning, and preparation are keys to the success of this annual school event. Counselors can help market the event during other contacts with parents. They should plan to greet the families as they arrive and prepare a formal presentation to explain their role in the school. Counselors will want to encourage parents to contact them and to participate in planned activities for parents held throughout the year. In addition, the counselor may want to have a display table of parent and community resource brochures and other items of interest to families.
- *New-families meeting.* Most new families have registered their children prior to the first day of school. Holding a new-families meeting during the week before school begins will enable the counselor to

connect with these families on a personal basis. The counselor might also give the families a tour of the school, introduce the families to the students' teachers, and answer other questions regarding school procedures and practices. This meeting can serve as a prelude to new-student group sessions held after the start of school.

- *School–parent compacts.* These are voluntary agreements between the home and school to define goals, expectations, and shared responsibilities of schools and parents as partners. Although this is a requirement of schools receiving federal Title I funds, it is a good practice for all schools to build partnerships that help students achieve high standards. Compacts need to be used in combination with other family involvement activities, not as the only way schools communicate with parents.
- *Positive phone calls and text messages.* Traditionally, parents have received a phone call from the school when there was a problem. Imagine the impact of a telephone call from the school that carries information that is positive! This kind of call opens lines of communication, helps parents feel hopeful, and encourages everyone to believe that all children can learn. To be most beneficial, parents need to receive at least two to three positive phone calls over the course of the school year. Counselors can assist and support teachers and administrators in this important effort.

VOICES FROM THE FIELD 14.2   **REPORT CARD TIME**

I work in an all-boys private high school. Usually after first-quarter interim grades are sent home, I will receive numerous phone calls from worried parents concerned about their sons' failing grades. Because we have a Web-based program that allows parents to track their sons' academic progress for each subject, I inquire whether or not they've been using this resource. If they have not, I recommend they do so. I encourage them to contact their sons' teachers through either e-mail or telephone. In most cases, these suggestions address the situation. However, there are occasions where I will recommend a parent conference to include all teachers because the issues are broad in scope, extending to most subjects. The purpose in arranging such a meeting is to allow all parties (e.g., parents, teachers, support staff, outside mental health professionals) an opportunity to share their insights. It is also a way to see if any problems are isolated to a particular teacher/subject or are common among all classes. My intention is that together we can identify the needs of the

student, develop a plan to meet those needs, and establish relationships that will allow for ongoing, effective communication.

I believe that parents are the primary teachers of their children, and therefore it is critical that they have an opportunity to share their knowledge, insights, and experience regarding their sons. Because it is extremely difficult to choose a time that ensures attendance of all parties, the parents and I decide on a date and time to meet. In most cases, the meeting begins 10 minutes after the end of the school day and is usually scheduled for a Tuesday, Wednesday, or Thursday. I have found that Mondays and Fridays are not conducive for gathering as many parties as possible. If a teacher cannot attend because of a scheduling conflict, I ask that he or she contact the parents directly.

We meet in the guidance conference room, which provides a professional environment devoid of interruptions. I begin by welcoming all to create a relaxed and hospitable

(Continued)

atmosphere. Invited members introduce themselves and state their relationship with the student. In advance, I inform the parents that they will speak first to give their impression of the issues, concerns, and needs regarding their son. Each teacher has an opportunity to discuss the student's academic progress regarding homework; tests and quizzes; class participation, which includes behavior; and any other general impressions regarding attitude. The first teacher provides for the parents a copy of the current academic progress report. The parents then have an opportunity to ask questions to seek clarification. After all questions have been thoroughly addressed, the next teacher does the same until all have had the opportunity to share. Teachers will relay to parents strategies that they will continue or introduce in the classroom to address any concerns that were raised. By listening to one another, teachers may be exposed to other effective strategies used by fellow teachers. Each teacher can decide with the parents how communication will occur regarding the student.

After all have shared, the teachers are thanked for their time and insights and are dismissed. The parents and I continue the meeting to discuss and process privately what has just transpired. I will ask them what insights they have gained, and we will discuss any common themes. I will share with the parents my insights regarding student performance and behavior. I will talk about my role and what services I can provide. For example, at one such meeting the student's need for organizational skills came to light. The following day I met with the student to discuss strategies with him such as time management, locker and book bag arrangement, use of a daily planner, and prioritization. I then follow up with all parties by sending an e-mail summarizing the points of concern, the strategies identified, and the format for evaluation and follow-up. I have found this process of parent–teacher conferences to be most effective.

Source: Charles J. Belzner, Professional School Counselor, Mount Saint Joseph High School, Baltimore, Maryland

Summary/Conclusion

It is unlikely that school resources are going to increase over time to the extent necessary to provide optimal professional school counselor-to-student ratios. The challenges facing counselors are many, with too many students to serve and too few resources. Through consultation, professional school counselors facilitate positive growth for students by working directly with teachers and family members and the systems within which these groups live and work. By helping to expand the skills and knowledge of these significant others, professional school counselors, as consultants, extend the reach of their services. Consultation efforts that focus on changing the nature and functioning of a system—be it a school or family system—provide the most promising prevention potential for large numbers of students.

Many professional school counselors have been trained primarily as direct service providers. Changing the mind-set—getting ready to enter the system as an agent of change—presupposes a change in orientation from direct to indirect service provider. A professional school counselor's primary focus is prevention, which can be accomplished most effectively by maximizing the consultation function.

Connecting school, family, and community continues to be a nationwide challenge. Professional school counselors are uniquely positioned to provide both traditional and innovative services to meet the needs of children and families. As we move forward in the 21st century, professional school counselors' use of technology and other innovative approaches will provide new opportunities and forums for schools and parents to connect and communicate.

Activities

1. Spend some time in a school setting. What examples of consultation and collaboration do you witness? How effective do these processes appear to be?
2. Imagine you are a professional school counselor and a teacher comes to you with concerns regarding one of her students, who has been acting out in class. Perform a consultation role play to come up with a plan of action for this teacher. What model of collaboration did you use? Why?

3. Pretend you are a new professional school counselor. Create a list of steps you would take to acclimate to your new school. With whom would you attempt to build relationships? Compare your list with that of another member of your class. What similarities and differences are evident between your lists? Discuss these with your partner.

Systemic Approaches to Counseling Students Experiencing Complex and Specialized Problems

Bradley T. Erford, Vivian V. Lee, and Elana Rock*

Editor's Introduction: Students experiencing academic failure and personal/social problems present a substantial dilemma for schools, families, and communities. This dilemma also presents an extraordinary example of how the transformed professional school counselor can collaborate with and coordinate school and community organizations and resources to benefit these students in need. After a brief introduction recapping the state of affairs for students in the United States, a case is made for professional school counselors as "coordinators of interdisciplinary resources" to collaborate and develop partnerships with community agencies and organizations providing overlapping services with school personnel. Specialized issues in working with specific populations of students also will be introduced (e.g., loss, divorce, dropout prevention, suicide, threat assessment). Perhaps most important, professional school counselors must help educators support students, rather than blaming and punishing them or their parents.

THE CHANGING NEEDS OF STUDENTS AND FAMILIES

American society and the world in general have changed so much in the past few decades that educators at all levels have struggled to keep pace. Although technological innovations and socially progressive movements have yielded many positive and exciting outcomes, the unintended consequences at times seem overwhelming. Rising levels of poverty, substance abuse, and domestic violence are but a few of the major problems presently affecting society (National Institutes of Health, 2014).

Society's fast-paced changes have resulted in myriad mental health dilemmas. Consider but a few of the staggering statistics. The U.S. Department of Health and Human Services (2008) reported that 20% of all children and adolescents have significant emotional impairment requiring treatment, but only about one out of five of these affected children and adolescents actually receives treatment. This is a particularly critical statistic, given that almost half of all students with emotional problems drop out of school. The American Psychiatric Association (APA, 2013) estimated that clinical depression afflicts 3 to 6 million children, contributing to widespread social and emotional problems, including suicide. Suicide continues to be the third leading cause of death among American adolescents. More than 2,000 adolescents kill themselves each year, and approximately 10,000 to 20,000 adolescents attempt suicide annually (National Institute of Mental Health, 2012). Finally, about 30% to 50% of school-aged children referred to community mental health agencies experience conduct problems and behavior disorders, the most common of which is Attention-deficit/Hyperactivity Disorder (AD/HD), which is estimated to exist in

---

*The first edition chapter, "A New Perspective on Counseling At-Risk Youth," was written by Fred Bemak, Rita Chi-Ying Chung, and C. Sally Murphy. Much of their outstanding work on systemic approaches to working with at-risk youth was continued in this fourth edition chapter.

3% to 5% of school-aged children (APA, 2013). Many children with AD/HD are served in the public schools either through special education or under Section 504 of the Rehabilitation Act of 1973; students with AD/HD constitute a large subgroup of the more than 5 million students who annually receive special education services (U.S. Department of Education, Office of Special Education and Rehabilitative Services, 2012).

All in all, there is an increasing trend toward mental and emotional problems among American students, perhaps stemming from rapid societal and technological changes. These problems have been compounded by government funding procedural changes and shortages of affordable community-based mental health services (National Institute of Mental Health, 2012). As so often has been the case, governments and citizens have turned to the schools to help resolve societal difficulties. Fortunately, professional school counselors can play an essential role in the amelioration of many of these mental health concerns.

Twenty-first-century society has the potential to learn from the past and improve on what has been done in previous centuries. This is especially true in light of technological innovations, globalization, dramatic improvements in health care, economic prosperity, and increased consciousness about cultural diversity. Yet, U.S. reports continue to show increasing numbers of youth who are alienated and disconnected from the positive aspects and opportunities of society and have difficult and negative experiences in schools, communities, and families. The result is an increasing quantity of youth who are struggling to mature and develop into contributing members of society.

In previous decades, students experiencing complex problems in the United States were identified as socially and culturally deprived, with a focus on impoverished and minority youth who were labeled as disadvantaged. As the realization dawned on policy makers and professionals working with youth, families, communities, and schools that children and adolescents experiencing complex problems came from all socioeconomic classes and ethnic and racial backgrounds, the characterization of this population changed to include those youth identified as disengaged and not connected to mainstream institutions and society at large. They were not just the minority or urban poor students. They originated in urban, suburban, and rural neighborhoods; were rich and poor; were immigrants and native born; had one or two parents living at home; and came from any racial and ethnic background. They came from the best schools and communities that the United States had to offer, as well as the poorest, most decayed neighborhoods. Anyone could be exposed to community, school, and family violence; family dysfunction; drugs and alcohol; teenage suicide; or problems with peers. It is critical to understand that in the United States, students who experience complex problems are quite diverse. Given the growing numbers of these youth, despite numerous programs to address their problems, it is clear that overall intervention and prevention strategies have been limited in their success.

The *ASCA National Model* (American School Counselor Association, 2012) proposes that the academic, career, and personal/social needs of all children be addressed through comprehensive school counseling programs that focus on systemic change, advocacy, leadership, and collaboration. Helping to address the holistic needs of children requires sound foundational skills in each of these primary areas. This chapter begins by presenting current perspectives and policy implications for working with students experiencing complex problems. The chapter goes on to review some new, innovative, and culturally responsive strategies for working with these students; examines reasons why the needs of this population have not been fully addressed; discusses the accountability for program failure; and provides systemic recommendations for professional school counselors. Finally, the chapter provides information for working with specific subpopulations of students experiencing problems, multicultural implications, and transition issues across grade levels.

RESILIENCY: FOCUSING ON WHAT'S RIGHT, RATHER THAN WHAT'S WRONG

Risk factors are characteristics of students that place them at higher risk of developing mental disorders, academic problems, or personal/social difficulties. It is important to realize that a single risk factor leads to only a slight increase in risk, whereas multiple factors exponentially increase one's risk status. Although risk factors are sometimes helpful when implementing prevention or early intervention models, resilience factors are ordinarily more important to assess because resilience involves characteristics that allow an individual to rebound from adversity or maintain equilibrium of positive functioning when exposed to traumatic events or environmental stressors. The Search Institute (2013) published a list of 40 developmental assets helpful to professional school counselors using a resilience-based or wellness approach to counseling, broken into eight organizing categories.

I. Support: (1) family support, (2) positive family communications, (3) other adult relationships, (4) caring neighborhood, (5) caring school climate, (6) parent involvement in schooling;

II. Empowerment: (7) community values youth, (8) youth as resources, (9) service to others, (10) safety;

III. Boundaries and Expectations: (11) family boundaries, (12) school boundaries, (13) neighborhood boundaries, (14) adult role models, (15) positive peer influence, (16) high expectations;

IV. Constructive Use of Time: (17) creative activities, (18) youth programs, (19) religious community, (20) time at home;

V. Commitment to Learning: (21) achievement motivation, (22) school engagement, (23) homework, (24) bonding to school, (25) reading for pleasure;

VI. Positive Values: (26) caring, (27) equality and social justice, (28) integrity, (29) honesty, (30) responsibility, (31) restraint;

VII. Social Competence: (32) planning and decision making, (33) interpersonal competence, (34) cultural competence, (35) resistance skills, (36) peaceful conflict resolution;

VIII. Positive Identity: (37) personal power, (38) self-esteem, (39) sense of purpose, (40) positive view of personal future.

Professional school counselors can help students develop increased resilience or protective factors by helping to build parent, peer, and school support mechanisms. Brooks (2006) proposed that resilience-enhancing school environments help students develop social competence, caring relationships, high expectations, and opportunities for meaningful interactions, while creating partnerships with families and communities. In short, school environments that surround students with nurturing, caring relationships help them to develop the sense of security and self-respect that foment the success experiences and positive outcomes that create resilience. Professional school counselors play a leadership role in creating the systemic changes that lead to nurturing, caring environments and educators (ASCA, 2012). Although we are well aware of the problems students encounter inside and outside schools, we are more concerned with pursuing solutions for students now and in the future, and resiliency models hold promise for helping students during current and future times of trouble.

IDENTIFYING AND CATEGORIZING STUDENTS WITH COMPLEX PROBLEMS

Although attempts to address at-risk youth have been long-standing, remarkably as we move into the 21st century, there is still ongoing debate and controversy over defining this population. For the purposes of this chapter, students are at risk when they lack the familial, community, cultural, institutional, and societal supports necessary to develop and grow in an environment that is safe, positive, healthy, and conducive to personal, social, cultural, intellectual, spiritual, economic, and physical development. The absence of these supports inhibits the potential for development as a person and the potential for choices and opportunities necessary to contribute as a productive member of society. Healthy growth and development for youth must include the context of the family and other social networks; environment; health and nutrition; opportunities for spiritual development; and a positive interaction with the surrounding community, society, and culture within which one lives. The quality of a child's or an adolescent's physical, mental, emotional, social, spiritual, and economic health significantly correlates to being at risk; therefore, prevention and intervention program design and implementation must include a holistic framework.

We prefer to avoid using the term *at-risk* when possible because use of that term leads to five potential problem areas. First, when using this term, there is a danger of discounting resiliency. Potential strengths, coping abilities, and strategies for handling the variables that constitute being at risk are disregarded with the shift in focus to pathology, problems, and weaknesses. Second, the label *at-risk* has strong negative associations and stigmatizes youth. Chances of moving out of an at-risk status are nominal, leaving many youth labeled for their entire childhood and adolescence. Third, when youth are identified as being at risk during adolescence, the prospect of being at risk is no longer a question, but becomes a fact. This leaves far less opportunity for designing prevention programs that would affect these youths' future, given the permanency associated with the label being designated during adolescence. It determines that being at risk, in essence, means "deep trouble," which has implications for how we regard, treat, and conceive of this population. A fourth problem with categorizing youth as at risk is that the term has been used as a catchall phrase that does not differentiate the risk level one is facing or the conditions, causes, or problem behaviors associated with that risk. This generalization of the term does not help in defining the problems or the strategies best employed to address them. Fifth, there is no sensitivity to or awareness of cultural differences related to at-risk behavior. For example, some cultures (including various cultural minorities in the United States) have far greater tolerance for youth behaviors than other cultures do. This has been differentiated as "broad socialization," or more open and tolerant practices that minimize social constraints, versus "narrow socialization," where obedience and conformity to community norms are demanded, thus reducing experimentation and sensation-seeking behaviors.

Cultures can be further differentiated as child centered and not child centered. In child-centered cultures, there is greater acceptance of children and support in developing personal, family, and community social skills within a social context, resulting in youth demonstrating higher levels of achievement and greater self-reliance. In contrast, non-child-centered cultures prioritize individuality over the family and community at large and have less tolerance for children. In non-child-centered cultures, children are shown to be more aggressive, to feel rejected and disengaged more often, and, subsequently, to be more independent. In turn, the adults in non-child-centered cultures exhibit greater hostility toward and less compassion for people in need, and their response to problems is in a reactive crisis mode that many of the schools, communities, and families in the United States face today. These problems contribute to confusion in characterizing and identifying youth with complex problems and are reflected in the lack of effective programming to reduce problems such as teenage pregnancy, substance abuse, violence, juvenile delinquency, gangs, school dropout, and school failure.

SYSTEMIC APPROACHES TO WORKING WITH STUDENTS EXPERIENCING COMPLEX PROBLEMS

Historically, the definition of *at-risk* has been based on one of four approaches: predictive, descriptive, unilateral, or school factors, with each approach having its flaws (Hixson & Tinzmann, 1990). For example, the predictive approach is based on a deficit model that emphasizes what is wrong or missing in the individual student, family, or community. The descriptive method focuses on after-the-fact reporting and therefore addresses the issue after the behavior has occurred. The unilateral technique assumes that all students are at risk by virtue of living in today's society. Finally, the school factors approach states that schools are solely accountable and therefore absolves parents of any responsibility.

To further illustrate, look more closely at the categorization of students solely by the criterion of academic achievement and success. When considering the large and growing number of immigrant and refugee students entering the United States, it is increasingly apparent that psychosocial adjustment, acculturation, and psychological well-being are not reflected solely by academic performance. Yet when complex problems experienced by students are standardized and measured by academic success, it is not reflective of the complex and demanding issues faced by this population. Designating immigrant and refugee students or any students by virtue of their

academic success automatically limits the area of concern to schools, neglecting other aspects of the students' lives, rather than examining the issues within a social context that would include collaboration with parents, community agencies, businesses, and government agencies. This, in turn, places the onus of responsibility for intervention and prevention strictly on school personnel, leading to the conclusion that problems are related only to the confines of the bricks and mortar of a school building. These assumptions are not only misleading, but also egregiously incorrect.

Helping students with complex problems cuts across several disciplines, including mental health, education, public health, substance abuse, business, social services, juvenile justice, and child and family services. Many professionals working within these various systems are disheartened by failures to reach these students. They are frustrated, burned out, and even angry at the lack of responsiveness to honest intervention attempts. These attitudes frequently result in schools, programs, and society giving up on those youth in most need and in trouble. In fact, a culture has emerged that blames the child in more subtle and sophisticated ways and molds itself into a 21st-century version of "blaming the victim." This defeatist attitude is observed in principals and other educators who want certain children out of their school, programs that identify children and adolescents as "too difficult" to benefit from their good services, families that are labeled and stigmatized as "unreachable," and neglected communities that are considered dangerous and "too far gone."

These negative attitudes toward students with complex problems are fueling the trend toward containment, punishment, and banishment, rather than treatment and prevention. The emphasis is on a "quick fix," rather than an in-depth examination of the problem from family, community, and societal perspectives. For example, Americans are more concerned with metal detectors than community prevention models, as demonstrated after the flurry of public school shootings in different parts of the United States. The emphasis on punishment not only results in resentment toward and disregard of the disenfranchised youth of today, but also marginalizes and segregates youth for whom there is little hope and on whom society has essentially given up. This is a dangerous proposition and will ultimately result in disenfranchised students who lead difficult and frustrating lives and who lack the skills and knowledge to participate in society in healthy, positive ways. Even more alarming is that a significant number of these youth will contribute to growing social problems and become an economic and social burden in the country.

Contrary to this subtle, but growing, movement is the contention that all children can be reached. But this requires a dramatic step in redefining the programs to fit the changing needs of youth in trouble. Rather than reject and abandon youth who do not respond to traditional programs, it is critical that professionals develop new and innovative strategies for working with families, communities, and schools to reach those children now regarded as unreachable. This requires support on multiple levels: new ways of training professionals at the university level to work with these students; innovative programming that goes beyond what we currently propose; policy changes; an emphasis on prevention and intervention, rather than crisis management; interdisciplinary cooperation to address the complexity of the problems that youth face; and a shift in attitude from control and punishment to intervention and prevention. Underlying this support is the firm belief and hope in the dignity and possibility of each child and adolescent.

SYSTEMS FAILURES: WHO IS TO BLAME?

There are a large number of facilities in the United States that have the potential to effectively serve at-risk youth. For example, there are more than 85,000 public and 25,000 private elementary and secondary schools; 400 national organizations (e.g., Boy Scouts, 4-H, YMCA); 17,000 community-based programs; and 6,000 libraries, recreational centers, and police departments that provide programs for youth. Even so, schools today, despite valiant efforts to prevent students from dropping out, still encounter a 7% dropout rate (U.S. Department of Education, National Center for Educational Statistics, 2012). The inability to reach these students reflects the inadequacy of programming strategies, rather than a belief that these students are hopeless and won't respond to programming.

For a number of years, at-risk youth have been blamed for their problems, whether done consciously or more subtly. The general consensus has been that youth fail our programs, rather than programs failing our youth. This has perpetuated a system of hopelessness and acceptance of failure and directly contradicts a reevaluation of current prevention and intervention methodologies that have a substantial rate of failure, yet continue to be funded. We contend that youth do not fail, but that programs and systems have a long-standing record of failing these students. By blaming children and adolescents who are already powerless, programs are not only negligent in protecting our youth, but also add to and perpetuate the existing problems faced by this population. If we truly want to help our youth engage in future opportunities, we can no longer blame the youth, but

must critically evaluate our intervention strategies and admit that they may not be effective; at the same time, we must move beyond the blame and work to redesign successful interventions.

To address the complexity of problems that interrelate with youth, peer groups, family, school, and community, it is critical that we not only reexamine our current strategies, but also redesign and develop new workable interventions. Service integration is a robust model that can address the complexity of interrelated problems facing youth. Many programs and interventions with students experiencing complex difficulties focus on problem areas that are categorized by distinct behaviors. This results in intensive and expensive programs that are aimed at specific issues such as substance abuse, teenage pregnancy, anger management, juvenile delinquency, school failure, or suicide risk.

Programs that are narrow in focus and aim to address isolated problems fail the students in need of services for more complex issues. It is important to adapt intervention strategies to the complex needs of the target population from the perspective of an interagency response that is not limited to schools. Furthermore, professional school counselors are in a pivotal position to lead this endeavor, given that they are based in schools. Schools have the potential to be the focal point for all youth during childhood and adolescence.

WHY HAVEN'T NEEDS OF STUDENTS EXPERIENCING COMPLEX PROBLEMS BEEN ADDRESSED?

There are five major reasons for the lack of commitment to the needs of students with complex problems. First, funding priorities have not been focused on this population within the broader context of multiple problems. Funding of intervention and prevention programs must be reevaluated, and cross-disciplinary, research-based, interagency funding must be supported. Simplifying the problems of youth with complex problems into discrete categories is insufficient, yet many funding initiatives remain limited in scope or breadth. Second, it is difficult to change systems. Professional school counselors and other professionals should study systems change theory and practice, learning how to move resistant systems that are set in their ways. Third, the nation does not have a consensual moral commitment to working with this population. As discussed previously, the current national trend in the United States emphasizes punishment and excommunication from one's community or society, rather than intervention strategies that aim to reengage youth into mainstream cultures.

A fourth reason for the lack of commitment to students with complex problems is the absence of societal, institutional, and community commitment to address these problems for a disengaged and essentially powerless population. Neither is there a true commitment reflected in school, state, and federal policies. For example, schools that are measured by student performance on standardized tests may prefer that problem students in jeopardy of failing those exams transfer to another school or leave school entirely. Essentially, this translates into education for some of our students, not all. Finally, graduate-level university training of professionals often lacks innovation and responsiveness to addressing modern-day concerns of students with complex problems as part of the curriculum. This can be seen in training for professional school counselors, which rarely focuses specifically on this population of students in courses such as career counseling, group counseling, individual counseling, family counseling, and human growth and development or during practicums and internships when counselors in training have the opportunity to work in agencies that serve this population. With these reasons in mind, the remainder of the chapter reviews some of the complex issues students may present to professional school counselors that lead to more complex problems and academic challenges.

CULTURAL REFLECTION 15.1

How might professional school counselors from diverse cultural backgrounds view the role of the professional school counselor working with youth with complex issues to support student educational achievement and opportunity? How might students, parents, and educators from diverse backgrounds view the leadership role of the professional school counselor when working with youth with complex issues? What cultural barriers and access points might exist?

WORKING WITH YOUTH WITH COMPLEX PROBLEMS

There are many issues that lead students to struggle academically or emotionally. This section identifies and addresses several of the more prominent issues that professional school counselors must prepare themselves to address, including crisis intervention, suicide, school violence, substance abuse, divorce, teen pregnancy, delinquency, dropout, and peer conflict. This list is by no means comprehensive, nor is the treatment given to each topic in this chapter. What follows is meant to educate and provide some strategies for assessing or intervening with students experiencing these complex issues.

Responding to Crisis Situations

During the past two decades, there has been a heightened awareness of the need for crisis intervention in schools. Crises in schools can affect anyone from a single student to the entire school community. Experiences of violence, disaster, and trauma can leave students without sufficient resources to cope. Crises that may affect the school community include suicide, loss, medical emergencies, family trauma, school shootings, gang activities, abuse, and natural disasters (e.g., hurricanes, floods, earthquakes, tornadoes). Professional school counselors play a key role in planning and implementing crisis response in schools. Consequently, professional school counselors need to understand what constitutes a crisis, know how to intervene effectively, and be able to help implement a response plan to schoolwide crises (Jackson-Cherry & Erford, 2014).

DEFINITION OF CRISIS The term *crisis* has been defined in many ways (e.g., James & Gilliland, 2013). The Chinese characters that represent *crisis* mean both "danger" and "opportunity." A crisis represents danger because it initially is experienced as an intolerable difficulty that threatens to overwhelm the individual. Unless the person obtains relief, the crisis potentially can cause severe psychological, cognitive, physical, and behavioral consequences. In contrast, the term represents opportunity because, during times of crisis, individuals are usually more receptive to help. Prompt, skillful interventions not only may prevent the development of sustained problems, but also may help individuals to develop new coping patterns, thereby increasing their ability to adapt and function in the future.

The concept of crisis is not simple or straightforward. With all crises, stress is a major component (Steigerwald, 2010a). However, individuals experience stress in different ways, with some students having stronger coping skills, resources, and support systems than others. An event that is perceived as relatively minor by one student, such as failing an exam or being "dumped" by a girlfriend, may be perceived as a crisis by another student. Also, the timing and intensity of the crisis, as well as the number of other stressors the student is experiencing, can impact the complexity of the crisis situation (Newsome & Gladding, 2014).

CRISIS INTERVENTION *Crisis intervention* differs from counseling in several ways. Crisis intervention refers to the immediate action a professional school counselor takes to "provide the support and direction that the student in crisis cannot provide for him or herself" (Steigerwald, 2010a, pp. 830–831). It is an action-oriented approach designed to help students cope with a particular life situation that has thrown them off course. Goals of crisis intervention include helping the student to defuse emotions, organize, and interpret what has happened; to integrate the traumatic event into his or her life story; and to interpret the event in a way that is meaningful. Crisis intervention is time limited and should not be confused with more long-term postcrisis counseling, which may be needed and which usually necessitates referral to other helping professionals. Trusty and Brown (2005, pp. 262–263), Jackson-Cherry and Erford (2014, Chapter 11), and Steigerwald (2010b, p. 840) suggested several guidelines for school counselors to follow in crisis counseling. These are summarized in Table 15.1

CRISIS RESPONSE PLANS At times, a crisis affects a large number of students, and a systematic response from the school is required (ASCA, 2012; Jackson-Cherry & Erford, 2014). Examples of crises that may dictate a systemic response include student homicide or suicide, unexpected death, and natural disasters. Although crises are, unfortunately, an uncontrollable aspect of school life, the manner in which school professionals respond to crisis can be controlled. Professional school counselors often play leadership roles in helping schools develop and implement a systemic crisis plan, which is comprehensive, is well planned, mobilizes resources, and operates quickly (Steigerwald, 2010b).

Crisis response plans should exist both on a district level and on an individual-school level. Professional school counselors may be members of the district and school critical response teams or solely members of the school-level response team. In either case, the professional school counselor takes a leadership role in the prevention, intervention, and postincident support of school critical responses (ASCA, 2012). In this role, professional school counselors provide individual and group counseling; consult with administrators, teachers, parents, and professionals; and coordinate services within the school and the community.

Crisis plans need to be put in place before a crisis occurs. Crisis response planning committees and crisis response teams (CRTs) are instrumental in planning for, coordinating, and implementing a systemic crisis response. James and Gilliland (2013) recommended the following minimum requirements for a school crisis plan:

- *Physical requirements:* Identify locations for temporary counseling offices. An operations/communications center should be identified where crisis intervention procedures are monitored, needs are

---

TABLE 15.1 Crisis Counseling Guidelines

1. *Respond immediately.* The longer students wait for counseling to occur, the more difficult it is to cope with the crisis.
2. *Be directive at first.* Environmental interventions may be necessary, especially when there are safety concerns. Being directive and caring provides structure, predictability, safety, and comfort to the students.
3. *Listen actively and nonjudgmentally as students tell their stories.* Attempt to view the crisis from their perspective. Pay close attention to feelings, and help normalize them. Emotions typically associated with crisis include confusion, sadness, loss of control, loss of self-worth, stigma, loneliness, fear of mortality, guilt, and anger.
4. *Follow a holistic approach.* Observe and assess the physical, behavioral, emotional, and cognitive domains of the student in crisis.
5. *Begin work where the student is experiencing the most impairment.*
6. *Get the facts surrounding the crisis.* The counselor needs to understand the situation to assess the students' reactions.
7. *Sustain relationships and resources.* Help students keep lines of communication open and use family, peer, school, and community resources for support. Watch for isolation behavior.
8. *Keep a multicultural awareness of the students' expressions of emotions, perspectives, and behaviors.*
9. *Do not offer false reassurance.* Students who have experienced crises face difficult tasks. Work toward generating realistic hope.
10. *Help students take action.* Helping students move from the victim role to the actor role is a key component of crisis counseling.
11. *Determine whether the effects are long-lasting and whether a referral for further assessment and counseling is needed.*
12. *Do not work in isolation.* Involve the student's support system and work with a consultant or supervisor.
13. *Continue to develop knowledge and skills in crisis intervention by reading current literature about the topic and by participating in crisis training workshops.* Such workshops are sponsored by the American Red Cross and the National Organization for Victim Assistance (NOVA).

assessed, and information for the media is disseminated. Also suggested are a break room, a first-aid room, and an information center designed to handle media personnel and to facilitate parent communication.

- *Logistics:* Address specific areas that need consideration as an intervention plan is implemented. For example, attention needs to be given to the manner in which on-site and off-site communication will take place. Other logistics that need attention include providing (a) procedural checklists to ensure that the intervention plan is being followed, (b) building plans for emergency personnel, and (c) food and drink for crisis personnel.

- *Crisis response:* A sequential plan for crisis response includes gathering and verifying the facts, assessing the impact of the crisis to determine what assistance is needed, providing triage assessment to determine who is most in need of immediate attention, providing psychological first aid as a first-order response, having a model in place, providing crisis intervention, and following through by briefing, debriefing, and demobilizing. (pp. 553–558)

It is essential for professional school counselors to be familiar with their district and school crisis response plans. If no such plan is in place, professional school counselors will want to work with administrators and other school personnel to create and implement a plan to respond to crises. Moreover, professional school counselors can be instrumental in leading workshops in the school and community to communicate the plan to others. A helpful resource that provides information and guidance for crisis planning is *The School Crisis Guide*, produced by the National Education Association (NEA, 2007).

THEORY INTO PRACTICE 15.1

CRISIS MANAGEMENT FOR THE HOLIDAYS

It was a Sunday evening, and I had just finished decorating my Christmas tree and wrapping the last Christmas gifts when I got a phone call from one of the principals with whom I work. She went on to explain, "Katie, we have a big problem. Mr. Smith just murdered Mrs. Smith and is on the loose. We don't have many more details, but we think that one of their children may have witnessed it."

My job as a professional school counselor is somewhat unique in that I am assigned to four nonpublic schools, but even with my high caseload, I never expected to have a crisis like this one on my hands. After taking a minute to digest the information that I had just received, I knew that I needed to get in touch with my supervisor to come up with a plan of how we could best help the school community that would be experiencing immeasurable shock and grief. This particular school is part of a very tightly knit community where it is rare to find a person whose grandfather or grandmother didn't also grow up in the town. We knew that there would be a ripple effect throughout not only the school, but also the community and that the rumor mill would be swirling.

Mr. and Mrs. Smith had three children together, and two of them attended my school. Along with their children, the Smiths had seven nieces and nephews and many more family friends who attended the same school. Mrs. Smith had been active with the Home and School Association, was a homeroom mother, and also volunteered lots of time working at the school. She was well known and loved by students and teachers alike. I knew

that I would need a lot of help from my colleagues in handling this situation. I am fortunate that I work for an organization that employs 19 professional school counselors, all of whom can be on call for crisis situations.

On Monday morning, eight additional counselors arrived at the school with me. We came up with a plan of how to respond. First thing in the morning, we would meet with all the teachers and staff members to answer any questions and let them know of our plan for the day. Two counselors went down to handle the parents who we knew would show up wanting their questions answered and reassurance that the children were safe at school, even though Mr. Smith was on the loose. Two counselors stayed in the office for any student, staff member, or parent who needed to talk. One counselor walked around and checked in with the teachers, maintenance man, lunch moms, and so on. The rest of us went around to the classrooms to dispel rumors and process what we could with the classes. The upper grades knew more and had heard more about the situation so it follows that more time was spent with the older students. In the Smith boys' classes, we discussed not only their feelings and concerns, but also what to do when the boys returned to school.

Needless to say, instead of going to my other schools that week, I spent every day at this school. On the day of the funeral, another counselor and I went to the viewing to be there for the students and teachers and to express our sorrow for the family. At the funeral, we had a counselor available to sit with each grade (1–8) in case anyone had to leave the chapel due to distress. Afterward, we went back into the classrooms to process any feelings that came up during the funeral. The funeral was the last day of school before Christmas break began. The Smith boys were due back at school after the break, so I arranged to be at the school on their first day back.

As I'm sure was true for many involved in this crisis, that Christmas was a difficult one for me. It was hard to leave what was happening at work behind. It was hard to stop thinking about the children whose mother was no longer there for them on Christmas morning because she was dead due to the actions of their father, who was now in jail.

In the weeks that followed, I got in touch with one of the local hospital's grief support programs to get resource information for the family. The mother of Mrs. Smith got custody of the Smith boys and wanted to do everything she could to help her grandchildren. I provided counseling referrals for the grandmother, as she had lost her daughter. I got in touch with a certified trauma specialist and arranged for her to do a training session with the faculty and staff so that they would know more about what grief looks like in children and learn ways that they could support the Smith boys. Many hours were spent on the phone speaking with parents who knew Mrs. Smith well. Some of my time was also spent consulting with the Smith children's teachers about the children's well-being and capacity for completing school work. I offered counseling to the students who were relatives or close family friends of the Smiths. For the second half of the school year, most of my one day per week at this school was spent responding to this crisis situation in one way or another.

Nearly 10 months later, it appears as if the school community is healing. When this crisis first happened, there was national media coverage of this case, and not all of it was accurate. Every once in a while the local news stations cover this story again, and this attention is difficult for the family and for the school community because it reopens the wounds that have begun to heal. I expect that when Mr. Smith's trial begins, the rumors will once again begin circulating throughout the school, and uncomfortable feelings will surface. There is a chance that the healing that this school community has achieved until this point may be halted or set back.

Source: Katie Young, Professional School Counselor, Pennsylvania

Suicide

Suicide is a real problem in schools, particularly high schools, and professional school counselors need to be prepared to assess suicidal ideation, behaviors, and risk, as well as be ready to intervene decisively. As discussed in Chapter 7, some states and many school systems require that professional school counselors inform parents or guardians of students demonstrating suicidal thoughts or behaviors. One is well advised to take all threats seriously and be very familiar with state laws and regulations, as well as local school system policies and procedures. Although the next section focuses on assessment of suicidal threat, a comprehensive explanation of how to intervene in cases of student suicidal threat is well beyond the scope of this text. While the student is in the school, it is common practice to be sure the student is in the company of an adult at all times and that contact is made with a parent or guardian as soon as possible. Many school systems require that the parent pick the child up from school. Professional counselors can be valuable consultants to parents, facilitating transitions to treatment with mental health professionals, community agencies, or psychiatric inpatient facilities. Professional school counselors are well advised to find out the scope of community services available to students in crisis to develop a referral network that can be acted on instantaneously.

ASSESSING SUICIDAL IDEATION AND BEHAVIORS

Professional school counselors should pay close attention to student suicidal ideation and behaviors during an initial interview and revisit the issue periodically during the course of treatment. Nearly all suicides are avoidable. A current and thorough understanding of the prevalence statistics across population demographics is essential to effective practice. A brief presentation can be found in Table 15.2, and professional counselors are encouraged to delve more deeply into this area of the literature.

Predicting who will attempt suicide is extremely difficult, which is why experienced professional school counselors take every student with suicidal ideation very seriously. Depressed, suicidal students may appear at minimal risk one day and the next day may experience a situational, environmental stressor or a frustrating, negative interpersonal encounter that leads to an attempted suicide. Pay particularly close attention to students with expressions of hopelessness and helplessness and alcohol or other substance use disorders.

In addition to assessing risk of suicide, professional school counselors should assess for resiliency and protective factors, activities, or people in a student's life that provide responsibilities, meaning, and hope for the student (Jackson-Cherry & Erford, 2014). Such factors may include significant supportive relationships (e.g., parents or relatives, friends, coworkers) or purpose (e.g., work or school, caregiving responsibilities).

TABLE 15.2 Demographic Parameters, Clinical Conditions, and Suicide Risk

Suicide is the 11th leading cause of death in the United States.

Suicide is the third leading cause of death in the 15- to 24-year-old range and the seventh leading cause of death in the 5- to 14-year-old range.

Females are more likely to attempt suicide; males are more likely to complete a suicide attempt, generally because they choose more lethal means (e.g., guns).

Seventy-three percent of all suicides are completed by White males. Of these, the highest prevalence occurs in the over-85-years-old category.

Married clients are at lower risk of suicide than single, divorced, or widowed clients.

Parents responsible for minor children are at lower risk.

Individuals who have attempted suicide are more likely to make future attempts.

Clients with depression who have experienced a recent loss (e.g., divorce, separation) are at greater risk of suicide.

Certain personality factors may increase risk (e.g., perfectionism, impulsivity, pessimism, aloofness, dependency).

Clients with personality disorders (e.g., Borderline PD, Antisocial PD) account for about one third of completed suicides.

Firearms account for nearly one half of all suicides. Hanging, strangulation, and suffocation are the next three most lethal means. Taking most poisons and medications have low levels of lethality.

Of counselors in professional practice, about 70% have treated a client who attempted suicide, and 28% had a client who committed suicide.

Source: National Institute of Mental Health (2012)

When assessing suicidal risk, it is essential to determine both the existence and the intensity of suicidal thoughts and behaviors and to respond quickly and decisively with a treatment plan to immediately address student needs and safety. Table 15.3 presents the seven areas Stelmacher (1995) recommended as the focus during an interview for determining suicidal risk.

Several instruments have been published that professional school counselors may find useful adjuncts to the interview when assessing suicidal ideation and behaviors. These include the Suicide Probability Scale (SPS; Cull & Gill, 1992), Beck Scale for Suicide Ideation (BSSI; Beck & Steer, 1991), Beck Hopelessness Scale (BHS; Beck & Steer, 1993), and Suicide Ideation Questionnaire (SIQ; Reynolds,

TABLE 15.3 Seven Facets of Suicidal Risk Determination and Some Related Brief, Important Queries

1. *Verbal communication.* Has the student verbalized suicidal thoughts overtly or subtly? Are there themes of escape, self-mutilation, or self-punishment? Has the student ever thought of hurting herself?

2. *Plan.* Does the student have a plan or idea about how he may kill himself? Is the plan concrete, detailed, and specific? Is it feasible? Does it contain provisions to prevent rescue?

3. *Method.* Has the student chosen a specific method of self-harm? Firearms are the most lethal and commonly used method by students who complete suicide.

4. *Preparation.* Has the student obtained the means to carry out the plan? Has he written a note or contacted others to resolve old business, put finances in order, given away possessions, or "said good-bye"? Preparation is a good index of the seriousness of a suicidal attempt.

5. *Stressors.* What are the student's past, present, and future stressors (e.g., loss, employment, illness)? What are important loss-related anniversary dates?

6. *Mental state.* What is the student's degree of hopelessness? Is the student impulsive, using alcohol, or both? Is the student despondent, angry, or distraught? Particular concern is warranted during periods of remission (e.g., uplifted spirits) because this may indicate a decision to commit suicide was made and the plan is progressing.

7. *Hopelessness.* What is the student's level of perceived hopelessness? To what degree is death viewed as the only way to relieve pain? This area is particularly important to assess when students do not verbalize suicidal thoughts.

Source: Based on "Assessing Suicidal Clients," by Z. T. Stelmacher, in *Clinical Personality Assessment: Practical Approaches,* edited by J. N. Butcher, 1995, New York: Oxford University Press, pp. 336–379

1988). The SIQ was specifically designed for use with school-aged youth. Professional school counselors who use these instruments must use caution because of the potential for clients to underreport the severity of suicidal thoughts and behaviors. In addition, checklists and rating scales rarely differentially weight suicide risks. Thus, at most, scores should be used as helpful guidelines. As with most psychological tests, students who respond openly and honestly generally yield accurate scores and interpretations; those who respond in a guarded or deceitful manner do not.

Violence and Threat Assessment

Several highly publicized school shootings have heightened public interest, and fears, related to school safety. Thankfully, such instances are rare, but unfortunately other types of school violence are not rare. Compared with a generation ago, students today are more likely to bring a weapon to school, fight on school grounds, and bully or harass other students.

BULLYING, HARASSMENT, ABUSE, AND DATING VIOLENCE One factor that heightens one's chances of being at-risk of academic problems is isolation from societal, cultural, school, family, or peer interactions and institutions. Such isolation may lead to victimization and perpetuation of violence in the forms of bullying and harassment, abuse and neglect, and suicide. A form of peer-on-peer abuse, bullying and harassment occur throughout American society and the world and may serve as a contributing factor to homicide and suicide (Borum, Cornell, Modzeleski, & Jimerson, 2010). Although these potentially devastating results have been infrequently observed, the more insidious long- and short-term influences of bullying and harassment may impact not only victims, but also perpetrators and bystanders.

Bullying and harassment are caused when an imbalance of power (e.g., social, physical, emotional) is created. It is maintained when others, including adults or peer bystanders, do not act to balance the inequalities. Failure of adults and bystanders to act encourages perpetuation of the abusers' reputation as strong individuals and the victims' reputation as weak. The quickest way to interrupt the cycle of bullying or harassment is for adults and peers to intervene. Thus, teaching adults and peers the importance of intervening and how to effectively intervene is a critical role the professional school counselor can undertake. Bullying and harassment have become so problematic in schools that a number of states have passed antibullying and antiharassment legislation or regulations prohibiting these behaviors—accompanied by stiff consequences for school system employees who do not intervene appropriately. This area of prevention and intervention becomes a huge opportunity for teaching advocacy skills. Importantly, this includes "indirect" forms of harassment and bullying, such as spreading vicious, hurtful rumors or socially excluding a victim—called relational aggression. Cyberbullying has become an insidious extension of relational aggression, where technology and social media are used to perpetuate relational aggression and destroy the social connectedness of students to the peer culture. Professional school counselors should ensure that school policies and procedures remain up to date to address newer forms of cyberbullying and relational aggression as they emerge. Technology allows for marvelous innovations and social accommodations, but can also be used to bully and disconnect students from the social fabric.

Physical and sexual abuse and neglect are also widespread problems in society, often resulting in devastating long-term emotional problems, including anxiety, depression, substance abuse, and other serious psychiatric disturbances. Emotional and social isolation is particularly problematic with individuals who have been abused or neglected—a result of the embarrassment and secrecy endemic to the acts. This social and emotional isolation is not restricted to children who are directly abused; children who witness domestic abuse, as when their mother is battered, have similar isolative reactions. But violence in significant or intimate relationships is no longer related only to the home and kept behind closed doors.

Dating violence has experienced an unfortunate rise over the past decade and affects many teenagers. McLeod, Muldoon, and Hays (2014) reported that about 9% of high school girls reported dating violence. The incidence jumps to nearly one third of college-attending females. Victims of dating violence displayed increased risks of suicidal thoughts and actions, substance use, depression, and risky sexual behavior (Howard & Wang, 2003; McLeod et al., 2014).

THREAT ASSESSMENT Violent acts committed on school property increased sharply during the 1980s, but contrary to popular opinion, they have been steadily declining since 1993 (Rollin, Kaiser-Ulrey, Potts, & Creason, 2003). Sensationalized school shootings in various parts of the United States have created a quite different public perception. One of the benefits of this attention is an increased research focus on the topic, both scholarly and governmental, particularly by the Federal Bureau of Investigation (FBI) and the U.S. Secret Service. Both of these agencies have developed protocols and procedures that have been used by school crisis management and public safety specialists. The FBI report can be accessed at http://www.fbi.gov/stats-services/publications/school-shooter. Although much of what follows was developed to understand school shooters, a great deal of the information generalizes to less drastic forms of school violence.

From the outset, it is important for professional school counselors to understand that there is no foolproof profile of violent youth or list of risk factors that allows certain identification of youth as violent. Indeed, the research is clear that the majority of youth who display multiple risk factors never become violent offenders. Likewise, many violent offenders do not display many of the risk factors commonly considered by experts to indicate increased risk. Violence, by its nature, is unpredictable. Also, an exclusive focus on identification, to the exclusion of prevention and intervention, is misguided. Threat assessment, developmental programming, prevention, and intervention are all part of a comprehensive school safety program. Threat assessment is an important facet that will be expounded on later. The developmental, prevention, and intervention facets will be addressed at the end of this section and later in this chapter in the section that deals with conflict resolution and peer mediation.

Historically, mental health practitioners have been no better at predicting violent behavior in clients than informed nonprofessionals have been; recent innovations have improved predictability somewhat, although the accuracy is very far from perfect. Importantly, violence is brought on by multiple factors, not just one, making it a complex problem, from both diagnostic and treatment perspectives.

Most violent students are not planful, although exceptions certainly exist. Violent students often feel desperate and panic stricken, fearing that others want to hurt them. Striking out violently is a means of defense and, at times, retribution. In general, males aged 15 to 24 have a higher risk of violence. Race is not ordinarily associated with violence risk, but students with lower socioeconomic status have higher associated risks. Students with thought disorders (e.g., hallucinations, delusions) and disorders of impulse (e.g., AD/HD, conduct disorder) present with higher degrees of risk. Of course, those with a history of violent acts are at greater risk for future violent acts (Wilson, 2004). Environmental risk factors include unstable family and peer relationships, association with criminal or sexual predators, association with antisocial peers, educational problems, and living in an urban environment.

Specific to school shooting incidences, motivation includes revenge for social isolation and bullying. The FBI reported that attackers frequently engage in "behaviors of concern," although not necessarily aberrant behaviors, prior to the incident. Most of the time, the attacker revealed his plan to at least one other person not involved in the attack, and most had access to guns and previous experience using guns. Finally, although the notion of a school shooter as a loner is often true, this is certainly not always the case.

The FBI defines a threat as intent to do harm or act out violently against someone or something. It classifies threats of violence into four categories.

1. *Indirect threats* are ambiguous and vague, but with implied violence. The phrasing of an indirect threat ordinarily suggests that a violent act may occur, not necessarily that it will occur.
2. *Veiled threats* do not specifically threaten violence, but strongly infer the possibility.
3. *Conditional threats* warn of violence if certain conditions or demands are not met (e.g., extortion).
4. *Direct threats* are clear, straightforward, and explicit warnings of a specific act against a specific target.

The FBI also presented guidelines for determining the seriousness of a threat. *Low-level threats* are vague and indirect, lack realism, and pose minimal risks to the victim or public. The specific content of a low-level threat ordinarily leads to the conclusion that the student is unlikely to carry out the threatened act of violence. *Medium-level threats* are somewhat more direct, concrete, and plausible than low-level threats are, but frequently they do not appear entirely realistic. Some evidence of rudimentary planning is often apparent (e.g., place, time, method), but the plan lacks detail, and preparations to fulfill the plan are absent. Often students making a medium-level threat will state "I mean it" to convey a seriousness to the threat. A *high-level threat* is direct, specific, and plausible, with a serious and imminent danger to the safety of the victim or public. Plans have been made and concrete steps have been taken to prepare for the act (e.g., obtaining weapon). High-level threats almost always require the involvement of law enforcement officials.

When assessing threat, the FBI suggests a four-pronged assessment model involving attention to the student's personality, family dynamics, school dynamics, and social dynamics. Table 15.4 provides specific facets of each of these areas that the professional school counselor should attend to during a threat assessment. The literature is replete with suggestions for helping to mitigate and minimize violence. Table 15.5 provides a short list.

The U.S. surgeon general reported that commitment to school, intelligence, intolerance toward deviance, and a positive social orientation were important protective factors (U.S. Department of Health and Human Services, U.S. Public Health Service, Office of Surgeon General, 2001). Adult mentoring programs have also had positive effects, as have programs designed to enhance positive social interaction, decision making, and problem solving. Finally, one cannot overemphasize the essential impact that a hopeful and rewarding future career can play in bolstering the motivations and attitudes of adolescents.

VOICES FROM THE FIELD 15.1   VERBAL THREATS AND THE LANGUAGE OF VIOLENCE

A greater use of violent language may also be considered a societal trend or crisis that professional school counselors will have to face. More and more students resort to the use of verbal threats to express their frustration and anger. If children are not taught appropriate ways to express anger, some may feel that the only way they can really express their strong emotions is to threaten violence against their entire class or specific groups of people. Others may "wish that they wouldn't wake up sometimes." I have had teachers and administrators report to me that students have said these things when they have been in trouble during class or when they are harassed by their peers. It amazes me that students realize that this language will result in grand amounts of attention. While assessing the severity of a threat, the majority of the time students tell me that they were just angry or that they didn't really mean what they said. Most students do not realize how seriously adults, and the school system as a whole, must interpret these comments.

Even after the realization of the consequences for this expression of anger or frustration, some students will repeatedly use these statements to express their anger.

When informing parents of their child's statements, parents usually seem to be extremely concerned. Some say they think it may be an attention-getting tactic. Whatever it may be, I reassure parents that this is not something that children typically say and that they may want to consider arranging for therapy outside school or having the child evaluated by another professional. Most parents are extremely receptive to this information, although I have encountered some who do not view the event to be significant enough to warrant additional mental health attention for their child. Along with the many types of harassment, threats seem to be more commonly used by today's youth.

Source: Lacey Wallace, Professional School Counselor, Manor View Elementary, Anne Arundel County Public Schools, Maryland

---

TABLE 15.4   The FBI's Four-Pronged Assessment Model for Conducting a Threat Assessment

Prong 1: Personality of the Student

- Leakage (intentional or unintentional revelation of clues to an impending violent act)
- Low tolerance for frustration
- Poor coping skills
- Lack of resiliency
- Failed love relationship
- "Injustice collector" (resentment over real or perceived injustices)
- Signs of depression
- Narcissism (self-centeredness)
- Alienation
- Dehumanizes others
- Lack of empathy
- Exaggerated sense of entitlement
- Attitude of superiority
- Exaggerated or pathological need for attention
- Externalizes blame
- Masks low self-esteem
- Anger-management problems
- Intolerance
- Inappropriate humor
- Seeks to manipulate others
- Lack of trust
- Closed social group
- Change in behavior
- Rigid and opinionated

(continued)

TABLE 15.4   The FBI's Four-Pronged Assessment Model for Conducting a Threat Assessment (*Continued*)

- Unusual interest in sensationalized violence
- Fascination with violence-filled entertainment
- Negative role models
- Behavior appears relevant to carrying out a threat

Prong 2: Family Dynamics

- Turbulent parent–child relationship
- Acceptance of pathological behavior
- Access to weapons
- Lack of intimacy
- Student "rules the roost"
- No limits or monitoring of TV and Internet

Prong 3: School Dynamics (from the student's perspective)

- Student's attachment to school
- Tolerance for disrespectful behavior (bullying)
- Inequitable discipline
- Inflexible culture
- Pecking order among students
- Code of silence
- Unsupervised computer access

Prong 4: Social Dynamics

- Media, entertainment, technology
- Peer groups
- Drugs and alcohol
- Outside interests
- The copycat effect

Source: From *The School Shooter: A Threat Assessment Perspective*, by the Federal Bureau of Investigation. Retrieved from http://www.fbi.gov/stats-services/publications/school-shooter

TABLE 15.5   Suggestions for Preventing Violence and Intervening with Violent Youth

1. Increase the quality and frequency of peer contacts.
2. Create a sense of hope and feelings of togetherness in the school and community.
3. Teach and role-play interpersonal and social skills in real-life situations.
4. Establish a clear districtwide policy for exploring and dealing with allegations of violence, bullying, harassment, abuse, and neglect.
5. Encourage participation in mentoring programs (e.g., Big Brother, Big Sister).
6. Develop and train a threat assessment team in each school.
7. Establish a peer mentoring program in the school to address needs of new and socially isolated students.
8. Collaborate with law enforcement, faith leaders, and representatives of social service agencies.
9. Create a school climate of trust between adults and students.
10. Help parents, guardians, and other adults in the life of the child make systematic connections in the community. Socially and emotionally isolated students often have socially and emotionally isolated caretakers.
11. Above all, provide supportive intervention services to potential offenders. This connection with a caring professional school counselor may make all the difference!

Substance Abuse

Substance abuse is a substantial problem in society and has reached an alarming level among children and adolescents. The Substance Abuse and Mental Health Services Administration (SAMHSA, 2012) estimated than nearly one third of youth aged 12 to 20 drank alcohol in the previous month, and as many as 10% of youth in this age group abused, or were dependent on, alcohol. Clients with substance abuse problems ranged between 12% and 30%, depending on the treatment setting. Whereas substance abuse counselors receive specialized training in the assessment, diagnosis, and treatment of substance disorders and professional school counselors may serve more as referral sources than as providers of actual treatment in the school context, professional school counselors must, at the very least, become proficient in substance abuse assessment to ensure that students get much-needed services. Similar to the assessment of suicidal thoughts and behaviors, assessment of substance abuse is best conducted early in the counseling process so that a comprehensive treatment program can be implemented.

Fortunately, self-reports of substance use are pretty reliable, although certainly not with all clients. During an initial interview, it is important to explore with the student any and all medications and substances being taken, including over-the-counter, prescription, alcohol, and illegal substances. Such a survey of substances helps the professional school counselor to understand potential for abuse, as well as whether use of such substances may cause side effects of concern. The most recent edition of the *Physician's Desk Reference* is an excellent source of information on drugs and side effects.

Because self-report of substance use is fairly reliable, professional school counselors often use a straightforward interviewing approach. Table 15.6 includes some commonly asked questions that professional school counselors can include in an initial interview to directly assess for substance use and abuse. Another brief, but classic interview method designed for alcohol abuse screening, but which can be easily adapted to other substances, uses the acronym CAGE (Mayfield, McLeod, & Hall, 1974):

C – Have you ever felt you need to **Cut down** on your drinking?

A – Have people **Annoyed** you by criticizing your drinking?

G – Have you ever felt bad or **Guilty** about drinking?

E – Have you ever had a drink first thing in the morning to steady your nerves or get rid of a hangover (**Eye opener**)?

Client responses to a brief screening device such as CAGE can lead the professional counselor to suspect alcohol or other drug abuse and use more formalized or systematic data collection procedures. Although there are a number of tests designed to assess for substance abuse issues, the most popular for use with adolescents is the Substance Abuse Subtle Screening Inventory–Adolescent 2 (SASSI–A2; Miller, 2001).

Grief Work and Children from Changing Families

Any time you experience a loss, you grieve. Sometimes the grief passes in a few moments, such as when a student gets an unexpected poor grade on an exam or when a teenage girl is informed she will not be allowed to carouse with her friends at the mall because Grandma is coming for a visit. Other times, the loss is so profound that recovery may take months, years, or longer. For example, when a parent or sibling dies or when parents separate or divorce, children and adolescents often experience a long emotional road before accepting the loss and moving on. Sometimes these youngsters never do recover properly. Professional school

---

TABLE 15.6 Useful Questions When Screening for Potential Substance Abuse

1. Do you take any over-the-counter medications? If yes . . . What is it called? What do you take it for? How much? How often? Side effects?

2. Do you take any prescription medications? If yes . . . What is it called? What do you take it for? How much? How often? Side effects?

3. Do you take any other drug or substances? If yes . . . What is it called? What effect does it have on you? How much? How often? Side effects? When did you start?

4. Do you drink alcohol? If yes . . . What kind? How much? How often? How does it affect you? When did you start?

5. With whom do you drink (take drugs)?

6. Has drinking (taking drugs) caused you problems (financial, legal, family, friends, at work)?

7. Has anyone ever suggested you have a problem with drinking (taking drugs)? Who? What makes them say this?

8. Have you ever tried to quit? Successful for how long? What happened (withdrawal, symptoms, relapse)?

counselors encounter children with grief reactions quite frequently, so some mention of strategies and interventions is appropriate. Most grief reactions share commonalities. This section will focus on helping mitigate grief reactions in youth from changing families, the grief-inducing circumstance most commonly encountered by school-aged youth. First, a review of relevant extant literature will be presented, followed by strategies and interventions. Importantly, most of the interventions are applicable to work with groups or individuals.

UNDERSTANDING THE EFFECTS OF DIVORCE   There is a large, rich literature base on children of divorce. A generally accepted conclusion of this research is that most children adjust well to divorce, although, on average, older children experience more negative outcomes (Amato, 2010). However, a number of risk and resiliency factors play into the mix, such as interparental conflict, gender, poor-quality parenting, and lack of contact with the father. It is essential to understand from the outset that these factors are family process variables, not family structure variables. That is, negative emotional and social outcomes can be expected of children from nondivorced families if many of these risk factors are evident. In other words, it is not difficult to imagine or conclude that many children growing up in an intact family in which the parents are in conflict, provide low-quality parenting, or have an uninvolved father would be at a disadvantage. Still, when compared to peers from nondivorced families, adolescents from divorced families demonstrate, on average, more depression, greater conflict with parents, poorer school performance, and higher levels of aggression and disruptive behavior.

Numerous resiliency and protective factors have been observed to ameliorate the potential negative effects of divorce (Vélez, Wolchik, Tein, & Sandler, 2011). Protective factors are characteristics or environmental facets that serve as buffers against stressors and harmful forces. In some ways, protective factors are on the opposite end of the spectrum from risk factors. Researchers have identified a number of resiliency or protective factors associated with positive outcomes for children of divorce, including interparental cooperation and diminished conflict following the divorce, competent parenting from custodial parents, and contact with and competent parenting from nonresidential parents (Amato, 2010). Relationships and activities outside the family also frequently serve as important buffers. Having a trusting relationship with a nonparental adult and peers and having positive school experiences may all play a protective role.

Although divorce continues to be a troubling societal issue and its effects on children can be grief inducing, emotionally draining, and even at times traumatic, it is critical for professional school counselors to understand that 75% to 80% of children and young adults from divorced families do not experience major psychological problems (e.g., depression), aspire to and achieve career or higher educational goals, and enjoy intimate relationships as adults (Amato, 2010). Indeed, some researchers (Vélez et al., 2011) have concluded that factors prior to the divorce, such as the degree of marital conflict or the child's ability to adjust to emotional and social circumstances, may be more indicative of long-term social adjustment and mental health.

A PRIMER ON GRIEF WORK   Various researchers and authors have discussed reactions to grief as a developmental process proceeding through stages similar to those discussed

---

VOICES FROM THE FIELD 15.2   **CUSTODY AND THE PROFESSIONAL SCHOOL COUNSELOR**

Although divorce is not a recently emerging societal issue, the experiences children face as a result of divorce are becoming more complex. In the past, the majority of children may have stayed together under the custody of one parent. Recently, children are more frequently separated among their parents, where a mother may have custody of one child and a father may have custody of two of the children. Sometimes these children may even be separated by thousands of miles. Children are no longer losing only a parent as a result of divorce; in some cases, they are also losing half of their once existing family. More and more fathers are gaining custody of children, whereas in the past we may have seen more mothers with custody, and parents are remarrying multiple times, which may lead to complicated step-sibling situations.

I have reviewed incoming folders of new students to find restraining orders against a parent due to violent threats or acts against the other parent. I have read restraining orders due to one parent's attempt to kidnap the children from the other parent. As a professional school counselor, it is extremely important to note the situations of these students to be sure that the number one duty is fulfilled, to keep children safe. These aggressive and threatening parental relationships can have a significant effect on a child's well-being.

Complex custody issues have made my job as a professional school counselor especially complicated. Because divorce is so common in our society, custody battles may be just as common. I find it extremely important to review divorce documents discussing custody to ensure that I do not divulge information to a noncustodial parent. As parents contact me on a daily basis, I have to be aware of which parent has access to educational information and the right to make educational decisions for their children.

Already, I have encountered a woman who has been remarried for all six years of her child's life, yet the stepfather is not the legal guardian. It is necessary to request that the mother be present when educational decisions are made or that legal documentation of the stepfather's guardianship be provided.

These are just a handful of the current issues that children may experience as a result of new trends of divorce. They bring about a number of cautionary practices that are necessary to ensure our students' safety. New interventions and practices must be employed to meet the needs of this student population.

Source: Lacey Wallace, Professional School Counselor, Manor View Elementary, Anne Arundel County Public Schools, Maryland

---

by Kübler-Ross (1969) in her classic work, *On Death and Dying*:

- *Stage 1: Shock and denial*—the individual is in disbelief that the event has occurred. Anxiety is heightened, but ordinarily decreases as fears are pinpointed.
- *State 2: Anger*—a period of rage is generally accompanied by an awareness of unfair treatment. Individuals often ask questions such as "Why me?" or "What did I do to deserve this?"
- *Stage 3: Guilt*—feelings arise that the individual may have contributed to the situation or done something to deserve it. Some may try to bargain with others (including God) to change what has happened. Generally, fear and anger decrease as fewer conditions for forgiveness are set.
- *Stage 4: Hopelessness/Depression*—individuals experience loneliness and feelings of sadness and hopelessness. This is often the longest stage and ordinarily becomes so uncomfortable that the individual becomes motivated to move on.
- *Stage 5: Acceptance*—the stage involves moving on from the event and readjusting to one's new life situation. Fears and anxieties are frequently harnessed and used as energy to propel the individual in new directions.

Many of the physical symptoms associated with grief reactions are similar to those of depression: fatigue, loss of or increase in appetite, loss of concentration, feelings of hopelessness and isolation, frequent sighing or breathlessness, and aches and pains. The intensity of the grief experience is usually determined by a combination of factors, including one's relationship to the person who was lost (e.g., parent, spouse, cousin, neighbor), the intensity of or ambivalence toward that relationship, the dependency or security provided by that relationship, how the loss occurred (e.g., single vs. multiple events, knowledge ahead of time), one's personality (e.g., hardiness, resilience, mental illness), history of dealing with grief experiences, and individual characteristics (e.g., sex, age, cultural determinants). A number of obstacles to effective grieving have been identified, including sudden loss (e.g., no warning, no chance to say good-bye), lack of finality or uncertain loss (possibility that things may still work out), lack of support, and the perception that grief is a weakness and should be avoided or denied.

Helping students deal with grief is a common service provided by professional school counselors. If the student is experiencing "complicated grief," specialized counseling services are usually required, and an immediate referral should be made. But in the context of developmental grief reactions, the professional school counselor should continuously remind the student that the symptoms and reactions are normal and that life and emotional health will get better in time. Professional school counselors can help students resolve the four primary tasks of grieving (Worden, 2009). The first task is to accept the reality of the loss, usually by talking about the loss and integrating the reality of the situation on both the intellectual and the emotional levels. The second task is to experience (not avoid) the pain of the grief. Worden referred to this task as the "bleeding stage" of grief, when the student must experience the pain of the grief reaction internally and externally. The third task is adjusting to life without the lost object or condition. This usually involves accepting help from others, acknowledging limitations, and performing new coping skills and activities on one's own. The final task involves emotionally relocating the loss and moving on with life. This requires students to reinvest energy from the lost relationship into new relationships or activities, as well as to find an appropriate place for the loss inside one's emotional psyche.

While helping students to resolve these tasks of grieving, professional school counselors should use good listening and communication skills, use questions sparingly, and honor silence when possible. Try to adjust to and connect with their mood or emotional state and be fully attentive to them. Help them to talk about the loss at a pace comfortable to them. Provide a safe place for and encourage emotional release (e.g., crying, raging, ranting, complaining), and offer assistance in practical as well as emotionally supportive ways. Help students to maintain helpful routines and encourage them to find a way to resolve the loss. Encourage social support (e.g., peers, caring adults), bibliotherapy, and journal writing. Also help the students keep busy in meaningful activities (including volunteering) and take care of their physical health. Finally, professional school counselors should always be alert for signs of complicated grief or other signs of trouble (e.g., extreme behavior changes, suicidal or homicidal ideation, changes in eating or sleeping habits, substance abuse). Refer these students to community mental health practices as appropriate.

THEORY INTO PRACTICE 15.2

IN TIMES OF CRISIS

Many of our students view school as "home." During times of hardship, school is the place where students feel a sense of structure, acceptance, and belonging. The faculty and staff work hard to help students feel connected to their school, and all of us (professional counselors, teachers, administrators, staff, custodians, nurse, psychologist, school resource officer, school probation officer) work together to ensure that all our students have at least one adult in the building who they feel a connection with and can approach in times of need. We also work with outside agencies that send clinical counselors into the school to meet with identified students and attend our meetings to report progress so that we can do our part to help the students achieve desirable goals.

On a schoolwide level, students are polled and asked to identify adults in the building with whom they feel a connection with and can go to in times of need. In addition, the faculty and staff are asked to identify students, from a list of the total school population of over 1,500 students, with whom they have a connection. Any students who are not identified are then recognized and looked in on by faculty members to help them establish some kind of connection.

In addition, as a school, we have set up programs to help students feel connected to their school. This year we had a freshmen connection day before the school year started and offered games, prizes, food, face painting, and so on to the freshmen who attended the event. We had a big turnout of students and faculty, and the event helped students meet other students and faculty members to help with the transition and ease the apprehension of attending high school.

Also, students have the same homeroom advisor each year in an effort to make nonacademic connections with adults. We provide remediation classes and after-school sessions for students who have not been successful with standardized tests needed as a graduation requirement, as well as academic tutoring for all students. Our pupil personnel worker has been instrumental in working with students who have high absentee rates, and as a result, our attendance rates have risen over the past couple of years. Furthermore, we work closely with our Parent Teacher Student Association (PTSA) so that teachers and parents can work together to help students stay on the path to success. All these strategies help students with complex problems persist in school, as well as forming a bond with someone in the school setting.

As a counselor at the high school level, my roles are very diverse. I embrace every opportunity I have to connect with students because most students want to know someone cares and will listen and help to steer them in the right direction. Many of my students who could benefit from treatment do not receive any outside the school setting, so I may be the first line of defense in helping to steer them in a direction to get the help that they need or in providing limited services within the school. Establishing rapport is key, and presenting lessons in the classroom, being present in the hallways and cafeteria, attending after-school activities, running groups, and meeting with students individually are all ways I connect with students and build a strong rapport. Providing career and vocational counseling and assisting with the college application process are important in helping students establish realistic goals. Also, I run a group with students with complex problems and incorporate creative arts into the counseling process. I have seen much success with these students, as the arts helps them express their feelings and thoughts so that we can work toward achieving individual goals, such as overcoming obstacles, being successful in school, and receiving a high school diploma.

In conclusion, many of our students turn to the school in times of crisis and look to the faculty and staff to assist during these times. A couple of years ago, a sibling of a former student was killed on her way to school. The deceased student's older brother, who had graduated several years earlier, came to school that day to find support and comfort from those members of the faculty with whom he had built a strong rapport. He is just one example of the many students who return to school for numerous reasons to visit faculty/staff members and maintain that connection that developed during the years they attended school. As a professional school counselor, I am an advocate for students and do what I can to empower students, offer them support, and connect them with resources available in the community to help them to overcome obstacles and reach their goals and become successful members of society.

Source: Tricia Uppercue, Professional School Counselor, Aberdeen High School, Harford County Public Schools, Aberdeen, Maryland

One complex issue children may be forced to deal with is the reality of a parent's deployment to another country to serve in war. Although war is not necessarily a new concept for the United States, it is something that our country has not had to face in a number of years. Wars in Iraq and Afghanistan have greatly affected us here at home, but one particular way in which it has affected our country is one that most may not think of on a daily basis. Working on a military base has provided me with ample opportunity to witness the effects of the war on the families and children of America. Not only is at least one student in every classroom experiencing this separation from a parent, but also they are experiencing the fear of losing a parent to death, on a daily basis.

There was a student who visited the nurse three times in one day, complaining of a stomach ache, but did not wish to go home sick. When the nurse called home to ask the parent if she thought it would be appropriate to pick her child up from school, she disclosed that her husband was scheduled to return home from Iraq two nights prior, yet they still had not heard any news. The nurse immediately approached me to discuss the situation. These psychosomatic symptoms are common for children who are experiencing stress of all different kinds. However, many children are not able to understand the connection between their mental and physical states. I spent some time with the student shortly afterward to "see how her year was going so far." During this time, she brought her father up a number of times. I asked a handful of open questions about her favorite memories with dad, what she loved most about him, and drew him a picture to send to Iraq. Later that day, I stopped into her classroom to see how she was feeling. I asked her how she was feeling, and she looked at me with a smile and chimed, "My stomach doesn't hurt any more." A precious memory, to be sure!

I have conversed with a handful of parents whose spouses were deployed. They report feelings of hopelessness and feel lost without their significant other. Parents request information to facilitate talking to their children about deployment and information about local parent support groups. Parents also request that I check in with their children to process the changes at home with them. As I have seen so far, most children are sad, yet extremely resilient. The parents may be the ones with greater concerns that also need to be tended to in every way possible. Parent support groups, workshops, and student groups are only a few of the avenues to attend to these needs of the community.

When parents return from war there are even more needs of both children and parents to be addressed. Soldiers may return with physical and mental wounds. A lack of medical and mental health attention may also be an issue. A parent with posttraumatic stress disorder (PTSD) can affect a child in many ways. A mother called me this year to inform me of her husband's violent streak due to PTSD. Her husband had become physically and verbally aggressive toward her, and her son had witnessed these acts. This boy was so confused about what had changed his father's demeanor from calm and passive to aggressive and argumentative. How can we expect children to understand the effects that war has on a person? These are just a few of the effects war has on the children and families of American soldiers.

The current issues facing today's youth reinforce the need for and importance of professional school counselors. Although working with this high-need population feels like a whirlwind at times, it is also an extremely fulfilling experience. The sense of making a difference in the lives of children is always apparent. Despite the frantic pace and the feeling that there are not enough hours in a day to address the needs of all of the students in my school, there is not a day that goes by that I have not addressed a serious issue that a child is very concerned about. What would these children do without a professional school counselor? That is the question that reminds me that the stress and busy days are worth it. After all, I am here for the children.

Source: Lacey Wallace, Professional School Counselor, Manor View Elementary, Anne Arundel County Public Schools, Maryland

Dropout Prevention

Because students who experience academic failure drop out at significantly high rates, a large part of successful programming involves dropout prevention. A number of factors contribute to or reduce dropout risk in students (Lehr, Johnson, Bremer, Cosio, & Thompson, 2004). Some risk factors are fixed and not subject to change. However, many of the factors associated with dropout risk are alterable, including high rates of absenteeism and tardiness, low grades, a history of course failure, limited parental support, low participation in extracurricular activities, alcohol or drug problems, negative attitudes toward school, high levels of mobility, and grade retention. In addition, there are factors that provide protection to students with other risk factors; these preventive factors relate to increased likelihood of persisting in school despite difficulties. Some preventive factors include more time in general education for students with disabilities, provision of tutoring services, training for competitive employment and independent living, and attendance at schools that maintain high expectations for all students. In addition, students with complex problems who remained in school reported participating in a "relevant" high school curriculum, receiving significant support from teachers, perceiving positive attitudes from teachers and administrators, and benefiting from improvements in curriculum and instruction (e.g., additional assistance, better teaching, more interesting classes, better textbooks).

Taking risk factors and preventive factors into account, most dropout interventions seek to enhance students' sense of belonging in school; foster the development of relationships with teachers, administrators, and peers; improve academic success; address personal problems through counseling; and provide skill-building opportunities in behavior and social skills. Reviews of effective dropout intervention programs found that most of these interventions could be categorized according to the following types (Lehr, Hansen, Sinclair, & Christenson, 2003).

- Personal/affective (e.g., retreats designed to enhance self-esteem, regularly scheduled classroom-based discussion, individual counseling, participation in an interpersonal relations class)
- Academic (e.g., provision of special academic courses, individualized methods of instruction, tutoring)
- Family outreach (e.g., strategies that include increased feedback to parents or home visits)
- School structure (e.g., implementation of school within a school, redefinition of the role of the home-room teacher, reduced class size, creation of an alternative school)
- Work related (e.g., vocational training, participation in volunteer or service programs)

Professional school counselors can help develop and implement schoolwide dropout prevention programs, using risk screenings to identify students at highest risk and promoting some of the key components related to school completion. Table 15.7 lists key intervention components synthesized from the research on dropout prevention and increasing school completion (Lehr et al., 2004) that are particularly appropriate for initiation or support by professional school counselors.

Conflict Resolution and Peer Mediation Program Development

Most schools implement some systemic or developmental program to help students mediate and resolve conflict. The development of any conflict resolution or peer mediation program or intervention should reflect the unique contextual needs of the school or district to be served. Climate assessment and strategies for systemic change are integral to program development, as are diversity considerations in the recruitment, selection, and training of peer mediators, in circumstances where a school system implements a peer mediation program.

ASSESSING CLIMATE Prior to proposing a conflict resolution–peer mediation program, careful assessment of school culture and climate is essential. It is particularly relevant to gain an understanding of the atmosphere of competition versus collaboration that characterizes most schools, as well as the systemic patterns, policies, and procedures that sustain and promote imbalances in power and the prejudice and discrimination directed at any disenfranchised population. It is also necessary to understand the structure of competition in the school. The ultimate goal of competition is to win, thus creating a loser. Winning rarely results in maintaining good relationships, understanding each other's perspectives, or accepting the legitimacy of others' needs and feelings. Conversely, in a cooperative win–win environment, there exists a commitment to developing mutual goals beneficial to all, while preserving positive relationships that honor and respect multiple perspectives.

The implementation of a cooperative school environment in which to manage conflict seems appropriate, given the positive effects of cooperative learning on cognitive and social development. However, opponents of school conflict resolution programs believe that these programs cover the real causes of conflict without focusing on the policies and practices of the adults who hold power. Essentially, the opponents of peer mediation and conflict resolution programs seem to be advocating attention to the issues that create intractable conflict (i.e., resolution resistant conflict). These issues are woven into the fabric of educational practices and contribute to the inequity that fuels the inevitable conflict of differing attitudes, values, and beliefs. For example, academic tracking and inconsistent policies and practices in attendance, discipline, and entrance into extracurricular activities can create inequities for students from low-income and underserved populations, based on policies that sort and select students, often diminishing access to and equity in educational opportunity. Student and parent/guardian awareness of these inequities causes conflict as students and parents/guardians strive to meet their needs satisfactorily.

Using Maslow's need theory, conflict theorists suggest that need is a motivating factor in intractable conflict and will go on indefinitely, as human needs are not negotiable (Conflict Information Consortium, 2013a). Most relevant to schools is conflict over the need for identity, a salient factor in racial, ethnic, gender, and family conflicts (Conflict Information Consortium, 2013b). Of additional concern are issues of dominance that reflect a power structure and hierarchy of "one up, one down" or "one group up, one group

---

TABLE 15.7   Key Dropout Prevention Interventions

Provide environmental support:

- Help provide a structured environment that includes clear and equitably enforced behavioral expectations.
- Monitor the occurrence of risk behaviors, regularly collect data, and measure the effects of timely interventions.

Provide counseling support:

- Provide individual behavioral assistance.
- Help students address personal and family issues through counseling and access to social services.
- Help students with personal problems (e.g., on-site health care, availability of individual and group counseling).
- Develop students' problem-solving skills and enhance skills to meet the demands of the school environment.
- Provide conflict resolution and violence prevention programs to enhance effective interpersonal skills.

Enhance relationships and affiliation:

- Incorporate personalization by creating meaningful and supportive bonds between students and teachers and among students.
- Create a caring and supportive environment (e.g., use of adult mentors, expanding role of homeroom teachers, organizing extracurricular activities).
- Promote additional opportunities for the students to form bonding relationships and include tutoring, service learning, alternative schooling, and out-of-school enhancement programs.
- Foster students' connections to school and sense of belonging to the community of students and staff (e.g., clubs, team activities, intraschool competition, retreats).

Provide/support vocational programming:

- Provide vocational education that has an occupational concentration.
- Provide career counseling and life-skills instruction.
- Coordinate the academic and vocational components of participants' high school programs.
- Communicate the relevance of education to future endeavors (e.g., offer vocational and career counseling, flexible scheduling, and work-study programs).

Bolster outside influences:

- Recognize the importance of families in the success of their children's school achievement and school completion.
- Link with the wider community through systemic renewal, community collaboration, career education, and school-to-work programs.

---

down." Students are keenly aware of inequities in power. When conflict arises and is peer mediated, the two disputants may come to an agreement to fight no more, but the underlying unmet needs have not been addressed. Unless students believe their needs can be met satisfactorily, the conflict will continue (Conflict Information Consortium, 2013c). However, if the issues that undergird intractable conflict are brought to light by a peer mediation program and are addressed from an institutional perspective, then the program takes an active role in institutional change, and the process becomes part of the framework of a transformed school climate and culture. This affords students a venue for meeting their needs while saving face (Conflict Information Consortium, 2013b). This process suggests the need for conflict resolution training for all members of the school community. Teachers cannot impart feelings and principles of empowerment to their students if they feel estranged from

their colleagues and the school in which they work. Transformation of school culture and climate is a slow process that requires careful assessment of the unique structure and assumptions of a school, but it is well worth the effort.

SYSTEMIC CHANGE   Resolving conflicts and preventing violence are interrelated. The relationship between initiatives addressing conflict resolution and youth violence reduction warrants attention to a systemic change model that targets youth violence. Successful school programs recognize violence as a developmental issue, with various grade-level interventions that are both preventive and remedial. Then, efforts to create a high level of personal and community awareness and participation in conflict resolution and peer mediation programs can stimulate collective power and share information about similarities and differences that is useful in formulating solutions. Efforts of the collective whole lead to change in daily patterns of the majority of the school, rather than isolated changes for only a few. Given that change is difficult, invitational strategies that involve all concerned stakeholders in planning and implementing change, address formal and informal policies, give attention to the needs of diverse constituents, and personalize and maintain involvement of all parties are essential. Student involvement in the change process broadens role expectation beyond the classroom setting. These opportunities encourage more-genuine renegotiated relationships and roles between students and school personnel. As teachers broaden their roles in systemic change initiatives, they become empowered and actively involved in redefining the school culture and climate.

Administrative support is vital to systemic change efforts, as principals are responsible for promoting the overall school mission through the efforts of school personnel. Therefore, administrators need to trust that change efforts will be carried out appropriately through a process defined by clear goals and objectives that foster and complement existing efforts and priorities. Because multilevel interventions reach beyond the school, the inclusion of families and the school community is essential.

DIVERSITY CONSIDERATIONS IN RECRUITMENT, SELECTION, AND TRAINING OF PEER MEDIATORS Peer mediation programs are used in many schools either as stand-alone programs or in conjunction with other initiatives. Because these programs put students in leadership roles, it is essential that peer mediators represent the multiple diversities of the school. In this way, programs demonstrate an appreciation for the dynamic worldview and cultural complexity of students and school personnel so that initiatives are inclusive and contribute to a balance in power as both an institutional and a programmatic objective. Specifically, when developing new programs and revising existing peer mediation programs to reflect the pluralistic composition of schools, examination of three factors—recruitment, selection, and training—is necessary. The diverse populations of schools—differentiated by age, race or ethnicity, disability, socioeconomic status, and academic ability—need to be reflected in programming. The basic goal in addressing difference is to assist students and school personnel in recognizing diversity as a resource, not a point of contention.

Empowering students to be leaders and role models is an essential step toward creating and maintaining a school environment that prevents harassment and violence (Wessler & Preble, 2003). Some groups of students who feel disenfranchised from the school community distance themselves from participation in extracurricular activities. As a result, traditional methods of recruitment prove unsatisfactory. Individual solicitations to students with low participation in school activities are advisable. Individual solicitation communicates

interest in a particular student or group and may be helpful coming from a teacher who has a close relationship with a student or group or from a teacher whom students respect. Moreover, enlisting the assistance of teachers helps to enlighten these teachers on the institutional issues that prevent some students from participating in school activities. On a cautionary note, only students who are likely to be selected should be encouraged because creating hopeless situations can be as detrimental as exclusion.

Selection of student mediators should reflect a cross section of the student population. Multiple criteria in terms of student attributes are suggested, including leadership skills, maturity, communication skills, responsibility, perspective taking, empathy, and problem-solving skills. High academic achievement is not necessarily a prerequisite for selection. Students with average grades and some who are considered at risk may well possess the desirable skills. A heterogeneous configuration of mediators makes the service more approachable.

The varying levels of racial or ethnic identity development among students are another salient factor to consider. It is critical that program coordinators be familiar with the stages of racial or ethnic identity development for students of color and White students. Coordinators need to be aware of and understand the impact of their own racial or ethnic identity development and the potential challenges that selecting for diversity may present to them and other members of the school community.

Throughout the literature, training is equated to the acquisition of lifelong skills that can be generalized beyond the school environment. Multicultural sensitivity should be integrated throughout the training process, as students should not always mediate conflicts between students from only their own racial or ethnic background. Training for awareness of ways members of different groups view conflict and mediation within a cultural, family, and community context is essential to understanding the pattern of behavior and avoiding inaccurate assumptions and conclusions. In addition, patterns of speech and issues specific to the special needs of non-English-speaking students or students for whom English is a second language must be considered in peer mediation training to avoid bias and discrimination, as well as to encourage the use of mediation services by all students.

PEER MEDIATION PROGRAM IMPLEMENTATION Regardless of the initiative or combinations of initiatives, implementation that is strategically planned, artfully carried out, and well documented is essential. This is especially important because the results of conflict resolution initiatives and peer mediation programs can be directly linked to schoolwide data as initiatives that assist in creating a safe school environment for learning. The specifics of implementation may vary from school to school and district to district, depending on who coordinates the initiatives. The professional school counselor may or may not coordinate the initiatives. Either way, program implementation can be conceptualized as a cyclical process including the development of a mission statement, the collection of data used to set goals, the prioritizing of goals, the provision of training for skill development, an implementation schedule, evaluation, and follow-up. In addition, careful examination of policies, practices, and procedures that affect the development and implementation of and access to these initiatives is important to ensure they reflect the spirit of the initiatives under construction. For example, inconsistencies in discipline referrals and patterns of punishments can undermine even carefully planned efforts to build peaceable schools and peer mediation programs.

Throughout every step of program revision or development, it is essential to enlist the input of all stakeholders. The use of multiple levels of input in a variety of venues that move beyond a onetime newsletter sent home, a community speaker, or several morning announcements can increase the level of ownership a school community feels in conflict resolution and peer mediation initiatives.

TRAINING FOR PROGRAM COORDINATORS   As with any important role in the school, the responsibility of coordinating peer mediation programs and conflict resolution initiatives requires specific training. Strategies and information that are practical, easy to use, and able to be directly applied include improving student success; preventing alcohol, tobacco, and other drug use; building school–community–parent partnerships; and resolving conflicts safely. Well-trained coordinators can take a leadership role and provide the school community with this practical information, as well as initiating appreciation of cultural diversity and challenging the beliefs of disenfranchised students.

STUDENT ACCESS TO SERVICES   As with other programs, careful examination of policies that govern program access helps ensure that programs serve the entire school community. For example, schoolwide policies establishing when and how mediation takes place should be publicized to all members of the school community. Individual teachers or staff members should not deny students access to the mediation process. Administrative support in establishing policy lends credibility to peer mediation as an integral part of the total school program and creates consistent student access. Moreover, it sends a message of the shared values, attitudes, and beliefs that form the foundation of the school culture and climate.

PROGRAM EVALUATION   The lack of empirical data documenting the consistent effectiveness of peer mediation and conflict resolution programs is problematic in schools where limited funds mandate programmatic outcomes such as student achievement. As the focus of accountability through concrete measure increases, it is incumbent on school-based peer mediation and conflict resolution coordinators to document results. The importance of conducting evaluations for conflict resolution and peer mediation programs cannot be overstated. As professional school counselors work to link school counseling programs to the mission of schools, evidence of concrete measures that contribute to creating a safe leaning environment is essential.

Regular program evaluation reports should be completed and presented to all school personnel. Program evaluations should specify the impact conflict and violence within the school have on the culture and climate of the school and student academic achievement (e.g., adequate yearly progress). Program evaluation reports should be completed regularly and presented to all school personnel to keep them up to date and informed.

MULTICULTURAL IMPLICATIONS OF CONFLICT RESOLUTION AND PEER MEDIATION PROGRAMS

According to the U.S. Department of Health and Human Services (2008), African-American and Hispanic males who attend large inner-city schools that serve very poor neighborhoods are at the greatest risk of becoming victims or perpetrators of school violence. Generally, racial-minority youth not only represent families from the lowest socioeconomic level, but also live in lower-income communities. Thus, these youth are much more vulnerable to the oppressions and negative afflictions plaguing society today. This can escalate the potential for these youths to adopt self-destructive, especially violent, attitudes and behaviors (Brinson, Kottler, & Fisher, 2004). But suburban and rural youth are no longer immune to school violence.

Some authors believe that to be truly effective, conflict resolution and violence prevention efforts must "adjust" to the diverse cultural, ethnic, and socioeconomic influences of society and involve every segment of society (e.g., families, neighborhoods, civic and social organizations, government and private institutions, businesses, cities, states, schools, justice systems, health professionals). Within the school setting, that translates into emphasizing the need to educate students in a global context and use education to bridge the divides between groups of people (Carter, 2004). Carter stated that "bridging the divides" between groups of people "requires attention not only to teaching about differences, such as language, culture, and religion, but also to exploring areas of deep cultural understanding" (p. 2). Brinson et al. (2004) asserted that there is also a lack of emphasis on cross-cultural conflict resolution, particularly within peer mediation and process curriculum approaches to conflict resolution. Therefore, not only must schools implement programs that educate and promote violence prevention, but also they must teach students how to manage and resolve conflicts through multiple contexts that move beyond merely tolerating diversity to seeking out and celebrating the rich dimensions of multiple diversities. All students need to learn alternatives to using violence for resolving their disputes and to learn to become peacemakers in a pluralistic society.

EFFECTIVE SYSTEMIC INTERVENTION FOR STUDENTS WITH COMPLEX PROBLEMS

Schools alone no longer have the capacity to handle the multileveled problems facing today's students with complex problems. The extent and degree of problems presented by these students require a multidisciplinary and multileveled response that goes beyond isolated school interventions and professional school counselors working solo. Complex problems of this nature require a redefined role for the professional school counselor, one that allows counselors to reach out to other resources in the community and in homes. We would term this aspect of the new role for the professional school counselor the coordinator of interdisciplinary resources (CIR) and shift the focus of the position from that of a primary intervention specialist to that of a facilitator of multiple resources.

There are nine key recommendations for shifting the role and responsibilities of the professional school counselor to ensure effective counseling of youth with complex problems:

1. *Develop authentic partnerships.* Although fostering partnerships with community agencies, businesses, families, universities, police departments, recreational centers, and so on is important, it oftentimes does not truly address the problems of at-risk youth. Partnerships have become fairly stable components of school outreach programs, but are frequently established merely for the sake of saying that schools have collaborative relationships. In fact, many of the partnership relationships retain the status quo, rather than developing new and innovative strategies to address the complex problems presented by youth at risk. Therefore, partnerships must be forged without traditional institutional boundaries and examine unique ways that multiple partners can cooperatively address the difficulties of children and adolescents who are experiencing problems.

2. *Facilitate interdisciplinary collaboration.* The modern-day problems of at-risk youth are far too complex to be addressed in any one system. Thus, to expand on the first recommendation, professional school counselors should assume the role of CIR to facilitate interdisciplinary school collaboration with community agencies, government, businesses, and families to generate comprehensive approaches to multifaceted problems. This requires moving beyond partnerships with one institutional or parental body and fostering cross-disciplinary collaboration.

3. *Maintain a strong multicultural focus.* Racial and ethnic demographics are changing in the United States, creating a growing ethnic minority population; therefore, problems manifested by youth must be considered from a cultural perspective. Too often, at-risk youth populations are defined and addressed by the nature of their problems, without considering the cultural distinctions among the youth when designing prevention and intervention programs. It is important to underscore the need for a concerted awareness of cultural differences in worldviews, especially when working with youth with complex problems.

4. *Be a systems change agent.* To better serve the needs of youth, professional school counselors must become change agents. Professional school counselors are in an ideal position to understand what needs to change to provide successful support and educational services for youth with problems. Rather than simply "hearing" about those problems from students and parents, we recommend that professional school counselors take an active role in challenging inequities, injustices, and harmful practices within the school context.

5. *Empower students.* Truly empowering students means that more powerful individuals must often give up power to equalize relationships. This is particularly important within the school setting when working with children and adolescents who are facing obstacles. Thus, professional school counselors should help empower students and their families while modeling and promoting collaboration.

6. *Look for short-term successes.* One way to ensure failure with students who face myriad problems is to demand unrealistic goals. This is done regularly in schools where students who are angry are told not to be angry, students who are not studying are told simply to study, and students with low grades are commanded to work harder and improve their grades. We argue that professional school counselors must pave the way in establishing short-term realistic goals as measures of success, particularly when working with at-risk youth. Building on these short-term positive experiences will provide a building block to longer-term success.

7. *Become an advocate.* Advocacy is a key ingredient in working with youth at risk. Traditionally, many of the disenfranchised youth are without anyone to fight

for their rights and dreams. The professional school counselor is in a unique position to intimately know the child or adolescent and the system. Furthermore, the professional school counselor has access to important systemic information regarding the child. Given their unique position, professional school counselors must assume the role of advocate, challenging policies, practices, and procedures that perpetuate failure for the at-risk population.

8. *Research and document outcomes.* It is not sufficient to justify the success of prevention and intervention programs with anecdotal reports. Professional school counselors must assume a leadership role in documenting and disseminating information on the efficacy of programs through publishing and presenting their findings, both within the school system and externally at state and national forums (Bemak, 2000). Clear outcomes and dissemination of findings will help tailor successful program strategies, create a base for future funding, and facilitate better job descriptions and responsibilities for professional school counselors.

9. *Assume responsibility for successes and failures.* It is important that professionals model the demands made on youth to assume responsibility for their lives. Professional school counselors, institutions, agencies, and other professionals must become more accountable for their work with these youth. It is important to acknowledge and accept when intervention strategies are flawed and therefore discontinue using such interventions. At the same time, professional school counselors need to recognize and implement effective intervention strategies. Although this sounds straightforward, there is a history of systems blaming the child or adolescent for failures and creating a culture of victimization, rather than assuming responsibility for ineffective interventions.

CULTURAL REFLECTION 15.2

How might professional school counselors from diverse cultural backgrounds view the role of the professional school counselor as coordinator of interdisciplinary resources to support student educational achievement and opportunity? How might students, parents, and educators from diverse backgrounds view the leadership role of the professional school counselor as coordinator of interdisciplinary resources? What cultural barriers and access points might exist?

Summary/Conclusion

It is clear that the issues encountered by youth with complex problems in the United States continue to present serious problems for schools, families, and communities. It is essential that professional school counselors design innovative service systems to effectively address the complex and multifaceted needs of these youth. It is clear that many of the existing prevention and intervention programs are ineffective and unsuccessful, given the high numbers of disengaged and marginalized youth. Therefore, a new approach to working with this population is critical.

The professional school counselor is in a unique position to assume a leadership role in more effectively working with children and adolescents with complex problems. As a CIR, advocate, social change agent, multicultural expert, and documenter of successful programs, the professional school counselor is well positioned to make a difference. Professional school counselors must shift the blame from the youth to ensure that the service system and programs assume responsibility and that youth are supported, rather than punished. These paradigm shifts will be critical in changing the trajectory of youths' lives. It is an opportune time to change the course of a growing number of youth in the United States, and the professional school counselor is an ideal professional to become a leader in this process.

Activities

1. Interview a high school counselor regarding his or her approach to working with students with complex problems. How does he or she identify these students? What techniques does he or she find to be helpful in dealing with these students?

2. Create a program for use in either a primary or a secondary school to reach at-risk youth. How would you define the population? How do you plan to reach your desired population? What messages would you try to convey to them? Why would such a program be important to implement in schools and communities?

3. Design an outline for a violence prevention program for an elementary, middle, or high school. What message would you attempt to convey to the students? What programs and activities would you ask the students to participate in?

4. Observe a school cafeteria during lunch hour. What types of conflicts do you notice? How are these conflicts resolved?

5. Conduct a role play involving a professional school counselor and two students who are involved in a conflict. What conflict resolution strategy was used? How well did it work?

16

The Professional School Counselor and Students with Disabilities

Elana Rock and Erin H. Leff*

Editor's Introduction: Advocating for the needs of all students is a primary responsibility of the transformed professional school counselor. For too long, students with special needs have been identified and served through special programs without appropriate attention given to their developmental academic, career, and personal/social needs. This chapter focuses on what professional school counselors can do to effectively advocate for and serve students with special needs.

IMPROVING OUTCOMES FOR STUDENTS WITH DISABILITIES

Professional school counselors are committed to helping all students realize their potential, and make adequate yearly progress regardless of challenges resulting from disabilities and other special needs. (American School Counselor Association [ASCA], 2010)

Since the passing of the Education for All Handicapped Children Act in 1975, public education has experienced unparalleled national progress in serving students with disabilities (U.S. Department of Education, Office of Special Education and Rehabilitative Services, 2010). Youth with disabilities are guaranteed access to a free appropriate public education (FAPE), a far cry from the days when more than two million children with disabilities were excluded from school programs. Along with enabling access to education and instruction, the delivery of special education has improved the educational outcomes for children and youth with disabilities. Subsequent reauthorizations and ammendments to special education law—now entitled The Individuals with Disabilities Education Act (IDEA)—have enabled students with disabilities to experience significant growth in achievement and academic performance, as well as steadily increasing rates of high school graduation and enrollment in post-secondary educational programs.

Despite the improvements in the past 35-plus years, students with disabilities continue to face a number of barriers to successful school and postschool outcomes. Significant academic achievement gaps persist between students with disabilities and students without disabilities, and especially among students with disabilities from racial and ethnic minority groups (National Council on Disability, 2011). In general, students with disabilities earn lower grades, are retained more often, and often fail to graduate with a diploma. In addition, more than 25% of students with disabilities drop out of school, a rate significantly higher than that of students without disabilities (U.S. Department of Education, Office of Special Education and Rehabilitative Services, Office of Special Education Programs, 2012). Regarding postschool outcomes, adults who were students with disabilities have lower rates of postsecondary educational involvement (including vocational training) and complete college at only half that of students without disabilities. Finally, these adults have higher rates of unemployment and underemployment throughout their lives (National Council on Disability, 2011).

---

*The authors acknowledge the significant contribution of Estes J. Lockhart to the first edition of this text chapter. May he rest in peace.

These poor outcomes are particularly disheartening when one considers the fact that, of the more than 6.6 million students receiving special education today, approximately 90% have "mild" or high-prevalence disabilities, including learning disabilities, language disorders, emotional/behavioral disorders, mild autism spectrum disorders, and other health impairments, including attention-deficit/hyperactivity disorder (U.S. Department of Education, Office of Special Education and Rehabilitative Services, Office of Special Education Programs, 2010, 2012). Most of these students have average cognitive ability and lack significant physical or sensory impairments that might further interfere with functioning. The great majority of students with disabilities are capable of positive school and adult outcomes, including college and competitive employment. Notably, nearly 95% of these children are educated in regular public schools, with more than half spending the majority of their time in typical classrooms. (U.S. Department of Education, Office of Special Education and Rehabilitative Services, Office of Special Education Programs, 2012).

In recognition of the poorer outcomes still experienced by students with disabilities, the U.S. Department of Education (USDOE) has mandated the ongoing evaluation and reporting of each state's compliance with special education law. In annual reviews of state performance plans and corresponding data, the USDOE ascertains the extent to which each state is meeting the requirements of IDEA. Most recently, only 14 of the total 60 states and U.S. territories were found to be meeting the compliance and outcome indicators required by IDEA (U.S. Department of Education, Office of Special Education and Rehabilitative Services, Office of Special Education Programs, 2012). This Continuous Improvement and Focused Monitoring System is a component of the most recent reauthorization of IDEA, which affirms that

> [d]isability is a natural part of the human experience and in no way diminishes the right of individuals to participate in or contribute to society. Improving educational results for children with disabilities is an essential element of our national policy of ensuring equality of opportunity, full participation, independent living, and economic self-sufficiency for individuals with disabilities. (Individuals with Disabilities Education Improvement Act of 2004)

SERVING STUDENTS WITH DISABILITIES

Students with disabilities are capable of becoming and expected to become contributing members of society,

providing they receive the appropriate supports necessary for positive school and adult outcomes. To achieve these ends, Congress mandated the delivery of special education and related services in the IDEA. In the 2004 reauthorization, Congress reported on the previous 30 years of research and experience, which demonstrated that the education of children with disabilities can be made more effective by

> having high expectations for such children and ensuring their access to the general education curriculum in the regular classroom, to the maximum extent possible, in order to . . . meet developmental goals and, to the maximum extent possible, the challenging expectations that have been established for all children; and . . . be prepared to lead productive and independent adult lives, to the maximum extent possible. (Individuals with Disabilities Education Improvement Act, 2004)

As a member of the multidisciplinary team developing and implementing special education programs and services, the professional school counselor may have many roles and potential responsibilities associated with programming and delivering services for children with disabilities. These responsibilities may be to the team (e.g., for assessment, development of the Individualized Education Program, implementation planning), directly to the child (e.g., counseling services, career development, transition planning), or indirectly to the child through work with others on the team (e.g., parent training, consultation with educators, schoolwide positive behavioral support, consultative services).

The American School Counselor Association (ASCA), in its position paper on students with special needs (2014a), asserts that the school counselor

> takes an active role in student achievement by providing a comprehensive school counseling program for all students. As a part of this program, professional school counselors advocate for students with special needs, collaborate with other educational professionals to promote academic achievement for all.

Furthermore, Owens, Thomas, and Strong (2011) made some specific suggestions (see Table 16.1) about how professional school counselors can help students with disabilities, and ASCA (2014a) delineated appropriate school counseling roles for the direct support of

---

TABLE 16.1 Recommendations for School Counselors to Assist Students with Disabilities

- Promote and support students' academic, social, and career development.
- Become an active voice during IEP team meetings and advocate on behalf of students with disabilities.
- Assist IEP teams in developing relevant goals for individual students.
- Identify realistic individual or group counseling interventions to help students meet their goals.
- Bring attention to students' nonacademic needs such as social development and personal skills.
- Assist students choosing the proper classes.
- Offer suggestions for career exploration.
- Focus on student strengths.
- Contact college admissions offices to inquire about accommodations and other support services.
- Assist in the coordination, development, and implementation of Section 504 plans.
- Monitor and update Section 504 plans.
- Monitor students for depression, conduct disorders, or substance abuse, which may relate to a diagnosis of a disability.
- Collaborate with special education teachers, general education teachers, outside community agencies, and the school administration.
- Teach students the necessary social skills to decrease social and/or personal deficits.
- Create a network of on-site school personnel that support, mentor, and advocate for students with disabilities.
- Stay current on special education laws and attend seminars and conferences on issues related to students with disabilities.

Source: Owens et al., 2011

---

children with disabilities or collaboration with other school staff:

- Providing classroom guidance, individual and/or group counseling to students with special needs within the scope of the comprehensive school counseling program
- Consulting and collaborating with staff and parents to understand the special needs of a student
- Advocating for students with special needs in the school and in the community
- Contributing to the school's multidisciplinary team, which identifies students who may need to be assessed to determine special education eligibility
- Collaborating with related student support professionals (e.g., physical therapists, occupational therapists, special education, speech and language pathologists) in the delivery of services
- Providing assistance with developing academic and transition plans for students in the Individualized Education Program (IEP) as appropriate

Despite clear expectations for the involvement of professional school counselors in supporting students with special needs by the American School Counseling Association and other professional organizations (e.g., American Academy of Pediatrics, Mental Health America), research indicates that many professionals feel underprepared to assume these roles effectively. In fact,

many professional school counselors report having completed little, if any, graduate-level coursework dealing with the needs of students with disabilities and often report feeling underprepared or unprepared for the delivery of services to the children with disabilities in their schools (Mynatt & Gibbons, 2011; Naugle, Campbell, Gray, 2010; Romano, Paradise, & Green, 2009). Our goal in this chapter is to provide the necessary foundation for professional school counselors to understand and assist in providing programs and services to children with disabilities in school settings.

Beginning with a review of the legal mandates and the special education service delivery process, this chapter will focus on the various roles, responsibilities, processes, and skills relevant to the delivery of counseling-related services and behavioral supports to children with disabilities, parents, and other school staff. Because many of the professional school counselors' responsibilities to students with disabilities are the same as or similar to their responsibilities to students without disabilities, emphasis in this chapter will be placed on those processes not discussed elsewhere in this text. Finally, we review best practices for the delivery of counseling-related services to school-aged students with disabilities, including focused recommendations for students with specific disabilities and identifying effective resources and programs for supporting students' school, postsecondary education, and vocational needs.

FEDERAL LEGISLATION

The federal laws that articulate and protect the rights of students with disabilities can be grouped into one of two categories: education laws or civil rights laws. The special education law most widely applied in schools is the IDEA (2004). It was originally entitled the Education for All Handicapped Children Act when it was first enacted in 1975. The IDEA provides federal funding and requires states to guarantee a free, appropriate public education (FAPE) to students who need special education and related services because of an eligible disability. There are other education laws that also affect the delivery of special education programs and services. Among them are Title I of the Elementary and Secondary Education Act (ESEA) and the No Child Left Behind Act of 2001 (NCLB; see U.S. Department of Education, 2002).

The most widely applied civil rights law is Section 504 of the Rehabilitation Act of 1973 (commonly referred to as Section 504). Although it provides no federal funding, Section 504 mandates that programs receiving federal funding under other laws may not exclude an otherwise qualified individual with a disability from participation in these programs. It also requires that individuals with disabilities be provided reasonable accommodations that will allow them to access these programs. The Americans with Disabilities Act (ADA) of 1990 (and amended in 2008) is another civil rights act whose school-related provisions are nearly identical to Section 504. The ADA extends the protection from discrimination because of disabilities to all public and private schools, except religious schools, whether or not they receive federal financial assistance.

Understanding the differences between the IDEA and Section 504 is of practical importance for the professional school counselor. Professional school counselors often act as consultants for school staff, family, and outside agency representatives to help them understand how the legal rights of a student with a disability are appropriately addressed within an educational setting. The major difference between the IDEA and Section 504 is one of focus. The IDEA focuses on educational remediation, whereas Section 504 focuses on prevention of discrimination. The IDEA attempts to address gaps in education-related skills or abilities by ensuring the provision of appropriate services, modified instruction, and other supports and services for students in need of special education. Section 504, on the other hand, attempts to level the playing field for those students whose disabilities may not directly affect their academic abilities but who may require accommodation to access their educational programs.

For example, a student with a learning disability served under the IDEA may require special instruction in reading, as well as related services such as speech therapy or counseling, to learn. In contrast, a student with cerebral palsy qualified under Section 504 may be achieving at grade level in all academics, but still need accommodations such as being allowed to dictate responses rather than write them, due to his or her limited fine motor skills.

Individuals with Disabilities Education Improvement Act (IDEA)

The IDEA is the major special education law governing identification, evaluation, program, placement, and the provision of a FAPE for students from birth to age 21 determined to have a disability falling in one of 13 identified categories. This law provides that eligible students receive "special education," which is defined as "specially designed instruction, at no cost to parents, to meet the unique needs of a child with a disability, including instruction conducted in the classroom, in the home, in hospitals and institutions, and in other settings" (IDEA, 2004). Table 16.2 includes

---

TABLE 16.2   Definitions of Disabilities Under the IDEA

Child with a Disability is defined as a child evaluated in accordance with IDEA as having one of the disabilities in the following list who, because of the disability, needs special education and related services. To be eligible, the disability must have *an adverse impact on the child's educational performance*.

1. **Autism**
   - a developmental disability
   - generally evident before age 3
   - causing significant impairment in verbal and nonverbal communication and social interaction
   - typically involving repetitive and stereotyped movements or behaviors, resistance to change, and unusual responses to sensory stimuli

2. **Deaf-Blindness**
   - concomitant hearing and visual impairments
   - causing severe communication, developmental, and educational need that cannot be addressed in programs for only one of the two disabilities

(Continued)

TABLE 16.2 Definitions of Disabilities Under the IDEA (*Continued*)

3. Deafness
- severe hearing impairment
- interferes with processing linguistic information through hearing, with or without amplification

4. Emotional Disturbance (also Emotional Disability)
- a condition exhibiting one or more of the following characteristics over a long period of time and to a marked degree
- an inability to learn that cannot be explained by intellectual, sensory, or health factors
- an inability to build or maintain satisfactory interpersonal relationships with peers or teachers
- inappropriate types of behavior or feelings under normal circumstances
- a general pervasive mood of unhappiness or depression
- a tendency to develop physical symptoms or fears associated with personal or school problems
- includes schizophrenia

5. Hearing Impairment
- an impairment in hearing
- may be permanent or fluctuating
- not included under the definition of deafness, above

6. Intellectual Disability (formerly Mental Retardation)
- significant subaverage general intellectual functioning
- concurrent deficits in adaptive behavior
- manifested during the developmental period

7. Multiple Disabilities
- co-existing impairments (excluding deaf-blindness)
- the combination of impairments causes such severe need that programs for one of the disabilities cannot adequately address the student's educational needs

8. Orthopedic Impairment
- a severe orthopedic impairment caused by congenital anomalies, disease, and other causes
- having limited strength, vitality, or alertness, or heightened alertness to environmental stimuli
- resulting in limited alertness with respect to the educational environment
- due to chronic or acute health problems such as asthma, diabetes, ADHD, epilepsy, Tourette syndrome etc.

9. Specific Learning Disability
- a disorder in one or more of the basic psychological processes involved in understanding or using language, spoken or written
- manifests in the imperfect ability to listen, think, speak, read, write, spell, or to do math calculations
- does not include learning problems that are primarily the result of visual, hearing, motor disabilities, mental retardation, emotional disturbance or of environmental, cultural, or economic disadvantage

10. Speech or Language Impairment
- a communication disorder
- includes stuttering, impaired articulation, a voice impairment, or language impairment

11. Traumatic Brain Injury
- an acquired injury to the brain caused by an external physical force
- resulting in impairments in one or more areas: cognition, language, memory, attention, reasoning, abstract thinking, judgment, problem-solving, psychosocial behavior, physical functions, information processing, speech and sensory, perceptual, and motor abilities
- does not include congenital or degenerative brain injuries or those caused by birth trauma

12. Visual Impairment Including Blindness
- an impairment in vision that, even with correction, affects educational performance
- includes partial sight and blindness.

Source: 34 CFR §300.8, 2007

the definitions of each of the categories of disabilities that may entitle a child to receive special education under the IDEA. As can be seen from the definitions in Table 16.2, the IDEA requires that the identified disabilities affect educational performance. Although a student with a disability may need, or at least benefit from, some interventions or special instruction, if the disability has minimal or no negative effect on learning, the student would not qualify as eligible for special education under the IDEA. However, he or she might be eligible for reasonable accommodations or supports under Section 504 if his or her impairment substantially limits a major life activity.

When a student is determined to be eligible for services under the IDEA, the school system is required to provide a FAPE. It is important to remember that the law specifically states that the education must be "appropriate." This standard has been adopted by most states. *Appropriate* does not mean *best*, and loosely using the term *best* when the school team means appropriate can cause significant problems. Although professional school counselors and other professionals will try to do their best in providing services, they will not always provide the maximum or most beneficial services to an individual student. When the word *best* is used, it can lead to parental expectations of a range of services that are not required under the law or necessary for the student to learn.

This increased level of services might be helpful in assisting the student to reach optimal performance; however, the IDEA does not require optimal programming, only appropriate programming that enables a child to make reasonable educational progress.

The provision of FAPE generally involves two types of services, special education and related services. Special education is provided by special educators, as well as general educators and paraprofessionals in consultation with special educators. The IDEA identifies a continuum of placements where students may receive their instructional services, related services, or both. They range from full-time regular class placement to part-time regular class placement to services provided in residential schools and hospitals, with most students educated in regular education classes for a majority of the school day (U.S. Department of Education, Office of Special Education and Rehabilitative Services, Office of Special Education Programs, 2012).

Once found eligible for special education, students are entitled to receive not only special education instruction, but also related services, accommodations, and supports that meet their needs and enable them to benefit from their educational program. In a few statutorily specified instances, some related services—for example, speech—can be considered special education instruction.

CASE STUDY 16.1

Disability Snapshots.

All the following snapshots were adapted from disability fact sheets available from the National Dissemination Center for Children with Disabilities (www.Nichcy.org).

Autism, Ryan's Story.

Ryan is a healthy, active 2-year-old, but his parents are concerned because he doesn't seem to be doing the same things that his older sister did at this age. He's not really talking, yet, although sometimes he repeats, over and over, words that he hears others say. He doesn't use words to communicate, though. It seems he just enjoys the sounds of them. Ryan spends a lot of time playing by himself. He has a few favorite toys, mostly cars, or anything with wheels on it! And sometimes, he spins himself around as fast as he does the wheels on his cars. Ryan's parents are really concerned, as he's started throwing a tantrum whenever his routine has the smallest change. More and more his parents feel stressed not knowing what might trigger Ryan's next upset.

Often, it seems Ryan doesn't notice or care if his family or anyone else is around. His parents just don't know how to reach their little boy, who seems so rigid and far too set in his ways for his tender young age. After talking with their family doctor, Ryan's parents call the Early Intervention office in their community and make an appointment to have Ryan evaluated.

When the time comes, Ryan is seen by several professionals who play with him, watch him, and ask his parents a lot of questions. When they're all done, Ryan is diagnosed with autism, one of the five disorders listed under an umbrella category of "autism spectrum."

As painful as this is for his parents to learn, the early intervention staff encourages them to learn more about the autism spectrum. By getting an early diagnosis and beginning treatment, Ryan has the best chance to grow and develop. Of course, there's a long road ahead, but his parents take comfort in knowing that they aren't alone, and they're getting Ryan the help he needs.

(Continued)

What Are the Characteristics of Autism Spectrum Disorder?

Each of the disorders on the autism spectrum is a neurological disorder that affects a child's ability to communicate, understand language, play, and relate to others. They share some or all of the following characteristics, which can vary from mild to severe and are typically evident before the age of 3 years:

- Communication problems (for example, with the use or comprehension of language);
- Difficulty relating to people, things, and events;
- Playing with toys and objects in unusual ways;
- Difficulty adjusting to changes in routine or to familiar surroundings; and
- Repetitive body movements or behaviors.

Children with autism or one of the other disorders on the autism spectrum can differ considerably with respect to their abilities, intelligence, and behavior. Some children don't talk at all. Others use language where phrases or conversations are repeated. Children with the most advanced language skills tend to talk about a limited range of topics and to have a hard time understanding abstract concepts. Repetitive play and limited social skills are also evident. Other common symptoms of a disorder on the autism spectrum can include unusual and sometimes uncontrolled reactions to sensory information—for instance, too loud noises, bright lights, and certain textures of food or fabrics.

Hearing Impairment: Caroline's Story

Caroline is 6 years old, with bright brown eyes and, at the moment, no front teeth, like so many other first graders. She also wears a hearing aid in each ear—and has done so since she was 3 years old, when she was diagnosed with a moderate hearing loss. For Caroline's parents, there were many clues along the way. Caroline often didn't respond to her name if her back was turned. She didn't startle at noises that made other people jump. She liked the TV on loud. But it was the preschool she started attending when she was 3 years old that first put the clues together and suggested to Caroline's parents that they have Caroline's hearing checked. The most significant clue to the preschool was Caroline's unclear speech, especially the lack of consonants like "d" and "t" at the end of words.

So Caroline's parents took her to an audiologist, who collected a full medical history, examined the little girl's ears inside and out, ran a battery of hearing tests and other assessments, and eventually diagnosed that Caroline's inner ear (the cochlea) was damaged. The audiologist said she had sensorineural hearing loss.

Caroline was immediately fitted with hearing aids. She also began receiving special education and related services through the public school system. Now in the first grade, she regularly gets speech therapy and other services, and her speech has improved dramatically. So have her vocabulary and her attentiveness. She sits in the front row in class, an accommodation that helps her hear the teacher clearly. She's back on track, soaking up new information like a sponge, and eager for more.

About Hearing Loss in Children

Hearing is one of our five senses. Hearing gives us access to sounds in the world around us—people's voices, their words, a car horn blown in warning, or a hello. When a child has a hearing loss, it is cause for immediate attention. That's because language and communication skills develop most rapidly in childhood, especially before the age of 3 years. When hearing loss goes undetected, children are delayed in developing these skills.

Recognizing the importance of early detection, the Centers for Disease Control and Prevention (CDC) recommends that every newborn be screened for hearing loss as early as possible, usually before they leave the hospital. Catching a hearing loss early means that treatment can start early as well and help the child develop lifelong communication and language skills.

Intellectual Disability: Matthew's Story

Matt is 15 years old. Because Matt has an intellectual disability, he has been receiving special education services since elementary school. These services have helped him tremendously because they are designed to fit his special learning needs. Last year he started high school. He, his family, and the school took a good hard look at what he wants to do when secondary school is over. Does he want more education? A job? Does he have the skills he needs to live on his own?

Answering these questions has helped Matt and the school plan for the future. He's always been interested in the outdoors, in plants, and especially in trees. He knows all the tree names and can recognize them by their leaves and bark. So this year he's learning about jobs like forestry, landscaping, and grounds maintenance. Next year he hopes to get a part-time job. He's learning to use public transportation, so he'll be able to get to and from the job. Having an intellectual disability makes it harder for Matt to learn new things. He needs things to be very concrete. But he's determined. He wants to work outside, maybe in the park service or in a greenhouse, and he's getting ready!

What Is an Intellectual Disability?

Intellectual disability is a term used when a person has certain limitations in mental functioning and in skills such as communicating, taking care of himself or herself, and social skills. These limitations will cause a child to learn and develop more slowly than a typical child.

Children with intellectual disabilities (sometimes called *cognitive disabilities* or *mental retardation*) may take longer to learn to speak, walk, and take care of their personal needs such as dressing or eating. They are likely to have trouble learning in school. They *will* learn, but it will take them longer. However, there may be some abstract things they cannot learn.

Learning Disability: Sara's Story

When Sara was in the first grade, her teacher started teaching the students how to read. Sara's parents were really surprised when Sara had a lot of trouble. She was bright and eager, so they thought that reading would come easily to her. It didn't. She couldn't match the letters to their sounds or combine the letters to create words.

Sara's problems continued into second grade. She still wasn't reading, and she was having trouble with writing, too. The school asked Sara's mom for permission to evaluate Sara to find out what was causing her problems. Sara's mom gave permission for the evaluation. The school conducted an evaluation and learned that Sara has a learning disability. She started getting special help in school right away.

Sara's still getting that special help. She works with a reading specialist and a resource room teacher every day. She's in the fourth grade now, and she's made real progress! She is working hard to bring her reading and writing up to grade level. With help from the school, she'll keep learning and doing well.

What Are Learning Disabilities?

Learning disability is a general term that describes specific kinds of learning problems. A learning disability can cause a person to have trouble learning and using certain skills. The skills most often affected are reading, writing, listening, speaking, reasoning, and doing math.

"Learning disabilities" is not the only term used to describe these difficulties. Others include *dyslexia*—which refers to difficulties in reading; *dysgraphia*—which refers to difficulties in writing; and *dyscalculia*—which refers to difficulties in math. All of these are considered learning disabilities.

Learning disabilities (LD) vary from person to person. One person with LD may not have the same kind of learning problems as another person with LD. Sara, in our example, has trouble with reading and writing. Another person with LD may have problems with understanding math. Still another person may have trouble in both of these areas, as well as with understanding what people are saying.

Researchers think that learning disabilities are caused by differences in how peoples' brains work and process information. Children with learning disabilities are not "dumb" or "lazy." In fact, they usually have average or above average intelligence. Their brains just process information differently. There is no "cure" for learning disabilities. They are lifelong. However, children with LD can be high achievers and can be taught ways to get around the learning disability. With the right help, children with LD can and do learn successfully.

Traumatic Brain Injury: Susan's Story

Susan was 7 years old when she was hit by a car while riding her bike. She broke her arm and leg. She also hit her head very hard. The doctors say she sustained a traumatic brain injury. When she came home from the hospital, she needed lots of help, but now she looks fine. In fact, that's part of the problem, especially at school. Her friends and teachers think her brain has healed because her broken bones have. But there are changes in Susan that are hard to understand. It takes Susan longer to do things. She has trouble remembering things. She can't always find the words she wants to use. Reading is hard for her now. It's going to take time before people really understand the changes they see in her.

(Continued)

What Is Traumatic Brain Injury?

A traumatic brain injury (TBI) is an injury to the brain caused by the head being hit by something or shaken violently. (The exact definition of TBI, according to special education law, is given in Table 16.2.) This injury can change how the person acts, moves, and thinks. A traumatic brain injury can also change how a student learns and acts in school. The term TBI is not used for a person who is born with a brain injury. It also is not used for brain injuries that happen during birth. Rather, the term TBI is used for head injuries that can cause changes in one or more areas, such as thinking and reasoning, understanding words, remembering things, paying attention, solving problems, thinking abstractly, talking, behaving, walking and other physical activities, seeing and/or hearing, and learning.

Attention-Deficit/Hyperactivity Disorder (AD/HD): Mario's Story

Mario is 10 years old. When he was 7 years old, his family learned he had AD/HD. At the time, he was driving everyone crazy. At school he couldn't stay in his seat or keep quiet. At home he didn't finish his homework or his chores. He did scary things, too, like climb out of his window onto the roof or run across the street without looking.

    Things are much better now. Mario was tested by a trained professional to find out what he does well and what gives him trouble. His parents and teachers came up with ways to help him at school. Mario has trouble sitting still, so now he does some of his work standing up. He's also the student who tidies up the room and washes the chalkboard. His teachers break down his lessons into several parts. Then they have him do each part one at a time. This helps Mario keep his attention on his work.

    At home, things have changed, too. Now his parents know why he's so active. They are careful to praise him when he does something well. They even have a reward program to encourage good behavior. He earns "good job points" that they post on a wall chart. After earning 10 points he gets to choose something fun he'd like to do. Having a child with AD/HD is still a challenge, but things are looking better.

What Is AD/HD?

Attention-Deficit/Hyperactivity Disorder (AD/HD) is a condition that can make it hard for a person to sit still, control behavior, and pay attention. These difficulties usually begin before the person is 7 years old. However, these behaviors may not be noticed until the child is older. Doctors do not know just what causes AD/HD. However, researchers who study the brain are coming closer to understanding what may cause AD/HD. They believe that some people with AD/HD do not have enough of certain chemicals (called *neurotransmitters*) in their brain. These chemicals help the brain control behavior. Parents and teachers do not cause AD/HD. Still, there are many things that both parents and teachers can do to help a child with AD/HD.

Orthopedic Impairment: Jennifer's Story

Jen was born 11 weeks early and weighed only 2½ pounds. The doctors were surprised to see what a strong, wiggly girl she was. But when Jen was just a few days old, she stopped breathing and was put on a ventilator. After 24 hours she was able to breathe on her own again. The doctors did a lot of tests to find out what had happened, but they couldn't find anything wrong. The rest of Jen's time in the hospital was quiet, and after 2 months she was able to go home. Everyone thought she would be just fine.

    At home, Jen's mom noticed that Jen was really sloppy when she drank from her bottle. As the months went by, Jen's mom noticed other things she didn't remember seeing with Jen's older brother. At 6 months, Jen didn't hold her head up straight. She cried a lot and would go stiff with rage. When Jen went back for her 6-month checkup, the doctor was concerned by what he saw and what Jen's mom told him. He suggested that Jen's mom take the little girl to a doctor who could look closely at Jen's development. Jen's mom took her to a *developmental specialist* who finally put a name to all the little things that hadn't seemed right with Jen—*cerebral palsy*.

What Is CP?

Cerebral palsy (CP) is a condition caused by injury to the parts of the brain that control our ability to use our muscles and bodies. Cerebral means having to do with the brain. Palsy means weakness or problems with using the muscles. Often the injury happens before birth, sometimes during delivery, or, like Jen, soon after being born. CP can be mild, moderate, or severe. Mild CP may mean a child is clumsy. Moderate CP may mean the child walks with a limp. He or she may need a special leg brace or a cane. More severe CP can affect all parts of a child's physical abilities. A child with moderate or severe CP may have to use a wheelchair and other special equipment.

Sometimes children with CP can also have learning problems, problems with hearing or seeing (called *sensory problems*), or intellectual disabilities. Usually, the greater the injury to the brain, the more severe the CP. However, CP doesn't get worse over time, and most children with CP have a normal life span.

In these circumstances, the child can receive an IEP that includes only the related services. In general, however, a child must need special education instruction to be found eligible under the IDEA.

For a child to receive special education and related services under the IDEA, a multidisciplinary team must complete a multistep process. The process involves a series of statutorily defined steps, including identification, screening, notification and consent, assessment, eligibility determination, IEP development, and implementation. Table 16.3 provides an outline of the special education process.

TABLE 16.3 Outline of Steps in the Special Education Process

1. *Identification.* A parent, guardian, state educational agency, other state agency, or local school system may initiate a request for initial evaluation for eligibility for special education (referral).

   - Referral must be made to the IEP team of the child's home school (the public school to which the child is zoned), even if he or she attends another public or a private school.
   - Referral should be in writing and clearly specify that it is a referral for special education services. It should provide parents' and child's names, address, and phone number.
   - Referral should include area(s) of concern—for example, problems with reading, problems attending and learning, and so forth.

2. *Screening.* A multidisciplinary team (e.g., parent, guardian, regular educator, special educator, administrator) reviews the records and history of the child's learning problem(s) to determine if there is a need for individualized assessment.

   - The parent will be asked to provide basic and historical information to determine possible areas of impairment.
   - The parent will be asked to allow review of records (e.g., medical, school) and sign consents to obtain any needed information.
   - The parent will be asked to complete screening interviews or data forms.
   - The evaluation team will determine if assessments are needed and in what areas.
   - If the team does not believe assessment is necessary, the parent may request mediation or due process.

3. *Notification and consent.* If screening identifies a need for further assessment, the team notifies parents and requests written consent for all areas to be assessed.

   - Parents must be notified in advance of any possible assessments.
   - Parents must sign written consent for all assessments.
   - Parents must receive 10 days' notice of all meetings.

4. *Assessment.* Professionals (e.g., special educators, psychologists, audiologists) administer tests individually to the student in a nondiscriminatory manner (considering dominant language, etc.).

   - Assessments should be completed in every area of suspected problem(s).
   - Assessments typically include educational and other areas (e.g., psychological, related health, visual acuity).
   - For each area of suspected disability, particular assessments are usually required, and these assessments are performed by assessment-specific evaluators. For example, a suspected learning disability requires at least an educational assessment and a psychological (cognitive) assessment, with the possible need for a speech-language or other assessment. The required evaluators are a special educator, psychologist, and speech-language pathologist, respectively.
   - If a parent disagrees with the results of an assessment, the parent may request that the school fund an independent evaluation.
   - Initial assessments are to be completed within 60 days of receipt of parental consent.

(Continued)

TABLE 16.3 Outline of Steps in the Special Education Process (*Continued*)

5. *Eligibility Determination.* The multidisciplinary team considers all assessment results and determines if the child meets the criteria for a disability under one of the eligible categories.

   • The team (including parent) reviews all assessment results.
   • With parent input, the team determines whether the child meets eligibility criteria for one (or more) disability areas.
   • If the team determines that the child does not meet eligibility requirements and the parent disagrees, the parent can request mediation or due process.

6. *IEP Development.* The team (including the parent) collaboratively: (1) develops goals to meet the student's needs and (2) determines all required services and supports needed to provide FAPE. IEPs must include

   • Present levels of performance in academic and functional areas.
   • A statement of measurable annual goals.
   • A description of how the child's progress toward meeting the goals will be measured.
   • A statement of the special education and related services and supplementary aids and services to be provided.
   • An explanation of the extent, if any, to which the child will not participate with nondisabled children in regular classes and activities.
   • A statement of any appropriate accommodations.
   • The start date for services.
   • The anticipated frequency, location, and duration of services and modifications.
   • Beginning not later than age 16 years, transition goals.

7. *Implementation.* The team, including the parent, determines the least restrictive environment (LRE) in which the student's IEP can be implemented. A school district is required to have a continuum of services available ranging from the least restrictive, general education classroom to the most restrictive, instruction in hospitals and institutions.

   • This occurs only after all the components of the IEP, described earlier, have been developed.
   • Each successive removal from a less restrictive placement to a more restrictive placement (e.g., from full-time regular class placement to part-time resource room) needs to be justified.
   • Placement in LRE includes placing the student, if at all possible, in the home school. It also means placement with nondisabled, age-appropriate peers to the maximum extent possible.
   • Students need not be assigned to a particular placement to obtain a service. Any service can be provided in any placement.
   • LRE is individually determined for each child—not by disability type, severity, program availability, or cost. It is based on his/her needs as reflected in the IEP.

Section 504 and the Americans with Disabilities Act (ADA)

Section 504 specifically focuses on students with disabilities in school and their right to access all services and programs available to students without disabilities (U.S. Department of Education, Office of Civil Rights, 2005). A student is eligible under Section 504 if the student has a physical or mental impairment that substantially limits one or more major life activities. Major life activities include caring for oneself, walking, talking, seeing, hearing, performing manual tasks, breathing, learning, and working. Thus, for example, students who are educationally able but physically disabled, such as typically achieving students with severe asthma or cerebral palsy, would be qualified individuals under Section 504. All students found eligible for services under the IDEA, then, are also qualified individuals under Section 504 because they have a

substantial impairment of a major life function—learning. This is important because this means that special education students may not be excluded from school activities such as assemblies, field trips, vocational programs, sports teams, or clubs because they have disabilities.

A student is also qualified under Section 504 if he or she has a record of having such an impairment or is regarded as having such an impairment. To "have a record of having, or be regarded as having such an impairment," means that the student has had a disability or has been believed to have a disability for a significant period of time even though the student no longer has a disability or did not, in fact, ever have a disability. An example would be someone who does not meet the criteria for autism, but who has been classified as having autism in the past.

To determine whether a student is protected under Section 504, an evaluation is conducted or existing records are reviewed. Public school districts receiving federal financial assistance are required by Section 504 regulations to provide a FAPE, parallel to the IDEA requirement, to students with disabilities in their jurisdiction. A FAPE under Section 504 consists of "regular or special education and related aids and services that . . . are designed to meet individual educational needs of handicapped persons as adequately as the needs of nonhandicapped persons are met" and are provided in accordance with Section 504 requirements relevant to educational setting, evaluation and placement, and procedural safeguards (34 C.F.R. Reg. 104.33(b)(1)). Although there is a clear overlap regarding the use of the words *special education* in both the IDEA and Section 504, in practice, students who require special education are served under the IDEA, and students who require only accommodations and support are typically served under Section 504.

Decisions about what educational and related services are appropriate for a child under Section 504 must be made by a placement group that includes persons knowledgeable about the child, the meaning of evaluation data, and placement options (IDEA, 2004). Students who are found eligible under Section 504 receive a Section 504 Plan. A Section 504 Plan is frequently patterned after an IEP, although it tends to contain less detail. The Section 504 Plan describes both the services the student is to receive and the accommodations the student needs to access the educational program. The services that may be provided under Section 504 include counseling services, physical recreational athletics, transportation, health services, recreational activities, special-interest groups or clubs sponsored by the recipients, referrals to agencies that provide assistance to handicapped persons, and employment of students, including both employment by the recipient and assistance in making available outside employment.

Section 504 is a civil rights statute that addresses discrimination in access to programs and services, not remediation of learning. Eligibility under Section 504 is not limited to a specific list of disabilities as for IDEA, nor is there a defined list of educational requirements and related services. In this sense, Section 504 covers a broader range of students in that any physical or mental impairment could potentially create eligibility. Impairments frequently resulting in eligibility under Section 504 are AD/HD (the most often cited diagnosis in schools under Section 504), medical conditions, physical impairments, behavioral or emotional disorders, addictions, communicable diseases, and chronic medical conditions. Examples of students who might be covered under Section 504, but not the IDEA, include students with alcohol or drug problems who are not currently using or abusing substances, as well as students with allergies or asthma, environmental illnesses, communicable diseases, and conduct disorders.

A useful resource entitled "Frequently Asked Questions about Section 504 and the Education of Children with Disabilities" is available at the U.S. Office for Civil Rights website at http://www2.ed.gov/about/offices/list/ocr/504faq.html. In addition, many states have developed comprehensive implementation guides for teachers and administrators such as the one available at http://doe.sd.gov/oess/documents/sped_section504_Guidelines.pdf.

Family Educational Rights and Privacy Act (FERPA)

In the role of case manager, professional school counselors are likely to encounter issues regarding confidentiality of records and other communications referred to them. Family Educational Rights and Privacy Act (FERPA), a federal law, defines access to and confidentiality of student educational records. FERPA also is sometimes referred to as the Buckley Amendment, in honor of its sponsor, Senator James Buckley. Under FERPA, parents have rights to control access to academic records until the student is 18 years old, at which time the rights are transferred to the student. Thus, under FERPA, an 18-year-old student must sign a release of information for a professional school counselor to share written records with anyone, including a service provider outside the system. In some states parents continue to control access to academic records until the student graduates. It is important to check your state's law regarding pupil records to determine which standard applies to you.

For the professional school counselor serving students with disabilities, three issues in FERPA are of particular importance:

1. Parents and adult students have a right to inspect and review all educational records of the student. Essentially, once a written document from any source is placed in the school file, parents and adult students have a right to inspect it. Further, they have a right to decide if the school may share the report in the future. In general, written permission must be obtained before an educational record can be shared.
2. FERPA defines what an educational record is and what a professional school counselor or anyone else may call a personal confidential file. Virtually every piece of paper, or other form of records such as audio or visual recordings, including all professional mental health reports, relating to a student in a school is an educational record if the information in it has been made available to anyone other than its creator. For professional school counselors to call any written documents in their possession "personal confidential notes," they must not have shared the information in the report with anyone at any time. For example, if a professional school counselor at a multidisciplinary meeting pulls out his or her notes

and reads from them, the notes become educational records and cease to be confidential counselor notes.

3. Under FERPA, the parent or adult student has a right to challenge what is in the school records and to have any information that can be proven to be inaccurate or misleading removed. They also can add explanatory notes to records.

Another issue of confidentiality facing professional school counselors who keep records on students with disabilities is that of safekeeping for the confidential files. Most counselors may believe that the files are safe in their offices. It is important, however, for the counselor to ensure that the records are locked up and that only the counselor (and supervisor) has keys that will allow access to the records. A good website that provides information and excellent copyright-free materials on all of the specific disabilities, education laws and regulations, parent rights and responsibilities, and other resources is www.nichcy.org.

RELATED SERVICES FOR STUDENTS WITH DISABILITIES UNDER THE IDEA AND SECTION 504

Students may receive related services under either Section 504 or the IDEA. Related services are noninstructional, ancillary services that are not part of the regular instructional program, but may be required for the successful implementation of a student's instructional program under the IDEA or Section 504. The IDEA (2004) definition of related services is "transportation, and such developmental, corrective, and other supportive services . . . as may be required to assist a child with a disability to benefit from special education" (20 USC 1400 § Title I(A)(602)(26)). These services include audiology, counseling, early identification and assessment, interpreting services, medical services (for diagnostic and evaluation purposes only), occupational therapy, orientation and mobility services, parent counseling and training, physical therapy, psychological services, recreation, rehabilitation counseling, school nurse services, social work services, speech-language services, and transportation (IDEA, 2004). In some instances, individual aides also are provided to assist students with school functioning.

School counseling services, when provided under the IDEA or Section 504, are listed on the IEP or Section 504 Plan as a related service. Related services can be provided on a direct basis, or they can be delivered indirectly using a consultation model with a teacher or family member. For example, the professional school counselor might instruct the teacher in how to reinforce social skills in class, rather than holding social skills training sessions individually with the student. The professional school counselor also might consult with the classroom teacher on how best to preempt or defuse the angry outbursts of a student with disabilities.

The need for counseling services in schools is as high as ever (see Table 16.4). Although mental health services may be provided by a number of different professionals in schools (e.g., psychologists, social workers, professional school counselors, mental health assistants, behavioral specialists), professional school counselors are increasingly being considered important resources in the delivery of services to students with emotional, behavioral, or social needs affecting their learning.

The IDEA (2004) specifically includes as related services for students with disabilities the following three service areas that are often performed by professional school counselors: counseling services, parent counseling and training, and rehabilitation counseling services. The information that follows on these three related service areas is provided by the National Dissemination Center for Children with Disabilities (2001) in collaboration with the U.S. Department of Education's Office of Special Education Programs.

Counseling Services

Counseling services, according to the ASCA (2014a), focus on the needs, interests, and issues related to various stages of student growth. Professional school counselors may help students with personal and social concerns such as developing self-knowledge, making effective decisions, making healthy choices, and improving responsibility. Counselors may also help students with future planning related to setting and reaching academic goals, developing a positive attitude toward learning, and recognizing and using academic strengths. Other counseling services may include parent counseling and training and rehabilitation counseling (i.e., counseling specific to career development and employment preparation). Counseling services are services provided by qualified social workers, psychologists, professional school counselors, or other qualified personnel (IDEA, 2004).

Parent Counseling and Training

Parent counseling and training is an important related service that can help parents enhance the vital role they play in the lives of their children. When necessary to help an eligible student with a disability benefit from the educational program, parent counseling and training can include

> assisting parents in understanding the special needs of their child, providing parents with information about child development, and helping parents to acquire the necessary skills that will allow them to support the implementation of their child's IEP or IFSP [individualized family service plan]. (IDEA, 2004)

TABLE 16.4	**The need for counseling services in schools**

Recent data on the mental health needs of children in schools reveal the following dismal status (Center for School Mental Health [CSMH], 2012):

- Between 14 and 20% of children and adolescents experience a mental, emotional, or behavioral disorder each year.
- Despite the widely documented need, the mental health needs of students are largely unmet.
  - Mental health services for preschool children are often limited and difficult to access.
  - Approximately 70% of school-aged children with a diagnosable mental illness do not receive treatment.

Recommendations for addressing the problem include

- It is critical to provide mental health care in natural settings, such as schools, and effectively partner with caregivers and communities.
- School mental health programs have significantly greater access to children and adolescents relative to community mental health centers, as evidenced by:
  - Of the children and adolescents who receive mental health services, 70% to 80% access services in the school setting.
  - Approximately 96% of children follow through with school mental health services after the initial referral; whereas only 13% of children follow through with referrals to community mental health centers.
  - Twenty percent of all students receive some form of school mental health services.
  - School mental health programs decreased barriers to care, as well as the stigma of help seeking, which has resulted in dramatic improvements in access to care.

Benefits of School Mental Health

- Integrating mental health services within schools promotes an ecologically grounded, comprehensive approach to helping children and families by addressing their educational and concomitant emotional, behavioral and developmental needs.
- A comprehensive literature review indicates that the most effective interventions are those that target the ecology or environments of the child and are well-integrated into the learning environment.
- School mental health programs promote the generalization and maintenance of treatment gains, enhance capacity for prevention and mental health promotion and foster clinical efficiency and productivity.
- Beyond just students with diagnosable disorders, all youth in schools can benefit from school mental health policies and programs that successfully promote social, emotional, and behavioral health, build positive school climate, and prevent school violence and dropout.
- When school mental health programs are successful in reaching the whole school, students and teachers feel that they are in a positive learning environment and there are fewer referrals to special education based on emotional/behavioral problems.

Evidence for the Positive Impact of School Mental Health on Educational and Emotional/Behavioral Outcomes

- School mental health programs have an impact across a variety of emotional and behavioral problems in children and adolescents. Addressing mental health issues in youth helps reduce nonacademic barriers to learning and can lead to the academic gains.
- Effective school mental health programs enable students to be more engaged and feel connected to the school, and led to lower rates of identified emotional and behavioral disorders such as attention deficit/hyperactivity disorder, depression, and conduct disorder.

Source: CSMH, 2012

Rehabilitation Counseling Services

Rehabilitation counseling services are

> services provided by qualified personnel in individual or group sessions that focus specifically on career development, employment preparation, achieving independence, and integration in the workplace and community. . . . The term also includes vocational rehabilitation

services provided to a student with disabilities by vocational rehabilitation programs funded under the Rehabilitation Act of 1973, as amended. (IDEA, 2004)

According to the Council on Rehabilitation Education (CORE; 2003–2004), a rehabilitation counselor is a counselor who possesses the specialized knowledge, skills, and attitudes needed to collaborate in a professional relationship with people who have disabilities to help them to achieve their personal, social, psychological, and vocational goals. To this end, rehabilitation counseling services generally may include assessment of a student's attitudes, abilities, and needs; vocational counseling and guidance; vocational training; and identifying job placements.

TRANSITION SERVICES UNDER THE IDEA

The professional school counselor may have a variety of responsibilities in providing transition services to students with disabilities. According to the IDEA (2004), the term *transition services* means a coordinated set of activities for a child with a disability that:

- Is designed to be within a results-oriented process that is focused on improving the academic and functional achievement of the child with a disability in order to facilitate the child's movement from school to postschool activities, including postsecondary education, vocational education, integrated employment (including supported employment), continuing and adult education, adult services, independent living, or community participation;
- Is based on the individual child's needs, taking into account the child's strengths, preferences, and interests; and
- Includes instruction, related services, community experiences, the development of employment and other postschool adult living objectives, and when appropriate, acquisition of daily living skills and the provision of a functional vocational evaluation.

Beginning not later than the first IEP to be in effect when the child is 16 years old, and updated annually thereafter, each student's IEP must include

- Appropriate, measurable postsecondary goals based on age-appropriate transition assessments related to training, education, employment, and, where appropriate, independent living skills;
- The transition services (including courses of study) needed to assist the child in reaching those goals; and
- Beginning not later than 1 year before the child reaches the age of majority under state law, a statement that the child has been informed of the child's rights under the IDEA, if any, that will transfer to the child on reaching the age of majority.

In addition to the provision of programming for transition services and of related services as described earlier, there are other support services required for students with disabilities that may involve the professional school counselor. These areas include some types of assessment, interpretation of assessments, positive behavioral support services, case management,

advocacy, collaboration with other pupil support specialists, social skills training, activities to improve self-esteem, support for high school completion, dropout prevention, self-determination training, vocational programming, career development, evaluation of college options, and referral to outside agencies. These support services and other IEP responsibilities are defined briefly in Table 16.5.

PROVIDING SERVICES TO SUPPORT STUDENTS WITH DISABILITIES

Professional school counselors have many responsibilities, which can be roughly divided into four main categories. First are the counselor's responsibilities in developing and implementing a response to intervention (RTI) process to identify students at risk. The second category includes counselors' responsibilities to the IEP team in providing assessments, collaborating on the eligibility decision-making process, and developing counseling goals and objectives. The third category of responsibilities involves the provision of direct services to children with disabilities, including counseling services, vocational guidance, and transition programming. Finally, professional school counselors have indirect responsibilities to support the child by providing case management, consulting with teachers, training parents, and/or developing community-based resources that can assist the child after his or her graduation.

Developing and Using Response to Intervention

According to a 2008 position statement, the ASCA views professional school counselors as stakeholders in the development and implementation of the RTI process. RTI is a multitier approach to help students in both general and special education who are struggling academically and behaviorally through early identification and support. All children begin the RTI process by participating in high-quality instruction coupled with screening for potential problems in the regular education classroom. Learners experiencing academic and behavioral problems then receive interventions at increasing levels of intensity to address problems and return their learning trajectory to normal levels. These early intervention services are provided by school personnel from various disciplines, including classroom teachers, special educators, and specialists. Student progress is monitored and assessed to determine both performance and learning rate. Duration and intensity of interventions are based on each student's response to the interventions and outcomes data.

Professional school counselors address the needs of struggling students by designing and implementing inter-

TABLE 16.5   Definitions of Typical Services Performed by Professional School Counselors for Children with Disabilities as Required Under the IDEA

Advocacy. Actively supporting the rights of individual children with disabilities, including referral, active participation in team processes, promotion of the rights and needs of students, and support for service delivery by self and others.

Assessment. Determining current performance and identifying areas of need for social or emotional functioning in school; evaluation in other areas, including substance abuse, social skills, self-determination, self-esteem, and career development.

Career counseling. The process of assisting individuals in the development of a life-career with focus on the definition of the worker role and how that role interacts with other life roles (National Career Development Association [NCDA], 2009).

Clinical case management. Coordinating counseling and delivery of other services for students with disabilities. Note that in its 2004 position statement, the ASCA (2014a) recommended against serving as case manager for students for whom a counselor is not delivering direct services.

Clinical support. Providing supervision and support of certified or trained assistants who are assisting in the delivery of related services, including mental health associates, interns, special educators, paraprofessionals, assistants, or others.

Collaboration. Working with other team members (e.g., educators, parents, other related service personnel) to deliver required services and supports to students with disabilities.

Crisis intervention. Providing intervention for emergent situations, including acting out behavior, suicide risk, panic attacks, or other urgent needs.

Decision making. Contributing to team consensus on the eligibility of a child for special education services under the current federal definitions of disability categories. Working with the team to determine required services and supports or accommodations as well as LRE where the student can receive an appropriate education.

Discipline and manifestation determination. Responding to serious discipline issues warranting possible suspension and expulsion. In cooperation with the multidisciplinary team, determining whether the behavior at issue was a manifestation of the disability and the need for alternative placement or supports.

Dropout prevention. Identifying students at high risk for dropping out and providing interventions aimed at engaging these students in school activities, promoting attendance, improving school functioning, and accessing other supports (e.g., mentors) as appropriate.

Direct services. Providing counseling to individuals or groups of students to address specific behavioral or emotional needs. May include social skills training, self-determination, career development, clinical support, grief work, and brief family counseling.

IEP development. Participating in designing measurable goals and identifying services and supports to address each area of need that interferes with functioning in school.

IEP team membership. Participating in screening, assessment, eligibility determination, IEP development, and progress monitoring for students with disabilities on the counselor's case load. Attending IEP meetings or providing written recommendations concerning the nature, frequency, and amount of counseling service to be provided to the child.

Parent counseling and training. Helping families access services in the school and community providing information on disability and disability management and supporting the implementation of their child's IEP. This may also involve helping the parent gain skills needed to support IEP goals and objectives at home.

Positive behavioral support. Collecting data on a student's interfering behaviors to determine patterns of occurrence and to identify the function of the behavior. Generation of strategies designed to replace inappropriate behavior with more appropriate behaviors meeting the same function. Devising a system of prevention and intervention emphasizing positive behavior change methods.

Referral. Completing screening or other identification procedures to help identify students in need of special education. Referring individual children, as needed, to the multidisciplinary special education team for eligibility determination.

Safekeeping of confidential records. Ensuring compliance with the IDEA and other laws (e.g., FERPA) concerning access to and contents of confidential records of students receiving special education.

Self-determination training. Helping students acquire the skills necessary to direct their own lives. Skills in this area include self-awareness; identification of strengths, limitations, and interests; identification and programming of goals; self-advocacy; and goal-directed activity.

Transition program planning. Participating in the development and implementation of a transition plan for caseload students with disabilities who are 14 years old or older, including an individual's and family's postschool goals specific to postsecondary education, employment, and independent living. Providing linkages to adult services, supported employment, independent living options, and postsecondary education supports as appropriate.

vention plans and assess the effectiveness of these interventions by collecting outcomes data. Professional school counselors assist in the RTI process by:

- Providing all students with a standards-based guidance curriculum to address universal academic, career, and personal/social development
- Analyzing academic and behavioral data to identify struggling students
- Identifying and collaborating on research-based intervention strategies that are implemented by school staff
- Evaluating academic and behavioral progress after interventions
- Revising interventions as appropriate
- Referring to school and community services as appropriate
- Collaborating with administrators about RTI design and implementation
- Advocating for equitable education for all students and working to remove systemic barriers (ASCA, 2008)

SCHOOLWIDE SYSTEMS OF PBS The Response to Intervention approach includes both academic supports and behavioral supports. The prevention and increasingly intensive tiers for student behavior is often referred to as Positive Behavior Support (PBS) or Positive Behavior Intervention Strategies (PBIS). The first approach for providing PBS is the establishment of general, schoolwide policies and procedures that promote positive behavior among all students, commonly referred to as schoolwide positive behavior support. According to the National Technical Assistance Center on Positive Behavioral Interventions and Supports (U.S. Department of Education, Office of Special Education Programs, 2005), the SWPBS process emphasizes the creation of systems

that support the adoption and durable implementation of evidence-based practices and procedures that fit within ongoing school reform efforts.

Comprehensive behavior management systems are very effective at improving school climate, decreasing instances of office referral by 50%, and preventing 80% of problematic student behaviors, including antisocial behavior; vandalism; aggression; later delinquency; and alcohol, tobacco, and other drug use. In addition, positive changes in academic achievement and school engagement have been documented using an SWPBS approach in concert with other prevention interventions (Sprague & Walker, 2004).

There are several major components in the development of effective schoolwide systems. These crucial elements are often constructed in a staff development program or incorporated into a model system that is developed, implemented, evaluated, and modified on a regular basis by school staff. Data are collected regularly and used to evaluate progress and monitor system implementation. The seven components are as follows:

1. An agreed-on and common approach to discipline,
2. A positive statement of purpose,
3. A small number of positively stated expectations for all students and staff,
4. Procedures for teaching these expectations to students,
5. A continuum of procedures for encouraging displays and maintenance of these expectations,
6. A continuum of procedures for discouraging displays of rule-violating behavior, and
7. Procedures for monitoring and evaluating the effectiveness of the discipline system on a regular and frequent basis. (U.S. Department of Education, Office of Special Education Programs, 2005)

THEORY INTO PRACTICE 16.1

THE PROFESSIONAL SCHOOL COUNSELOR AND RESPONSE TO INTERVENTION

Professional school counselors are stakeholders in the development and implementation of the Response to Intervention (RTI) process. Professional school counselors align with the RTI process through the implementation of a comprehensive school counseling program designed to improve student achievement and behavior.

The Rationale

Response to Intervention (RTI) is a multitiered approach to help struggling learners. Guided by student outcome data, RTI can be used to make decisions about general, compensatory, and special education, assisting in the creation of a well-integrated

and seamless system of instruction and intervention. Professional school counselors implement a data-driven comprehensive school counseling program that meets the needs of all students and includes the identification of students who are at-risk for not meeting academic and behavioral expectations. Professional school counselors design and implement plans to address the needs of struggling students and collect results data based on the effectiveness of the interventions.

The Professional School Counselor's Role

Professional school counselors assist in the academic and behavioral development of students through the implementation of a comprehensive developmental school counseling program based on the *ASCA National Model* by:

- Providing all students with a standards-based guidance curriculum to address universal academic, career, and personal/social development
- Analyzing academic and behavioral data to identify struggling students
- Identifying and collaborating on research-based intervention strategies that are implemented by school staff
- Evaluating academic and behavioral progress after interventions

- Revising interventions as appropriate
- Referring to school and community services as appropriate
- Collaborating with administrators about RTI design and implementation
- Advocating for equitable education for all students and working to remove systemic barriers

Table 16.6 demonstrates how the American School Counseling Association views the alignment of comprehensive school counseling programming with the RTI process (ASCA, 2008).

TABLE 16.6   Role of the professional school counselor in the RTI process

RTI Process	Role of the Professional School Counselor
Tier 1: Universal Core Instructional Interventions: All Students, Preventative and Proactive	1. Standards and Competencies (Foundation) 2. Guidance Curriculum (Delivery System) 3. Individual Student Planning (Delivery) 4. Curriculum Action Plan (Management) 5. Curriculum Results Report (Accountability)

Tier 2: Supplemental/ Strategic Interventions: Students at Some Risk	1. Standards and Competencies (Foundation)
	2. Individual Student Planning (Delivery)
	   a. Small-group appraisal and b. Small-group advisement
	3. Responsive Services (Delivery)
	   a. Consultation; b. Individual counseling; and c. Small-group counseling
	4. Closing the Gap Action Plan (Management)
	5. Closing the Gap Results Report (Accountability)

Tier 3: Intensive, Individual Interventions: Students at High Risk	1. Standards and Competencies (Foundation) 2. Responsive Services (Delivery) a. Consultation; b. Individual counseling; c. Small-group counseling; and d. Referral to school or community services 3. Closing the Gap Action Plan (Management) 4. Closing the Gap Results Report (Accountability)

(*Source:* ASCA, 2008)

The Professional School Counselor and the Identification, Prevention, and Intervention of Behaviors That Are Harmful and Place Students At Risk (*ASCA, 2008*)

The professional school counselor provides proactive leadership in identifying, preventing, and intervening with student behaviors. Using data to develop and evaluate preventive and responsive services to address these risks is an integral part of a comprehensive school counseling program. The professional school counselor collaborates with staff, schoolwide teams, parents/guardians, and the community to identify students who are participating in behaviors and intervenes with these students to limit or

eliminate the risk of harm or negative consequences. White and Kelly (2010) delineated many evidence-based practices professional school counselors can use to address protective and risk factors. Professional school counselors take a leadership role in enhancing students' strengths and reducing their risk factors by:

- enhancing social support through a peer mentoring or buddy system
- assigning adults as monitors or mentors for students
- providing classroom guidance lessons to increase student knowledge and awareness of the dangers of harmful behaviors, as well as promoting resiliency and success skills

(*Continued*)

- providing responsive services, including short-term individual and group counseling
- referring students and families to appropriate support services and community agencies
- collaborating with school staff to identify and assist students in crisis
- conducting staff development for school and district staff
- providing information, consultation, and support to parents/guardians to increase familial involvement

- advocating for changes in the school and community to promote resilience, success, and equitable access to needed resources

In summary, by implementing a comprehensive school counseling program, professional school counselors collaborate with other educators and stakeholders to provide prevention, early identification, and intervention for all students to minimize or eliminate harmful behaviors that place students at risk.

It is beyond the scope of this chapter to describe the development of a schoolwide Positive Behavior Support System. However, the Office of Special Education Programs has developed a Technical Assistance Center on Positive Behavioral Interventions and Supports (PBIS) in collaboration with the U.S. Department of Education and 11 technical assistance units across the United States. Resources on this site include everything necessary to develop a comprehensive schoolwide (or districtwide) PBIS system, including planning and training materials, videos examples, and evaluation materials. All resources can be accessed for free at http://www.pbis.org/school/rti.aspx.

Multidisciplinary Team Responsibilities

ASSESSING STUDENTS WITH DISABILITIES Professional school counselors serving students with disabilities often provide wide-ranging assessment services (see Table 16.7). In addition, professional school counselors may be asked to explain the assessments conducted by others. Usually, the reason professional school counselors are asked to review the assessment reports of others is because of time conflicts preventing the assessor from attending meetings. The professional school counselor can prepare for this eventuality through training or by asking the report writer, usually the

school psychologist or educational diagnostician, for a briefing on the specific report prior to the day of the multidisciplinary meeting. The professional school counselor also needs to determine the policy in the school district regarding who may interpret another professional's report during a meeting.

Professional school counselors sometimes perform a complete assessment or a portion of an assessment. The professional school counselor must be trained in the administration of any assessment instruments used. IDEA requires any person assessing an individual student to obtain written parental consent prior to performing any assessment. Professional school counselors also need to be aware that in school systems, disagreements over who may use a testing instrument may arise among professionals who do assessments. Professional school counselors who find themselves in such conflicts will have to determine whether administering a specific assessment instrument is worth being in conflict with a colleague.

Professional school counselors often do assessments of social skills and career skills and frequently deliver or consult on the delivery of training for these skills. In assessing social skills, most programs have a preintervention screening measure, or pretest. Using the pretest along with implementing the social skills program provides an indicator of the treatment success.

TABLE 16.7 **Assessment Functions of Professional School Counselors Serving Students with Disabilities**

1. Carry out and/or interpret functional behavioral assessments.
2. Interpret educational skill assessments.
3. Carry out and/or interpret curriculum-based assessments.
4. Explain psychological testing, including cognitive ability, emotional status, and behavior measures.
5. Carry out and/or interpret counseling assessments, including social skill, emotional status, and behavioral measures.
6. Carry out structured observations of the student.
7. Carry out a student records review.
8. Help stress the need for assessing student strengths.
9. Assess peer attitudes toward students with disabilities.
10. Collaborate with others using portfolio-, performance-, and curriculum-based assessments.

In particular, the professional school counselor may be asked to assess a student's social, emotional, or behavioral functioning in school. One method is to use a behavior checklist that has parent, teacher, and student forms. The results of the assessment are the answers given by the parent, teacher, and student that the professional school counselor may then interpret, report, or both.

An example of this type of assessment instrument is the Child Behavior Checklist (CBCL), part of the Achenbach System of Empirically Based Assessment (ASEBA) by Achenbach and Rescorla (2001). The CBCL has become one of the most widely used instruments for assessing children's behavior, with separate norms for males and females and for different age groups from age 6 to 18 years. A direct observation form, teacher rating form, semistructured interview form, and youth self-report are also available. The CBCL has six scales—Affective Problems, Anxiety Problems, Somatic Problems, Attention Deficit/Hyperactivity Problems, Oppositional Defiant Problems, and Conduct Problems—oriented to the American Psychiatric Association's (2013) *Diagnostic and Statistical Manual of Mental Disorders.* In addition, the CBCL provides descriptive measures in nine observable behavioral areas.

Other instruments are available to address more specific areas of social, emotional, or behavioral functioning. For example, there are substance abuse, depression, social skills, self-esteem, and anxiety rating scales available. Most of these instruments require only training on the instrument for the professional school counselor to become adept at using them, as long as they are not being used to evaluate or diagnose, but rather to describe how the student perceives the situation or how others perceive the student's situation.

The Center for School Mental Health (CSMH) at the University of Maryland Medical School has compiled many useful resources for school-based clinicians available at http://csmh.umaryland.edu/Resources/ClinicianTools /index.html. In addition to information and resources on children's mental health awareness and dealing with trauma in school, CSMH provides a list of assessment measures for clinicians that are available for free online. Many of the recommended clinical measures can be used in school mental health programs to help assess symptoms of clinical disorders (e.g., depression, anxiety, ADHD), as well as measures to assess school climate and student attitudes.

Two other assessments are seeing increased usage because of changes to the IDEA. When disciplinary actions by school personnel will result in extended periods of removal from school for a student (i.e., after the first removal beyond 10 cumulative school days in a school year or after a removal that constitutes a change in placement), the IDEA requires that the IEP team meet within 10 days to make a *manifestation determination.* If a manifestation is evident, the team must then conduct a functional behavioral assessment (FBA) and develop a behavior intervention plan (BIP). If a behavior intervention plan already exists, the team must review and revise it as necessary to ensure that it addresses the behavior on which disciplinary action is predicated. The FBA and the development of BIPs are discussed in detail following. Figure 16.1 provides a helpful resource for understanding and conducting an SOP.

Purpose: The Summary of Functional Performance (SOP) is required under the reauthorization of the Individuals with Disabilities Education Act of 2004. The language as stated in IDEA 2004 regarding the SOP is as follows:

For a child whose eligibility under special education terminates due to graduation with a regular diploma, or due to exceeding the age of eligibility, the local education agency "shall provide the child with a summary of the child's academic achievement and functional performance, which shall include recommendations on how to assist the child in meeting the child's postsecondary goals" Sec. 300.305(e){3}.

The Summary of Functional Performance, with the accompanying documentation, is important to assist the student in the transition from high school to higher education, training and/or employment. This information is necessary under Section 504 of the Rehabilitation Act and the Americans with Disabilities Act to help establish a student's eligibility for reasonable accommodations and supports in postsecondary settings. It is also useful for the Vocational Rehabilitation Comprehensive Assessment process. The information about students' current level of functioning is intended to help postsecondary institutions consider accommodations for access. *These recommendations should not imply that any individual who qualified for special education in high school will automatically qualify for services in the postsecondary education or the employment setting. Postsecondary settings will continue to make eligibility decisions on a case-by-case basis.*

The SOP is most useful when linked with the IEP process, and the student has the opportunity to actively participate in the development of this document.

The SOP must be completed during the final year of a student's high school education. The timing of completion of the SOP may vary depending on the student's postsecondary goals. If a student is transitioning to higher education, the

(Continued)

FIGURE 16.1 Summary of Functional Performance.

SOP, with additional documentation, may be necessary as the student applies to a college or university. Likewise, this information may be necessary as a student applies for services from state agencies such as vocational rehabilitation. In some instances, it may be most appropriate to wait until the spring of a student's final year to provide an agency or employer the most updated information on the performance of the student.

Part 1: Background Information—Complete this section as specified. Please note this section also requests that you attach copies of the most recent formal and informal assessment reports that document the student's disability or functional limitations and provide information to assist in post-high school planning.

Part 2: Student's Postsecondary Goals—These goals should indicate the post-school environment(s) the student intends to transition to upon completion of high school.

Part 3: Summary of Performance—This section includes three critical areas: Academic, Cognitive, and Functional levels of performance. Next to each specified area, please complete the student's present level of performance and the accommodations, modifications and assistive technology that were essential in high school to assist the student in achieving progress. Please leave blank any section that is not applicable.

An **Accommodation** is defined as a support or service that is provided to help a student fully access the general education curriculum or subject matter. Students with impaired spelling or handwriting skills, for example, may be accommodated by a note taker or permission to take class notes on a laptop computer. An accommodation *does not change the content* of what is being taught or the expectation that the student meet a performance standard applied for all students. A **Modification** is defined as a change to the general education curriculum or other material being taught, which alters the standards or expectations for students with disabilities. Instruction can be modified so that the material is presented differently and/or the expectations of what the student will master are changed. Modifications are not allowed in most postsecondary education environments. **Assistive Technology** is defined as any device that helps a student with a disability function in a given environment, but does not limit the device to expensive or "high-tech" options. Assistive technology can also include simple devices such as laminated pictures for communication, removable highlighter, tapes, Velcro, and other "low-tech" devices.

The completion of this section may require input from a number of school personnel including the special education teacher, regular education teacher, school psychologist or related services personnel. It is recommended, however, that one individual from the IEP Team be responsible for gathering and organizing the information required on the SOP.

Part 4: Recommendations to assist the student in meeting postsecondary goals—This section should present suggestions for accommodations, adaptive devices, assistive services, compensatory strategies, and/or collateral support services, to enhance access in a post-high school environment, including higher education, training, employment, independent living and/or community participation.

Part 5: Student Input (Highly recommended)—It is highly recommended that this section be completed and that the student provide information related to this Summary of Performance. The student's contribution can help (a) secondary professionals complete the summary, (b) the student to better understand the impact of his/her disability on academic and functional performance in the post-secondary setting, (c) postsecondary personnel to more clearly understand the student's strengths and the impact of the disability on this student. This section may be filled out independently by the student or completed with the student through an interview.

Part 1: Background Information

Student Name: _____ DOB:_____ Year of Graduation/Exit: _____

Address: _____ _____
                (Street)   (Town, state)   (Zip code)

Telephone Number: _____ Primary Language: _____
Current School: _____ City/State: _____
Student's primary disability (diagnosis): _____
Student's secondary disability, if applicable: _____
When was the student's disability (or disabilities) formally diagnosed?
If English is not the student's primary language, what services were provided for this student as an English language learner?
Date of most recent IEP or most recent 504 plan: _____

Date this Summary was completed: _____

This form was completed by: Name: _____ Title: _____

School: _____ E-mail: _____ Telephone: _____

Please check and include the most recent copy of assessment reports that you are attaching that diagnose and clearly identify the student's disability or functional limitations and/or information that will assist in postsecondary planning.

- Psychological/cognitive
- Neuropsychological
- Medical/physical
- Achievement/academics
- Adaptive behavior
- Social/interpersonal skills
- Community-based assessment
- Self-determination
- Informal assessment:_____
- Other:_____

- Response to Intervention (RTI)
- Language proficiency assessments
- Reading assessments
- Communication
- Behavioral analysis
- Classroom observations (or in other settings)
- Career/vocational or transition assessment
- Assistive technology

Part 2: Student's Postsecondary Goals

1.
2.
3.

If employment is the primary goal, the top three job interests:

_____
_____
_____

Part 3: Summary of Performance (Complete all that are relevant to the student)

Academic Content Areas	Present Level of Performance (grade level, standard scores, strengths, needs)	Essential accommodations, modifications, or assistive technology used in high school & why needed
Reading (Basic reading/decoding, reading comprehension, reading speed)		
Math (Calculation skills, algebraic problem solving, quantitative reasoning)		
Language (written expression, speaking, spelling)		
Learning Skills (class participation, note taking, keyboarding, organization, homework management, time management, study skills, test-taking skills)		
COGNITIVE AREAS	**Present Level of Performance** (grade level, standard scores, strengths, needs)	**Essential accommodations, modifications, assistive technology used in high school, why needed**
General Ability and Problem Solving (reasoning/processing)		

(Continued)

FIGURE 16.1 (*Continued*)

Attention and Executive Functioning (energy level, sustained attention, memory functions, processing speed, impulse control, activity level)		
Communication (speech/language, assisted communication)		

FUNCTIONAL AREAS	Present Level of Performance (strengths and needs)	Essential accommodations, modifications, assistive technology used in high school, why needed
Social Skills and Behavior (Interactions with teachers/peers, level of initiation in asking for assistance, accommodations, degree of involvement in extracurricular activities, confidence and persistence as a learner)		
Independent Living Skills (Self-care, leisure skills, personal safety, transportation, banking, budgeting)		
Environmental Access/Mobility (assistive technology, mobility, transportation)		
Self-Determination /Self-Advocacy Skills (Ability to identify and articulate postsecondary goals, learning strengths and needs)		
Career-Vocational/ Transition/ Employment (Career interests, career exploration, job training, employment experiences and supports)		
Additional important considerations that can assist in making decisions about disability determination and needed accommodations (e.g., medical problems, family concerns, sleep disturbance)		

Part 4: Recommendations to assist the student in meeting postsecondary goals
Suggestions for accommodations, adaptive devices, assistive services, compensatory strategies, and/or collateral support services, to enhance access in the following post-high school environments (only complete those relevant to the student's postsecondary goals).

Higher Education or Career-Technical Education:

Employment:

Independent Living:

Community Participation:

Part 5: Student Input (Highly Recommended)

SUMMARY OF PERFORMANCE: STUDENT PERSPECTIVE
  A. How does your disability affect your schoolwork and school activities (such as grades, relationships, assignments, projects, communication, time on tests, mobility, extracurricular activities)?
  B. In the past, what supports have been tried by teachers or by you to help you succeed in school (aids, adaptive equipment, physical accommodations, other services)?
  C. Which of these accommodations and supports has worked best for you?
  D. Which of these accommodations and supports have not worked?
  E. What strengths and needs should professionals know about you as you enter the postsecondary education or work environment?

I have reviewed and agree with the content of this *Summary of Performance.*

Student Signature: _____   Date: _____

Note. This template was developed by the National Transition Documentation Summit © 2005 based on the initial work of Stan Shaw, Carol Kochhar-Bryant, Margo Izzo, Ken Benedict, and David Parker. It reflects the contributions and suggestions of numerous stakeholders in professional organizations, school districts, and universities. The model template has been developed with participation of the Council for Exceptional Children (CEC), as well as several of its divisions—including the Division on Career Development and Transition (DCDT), Division on Learning Disabilities (DLD), and Council on Educational Diagnostic Services (CEDS)—the Learning Disability Association (LDA), the Higher Education Consortium for Special Education (HECSE), and the Council for Learning Disabilities (CLD). *It is available to be freely copied or adapted for educational purposes.*

COLLABORATION AND GROUP DECISION MAKING

Professional school counselors often will serve on multidisciplinary teams for determining eligibility and planning programs for students with disabilities. Although the laws are different with regard to the formation, membership, and responsibilities of multidisciplinary teams under the IDEA and Section 504, the professional school counselor's role is the same whether at a meeting operating under the IDEA or under Section 504. The professional school counselor must be a supportive member of a group decision-making process whose goal is to enable a student with a disability to learn. A primary task of the professional school counselor is to help the multidisciplinary team understand the whole student, especially the individual assets of the student that are sometimes not readily apparent in paper reviews. Assets such as good character, perseverance, mood, gross- or fine-motor coordination, special talents, desire to help others, motivation, sports skills, leadership qualities, unique experiences, supportive relationships, enriching hobbies, vocational experiences, close family ties, and membership in organizations need to be brought before the multidisciplinary group planning an individualized program for the student. In addition, school counselors are advised to avoid overstepping their required roles or assuming responsibilities, which would interfere with their ability to provide core counseling services. According to ASCA (2012), *inappropriate* administrative

or supervisory responsibilities for the professional school counselor include, but are not limited to:

- making singular decisions regarding placement or retention
- serving in any supervisory capacity related to the implementation of the Individuals with Disabilities Education Act (IDEA)
- serving as the school district representative for the team writing the IEP
- coordinating, writing, or supervising a specific plan under Section 504
- coordinating, writing, or supervising the implementation of the IEP.

All professional school counselors should consider whether peer tutoring or other generally available services would address the student's needs without the student's having to be labeled as having a disability. Most schools use some type of prereferral team process that attempts to address the student's performance problems prior to seeking eligibility for special services. On the other hand, no student may be refused the opportunity to receive special education under the IDEA when qualified, nor should the prereferral process be used to delay the determination of a student's eligibility for special education and related services under IDEA. Professional school counselors should always keep in mind the fact that the student's learning needs are the main focus of the multidisciplinary meeting.

Once a student has been deemed eligible, the IEP team determines the appropriate constellation of services to address the student's needs. If a student needs counseling services, this responsibility sometimes will be assigned to the professional school counselor. In other situations, a psychologist or social worker will provide the services. Sometimes the goals are written so that any one of these three professionals can provide the service, and the professionals determine among themselves who will take the responsibility. It is important that the provider of the service have the necessary training and availability to provide the service as specified on the student's IEP.

POSITIVE BEHAVIORAL SUPPORTS A significant percentage of students identified as having an emotional disturbance, behavioral disorder, or AD/HD demonstrate behaviors that interfere with their learning or the learning of their peers. Under the IDEA, the IEP team is charged with specific responsibilities in relation to the support of such students and others with similarly disruptive or problematic behaviors (e.g., students with autism, traumatic brain injury, mental retardation, learning disabilities).

There are three primary occasions that require the provision of *positive behavioral supports* (PBSs) under the IDEA: (a) the development of schoolwide systems of PBS, (b) PBS to individual students, and (c) PBS after a serious behavior (IDEA, 2004). The professional school counselor has roles in each area. In the creation of schoolwide systems of PBS, the counselor can serve on the school improvement team, help provide staff development activities, or otherwise provide assistance in general school programming for student well-being. By taking a leadership role in developing systems of schoolwide support, the school counselor can facilitate improvement for all students in the building in areas of appropriate behavior and reduction of problem behaviors (e.g., substance abuse, vandalism, bullying) and can help support increased learning for all.

In the second and third areas for providing PBS, the counselor is likely to be more directly involved in the collection of information for the FBA and the development of the BIP. In some schools, psychologists or behavior specialists typically conduct FBAs; in other systems, a behavioral support team collaboratively conducts them. This team is usually composed of a special education teacher, a regular teacher, a professional school counselor, a school psychologist, and an administrator. Sometimes professional school counselors are given the role of carrying out or interpreting FBAs. In these cases, the professional school counselor will want to attend training on the process. Most school systems provide their own training and have a required process for carrying out assessments. A general description of the process is provided later.

Positive behavioral supports are specifically required when an individual student's behavior interferes with his or her learning or that of others. When a student with a disability exhibits disruptive or problematic behavior, the IEP team must consider the need for a targeted intervention that includes appropriate strategies and support systems. This targeted intervention involves the completion of an FBA and the development of a BIP to address the specific target behaviors. The rationale for an FBA is that identifying the function of a student's behavior—specifically what the student seeks to receive or avoid by engaging in the behavior—helps the IEP team develop proactive instructional strategies (such as a positive behavior management program or strategies) that address behaviors interfering with learning. The use of BIPs has wide applicability to individuals with serious challenging behaviors and has been demonstrated to reduce problem behavior by 80% in two thirds of the cases. The FBA/BIP process has also been used to successfully reduce disruptive classroom behaviors in students with mild and moderate disabilities in both general education and self-contained classrooms (Goh & Bambara, 2012).

Unlike with other types of assessment, the goal of an FBA is the identification of the function of a student's misbehavior and the development of information on the conditions that give rise to the behavior, as well as the conditions likely to sustain or decrease the behavior. This information is directly applicable to the generation of strategies to prevent the occurrence of the behavior and to substitute more appropriate behaviors when similar conditions arise. The steps in the FBA process include: (a) the clear identification and description of the problematic behavior, (b) the identification of the conditions and settings in which the behavior does and does not occur, (c) the generation of a hypothesis regarding the "function" of the behavior for the child, and (d) the testing of the hypothesized function of the behavior by manipulating the environmental antecedents and consequences. An excellent overview of the FBA process, including completed samples, is available on the Multimodal Functional Behavioral Assessment website (www.mfba.net).

To document the existence of the target behavior, team members first collect data on the occurrences of the behavior in a variety of environments and under a number of differing conditions. Data need to be collected on the situation in which the behavior is demonstrated, such as the setting, time of day, environmental conditions, and group membership (situation demands). Data also need to be collected on the specific requirements expected of the child at that point in time (setting demands). Data are typically collected via an ABC log, which is a narrative listing of antecedents (what occurs immediately before the target behavior), the description of the behavior, and consequences (what occurs immediately after the behavior). When conducting ABC observations, it is important to identify class or setting demands, describe what is occurring, describe student behavior, describe the response (from teacher or environment), identify next antecedent (and repeat), and take copious anecdotal notes (see Table 16.8). It also helps to compute percentage of time on task or percentage of work completed, if possible.

The ABC data in Table 16.8 allow for the clear examination of the student's behavior. The ABC log reveals that some of Jeri's problematic behavior can be described as "calling out answers" and "arguing with teacher," both more objective targets than "disruptive behavior." Other data to collect include amount of work turned in, discipline referrals, grade report, frequency of time-outs or direct intervention, and educational history regarding the demonstration of similar behaviors.

In addition to the ABC data collection, a variety of individuals are asked to complete an interview regarding the possible behavioral targets. Parents, teachers, and other school staff would be asked questions about problematic behavior that occurs in their interaction with the student, the conditions under which it occurs, and what the individual has done to address the behavior in the past. In addition, the student should be interviewed to examine his or her perception of the behavior and its benefit to him or her. Interview data should include a description of the problematic behavior, settings where it occurs, frequency, intensity, duration, previous interventions used, and effect on the student. The Center for Effective Collaboration and Practice (http://cecp.air.org/fba/) has copyright-free samples of interview instruments available for FBAs, along with ABC charts and scatterplots to record frequency of behavior. Additional forms and completed FBA samples and other useful resources are available from the Technical Assistance Center on Social Emotional Intervention for Young Children (TACSEI; http://www.challengingbehavior.org /explore/webinars/12.14.2012_tacsei_webinar/prevent.pdf) and Special Connections, at the University of Kansas (www .specialconnections.ku.edu).

To select a specific target behavior to address, the team considers the existing problems that were revealed from the interviews and ABC data. Potential target behaviors must be described objectively and must be repeatable, controllable, and measurable. These elements are essential for verifying that the behavior is within the conscious control of the student, as well as quantifiable by the observer. To be measurable, a behavior typically must have a clear beginning and end point, contain movement, or produce a product that can be measured. Therefore, "throwing objects" would be an appropriate target behavior, whereas "aggressive behavior" would not. Similarly, "laziness, off-task behavior, and daydreaming" are not measurable targets, but "failure to complete work" or "completing work" can be measured. Only one or two behaviors are targeted at any one time. If necessary, the team can generate a list of behaviors and ask members to rank-order them by priority level. A useful hierarchy is Severity Level I: Physically dangerous to self or others; Severity Level II: Interfering with work or learning of self or others; and Severity Level III: Inappropriate for age or grade placement or likely to cause increasing problems in the future.

TABLE 16.8 ABC Log for Jeri, a Student with Disruptive Classroom Behaviors

Time:	9:30 a.m.
Setting:	Social studies class with Mr. Peters
Setting demands:	Group discussion with teacher-directed questioning
Participants:	Class of 28 students in Grade 4

Antecedent	Behavior	Consequence
Teacher (T) asks question.	Jeri says, "Ooh, ooh" and waves hand.	T calls on Jeri.
T asks another question.	Jeri calls out answer.	T says, "Raise your hand," and says answer is correct.
Jon (student) asks question.	Jeri calls out answer.	T says, "Jeri, that is incorrect."
T says, "Jeri, that is incorrect."	Jeri argues with T that she read it in a book.	T says, "You are wrong. The correct answer is _____."
T says, "The correct answer is _____."	Jeri says sarcastically, "Like you know anything, Peters!"	T says, "You've disrupted class one too many times. Go to the principal's office!"

Next, by examining situations where the target behavior does and does not occur, team members can identify variables that may predict the behavior (e.g., from Jeri's example in Table 16.8, the teacher asking a general question to the class) or consequences that may sustain it (e.g., the teacher paying attention to Jeri's call-outs and arguing with her). In addition, by seeing where the behavior does *not* occur, the team can explore possible functions for the student. For example, in other data collections conducted with different teachers and in different instructional settings, it became obvious that Jeri did not call out in class activities that included cooperative learning groups, and instead actively assumed a group leadership role).

The next step is to synthesize the available data to determine the possible function of the behavior for the student. Functions of behavior may relate to involvement with others (interactive functions), such as requests for attention (e.g., social interaction, play interaction, affection, permission to engage in an activity, action by receiver, assistance, information/clarifications, objects, food); negations/protests (e.g., cessation, refusal); declarations/comments about events or actions (e.g., about objects/persons, about errors/mistakes, affirmation, greeting, humor); or declarations about feelings/anticipation (e.g., boredom, confusion, fear, frustration, hurt feelings, pain, pleasure). Functions of behavior also may be noninteractive in that they provide internalized effects. For example, noninteractive functions can be habitual or for self-regulation, rehearsal, pleasure, or relaxation or tension release.

In our example, interview data were collected from Jeri as well as from her divorced parents. Her mother reported extreme difficulty getting Jeri to follow directions without a struggle. Her father reported no difficulty, as he "laid down the law" with no room for negotiation or discussion. He reported that he was surprised her male teacher had problems with her, as Jeri should respond immediately to the teacher as she does her father. Based on the synthesis of all of the available data, the team hypothesized that the function of her behavior may be to seek power or control.

Once the function of the behavior is hypothesized, the next step is to manipulate the environment to test the hypothesis. For example, if a student's behavior was hypothesized as seeking attention from peers, the team might construct a strategy to collect data at times where peer response was or was not forthcoming and to determine if the hypothesis was supported.

Once the function of the behavior is identified, the team can begin to craft a BIP. This document is used to provide information to educators and parents to address the student's target behavior. Typically, problematic behavior is addressed by (a) identifying ways to prevent or minimize the occurrence of the behavior, (b) providing appropriate methods to change the behavior, and (c) assisting the student in building more appropriate behaviors to meet the same function as the inappropriate behaviors did.

To reduce instances or prevent the occurrence of the behavior, strategies may be provided to help teachers and parents restructure the setting demands where the behavior occurs. For example, a teacher may use "Every Student Responds" (whole-class response) techniques to reduce the times when he or she calls on a single student for a response. Similarly, a parent may be advised to tell a child, "Come to the table now," instead of asking, "Are you ready for dinner?"

Next, the BIP often includes a specific behavior change plan to address problem behavior as it occurs. For example, Jeri's BIP might include the use of extinction procedures for call-outs to be combined with a DRL (differential reinforcement of lower rates of behavior) strategy. By ignoring the call-outs, Jeri's teacher stops reinforcing problem behavior, and the DRL provides reinforcement to Jeri as she meets preset (and increasingly lower) goals for number of call-outs per time period.

Finally, the BIP typically includes strategies to help the student learn more appropriate ways to achieve the same objective. For example, a student like Jeri who seeks control or power may be provided with choices and opportunities for appropriate leadership within the classroom or in other school activities. An excellent resource for developing and evaluating BIPs that includes methods for addressing skill deficits, addressing performance deficits, modifying the learning environment, and providing additional supports is available at the Center for Effective Collaboration and practice (http://cecp.air.org/fba/ under Part III—Creating Positive Behavioral Intervention Plans and Supports).

STUDENT SUSPENSION OR EXPULSION Another situation requiring the use of PBS is when a student has been suspended or expelled because of problem behavior. According to the IDEA, FBAs and BIPs are required in connection with disciplinary removals of students receiving special education services or for any combination of school removals totaling more than 10 days in a school year. The IEP team must meet within 10 days of the removal that results in the student being excluded for more than 10 days to determine whether the removal constitutes a change of placement. If so, the team must determine whether the behavior resulting in the disciplinary removal is a manifestation of the student's disability (discussed later). If it is determined that the behavior is a manifestation, the team must ensure an FBA is conducted and formulate a BIP. If a BIP already exists, the team must review and revise it as necessary to ensure that it addresses the behavior on which the disciplinary action is predicated. This process follows the same series of steps described earlier, but it is obviously less preventive in nature, as the student has already demonstrated seriously problematic behavior, warranting the school removal.

PARTICIPATION IN MANIFESTATION MEETINGS Manifestation meetings are multidisciplinary team meetings convened because a student has been excluded for disciplinary reasons from his or her educational program for more than 10 days during a school year. The meeting must occur within 10 days of the student's removal from school. The purpose of the manifestation meeting is for the team to determine whether the student's behavior was caused by, or had a direct and substantial relation to, the student's disability. It is important to remember that the student's competency is not at issue in a manifestation meeting. In other words, manifestation is not a determination of whether the student understood if his or her actions were right or wrong; rather, the meeting is purely intended to determine whether there was a causal connection between the student's disability and the behavior.

If the team decides that the behavior was caused by, or was directly related to, the student's disability, the student is not suspended and should return to his or her school program unless the team and the parent agree to change the student's placement. If the team determines that the student's disability did not cause the behavior, the student may be suspended or expelled unless the team finds one of two situations occurred: (a) if the student's IEP was not properly implemented or (b) if the team determines that the IEP did not provide the student with a FAPE (and therefore additional or different services should be included in the IEP). In addition, the student may not be suspended if it is determined his or her IEP was not implemented.

Under the IDEA, if a student with a disability is removed from school for more than 10 days in a school year, he or she must continue to receive programs and services that will allow him or her to progress toward meeting the goals on the IEP and in the general curriculum even when suspended or expelled. These programs and services may be provided through home teaching or, if the suspension is for an extended period of time, at a different location, such as an alternative education setting. Under Section 504, if the problem behavior is not a result of the student's disability, then the student may be excluded, and there is no requirement to continue his or her educational services during the period of exclusion unless the school provides educational services to any student excluded for the same reason.

In some instances, a student's behavior may be directly related to the disability and still result in a removal from school for up to 45 school days. This can occur if: (a) the student is involved in a drug offense, (b) the student is involved in a weapons offense, or (c) the student's behavior inflicted serious bodily injury.

The professional school counselor can be an important player in the manifestation determination meeting, particularly when the student's disability is emotionally based or has strong emotional or behavioral aspects (e.g., AD/HD, emotional disturbance, autism). The team may look to the professional school counselor to help it better understand the nature of the emotionally or behaviorally based disability. This can place the professional school counselor in a difficult position if other staff members disagree with the counselor's perspective. For example, the student might have physically or verbally assaulted a staff member in a fairly serious manner. When this happens, the counselor can lose the trust or respect of staff by simply focusing on the manifestation issue without acknowledging the effect of the assault on the staff member, whether or not it was a manifestation of the student's disability.

DETERMINING NEED FOR COUNSELING SERVICES FOR STUDENTS WITH DISABILITIES When considering individual counseling for a student, the professional school counselor should work with the family and staff to construct a list of the social, emotional, or behavioral issues and concerns affecting the student's educational performance. Assessments (including the FBA, if available) and interviews can provide important information on the extent and nature of the problems. A review and prioritization of this information can help the team to clarify the problem, identify ways to involve parents and other staff (e.g., teachers, other related service providers), recognize the need for implementation in multiple settings, and reveal the extent of this need and its impact on the types and amounts of services needed.

It is important for the professional school counselor to help the team remain focused on the purpose of school counseling as a related service for children with disabilities—that is, to enable the student to learn. It is easy to slip into discussing counseling interventions that might be helpful for the student, but that are not required for the student to learn. For example, the parents of a child with a learning or emotional disability might feel that counseling could reduce the child's anxiety. However, unless such a reduction in anxiety is needed for the child to be able to learn, it should not be included in the IEP.

Counseling goals usually fall under the area of social-emotional or behavioral needs, though they may include transition goals as mandated by law for students over age

16 years. Typical areas addressed by counseling goals include anger management, stress/anxiety management, respect for authority, compliance with school rules, self-determination/life planning, career awareness/vocational development, coping skills/frustration tolerance, interpersonal skills, family issues regarding postschool outcomes, and self-esteem.

Provision of Direct Services to Children with Disabilities

PROVIDING IEP COUNSELING SERVICES The IEP team, as a group, determines what services the student is to receive, the frequency of the services, and who is to provide the services. No one individual can change the components of an IEP. Sometimes the professional school counselor may feel the IEP does not identify the appropriate amount of time to provide the service, the appropriate services to provide, or the training necessary to carry out the task appropriately. Any of these issues could produce an ethical

dilemma for the professional school counselor. In these situations, the professional school counselor must follow the IEP as written until it is changed at an IEP meeting. At a meeting to revise the IEP, the concerns can be raised, and the team will have the opportunity to revise the IEP to appropriately address them. Under the 2004 provisions of the IDEA, nonsubstantive changes can be made to the IEP without another meeting. But this provision was merely intended to allow editing of typographical or similar errors.

It is also important that professional school counselors remain cognizant of the limits of their role and ensure that they do not perform activities outside their area of qualification. In particular, counselors should be careful not to assume responsibilities that are typically within the purview of psychologists or social workers or that are specifically assigned to others by the IEP. In some instances, IEP counseling goals will indicate that the counselor, psychologist, or social worker may provide the service. In that situation, the providers can decide who will implement the IEP. If a student's IEP calls for counseling

TABLE 16.9 Five Required Components of IEP Goals

1. *Direction* of change desired (may be *increase*, *decrease*, or *maintain*)	*Increase* (would be used for social skills, impulse control, self-determination, etc.)	*Decrease* (used for hitting, temper tantrums, call-outs, days absent, etc.)	*Maintain* (for example with attention span, attendance).
2. *Deficit* or *excess*	The general area that is identified as needing special attention	Deficit examples: work completion, ability to follow staff directions, frustration tolerance, coping, impulse control, and peer relationships	Excess examples: physical aggression, activity level, talking out, and anxiety level.
3. *Present* level	A description of what the student does now in the area of deficit or excess	Student's present performance level; ("from" _____)	Examples: working with a peer for 2 minutes, completing 40% of class work, arguing with teacher when corrected, remaining on task with direct adult supervision, and following directions with repeated prompts.
4. *Expected* level	Where the student can reasonably be expected to be, or what he or she can reasonably be expected to attain, at the end of one year ("to" _____)	Must be specific to the individual student and based on present level and what is realistic to expect in a year's time if the needed resources are provided	Examples: working with a peer cooperatively for 10 minutes, following teacher directions the first time given, responding appropriately to redirection/correction, remaining on task for 15 minutes with no reminders, using appropriate language in school, and asking for help or a break when needed.
5. *Resources* needed	The special methods, techniques, materials, situations, equipment, etc. that will be needed to enable the student to reach the expected levels of performance	Note: Do not name proprietary programs, devices, or equipment; rather, provide a description of the nature of the method	Examples: positive reinforcement, a point system, individual counseling, parent training, and job coaching.

services and the professional school counselor is unable to provide these services, the school may contract with another counselor to provide the services or may rewrite the IEP so that a psychologist can provide the services.

Goals are the core components of an IEP. They are intended to establish what the IEP team—including the parent and the child, when appropriate—thinks the student should accomplish in a year. These goals are based on the needs of the student as determined by relevant assessments and on the student's present levels of academic achievement and functional performance. The IDEA requires goals to address all areas of identified need in academic and functional skill areas. Functional skills may include adaptive skills, classroom behavior, social-interpersonal skills, self-determination, and vocational skills. The IDEA specifically requires the IEP team, in developing goals, to consider the strengths of the child; the concerns of the parents for enhancing the education of their child; the results of the initial or most recent evaluation of the child; and the academic, developmental, and functional needs of the child. The goals are to be designed to enable the student to be involved in and make progress in the general education curriculum and to address the student's other educationally related needs that result from the disability. Because goals are focused on the student's expected achievement in one year's time, goals are generally written in broad, measurable terms, but as required by the IDEA.

For each area of identified need, at least one goal should be written. If there are multiple areas, the team may decide to prioritize the issues and first address those issues it considers most important. Table 16.9 provides guidelines on how to develop effective goals.

The sample goals listed in Table 16.10 incorporate all five essential goal components. IDEA 2004 no longer includes the requirement for short-term or benchmark objectives; however, many state laws continue to require the provision of objectives. In addition, parents are entitled to request the provision of benchmarks to ascertain their child's progress in meeting goals. Therefore, we provide examples of appropriate, measurable objectives in Table 16.11.

EVALUATION PROCEDURES   IEPs must include evaluation procedures and schedules for determining, at least on an annual basis, whether the goals and objectives are being achieved. The evaluation procedure selected must be appropriate for the behavior or skill in question. Put another way, not every behavior or skill can be evaluated through "teacher or therapist observation." Some of the evaluation procedures that might be used for different objectives include direct observation, formal or informal assessments, and permanent products.

Direct observation by counselors and teachers provides a continuous and potentially valuable source of assessment information regarding student performance and may be used in all areas, including academic and social behavior. Observation can vary in its degree of formality and specificity, but when used to evaluate student progress it must be objective. Observational methods that are both objective and structured include event recording (e.g., number of call-outs), duration recording (e.g., time on task), interval recording (e.g., whether the student kept his hands to himself for each 15-minute period), and time sampling (e.g., whether the student was in her seat each time the timer went off). Evaluation methods may also use formal and informal tests (e.g., the ARC's Self-Determination Scale) or permanent products (e.g., a point sheet, percent work completed, homework returned, attendance record).

The frequency of data collection should be determined by (a) the importance of the objective in question and (b) the amount of additional staff time that it takes. As a guideline, evaluative data should generally be collected at

---

TABLE 16.10   Sample Goal Statements

1. Jon will decrease destructive behavior from an average of five incidents per week to no destructive acts through reinforcement of positive behavior and individual counseling.
2. Chandra will increase coping skills from screaming and crying to asking for help appropriately through modeling, strategy instruction, and positive reinforcement.
3. Lin will increase ability to follow class and school rules from 30% compliance to 90% compliance through group counseling, positive reinforcement (point sheet), and the use of a peer buddy.
4. Keith will increase peer relationships from rejection by peer group members to inclusion in group activities through social skills training and the use of group contingencies.
5. Davon will decrease arguing with adults and peers from a mean of 13 times per day to zero times through the use of extinction and individual or group counseling.
6. Keisha will increase social behavior from daily hitting, kicking, and throwing objects to no hitting, kicking, or throwing objects through modeling, positive reinforcement for appropriate social behaviors, and structured, small-group interaction.

TABLE 16.11   Sample Objectives

1. Given a 10-minute cooperative learning activity, Rodney will participate with peers without leaving the group in two of three consecutive trials. Evaluation procedure: Peer group log; Schedule: Daily.
2. Given a verbal direction from the teacher, Jay will comply within 1 minute 80% of the time. Evaluation procedure: "Follows Directions" points on point sheets; Schedule: Weekly.
3. When included in a small group of peers, Julie will exhibit consideration for others by taking turns, sharing, and refraining from physical aggression in three of four opportunities. Evaluation procedure: "Peer" points on daily point sheet; Schedule: Weekly.
4. Given bus tokens, Jose will arrive for school on time 95% of school days. Evaluation procedure: Attendance record review; Schedule: Weekly.
5. When demonstrating signs of anxiety and prompted by a teacher, Thomas will verbally identify the cause of his distress and at least one strategy for resolution. Evaluation procedure: Event recording; Schedule: Weekly.

least every week. It is these data that must be reported on regular IEP report cards. Table 16.11 provides examples of objectives written in measureable terms that include evaluation procedure and schedule.

SPECIFYING IEP SERVICES   The IDEA further requires that the IEP include a statement of the special education and related services and supplementary aids and services, based on scientifically based practices, to the extent practicable, to be provided to or on behalf of the child. In addition, the IEP must describe the student's participation in regular education programs, a list of the projected dates for the initiation of services, and the anticipated duration of services.

The frequency and intensity of counseling sessions are determined at the IEP meeting. Service frequency will vary significantly according to an individual child's needs.

Sometimes, for example, a student's needs require weekly sessions, either to help the student learn a new coping skill or to help the student stay emotionally stable and support his or her access to education. In other situations, the student may need to be seen less frequently, for monitoring only. In any counseling relationship, there also may be situations requiring that the counselor see the student when in crisis in addition to the time allotted on the IEP. IDEA permits a counselor to provide more services than the IEP dictates, but not less.

With the professional school counselor's input, the IEP team may also determine whether required services are provided individually or in group sessions. In other situations, the team will leave that decision to the judgment of the service provider. Also, the IEP team determines whether the service is delivered directly or via consultation with another staff member or parent.

THEORY INTO PRACTICE 16.2

STRATEGIES FOR COUNSELING STUDENTS WITH DYSLEXIA/LEARNING DISABILITIES
(ADAPTED FROM FALZON & CAMILLERI, 2010)

1. Don't underestimate students due to a varied cognitive profile, sloppy handwriting, poor spelling, or weak oral/written sentence structure.
2. Accommodate for:
   • Problems sequencing/organizing language.
   • Short-term memory challenges (use visuals).
   • Difficulty remembering instructions (use visuals).
3. Tips:
   • Use visuals to help with short-term memory, especially for instructions.
   • Keep writing as concise as possible.
   • Write in a large font and manuscript.
   • Pause frequently when speaking to allow for language processing.
   • Ensure comprehension.

4. Consider the following specific techniques:
   • Use cognitive behavioral therapy to help clients reflect on challenges, abilities and plans of action, through techniques such as motivational interviewing.
   • Teach assertiveness training for self-advocacy in the classroom (e.g., Rogerian techniques, role play, and/or empty chair technique).
   • Extend and explain therapy techniques to teachers, special educators, and parents.
   • Use psychodynamic group therapy for awareness of others with similar difficulties and mutual support to enable students to experience self- and other-empowerment.

Individualized Transition Program Planning

As noted earlier, the IDEA requires the IEP team to create a transition plan for a student with a disability by the time the student is 16 years old. Section 504 has no transition requirements. Students must be invited to IEP meetings where their transition plans are to be discussed. Representatives of programs such as vocational rehabilitation services also are to be invited to transition planning meetings if the parent consents to their being invited. If the parent does not consent to inviting the representatives of these outside programs to IEP meetings, including them could be a FERPA violation. Sometimes the state's department of rehabilitation services can provide diagnostic services while the student is in school and can then offer training for a career, money to assist in obtaining educational or support services, or linkages to adult services as needed after graduation.

The transition plan is intended to address all areas of the student's life after high school, including postsecondary education, career, independent living, recreation, and community involvement. Counselors can help the team by assessing student career interests; developing appropriate transition goals; providing resources and connections to adult services as needed; and helping the student with personal adjustment, self-concept development, self-determination training, career exploration, and job coaching. Professional school counselors also might help plan and implement a school-to-work program or internship for the student.

Because a transition plan focuses on the individual student's present needs and stated preferences, assessment is required. Typically, the assessment includes interest inventories, interviews of the student and parents (to determine expectations regarding employment, education, and living arrangements after high school), review of work history and work habits, review of progress toward graduation and postsecondary acceptance, self-determination assessment, and other information specific to the individual student needs (e.g., assessment of functional living skills, vocational assessment, interpersonal skill assessment). In many schools, the professional school counselor provides some or most of this assessment information to the team, which uses it to develop the individualized transition plan, which becomes part of a student's IEP. For example, the goals and needs addressed in a transition plan for Ryan, a 16-year-old, 11th-grade student with learning and behavioral disorders, might include

- Obtaining a part-time paid job in the community;
- Selecting and applying to a 2-year college or vocational program;
- Shadowing workers in three areas of career interest: elevator maintenance, cable installation, and computer networking;

- Identifying community-based counseling agencies to assist in addressing life stresses after high school; and
- Participating in church-related youth activities on a monthly basis.

Transition planning may also include goals relating to personal development, independence, self-determination, social skill development, or other needs for adult independent functioning (e.g., self-care, accepting criticism, cooking, resume development). For example, if a student plans to live independently in an apartment, then he or she may need goals in some or all of the following areas:

- Identify living options in the community;
- Describe processes and requirements for renting an apartment;
- Secure employment to financially support the goal;
- Budget for the cost of living by oneself;
- Demonstrate skills for maintaining an apartment; and
- Identify and access needed community resources.

Secondary Transition Programming

Although research continues to focus on ways to improve outcomes for students with disabilities, numerous programs and methods have been studied for their efficacy and outcomes. The following list of environmental supports, synthesized from the "best practice" literature, may be integrated into secondary programs serving students with disabilities (Stewart et al., 2013):

- Preprogramming/planning; high-quality programming; gender differences addressed in service delivery; and adult mentors as key supports;
- Collaborative team planning;
- Supportive community systems such as housing and policy/legislative supports, including financial and insurance aid;
- Peer networks and mentoring/personal advisor/navigator relationships to provide the support to youth and parents to access opportunities and experiences; and
- Flexibility and individualized supports to youth entering employment.

Although there are many school personnel involved in the successful transition of students with disabilities, a significant number of recommended services and strategies may involve the secondary school counselor. An overview of practices used in schools and demonstrated to promote successful transition is presented in Table 16.12.

An excellent resource for schools and professionals serving secondary students with disabilities is the National Alliance for Secondary Education and Transition (NASET). NASET is a voluntary coalition of 40 national organizations representing general education, special education, career and

TABLE 16.12   Research to Practice: Evidence-Based In-School Predictors of Postschool Success

Career Awareness	Employment-related skills learned through career or vocational education, including job search skills, interview skills, and job-specific skills
Community Experiences	Skills learned in nonschool environments, including mobility in the community and transportation, daily living skills, recreational and leisure skills, and workplace skills
High School Diploma Status	Standard high school diploma track (as opposed to alternative or occupational diploma)
Inclusion in General Education	Higher levels of enrollment in regular academic classes
Independent Living Skills	Instruction in leisure skills, social skills, self-care skills, and other adaptive behavior skills
Interagency Collaboration	Developing relationships with multiple parties, including students, parents, other family members, special educators, general educators, vocational rehabilitation counselors, independent living counselors, and/or other adult service providers
Occupational Courses	Participation in coursework designed to help students learn functional skills, independent living skills, and work skills
Paid Employment/ Work Experience	Having a paying job while in high school
Parental Involvement	Parents contributing actively during a student's transition years
Program of Study	Involvement in one of the following: (a) career major (i.e., sequence of courses based on occupational goal); (b) cooperative education (i.e., combines academic and vocational studies with a job in a related field); (c) school-sponsored enterprise (i.e., involves the production of goods or services by students for sale to or use by others); and (d) technical preparation (i.e., a planned program of study with a defined career focus that links secondary and postsecondary education)
Self-Determination	Developing skills in choice making, problem solving, decision making, goal setting and attainment, self-regulation, self-awareness, self-efficacy, and self-advocacy
Social Skills	Acquiring social skills to interact successfully with others both during school and after graduation
Student Support	Students with high levels of satisfaction in the support of their friends, family, teachers, and others during high school
Transition Program	Receiving comprehensive instruction and services to help work toward completing postschool goals in education, employment, or independent living
Vocational Education	Learning skills needed for choosing and preparing a career, skills and work habits, including skills such as interviewing, writing resumes, and completing applications needed for acceptance into college, or other postsecondary training, or to the workforce
Work Study	Spend a part of the school day taking traditional courses on-campus and the remaining part of the day at a job site working for pay or credit hours

Source: Adapted from Test & Cease-Cook, 2012

technical education, youth development, postsecondary education, workforce development, and families. Promoting high-quality and effective secondary education and transition services, NASET advocates for identifying what youth need to achieve success in postsecondary education and training, civic engagement, meaningful employment, and adult life. NASET has identified benchmarks that reflect quality secondary education and transition services for all students in its *Standards for Secondary Education and Transition*. The standards focus on five areas relating to the transition of students with disabilities to adult living: schooling, career preparatory experiences, youth development and youth leadership, family involvement, and connecting activities. A complete transition toolkit, which includes the standards and indicators, supporting evidence and research, and tools for self-assessment, priority setting, and action planning are available for free download at http://www.nasetalliance.org/toolkit/.

The National Secondary Transition Technical Assistance Center website (http://www.nsttac.org/) provides an extensive compilation of transition resources including training webinars and presentations, comprehensive transition toolkits, a directory of evidence-based practices and predictors, fact sheets, lesson plan starters for various transition skill areas, parent and student materials, and assessment and evaluation instruments. All of these resources are free and available for download.

HIGH SCHOOL PROGRAMMING The professional school counselor has an essential role in providing support for appropriate curricular programming for secondary students with disabilities. Students with disabilities have increased significantly the number of academic courses they are taking in mathematics, science, and foreign language. This is likely a positive effect of the increased requirements for access to the general curriculum under NCLB and IDEA. It is unknown whether this access, in and of itself, will be sufficient to enable students with disabilities to pass high-stakes testing for graduation, now required in every state. It will be essential to monitor student progress carefully over the next few years to determine what additional supports and services are required to enable students with disabilities to graduate with a standard diploma.

Another concern recently noted has been the significant decrease in the numbers of students taking vocational courses. This is likely a result of the increase in courses taken in the general curriculum by students with disabilities. This is a large concern, however, as vocational programming can significantly increase positive postsecondary outcomes. Professional school counselors should advocate for curricular programming to address individual student needs and help families to realistically determine whether goals should relate primarily to postsecondary education or to employment and independent living.

POSTSECONDARY EDUCATIONAL PROGRAMMING As noted earlier, students with disabilities attend college and other postsecondary educational programs at rates far below those of their nondisabled peers. One of the greatest needs for these students is to have others hold high expectations for their continued education, including attendance at 4-year universities, technical schools, and community colleges. There are excellent resources available to help students identify appropriate colleges, seek reasonable accommodations, and access support services (e.g., mental health services) while attending postsecondary educational programs. Some examples include the following:

1. DO-IT (Disabilities, Opportunities, Internetworking, and Technology), at the University of Washington (www.washington.edu/doit/Resources/postsec.html)
2. Post-ITT (Postsecondary Innovative Transition Technology), supported by the U.S. Department of Education's Office of Special Education and Rehabilitative

Services (http://azassist.com/wp-content/uploads/2012/06/Post-ITT-Guidance-Activities.pdf)
3. HEATH Resource Center (Higher Education and Adult Training for People with Disabilities), a national clearinghouse on postsecondary education for individuals with disabilities (www.heath.gwu.edu)

In March 2010, the Obama administration released recommendations for the reauthorization the Elementary and Secondary Education Act, entitled "Blueprint for Reform" asserting that "every student should graduate from high school ready for college and a career." Along with promoting a national consensus on core academic standards (referred to as the Common Core Standards), the National Governors Association Center has coordinated the development of curriculum standards for college and career readiness to formulate the "knowledge and skills students should have within their K–12 education careers so that they will graduate high school able to succeed in entry-level, credit-bearing academic college courses and in workforce training programs." Regarding college readiness, these standards articulate key curriculum content in four major aspects of college readiness including (a) key cognitive strategies, (b) academic knowledge and skills, (c) academic behaviors, and (d) contextual skills and awareness (Test, Cease-Cook, Fowler, & Bartholomew, 2012). The mapping of the college readiness standards onto specific common core academic standards enables secondary school personnel to ensure access to and acquisition of essential skills needed for successful transition to postsecondary education settings for students with disabilities.

Professional school counselors can help students with disabilities by providing them and their parents specialized information regarding readiness for college, including accommodations for the SAT-I or ACT exams, information on disability disclosure during the application process, methods to interview effectively, ways to document a disability at the postsecondary level, information on how to identify available accommodations at various colleges, and tips for finding a "good match" for a specific student's special needs. Following are general tips on supporting students with learning disabilities in the transition to college:

1. Teach students about their disability and compensatory strategies. Students should understand the nature of their learning problems. Specifically, they should be aware of their academic strengths and weaknesses, accommodations that allow them to circumvent their learning problems, and other study skills and learning strategies.
2. Teach students to self-advocate. Students become self-advocates when they (a) demonstrate an understanding of their disability, (b) are aware of their

legal rights, and (c) can competently and tactfully advocate for their rights and needs to those in positions of authority.

3. Teach students about the law. After high school, students with disabilities are no longer entitled to special services, only equal access. Students need to know that it is their responsibility to self-identify and provide documentation supporting their need for accommodations. They must request necessary accommodations, be familiar with college requirements, make programming decisions with the assistance of an advisor, monitor their own progress, request assistance when needed, and meet the same academic standards as all other students.

4. Help students select postsecondary schools wisely. Although choosing the right college is important for any student, it takes on added significance when the student has a learning disability.

THEORY INTO PRACTICE 16.3

HELPING STUDENTS WITH EMOTIONAL/BEHAVIORAL DISORDERS TRANSITION TO COLLEGE

Principles:

- Use Hettler's (1984) Wellness Model to help students to develop balance in six dimensions of healthy functioning: physical, emotional, social, intellectual, occupational, and spiritual adjustment.
- Can be used with students on an individual or group basis.
- Employ the Wellness Model as a structure to foster communication between the school and families and facilitate open discussion about difficult topics.
- Plan early and take a long-term, health-based approach.
- Use efficient, targeted interventions and tools to disseminate information to students and parents.
- Assist the student and their college service providers to take a developmental, future-focused approach to college rather than a crisis management, illness-focused approach.

Intellectual wellness:

- Emphasize a foundation of adequate study skills and learning strategies, effective time management.
- Help students develop a workable schedule that stresses balance between time for academics and other activities.
- Encourage students to use technology and maintain precollege hobbies and interests.
- Prepare students to recognize the effects of stress on attention, concentration, memory, organization, and communication skills, as well as the exacerbation of psychiatric disabilities.
- Help students to focus on academics right away.

Physical wellness:

- Include regular exercise, sleep, and balanced nutrition.
- Discuss drugs, sex, alcohol, peer pressure, and consequences of risk-taking.
- Discourage students from discontinuing their psychiatric medication.

- Caution about mixing alcohol or drugs with prescribed medications.
- Discuss options for living arrangements (roommate, location).

Emotional wellness:

- Discuss the possibility of experiencing an increase in anxiety and a more difficult transition to college than other students.
- Encourage students and families to find out about available counseling and psychiatric care, even in community colleges.
- If possible, set up counseling and other support resources prior to the student starting college.
- Help students obtain emergency contact information and a safety plan (with local connections) outlining what should be done and who should be contacted in crisis situations.
- Remind families to ascertain their insurance coverage for care providers in the college community or if the student drops below 12 credits.

Social wellness:

- Discuss the importance of face-to-face social connections beyond the use of technology.
- Explain how developing *new* peer relationships and identity development impact successful college transition.
- Help students recognize and expect changes in social status.
- Encourage parents to provide a moderate/balanced level of support.

Occupational wellness:

- Discuss the role of the disability services office at colleges.
- Encourage parents and students to research and visit schools to determine available resources.
- Encourage students to seek good advising.

- Discuss an appropriate course load during the first semester.
- Help parents and students evaluate available services by arranging opportunities to talk with staff at disability services.
- Provide information about vocational rehabilitation services and encourage families to connect with them, if eligible.
- Explain the need to document a *DSM*-diagnosed disability to obtain accommodations in college.
- If possible, encourage students to arrange accommodations before starting college.
- Encourage greater self-advocacy.

Wellness:

- Encourage students to consider spiritual/religious practices and establishing a connection to a campus faith-based organization.
- Illustrate the role that access to nature plays in general health and well-being.
- Suggest students consider volunteer opportunities on campus and in the greater community.
- Discuss the importance of relaxation and its various methods of practice.

Source: Adapted from Fier & Brzezinski, 2010

CAREER COUNSELING Career counseling for students with disabilities requires the professional school counselor to understand the implications of the disability for a potential career. The school counselor must encourage and support, while remaining realistic. Computerized career programs can easily be used with assistive technology screen readers to enable students with disabilities to explore various career possibilities and requirements independently. The professional school counselor who is knowledgeable about training opportunities through private and public agencies and about resources in general, including financial resources, can be helpful to students with disabilities. There are excellent resources for career exploration online, including these:

1. Kids & Youth Pages from the U.S. Department of Labor at www.dol.gov/dol/audience/aud-kidsyouth.htm
2. Occupational Outlook Handbook at www.bls.gov/oco
3. Teenager's Guide to the Real World—Careers at www.bygpub.com/books/tg2rw/careers.htm
4. Job and Career Resources for Teenagers at www.quintcareers.com/teen_jobs.html

In addition to the websites intended for the general population, there are a number of excellent resources specifically developed for students with disabilities. Partners in Employment is a free online course designed to help people with developmental disabilities find meaningful jobs and plan a career. In this course, available at www.partnersinpolicymaking.com/employment/index.html, participants create a resume or portfolio of their strengths, skills, and interests; learn how to network and identify potential employers; prepare for an interview; and gain an understanding of the hiring process.

VOCATIONAL/CAREER PLANNING In many school systems today, online programs and software are used to assist students in career planning. Typically, they include interest inventories and career-trait surveys. In addition, some programs provide decision-making support to students to help them identify job values, personal strengths, and coursework related to professions of interest. There are also online tools that assess student interests, aptitudes, and personality styles. A good resource is www.QuintCareers.com, which provides reviews of free and low-cost online career assessment tools, including the name and link to each assessment, the measures obtained, the relative ease of use, and the level of detail of the results. In addition, QuintCareers provides a qualitative rating of the overall utility of each assessment based on personal and clients' experiences.

In addition to computerized testing for vocational interests, either school system or local agency staff members are generally available to do vocational aptitude testing of students with disabilities. In fact, in many school systems, all secondary students with IEPs complete a lengthy vocational assessment at a vocational school or center.

Other information necessary for vocational/career planning includes interview data from parents regarding their expectations and dreams for their child, the student's stated career goal and history of work experience, reports of the student's work habits and behaviors, and observation of the student's functioning at the work site.

The involvement of staff from the state office of rehabilitative services is essential in obtaining linkages to adult services, determining funding for postsecondary educational or vocational programs, and assisting families with ongoing transition needs beyond high school. For some students with disabilities (including even those who are high functioning), providing information on how to access Social Security Insurance and Social Security Disability Insurance (www.ssa.gov) can allow these students to attend adult vocational training programs, access job coaching and other adult services (e.g., Ticket to Work Program), pay for college, or defer income to pay for disability-related expenses (e.g., Plan for Achieving Self-Support [PASS]).

VOCATIONAL TRAINING Another strategy employed to improve outcomes after high school for individuals with disabilities is vocational training. The School-to-Work Opportunities Act, passed in 1994, focuses on coordinated efforts between schools and the community to design and provide an appropriate, individualized education for individuals with disabilities, including those with emotional and behavior disorders, that smoothly and successfully moves them from the school environment to the work environment. This act and other school efforts focus on providing students with the skills that employers seek. Thus, while still in school, students are provided with specific job training and experiences through vocational work placements, job coaching, and other related activities.

SELF-DETERMINATION The Division on Career Development and Transition of the Council for Exceptional Children (CEC) defines *self-determination* as a combination of skills, knowledge, and beliefs that enable a person to engage in goal-directed, self-regulated, autonomous behavior. These skills enhance individuals' abilities to take control of their lives and assume the role of successful adults. Research has found that helping students acquire and exercise self-determination skills is a strategy that leads to more positive educational outcomes, including higher rates of employment, postsecondary education, and independent living (see Wehmeyer et al., 2012).

Elements of self-determination include self-awareness, self-evaluation, choice and decision making, goal setting and attainment, problem solving, self-advocacy, and IEP planning. Professional school counselors can use some of the following strategies to assist students in developing self-determination skills:

- Use a structured curriculum to directly teach skills and attitudes. A good compilation of curriculum descriptions can be found on the Self-Determination Synthesis Project website at www.uncc.edu/sdsp/sd_curricula.asp.
- Use assessments to determine student needs (e.g., the ARC's Self-Determination Scale is available free online at the Beach Center on Disability of the University of Kansas, at www.beachcenter.org).

- Prepare students for the IEP planning and implementation process. Expect and support active student participation and leadership in their IEPs. Resources for student participation in the IEP process are available through the National Dissemination Center for Children with Disabilities at www.nichcy.org.
- Meet with students weekly to discuss their goal attainment and help them to implement strategies.
- Provide students with information on their disabilities. Help students to describe their needs to others and appropriately request needed accommodations.
- Help students to access available resources, especially online, to assist with college, career, leisure, and living planning (e.g., the National Center on Secondary Education and Transition at www.youthhood.org).
- Help students adjust strategies, schedules, or supports in collaboration with their teachers or family members to help them to attain their goals.
- Encourage families to promote choice and decision making.
- Allow for student selection of course electives and program of study.

There are excellent resources, including staff development materials, curricula, and lesson plans available online to promote self-determination in students with disabilities. Following are some examples of electronic resources:

- The Person-Centered Planning Education Site (PCPES) at www.ilr.cornell.edu/ped/tsal/pcp was developed by the Employment and Disability Institute at Cornell University. The PCPES provides coursework and staff development activities in such areas as transition planning, community membership, and self-determination.
- The Self-Determination Synthesis Project (www.uncc.edu/sdsp), at the University of North Carolina, provides information on exemplary programs, reviews existing research on self-advocacy models for students with disabilities, and develops and disseminates an array of products, including a directory of self-advocacy model programs.

VOICES FROM THE FIELD 16.1 **ADVOCACY FOR STUDENTS WITH DISABILITIES**

The role of the professional school counselor encompasses many areas of the educational experience. As a professional school counselor, it is important to advocate for the needs of all students, which includes students with disabilities. This sometimes creates the feeling of a "baptism by fire" in the first year of practice for a new professional

school counselor. Many times the counselor is unclear about his or her responsibilities, or the child study (special education) team is unclear in communicating their expectations. However, it is the responsibility of the professional school counselor to be able to have an honest and courageous dialogue to understand the team's expectations.

Quite often both the professional school counselor and the team members have the same goals in mind, but go about a plan of attack in *very* different ways. Once the professional school counselor and the team are in synch with each other, the effectiveness of the team can grow exponentially.

The professional school counselor is the consistent common bond between the family of a student with a disability and the school community. It is the responsibility of the professional school counselor to create a relationship with the student and synthesize that relationship with the student's educational needs. The professional school counselor advocates for that student's needs within the team process and throughout every school day. When the special education team meets, it expects the professional school counselor to be familiar with the student in and out of the classroom, as well as with the student's personal or family concerns. Many times it is the information provided by the professional school counselor that explains behaviors or reactions that members of the team would not necessarily see because they lack context.

When the special education process begins, the counselor may be the only professional in the meeting with prior knowledge of the student. It is the professional school counselor who must inform the team of the student's strengths and weaknesses. It is also the role of the school counselor to understand the criteria the team must use to evaluate the student's placement in special education. The school counselor needs to be able to see from both viewpoints—the observed qualities of the student versus the actual special education criteria—and translate that vision into a well-thought-out conclusion. Many times the team will look to the professional school counselor as the person to span the gap between home and school and to deliver appropriate information to the family. The professional school counselor has the ability to integrate the special education information into a more "user friendly" explanation for families and students. It is for this reason that the professional school counselor must understand the special education process, in addition to NCLB and the IDEA.

When the professional school counselor has a strong relationship with students with special needs, it makes the IEP process more cohesive. The goals and objectives that each child has on an IEP can be supported by the professional school counselor and evaluated for effectiveness. Also, there may be goals that need to be met with the help of the professional school counselor, such as individual counseling, group counseling, and transition planning. The professional school counselor can implement a number of strategies to become an effective supporter of that student. Sometimes the professional school counselor is integral in providing education to the school community regarding certain disabilities, rather than providing a direct service to the student; other times the professional school counselor does both. Regardless of the role that the professional school counselor needs to adopt, it is in the best interest of the student that the responsibility be met efficiently and effectively and with empathy.

As you become a professional school counselor, it is important to understand your role as an advocate for all students. Many times you will be called on to be the expert: the advocate, the translator, the supporter, and the policy specialist. However, it is within these roles that we support our school and the community. As a professional school counselor, you may be involved in the team process of writing IEPs and BIPs or of sitting in on manifestation meetings; the perspective that the counselor has is fundamental for these documents to be effective. In my professional school counseling career, I have had many positive moments working with the special education team and the parents for the good of the student. As you move into this role, my hope is that you can maximize the capacity of the team in your building that supports students with special needs in all domains and that you can witness the immense growth of students who are supported by this process.

Source: Maryellen Beck, Professional School Counselor, George Fox Middle School, Anne Arundel County Public School System, Maryland

GENERAL ISSUES FOR PROFESSIONAL SCHOOL COUNSELORS SERVING STUDENTS WITH DISABILITIES

Clearly, there are numerous ways in which professional school counselors will come into contact with students with disabilities. Although there are significant similarities in serving students with and without disabilities in schools, there are a few areas where special sensitivity is required or where special considerations are necessary in serving youth with disabilities.

Cultural Considerations

High stress can be felt by the parents of a child with a disability in families from all cultural backgrounds. However, the professional school counselor needs to be sensitive to cultural considerations because families from different cultures may approach identification of a child with a disability differently, particularly regarding the level of protection and independence afforded.

In some cultures, the disability of a family member is too private to share, and some families feel that discussion about the disability with anyone outside the family would be shameful. In other cultures, a high value on learning and achievement may create added pressure on a student. In still other cultures, those identified by mainstream society as having disabilities are not seen as disabled. Sometimes attempting to physically help a child with a disability can present a challenge because in some cultures the degree of physical touch implies respect or disrespect.

When collaborating with or counseling families of students from different cultures, the professional school counselor must consider the language differences and the cultural views of those involved. This process can be improved with the help of a friend of the family who is from the same culture, who can be an interpreter of both the language and the culture. It is critical for the professional school counselor to hear the "real" needs and priorities of the family and attempt to address them. To the extent possible, professional school counselors must place themselves in the position of the families. Before the professional can begin to meet the needs of families and children with disabilities, he or she must understand how family needs are shaped by the context of their subculture.

In addition to cultural response to disability, evidence indicates that students from minority and disadvantaged groups have limited access to mental health services in schools. If these students are able to access services, they often receive poorer quality care. School systems must be responsive to shifting demographics and provide culturally sensitive and competent school mental health policies, programs, and practices. Evidence suggests that school mental health programs help to close the gap in services for ethnic minority youth (Center for School Mental Health, 2012)

The professional school counselor can also help the family of diverse students cope with the maze of bureaucracy that public education may present to someone from another culture. For parents of a student with a disability, fears often exist because of language issues; those in the school system may not understand the needs of their child, and the parents may not understand how best to acquire services for their child. The CEC (www.cec.sped.org) has a Division for Culturally and Linguistically Diverse Exceptional Learners that can be a resource for the professional school counselor addressing the needs of a student with a disability from another culture. The American Counseling Association maintains a division of multicultural counseling, the Association for Multicultural Counseling and Development, which could also provide resources. Finally, Table 16.13 provides additional information on professional associations and other Internet-based resources the professional school counselor may find helpful in the quest to serve all students, including those with special needs.

TABLE 16.13 Professional Organizations and Other Web Resources

Organization	URL	Audience(s)	Description and Contents
National Information Center for Children and Youth with Disabilities (NICHCY)	Nichcy.org	Parents, teachers, related service providers, administrators	Website contents include information and fact sheets on specific disabilities, early intervention services for infants and toddlers, special education and related services for children in school, research on effective educational practices, resources and connections in every state, IEPs, parent materials, disability organizations, professional associations, education rights and what the law requires, transition to adult life and much, much more!
NICHCY is part of the Technical Assistance and Dissemination network, otherwise known as the TA&D network. The network consists of more than 40 projects funded by the Office of Special Education and Rehabilitative Services (OSERS) of the U.S. Department of Education. These projects offer information and technical assistance on a broad range of disability and special education issues.			
The IRIS Center for Training Enhancements	iris.peabody .vanderbilt.edu	University faculty, students, educators, and related service providers	Provides free online interactive resources that translate research about the education of students with disabilities into practice. Materials cover a wide variety of evidence-based topics, including behavior, RTI, learning strategies, and progress monitoring.
The IRIS Center at Peabody College of Vanderbilt University is a national center that aims to provide high-quality resources for college and university faculty and professional development providers about students with disabilities. IRIS seeks to obtain this goal by providing free, online, interactive training enhancements that translate research about the education of students with disabilities into practice.			

Organization	URL	Audience(s)	Description and Contents
Building the Legacy: IDEA 2004, U.S. Department of Education	idea.ed.gov	Teachers, administrators, parents, related service providers	Contents include IDEA regulations, statute, training materials, model forms, video clips, webcast, presentations, dialogue guides, and Q&A documents.

The IDEA website was created to provide a "one-stop shop" for resources related to IDEA and its implementing regulations, released on August 3, 2006. It is a "living" website and will change and grow as resources and information become available. When fully implemented, the site will provide searchable versions of IDEA and the regulations, access to cross-referenced content from other laws (e.g., the No Child Left Behind Act [NCLB], the Family Education Rights and Privacy Act [FERPA]), video clips on selected topics, topic briefs on selected regulations, links to OSEP's Technical Assistance and Dissemination (TA&D) Network and a Q&A Corner where you can submit questions, and a variety of other information sources. As items are completed and added to this site, we invite you to grow and learn with us as we implement these regulations.

Organization	URL	Audience(s)	Description and Contents
Council for Exceptional Children	cec.sped.org	Parents, teachers, related service providers	CEC's Special Education Topics are a comprehensive resource for special educators and others who work with children and youth with disabilities and/or gifts and talents. It includes information about the different exceptionality areas; international special education; hot topics in special education; and professional practice topics such as assessment, evidence-based practices, and inclusion.

The Council for Exceptional Children (CEC) is the largest international professional organization dedicated to improving the educational success of individuals with disabilities and/or gifts and talents. CEC advocates for appropriate governmental policies, sets professional standards, provides professional development, advocates for individuals with exceptionalities, and helps professionals obtain conditions and resources necessary for effective professional practice.

Organization	URL	Audience(s)	Description and Contents
The Office of Special Education Programs (OSEP)	www.ed.gov /about/offices /list/osers/osep	Administrators, researchers, educators, parents	Includes information on programs and projects, federal grants and funding, legislation and policy, publications and products, research and statistics, national studies, state monitoring, the Special Education Technical Assistance and Dissemination Network, FAQs, and teaching resources.

The Office of Special Education Programs (OSEP) of the U.S. Department of Education is dedicated to improving results for infants, toddlers, children, and youth with disabilities ages birth through 21 years by providing leadership and financial support to assist states and local districts.

Organization	URL	Audience(s)	Description and Contents
The PACER Center	www.pacer .org	Parents and families	Offers over 40 specialty projects created to provide assistance to families of children with disabilities on a variety of special issues, including children with special health needs, assistive technology, social inclusion for children with disabilities, bullying prevention, transition issues, and much more.

PACER Center is a parent training and information center for families of children and youth with all disabilities from birth through 21 years old. Located in Minneapolis, Minnesota, it serves families across the nation. Parents can find publications, workshops, and other resources to help make decisions about education, vocational training, employment, and other services for their children with disabilities. PACER's National Bullying Prevention Center provides resources designed to benefit all students, including those with disabilities. The mission of PACER Center is to expand opportunities and enhance the quality of life of children and young adults with ALL disabilities and their families, based on the concept of parents helping parents.

(Continued)

TABLE 16.13 Professional Organizations and Other Web Resources (*Continued*)

Organization	URL	Audience(s)	Description and Contents
Schoolmentalhealth .org	http://www .schoolmental health.org	Mental Health clinicians, educators, parents, students	Offers school mental health resources not only for clinicians, but also for educators, administrators, parents/caregivers, families, and students. The resources on this site emphasize practical information and skills based on current research, including prominent evidence-based practices, as well as lessons learned from local, state, and national initiatives.

This website is a central feature of the Baltimore School Mental Health Technical Assistance and Training Initiative. The initiative is funded through the support of The Baltimore City Health Department and is administered by The University of Maryland's Center for School Mental Health.

Summary/Conclusion

The professional school counselor's role with the student who has a disability is still emerging, even though the laws addressing students with disabilities have been around since the early to mid-1970s. Professional school counselors have always served students with disabilities; however, it was usually with services similar to those given to regular education students who might be experiencing a problem. When professional school counselors addressed the clinical needs of students with disabilities, it was most often to provide appropriate referral sources. Today, professional school counselors are being called on to play a major role in delivering a broad array of counseling services to students with disabilities. Thus, professional school counselors must have a clear understanding of the laws that govern eligibility of and service delivery to those students.

Professional school counselors are well trained to provide counseling services to students with disabilities and their families—in part because professional school counselors have a strong tradition of training in developmental counseling. Counselors have traditionally focused on integrating social and academic skills and prefer working collaboratively, rather than in isolation. Increasingly, counselors are seeking additional training and taking on greater mental health and case management roles. The ASCA (2014a) has responded by issuing a position paper on appropriate and inappropriate roles for professional school counselors serving students with disabilities. One of the main concerns of the ASCA is that counselors not be put in positions that will harm their counseling relationships and thus their effectiveness. The ASCA leaves open the opportunity for professional school counselors to address any issue that falls in the counselor's arena, and it seeks to promote a role for the school counselor to work collaboratively and in a transdisciplinary mode when serving students with disabilities. It is possible that a new subspecialty in school counseling could develop in response to the increasing needs of students with disabilities. For example, perhaps special education and student services may jointly fund positions providing a school team with a professional school counselor specially trained in the areas discussed in this chapter.

The number of students with disabilities has grown, and counseling services will be essential for many of them. In addition, the passing of the Patient Protection and Affordable Care Act (ACA) in 2010 creates a unique opportunity to expand mental health services for children. According to recent study (Green et al., 2013), health-care reform has significant implications for the future of health and mental health care provided to children and youth in school-based settings. With greater numbers of children and families seeking accessible health and mental health care, school-based providers are likely to see an increase in demand for their services. In addition, a provision of the ACA authorizes funding to establish and expand school-based health centers, which will significantly increase and enhance access to mental health services in schools. Schools have already become de facto providers of mental health services to children and adolescents, related to several barriers to accessing traditional community-based care, including lack of available specialists, insurance restrictions, appointment delays and mental health stigma.

Preventative care and early intervention services are essential components of comprehensive support for children and adolescents at risk. Given the recent national focus on providing mental health services in schools and the significant federal, state, and local support being directed toward school programs, there is likely to be increasing demand for professional school counselors who are knowledgeable and skilled in the delivery of school mental health services to children with and without identified disabilities.

Activities

1. Discuss how the IEP process enhances the participation of parents and students in educational programs. If possible, invite a parent to discuss his or her experience with the IEP process. The Arc, Learning Disabilities Association of America (LDA), or a self-advocacy group could be a good source of volunteers to invite. There may be a student with a disability or the family member of a student with a disability in your class who is willing to serve as an "expert" during this activity.

2. Interview parents to discover ways to promote a greater feeling of welcome at their child's school. Develop a school plan for making a school more inviting for families and more reflective of the cultures and traditions of the local community.

3. Interview a school administrator or teacher about the SWPBS system at his/her school. What positive expectations are conveyed to all students and staff? How are positive behaviors encouraged and negative behaviors discouraged? How is the effectiveness of the program monitored and revised?

4. Interview a special education teacher to learn what he or she thinks are the supports and barriers to effective special education in his/her school. Ask him/her what a school counselor could do that would improve special education in the school.

5. Arrange to attend a due process hearing and talk to the hearing officer after the hearing. Ask him/her about the process and how s/he thinks it affects students, parents and schools.

6. Bobby is a fourth-grade student identified with a serious emotional disturbance. He is aggressive and having difficulty getting along with peers. Create three sample goal statements that could be included on his IEP.

Helping Students with Mental and Emotional Disorders

Bradley T. Erford*

Editor's Introduction: Whereas the historical roots of professional school counseling lie in developmental counseling theories, societal changes are contributing to substantial increases in psychopathology among school-aged children. A professional school counselor's ability to treat students with emotional disorders depends on education, training, and experience, as well as local school board policies and procedures; however, all future professional school counselors living the transformed role must know the characteristics and diagnostic criteria for common disorders of childhood and adolescence. Such knowledge is essential to one's ability to make timely and appropriate referrals, as well as to facilitate school-based services to supplement mental health treatment. This chapter introduces the vast array of mental disorders that professional school counselors may encounter in their work with students. In addition, each section addresses common treatment interventions and discusses their relevance to the professional school counselor. Whether referring, treating, collaborating, or advocating, professional school counselors must be aware of this information to interface with and make appropriate referrals to the medical and mental health communities and help the students to achieve academic and social success at school.

Professional school counselors are not long-term therapists. Professional school counselors do not diagnose and treat serious mental disorders. The professional school counselor's primary responsibility is to support the educational mission of schools—to help all students be academically successful. Often, professional school counselors need to educate parents, teachers, students, and others about these restrictions to practice, so that others do not expect the professional school counselor to initiate long-term therapy, or pick up where a mental health clinician in private practice leaves off.

The No Child Left Behind Act (NCLB) of 2001, Reach for the Top, and other school reform movements have increased the pressure on schools to focus on academic performance and achievement for *all* students. Unfortunately, a number of factors interfere with the achievement of that goal. Environmental and mental health issues affect children and make it difficult for schools to provide them an appropriate education. As a result, schools are increasingly expected to deal with the emotional and mental health concerns of students.

This chapter will briefly review the history of the professional school counselor's role in serving students with mental and emotional disorders, the role professional school counselors can play in identification and intervention for students with mental disorders in light of the transformation of the school counseling profession, the nature and prevalence of mental disorders most often diagnosed in students, and the implications for future practice.

---

*The first two editions of this chapter were coauthored by Dr. Linda Seligman, may she rest in peace. I gratefully acknowledge the contributions of Carol J. Kaffenberger to the first three editions of this chapter.

PREVALENCE OF MENTAL HEALTH ISSUES IN YOUTH

The prevalence of mental health issues in children and adolescents is increasing and is considered a mental health crisis in the United States (American Psychological Association, 2004) and around the world (Kessler, Berglund et al., 2005), where almost half of all people qualify for a mental disorder diagnosis at some point during their lives. One in five children and adolescents has a mild to moderate mental health issue, and 1 in 20 has a serious mental or emotional illness (U.S. Department of Health and Human Services, 2008). Unfortunately, of the children between the ages of 9 and 17 who have a serious emotional illness, only 20% receive mental health services (Kazdin, 2008, 2011; U.S. Department of Health and Human Services, 2008). In addition to the increased prevalence of mental illness, children are presenting with mental health concerns at a younger age. The rate of unmet needs among Latino youth and uninsured children is even greater than that among White and publicly insured youth (Kataoka, Zhang, & Wells, 2002), and the needs of children living in rural areas are also largely unmet due to lack of access and availability of convenient quality mental health services (Mohatt, Adams, Bradley, & Morris, 2006).

Adolescent suicide rates are another indicator of the severity of mental health concerns. Suicide is the third leading cause of death for adolescents, after accidents and homicide (National Institute of Mental Health, 2012). After a 28.5% decline between 1990 and 2003, the incidence of suicide began a slight increase (Lubell, Kegler, Crosby, & Karch, 2008). It is estimated that 7% of adolescents who develop a major depressive disorder will commit suicide (National Institute of Mental Health, 2012) and that 90% of teens who commit suicide have a mental disorder and or substance use disorder. Adolescents who use alcohol or illicit drugs are three times more likely than nonusing adolescents to attempt suicide (Substance Abuse and Mental Health Services Administration, 2012).

FACTORS CONTRIBUTING TO THE HIGH INCIDENCE OF EMOTIONAL DISTURBANCE

Environmental factors such as the breakdown of the family, homelessness, poverty, and violence in the community place increased stress on families and contribute to an increase in mental health needs. The number of children living in poverty has steadily increased. It is estimated that 23% of all homeless families include children and that the number of homeless children is in excess of 1 million (National Coalition for the Homeless, 2008). Poverty, as well as exposure to violence and substance use in the community, puts children at greater risk for developing mental disorders and experiencing emotional difficulties, thus making it more difficult for them to attend school regularly and succeed academically (U.S. Department of Health and Human Services, 2008).

Particularly at risk are children from diverse ethnic and cultural groups, who have a higher incidence of mental disorders and are overrepresented in special education programs (Santos de Barona & Barona, 2006). Children and adolescents of color have been unserved or underserved and have had their emotional difficulties overlooked or misdiagnosed (Kress, Erikson, Rayle, & Ford, 2005). Diagnostic tools and procedures that have been developed for Euro-American populations may not be appropriate for diagnosing emotional difficulties in children from other cultures.

Low-cost mental health services available in the community are limited, thereby putting added pressure on schools to provide those services. In addition, lack of transportation, poor insurance coverage, limited after-school office hours, and understaffing at mental health agencies all serve as barriers to young people receiving mental health services (Kazdin, 2008). Services that are available often are fragmented, and typically no one agency takes responsibility for providing or coordinating care.

The Individuals with Disabilities Education Improvement Act (IDEA) was originally authorized in 1975 (as the Education for All Handicapped Children Act) to ensure that all children with disabilities would have their educational needs met in schools (Cortiella, 2006). Changes introduced in 2004, when the IDEA was reauthorized, require that students be served in regular education classrooms and that expectations for students with disabilities be increased. Under the IDEA, the process of identifying students with disabilities is now called response to research-based interventions (RTI; Burns, Jacob, & Wagner, 2008). RTI requires that research-based teaching strategies be used and documented for all children and that student progress be monitored, allowing for more intense services for students who do not make adequate progress. The American School Counselor Association (ASCA, 2008) position statement on RTI identifies a significant role for professional school counselors in providing research-based interventions through classroom guidance, small-group and individual counseling, consultation, and data-gathering activities. Theory into Practice 17.1 provides an example of how school counselors can be involved with RTI.

THEORY INTO PRACTICE 17.1

SCHOOL COUNSELOR INVOLVEMENT WITH RESPONSE TO INTERVENTION

Ms. Houseman, the school counselor, participated in a Child Study Committee meeting to discuss Jimmy Rodriquez's progress in the second grade. Jimmy's progress has been monitored since first grade, when his teacher grouped him with others who were struggling with learning letters and sounds and with word recognition. Jimmy made some progress with Tier I classroom interventions. Now in grade 2, by the end of the first marking period Jimmy's progress seems to have slowed down. Not only is Jimmy struggling with reading skills and basic classroom performance skills, but also he is having some trouble getting along with others. The Child Study

Committee determined that Jimmy's failure to make adequate progress requires a Tier II intervention. Jimmy will see the reading teacher once a week and will be put in a small group with Ms. Houseman. Before Ms. Houseman begins to work with Jimmy, she reviews evidence-based counseling interventions and chooses one that she believes will help Jimmy with his attitude toward school, learning, and problems he is experiencing with peers. Ms. Houseman and the reading teacher will both document Jimmy's progress throughout the second and third marking periods and report back to the Child Study Committee in April.

Professional school counselors are often members of the school's special education team and should be involved with the RTI process for all children (Burns et al., 2008; Santos de Barona & Barona, 2006). The IDEA requires that school counselors be well versed in the nature of, and requirements for, psychological assessment and services.

Section 504 of the Rehabilitation Act of 1973 protects students who have a physical or mental disability that substantially limits a major life activity (U.S. Department of Health and Human Services, 2006). Section 504 provides program modifications that are different from special education services. This legislation, too, has increased professional school counselors' involvement with students' mental health needs. Students who are eligible for Section 504 accommodations require modifications to their learning environment so that they will have access to educational opportunity. Examples of students who might be eligible for Section 504 services include a student with leukemia who requires a shorter school day and homebound instruction; a student with AD/HD who might benefit from modifications to assignments, special seating, and permission to take frequent breaks; and a child with dysgraphia who requires special testing accommodations. In some school districts, professional school counselors collaborate with the Section 504 committee and are responsible for working with parents, teachers, and students to develop and implement appropriate accommodations (ASCA, 2014a).

Failure to address the emotional and mental health concerns of students has a cost. Most mental health issues in adulthood are known to begin during childhood or adolescence (Berglund, Demler, Jin, Merikangas, & Walters, 2005). Estimates suggest that 48% of students with emotional

problems drop out of school and that students with severe emotional problems miss more days of school than students in any other disability category. Children with mental or emotional disorders are at an increased risk of substance abuse (Substance Abuse and Mental Health Services Administration, 2008). Forty-three percent of children using mental health services also have a substance abuse disorder, and it is estimated that 66% of males and 75% of females in the juvenile justice system have one or more mental disorder diagnoses (President's New Freedom Commission on Mental Health, 2003).

CULTURAL REFLECTION 17.1

How might professional school counselors from diverse cultural backgrounds view the role of the professional school counselor when helping students with emotional issues? How might students, parents, and educators from diverse backgrounds view the role of the professional school counselor when helping students with emotional issues? What cultural barriers and access points might exist?

THE PROFESSIONAL SCHOOL COUNSELOR'S ROLE

The role of professional school counselors is in a period of transformation (ASCA, 2012). Part of the ongoing debate focuses on how professional school counselors should address the mental health and emotional issues of students and how that role fits into a systemic and comprehensive school counseling program as framed by *The ASCA National Model.* The mental health needs of students have not always been the concern of professional school counselors. School counseling in the 1950s and 1960s emphasized a personal growth model that promoted individual development (Tang & Erford, 2010). Currently, most school counseling programs are based on a comprehensive developmental model that focuses on prevention and meeting the needs of the whole child and that emphasizes the educational goals of counseling services and programs.

Although many professional school counselors, influenced by the direction of ASCA, the National Office for School Counseling Advocacy at the College Board, and the Transforming School Counseling Initiative at the Education Trust, affirm the educational goals of their school counseling programs, others argue that professional school counselors are not doing enough to meet the complex needs of children who are at risk (see Chapter 15). They claim that professional school counselors are not allowing sufficient individualization of services and are focused on student competencies, rather than individual mental health needs (Gysbers & Henderson, 2012). Leaders in the counseling field argue that the role of school counselors is still evolving, whereas others believe that new delivery systems for providing school-based mental health services are required (Bemak, Murphy, & Kaffenberger, 2005).

Barriers to Providing Mental Health Services in Schools

The ability of professional school counselors to meet the needs of students with mental health issues is limited by several factors, including workload ratio of students to counselors, local policy, fragmented programs, and lack of expertise. The first barrier is the number of noncounseling duties that professional school counselors are asked to shoulder (ASCA, 2012). Overworked professional school counselors with a host of other school responsibilities, both of a counseling and of a noncounseling nature, are unable to provide adequate counseling services or consult with parents and mental health professionals to serve students with chronic and serious mental health needs.

The second barrier that interferes with a counselor's ability to serve the mental health needs of students is the fragmentation and duplication of services and programs (Bemak et al., 2005; also see Chapter 15). School- and community-based services and programs often have been developed in isolation, without consideration of existing services and programs. Lacking knowledge and awareness of collaborative opportunities, both school and community settings miss the opportunity to provide comprehensive and coordinated services.

The third barrier is the discrepancy that exists between professional school counselors' need to understand mental disorders and their knowledge base (Seligman, 2004). Not all professional school counselors possess the knowledge, experience, and expertise needed to recognize and address the mental health needs of students. Counselor education programs have typically prepared professional school counselors to understand the developmental needs of students, but have not provided the training required to recognize and intervene in mental disorders affecting children, adolescents, and their families.

Despite these barriers that schools and professional school counselors encounter when addressing the mental health needs of students, the reality is that the most common point of entry into the mental health system is through the schools. One study found that 60.1% of all youth who received mental health services entered the system through the school (Farmer, Burns, Phillips, Angold, & Costello, 2003). Unfortunately, this same study found that entering the mental health services system through the schools was also least likely to result in involvement with other services, such as community mental health or private care.

Current and Future Trends in the Way Services Are Provided

If schools are to achieve their educational mission, new service models will be required of professional school counselors (ASCA, 2012; Bemak et al., 2005). The way mental health services are provided for children and the role of the professional school counselor are beginning to change. The U.S. Department of Education, the U.S. Department of Health and Human Services (2008), and private managed health-care organizations are encouraging preventive health care as a way of ultimately reducing the need for future costly care, remediation, and intervention. Schools are the logical place for programs that seek to both prevent and ameliorate mental health problems in students and their families. As a growing number of public schools privatize, various counseling service models have been developed. In increasing numbers of schools, the counseling functions are either shared between the professional school counselor and outside agencies or contracted out completely.

The effectiveness of new community-based mental health services and comprehensive guidance programs is being assessed. One study evaluated the effectiveness of high school counseling programs statewide and found that students who attend schools with fully implemented mental health programs are more academically successful and have a greater sense of belonging and safety than do those who do not (Lapan, Gysbers, & Sun, 1997). Another study showed that comprehensive community-based services to children cut state hospital admissions and inpatient bed days by between 39% and 79% and reduced average days of detention by 40% (Substance Abuse and Mental Health Services Administration, 1995).

The discussion of how best to provide services to students is ongoing. What is clear is that, to efficiently and effectively use the limited resources available to meet the needs of students, a high level of collaboration will be required (Bemak et al., 2005). Collaboration among mental health professionals is even more important when fiscal concerns threaten to reduce services to students. To maximize their effectiveness, professional school counselors need to develop interdisciplinary and interagency relationships and practices and a working knowledge of the role and function of the other mental health professions in schools and in the community (Bemak et al., 2005; Farmer et al., 2003).

Professional school counselors must increase their knowledge, skills, and expertise regarding mental health issues of students to assume a more collaborative role (see Chapter 14–Chapter 15). They must be knowledgeable about the criteria in the fifth edition of the *Diagnostic and Statistical Manual of Mental Disorders* (*DSM–5*; American Psychiatric Association, 2013) and appropriate treatment recommendations for all children, including the culturally and linguistically diverse (Santos de Barona & Barona, 2006; Seligman, 2004). Professional school counselors must understand psychological evaluation processes, be able to explain them to school staff, and communicate with other mental health professionals.

WHAT PROFESSIONAL SCHOOL COUNSELORS NEED TO KNOW ABOUT MENTAL AND EMOTIONAL DISORDERS

With the increased prevalence of mental health and emotional issues in children and adolescents, professional school counselors need to take an increasingly active role in understanding these disorders and facilitating services. The professional school counselor is often the first person contacted by parents or teachers when concerns about children arise. Professional school counselors must understand normal social, emotional, cognitive, and physical development. In addition, it is essential that they possess a working knowledge of the range of mental disorders and mental health issues affecting young people. Professional school counselors need to be familiar with the diagnostic criteria for those mental disorders that are commonly found in young people, even though professional school counselors may not be responsible for diagnosing and treating mental disorders. Professional school counselors will need to be knowledgeable about diagnostic tools and

intervention strategies appropriate for culturally and ethnically diverse students (Santos de Barona & Barona, 2006). Professional school counselors can play a pivotal role in raising awareness concerning mental disorders, identifying students who are experiencing significant emotional difficulties, collaborating with the child study team on response-to-intervention strategies, recommending school-based interventions, interpreting diagnostic information for parents, and making referrals. Counselors' awareness of diagnostic information also will be invaluable to parents, teachers, and administrators as initial treatment decisions are being made.

Mental health professionals, including psychologists, psychiatrists, social workers, and licensed professional counselors, regularly use the *DSM–5* (American Psychiatric Association, 2013) to diagnose emotional, behavioral, and mental disorders in children and adolescents. In general, school psychologists did not use the *DSM* until the 1987 publication of the revised third edition, the *DSM–III–R*, but for the last 20 or so years, they have viewed diagnosis as one of their essential skills. By 1994, when the fourth edition of the *DSM* was published, the expectations of the school's role in the diagnostic process had increased, and many professional school counselors recognized that they, too, needed to be familiar with the diagnostic criteria for mental disorders in young people. Changes in the way mental health services were provided to children and increased pressure to provide special education services to children required that schools develop more sophisticated ways of diagnosing educational and behavioral disorders. *DSM* criteria are now accepted as the standard, and workshops, training, and textbooks guiding the use of *DSM* criteria proliferate.

Although the *DSM* is gaining greater credibility among mental health professionals, a debate about the relevance of *DSM* criteria to people of other cultures and ethnicities is increasing (Kress et al., 2005; Santos de Barona & Barona, 2006). Despite good-faith efforts on the part of those who prepare the *DSM*, working groups, collaborative task forces, and independent researchers found the previous version, the *DSM–IV–TR*, does not reflect "cultural or racial difference in symptoms, syndromes" (Dana, 2001, p. 131). The *DSM–5* (American Psychiatric Association, 2013) addressed a number of ethnic and cultural considerations and warned that *DSM* diagnostic criteria may not be appropriately assessed unless the cultural frame of reference is considered. In this edition of the *DSM*, the American Psychiatric Association also provided three types of information related to cultural considerations: (a) descriptions of known cultural variance for each disorder, (b) culture-bound syndromes, and (c) an outline of cultural formation.

Professional school counselors are not expected to, nor have most been trained to, make diagnoses using the

DSM criteria. Although professional school counselors may not make formal diagnoses and will probably not provide primary services to students diagnosed with a mental disorder, professional school counselors often are expected to identify young people in need of mental health services; to consult with other school-based mental health professionals such as school psychologists and social workers; to make referrals to outside community agency resources such as psychiatrists, psychologists, social workers, and mental health counselors; and to decipher mental health reports for school personnel and parents. Once an outside referral has been made, professional school counselors, with the parents' permission, may be asked to provide input from the school, including observations, behavioral checklists, and sample school-work. When parents, professional school counselors, teachers, and mental health therapists work together successfully, the results can be very beneficial for children. Although professional school counselors typically will not provide therapeutic services to students with severe mental disorders, having a working knowledge of the diagnosis of mental disorders and understanding ways that diagnostic criteria may not be relevant to students from other cultures or students of color can greatly enhance the effectiveness of professional school counselors' interactions with students, teachers, and parents (Gardner & Miranda, 2001).

Diagnosis and Treatment Planning

The *DSM–5* (American Psychiatric Association, 2013) includes a system of diagnosis that involves an assessment of a person's mental and emotional functioning to describe clinical disorders such as conduct disorders, eating disorders, anxiety disorders, and mood disorders. This approach to assessment is used to facilitate a comprehensive and systematic evaluation of a person.

Professional school counselors usually will not be involved in the assessment process, but will benefit from understanding how the multiaxial system is used in the diagnosis of an emotional or mental disorder. For example, when assessing an adolescent for depression, the clinician should know about all areas of this young person's life. This adolescent might have a medical condition such as cancer, or the adolescent's parents may have recently been divorced. It is helpful to be able to assess the child or adolescent for various issues other than the primary diagnosis to create a treatment plan that is tailored for the individual's issues and experiences, rather than just for "depression." A sample *DSM* diagnosis is presented in Case Study 17.1. What follows throughout the remainder of this chapter is a description of those disorders most likely to be encountered in school-aged children. Specific characteristics of each disorder, intervention strategies, prognosis, and relevance to the professional school counselor are presented.

CASE STUDY 17.1

Demonstrating a *DSM–5* Diagnosis

Anna, a 7-year-old girl, was evaluated for an episode of depressed mood, sleeping problems, irritability, loss of weight, and reduced energy level. Anna's symptoms had been present for nearly 2 months. Her parents could hardly get her to wake up in the morning. She refused to dress or bathe and had been absent from school for 2 weeks. On further evaluation, it was discovered that Anna's dog, Max, was killed about 2 months ago, right around the time that Anna's symptoms began. Recently, Anna had begun to tell her parents that she wished the car could have hit her also so that she could be with Max. Anna's diagnosis is 296.22 Major Depressive Disorder, Single Episode, with Melancholic Features.

NEURODEVELOPMENTAL DISORDERS: DISORDERS ORDINARILY DIAGNOSED IN SCHOOL-AGED CHILDREN OR ADOLESCENTS

Intellectual Developmental Disorder

Intellectual developmental disorder (IDD; formerly known as mental retardation) typically is described in terms of a person's failure to demonstrate skills that are age-, culture-, and situation-appropriate, reflected by an intelligence quotient (IQ) that is much lower than that found in the normal population (APA, 2013). IDD has a pervasive impact on cognitive, emotional, and social development (Seligman & Reichenberg, 2011). It is diagnosed from results of individual intelligence tests, such as the Wechsler Intelligence Scale for Children, Fourth Edition (WISC–IV; Wechsler, 2001) or the Stanford-Binet Intelligence Scale, Fifth Edition (SBIS–5; Roid, 2003). According to the *DSM–5*, the criteria for diagnosis of mental retardation includes onset prior to age 18; subaverage intellectual functioning reflected by an IQ two standard deviations below the mean (WISC–IV or SBIS–5 full scale IQ of 70 or less); and impaired adaptive functioning in at least two areas, such as communication, social skills, interpersonal skills, self-direction, leisure, functional academic skills, safety, and work (APA, 2013). Although people with an IQ that is in the 71–84 range are not typically diagnosed with mental retardation, they, too, are likely to have academic and other difficulties related to their below-average intellectual abilities. The *DSM–5* describes people in this group as having a condition called borderline intellectual functioning.

The impact of IDD is directly related to the degree of intellectual impairment. Four degrees of retardation are defined by the *DSM* as follows: Mild is diagnosed when the IQ score is in the range of 50–55 to 70, moderate is diagnosed when the IQ score is in the range of 35–40 to 50–55, severe is diagnosed when the IQ score is in the range of 20–25 to 35–40, and profound is diagnosed when the IQ score is below 20–25.

The American Association of Intellectual and Developmental Disabilities (AAIDD) has recently modified the classification of IDD. The new system advocates a multidimensional approach to identification, involving intellectual functioning and adaptive skills, psychological and emotional considerations, and etiology, as well as environmental considerations. The language used for students with IDD has also been modified to be more sensitive to the negative connotation of the term *retarded* and to encourage such terms as *developmental* or *cognitive disabilities*.

Intellectual Developmental Disability is usually diagnosed in infancy or early childhood, although mild IDD may not be identified until the child reaches school age. It is estimated that 1% to 2% of the general population can be diagnosed with an IDD, although estimates can vary depending on definitions and populations studied (American Psychiatric Association, 2013). Of those people meeting the criteria for IDD, about 85% are diagnosed with mild IDD. Boys are three times more likely than girls to be diagnosed with this disorder.

Approximately 25% to 30% of people with IDD have identifiable biological causes of the disorder, such as genetic and chromosomal abnormalities, prenatal and perinatal difficulties, or acquired childhood diseases. Down syndrome is the most widely known genetic type of mild or moderate IDD (Davis, 2008). Severe and profound degrees of the disorder commonly have a neurological origin and may be associated with more than 200 physical disorders, including cerebral palsy, epilepsy, and sensory disorders. When mental retardation lacks identifiable biological causes, it is thought to be the result of some combination of inherited cognitive impairment and environmental deprivation.

Children and adolescents diagnosed with mental retardation usually receive special education services under the IDEA. Prior to the passage of Public Law 94-142 (the precursor to IDEA) in the 1970s, children who had previously been categorized as trainable and custodial were excluded from free public education. Today, public education is available to all children, regardless of the nature and degree of their impairment; thus, many children with mild degrees of IDD are found in the public schools.

The characteristics of children, adolescents, and adults with IDD vary greatly, depending on their level of impairment and on their environment. These clients often present with aggressive, overactive, or self-injurious behaviors. Although children with Down syndrome display fewer behavior problems overall than other children with IDD do, these children still exhibit maladaptive behaviors, particularly stubbornness (Ly & Hodapp, 2002). Because of their cognitive limitations, they tend to be concrete in their thinking, reasoning, and problem solving. Developmental delays are common, with such milestones as walking and talking generally reached later than average. Learning new tasks requires more practice and guidance for people with mental retardation than for their chronological counterparts (Seligman & Reichenberg, 2011).

Children with mild disabilities present with a wide variety of cognitive abilities and need to be evaluated with these differences in mind (Davis, 2008). Inclusion requires that most children with mild disabilities be educated in the regular classroom. Many students with mild disabilities are academically successful in the regular classroom, but lack the social skills needed to interact with peers and adults.

INTERVENTION STRATEGIES Early intervention is essential for treatment of children with an intellectual developmental disorder (Seligman & Reichenberg, 2011). Early intervention includes systems, services, and supports designed to enhance the development of young children, minimize the potential of developmental delays and the need for special education services, and enhance the capacities of families as caregivers (Baker & Feinfield, 2003). Family, group, and individual counseling can be effective in promoting the child's or adolescent's positive self-regard and in improving social, academic, and occupational skills. Behavior modification has long been the treatment modality of choice for people with IDD (Baumeister & Baumeister, 2000).

PROGNOSIS Intellectual developmental disorder has implications for a person's entire life span (Seligman & Reichenberg, 2011). Adults with a mild level of IDD often live independently and maintain a job with minimal supervision. People with a moderate level of IDD may be able to live independently in group-home settings and gain employment in sheltered workshops. Those with severe and profound degrees of IDD often reside in public and private institutions.

RELEVANCE TO SCHOOL COUNSELORS Professional school counselors are often members of multidisciplinary teams that attempt to develop appropriate educational plans for students with IDD. In so doing, they may engage in advocacy, consultation, diagnosis, assessment, development of a delivery system, and provision of support services for students, parents, and teachers (Wood Dunn & Baker, 2002). Professional school counselors may play a role in helping families understand and accept the diagnosis and make the transition to an appropriate school program. Professional school counselors may be asked to provide social skills training for students with IDD. It also is important for professional school counselors to help educate the other students about IDD to promote their understanding and tolerance. It is suggested that professional school counselors be familiar with the overall procedural safeguards of the IDEA and characteristics unique to students with disabilities. Professional school counselors who are more able to understand the challenges for students with disabilities are also able to provide the students, parents, and teachers with accurate information.

Specific Learning, Motor, and Communication Disorders

Specific learning disorder, motor disorders, and communication disorders are diagnosed in children when they are functioning significantly below expectations in a specific area, based on their age, cognitive abilities, and education, and when their level of functioning is interfering with daily achievement and functioning (Seligman & Reichenberg, 2011). Significant discrepancies between functioning and performance are typified by achievement in a given area that is 20 to 30 standard score points below the child's intelligence as measured by standardized achievement tests and intelligence tests. Diagnosis of these disorders also requires that other factors that may be primary contributors to the learning problems, such as lack of educational opportunity, poor teaching, impaired vision or hearing, and intellectual developmental disorders, be ruled out (Young & Beitchman, 2002). Specific learning disabilities (SLDs) reflect a disorder in one or more of the basic learning processes, which may manifest itself in an impaired ability to listen, think, speak, read, write, spell, or do mathematical calculations. SLDs, referred to as learning

disorders in the *DSM–5*, are believed to affect approximately 10% of the population, but are diagnosed in only about 5% of students in public schools in the United States (APA, 2013). The *DSM–5* identified only one type of learning disorder (i.e., specific learning disorder), which can be manifested in: mathematics, reading, or written expression, characterized by significant difficulties in academic functioning in each of those areas. A disorder in reading is diagnosed in approximately 4% of the school-aged population; 60% to 80% are boys. Children with reading disorder have difficulty decoding unknown words, memorizing sight-word vocabulary lists, and comprehending written passages. Estimates of the prevalence of mathematics disorder range from 1% to 6% of the population (American Psychiatric Association, 2013). Children with mathematics disorder have difficulty with problem solving, calculations, or both (Seligman & Reichenberg, 2011). A learning disorder in written expression is rarely found in isolation; in most cases, another learning disorder is also present (American Psychiatric Association, 2013). Children with a learning disorder of written expression often have difficulty with handwriting, spelling, grammar, and the creation of prose (Seligman & Reichenberg, 2011). Care must be taken to distinguish these disorders from underachievement, poor teaching, lack of opportunity, and cultural factors.

Communication disorders are defined as speech and language impairment. This category is narrowly defined as impairments in language, voice, fluency, or articulation that are not a result of sensory impairment or developmental delay (Johnson & Slomka, 2000). Three communication disorders are identified in the *DSM–5*: language disorder, speech disorder, and social communication disorder. Like nearly all sections in the *DSM–5*, this section also includes a not otherwise classified diagnosis for disorders that belong in this category, but do not fully meet the diagnostic criteria for any of the specific disorders. Language disorder is diagnosed when language skills are significantly below expectations based on nonverbal ability and interfere with academic progress. Speech disorder involves an inability to use developmentally appropriate speech sounds (American Psychiatric Association, 2013). Professional school counselors should be sure that an unusual speech pattern is not primarily the result of an inadequate education or a family or cultural environment before diagnosing a communication disorder. A referral to a speech and language specialist can facilitate this discrimination.

Specific learning, motor, and communication disorders are currently thought to involve perinatal or neonatal causes (Johnson, 1995). Other causes for these disorders are being investigated. Changes in the communication skills of individuals with the human immunodeficiency virus (HIV) and the resultant disease, the acquired immunodeficiency syndrome (AIDS), are being recognized and studied (McCabe, Sheard, & Code, 2002). Lead poisoning or head trauma in childhood might also contribute to learning disorders. Specific infections, such as a particular type of meningitis, have also been related to later learning difficulties (Johnson & Slomka, 2000). Approximately 35% to 40% of boys with learning disorders have at least one parent who had similar learning problems (Snowling, 2002; Young & Beitchman, 2002). Learning disorders are also associated with low socioeconomic status, poor self-esteem, depression, and perceptual deficiencies. Children with these disorders often are unhappy in school, have negative self-images and social difficulties, and show increased likelihood of dropping out of school (Seligman & Reichenberg, 2011). High school students with learning disabilities are reported to have lower educational and career aspirations than do their peers (Young & Beitchman, 2002). Depression, anxiety, AD/HD, and disruptive behavior disorders often coexist with learning disorders. In addition, a wide assortment of social skill deficits has been found in children with learning and communication disorders (Barnes, Friehe, & Radd, 2003; Young & Beitchman, 2002).

INTERVENTION STRATEGIES The primary educational strategies for these disorders include behavioral, cognitive behavioral, and psychoeducational interventions (Seligman & Reichenberg, 2011). Children who demonstrate a significant discrepancy between intelligence and achievement, with achievement usually being 20 to 30 standard score points below measured intelligence, may be eligible to receive special education services. An Individualized Education Program (IEP) is developed by the school according to the requirements of the IDEA (Cortiella, 2006; Individuals with Disabilities Education Improvement Act, 2004). The IEP specifies areas of weakness, strategies for addressing the deficit areas, measurable behavioral goals, and criteria for determining whether goals have been successfully met. Young and Beitchman (2002) suggested teaching strategies that include paying attention to sequencing; using drill-repetition-practice; segmenting information into parts or units for later synthesis; controlling task difficulty using prompts and cues; making use of technology (e.g., computers); systematically modeling problem-solving steps; and using small, interactive groups. Frequently, social and emotional goals such as improved interpersonal relations and increases in motor or attention on-task behaviors are included in the IEP, and interventions, including counseling, individualized teaching strategies, accommodations, and social skills training can lead to positive outcomes.

PROGNOSIS Specific learning disorders continue to have an impact on people's lives throughout adolescence and adulthood (Seligman & Reichenberg, 2011). When learning disorders are undiagnosed and untreated, they can lead to extreme frustration, loss of self-esteem, inadequate education, underemployment, and more serious mental disorders. Functioning of the family affects the prognosis of a child with learning problems. A "healthy" family may cope adequately in parenting a child with a learning disorder; however, families described as "disorganized" and "blaming" have more difficulty responding to the child's needs and providing appropriate support and intervention (Johnson & Slomka, 2000).

RELEVANCE TO PROFESSIONAL SCHOOL COUNSELORS Professional school counselors frequently serve on child study and IEP committees tasked with screening and determining eligibility for children with a specific learning disorder. Through their contact with children, teachers, and parents, professional school counselors are often the first to be aware of how learning problems are affecting the child's performance in the classroom, in the home, and with peers. Professional school counselors may be required by the IEP to provide some individual or small-group counseling to the child, to help parents and children understand and cope with the diagnosis of a learning disorder, and to implement accommodations. Because children with learning disorders frequently have coexisting issues such as poor social skills, low self-esteem, negative attitudes toward school, behavioral difficulties, and family problems, professional school counselors can expect to be involved with students, teachers, and parents in a collaborative role.

Collaboration between professional school counselors and speech and language pathologists is important when helping students with communication disorders. It is suggested that the professional school counselor and speech and language pathologist work together to develop appropriate accommodations, such as in materials, activities, and instructional discourse, for these students during classroom group guidance lessons. Professional school counselors can also coordinate support groups for students with communication disorders, as well as see these students individually and meet with families (Barnes et al., 2003).

Autism Spectrum Disorders

The increase in the diagnosis of Autism Spectrum Disorders (ASD) is attributed to many factors. Some of these factors include more sensitive diagnostic procedures, a rise in appropriate referrals, ambiguity in diagnostic criteria, administrative mandates to use psychiatric diagnoses to ensure reimbursement for professional services in medical settings, categorical funding for children with autism by state and county health and social service agencies, and educational placement in categorical programs, as well as changing biological and environmental influences on the etiology of developmental disorders (Mulick & Butter, 2002). ASDs are diagnosed in approximately 1 in 88 people (CDC, 2012). Males with these disorders outnumber females by a ratio of approximately 2.5:1. Formerly there were up to five subtypes of pervasive developmental disorders (APA, 2000), including autistic, Asperger's, childhood disintegrative, Rett's, and PDD–NOS, but these have all been collapsed onto a single spectrum in the *DSM-5* (APA, 2013).

Children with ASD are characterized by impaired social behavior and impaired communication, as well as abnormalities of routine behavior (APA, 2013). They usually exhibit a flat affect (lack of facial expression; emotionless), poor eye contact, and minimal social speech. In addition, these children often show repetitive, stereotyped body movements such as rocking, waving, or head banging. They generally do not seek parental attention or involvement with peers and rarely engage in imitative or interactive play. Language impairment is present in most people with ASD.

PROGNOSIS For most children, ASD will last a lifetime. Although early intervention for many young children with ASD has produced major developmental changes, the technology and knowledge of effective treatment approaches have not yet reached the point where the majority of children diagnosed with ASD make the degree of change that allows them to blend imperceptibly into their peer group (APA, 2013). Those on the mild end of the ASD continuum have the best prognosis; many succeed in becoming self-sufficient (Seligman & Reichenberg, 2011). Often, children and adults on the severe end of the ASD continuum are likely to be placed in residential treatment facilities due to the progressive nature of these disorders. Early intervention seems to be the most important factor for a positive outcome.

INTERVENTION STRATEGIES Children with ASD often need a combination of special education services that may include speech and language therapy, and sometimes physical therapy. Children on the severe end of the spectrum may also require the services of neurologists, medical specialists, and behavioral therapists. Although these children could benefit from social and communication skills, there are some difficulties in having children with ASD in social skills groups. For example, there are the anxieties intrinsic in group learning situations, the natural difficulty of the subject matter (i.e., social interaction and social

understanding), and the typically high oral language load in social skills group work, compounded by the difficulties that the children have in generalizing their new skills into their real-life experiences. Instead, Smith (2001) suggested using social stories, a short-story form (20–150 words), to inform and advise the child about a social situation. Some of the benefits of social stories are that they focus on immediate social difficulties, they can be more personalized than a traditional social skills group, they are easily produced and shared by those involved with the child, and they focus on real-life situations. Behavioral treatments, social skills, and social communication training have been found to be particularly effective in helping children with ASD.

RELEVANCE TO PROFESSIONAL SCHOOL COUNSELORS Having a child with ASD in the family places a considerable strain on every family member. Siblings typically have problems with friends, feel lonely, and worry about their sibling. Marital problems in the parents are also common. Most children with ASD will receive special education services; however, the professional school counselor may play an important role in helping siblings cope, as well as helping parents access supportive resources. The professional school counselor can help teachers make classroom modifications and help students with milder forms of ASD learn the routines that will contribute to their success in the classroom. Parents may also benefit from structured behavioral training programs that help them learn how to help their child.

In addition, professional school counselors may need to provide educators with resources as the expectation that students with ASD will be included in regular education classrooms increases. In-service training for teachers can provide time for learning about the nature of the ASD; for discovering the preferences, priorities, and concerns of the children with ASD; and for adapting curriculum and instruction to match the learning strengths, needs, and interests of these students (Dow & Mehring, 2001).

Attention-Deficit/Hyperactivity Disorder

Attention-deficit/hyperactivity disorder (AD/HD) is found in as many as 50% of children seen for counseling or psychotherapy. The *DSM–5* (APA, 2013) divides AD/HD into predominately hyperactive-impulsive presentation and predominately inattentive presentation, although an individual can be diagnosed with both presentations. By definition, AD/HD has an onset prior to age 7 years; is present in two or more settings (such as home and school); and interferes with social, academic, or occupational functioning. For a diagnosis of AD/HD predominantly inattentive presentation, symptoms need to be present for at least

6 months and may include failure to give close attention to details, difficulty sustaining attention, poor follow-through on instructions, failure to finish work, difficulty organizing tasks, misplacement of things, distraction by extraneous stimuli, and forgetfulness. Children with hyperactive-impulsive presentation are usually diagnosed at a younger age than are children with symptoms of the inattentive presentation. The diagnosis of AD/HD is made through medical, cognitive, and academic assessments, as well as parents' and teachers' input on behavioral rating scales such as the Conners-3 (Conners, 2008).

The current prevalence rates for AD/HD range from 3% to 7% of children (American Psychiatric Association, 2013; CDC, 2005). AD/HD is typically diagnosed early and more commonly in males (Zahn-Waxler, Shirtcliff, & Maraceau, 2008). AD/HD is diagnosed in boys two to nine times more frequently than in girls (American Psychiatric Association, 2013) and is diagnosed in nearly half of children receiving special education services. A meta-analysis of gender differences has also pointed to diagnostic differences. Girls with AD/HD had lower ratings on hyperactivity, inattention, impulsivity, and externalizing of problems and greater intellectual impairment and internalizing of problems than boys did (Gershon, 2002). However, more research is needed to clarify gender and ethnic differences in students with AD/HD.

The diagnosis and treatment of AD/HD remain controversial. Dramatic increases in diagnostic rates of AD/HD have raised questions about the accuracy of the diagnoses and have led to particular concern that lively and active boys may often be misdiagnosed with this disorder (Seligman & Reichenberg, 2011). Correspondingly, concerns have been raised about whether stimulant medication prescribed for treatment of this disorder is overused (Gruttadaro & Miller, 2004). One study of children diagnosed with AD/HD in four communities concluded that of the 5.1% of the population of children meeting the AD/HD criteria, only 12.5% were being treated with psychostimulant medication (Jensen et al., 1999). However, this study also found that a number of children not meeting the AD/HD criteria were being treated with medication. This study supports the conclusion that children are both undermedicated and overmedicated for AD/HD. Adding further support to this view is a study by Hoagwood, Kelleher, Feil, and Comer (2000) that found that only 50% of the children diagnosed with AD/HD were receiving adequate and appropriate care.

PROGNOSIS The prognosis for improvement of children with AD/HD via treatment is good. Behavioral interventions allow most children with AD/HD to reduce off-task and distractible behaviors. The effectiveness of psychostimulant medications such as methylphenidate (Ritalin or Concerta), Adderall, Strattera, and dextroamphetamine (Dexadrine) continues to be supported by research despite an ongoing debate concerning the use of these medications.

INTERVENTION STRATEGIES The most commonly used interventions with children diagnosed with AD/HD are behavioral strategies and the use of stimulant medication (Seligman & Reichenberg, 2011). Cognitive-behavioral strategies have been used to improve social skills in children with AD/HD and to address on-task behaviors. Social skills training programs focus on such skills as improving awareness of appropriate interpersonal distance, starting and maintaining a conversation, identifying the main idea of a conversation, and accepting and giving compliments. Group therapy has also been used effectively to help children with AD/HD improve self-esteem and communication and develop social skills.

Training for parents is considered to be essential to successfully addressing AD/HD in children. Training involves helping parents recognize and encourage socially competent behaviors, teach self-evaluation strategies, model good communication skills, establish appropriate limits, and provide consistent rewards and consequences (Anastopoulos & Farely, 2003). Programs like Systematic Training for Effective Parenting (STEP; Dinkmeyer, 1975) and support groups like Children and Adults with Attention-Deficit/Hyperactivity Disorder (CHADD) may also be useful (Seligman & Reichenberg, 2011). Multifaceted approaches such as school-based community support programs (Hussey & Guo, 2003) that target elementary-aged students and aim to increase family involvement and support of the school and to improve social and behavioral functioning, as well as attendance and academic achievement, also seem to be effective in reducing AD/HD behaviors. Ultimately, the goal for children with AD/HD is to learn self-monitoring behaviors (Seligman & Reichenberg, 2011). Self-monitoring is encouraged through behavioral strategies such as praise to reinforce desirable behaviors, proximity (standing near the student), and the use of token economies. Token economies consist of providing children with tokens or points for appropriate behaviors that can be exchanged later for rewards (Erford, Eaves, Bryant, & Young, 2010).

One of the most controversial strategies for treating AD/HD is the use of psychostimulant medication. Effective medications are thought to stimulate the production of the neurochemicals that facilitate brain functioning (Seligman & Reichenberg, 2011). Contrary to the misconception that these children are hypersensitive or hyperattentive, neurodevelopmental research suggests that AD/HD is actually a problem of underarousal. Methylphenidate (Ritalin) and dextroamphetamine (Dexadrine) are the most frequently prescribed medications. Medications such as Adderall, which is long acting and has less drop-off action; a sustained release version of methylphenidate (Concerta); and a stimulant-free medication, Strattera, are also being used. The National Alliance on Mental Illness (NAMI) concluded after conducting a task force investigation that psychotropic medications should be used to treat children only when the benefits outweigh the risks (Gruttadaro & Miller, 2004). The task force went on to recommend that evidence-based treatments be identified, through research, and used to treat mental disorders in children.

Tic Disorders

The *DSM–5* identifies four tic disorders: Tourette's disorder, chronic motor or vocal tic disorder, provisional tic disorder, and tic disorder not otherwise classified. Tics are defined as recurrent, nonrhythmic series of movements and sounds (of a nonvoluntary nature) in one or several muscle groups. Tics are usually divided into simple and complex tics of a motor, sensory, or vocal nature (American Psychiatric Association, 2013). Examples of motor tics are eye blinking, neck jerking, facial grimacing, and shrugging. Vocal tics include coughing, clearing one's throat, grunting, sniffing, and barking. Tic symptoms are typically worse under stress, are less noticeable when the child is distracted, and diminish entirely during sleep (Seligman & Reichenberg, 2013). Tic disorders are more common in boys and have an elevated incidence in children with other disorders such as AD/HD, specific learning disorders, ASD, anxiety disorders, and obsessive-compulsive disorder (Gadow, Nolan, Sprafkin, & Schwartz, 2002; Kurlan et al., 2002).

Tourette's disorder is characterized by a combination of multiple motor tics and one or more vocal tics that have been present for at least 1 year. Tourette's disorder often begins with simple eye blinking. Over time, the tic behaviors become persistent and occur at multiple sites in the body. These tics commonly interfere with academic performance and social relationships. Tourette's is diagnosed in 4 or 5 children per 10,000 and tends to run in families.

Budman, Bruun, Park, Lesser, and Olson (2000) reported sudden, explosive outbursts of behavior in children and adolescents with Tourette's disorder. These explosive outbursts are recognizable by their stereotypic features, which include the abrupt onset of unpredictable and primitive displays of physical aggression, verbal aggression, or both that are grossly out of proportion to any provoking stimuli, often threatening serious self-injury or harm to others. Explosive outbursts in children can be distinguished from the more common "temper tantrum" by their magnitude and intensity. These outbursts occur at an age when such symptoms are no longer regarded as age appropriate.

PROGNOSIS Tic severity usually peaks at approximately 10 to 11 years and declines in early adolescence (Coffey et al., 2000). One study of the treatment of tic disorders compared the effectiveness of behavioral interventions with that of medication (Peterson, Campise, & Azrin, 1994). Habit-reversal techniques showed a 90% reduction in tics as compared to medication, which showed only a 50% to 60% reduction. Coffey et al. (2000) conducted a study examining whether a substantial decline in the prevalence rate of tic disorders occurs from childhood to adulthood, suggesting that tic disorders may follow a remitting course. Results of this study found that early adolescence is the time of remission of tics and Tourette's disorder–associated impairment.

INTERVENTION STRATEGIES The treatment of tic disorders currently includes identification of any underlying stressors; cognitive-behavioral methods for stress management; education of children and families about the disorder; advocacy with education professionals; and collaborative work with physicians, if pharmacological interventions are necessary. The first steps include gathering enough information about the symptoms to make an accurate diagnosis and educating the parents and the child about the course of the disorder and the influence of stress. Behavioral strategies such as self-monitoring, relaxation training, and habit-reversal training may be recommended after baseline data concerning the nature and frequency of the tic are collected. The current psychological treatment of choice for tics is habit reversal, which essentially addresses the tic as a behavior. Social skills training has also been used successfully to offset the negative impact of tic disorders on peer relationships. Pharmacological treatment is used only for children who do not respond to behavioral strategies.

RELEVANCE TO PROFESSIONAL SCHOOL COUNSELORS The professional school counselor may be the first professional consulted about the development of tic behaviors in a child. A counselor who is knowledgeable about this disorder will be able to provide sources of referral and information to parents and teachers during the diagnostic period. Once the diagnosis has been made, the professional school counselor can provide suggestions concerning classroom modifications to reduce stress, rewards for behavioral control, and adjustment of academic expectations. Professional school counselors may also be able to provide the social skills training to help children deal with the peer relationship problems that frequently result from tic disorders.

DISRUPTIVE BEHAVIOR DISORDERS

The *DSM–5* describes two disruptive behavior disorders that occur primarily in childhood: conduct disorder (CD) and oppositional defiant disorder (ODD). Prevalence rates for all disruptive behavior disorders are approximately 10% (Tynan, 2008). For CD, the prevalence is 6% to 16% of males and 2% to 9% of females under the age of 18 years (American Psychiatric Association, 2013; Tynan, 2006). Prevalence rates for ODD are 2% to 16% for males and females.

CD is a more serious disruptive behavior disorder than ODD. Left untreated, ODD may develop into a conduct disorder. A diagnosis of CD requires the presence of repeated and persistent violations of the basic rights of others or violations of major age-appropriate societal norms or rules (Seligman & Reichenberg, 2011). CD is diagnosed when students display aggression against people and animals, destruction of property, deceitfulness or theft, or serious violations of rules. CD is divided into childhood-onset and adolescent-onset types. The adolescent-onset type is diagnosed when no symptoms are present before the age of 10 years, whereas the childhood-onset type is diagnosed if symptoms appear before that age. The prognosis for the childhood-onset type is worse than for the adolescent-onset type. If the symptoms of CD have not remitted by age 18 years, the diagnosis of CD is usually replaced with the diagnosis of antisocial personality disorder. Approximately 50% of children with CD are also diagnosed with AD/HD (Tynan, 2006). Mood disorders, anxiety disorders, substance use, low verbal intelligence, learning disorders, dropping out of school, delinquency, and violent behavior are common in young people with CD (Tynan, 2008).

ODD is described as a pattern of negativistic, hostile, and defiant behaviors lasting at least 6 months. According to the *DSM–5*, characteristic behaviors include losing one's temper, arguing with adults, defying or refusing to comply with adults' requests, deliberately annoying people, being angry and resentful, being easily annoyed by others, blaming others for one's own negative behavior, and being vindictive. Younger children may have temper tantrums, engage in power struggles, have low tolerance for frustration, and be disobedient (Tynan, 2008). Older children will argue, threaten, show disrespect for adults, destroy property in a rage, and refuse to cooperate. The presence of ODD is positively correlated with having low socioeconomic status and growing up in an urban location. ODD is more common in boys, and the symptoms first appear by the age of 8.

Prognosis

Disruptive behavior disorders are difficult to treat, and even with the use of evidence-based treatment, young people with this diagnosis often experience long-term consequences (Tynan, 2008). However, the prognosis for ODD is more promising than for CD. Prognoses for disruptive behavior disorders appear to be best when there has been late onset, early intervention, and long-term intervention. The most critical element of successful treatment is parents' support and participation.

CASE STUDY 17.2

Defiance in the Teenage Years

A 15-year-old female was brought to counseling by her parents. They reported that over the past year or so, she had changed; she has a quick temper and is hostile and argumentative; she has disobeyed her parents repeatedly to meet her boyfriend at a local shopping mall; she blames her teachers for her poor grades in some subjects, but will not ask them for help; and she has even been teasing her 4-year-old sister, whom she used to adore. Family, as well as teachers, report that she is difficult and uncooperative, but cannot provide an explanation for the change. A physical examination revealed no medical problems. Principal Diagnosis: Oppositional Defiant Disorder

Intervention Strategies

Intervention for children with disruptive behavior disorders should be multifaceted. Four types of intervention strategies are suggested: individual counseling, family interventions, school-based interventions, and community interventions (Cooley, 2007; Tynan, 2006). Residential or day treatment programs may be recommended when the child or adolescent poses a danger to self or others. School-based interventions include early education, classroom guidance units, classroom instruction, home visits, and regular meetings with parents.

Relevance to Professional School Counselors

Classroom teachers and other school personnel, as well as parents, may look to the professional school counselor for guidance concerning how to effectively work with children diagnosed with these disorders. Children are not usually diagnosed with disruptive behavior disorders until they enter school. Teachers and professional school counselors will want to work closely with parents to help them understand these disorders and make appropriate referrals to medical and mental health professionals who can make the diagnosis. Because AD/HD and disruptive behavior disorders frequently coexist, the diagnosis and decisions about interventions will require a high degree of collaboration among physicians, psychologists, classroom and special education teachers, professional school counselors, and parents. Children with disruptive behavior disorders may qualify for special education or Section 504 services.

Studies have examined the relationship between low reading achievement and the development of CD in young children (Bennett, Brown, Boyle, Racine, & Offord, 2003) and the relationship of perceived school culture, self-esteem, attachment to learning, and peer approval to the development of disruptive behavior problems in adolescents (DeWit et al., 2000). This research is encouraging the development of a range of school-based and family-focused prevention programs targeting young children (Webster-Stratton & Taylor, 2001). There are two approaches to early prevention. One is to provide social skills, problem-solving, and anger management training to the entire school population through a developmental curriculum. Second Step: A Violence Prevention Curriculum (Committee for Children, 2002b) is an example of such a developmental program. The second approach to prevention is to identify high-risk students and provide a small-group curriculum for them. Fast Track (Bierman et al., 2002) is an example of a research-based program delivered to identified high-risk first graders. By the end of the third grade, 37% of the program participants were free of serious conduct-problem dysfunctions. The efficacy of both of these approaches will continue to be evaluated, but the implications for professional school counselors are clear. Using either approach, the professional school counselor will play a central role in the delivery of such programs. Theory into Practice 17.2 provides an example of the professional school counselor's role in supporting students with a disruptive behavior disorder.

THEORY INTO PRACTICE 17.2

THE SCHOOL COUNSELOR'S ROLE IN DETERMINING THE EXTENT OF DISRUPTIVE BEHAVIOR

Robert's seventh-grade homeroom teacher has come to talk with the professional school counselor about Robert's behavior. By midterm in the first marking period, Ms. Sandhouse has already documented a series of behavioral issues, including Robert being argumentative with teachers, not getting along with peers, annoying students he sits next to, and not taking responsibility for his behavior. Ms. Sandhouse has spoken with Robert's parents by phone and concluded that they do not know how to control Robert's anger other than to punish him and were unable to help the teacher come up with a plan. The professional school counselor listens carefully to the teacher's report and considers a variety of explanations. Robert could be having trouble adjusting to middle school, or perhaps something is going on at home. After speaking with the school counselor, the teacher will implement a more consistent behavior plan with Robert to see if that will make a difference. The school counselor offers Ms. Sandhouse suggestions on how to avoid power struggles and help Robert to increase his self-control. The teacher will also keep a log of Robert's outbursts, noting what has worked and what the triggers seem to be, and establish a behavior contract. They will also meet in person with the parents to share their concerns and ask for parent support for the plans they are implementing. The professional school counselor will ask for parent permission to work with Robert on research-based anger management strategies and will begin by building a positive alliance with Robert. The school counselor considers that Robert may have a disruptive behavior disorder, but before such a diagnosis can be made, the efforts of the teacher and school counselor will need to be documented. Once the teacher and school counselor have more information, they will consider the possibility of asking for a Child Study Team meeting and recommending a psycho-educational evaluation.

EATING DISORDERS IN CHILDREN AND ADOLESCENTS

Feeding and eating disorders of early childhood include two disorders that can interfere with a child's development, social functioning, or nutritional health: pica and rumination disorder. Pica and rumination disorder are especially likely to be diagnosed in children with intellectual disabilities and are often associated with ASD. Typically, these disorders will be diagnosed before a child enters school, but professional school counselors should be aware of them nonetheless.

Pica is characterized by the ingestion of nonfood substances (APA, 2013). Mouthing and eating nonnutritive substances is not uncommon in children under the age of 2; therefore, the diagnosis of pica should not be made before that age unless the behavior is judged to be problematic. Rumination disorder is characterized by persistent regurgitation and rechewing of food. Typically, rumination disorder is diagnosed in infants and very young children after a period in which a normal eating pattern has been established. Prevalence rates and risk factor assessments have been established based on samples of Caucasian adolescents and, therefore, do not accurately reflect the nature of eating disorders in other ethnic populations (Jacobi, Hayward, de Zwaan, Kraemer, & Agras, 2004).

Anorexia nervosa and bulimia nervosa are eating disorders that are diagnosed in adults, as well as in children and adolescents. Women are identified with these disorders at least three times more frequently than men. Lifetime prevalence rates for anorexia nervosa are 0.9% for women and 0.3% for men; for bulimia nervosa lifetime prevalence rates are 1.5% for women and to 0.5% for men (Hudson, Hiripi, Pope, & Kessler, 2007). Prevalence rates for anorexia nervosa and bulimia nervosa have increased during the last 50 years both in the United States and in other developed countries, and the incidence of eating disorders among elementary-aged children is also increasing. Approximately 95% of people with eating disorders are between the ages of 12 and 26 (National Association of Anorexia Nervosa and Associated Disorders [ANAD], 2014). The most common risk factors for eating disorders in adolescence include early childhood eating and gastrointestinal problems, body dissatisfaction, depression or anxiety, and low self-esteem. Other factors sometimes associated with eating disorders are environmental stressors, cognitive distortions such as obsessive thoughts, and weak identity formation. Caution must be used in the application of these risk factors to diverse cultural groups. The causes of eating disorders and the role culture plays in the manifestation of eating disorders are being debated. Keel and Klump (2003) challenged the belief that eating disorders are culture-bound syndromes, concluding that a strong genetic link exists. People in occupational or avocational roles that require low weight, such as in ballet, theater, and many sports, are at an elevated risk of developing an eating disorder.

Anorexia nervosa, according to the *DSM–5* (American Psychiatric Association, 2013), involves a person's refusal to maintain normal body weight or failure to gain weight at what would be an expected rate. For adolescents diagnosed with anorexia nervosa, the *DSM–5* criteria specify a body weight that is 85% or less than the normal weight for the person's age and size. Other symptoms include great fear of becoming overweight, a disturbed body image, dread of loss of control, and in females, the cessation of menstrual cycles. In prepubescent girls, the disorder may be associated with apprehension about puberty. Two types of anorexia nervosa have been identified: restricting type (more common) and binge-eating/purging type. The restricting type is associated with dieting, fasting, or excessive exercise. The binge-eating/purging type is associated with binge eating, purging, or both, accompanied by a very low weight. Purging is accomplished through self-induced vomiting or the misuse of laxatives, diuretics, or enemas. Physiological consequences of anorexia nervosa include dry skin, edema, low blood pressure, metabolic changes, potassium loss, and cardiac damage that can result in death.

Individuals diagnosed with bulimia nervosa engage in behaviors similar to those of persons with the binge-eating/purging type of anorexia nervosa, but do not meet the full criteria for that disorder, usually because their weight is more than 85% of normal. According to the *DSM–5* (American Psychiatric Association, 2013), bulimia nervosa involves an average of two episodes a week of binge eating (usually accompanied by compensatory behavior such as vomiting, fasting, laxative use, or extreme exercise) for at least 3 months. Physiological reactions to purging include dental cavities and enamel loss, electrolyte imbalance, cardiac and renal problems, and esophageal tears (ANAD, 2014). Bingeing is associated with dysphoric mood, stress, and unstructured time. People usually binge alone and can consume 3,000 calories in a single binge.

Prognosis

The prognosis for women with anorexia nervosa is mixed (Hudson et al., 2007). Nearly half completely recover, and another quarter of patients improve significantly. About a quarter of clients with anorexia nervosa are not helped or deteriorate, and approximately 5% of people with anorexia nervosa die as a result of the disorder. The prognosis for bulimia nervosa is somewhat better. Treatment that follows recommended guidelines can have a positive impact on eating patterns, typically reducing binge eating and purging by a rate of at least 75% (Seligman & Reichenberg, 2011). A positive prognosis is associated with the following factors: good functioning prior to occurrence of the disorder, a positive family environment, the client's acknowledgment of hunger, greater maturity, higher self-esteem, higher educational level, earlier age of onset, lower weight loss, shorter duration of the disease, little denial of the disorder, and absence of coexisting mental disorders.

CASE STUDY 17.3

Eating Disorders and Other Complex Treatment Issues in Childhood

Marie, age 11, aspired to be a model. She exercised daily and ate very little. Her weight had dropped from 120 lb to 95 lb; at 5 ft 5 in., she looked gaunt and tired. Nevertheless, she continued to perform well at school and at home and was never disobedient. She had few friends, but reported that she was so busy studying that she had little time for socializing. Part of her reluctance to socialize with others stemmed from some unusual behaviors she manifested. She would often wave her arm as though she were swatting flies. She also spontaneously emitted sounds and words, including obscenities. Marie reported that she could not control these behaviors. Marie was in a special class because of severe difficulty with reading; her reading ability was nearly 2 standard deviations below the norm for her age. Diagnoses: Anorexia nervosa, Tourette's disorder, and a specific learning disorder in reading.

Intervention Strategies

Primary intervention strategies for eating disorders involve a complete medical assessment and multifaceted therapy (Seligman & Reichenberg, 2011). Behavioral therapy has been effective in promoting healthy eating and eliminating purging and other destructive behaviors. Cognitive therapy can help the individual gain an understanding of the disorder, improve self-esteem, and gain a sense of control. Group therapy has been used effectively to treat people diagnosed with anorexia nervosa and bulimia nervosa, with family therapy included as an important component of the treatment plan, especially for children and adolescents.

Relevance to Professional School Counselors

Given that 86% of adults with eating disorders report that the disorder began before age 20, professional school counselors will need to have knowledge of the risk factors and symptoms of eating disorders and will need to consider how culture may influence the development of an eating disorder (ANAD, 2014). Prevention programs and early detection in elementary and middle school may be the best defense against the development of an eating disorder during adolescence. Professional school counselors can enlist the help of classroom teachers by increasing their knowledge of eating disorder risk factors and encouraging strategies that promote healthy behaviors (Piran, 2004). Schoolwide antibullying programs can go a long way in protecting students' self-esteem, body image, and identity development.

Professional school counselors may become aware of students who are regularly eating little or no lunch, engaging in ritualized eating patterns, or purging. It is not uncommon in schools to have other students, influenced by the weight loss of youth with anorexia or bulimia nervosa, begin to experiment with restricted eating patterns. Working with classroom teachers, the school nurse, and the parents, the professional school counselor can help students and their families become aware of dangerous eating patterns and the long-term consequences of eating disorders. Children and adolescents who are diagnosed with eating disorders will need to have long-term medical and mental health interventions. However, professional school counselors can assist these students in school, support the efforts of their mental health counselors, and help parents and families find resources.

ELIMINATION DISORDERS: ENCOPRESIS AND ENURESIS

Encopresis and enuresis are characterized by inadequate bowel or bladder control in children whose age and intellectual level suggest they can be expected to have adequate control of these functions. Many children diagnosed with these disorders have no coexisting mental disorders. For the diagnosis to be made, the encopresis or enuresis cannot be associated with a general medical condition, with the exception of constipation (Seligman & Reichenberg, 2011).

Encopresis is the voluntary or involuntary passage of feces in inappropriate places (American Psychiatric Association, 2013). This diagnosis would not be made in a child younger than 4 years. There sometimes is an association between encopresis and ODD or CD. Sexual abuse and family pressure have also been associated with this disorder. The most effective treatment strategies involve medical, educational, and therapeutic interventions. Encopresis may continue for some time, but it is rarely chronic. Educational, behavioral, dietary, and physiological components comprise primary treatment modalities.

Enuresis is the involuntary or intentional inappropriate voiding of urine, occurring in children over the age of 5 years (Butler, 2004). The nocturnal-only subtype is the most common form of this disorder. Nocturnal enuresis can be caused by high fluid intake at night before bedtime, urinary tract infection, emotional stress, sexual abuse, chronic constipation, or a family history of enuresis (Silverstein, 2004). Traumatic events during a sensitive stage in the development of bladder control (2 to 3 years of age) have been found to be related to the later development of nocturnal enuresis (Butler, 2004). Behavioral interventions are the most successful (Seligman & Reichenberg, 2011). Behavioral treatment in the form of a bell-and-pad method of conditioning is usually considered a first line of intervention. Spontaneous remission occurs in many children.

Relevance to Professional School Counselors

Parents are likely to consult professional school counselors about their child's enuresis, most often manifested as bedwetting. Parents will need information and education about the nature of this disorder and how to deal with it. Education may help alleviate parents' anxiety about the course of the disorder (Seligman & Reichenberg, 2011). Parents should be encouraged to rule out medical causes of the bedwetting; if a diagnosis of enuresis is made, professional school counselors can help parents cope. Encopresis is a less common, but often more serious disorder than enuresis. Counselors suspecting this diagnosis in a student should recommend a medical evaluation as the first step in treatment.

MOOD DISORDERS

Although the diagnostic criteria for depressive disorders in adults and children are the same, children and adolescents diagnosed with mood disorders typically have symptoms that differ from those of adults (Seligman & Reichenberg, 2011). Rather than manifesting the classic symptoms of depression, children tend to externalize their feelings and may be irritable, often presenting with somatic complaints. Adolescents are more likely to present with the more familiar symptoms of depression, similar to those of adults, including feelings of sadness and guilt, social withdrawal, and perhaps even thoughts of suicide.

Suicide is rare in children, but increases in prevalence through adolescence, and as many as one out of five students seriously considers taking his or her own life (Seligman & Reichenberg, 2011). The rate of suicide among African Americans has always been lower than that among Whites, but has been increasing in adolescent males. Attempted suicide is greater among Hispanic adolescents than among African Americans and Whites. Native American adolescents have a very high rate of suicide. Depressive disorders, disruptive behavior disorders, and anxiety disorders increase the risk of suicidal ideation and attempts in both sexes. Approximately 90% of adolescents who commit suicide had been diagnosed with a psychiatric disorder for at least 2 years. Given the high correlation of mood disorders and suicide attempts, it is important to identify young people with mood disorders and begin treatment. Yet it is estimated that 70% of children and adolescents with serious mood disorders are either undiagnosed or inadequately treated.

CASE STUDY 17.4

Depression in Adolescence

A 17-year-old girl was evaluated for an episode of depressed mood, sleeping problems, irritability, loss of weight, and reduced energy level. Symptoms had been present for nearly a month, since her best friend was killed by a car. Her parents could hardly get her up in the morning. She refused to dress or bathe and had been absent from school for 2 weeks. She repeatedly told her parents that she wished she could die so that she could be with her friend. No previous emotional difficulties were reported. Principal Diagnosis: Major depressive disorder, single episode.

Major depressive disorder, characterized by at least 2 weeks of severe depression, has a lifetime prevalence rate of about 18% (Kessler, Chiu, Demler, & Walters, 2005). Dysthymic disorder, a milder, but more pervasive form of depression that lasts for at least 1 year, is diagnosed in about 1% of children and 2% to 8% of adolescents (APA, 2013). Bipolar disorder, characterized by episodes of depression and episodes of mania or hypomania, is difficult to diagnose in children and adolescents. Prevalence rates for adolescents are thought to be as high as 1%, but the estimates for young children are likely lower.

Prognosis

Psychotherapy and psychoeducational interventions have been shown to be effective in treating depression in children and adolescents. A cognitive-behavioral group treatment intervention, Coping with Depression for Adolescents (CWDA), has demonstrated significant positive outcomes (Clark, DeBar, & Lewinsohn, 2003). A meta-analysis conducted by Erford et al. (2010) found that counseling was effective in alleviating the symptoms of children and adolescents diagnosed with depression at both termination and follow-up.

Intervention Strategies

Treatment of children and adolescents with mood disorders is similar to that of adults; cognitive and behavioral interventions are emphasized (Seligman & Reichenberg, 2011). Psychoeducational programs focus on improving social skills and encouraging rewarding activities. Although medications are used successfully to treat depression in adults, the effective and safe use of antidepressant medications with children and adolescents has not been established. Nevertheless, medication is often used with children and adolescents to relieve depression.

Relevance to Professional School Counselors

Professional school counselors will encounter many sad children and adolescents. It will be particularly important for counselors to understand the diagnostic criteria for mood disorders so they can distinguish situational sadness from a mental disorder, especially given the differences between adult and childhood depression. Mood disorders in children are frequently overlooked and misdiagnosed (Erford et al., 2010; Seligman & Reichenberg, 2011). Given the increased risk of suicide behavior linked to mood disorders, this is a diagnosis that professional school counselors will need to be educated about. Professional school counselors will want to consult with parents, teachers, and other mental health professionals if a diagnosis of a mood disorder is suspected, given the evidence that early diagnosis and treatment are associated with better outcomes.

SUBSTANCE USE AND ADDICTIVE DISORDERS

Professional school counselors and other mental health professionals generally have considerable concern about the use of alcohol, tobacco, and other harmful substances by children and adolescents. Children who live with parents with substance use and addictive disorders are at particularly high risk of developing these disorders themselves. Professional school counselors need to have current and accurate information about substance use, abuse, and dependence to work effectively with students, teachers, and parents.

Substance-use disorders are unlike most other mental disorders in at least two ways. First, drug abuse and dependence rely on an external agent (the drug) and vary depending on the availability of drugs. Second, substance-use disorders always involve a willing host (the user), who is an active instigator and participant in creating the disorder. Substance use and addictive disorders, according to the *DSM–5* (American Psychiatric Association, 2013), include a variety of substances, such as marijuana, cocaine, heroin, and amphetamines. Substance abuse is characterized by maladaptive use of substances, leading to significant impairment or distress. People may fail to fulfill their obligations or may have social or legal problems related to their substance use.

Determining whether a young person is using substances is often difficult. Children and adolescents commonly deny substance use for fear of punishment. Substance-use disorders have a high comorbidity with other mental disorders, such as mood disorders, impulse control disorders, and learning disorders in children and adolescents (American Psychiatric Association, 2013). Consequently, diagnosing substance use and addictive disorders in young people may be complicated by a pre- or coexisting condition.

Prognosis

Many factors are related to a good prognosis for substance use and addictive disorders (Seligman & Reichenberg, 2011). A stable family situation, early intervention, the lack of accompanying antisocial behavior, and no family history of alcohol use are indicators of a positive outcome. However, Newcomb and Richardson (2000) suggested several areas that work together to influence drug use: cultural, societal environment (i.e., school, peers, and family);

psychobehavioral factors (i.e., personality, attitudes, and activities); and biogenetic factors. Furthermore, Lambie and Rokutani (2002, p. 355) proposed 10 risk factors that predict or precipitate substance use disorders: (a) poor parent–child relationships; (b) mental disorders, especially depression; (c) a tendency to seek novel experiences or take risks; (d) family members or peers who use substances; (e) low academic motivation; (f) absence of religion/religiosity; (g) early cigarette use; (h) low self-esteem; (i) being raised in a single-parent or blended family; and (j) engaging in health-compromising behaviors. It has been found that adolescents who concurrently possess five or more of these qualities are at an extremely high risk for developing substance-use problems. Childhood anxiety disorders and depression have also been identified as potential risk factors affecting the development and course of substance-use disorders (Kendall, Safford, Flannery-Schroeder, & Webb, 2004). According to Wu et al. (2004), there is a strong association between alcohol abuse and suicide attempts. This relationship may involve the disinhibitory effects of acute alcohol intoxication, the increase in vulnerability for depression resulting from chronic alcohol abuse, and the possible use of drugs or alcohol as self-medication for depressive symptoms. Abusing substances poses significant health risks such as overdose, suicide, aggression, violent behavior, and other psychopathology (McClelland, Elkington, Teplin, & Abram, 2004).

Intervention Strategies

Prevention through substance-abuse education, recognition of risk factors, and early detection and treatment are the most important strategies for dealing with substance-use disorders in children and adolescents (Rongione, Erford, & Broglie, 2011). Accurate screening for substance use is the first step in intervention. Home drug-test kits are available to parents who wish to assess their child's drug use. The presence of other mental disorders should be assessed as part of any intervention (Seligman & Reichenberg, 2011). Treatment models vary and may be distinguished by their duration, intensity, goals, degree of restrictiveness, and participant membership. Contemporary treatments may be viewed on a continuum that ranges from brief outpatient therapy to intensive inpatient treatment (Newcomb & Richardson, 2000). Treatment may include detoxification, contracting, behavior therapy, self-help groups, family therapy, change in a person's social context, social skills training, and nutritional and recreational counseling. Rongione et al. (2011) reported small to moderate effects of alcohol and drug treatment at termination, but no to small effects of treatment at follow-up. In addition, McClelland et al. (2004) suggested

that treatment programs for youth target the specific needs of adolescents: level of cognitive development, family situation, and educational needs. Treatment programs must target all substances of abuse, especially marijuana, and address comorbid mental disorders.

Relevance to Professional School Counselors

Professional school counselors have an important role to play in the prevention of substance use. The turning-point year, marking the most dramatic increase in exposure and drug use, is 12 to 13, primarily because of the immense availability of drugs and alcohol during the middle school years. There is a continued need for proactive substance-use educational programs at the elementary and middle school levels, as well as an aggressive parent education component in these programs (Rongione et al., 2011). To serve as a resource to school personnel and parents in the detection and treatment of substance use and to be a credible resource to students, professional school counselors will need to obtain accurate and up-to-date information about levels of substance use in their community, detection of substance use, and available community resources.

Lambie and Rokutani (2002) suggested that professional school counselors can be the first line of defense in detecting student troubles that may require specialized treatment not offered in the school setting. Some visible indicators of possible substance-related problems are deterioration of academic performance, increased absenteeism and truancy, fighting, verbal abuse, defiance, and withdrawal. Professional school counselors have four functions in working with students with possible substance-abuse issues: (a) identify the possible warning signs of student substance abuse; (b) work with the youth to establish a therapeutic relationship; (c) support the family system to promote change; and (d) be a resource for and liaison among the student, the family, the school, and community agencies and treatment programs.

SCHIZOPHRENIA SPECTRUM AND OTHER PSYCHOTIC DISORDERS

Psychotic disorders in children are rare (Seligman & Reichenberg, 2011). Approximately 1 child in 10,000 is diagnosed with schizophrenia. These disorders have both internalizing features (e.g., flat affect, social withdrawal) and externalizing features (e.g., impulsivity, inattention). The symptoms of psychotic disorders in children are the same as in adults: hallucinations, delusions, loose associations, and illogical thinking. The most common symptoms of schizophrenia in childhood are auditory hallucinations and delusions, along with illogical conversation and thought patterns (McClellan, McCurry, Speltz, & Jones, 2002). Schizophrenia in children and adolescents is difficult to diagnose because of the comorbidity with other disorders such as mood and cognitive (organic) mental disorders. Given the complexities of psychotic disorders, children and adolescents with these disorders are often difficult to identify, leading to possible delays in treatment. Psychotic disorders are commonly misdiagnosed in youths, due in part to clinicians not following the diagnostic criteria and in part to the relative rarity of these disorders in children.

Prognosis

The prognosis for young people diagnosed with psychotic disorders is good when they are treated with a combination of family therapy and medication. Seventeen percent of children who received both family therapy and medication relapsed, as compared to 83% of children receiving only medication. Biederman, Petty, Faraone, and Seidman (2004) found that psychotic symptoms lasted an average of 3 years and were present during an average of 27% of the children's and adolescents' lives.

Intervention Strategies

Asarnow, Tompson, and McGrath (2004) suggested two phases within the treatment process: (a) acute and (b) stabilization and maintenance. The acute phase emphasizes pharmacological treatment. The stabilization and maintenance phase emphasizes the continuation of medication management supplemented with psychosocial and community treatment strategies. These include family psychoeducational interventions, individual psychotherapy, social skills training, and cognitive remediation. Treatment for children and adolescents with psychotic disorders should include family therapy, medication, counseling, and special education (Seligman & Reichenberg, 2011). Social skills training, including the teaching of appropriate behaviors, interpersonal interactions, playing with peers, and effective communication, should be included as part of treatment. Working with the family will also be important to promote a positive attitude, make modifications to the home environment, and teach parents effective coping skills. A positive and encouraging home environment can reduce the likelihood that a psychotic disorder will recur.

Relevance to Professional School Counselors

Due to the small number of children diagnosed with psychotic disorders, it is unlikely that professional school counselors will encounter many children with these disorders. It is important for professional school counselors to remember that loose associations in speech and illogical thinking are not unusual before the age of 7 years and probably are not indicative of the symptoms of psychosis. However, professional school counselors do need to be aware that the frequency of schizophrenia increases from age 11 years to late adolescence, when it reaches adult prevalence rates (American Psychiatric Association, 2013). Professional school counselors may be involved in the implementation and delivery of special education services as part of an IEP for young people with psychotic disorders that may include social and emotional goals.

OBSESSIVE-COMPULSIVE DISORDER

OCD is more common in children than in adults (about 0.5%; Gothelf, Aharonovsky, Horesh, Carty, & Apter, 2004). Although the symptoms for children are the same as for adults, most children with OCD present with obsessions about germs, external threats, or disease and exhibit rituals of washing or checking. Other common compulsions include touching, counting, hoarding, and repeating. A high rate of comorbidity between OCD and tic disorders, anxiety disorders, and bipolar disorder (Masi, Mucci, & Millepiedi, 2001) has been reported.

Intervention Strategies

Children with OCD respond to cognitive-behavioral interventions. The primary intervention strategy is exposure to obsessions, with accompanying prevention of compulsions, to promote systematic desensitization. Medication also is often used as part of the treatment plan. The family should be included in treatment because the family may have developed maladaptive coping strategies for dealing with the distressed child (Seligman & Reichenberg, 2011).

Relevance to Professional School Counselors

Professional school counselors may be the first consulted by teachers and parents concerning the symptoms of OCD. Counselors can provide information about the disorder and may be instrumental in helping parents determine whether a referral is warranted. When a diagnosis of OCD is made, professional school counselors can help structure the school modifications and interventions.

TRAUMA AND STRESSOR-RELATED DISORDERS

Reactive Attachment Disorder

Reactive Attachment Disorder (RAD) is an uncommon disorder that begins before the age of 5 years and is characterized by children manifesting severe disturbances in social relatedness (Seligman & Reichenberg, 2011). The style of social relating among children with RAD typically occurs in one of two extremes: (a) indiscriminate and excessive attempts to receive comfort and affection from any available adult, even relative strangers, or (b) extreme reluctance to initiate or accept comfort and affection, even from familiar adults and especially when distressed (Haugaard & Hazan, 2004). Children with this disorder are those whose attachments to their primary caregivers have been disrupted, leading to impairment of future relationships. Neglect, abuse, or grossly inadequate parenting, otherwise known as pathogenic care, is thought to cause this disorder (Coleman, 2003; Haugaard & Hazan, 2004; Sheperis, Renfro-Michel, & Doggett, 2003). Studies have considered the relationship between RAD and behavioral problems among preschool children. In older children and adolescents, the behaviors associated with RAD present as withdrawing from others, acting out aggressively toward peers, being socially awkward, and exhibiting sexual promiscuity, as well as being the frequent victim of bullying (Haugaard & Hazan, 2004). According to Sheperis et al. (2003), some additional symptoms of RAD include low self-esteem; lack of self-control; antisocial attitudes and behaviors; aggression and violence; and a lack of ability to trust, show affection, or develop intimacy. Behaviorally, these children are often self-destructive, suicidal, self-mutilative, and self-defeating (Sheperis et al., 2010). Coleman (2003) suggested that behaviors such as tantrums, recklessness, risk taking, bullying, stealing, abuse of pets, hoarding of food, and deception are also believed to be associated with RAD; however, these problem behaviors are not currently considered a part of the *DSM–5* criteria.

INTERVENTION STRATEGIES Early intervention is the key to treating RAD. Recent research based on Bowlby's theory of attachment has focused on the ways in which secure and insecure attachment patterns evolve and affect children (Seligman & Reichenberg, 2011). Bowlby and others have found that without treatment, failure to achieve a secure and rewarding attachment during the early years can impair people's ability to form rewarding relationships throughout their lives.

Once the medical needs of the child are addressed, behavioral programs to improve feeding, eating, and caregiving routines can be implemented (Seligman & Reichenberg, 2011). It will be important to provide caregivers with training so that they know how to provide infants and children with a nurturing environment. Speltz (1990), for example, developed a parental training program based on behavioral and attachment theory that might be useful to parents of children with RAD. Beneficial treatments of RAD should include (a) proper

diagnosis at an early age; (b) placement in a secure and nurturing environment; (c) instruction for the parents in empirically based parenting skills; (d) emphasis on family functioning, coping skills, and interaction; and (e) working within the child's and family's more naturalistic environments, as opposed to their more restrictive and intrusive settings (Sheperis et al., 2003).

RELEVANCE TO PROFESSIONAL SCHOOL COUNSELORS
Professional school counselors will need to be aware of the diagnostic criteria for RAD because a connection has been found between insecure attachment and both subsequent behavior and impulse-control problems and poor peer relationships in young children. RAD may be associated with eating problems; developmental delays; and abuse, neglect, and other parent–child problems. In addition, it is important to distinguish RAD from other diagnoses with related symptoms, such as CD and depression, because effective treatment for RAD and these other disorders can be quite different (Haugaard & Hazan, 2004).

Posttraumatic Stress Disorder

The criteria for Posttraumatic Stress Disorder (PTSD) are the same for children as for adults, although the disorder may be manifested differently due to differences in cognitive and emotional functioning (Seligman & Reichenberg, 2011). The essential feature of PTSD is symptom development following direct personal experience of a traumatic event, witnessing a traumatic event, or learning of such an experience with someone interpersonally close (Cook-Cottone, 2004). The *DSM–5* (American Psychiatric Association, 2013) describes the following criteria for a diagnosis of PTSD: great fear and helplessness in response to the event; persistent reexperiencing of the event; loss of general responsiveness; and symptoms of arousal and anxiety, such as sleep disturbances, anger, or irritability. Children might have nightmares, present with a flat affect, or act withdrawn. It is often difficult for children to express their feelings about the traumatic experience except through play.

Traumatic stressors can be naturally occurring (e.g., a hurricane) or man-made (e.g., terrorism). Trauma can occur in intimate physical and emotional proximity, occur physically distant and strike emotionally close (e.g., *Challenger* tragedy, September 11), or occur physically close and emotionally distant (witnessing the fatal accident of a stranger). The stress can be acute, as in a rape, or chronic, as through years of repeated sexual abuse (Cook-Cottone, 2004).

In the past, children were thought to be resilient to the impact of traumatic events. Much has been learned about PTSD in the last 10 years through research focused on children who have been victims of natural disasters, war, violent crime, community violence, and sexual abuse (Cooley-Quille, Boyd, Frantz, & Walsh, 2001; Thabet, Abed, & Vostanis, 2004). Although adolescents exhibit symptoms of PTSD similar to those of adults, including depression, anxiety, and emotional disturbance, children's symptoms are more likely to be behavioral or physical (Cook-Cottone, 2004). Children who have experienced sexual abuse often exhibit inappropriate sexual behaviors. Preschoolers' PTSD symptoms are expressed in nonverbal channels, which include acting out or internalized behaviors, nightmares and disturbed sleep patterns, developmental regression, and clinging behavior. In school-age children, symptoms continue to be expressed behaviorally and may include regressions, anxious attachment, school refusal, weak emotional regulation, and an increase in externalizing or internalizing behavioral expression (e.g., fighting with peers, withdrawal from friends, poor attention, decline in academic performance). Physiological complaints such as stomachaches and headaches are also common in children. Adolescents often present with a sense of foreshortened future, self-injurious behaviors, suicidal ideation, conduct problems, dissociation, depersonalization, and possibly substance abuse (Cook-Cottone, 2004).

PROGNOSIS Symptoms of trauma-related disorders often decrease without treatment within 3 months of the event (Seligman & Reichenberg, 2011). With treatment, the prognosis usually is also very good for recovery from symptoms that have not spontaneously remitted, especially for people whose functioning was positive before exposure to trauma, whose onset of symptoms was rapid, whose symptoms have lasted less than 6 months, whose social supports are strong, and who have received early treatment. According to Ozer and Weinstein (2004), children who perceive that they have strong social support, who are able to talk about the traumatic event and feelings associated with the event, and who have safe schools and cohesive family environments have a better chance at decreasing their PTSD symptoms more quickly.

INTERVENTION STRATEGIES Effective treatment for children and adolescents is similar to treatment for adults diagnosed with PTSD. Treatment should begin as soon as possible after the event (Seligman & Reichenberg, 2011). Preventive treatment, even before symptoms emerge, is recommended. When treatment for PTSD is required, a multifaceted approach emphasizing cognitive-behavioral strategies seems to work best. The goal of treatment is to help the person process the trauma, express feelings, increase coping and control over memories, reduce cognitive distortions and self-blame, and restore self-concept and previous levels of functioning. Group therapy involving people who have had similar traumatic experiences can be especially helpful in reducing feelings of being isolated and being different. However, the group leader should ensure that the sharing of memories does not have a retraumatizing effect. In addition, therapeutic interventions should be based within the school setting only when (a) comprehensive assessment has been completed; (b) it is determined that school-based support is the appropriate, least restrictive level of intervention; (c) parents have been informed of all treatment options; (d) the child is experiencing adequate adjustment and academic success with intervention; and (e) consultation, supervision, and referral are readily utilized by the professional school counselor (Cook-Cottone, 2004).

RELEVANCE TO PROFESSIONAL SCHOOL COUNSELORS Professional school counselors will be called on to provide support to students, staff, and parents in the event of a trauma that affects individuals and school communities. When a student or teacher or parent dies, when there is a natural disaster in the community, or when a violent crime has been committed, professional school counselors will be called on to provide group and individual interventions that offer accurate information, give people a place to ask questions and talk about the trauma, and screen for symptoms of PTSD. Professional school counselors will need to be aware of the differences between unhealthy and healthy responses to traumatic events and to be able to provide resources to students and families when a therapeutic intervention is deemed necessary or is requested. Professional school counselors should encourage and lead school administrators to develop crisis intervention plans to deal with traumatic events affecting school communities. The professional school counselor should have a solid working knowledge of the etiological and diagnostic implications of PTSD, the therapeutic options, and, when needed, ways to facilitate school reintegration of a child who has suffered a traumatic event (Cook-Cottone, 2004).

Adjustment Disorders

Adjustment disorders are fairly common in adults, as well as in young people (American Psychiatric Association, 2013). Adjustment disorders are characterized by a relatively mild maladaptive response to a stressor that occurs within 3 months of that event. Stressors may include experiences such as changing schools, parental separation, or illness in the family. The maladaptive response may include anxiety or depression, as well as behavioral changes. This diagnosis can be maintained only for 6 months beyond the termination of the stressor or its consequences. If symptoms remain after that time, the diagnosis must be changed.

PROGNOSIS The short-term and long-term prognoses for an adjustment disorder are quite good if the disorder stands alone. When other disorders are also diagnosed, the prognoses are less optimistic.

INTERVENTION STRATEGIES Most adjustment disorders improve spontaneously without treatment when the stressor is removed or attenuated. However, counseling can facilitate recovery (Seligman & Reichenberg, 2011). Treatment should focus on teaching coping skills and adaptive strategies to help people avert future crises and minimize poor choices and self-destructive behaviors.

RELEVANCE TO PROFESSIONAL SCHOOL COUNSELORS Professional school counselors are in an excellent position to provide students with the supportive strategies required to cope with the symptoms of an adjustment disorder. Professional school counselors regularly are asked to provide crisis intervention to students dealing with the death of a loved one, a divorce, or some other family crisis. Professional school counselors can also help parents understand the effect the stressor is having on their children.

ANXIETY DISORDERS

Separation Anxiety Disorder

Separation Anxiety Disorder is diagnosed in 4% to 5% of children and young adolescents (American Psychiatric Association, 2013). Separation anxiety disorder is diagnosed only in children and adolescents under the age of 18 years. This disorder is characterized by excessive distress on separation from primary attachment figures. Children diagnosed with separation anxiety disorder must have three or more qualifying symptoms present for at least 4 weeks prior to age 18 years: worry about caregivers' safety, reluctance or refusal to go to school or be separated from caregivers, fear about being alone, repeated nightmares involving separation themes, and somatic complaints. Separation anxiety disorder is more common in girls than boys, and these children typically spend a great deal of time in the school clinic complaining of minor illnesses, will ask to go home, and have more negative thoughts and lower estimations of their ability to cope than do children without this disorder (Bögels, Snieder, & Kindt, 2003). School refusal is a prominent symptom in the majority of children diagnosed with the disorder. Children with a history of SAD are at a 20% increased risk

of developing adolescent panic attacks (Hayward, Wilson, Lagle, Killen, & Taylor, 2004).

PROGNOSIS The vast majority of students with separation anxiety disorder recovery fully with treatment. A history of the disorder is reported by many adults being treated for other disorders. Childhood separation anxiety disorder may be a precursor to early-onset panic disorder (Goodwin, Lipsitz, Chapman, Mannuzza, & Fyer, 2001), adult anxiety and mood disorders. In addition, a family history of emotional disorders seems to be related to a poor prognosis for children with separation anxiety disorder (Kearney, Sims, Pursell, & Tillotson, 2003).

INTERVENTION STRATEGIES Treatment strategies can best be determined when the underlying cause of the disorder is understood, particularly whether it stems from insecurity and change in the home environment or is linked to negative experiences in the school setting. The first treatment strategy should be psychoeducational, involving the education of the parents and child (if he or she is old enough) about the symptoms, consequences, and management strategies. Encouraging the child to face new situations and being positive may be enough to allow the child to return to school and participate in anxiety-producing situations.

Separation anxiety disorder is considered a type of phobia; therefore, behavioral strategies such as systematic desensitization may be the most effective treatment (Seligman & Reichenberg, 2011). Because getting the child back in school is frequently the goal, an effective strategy would involve rewarding the child for being driven to the school, then entering the school, and finally going into the classroom. Working closely with the parents and school personnel on consistent strategies will be essential. Family therapy may also be necessary, especially when family enmeshment is present.

RELEVANCE TO PROFESSIONAL SCHOOL COUNSELORS Professional school counselors will most likely encounter children with separation anxiety disorder through referrals from teachers, school nurses, or other personnel in the school clinic. Parents also may be aware of the symptoms of this disorder and may seek the counselor's help. Children are more likely to demonstrate symptoms of the disorder during the first few weeks of school and particularly in the early years of school (kindergarten and the primary grades). Professional school counselors can help parents distinguish between mild and transient symptoms associated with difficulty adjusting to school and true SAD. When SAD, the symptoms of school refusal, or both are present, professional school counselors can play an important role in helping to plan and implement systematic desensitization. Professional school counselors can also provide parents with encouragement and support to leave their children at school and provide children with the help they need to stay in school.

Generalized Anxiety Disorder

The diagnosis formerly known as overanxious disorder of childhood is now included in the diagnosis of Generalized Anxiety Disorder (GAD) because the symptoms of pervasive anxiety are the same regardless of the person's age. GAD is characterized by feelings of worry or anxiety about many aspects of the person's life and is reflected in related physical symptoms such as shortness of breath and muscle tension that are difficult to control (Wicks-Nelson & Israel, 2003). To meet the diagnostic criteria, symptoms of this disorder must persist for a minimum of 6 months (American Psychiatric Association, 2013) and must have a significant impact on the person's functioning. Comorbidity of GAD with other disorders is common. A child with GAD usually experiences anticipatory anxiety that is generalized to include situations requiring appraisal or performance, but is not associated with a specific stimulus. GAD is the most common anxiety disorder in adolescents.

VOICES FROM THE FIELD 17.1   **HELPING ELEMENTARY SCHOOL STUDENTS WITH MENTAL AND EMOTIONAL DISORDERS**

I believe that the professional school counselor is crucial to the success of students with mental health issues. Despite the increasing need and the IDEA mandates for mental health services within the school system, no additional funding or personnel have been supplied to meet student needs. I believe that through a comprehensive school counseling program, I am the ideal provider and coordinator for students with mental health issues. I regularly work with students with a variety of mental health issues, including anxiety, depression, attention-deficit/hyperactivity disorder, autism spectrum disorders, and other mental health issues. I use a variety of strategies to promote the success of students with mental health issues, including prevention activities, early intervention activities, coordination (e.g., resource identification, education, advocacy, collaboration), and direct treatment. The school environment is ideal for the implementation of mental health services due to student access, the existing student–counselor relationship, and the ability to monitor and follow up on these services.

As a first step to promote positive mental health, I teach children appropriate social, emotional, academic, and career skills through classroom, small-group, and individual lessons. These prevention services can assist students in modifying behaviors, thoughts, and feelings that will lead to building relationships, career development, educational fulfillment, and personal success. As a professional school counselor, I am often the first person to be asked about a student concern by school staff and parents. With an understanding of common mental health issues and typical child development, I can help to identify and provide referrals for the assessment of mental health issues. Early intervention will lead to improved outcomes for students with mental health issues. I can monitor the student's progress and facilitate the ongoing referral, coordination, and transition of services as necessary among schools and settings.

As a professional school counselor, I can provide support, advocacy, and education for the child, family, and educators as they participate in assessments by explaining results and any mental health issues. With the knowledge of both educational and mental health issues, I can identify and advocate for the child to receive the best services, both within and outside the school system, as early as possible. I can also identify possible educational, social, and emotional accommodations; provide research-based treatment approaches and strategies; and coordinate treatment with other professionals. The services that the child will receive require coordination by a professional that understands both the mental health and the educational areas to promote the best treatment possible.

I believe that the professional school counselor can provide treatment for children with mental health issues. I can select research-based treatments to help students with and without disabilities learn new appropriate skills and practice those skills in the school setting, and I can provide these treatments early and often for children in a naturalistic setting. As a school counselor, I am a familiar person, and unlike other mental health professionals, I am on-site, at school, and able to handle many day-to-day student needs and personal crises. Although school counselors will still need to refer more serious mental health issues for assessment, many mental health services can be provided by the professional school counselor in the school setting.

Source: Judy Trigiani, Professional School Counselor, Spring Hill Elementary School, McLean, Fairfax County Public Schools, Virginia

PROGNOSIS People who receive cognitive-behavioral therapy for GAD frequently show significant and consistent improvement, although few will be free of all symptoms. Erford, Kress, Giguere, Cieri, and Erford (in press) conducted a meta-analysis of anxiety treatment clinical trials in children and youth and found consistent, robust, moderate effect sizes at both termination and follow-up.

INTERVENTION STRATEGIES As with other anxiety disorders, cognitive-behavioral strategies are the most effective treatments (Erford et al., in press). The goal of treatment is to lessen the extent of the anxiety and the overarousal that accompanies it by teaching children to cope with anxiety using a variety of strategies such as identification and modification of anxious self-talk, modeling, education about emotions, relaxation techniques, and homework.

RELEVANCE TO PROFESSIONAL SCHOOL COUNSELORS
Professional school counselors will undoubtedly encounter students exhibiting symptoms of GAD. Professional school counselors may be able to suggest stress management strategies to students and can help parents understand this disorder. Professional school counselors can offer guidance units and small-group counseling sessions to students coping with anxiety, as well as workshops to help their parents. Used in collaboration with treatment by mental health professionals, these psychoeducational strategies may afford considerable ongoing help to students coping with GAD.

Summary/Conclusion

Clearly, professional school counselors need to increase their knowledge of the symptoms, diagnosis, and treatment of mental disorders to meet the needs of all students. Requirements of the IDEA and Section 504 regulations, an increased number of students with mental health concerns, and the school reform movement demand that professional school counselors expand their repertoire of diagnostic skills and knowledge and work collaboratively with other educational and mental health professionals in schools and the community (ASCA, 2012; Santos de Barona & Barona, 2006). Additional training in special education procedures, Section 504 regulations, diagnostic assessment, multiculturalism, and the *ASCA National Model* will enhance professional school counselors' clinical knowledge and skills (ASCA, 2012; Santos de Barona & Barona, 2006; Wicks-Nelson & Israel, 2003). Currently, to qualify for endorsement by the Council for Accreditation of Counseling and Related Educational Programs (CACREP), counselor education programs must include coursework that covers issues related to the development and functioning of children and adolescents, such as eating disorders, abuse, attention-deficit disorders, and depression (CACREP, 2009).

The role of the professional school counselor is changing. Counselor education programs, as well as school districts, need to continue to be responsive to the changing nature of school counseling programs and the clinical challenges professional school counselors face. For professional school counselors to expand their role to include greater application of clinical knowledge and skills and increased collaboration with community and other mental health treatment programs, school districts may need to reconceptualize the role of the professional school counselor. Recognition of the importance of the clinical aspect of the professional school counselor's role may necessitate realignment of duties, affording counselors the opportunity to use their clinical skills to more effectively help their students and families. In addition, professional school counselors must continue to make appropriate referrals to medical and mental health practitioners and to work with teachers, parents, and students to help students achieve and develop despite clinical issues.

Activities

1. Choose one of the mental or emotional disorders found in the *DSM–5*, and find several current research articles that describe the school's role in helping students who have this disorder.
2. Interview a school psychologist or special educator in a local school. Find out the percentage of students in the school that have been diagnosed with mental or emotional disorders. Also inquire about how these students are handled within the system (i.e., inclusion, separate classes all day).
3. Home drug-testing kits are often easy to locate. Examine a home drug-testing kit and determine if it would be simple for parents to use when they suspect their child of using drugs.
4. Interview a professional school counselor about his or her involvement with students with mental disorders or learning problems. Ask about the counselor's role with child study, local screening, and Section 504. Determine how the school counselor supports parents and teachers that have students with mental health and learning disorders.

REFERENCES

Achenbach, T. M., & Rescorla, L. A. (2001). *Manual for the Achenbach System of Empirically Based Assessment (ASEBA)*. Burlington: University of Vermont, Research Center for Children, Youth, and Families.

Achieve, Inc. (2004). *American Diploma Project: Ready or not, creating a high school diploma that counts*. Washington, DC: Author.

Achieve, Inc. (2005). *Rising to the challenge: Are high school graduates prepared for college and work?* Washington, DC: Peter D. Hart Research Associates/Public Opinion Strategies.

Achieve, Inc. (2012). *Implementing the common core state standards: The role of the school counselor*. Retrieved from http://www.achieve.org/files/RevisedCounselorActionBrief_Final_Feb.pdf

ACT. (2013). *ACT, Aspire, Explore, Plan*. Retrieved from www.act.org

Adelman, C. (2006). *The toolbox revisited*. Washington, DC: U.S. Department of Education.

Akos, P., & Galassi, J. P. (2004). Middle and high school transitions as viewed by students, parents, and teachers. *Professional School Counseling, 7*, 212–221.

Akos, P., Goodnough, G. E., & Milsom, A. S. (2004). Preparing school counselors for group work. *Journal for Specialists in Group Work, 29*, 127–136.

Akos, P., & Martin, M. (2003). Transition groups for preparing students for middle school. *Journal for Specialists in Group Work, 28*, 139–154.

Alexander, K. P., & Hirsch, B. J. (2012). Marketable job skills for high school students: What we learned from an evaluation of After School Matters. *New Directions for Youth Development, 134*, 55–63.

Amato, P. R. (2010). Research on divorce: Continuing trends and new developments. *Journal of Marriage and Family, 72*, 650–666. doi: 10.1111/j.1741-3737.2010.00723.x

American Bar Association. (2009). *Kinship care may lead to increased behavioral well-being*. Retrieved from www.abanet.org/child/sept08.pdf

American Counseling Association (ACA). (1997, May 31). *Know your rights: Mental health, private practice and the law* [ACA national videoconference]. Alexandria, VA: Author.

American Counseling Association (ACA). (2005). *ACA code of ethics*. Alexandria, VA: Author.

American Counseling Association (ACA). (2010). *Definition of counseling*. Retrieved from http://www.counseling.org/20-20/definition.aspx

American Counseling Association (ACA). (2013). *Common Core State Standards: Essential information for school counselors*. Retrieved from http://www.counseling.org/docs/resources---school-counselors/common-core-state-standards.pdf?sfvrsn=2

American Counseling Association. (2014). *Public awareness ideas and strategies for professional counselors*. Alexandria, VA: Author.

American Institutes for Research. (2005, November 22). *New study finds US math students consistently behind their peers around the world*. Retrieved from http://www.air.org/news/index.cfm?fa=viewContent&content_id=451

American Psychiatric Association. (2000). *Diagnostic and statistical manual of mental disorders* (4th ed., Text rev.). Washington, DC: Author.

American Psychiatric Association. (2013). *Diagnostic and statistical manual of mental disorders* (5th ed.). Washington, DC: Author.

American Psychological Association. (2004). *Report on the Task Force on Psychology's agenda for child and adolescent mental health*. Washington, DC: Author.

American School Counselor Association. (1999). *Role statement*. Retrieved from www.schoolcounselor.org/role.htm

American School Counselor Association. (2003). *The ASCA national model: A framework for school counseling programs*. Alexandria, VA: Author.

American School Counselor Association. (2005). *The ASCA national model: A framework for school counseling programs* (2nd ed.). Alexandria, VA: Author.

American School Counselor Association. (2008). *Position statement: Response to intervention*. Retrieved from http://asca2.timberlakepublishing.com/content.asp?contentid=557

American School Counselor Association. (2009). *ASCA website*. Retrieved from www.schoolcounselor.org

American School Counselor Association. (2010). *Ethical standards for school counselors*. Retrieved from www.schoolcounselor.org/files/EthicalStandards2010.pdf

American School Counselor Association. (2012). *ASCA national model: A framework for school counseling programs* (3rd ed.). Alexandria, VA: Author.

American School Counselor Association. (2013). *The professional school counselor and comprehensive school counseling programs*. Retrieved from http://www.schoolcounselor.org/files/PS_ComprehensivePrograms.pdf

American School Counselor Association. (2014a). *The professional school counselor and students with special needs.* Retrieved from http://www.schoolcounselor.org/files/PS_SpecialNeeds.pdf

American School Counselor Association. (2014b). Student to counselor ratio by state: 2009–10. Retrieved from http://www.schoolcounselor.org/files/Ratios09-10.pdf

Amundson, N. (2005). The potential impact of global changes in work for career theory and practice. *International Journal for Educational and Vocational Guidance, 5*(2), 91–99. doi: 10.1007/s10775-005-8787-0

Amundson, N. (2006). Challenges for career interventions in changing contexts. *International Journal for Educational and Vocational Guidance, 6*(1), 3–14. doi: 10.1007/s10775-006-0002-4

Anastopoulos, A. D., & Farely, S. E. (2003). A cognitive-behavioral training program for parents of children with attention-deficit/hyperactivity disorder. In A. E. Kazdin & J. R. Weisz (Eds.), *Evidence-based psychotherapies for children and adolescents* (pp. 187–203). New York, NY: Guilford Press.

Ancis, J. R., & Rasheed, S. A. (2005). Multicultural counseling training approaches: Implications for pedagogy. In C. Z. Enns & A. L. Sinacore (Eds.), *Teaching and social justice: Integrating multicultural and feminist theories in the classroom* (pp. 85–97). Washington, DC: American Psychological Association.

Anderson, D. (2007). Multicultural group work: A force for developing and healing. *Journal of Specialists in Group Work, 32,* 224–244.

Arnold, M. S., Chen–Hayes, S. F., & Lewis, J. (2002, June). *Unlearning oppression: Learning skills to challenge the barriers of racism, classism, and other "-isms."* Paper presented at the Education Trust Summer School Counseling Academy, Chicago, IL.

Arredondo, P., & D'Andrea, M. (1995, September). AMCD approves multicultural counseling competency standards. *Counseling Today,* 28–32.

Arredondo, P., Toporek, R., Brown, S., Jones, J., Locke, D. C., Sanchez, J., & Stadler, H. (1996). *Operationalization of the multicultural counseling competencies.* Alexandria, VA: Association for Multicultural Counseling and Development.

Asarnow, J. R., Tompson, M. C., & McGrath, E. P. (2004). Annotation: Childhood-onset schizophrenia: Clinical and treatment issues. *Journal of Child Psychology and Psychiatry, 45,* 180–194.

Aseltine, R. H., James, A., Schilling, E., & Glanovsky, J. (2007). Evaluating the SOS suicide prevention program: A replication and extension. *BMC Public Health, 7*(161). Retrieved from http://www.biomedcentral.com/1471-2458/7/161

Asner-Self, K. K., & Feyissa, A. (2002). The use of poetry in psychoeducational groups with multicultural and multilingual clients. *Journal of Specialists in Group Work, 27,* 136–160.

Association for Specialists in Group Work. (2000). Association for Specialists in Group Work: Professional standards for the training of group workers. *Journal for Specialists in Group Work, 25,* 327–342.

Association for Specialists in Group Work. (2012). *ASGW principles for diversity-competent group workers.* Retrieved from http://www.asgw.org/diversity.htm

Baba, M. L., & Darga, L. L. (1981). The genetic myth of racial classification. In M. S. Collins, I. W. Wainer, & T. A. Bremmer (Eds.), *Science and the question of human equality* (pp. 1–19). Boulder, CO: Westview Press.

Bailey, D. F., & Bradbury-Bailey, M. (2004). Respecting differences: Racial and ethnic groups. In R. Perusse & G. E. Goodnough (Eds.), *Leadership, advocacy, and direct service strategies for professional school counselors* (pp. 157–186). Belmont, CA: Brooks/Cole-Thomson Learning.

Bailey, D. F., & Bradbury-Bailey, M. E. (2007). Promoting achievement for African American males through group work. *Journal for Specialists in Group Work, 32,* 83–96.

Baker, B. L., & Feinfield, K. A. (2003). Early intervention. *Current Opinion in Psychiatry, 16,* 503–509.

Baker, S. B., & Gerler, E. R., Jr. (2008). *School counseling for the twenty-first century* (5th ed.). Upper Saddle River, NJ: Pearson Prentice Hall.

Balfanz, R., Bridgeland, J. M., Bruce, M., & Fox, J. H. (2012). *Building a grad nation: Progress and challenge in ending the high school dropout epidemic.* Retrieved from http://www.americaspromise.org/~/media/Files/OurWork/GradNation/BuildingGradNation/BuildingAGRAdNation2012.ashx

Bandura, A. (2001). Social cognitive theory: An agentic perspective. *Annual Review of Psychology, 52,* 1–26. doi: 10.1146/annurev.psych.52.1.1

Banks, J. A., & Banks, C.A. M. (2010). *Multicultural education: Issues and perspectives.* Hoboken, NJ: Wiley.

Barnes, P. E., Friehe, M. J. M., & Radd, T. R. (2003). Collaboration between speech-language pathologists and school counselors. *Communication Disorders Quarterly, 24*(3), 137–142.

Barton, P. E., & Coley, R. J. (2009). *Parsing the achievement gap II.* Princeton, NJ: Educational Testing Service, Policy Information Center.

Baskin, T. W., Slaten, C. D., Crosby, N. R., Pufahl, T., Schneller, C. L., & Ladell, M. (2010). Efficacy of counseling and psychotherapy in schools: A meta-analytic review of treatment outcome studies. *The Counseling Psychologist, 38,* 878–903.

Baumberger, J. P., & Harper, R. E. (2007). *Assisting students with disabilities: A handbook for school counselors* (2nd ed.). Thousand Oaks, CA: Corwin.

Baumeister, A. A., & Baumeister, A. A. (2000). Mental retardation: Causes and effects. In M. Hersen, & R. T. Ammerman

(Eds.), *Advanced abnormal child psychology* (2nd ed.). Mahwah, NJ: Erlbaum.

Beale, A. V., & Scott, P. C. (2001). "Bullybusters": Using drama to empower students to take a stand against bullying behavior. *Professional School Counseling, 4*, 300–305.

Beck, A. T., & Steer, R. A. (1991). *Beck Scale for Suicide Ideation (BSSI) manual.* San Antonio, TX: Psychological Corporation.

Beck, A. T., & Steer, R. A. (1993). *Beck Hopelessness Scale (BHS) manual.* San Antonio, TX: Psychological Corporation.

Bemak, F. (2000). Transforming the role of the counselor to provide leadership in educational reform through collaboration. *Professional School Counseling, 3*, 323–331.

Bemak, F., & Chung, R. C.-Y. (2005). Advocacy as a critical role for urban school counselors: Working toward equity and social justice. *Professional School Counseling, 8*, 196–202.

Bemak, F., & Chung, R. C.-Y. (2008). New professional roles and advocacy strategies for school counselors: A multicultural/social justice perspective to move beyond the nice counselor syndrome. *Journal of Counseling and Development, 86*, 372–381.

Bemak, F., Murphy, S., & Kaffenberger, C. (2005). Community-focused consultation: New directions and practice. In C. Sink (Ed.), *Contemporary school counseling: Theory, research and practice* (pp. 206–228). Boston, MA: Houghton Mifflin.

Bennett, K. J., Brown, K. S., Boyle, M., Racine, Y., & Offord, D. (2003). Does low reading achievement at school entry cause conduct problems? *Social Science and Medicine, 56*, 2443–2448.

Benson, F. (2004). *Empowering teachers with best instructional practices.* New York, NY: New Millenium.

Berg, I. K., & Miller, S. (1992). *Working with the problem drinker.* New York, NY: Norton.

Berg, I. K., & Steiner, T. (2003). *Children's solution work.* New York, NY: Norton.

Bergan, J., & Kratochwill, T. (1990). *Behavioral consultation and therapy.* New York, NY: Plenum Press.

Berger, E. H. (2000). *Parents as partners in education.* Upper Saddle River, NJ: Merrill.

Bergin, J. J. (2004). Small-group counseling. In A. Vernon (Ed.), *Counseling children and adolescents* (3rd ed., pp. 355–390). Denver, CO: Love.

Berglund, P. A., Demler, O., Jin, R., Merikangas, K. R., & Walters, E. E. (2005). The nature of panic disorders and agoraphobia. In D. H. Barlow, & M. G. Craske (Eds.), *Mastery of your anxiety and panic* (pp. 21–32). New York, NY: Oxford University Press.

Berk, L. (2010). *Development through the lifespan* (5th ed.). Boston, MA: Pearson Allyn & Bacon.

Berthelson, D., & Walker, S. (2008). Parents' involvement in their children's education. *Family Matters, 79*, 34–41.

Biederman, J., Petty, C., Faraone, S. V., & Seidman, L. (2004). Phenomenology of childhood psychosis: Findings from a large sample of psychiatrically referred youth. *Journal of Nervous and Mental Disease, 192*, 607–613.

Bierman, K. L., Coie, H. D., Dodge, K. A., Greenberg, M. T., Lochman, J. E., McMahon, R. J., & Pinderhughes, E. E. (2002). Evaluation of the first 3 years of the Fast Track prevention trial with children at high risk for adolescent conduct problems. *Journal of Abnormal Child Psychology, 30*, 19.

Blackhurst, A. E., Auger, R. W., & Wahl, K. H. (2003). Children's perceptions of vocational preparation requirements. *Professional School Counseling, 7*, 58–67.

Bloomfield, M. (1915). *Readings in vocational guidance.* Cambridge, MA: Harvard University Press.

Blue-Banning, M., Summers, J. P., Frankland, H. C., Nelson, L. L., & Beegle, G. (2004). Dimensions of family and professional partnerships: Constructive guidelines for collaboration. *Exceptional Children, 70*, 167–184.

Bögels, S. M., Snieder, N., & Kindt, M. (2003). Specificity of dysfunctional thinking in children with symptoms of social anxiety, separation anxiety, and generalized anxiety. *Behavior Change, 20*, 160–169.

Bolman, L. G., & Deal, T. E. (1997). *Reframing organizations: Artistry, choice, and leadership* (2nd ed.). San Francisco, CA: Jossey-Bass.

Borders, L. D., & Drury, S. M. (1992). Comprehensive school counseling programs: A review for policymakers and practitioners. *Journal of Counseling and Development, 70*, 487–498.

Borum, R., Cornell, D. G., Modzeleski, W., & Jimerson, S. R. (2010). What can be done about school shootings: A review of the evidence. *Educational Researcher, 39*, 27–37. doi: 10.3102/0013189X09357620

Boyer, E. L. (1983). *High school: A report on secondary education in America.* New York. NY: Harper & Row.

Bratton, S. C., Ray, D., Rhine, T., & Jones, L. (2005). The efficacy of play therapy with children: A meta-analytic review of treatment outcomes. *Professional Psychology: Research and Practice, 36*, 376–390.

Brewer, J. M. (1942). *History of vocational guidance.* New York, NY: Harper & Brothers.

Brigman, G., & Campbell, C. (2003). Helping students improve academic achievement and school success behavior. *Professional School Counseling, 7*, 91–98.

Brigman, G. A., Webb, L. D., & Campbell, C. (2007). Building skills for school success: Improving the academic and social competencies of students. *Professional School Counseling, 10*, 279–288.

Bringman, N., & Lee, S. M. (2008). Middle school counselors' competence in conducting developmental classroom lessons:

Is teaching experience necessary? *Professional School Counseling, 11*, 380–385.

Brinson, J. A., Kottler, J. A., & Fisher, T. A. (2004). Cross-cultural conflict resolution in the schools: Some practical intervention strategies for counselors. *Journal of Counseling and Development, 82*, 294–301.

Brooks, J. (2006). Strengthening resilience in children and youths: Maximizing opportunities through the schools. *Children and Schools, 28*, 69–76.

Brown, A., & Mistry, T. (1994). Group work with mixed membership groups: Issues of race and gender. *Social Work with Groups, 17*, 5–21.

Brown, D. B., & Trusty, J. (2005a). School counselors, comprehensive school counseling programs, and academic achievement: Are school counselors promising more than they can deliver? *Professional School Counseling, 9*, 1–8.

Brown, D. B., & Trusty, J. (2005b). *Designing and leading comprehensive school counseling programs: Promoting student competence and meeting student needs.* Belmont, CA: Thomson Brooks/Cole.

Brown, D., & Trusty, J. (2005c). The ASCA national model, accountability, and establishing causal links between school counselors' activities and student outcomes: A reply to Sink. *Professional School Counselor, 9*, 13–15.

Bruce, A., Getch, Y. Q., & Daigle, J. Z. (2009). Closing the gap: A group counseling approach to improve test performance of African-American students. *Professional School Counseling, 12*, 450–457.

Bryan, J., & Holcomb-McCoy, C. (2004). School counselors' perceptions of their involvement in school–family–community partnerships. *Professional School Counseling, 7*, 162–171.

Bryan, J., Holcomb-McCoy, C., Moore-Thomas, C., & Day-Vines, N. (2009). Who sees the school counselor for college information? A national study. *Professional School Counseling, 12*, 280–291.

Bryan, J., Moore-Thomas, C., Day-Vines, N., & Holcomb-McCoy, C. (2011). School counselors as social capital: The effects of high school college counseling on college application rates. *Journal of Counseling & Development, 89*, 190–199.

Budman, C. L., Bruun, R. D., Park, K. S., Lesser, M., & Olson, M. (2000). Explosive outbursts in children with Tourette's disorder. *Journal of the American Academy of Child and Adolescent Psychiatry, 39*, 1270–1276.

Burns, M. K., Jacob, S., & Wagner, A. (2008). Ethical and legal issues associated with using response-to-intervention to assess learning disabilities. *Journal of School Psychology, 46*, 263–279.

Butler, R. J. (2004). Childhood nocturnal enuresis: Developing a conceptual framework. *Clinical Psychology Review, 24*, 909–931.

Campbell, C. A., & Brigman, G. (2005). Closing the achievement gap: A structured approach to group counseling. *Journal for Specialists in Group Work, 30*, 67–82.

Campbell, C., & Dahir, C. (1997). *The national standards for school counseling programs.* Alexandria, VA: American School Counselor Association.

Campbell, D. T., & Stanley, J. C. (1963). *Experimental and quasi-experimental designs for research.* Boston, MA: Houghton Mifflin.

Career Readiness Partner Council. (2012). *What is career readiness?* Retrieved from www.careerreadynow.org/wp/sample-page/

Career Technical Education (CTE). (2013a). *Career clusters & pathways.* Retrieved from http://www.careertech.org/career-clusters/glance/clusters-occupations.html

Career Technical Education (CTE). (2013b). *Common Career Technical Core (CCTC).* Retrieved from http://www.careertech.org/career-technical-education/cctc/

Carey, J. (2006, November). *Evaluation is not a four letter word: How to know whether or not what you are doing is working.* Paper presented at the Colorado School Counselors Association, Denver, CO.

Carey, J., & Dimmitt, C. (2006). Resources for school counselors and counselor educators: The Center for School Counseling Outcome Research. *Professional School Counseling, 9*, 416–420.

Carey, J., & Dimmitt, C. (2012). School counseling and student outcomes: Summary of six statewide studies. *Professional School Counseling, 16*, 146–153.

Carey, J. C., Dimmitt, C., Hatch, T. A., Lapan, R. T., & Whiston, S. C. (2008). Report of the national panel for evidence-based school counseling: Outcome research coding protocol and evaluation of student success skills and second step. *Professional School Counseling, 11*, 197–206.

Carmichael, S. H., & Erford, B. T. (2014). Outcomes research in counseling. In B. T. Erford (Ed.), *Orientation to the counseling profession: Advocacy, ethics, and essential professional foundations* (2nd ed., pp. 484–512). Columbus, OH: Pearson Merrill.

Carrell, S. E., & Carrell, S. A. (2006). Do lower student to counselor ratios reduce school disciplinary problems? *Contributions to Economic Analysis and Policy, 5*(1), 1–12.

Carter, G. R. (2004, February). *Connecting the world of education: Is it good for the kids?* (Editorial). Retrieved from www.ascd.org

Castillo, L. G., Brossart, D. F., Reyes, C. J., Conoley, C. W., & Phoummarath, M. J. (2007). Perceived multicultural competencies and implicit racial prejudice. *Journal of Multicultural Counseling and Development, 35*, 243–254.

Center for Excellence in School Counseling and Leadership. (CESCAL). (2013). *About us.* Retrieved from www.cescal.org

Center for Public Education. (2011). *Back to school: How parent involvement affects student achievement (full report).* Retrieved from http://www.centerforpubliceducation.org/Main-Menu/Public-education/Parent-Involvement/Parent-Involvement.html

Center for School Mental Health. (2012). *The impact of school mental health: Educational, emotional, and behavioral outcomes.* Retrieved from http://csmh.umaryland.edu/Resources/OtherResources/ChildrensMHAwareness

Centers for Disease Control and Prevention (CDC). (2005). Mental health in the United States: Prevalence of diagnosis and medication treatment for Attention-deficit/Hyperactivity Disorder—United States, 2003. *Morbidity and Mortality Weekly Report, 54,* 842–847.

Centers for Disease Control and Prevention (CDC). (2008). *Autism spectrum disorders overview.* Retrieved from www.cdc.gov/ncbddd/autism/overview.htm

Centers for Disease Control and Prevention (CDC). (2012). *Autism spectrum disorders: Data and statistics.* Retrieved from http://www.cdc.gov/ncbddd/autism/data.html

Chall, J. S. (1996). *Learning to read: The great debate* (3rd ed.). New York, NY: McGraw-Hill.

Charles, C. M., & Senter, G. W. (2005). *Building classroom discipline.* New York, NY: Longman.

Charlesworth, J. R., & Jackson, C. M. (2010). Solution-focused brief counseling: An approach for school counselors. In B. T. Erford (Ed.), *Professional school counseling: A handbook of theories, programs, and practices* (pp. 139–148). Austin, TX: PRO-ED.

Charney, R. S. (2002). *Teaching children to care* (2nd ed.). Greenfield, MA: Northeast Foundation for Children.

Chen-Hayes, S. F. (2007). The ACCESS Questionnaire: Assessing school counseling programs and interventions to ensure equity and success for every student. *Counseling and Human Development, 39*(6), 1–10.

Chen-Hayes, S. F. (2009). Types of oppression. In American Counseling Association (Ed.), *American Counseling Association encyclopedia of counseling* (pp. 383–384). Alexandria, VA: American Counseling Association.

Chen-Hayes, S. F. (2013). Empowering members of underrepresented groups in college readiness and admission. In National Association for College Admission Counseling (Ed.), *Fundamentals of college admission counseling* (3rd ed., pp. 150–174). Arlington, VA: Editor.

Chen-Hayes, S. F., Chen, M., & Athar, N. (2000). Challenging linguicism: Action strategies for counselors and client-colleagues. In J. Lewis & L. Bradley (Eds.), *Advocacy in counseling: Counselors, clients, and community* (pp. 25–36). Greensboro, NC: CAPS & ERIC/CASS.

Chen-Hayes, S. F., Ockerman, M., & Mason, E. C. M. (2013). *101 solutions for school counselors and leaders in challenging times.* Thousand Oaks, CA: Corwin.

Cinamon, R. G. (2010). Anticipated work–family conflict: Effects of role salience and self-efficacy. *British Journal of Guidance & Counselling, 38*(1), 83–99. doi: 10.1080/03069880903408620

Clark, G. N., DeBar, L. L., & Lewinsohn, P. M. (2003). Cognitive-behavioral group treatment for adolescent depression. In A. E. Kazdin & J. R. Weisz (Eds.), *Evidence-based psychotherapies for children and adolescents* (pp. 120–134.). New York, NY: Guilford Press.

Clark, L. A. (1987). Mutual relevance of mainstream and cross-cultural psychology. *Journal of Consulting and Clinical Psychology, 55,* 461–470.

Clark, M. A., & Breman, J. C. (2009). School counselor inclusion: A collaborative model to provide academic and social-emotional support in the classroom setting. *Journal of Counseling and Development, 87,* 6–11.

Clark, M. A., & Stone, C. (2000, May). Evolving our image: School counselors as educational leaders. *Counseling Today, 21* & 46.

Coalition of Essential Schools. (2008). *CES school benchmarks: Transformational leadership.* Retrieved from www.essentialschools.org/cs/cestop/print/ces_docs/643?x-r=disp

Cobia, D. C., & Henderson, D. A. (2007). *Handbook of school counseling* (2nd ed.). Upper Saddle River, NJ: Merrill/Prentice Hall.

Code, M. N., Bernes, K. B., Gunn, T. M., & Bardick, A. D. (2006). Adolescents' perceptions of career concern: Student discouragement in career development. *Canadian Journal of Counselling, 40*(3), 160–174.

Coffey, B. J., Biederman, J., Geller, D. A., Spencer, T. J., Kim, G. S., Bellordre, C. A., … & Mariola, M. S. (2000). Distinguishing illness severity from tic severity in children and adolescents with Tourette's disorder. *Journal of the American Academy of Child and Adolescent Psychiatry, 39,* 556–561.

Cohen, J. (1988). *Statistical power analysis for the behavioral sciences* (2nd ed.). Hillsdale, NJ: Erlbaum.

Coker, J. K. (2004). Alcohol and other substance abuse: A comprehensive approach. In R. Perusse, & G. E. Goodnough (Eds.), *Leadership, advocacy, and direct service strategies for professional school counselors* (pp. 284–327). Belmont, CA: Brooks/Cole-Thomson Learning.

Coleman, H. L. K., & Yeh, C. J. (Eds.). (2008). *Handbook of school counseling.* New York, NY: Routledge.

Coleman, P. K. (2003). Reactive attachment disorder in the context of the family: A review and call for future research. *Emotional and Behavioral Difficulties, 8,* 205–216.

College Board. (2008a). *The NOSCA components of college counseling: Preparation, planning and admissions.* Washington, DC: Author.

College Board. (2008b). *Inspiration and innovation: 10 effective counseling practices from the College Board's Inspiration Awards schools.* Washington, DC: Author.

College Board. (2009). *National Office for School Counselor Advocacy equity belief statement.* Retrieved from http://apcentral.collegeboard.com/apc/public/homepage/22794.html

College Board. (2012a). *The 8th annual AP report to the nation.* Retrieved from http://media.collegeboard.com/digital Services/public/pdf/ap/rtn/AP-Report-to-the-Nation.pdf

College Board. (2012b). *National survey of school counselors and administrators.* Retrieved from http://media.collegeboard.com/digitalServices/pdf/nosca/Barriers-Supports_TechReport_Final.pdf

The College Board. (2012c). *College counseling sourcebook: Advice and strategies from school counselors* (7th ed.). New York, NY: Author.

The College Board. (2013a). *AP students.* Retrieved from https://apstudent.collegeboard.org/exploreap

The College Board. (2013b). *College Board tests.* Retrieved from www.collegeboard.com/testing/

College Board Advocacy and Policy Center. (2012). *2012 national survey of school counselors: Counseling at a crossroads.* New York, NY: Author.

College Board National Office for School Counselor Advocacy. (2011). *School counselors literature and landscape review: The state of school counseling in America.* Retrieved from http://advocacy.collegeboard.org/sites/default/files/11b_4045_LitReview_BOOKLET_WEB_111104.pdf

College Results Online. (2013). *About us.* Retrieved from www.collegeresultsonline.org

Collins, N. M., & Pieterse, A. L. (2007). Critical incident analysis based learning: An approach to training for active racial and cultural awareness. *Journal of Counseling & Development, 85,* 24–29.

Commission on Chapter 1. (1992). *Making schools work for children in poverty.* Washington, DC: Author.

Committee for Children. (2002a). *Second Step: A violence prevention curriculum* (3rd ed.). Seattle, WA: Author.

Committee for Children. (2002b). *Second Step: A violence prevention program.* Available at www.cfchildren.org

Common Core State Standards Initiative. (2013). Frequently asked questions: Overview. Retrieved from http://www.corestandards.org/resources/frequently-asked-questions

Conant, J. B. (1959). *The American high school today: A first report to interested citizens.* New York, NY: McGraw-Hill.

Conflict Information Consortium. (2013a). *Denial of identity.* Retrieved from www.colorado.EDU/conflict/peace/problem/denyid.htm

Conflict Information Consortium. (2013b). *Treatment list 2: Treating core conflict problems.* Retrieved from www.colorado.EDU/conflict/peace/!treating_core.htm

Conflict Information Consortium. (2013c). *The denial of other human needs.* Retrieved from www.colorado.EDU/conflict/peace/problem/needs.htm

Conley, D. T. (2011). *College and career ready: Helping all students succeed beyond high school.* San Francisco, CA: Jossey-Bass.

Conners, C. K. (2008). *Manual for the Conners-3 Rating Scales.* North Tonawanda, NY: Multi- Health Systems.

Constantine, M. G. (2001). Predictors of observer ratings of multicultural counseling competence in Black, Latino, and White American trainees. *Journal of Counseling Psychology, 48,* 456–462.

Cook-Cottone, C. (2004). Childhood posttraumatic stress disorder: Diagnosis, treatment, and school reintegration. *School Psychology Review, 33*(1), 127–139.

Cooley, M. L. (2007). *Teaching kids with mental health and learning disorders in the regular classroom: How to recognize, understand and help challenged (and challenging) students succeed.* Minneapolis, MN: Free Spirit Publications.

Cooley-Quille, M., Boyd, R. C., Frantz, E., & Walsh, J. (2001). Emotional and behavioral impact of exposure to community violence in inner-city adolescents. *Journal of Clinical Child Psychology, 30*(1), 199–206.

Corey, G., Corey, M. S., & Callanan, P. (2006). *Issues and ethics in the helping professions* (5th ed.). Pacific Grove, CA: Brooks/Cole.

Corey, M. S., Corey, G., & Corey, C. (2010). *Groups: Process and practice* (8th ed.). Pacific Grove, CA: Brooks/Cole-Cengage Learning.

Cornett, C. E., & Cornett, C. F. (1980). *Bibliotherapy: The right book at the right time.* Bloomington, IN: Phi Delta Kappa Educational Foundation.

Cortiella, C. (2006). *NCLB and IDEA: What parents of students with disabilities need to know and do.* Minneapolis: University of Minnesota, National Center on Educational Outcomes.

Cottone, R. R., & Tarvydas, V. M. (2007). *Ethical and professional issues in counseling* (3rd ed.). Upper Saddle River, NJ: Merrill/Prentice Hall.

Council for Accreditation of Counseling and Related Educational Programs. (2009). *CACREP accreditation standards and procedures manual.* Alexandria, VA: Author.

Council on Rehabilitation Education. (2003–2004). *Accreditation manual.* Available from www.core-rehab.org

Cowley, W. H. (1937). Preface to the principles of student counseling. *Educational Record, 18,* 218–234.

Cremin, L. A. (1964). The progressive heritage of the guidance movement. In E. Landy & L. Perry (Eds.), *Guidance in American education: Backgrounds and prospects* (pp. 11–19). Cambridge, MA: Harvard University Graduate School of Education.

Crethar, H. C., Rivera, E. T., & Nash, S. (2008). In search of common threads: Linking multicultural, feminist, and social justice counseling paradigms. *Journal of Counseling and Development, 86*, 269–278.

Crites, J. O. (1978). *Theory and research handbook for the Career Maturity Inventory.* Monterey, CA: CTB-McGraw Hill.

Cuijpers, P. (2002). Effective ingredients of school-based drug prevention programs: A systematic review. *Addictive Behavior, 27*, 1009–1023.

Cull, J. G., & Gill, W. S. (1992). *Suicide Probability Scale.* Los Angeles, CA: Western Psychology Service.

Dana, R. H. (2001). Clinical diagnosis of multicultural populations in the United States. In L. A. Suzuki, J. G. Ponterotto, & P. J. Meller (Eds.), *Handbook of multicultural assessment: Clinical, psychological, and educational applications* (2nd ed., pp. 101–132). San Francisco, CA: Jossey-Bass.

D'Andrea, M., & Daniels, D. (1995). Helping students to learn to get along: Assessing the effectiveness of a multicultural developmental guidance project. *Elementary School Guidance and Counseling, 30*, 143–154.

D'Andrea, M., & Heckman, E. F. (2008). Contributing to the ongoing evolution of the multicultural counseling movement: An introduction to the special issue. *Journal of Counseling and Development, 86*, 259–260.

Danziger, S., & Ratner, D. (2010). Labor market outcomes and the transition to adulthood. *Future of the Children, 20*(1), 133–158

Darling, S., & Westberg, L. (2004). Parent involvement in children's acquisition of reading. *Reading Teacher, 57*, 774–776.

Davis, A. S. (2008). Children with Down syndrome: Implications for assessment and intervention in the school. *School Psychology Quarterly, 23*, 271–281.

DeLucia-Waack, J. L., DiCarlo, N. J., Parker-Sloat, E. L., & Rice, K. G. (1996). Multiculturalism: Understanding at the beginning of the process, rather than the ending. In J. DeLucia-Waack (Ed.), *Multicultural counseling competencies: Implications for training and practice* (pp. 237–243). Alexandria, VA: Association for Counselor Education and Supervision.

de Shazer, S. (1985). *Keys to solution in brief therapy.* New York, NY: Norton.

DeWit, D. J., Offord, D. R., Sanford, M., Rye, B. J., Shain, M., & Wright, R. (2000). The effect of school culture on adolescent behavior problems: Self-esteem, attachment to learning, and peer approval of deviance as mediating mechanisms. *Canadian Journal of School Psychology, 16*, 15–38.

Diemer, M. A., & Blustein, D. L. (2006). Critical consciousness and career development among urban youth. *Journal of Vocational Behavior, 68*, 220–232.

Dimmitt, C. (2007). *The Real Game evaluation results.* Amherst, MA: Center for School Counseling Outcome Research.

Dimmitt, C., Carey, J. C., & Hatch, T. (2007). *Evidence-based school counseling: Making a difference with data-driven practices.* Thousand Oaks, CA: Corwin Press.

Dinkmeyer, D. (1975). *Systematic training for effective parenting.* Circle Pines, MN: American Guidance Service.

Dinkmeyer, D., & McKay, G. (1980). *Systematic training for effective teaching.* Circle Pines, MN: American Guidance Service.

Dollarhide, C. T. (2003). School counselors as program leaders: Applying leadership contexts to school counseling. *Professional School Counseling, 6*, 204–208.

Dollarhide, C. T., Gibson, D. M., & Saginak, K. A. (2008). New counselors' leadership efforts in school counseling: Themes from a year-long qualitative study. *Professional School Counseling, 11*, 262–271.

Dow, M. J., & Mehring, T. A. (2001). Inservice training for educators of individuals with autism. *Autistic Spectrum Disorders: Educational and Clinical Interventions, 14*, 89–107.

Driekurs, R., & Cassell, P. (1974). *Discipline without tears.* New York, NY: Hawthorne Books.

Dumont, F., & Carson, A. (1995). Precursors of vocational psychology in ancient civilizations. *Journal of Counseling and Development, 73*, 371–378.

Duncan, G. J., & Murnane, R. J. (Eds.). (2011). *Whither opportunity? Rising inequality, schools, and children's life chances.* New York, NY: Russell Sage Foundation.

Durlak, J. A., Weissberg, R. P., Dymnicki, A. B., Taylor, R. D., & Schellinger, K. B. (2011). The impact of enhancing students' social and emotional learning: A meta-analysis of school-based universal interventions. *Child Development, 82*, 405–432.

Education Trust. (1996). *National Center for Transforming School Counseling.* Retrieved from www.edtrust.org

Education Trust. (1997). *The national guidance and counseling reform program.* Washington, DC: Author.

Education Trust. (1999). *Dispelling the myth: High poverty schools exceeding expectations.* Washington, DC: Author.

Education Trust (2004). *Edwatch online 2004 state summary reports.* Retrieved from www2.edtrust.org/edtrust /summaries2004/USA.pdf

Education Trust. (2005). *Achievement in America: 2005* [Computer diskette]. Washington, DC: Author.

Education Trust. (2011). *Parents want to know about America's schools.* Retrieved from http://www.edtrust.org/sites/edtrust .org/files/publications/files/Parents_Want_to_Know.pdf

Education Trust. (2013). *The Education Trust's National Center for Transforming School Counseling initiative.* Retrieved from www2.edtrust.org/EdTrust/Transforming1School1Counseling

Eisel v. Board of Education, 597 A.2d 447 (Md. Ct. App. 1991).

Elam, D., McCloud, B., & Robinson, S. (2007). *New directions for culturally competent school leaders: Practices and policy considerations* (Policy Brief). Tampa, FL: University of South Florida, David C. Anchin Center.

Epstein, J. L., & Associates. (2009). *School, family, and community partnerships: Your handbook for action* (3rd ed). Thousand Oaks, CA: Corwin.

Epstein, J. L., & Voorhis, F. L. (2010). School counselors' roles in developing partnerships with families and communities for student success. *Professional School Counseling, 14,* 1–14.

Erford, B. T. (2010). How to write learning objectives. In B. T. Erford (Ed.), *Professional school counseling: A handbook of theories, programs and practices* (2nd ed., pp. 279–286). Austin, TX: PRO-ED.

Erford, B. T. (Ed.). (2011). *Group work: Process and applications.* Columbus, OH: Pearson Merrill.

Erford, B. T. (2013). *Assessment for counselors* (2nd ed.). Belmont, CA: Cengage Wadsworth.

Erford, B. T. (Ed.). (2014). *Research and evaluation in counseling* (2nd ed.). Boston, MA: Cengage.

Erford, B. T. (Ed). (2015). *The odyssey: A lifespan adventure for professional counselors.* Boston, MA: Cengage.

Erford, B. T., Eaves, S. H., Bryant, E., & Young, K. (2010). *35 techniques every counselor should know.* Columbus, OH: Pearson Merrill Prentice Hall.

Erford, B. T., Kress, V., Giguere, M., Cieri, D., & Erford, B. M. (in press). Meta-analysis of counseling outcomes for youth with anxiety from 1990–2009.

Erikson, E. H. (1963). *Childhood and society.* New York, NY: Norton.

Erikson, E. H. (1968). *Identity: Youth and crisis.* New York, NY: Norton.

Eschenauer, R., & Chen-Hayes, S. F. (2005). The transformative individual school counseling model: An accountability model for urban school counselors. *Professional School Counseling, 8,* 244–248.

Espelage, D. L., & Poteat, V. P. (2012). School-based prevention of peer relationship problems. In E. M. Altmaier, & J. C. Hansen (Eds.), *The Oxford handbook of counseling psychology* (pp. 703–722). New York, NY: Oxford University Press.

Ezell, M. (2001). *Advocacy in the human services.* Belmont, CA: Wadsworth.

Falzon, R., & Camilleri, S. (2010). Dyslexia and the school counsellor: A Maltese case study. *Counselling and Psychotherapy Research, 10,* 307–315.

Family Educational Rights and Privacy Act (FERPA). (2013). *Family Educational Rights and Privacy Act; Final Rule.* Retrieved from http://www.ed.gov/legislation/FedRegister/finrule/2008-4/120908a.pdf

Farmer, E. M. Z., Burns, B. J., Phillips, S. D., Angold, A., & Costello, E. J. (2003). Pathways into and through mental health services for children and adolescents. *Psychiatric Services, 54*(1), 60–66.

Feagin, J. R. (2006). *Systemic racism: A theory of oppression.* New York, NY: Routledge/Taylor & Francis Group.

Federal Bureau of Investigation. (2005). *The school shooter: A threat assessment perspective.* Retrieved September 2, 2005, from www.fbi.gov/publications/school/school2.pdf

Fier, S. M., & Brzezinski, L. G. (2010). Facilitating the high school-to-college transition for students with psychiatric disabilities: Information and strategies for school counselors. *Journal of School Counseling, 8*(1), 1–40.

Fitch, T. J., & Marshall, J. L. (2004). What counselors do in high-achieving schools: A study on the role of the school counselor. *Professional School Counseling, 7,* 172–177.

Flannery, D. J., Vazsonyi, A. T., Liau, A. K., Guo, S., Powell, K. E., Atha, H., . . . Embry, D. (2003). Initial behavior outcomes for the PeaceBuilders universal school-based violence prevention program. *Developmental Psychology, 39,* 292–308.

Forester-Miller, H., & Davis, T. (1996). *A practitioner's guide to ethical decision making.* Retrieved from www.counseling.org/Content/NavigationMenu/RESOURCES/ETHICS/APRACTIONERSGUIDETOETHICALDECISIONMAKING/Practioner_s_Guide.htm

Fouad, N. A., & Byars-Winston, A. M. (2005). Cultural context of career choice: Meta-analysis of race/ethnicity differences. *Career Development Quarterly, 53,* 223–233.

Frankenberg, R. (1999). *White women, race matters: The social construction of whiteness.* Minneapolis: University of Minnesota Press.

Friesen, B., & Huff, B. (1990). Parents and professional school counselors as advocacy partners. *Preventing School Failure, 34,* 31–35.

Fullan, M. (2005). *Leadership and sustainability: Systems thinkers in action.* Thousand Oaks, CA: Corwin Press.

Furr, S. R. (2000). Structuring the group experience: A format for designing psychoeducational groups. *Journal for Specialists in Group Work, 25,* 29–49.

Gadow, K. D., Nolan, E. E., Sprafkin, J., & Schwartz, J. (2002). Tics and psychiatric comorbidity in children and adolescents. *Developmental Medicine and Child Neurology, 44,* 330–338.

Galassi, J. P., & Akos, P. (2007). *Strengths-based school counseling: Promoting student development and achievement.* Mahwah, NJ: Erlbaum.

Galassi, J. P., Griffin, D., & Akos, P. (2008). Strengths-based school counseling and the ASCA national model. *Professional School Counseling, 12*, 176–182.

Gardner, H. (1999). *The disciplined mind.* New York, NY: Simon & Schuster.

Gardner, R., & Miranda, A. H. (2001). Improving outcomes for urban African American students. *Journal of Negro Education, 70*, 255–263.

Gates, B. (2005, March 3). Fixing obsolete high schools. *Washington Post*, 3B.

Gay, L. R., Mills, G. E., & Airasian, P. (2011). *Educational research: Competencies for analysis and applications* (10th ed.). Upper Saddle River, NJ: Prentice Hall.

Gay Lesbian and Straight Education Network (GLSEN). (2008). *Involved, invisible, ignored: The experiences of lesbian, bisexual, gay, and transgender parents and their children in our nation's K–12 schools.* New York, NY: Author.

Gay Lesbian and Straight Education Network (GLSEN). (2009a). *Harsh realities: The experiences of transgender youth in our nation's schools.* New York, NY: Author.

Gay Lesbian and Straight Education Network (GLSEN). (2009b). *National school climate survey.* New York, NY: Author.

Gay Lesbian and Straight Education Network (GLSEN). (2009c). *Shared differences: The experiences of lesbian, gay, bisexual, and transgender students of color in our nation's schools.* New York, NY: Author.

Gay Lesbian and Straight Education Network (GLSEN). (2012). *Playgrounds and prejudice: Elementary school climate in the United States.* New York, NY: Author.

Gazda, G. M., Ginter, E. J., & Horne, A. M. (2008). *Group counseling and group psychotherapy: Theory and application* (2nd ed.). Boston, MA: Allyn & Bacon.

Geertz, C. (1983). *Local knowledge.* New York, NY: Basic Books.

Geltner, J. A., & Clark, M. A. (2005). Engaging students in classroom guidance: Management strategies for middle school counselors. *Professional School Counseling, 9*, 164–166.

Gere, J., & Helwig, C. C. (2012). Young adults' attitudes and reasoning about gender roles in the family context. *Psychology of Women Quarterly, 36*, 301–313. doi: 10.1177/0361684312444272

Gerler, E. R., Jr. (1992). Consultation and school counseling. *Elementary School Guidance and Counseling, 26*, 162.

Gerrity, D. A., & DeLucia-Waack, J. L. (2007). Effectiveness of groups in the schools. *Journal for Specialists in Group Work, 32*, 97–106.

Gershon, J. (2002). A meta-analytic review of gender differences in ADHD. *Journal of Attention Disorders, 5*(3), 143–154.

Getch, Y. Q., & Johnson, A. (2012). Counseling individuals with disabilities: Empowerment and advocacy. In G. Mcauliffe (Ed.), *Culturally alert counseling* (2nd ed., pp. 505–539). Thousand Oaks, CA: Sage.

Gibson, D. (2008*). Using career genograms in K–12 settings.* Retrieved from http://www.associationdatabase.com/aws /NCDA/pt/sd/news_article/5473/_PARENT/layout_details/false

Gibson, D. M. (2014). Advocacy counseling: Being an effective agent of change for clients. In B. T. Erford (Ed.), *Orientation to the counseling profession: Advocacy, ethics, and essential professional foundations* (2nd ed., pp. 294–320). Upper Saddle River, NJ: Prentice Hall.

Gilbert, A. (2003). Group counseling in an elementary school. In K. R. Greenberg (Ed.), *Group counseling in K–12 schools: A handbook for school counselors* (pp. 56–80). Boston, MA: Allyn & Bacon.

Gladding, S. T. (2011). *Counseling as an art: The creative arts in counseling* (4th ed.). Alexandria, VA: American Counseling Association.

Gladding, S. T. (2012). *Group work: A counseling specialty* (6th ed.). Upper Saddle River, NJ: Pearson Merrill.

Glasser, W. (1998). *Choice theory.* New York, NY: HarperCollins.

Glasser, W. (2000). *Reality therapy in action.* New York, NY: HarperCollins.

Glied, S., & Cuellar, A. E. (2003). Trends and issues in child and adolescent mental health. *Health Affairs, 22*(5), 39–50.

Goh, A. E., & Bambara, L. M. (2012). Individualized positive behavior support in school settings: A meta-analysis. *Remedial and Special Education, 33*, 271.

Goodenough, W. H. (1981). *Culture, language, and society.* Menlo Park, CA: Benjamin/Cummings.

Goodnough, G. E., & Lee, V. V. (2010). Group counseling in schools. In B. T. Erford (Ed.), *Professional school counseling: A handbook of theories, programs, and practices* (pp. 173–182). Austin, TX: PRO-ED.

Goodwin, R., Lipsitz, J. D., Chapman, T. F., Mannuzza, S., & Fyer, A. J. (2001). Obsessive-compulsive disorder, separation anxiety co-morbidity in early onset panic disorder. *Psychological Medicine, 31*, 1307–1310.

Gothelf, D., Aharonovsky, O., Horesh, N., Carty, T., & Apter, A. (2004). Life events and personality factors in children and adolescents with obsessive-compulsive disorder and other anxiety disorders. *Comprehensive Psychiatry, 45*, 192–198.

Gottfredson, D. C., & Wilson, D. B. (2003). Characteristics of effective school-based substance abuse prevention. *Prevention Science, 4*(1), 27–38.

Gottfredson, L. S. (1996). Gottfredson's theory of circumscription and compromise. In D. Brown & L. Brooks (Eds.),

Career choice and development: Applying contemporary theories to practice (3rd ed., pp. 179–232). San Francisco, CA: Jossey-Bass.

Green, A., & Keys, S. (2001). Expanding the school counseling paradigm: Meeting the needs of the 21st century student. *Professional School Counseling, 5*, 84–95.

Green, J. G., McLaughlin, K. A., Alegría, M., Costello, E. J., Gruber, M. J., Hoagwood, K., . . . Kessler, R. C. (2013). School mental health resources and adolescent mental health service use. *Journal of the American Academy of Child and Adolescent Psychiatry, 52*, 501–510. doi: 10.1016/j.jacc.2013.03.002

Greenberg, K. R. (Ed.). (2003). *Group counseling in K–12 schools: A handbook for school counselors.* Boston, MA: Allyn & Bacon.

Gruttadaro, D. E., & Miller, J. E. (2004). *NAMI Policy Research Institue task force report: Children and psychotropic medications.* Arlington, VA: Nation's Voice on Mental Illness.

Guillot-Miller, L., & Partin, P. W. (2003). Web-based resources for legal and ethical issues in school counseling. *Professional School Counseling, 7*, 52–60.

Guttmacher Institute. (2005). *State policies in brief: Sex and STD/HIV education.* Washington, DC: Author.

Guttmacher Institute. (2009). *State policies in brief: Minors' access to contraceptive services.* Washington, DC: Author.

Guttmacher Institute. (2013). *Guttmacher Institute state policies in brief: An overview of minor consent laws.* Retrieved from. http://www.guttmacher.org/statecenter/spibs/spib_OMCL.pdf

Gysbers, N. C., & Henderson, P. (2012). *Developing and managing your school guidance program* (5th ed.). Alexandria, VA: American Counseling Association.

Gysbers, N. C., Heppner, M. T., & Johnston, J. A. (2009). *Career counseling: Centers, processes, and techniques* (3rd ed.). Alexandria VA: American Counseling Association.

Gysbers, N. C., & Lapan, R. T. (2009). *Strengths-based career development for school guidance and counseling programs.* Ann Arbor, MI: Counseling Outfitters, LLC.

Gysbers, N. C., Lapan, R. T., & Blair, M. (1999). Closing in on the statewide implementation of a comprehensive guidance program model. *Professional School Counseling, 2*, 357–366.

Hall, D. T. (1996). Protean careers of the 21st century. *The Academy of Management Executive, 10*(4), 8–16.

Hall, K. R. (2006). Using problem-based learning with victims of bullying behavior. *Professional School Counseling, 9*, 231–237.

Halpern, R. (2012). Supporting vocationally oriented learning in the high school years: Rationale, tasks, challenges. *New Directions for Youth Development, 134*, 85–106.

Handel, S. J. (2009). *Community college counselor sourcebook* (2nd ed.). New York, NY: The College Board.

Harrow, A. (1972). *A taxonomy of the psychomotor domain: A guide for developing behavioral objectives.* New York, NY: McKay.

Hart, P. J., & Jacobi, M. (1992). *From gatekeeper to advocate: Transforming the role of the school counselor.* New York, NY: College Entrance Examination Board.

Hartline, J., & Cobia, D. (2012). School counselors: Closing achievement gaps and writing results reports. *Professional School Counseling, 16*, 71–79.

Hartung, P. J., Porfeli, E. J., & Vondracek, F. W. (2005). Child vocational development: A review and reconsideration. *Journal of Vocational Behavior, 66*, 385–419. doi: 10.1016/j.jvb.2004.05.006

Harvard Graduate School of Education and Center for Educational Policy Research. (2012). *Many high achievers do not attend college.* Retrieved from https://www.gse.harvard.edu/news-impact/2013/01/sdp-study-many-high-achieving-students-do-not-attend-college/

Hatch, T., & Chen-Hayes, S. F. (2008). School counselor beliefs about ASCA model school counseling program components using the SCPSCS. *Professional School Counseling, 12*, 34–42.

Haugaard, J. J., & Hazan, C. (2004). Recognizing and treating uncommon behavioral and emotional disorders in children and adolescents who have been severely maltreated: Reactive attachment disorder. *Child Maltreatment, 9*, 154–160.

Haycock, K. (2009, February). *Access and success in higher education: Can we do more?* Oklahoma Open Enrollment Conference, El Reno, OK. Retrieved February 20, 2009, from www2.edtrust.org/EdTrust/Product+Catalog/recent+presentations.htm

Hayes, R. L., Dagley, J. C., & Horne, A. M. (1996). Restructuring school counselor education: Work in progress. *Journal of Counseling and Development, 74*, 378–384.

Hayes, R. L., Nelson, J. L., Tabin, M., Pearson, G., & Worthy, C. (2002). Using school-wide data to advocate for student success. *Professional School Counseling, 62*, 86–95.

Hays, D. G., & Erford, B. T. (Eds.). (2014). *Developing multicultural counseling competency: A systems approach* (2nd ed.). Columbus, OH: Pearson Merrill.

Hayward, C., Wilson, K. A., Lagle, K., Killen, J. D., & Taylor, C. B. (2004). Parent-reported predictors of adolescent panic attacks. *Journal of the American Academy of Child and Adolescent Psychiatry, 4*, 613–620.

Hedges, L. V., & Olkin, I. (1985). *Statistical methods for meta-analysis.* Orlando, FL: Academic Press.

Hedrick, W. B., Harmon, J. M., & Wood, K. (2008). Prominent content vocabulary strategies and what secondary preservice teachers think about them. *Reading Psychology, 29*, 443–470.

Henderson, D. A., & Thompson, C. L. (2011). *Counseling children* (8th ed.). Belmont, CA: Brooks/Cole-Cengage Learning.

Henderson, P. A. (1987). Terminating the counseling relationship with children. *Elementary School Guidance and Counseling, 22*, 143–148.

Herlihy, B., & Corey, G. (2006). *ACA ethical standards casebook* (6th ed.). Alexandria, VA: American Counseling Association.

Herr, E. L. (1979). *Guidance and counseling in the schools: Perspectives on the past, present, and future.* Falls Church, VA: American Personnel and Guidance Association.

Herr, E. L. (1998). *Counseling in a dynamic society: Contexts and practices in the 21st century* (2nd ed.). Alexandria, VA: American Counseling Association.

Herr, E. L. (2002). School reform and perspectives on the role of school counselors: A century of proposals for change. *Professional School Counseling, 5*, 220–234.

Herr, E. L., Cramer, S. H., & Niles, S. G. (2004). *Career guidance and counseling through the lifespan* (6th ed.). Boston, MA: Allyn & Bacon.

Hess, R. S., Magnuson, S. L., & Beeler, L. M. (2012). *Counseling children and adolescents in schools: Practice and application guide.* Thousand Oaks, CA: Sage.

Hettler, W. (1984). Wellness: Encouraging a lifetime pursuit of excellence. *Health Values: Achieving High Level Wellness, 8*, 13–17.

Hines, P. L, Lemons, R. W., & Crews, K. D. (2011). *Poised to lead: How school counselors can drive college and career readiness.* Washington, DC: National Center for Transforming School Counseling.

Hirschi, A., Niles, S. G., & Akos, P. (2011). Engagement in adolescent career preparation: Social support, personality and the development of choice decidedness and congruence. *Journal of Adolescence, 34*(1), 173–82. doi: 10.1016/j.adolescence.2009.12.009

Hixson, J., & Tinzmann, M. B. (1990). *Essay: Who are the "at-risk" students of the 1990s?* Retrieved from www.ncrel.org/sdrs/areas/rpl_esys/equity.htm

Hoag, M. J., & Burlingame, G. M. (1997). Evaluating the effectiveness of child and adolescent group treatment: A meta-analytic review. *Journal of Clinical Child Psychology, 26*, 234–246.

Hoagwood, K., Kelleher, K. J., Feil, M., & Comer, D. M. (2000). Treatment services for children with AD/HD: A national perspective. *Journal of the American Academy of Child and Adolescent Psychiatry, 39*, 198–206.

Hoard, D., & Shepard, K. N. (2005). Parent education as parent-centered prevention: A review of school-related outcomes. *School Psychology Quarterly, 20*, 434–454.

Hobson, S. M., & Phillips, G. A. (2010). Educational planning. In B. T. Erford (Ed.), *Professional school counseling: A handbook of theories, programs, & practices* (2nd ed., pp. 325–340). Austin, TX: PRO-ED.

Hoffman, E. (2002). *Changing channels: Activities promoting media smarts and creative problem solving for children.* St. Paul, MN: Redleaf Press.

Holcomb-McCoy, C. (2007a). *School counseling to close the achievement gap: A social justice framework for success.* Thousand Oaks, CA: Corwin Press.

Holcomb-McCoy, C. (2007b). Transitioning to high school: Issues and challenges for African American students. *Professional School Counseling, 10*, 253–260.

Holcomb-McCoy, C., & Myers, J. E. (1999). Multicultural competence and counselor training: A national survey. *Journal of Counseling and Development, 77*, 294–302.

Holland, J. L. (1992). *Making vocational choices* (2nd ed.). Odessa, FL: Psychological Assessment Resources.

Hook, J. N., & Davis, D. E. (2012). Integration, multicultural counseling, and social justice. *Journal of Psychology & Theology, 40*, 102–106.

House, R. M., & Hayes, R. L. (2002). School counselors: Becoming key players in school reform. *Professional School Counseling, 5*, 249–256.

House, R. M., & Martin, P. J. (1998). Advocating for better futures for all students: A new vision for school counselors. *Education, 119*, 284–291.

Howard, D. E., & Wang, M. Q. (2003). Risk profiles of adolescent girls who were victims of dating violence. *Adolescence, 38*(149), 1–14.

Howard, K. A. S., & Walsh, M. E. (2010). Conceptions of career choice and attainment: Developmental levels in how children think about careers. *Journal of Vocational Behavior, 76*, 143–152. doi: 10.1016/j.jvb.2009.10.010

Hudson, J. I., Hiripi, E., Pope, H. G., Jr., & Kessler, R. C. (2007). The prevalence and correlates of eating disorders in the national comorbidity survey replication. *Biological Psychiatry, 61*, 348–358. doi: 10.1016/j.biopsych.2006.03.040

Hussey, D. L., & Guo, S. (2003). Measuring behavior change in young children receiving intensive school-based mental health services. *Journal of Community Psychology, 31*, 629–639.

Hutson, P. W. (1958). *The guidance function in education* (2nd ed.). New York, NY: Appleton-Century-Crofts.

Individuals with Disabilities Education Improvement Act of 2004. (2004). *20 USC 1400.* Retrieved from http://idea.ed.gov

Ingraham, C. L. (2000). Consultation through a multicultural lens: Multicultural and cross-cultural consultation in schools. *School Psychology Review, 29*, 320–343.

International Baccalaureate. (2013). *About us.* Retrieved from www.ibo.org

Israel, T. (2006). Marginalized communities in the United States: Oppression, social justice, and the role of counseling psychologists. In R. L. Toporek, L. H. Gerstein, N. A. Fouad, G. Roysircar, & T. Israel (Eds.), *Handbook for social justice in counseling psychology: Leadership, vision and action* (pp. 149–154). Thousand Oaks, CA: Sage.

Ivey, A. E., D'Andrea, M., Ivey, M. B., & Simek-Morgan, L. (2007). *Counseling and psycho-therapy: A multicultural perspective* (6th ed.). Boston, MA: Allyn & Bacon.

Jackson, M., & Grant, D. (2004). Equity, access, and career development: Contextual conflicts. In R. Perusse & G. E. Goodnough (Eds.), *Leadership, advocacy, and direct service strategies for professional school counselors* (pp. 125–153). Belmont, CA: Brooks/Cole-Thomson Learning.

Jackson-Cherry, L. R., & Erford, B. T. (Eds.). (2014). *Crisis assessment, intervention, and prevention* (2nd ed.). Columbus, OH: Pearson Merrill.

Jacobi, C., Hayward, C., de Zwaan, M., Kraemer, H., & Agras, W. S. (2004). Coming to terms with risk factors for eating disorders: Application of risk terminology and suggestions for a general taxonomy. *Psychological Bulletin, 130,* 19–65.

Jacobs, E. E., Masson, R. L., Harvill, R. L., & Schimmel, C. J. (2011). *Group counseling: Strategies and skills* (7th ed.). Belmont, CA: Brooks/Cole-Cengage Learning.

Jacobs, E., & Schimmel, C. (2005). Small group counseling. In C. Sink (Ed.), *Contemporary school counseling: Theory, research, and practice* (pp. 82–115). Boston, MA: Houghton Mifflin/Lahaska.

James, R. K., & Gilliland, B. E. (2013). *Crisis intervention strategies* (7th ed.). Belmont, CA: Books/Cole-Cengage Learning.

Janson, C. (2009). High school counselors' views of their leadership behaviors: A Q methodology study. *Professional School Counseling, 13,* 86–97.

Jensen, P. S., Kettle, L., Roper, M. T., Sloan, M. T., Dulcan, M. K., Hoven, C., . . . Payne, J. (1999). Are stimulants overprescribed? Treatment of AD/HD in four U.S. communities. *Journal of the American Academy of Child and Adolescent Psychiatry, 38,* 797–804.

Jenson, J. M., & Dieterich, W. A. (2007). Effects of a skills-based prevention program on bullying and bully victimization among elementary school children. *Prevention Science, 8,* 285–296.

Johnson, C. D., & Johnson, S. K. (2001). *Results-based student support programs: Leadership academy workbook.* San Juan Capistrano, CA: Professional Update.

Johnson, C. R., & Slomka, G. (2000). Learning, motor, and communication disorders. In M. Hersen, & R. T. Ammerman (Eds.), *Advanced abnormal child psychology* (2nd ed., pp. 371–385). Mahwah, NJ: Erlbaum.

Johnson, D. (1995). Specific developmental disorders. In M. Hersen & R. T. Ammerman (Eds.), *Advanced abnormal child psychology* (pp. 95–122). Washington, DC: American Psychiatric Press.

Johnson, J., Arumi, A. M., & Ott, A. (2006). *Reality check 2006: Is support for standards and testing fading?* Retrieved from www.publicagenda.org/files/pdf/rc0603.pdf

Johnson, S. D. (1990). Toward clarifying culture, race, and ethnicity in the context of multicultural counseling. *Journal of Multicultural Counseling and Development, 18,* 41–50.

Jones, A. J. (1934). *Principles of guidance* (2nd ed.). New York, NY: McGraw-Hill.

Jones, L. K. (2004). *The Career Key.* Retrieved from www.career-key.org

Judge, T. A, & Livingston, B. A. (2008). Is the gap more than gender? A longitudinal analysis of gender, gender role orientation, and earnings. *The Journal of Applied Psychology, 93,* 994–1012. doi: 10.1037/0021-9010.93.5.994

Kaffenberger, C. J., Murphy, S., & Bemak, F. (2006). School counseling leadership team: A statewide collaborative model to transform school counseling. *Professional School Counseling, 9,* 288–294.

Kahn, B. B. (2000). A model of solution-focused consultation for school counselors. *Professional School Counseling, 3,* 248–254.

Kalafat, J. (2003). School approaches to youth suicide prevention. *American Behavioral Scientist, 46,* 1211–1223.

Kaminski, J. W., Valle, L. A., Filene, J. H., & Boyle, C. L. (2008). A meta-analytic review of components associated with parent training program effectiveness. *Journal of Abnormal Child Psychology, 36,* 567–589.

Kataoka, S. H., Zhang, L., & Wells, K. B. (2002). Unmet need for mental health care among U.S. children: Variation by ethnicity and insurance status. *American Journal of Psychiatry, 159,* 1548–1555.

Kazdin, A. E. (2008). Evidence-based treatments and delivery of psychological services: Shifting our emphases to increase impact. *Psychological Services, 5,* 201–215.

Kazdin, A. E. (2011). Evidence-based treatment research: Advances, limitations, and next steps. *American Psychologist, 66,* 685–698.

Kearney, C. A., Sims, K. E., Pursell, C. R., & Tillotson, C. A. (2003). Separation anxiety disorder in young children: A longitudinal and family analysis. *Journal of Clinical Child and Adolescent Psychology, 32,* 593–598.

Keel, P. K., & Klump, K. L. (2003). Are eating disorders culture-bound syndromes? Implications for conceptualizing their etiology. *Psychological Bulletin, 129,* 747–769.

Kendall, P. C., Safford, S., Flannery-Schroeder, E., & Webb, A. (2004). Child anxiety treatment: Outcomes and impact on substance use and depression at 7.4-year follow-up. *Journal of Consulting and Clinical Psychology, 72,* 276–287.

Kessler, R. C., Berglund, P., Demler, O., Jin, R., Merikangas, K. R., & Walters, E. E. (2005). Lifetime prevalence and age-of-onset distributions of *DSM-IV* disorders in the National Comorbidity Survey Replication. *Archives of General Psychiatry, 62,* 593–602. doi: 10.1001/archpsyc.62.6.593

Kessler, R. C., Chiu, W. T., Demler, O., & Walters, E. E. (2005). Prevalence, severity, and comorbidity of twelve-month *DSM-IV* disorders in the National Comorbidity Survey Replication (NCS-R). *Archives of General Psychiatry, 62,* 617–627.

Keys, S. G., Bemak, F., Carpenter, S. L., & King-Sears, M. F. (1998). Collaborative consultants: A new role for counselors serving at-risk youth. *Journal of Counseling and Development, 76,* 123–133.

Kluckhohn, C. (1985). *Mirror for man: The relation of anthropology to modern life.* Tucson: University of Arizona Press.

Krathwohl, D. R., Bloom, B. S., & Masia, B. B. (1964). *Taxonomy of educational objectives: Book 2. Affective domain.* New York, NY: Longman.

Kress, V. E., Erikson, K. P., Rayle, A. D., & Ford, S. J. W. (2005). The *DSM–IV–TR* and culture: Consideration for counselors. *Journal of Counseling and Development, 83,* 97–104.

Kübler-Ross, E. (1969). *On death and dying.* New York, NY: Collier Books.

Kurlan, R., Como, P. G., Miller, B., Palumbo, D., Deeley, C., Andersen, E. M., . . . McDermott, M. P. (2002). The behavioral spectrum of tic disorders: A community-based study. *Neurology, 59,* 414–420.

Lachat, M. A. (2002). *Data-driven high school reform: The breaking ranks model.* Hampton, NH: Center for Resource Management.

LaFountain, R. M., & Garner, N. E. (1998). *A school with solutions: Implementing a solution-focused/Adlerian-based comprehensive school counseling program.* Alexandria, VA: American School Counselor Association.

Lambert, M. J. (1991). Introduction to psychotherapy research. In L. E. Beutler, & M. Crago (Eds.), *Psychotherapy research: An international review of programmatic studies* (pp. 1–23). Washington, DC: American Psychological Association.

Lambie, G. W., & Rokutani, L. J. (2002). A systems approach to substance abuse identification and intervention for school counselors. *Professional School Counseling, 5,* 353–359.

Landreth, G. (2002). *Play therapy: The art of the relationship* (2nd ed.). New York, NY: Brunner-Routledge.

Lapan, R. T. (2004). *Career development across the K–16 years: Bridging the present to satisfying and successful futures.* Alexandria, VA: American Counseling Association.

Lapan, R. T. (2012). Comprehensive school counseling programs: In some schools for some students but not in all schools for all students. *Professional School Counseling 16,* 84–88.

Lapan, R. T., Aoyagi, M., & Kayson, M. (2007). Helping rural adolescents make successful postsecondary transitions: A longitudinal study. *Professional School Counseling, 10,* 266–272.

Lapan, R. T., Gysbers, N. C., Bragg, S., & Pierce, M. E. (2012). Missouri professional school counselors: Ratios matter, especially in high-poverty schools. *Professional School Counseling, 16,* 117–124.

Lapan, R. T., Gysbers, N. C., & Petroski, G. F. (2003). Helping seventh graders be safe and successful: A statewide study of the impact of comprehensive guidance and counseling programs. *Professional School Counseling, 6,* 186–197.

Lapan, R. T., Gysbers, N. C., & Sun, Y. (1997). The impact of more fully implemented guidance programs on the school experiences of high school students: A statewide evaluation study. *Journal of Counseling and Development, 75,* 292–302.

Lapan, R. T., Whitcomb, S. A., & Aleman, N. M. (2012). Connecticut professional school counselors: College and career counseling services and smaller ratios benefit students. *Professional School Counseling 16,* 117–124.

Lee, C. C. (2001). Culturally responsive school counselors and programs: Addressing the needs of all students. *Professional School Counseling, 4,* 257–261.

Lee, C. C., & Hipolito-Delgado, C. P. (2007). Introduction: Counselors as agents of social change. In C. C. Lee (Ed.), *Counseling for social justice* (2nd ed., pp. xiii–xxviii). Alexandria, VA: American Counseling Association.

Lee, J. M., & Ransom, T. (2011). *The educational experience of young men of color: A review of research, pathways, and progress.* New York, NY: The College Board Advocacy and Policy Center.

Lee, V. V. (2005, August). *Teaming and collaborating to challenge the realities that impact student success.* Washington, DC: College Board.

Lee, V. V. (2006, June). *Using data to build equitable access, achievement and attainment in AP, IB, honors and college preparatory courses.* Paper presented at the 2006 Education Trust Summer Academy, Deerfield Beach, FL.

Lee, V. V., & Goodnough, G. E. (2006, October). *Systemic advocacy: A model for school counseling practice and supervision.* Paper presented at the North Atlantic Regional Counselor Education and Supervision Conference, Lake George, NY.

Lehr, C. A., Hansen, A., Sinclair, M. F., & Christenson, S. L. (2003). Moving beyond dropout prevention to school completion: An integrative review of data-based interventions. *School Psychology Review, 32,* 342–364.

Lehr, C. A., Johnson, D. R., Bremer, C. D., Cosio, A., & Thomson, M. (2004). *Essential tools—Increasing rates of school completion: Moving from policy and research to practice: A manual for policymakers, administrators, and educators.* Retrieved August 28, 2005, from www.ncset.org/publications/essentialtools/dropout/default.asp

Lemov, D. (2010). *Teach like a champion: 49 techniques that put students on the path to college.* San Francisco, CA: Jossey-Bass.

Lewis, J. A., & Bradley, L. (Eds.). (2000). *Advocacy in counseling: Counselors, clients, and community.* Greensboro, NC: CAPS & ERIC/CASS.

Linde, L. E. (2014). Ethical and legal issues in counseling. In B. T. Erford (Ed.), *Orientation to the counseling profession: Advocacy, ethics, and essential professional foundations* (2nd ed., pp. 66–112). Columbus, OH: Pearson Merrill.

Littrell, J. M., Malia, J. A., & Vanderwood, M. (1995). Single session brief counseling in a high school. *Journal of Counseling and Development, 73*, 451–458.

Locke, D. C. (1990). A not so provincial view of multicultural counseling. *Counselor Education and Supervision, 30*, 18–25.

Lubell, K. M., Kegler, S. R., Crosby, A. E., & Karch, D. (2008). Suicide trends among youths and young adults aged 10–24 years—United States, 1900–2004. *Journal of the American Medical Association, 299*, 283–284.

Lundahl, B. W., Nimer, J., & Parsons, B. (2006). Preventing child abuse: A meta-analysis of parent training programs. *Research on Social Work Practice, 16*, 251–262.

Ly, T. M., & Hodapp, R. M. (2002). Maternal attribution of child noncompliance in children with mental retardation: Down syndrome versus other causes. *Journal of Developmental and Behavioral Pediatrics, 23*, 322–329.

Manese, J. E., Wu, J. T., & Nepomuceno, C. A. (2001). The effect of training on multicultural counseling competencies: An exploratory study over a ten year period. *Journal of Multicultural Counseling and Development, 29*, 31–40.

Markus, H. R. (2008). Pride, prejudice, and ambivalence: Toward a unified theory of race and ethnicity. *American Psychologist, 63*, 651–670.

Marshak, L. E., Dandeneau, C. J., Prezant, F. P., & L'Amoreaux, N. A. (2009). *The school counselor's guide to helping students with disabilities.* San Francisco, CA: Wiley Jossey-Bass.

Marshall, P. L. (2002). *Cultural diversity in our schools.* Belmont, CA: Wadsworth/Thomson Learning.

Marsico, M., & Getch, Y. Q. (2009). Transitioning Hispanic seniors from high school to college. *Professional School Counseling, 12*, 458–462.

Martin, P. J., & House, R. M. (2002). *Transforming school counseling in the Transforming School Counseling Initiative.* Washington, DC: Education Trust.

Masi, G., Mucci, M., & Millepiedi, S. (2001). Separation anxiety disorder in children and adolescents: Epidemiology, diagnosis and management. *CNS Drugs, 15*, 94–104.

Mason, E. C. M., & McMahon, H. G. (2009). Leadership practices of school counselors. *Professional School Counseling, 13,* 107–115.

Mason, E. C. M., Ockerman, M. S., & Chen-Hayes, S. F. (2013). Change agent for equity (CAFE) model: A framework for school counselor identity. *Journal of School Counseling, 11*(4).

Mattingley, D. J., Prislin, R., McKenzie, T. L., Rodriquez, J. L., & Kayzar, R. (2002). Evaluating evaluations: The case of parental involvement programs. *Review of Educational Research, 72*, 549–576.

Mayfield, D., McLeod, G., & Hall, P. (1974). The CAGE questionnaire: Validation of a new alcoholism screening instrument. *American Journal of Psychiatry, 131*(10), 1121–1123.

McCabe, P., Sheard, C., & Code, C. (2002). Acquired communication impairment in people with HIV. *Journal of Medical Speech-Language Pathology, 10*, 183–199.

McClellan, J., McCurry, C., Speltz, M. L., & Jones, K. (2002). Symptom factors in early-onset psychotic disorders. *Journal of the American Academy of Child and Adolescent Psychiatry, 41*, 791–798.

McClelland, G. M., Elkington, K. S., Teplin, L. A., & Abram, K. M. (2004). Multiple substance use disorders in juvenile detainees. *Journal of the American Academy of Child and Adolescent Psychiatry, 43*, 1215–1224.

McGannon, W. M., Carey, J., & Dimmitt, C. (2005). *The current status of school counseling outcome research.* Amherst, MA: Center for School Counseling Outcome Research.

McKillip, M., Rawls, A., & Barry, C. (2012). Improving college access: A review of research on the role of high school counselors. *Professional School Counseling, 16*, 49–58.

McLeod, A. L., Muldoon, J., & Hays, D. G. (2014). Intimate partner violence. In L. R. Jackson-Cherry & B. T. Erford (Eds.), *Crisis assessment, intervention, and prevention* (2nd ed., pp. 157–192). Columbus, OH: Pearson Merrill.

McMahon, H. G., Mason, E. C. M., & Paisley, P. O. (2009). School counselor educators as educational leaders promoting systemic change. *Professional School Counseling, 13,* 116–124.

Merriam-Webster's Collegiate Dictionary. (12th ed.). (2012). Springfield, MA: Merriam-Webster.

Metcalf, L. (2008). *Counseling toward solutions: A practical solution-focused program for working with students, teachers, and parents* (2nd ed.). West Nyack, NY: Center for Applied Research.

MetLife Survey of the American Teacher, Student Life—School, Home and Community. (2002). Retrieved from https://www .metlife.com/metlife-foundation/what-we-do/student-achievement/survey-american-teacher.html?WT.mc_id=vu1101

Miller, C. H. (1961). *Foundations of guidance.* New York, NY: Harper & Brothers.

Miller, D. N., Eckert, T. L., & Mazza, J. J. (2009). Suicide prevention programs in schools: A review and public health perspective. *School Psychology Review, 38*(2), 168–188.

Miller, F. G. (2001). *The SASSI-A2 manual.* Springfield, IN: SASSI Institute.

Milsom, A., & Dietz, L. (2009). Defining college readiness for students with learning disabilities: A Delphi study. *Professional School Counseling, 12,* 315–323.

Mohatt, D. F., Adams, S. J., Bradley, M. M., & Morris, C. D. (Eds). (2006). *Mental health and rural America: 1994–2005.* Washington, DC: U.S. Department of Health and Human Services, Health Resources and Services Administration, Office of Rural Health Policy.

Mulick, J. A., & Butter, E. M. (2002). Educational advocacy for children with autism. *Behavioral Interventions, 17,* 57–74.

Murphy, G. (1955). The cultural concept of guidance. *Personnel and Guidance Journal, 34,* 4–9.

Murphy, J. J. (2008). *Solution-focused counseling in middle and high schools* (2nd ed.). Alexandria, VA: American Counseling Association.

Mynatt, B. S., & Gibbons, M. M. (2011). *Preparing students with disabilities for their future careers.* Retrieved from http://counselingoutfitters.com/vistas/vistas11/Article_08.pdf

Myrick, R. D. (2003a). *Developmental guidance and counseling: A practical approach* (4th ed.). Minneapolis, MN: Education Media Corporation.

Myrick, R. D. (2003b). Accountability: Counselors count. *Professional School Counseling, 6,* 174–179.

National Association of Anorexia Nervosa and Associated Disorders. (2014). E*ating disorder statistics.* Retrieved from http://www.anad.org/get-information/about-eating-disorders/eating-disorders-statistics/

National Association for College Admission Counseling. (2012). *Statement of professional good practice.* Arlington, VA: Author.

National Association for College Admission Counseling. (2013). *Fundamentals of college admission counseling* (3rd ed.). Arlington, VA: Author.

National Career Development Association. (2009). *Career counseling competencies.* Retrieved from http://www.ncda.org/aws/NCDA/pt/sd/news_article/37798/_self/layout_ccmsearch/true

National Center for Transforming School Counseling. (2013). *The new vision for school counseling.* Retrieved from http://www.edtrust.org/dc/tsc/vision

National Coalition for the Homeless. (2008). *Homeless families and children* (NCH Fact Sheet #12). Retrieved from www.nationalhomeless.org/publications/facts/families.html

National Commission on Excellence in Education. (1983). *A nation at risk: The imperative for educational reform.* Retrieved from www.ed.gov/pubs/NatAtRisk/index.html

National Council on Disability. (2004). *Improving educational outcomes for students with disabilities.* Retrieved from www.ncd.gov/newsroom/publications/2004educationoutcomes.htm

National Council on Disability. (2011, October 31). *National disability policy: A progress report.* Retrieved from http://www.ncd.gov/progress_reports/Oct312011

National Dissemination Center for Children with Disabilities. (2001). *Related services: News digest 16* (2nd ed.). Retrieved from www.nichcy.org/pubs/newsdig/nd16txt.htm

National Education Association. (2007). *The school crisis guide.* Retrieved from http://www.crisisguide.neahin.org/crisisguide/

National Institute of Mental Health. (2012). *Suicide in the U.S.: Statistics and prevention.* Retrieved from http://www.nimh.nih.gov/health/publications/suicide-in-the-us-statistics-and-prevention/index.shtml

National Institutes of Health. (2014). *The national children's study.* Retrieved from www.nationalchildrensstudy.gov

National Office for School Counselor Advocacy (NOSCA). (2010). *Eight components of college and career readiness counseling.* Washington, DC: The College Board.

National Office for School Counselor Advocacy (NOSCA). (2011). *Young men of color initiative journal.* New York, NY: Author.

National Office for School Counselor Advocacy (NOSCA). (2012). *2012 national survey of school counselors—True north: Charting the course to college and career readiness.* New York, NY: Author.

National Registry of Effective Prevention Programs. (2012). *About us.* Retrieved from http://nrepp.samhsa.gov/SearchLegacy.aspx

Naugle, K., Campbell, T. A., & Gray, N. D. (2010). Postsecondary transition model for students with disabilities. *Journal of School Counseling, 8*(40). Retrieved from http://www.jsc.montana.edu/articles/v8n40.pdf

Nelson, D. E., Fox, D. G., Haslam, M., & Gardner, J. (2007). *An evaluation of Utah's comprehensive guidance program: The fourth major study of Utah's thirteen-year program.* Retrieved from www.schools.utah.gov/cte/documents/guidance/publications/Research_AnEvaluationUtahsCCGP2007.pdf

Nelson, D. E., Gardner, J. L., & Fox, D. G. (1998). *Contrast between students in high implementation and low implementation high schools in the Utah Comprehensive Guidance Program.* Salt Lake City, UT: Institute for Behavioral Research in Creativity.

Newcomb, M. D., & Richardson, M. A. (2000). Substance-use disorders. In M. Hersen & R. T. Ammerman (Eds.), *Advanced abnormal child psychology* (2nd ed., pp. 467–492). Mahwah, NJ: Erlbaum.

Newman-Carlson, D., & Horne, A. M. (2004). Bully busters: A psychoeducational intervention for reducing bullying behaviors in middle school students. *Journal of Counseling and Development, 82,* 259–267.

Newsome, D. W., & Gladding, S. T. (2014). *Clinical mental health counseling in community and agency settings* (4th ed.). Upper Saddle River, NJ: Pearson Merrill.

Nicoll, W. G. (1994). Developing effective classroom guidance programs: An integrative framework. *School Counselor, 41,* 360–364.

Niedringhaus, J. J. (2000). *Counseling children: Some practical suggestions.* Unpublished manuscript.

Nieto, S. (2004). *Affirming diversity: The sociopolitical context of multicultural education* (4th ed.). Boston, MA: Pearson/Allyn & Bacon.

Niles, S. G., Amundson, N. E. & Neault, R. A. (2010). *Career flow: A hope-centered approach to career development.* Boston, MA: Pearson Education.

Niles, S. G., & Harris-Bowlsbey, J. (2013). *Career development interventions in the 21st century* (4th ed.). Upper Saddle River, NJ: Prentice Hall.

Niles, S. G., Yoon, H. J., Balin, E., & Amundson, N. E., (2010). Using a hope-centered model of career development in challenging times. *Turkish Psychological Counseling & Guidance Journal, 4*(34), 101–108.

Nims, D., James, S., & Hughey, A. (1998). The challenge of accountability: A survey of Kentucky school counselors. *Kentucky Counseling Association Journal, 17,* 31–37.

O'Hanlon, W. H., & Weiner-Davis, M. (1989). *In search of solutions: A new direction in psychotherapy.* New York, NY: Guilford Press.

Ohrt, J. H., Lambie, G. W., & Ieva, K. P. (2009). Supporting Latino and African-American students in Advanced Placement courses: A school counseling program's approach. *Professional School Counseling, 13,* 59–63.

Oliver, B. (2012). An innovative approach to tackling truancy. *Counseling Today, 55,* 10–11.

Oliver, L. W., & Spokane, A. R. (1988). Career-intervention outcome: What contributes to client gain? *Journal of Counseling Psychology, 35,* 447–462.

Olweus, D. (2005). A useful evaluation design, and effects of the Olweus bullying prevention program. *Psychology, Crime, and Law, 11,* 389–402.

Organisation for Economic Cooperation and Development (OECD). (2010). *Learning for jobs: Synthesis report of the OECD reviews of vocational education and training.* Paris, France: Author.

Orpinas, P., & Horne, A. M. (2006). *Bullying prevention: Creating a positive school climate and developing social competence.* Washington, DC: American Psychological Association.

Orton, G. L. (1997). *Strategies for counseling with children and their parents.* Pacific Grove, CA: Brooks/Cole.

Osborne, J. L., Collison, B. B., House, R. M., Gray, L. A., Firthe, J., & Lou, M. (1998). Developing a social advocacy model for counselor education. *Counselor Education and Supervision, 37,* 190–202.

Owens, D., Thomas, D., & Strong, L. A. (2011). School counselors assisting students with disabilities. *Education, 132,* 235–240.

Ozer, E. J., & Weinstein, R. S. (2004). Urban adolescents' exposure to community violence: The role of support, school safety, and social constraints in a school-based sample of boys and girls. *Journal of Clinical Child and Adolescent Psychology, 33,* 463–476.

Pack-Brown, S. P., Thomas, T. L., & Seymour, J. M. (2008). Infusing professional ethics into counselor education programs: A multicultural/social justice perspective. *Journal of Counseling and Development, 86,* 296–302.

Paisley, P. O., & Milsom, A. (2007). Group work as an essential contribution to transforming school counseling. *Journal for Specialists in Group Work, 32,* 9–17.

Parsons, F. (1909). *Choosing a vocation.* Boston, MA: Houghton Mifflin.

Perna, L. W., Rowan-Kenyon, H. T., Thomas, S. L., Bell, A., Anderson, R., & Li, C. (2008). The role of college counseling in shaping college opportunity: Variations across high schools. *Review of Higher Education, 31,* 131–159.

Perusse, R., & Goodnough, G. E. (Eds.). (2004). *Leadership, advocacy, and direct service strategies for professional school counselors.* Belmont, CA: Brooks/Cole-Thomson Learning.

Peterson, A. A., Campise, R. L., & Azrin, N. H. (1994). Behavioral and pharmacological treatments for tic and habit disorders: A review. *Journal of Developmental and Behavioral Pediatrics, 15,* 430–441.

Peterson, J. (2004). The individual counseling process. In A. Vernon (Ed.), *Counseling children and adolescents* (3rd ed., pp. 35–74). Denver, CO: Love.

Peterson, J. S., Goodman, R., Thomas, K., & McCauley, A. (2004). Teachers and non-teachers as school counselors: Reflections on the internship experience. *Professional School Counseling, 7,* 246–255.

Piaget, J. (1963). *The origins of intelligence in children.* New York, NY: Norton.

Piran, N. (2004). Teachers: On "being" (rather than "doing") prevention. *Eating Disorders, 12,* 1–9.

Ponec, D. L., Poggi, J. A., & Dickel, T. A. (1998). Unity: Developing relationships between school and community counselors. *Professional School Counseling, 2,* 95–102.

Ponterotto, J. G., Casas, J. M., Suzuki, L. A., & Alexander, C. M. (Eds.). (2010). *Handbook of multicultural counseling* (3rd ed.). Thousand Oaks, CA: Sage.

Porfeli, E. J., Hartung, P. J., & Vondracek, F. W. (2008). Children's vocational development: A research rationale. *The Career Development Quarterly, 57,* 25–37.

President's New Freedom Commission on Mental Health. (2003). *Final report to the President.* Retrieved from www .mentalhealthcommission.gov/reports/FinalReport /FullReport-03.htm

Prout, H. T., & DeMartino, R. A. (1986). A meta-analysis of school-based studies of psychotherapy. *Journal of School Psychology, 24,* 285–292.

Prout, S. M., & Prout, H. T. (1998). A meta-analysis of school-based studies of counseling and psychotherapy: An update. *Journal of School Psychology, 36,* 121–136.

Ramirez, S. Z., & Smith, K. A. (2007). Case vignettes of school psychologists' consultations involving Hispanic youth. *Journal of Educational and Psychological Consultation, 17,* 79–93.

Randolph, D. L., & Masker, T. (1997). Teacher certification and the counselor: A follow-up survey of school counselor certification requirements. *ACES Spectrum, 57*(4), 6–8.

Rappaport, J. (1987). Terms of empowerment/examples of prevention: Toward a theory for community psychology. *American Journal of Community Psychology, 15,* 121–144.

Ratts, M. J., DeKruyf, L., & Chen-Hayes, S. F. (2007). The ACA advocacy competencies: A social justice advocacy framework for professional school counselors. *Professional School Counselors, 11,* 90–97.

Reese, R. J., Prout, H. T., Zirkelback, E. A., & Anderson, C. R. (2010). Effectivenss of school-based psychotherapy: A meta-analysis of dissertation research. *Psychology in the Schools, 47,* 1035–1045.

Remley, T., & Herlihy, B. (2010). *Ethical, legal, and professional issues in counseling* (3rd ed.). Upper Saddle River, NJ: Merrill/ Prentice Hall.

Reynolds, W. M. (1988). *Suicide Ideation Questionnaire.* Lutz, FL: Psychological Assessment Resources.

Rhodes, R. L., Ochoa, S. H., & Ortiz, S. O. (2005). *Assessing culturally and linguistically diverse students: A practical guide.* New York, NY: Guilford Press.

Ripley, V. V. (2001, October). *From position to program: Supervision in context.* Paper presented at North Atlantic Region Association for Counselor Education and Supervision National Conference, Amherst, MA.

Ripley, V. V., & Goodnough, G. E. (2001). Planning and implementing group counseling in a high school. *Professional School Counseling, 5,* 62–65.

Riva, M. T., & Haub, A. L. (2004). Group counseling in the schools. In J. L. DeLucia-Waack, D. A. Gerrity, C. R. Kalodner, & M. T. Riva (Eds.), *Handbook of group counseling and psychotherapy* (pp. 309–321). Thousand Oaks, CA: Sage.

Rivera, L. M., & Schaefer, M. B. (2008). The career institute: A collaborative career development program for traditionally underserved secondary (6–12) school students. *Journal of Career Development, 35,* 406–426. doi: 10.1177/ 0894845308327737

Roache, M., Shore, J., Gouleta, E., & de Obaldia Butkevich, E. (2003). An investigation of collaboration among school professionals in serving culturally and linguistically diverse students with exceptionalities. *Bilingual Research Journal, 27,* 117–136.

Roberts, P., Kellough, R., & Moore, K. (2010). *A resource guide for elementary school teaching: Planning for competence.* Upper Saddle River, NJ: Prentice Hall.

Roderick, M., Nagaoka, J., & Coca, V., (2009). College readiness for all: The challenge for urban high schools. *The Future of Children, 19,* 185–210.

Roderick, M., Nagaoka, J., Coca, V., & Moeller, E. (2008). *From high school to the future: Potholes on the road to college.* Retrieved from http://www.diversityweb.org/research_and_trends/ research_evaluation_impact/student_learning_outcomes/ documents/FromHighSchooltotheFuturePotholestoCollege.pdf

Rogers, C. R. (1942). *Counseling and psychotherapy: Newer concepts in practice.* New York, NY: Houghton Mifflin.

Rogers, M. R. (2000). Examining the cultural context of consultation. *School Psychology Review, 29,* 414–418.

Roid, G. H. (2003). *The Stanford-Binet Intelligence Scale–5th Edition (SBIS).* Itasca, IL: Riverside.

Rollin, S. A., Kaiser-Ulrey, C., Potts, I., & Creason, A. H. (2003). A school-based violence prevention model for at-risk eighth grade youth. *Psychology in the Schools, 40,* 403–416.

Romano, D., Paradise, L., & Green, E. J. (2009, November 20). School counselor's attitudes towards providing services to students receiving Section 504 classroom accommodations: Implications for school counselor educators. *Journal of School Counseling, 7*(37). Retrieved from http://www.jsc .montana.edu/articles/v7n37.pdf

Rongione, D., Erford, B. T., & Broglie, C. (2011). Alcohol and other drug counseling outcomes for school-aged youth: A meta-analysis of studies from 1990-2009. *Counseling Outcome Research and Evaluation, 2,* 1–17. doi: 10.1177/2150137811400595

Rosenbaum, J. E., Stephan, J. L., & Rosenbaum, J. E. (2010). Beyond one-size-fits-all college dreams: Alternative pathways to desirable careers. *American Educator, 34*(3), 2–13.

Rowley, W. J., Sink, C. A., & MacDonald, G. (2002). An experiential and systemic approach to encourage collaboration and community building. *Professional School Counseling, 5,* 360–365.

Rowley, W. J., Stroh, H. R., & Sink, C. A. (2005). Comprehensive guidance and counseling programs' use of guidance curricula materials: A survey of national trends. *Professional School Counseling, 8,* 296–304.

Ryan, C., & Chen-Hayes, S. F. (in press). Educating and empowering families of LGBT K–12 students. In E. Fisher & K. Komosa-Hawkins (Eds.), *Creating school environments to support lesbian, gay, bisexual, transgender, and questioning students and families.* New York, NY: Routledge.

Saenz, R. (2009). *Latinos and the changing face of America.* Washington, DC: Population Reference Bureau. Retrieved from www.prb.org/Articles/2004/LatinosandtheChanging FaceofAmerica.aspx

Santos de Barona, M. S., & Barona, A. (2006). School counselors and school psychologists: Collaborating to ensure minority students receive appropriate consideration for special educational programs. *Professional School Counseling, 10,* 3–13.

Saphier, J., King, M., & D'Auria, J. (2006). Three strands form strong school leadership. *Journal of Staff Development, 27,* 51–57.

Savickas, M. L. (1989). Career style assessment and counseling. In T. Sweeney (Ed.), *Adlerian counseling: A practical approach for a new decade* (3rd ed., pp. 289–320). Muncie, IN: Accelerated Development.

Savickas, M. L. (1997). Career adaptability: An integrative construct for life-span, life-space theory. *The Career Development Quarterly, 45,* 247–259.

Savickas, M. L. (1999). The transition from school to work: A developmental perspective. *Career Development Quarterly, 47,* 326–336.

Savickas, M. L. (2005). The theory and practice of career construction. In S. D. Brown, & R. W. Lent (Eds.), *Career development and counseling: Putting theory and research to work* (pp. 42–70). Hoboken, NJ: Wiley.

Savickas, M. L. (2011). New questions for vocational psychology: Premises, paradigms, and practices. *Journal of Career Assessment, 19,* 251–258. doi: 10.1177/1069072710395532

Savickas, M. L. (2012). Life design: A paradigm for career intervention in the 21st century. *Journal of Counseling & Development, 90,* 13–20.

Savitz-Romer, M., & Bouffard, S. (2012). *Ready, willing, & able: A developmental approach to college access and success.* Boston, MA: Harvard University Educational Press.

Schein, E. (1969). *Process consultation: Its role in organizational development.* Reading, MA: Addison-Wesley.

Schlossberg, S. M., Morris, J. D., & Lieberman, M. G. (2001). The effects of a counselor-led guidance intervention on students' behaviors and attitudes. *Professional School Counseling, 4,* 156–174.

Schmidt, J. J. (2008). *Counseling in schools: Comprehensive programs of responsive services for all students* (5th ed.). Boston, MA: Allyn & Bacon.

Scottham, K. M., & Smalls, C. P. (2009). Unpacking racial socialization: Considering female African American primary caregivers' racial identity. *Journal of Marriage and Family, 71,* 807–818.

Scruggs, M. Y., Wasielewski, R. A., & Ash, M. J. (1999). Comprehensive evaluation of a K–12 counseling program. *Professional School Counseling, 2,* 244–247.

Search Institute. (2013). *Developmental assests.* Retrieved from http://www.search-institute.org/developmental-assets

Selekman, M. D. (1997). *Pathways to change: Brief therapy solutions with difficult adolescents.* New York, NY: Guilford Press.

Seligman, L. (2004). *Diagnosis and treatment planning in counseling* (3rd ed.). New York, NY: Kluwer.

Seligman, L., & Reichenberg, L. W. (2011). *Selecting effective treatments: A comprehensive, systematic guide to treating mental disorders* (4th ed.). San Francisco, CA: Wiley.

Sheperis, C. J., Renfro-Michel, E. L., & Doggett, R. A. (2003). In-home treatment of reactive attachment disorder in a therapeutic foster care system: A case example. *Journal of Mental Health Counseling, 25,* 76–88.

Silverstein, D. M. (2004). Enuresis in children: Diagnosis and management. *Clinical Pediatrics, 43,* 217–221.

Sink, C. (Ed.). (2005). *Contemporary school counseling: Theory, research, and practice.* Boston, MA: Houghton Mifflin/ Lahaska.

Sink, C. A., & Stroh, H. R. (2003). Raising achievement test scores of early elementary school students through comprehensive school counseling programs. *Professional School Counseling, 6,* 350–364.

Skiba, R., & Fontanini, A. (2000). *Bullying prevention: What works in preventing school violence.* Bloomington, IN: Indiana Education Policy Center. (ERIC Document Reproduction Service No. ED470431)

Sklare, G. B. (2005). *Brief counseling that works: A solution-focused approach for school counselors and administrators* (2nd ed.). Thousand Oaks, CA: Corwin Press.

Smith, C. (2001). Using social stories to enhance behavior in children with autistic spectrum difficulties. *Educational Psychology in Practice, 17,* 337–345.

Smith, J. D., Schneider, B. H., Smith, P. K., & Ananiadou, K. (2004). The effectiveness of whole-school antibullying programs: A synthesis of evaluation research. *School Psychology Review, 33,* 547–560.

Smith, J. S., Feldwisch, R., & Abell, A. (2006). Similarities and differences in caregivers' and students' perceptions of the transition to high school. *Research on Middle Level Education Online, 29*(10), 1–9.

Smith, S. D., & Chen-Hayes, S. F. (2004). Leadership and advocacy for lesbian, bisexual, gay, transgendered, and questioning (LBGTQ) students: Academic, career, and interpersonal success strategies. In R. Perusse & G. E. Goodnough (Eds.), *Leadership, advocacy, and direct service strategies for professional school counselors* (pp. 187–221). Belmont, CA: Brooks/Cole-Thomson Learning.

Snowling, M. J. (2002). Reading and other learning difficulties. In M. Rutter, E. Taylor, & L. Hersov (Eds.), *Child and adolescent psychiatry: Modern approaches* (4th ed., pp. 682–696). Cambridge, MA: Blackwell.

Snyder, C. R. (2002). Hope theory: Rainbows in the mind. *Psychological Inquiry, 13*, 249–275. doi: 10.1207S15327965PLI1304_01.

Southern Region Educational Board. (2013). *The next generation of school accountability: A blueprint for raising high school achievement and graduation rates in SREB states.* Atlanta, GA: Author.

Spanierman, L. B., Poteat, V., Wang, Y., & Oh, E. (2008). Psychosocial costs of racism to White counselors: Predicting various dimensions of multicultural counseling competence. *Journal of Counseling Psychology, 55*, 75–88.

Spaulding, F. E. (1915). Problems of vocational guidance. In M. Bloomfield (Ed.), *Readings in vocational guidance.* Cambridge, MA: Harvard University Press.

Speight, S. L., Myers, L. J., Cox, C. E., & Highlen, P. S. (1991). A redefinition of multicultural counseling. *Journal of Counseling & Development, 70*, 29–36.

Speltz, M. (1990). The treatment of preschool conduct problems: An integration of behavioral and attachment concepts. In M. Greenburg, D. Cicchetti, & E. M. Cummings (Eds.), *Attachment in the preschool years* (pp. 399–426). Chicago, IL: University of Chicago Press.

Sprague, J. R., & Walker, H. M. (2004). *Safe and healthy schools: Practical prevention strategies.* New York, NY: Guilford Press.

Stathakow, P., & Roehrle, B. (2003). The effectiveness of intervention programmes for children of divorce—A meta-analysis. *International Journal of Mental Health Promotion, 5*, 31–37.

Steele, C. M. (2007). A threat in the air: How stereotypes shape intellectual identity and performance. *American Psychologist, 52*, 613–629.

Steen, S., Bauman, S., & Smith, J. (2007). Professional school counselors and the practice of group work. *Professional School Counseling, 11*, 72–80.

Steen, S., & Kaffenberger, C. J. (2007). Integrating academic interventions into small group counseling in elementary school. *Professional School Counseling, 10*, 516–519.

Steigerwald, F. (2010a). Crisis intervention with individuals in the schools. In B. T. Erford (Ed.), *Professional school counseling: A handbook of theories, programs, and practices* (2nd ed., pp. 829–841). Austin, TX: PRO-ED.

Steigerwald, F. (2010b). Systemic crisis intervention in the schools. In B. T. Erford (Ed.), *Professional school counseling:*

A handbook of theories, programs, and practices (2nd ed., pp. 843–849). Austin, TX: PRO-ED.

Stelmacher, Z. T. (1995). Assessing suicidal clients. In J. N. Butcher (Ed.), *Clinical personality assessment: Practical approaches* (pp. 366–379). New York, NY: Oxford University Press.

Stephens, W. R. (1970). *Social reform and the origins of vocational guidance.* Washington, DC: National Career Development Association.

Stewart, D., Freeman, M., Law, M., Healy, H., Burke-Gaffney, J., Forhan, M., Young, N., & Guenther, S. (2013). Transition to adulthood for youth with disabilities: Evidence from the literature. In J. H. Stone & M. Blouin (Eds.), *International encyclopedia of rehabilitation.* Retrieved from http://cirrie.buffalo.edu/encyclopedia/en/article/110/

Stice, E., Marti, C. N., Shaw, H., & Jaconis, M. (2009). An 8-year longitudinal study of the natural history of threshold, subthreshold, and partial eating disorders from a community sample of adolescents. *Journal of Abnormal Psychology, 118*, 587–597. doi: 10.1037/a0016481

Stone, C. B. (2004). School counselors as leaders and advocates in addressing sexual harassment. In R. Perusse & G. E. Goodnough (Eds.), *Leadership, advocacy, and direct service strategies for professional school counselors* (pp. 353–380). Belmont, CA: Brooks/Cole-Thomson Learning.

Stone, C. B. (2009). *School counseling and principles: Ethics and law* (2nd ed.). Alexandria, VA: American School Counselor Association.

Stone, J. R., III, & Lewis, M. V. (2012). *College and career ready in the 21st century: Making high school matter.* New York, NY: Teachers College Press.

Stone, L. A., & Bradley, F. O. (1994). *Foundations of elementary and middle school counseling.* White Plains, NY: Longman.

Stroh, H. R., & Sink, C. A. (2002). Applying APA's learner-centered principles to school-based counseling. *Professional School Counseling, 6*, 71–78.

Substance Abuse and Mental Health Services Administration. (1995). *Cost of addictive and mental disorders and effectiveness of treatment.* Washington, DC: Author.

Substance Abuse and Mental Health Services Administration (SAMHSA). (2008). *Facts on children's mental health.* Retrieved from www.samhsa.gov/reports/congress2002/chap1ucod.htm#3

Substance Abuse and Mental Health Services Administration (SAMHSA). (2012). *Results from the 2010 National Survey on Drug Use and Health: Mental health findings,* NSDUH Series H-42, HHS Publication No. (SMA) 11-4667. Rockville, MD: Substance Abuse and Mental Health Services Administration. Retrieved from http://www.samhsa.gov/data/nsduh/2k10MH_Findings/2k10MHResults.htm

Sue, D. W., Arredondo, P., & McDavis, R. J. (1992). Multicultural competencies/standards: A pressing need. *Journal of Counseling and Development, 70*, 477–486.

Sue, D. W., & Torino, G. (2005). Racial-cultural competence: Awareness, knowledge, and skills. In R. T. Carter (Ed.), *Handbook of racial-cultural psychology and counseling: Vol. 2. Training and practice* (pp. 3–18). Hoboken, NJ: Wiley.

Sue, S. (1998). In search of cultural competence in psychotherapy and counseling. *American Psychologist, 53,* 440–448.

Super, D. E. (1957). *A psychology of careers.* New York, NY: Harper & Row.

Super, D. E. (1977). Vocational maturity in midcareer. *Vocational Guidance Quarterly, 25,* 294–302.

Super, D. E. (1980). A life span, life space approach to career development. *Journal of Vocational Behavior, 16,* 282–298.

Super, D. E. (1990). Career and life development. In D. Brown & L. Brooks (Eds.), *Career choice and development: Applying contemporary theories to practice* (2nd ed., pp. 197–261). San Francisco, CA: Jossey-Bass.

Super, D. E., & Knasel, E. G. (1981). Career development in adulthood: Some theoretical problems and a possible solution. *British Journal of Guidance & Counselling, 9,* 194–201.

Super, D. E., Savickas, M. L., & Super, C. M. (1996). The life span, life-space approach to careers. In D. Brown, & L. Brooks (Eds.), *Career choice and development: Applying contemporary theories to practice* (3rd ed., pp. 121–178). San Francisco, CA: Jossey-Bass.

Super, D. E., Thompson, A. S., & Lindeman, R. H. (1988). *Adult Career Concerns Inventory: Manual for research and exploratory use in counseling.* Palo Alto, CA: Consulting Psychologists Press.

Sweeney, T. J. (2001). Counseling: Historical origins and philosophical roots. In D. C. Locke, J. Myers, & E. L. Herr (Eds.), *The handbook of counseling* (pp. 1–13). Thousand Oaks, CA: Sage.

Tang, M. & Erford, B. T. (2010). The history of school counseling. In B. T. Erford (Ed.), *Professional school counseling: A handbook of theories, programs, and practices* (2nd ed., pp. 9–22). Austin, TX: PRO-ED.

Tarasoff v. Regents of the University of California, 17 Cal. 3d 425, 551 P.2d 334 (Cal. 1976).

Teachers for a New Era. (2001). *Announcement and prospectus and executive summary.* Retrieved from teachersforanewera .org/index.cfm?fuseaction=home.prospectus

Terry, N. P., & Irving, M. A. (2010). Cultural and linguistic diversity: Issues in education. In R. P. Colarusso & C. M. O'Rourke (Eds.), *Special education for all teachers* (pp. 110–132). Dubuque, IA: Kendall Hunt Publishing.

Test, D. W., & Cease-Cook, J. (2012). Evidence-based secondary transition practices for rehabilitation counselors. *Journal of Rehabilitation, 78*(2), 30–38.

Test, D. W., Cease-Cook, J., Fowler, C. H., & Bartholomew, A. (2012, October). *College and career ready standards and secondary transition planning for students with disabilities: 101.* Retrieved from http://nsttac.org/content/students-w-disabilities-and-collegecareer-readiness-101-documents

Thabet, A. A. M., Abed, Y., & Vostanis, P. (2004). Comorbidity of PTSD and depression among refugee children during war conflict. *Journal of Child Psychology and Psychiatry, 45,* 533–542.

Thomas, R. M. (2005). *Comparing theories of child development* (6th ed.). Belmont, CA: Wadsworth.

Thompson, R., & Littrell, J. M. (1998). Brief counseling for students with learning disabilities. *Professional School Counseling, 2,* 60–67.

Tomlinson, C. A, & Allan, S. D. (2000). *Understanding differentiated instruction: Building a foundation for leadership. Leadership for differentiated schools and classrooms.* Retrieved from http://www.ascd.org/publications/books/100216/chapters /Understanding-Differentiated-Instruction@-Building-a-Foundation-for-Leadership.aspx

Toporek, R. L. (1999, June). Advocacy: A voice for our clients and communities: Developing a framework for understanding advocacy in counseling. *Counseling Today,* 34–35, 39.

Traxler, A. E., & North, R. D. (1966). *Techniques of guidance.* New York, NY: Harper & Row.

Trolley, B. C., Haas, H. S., & Patti, D. C. (2009). *The school counselor's guide to special education.* Thousand Oaks, CA: Corwin.

Trusty, J., & Brown, D. (2005). Advocacy competencies for professional school counselors. *Professional School Counseling, 8,* 259–265.

Trusty, J., & Niles, S. G. (2003). High-school math courses and completion of the bachelor's degree. *Professional School Counseling, 7,* 99–107.

Trusty, J., & Niles, S. G. (2004). Realized potential or lost talent: High-school variables and bachelor's degree completion. *Career Development Quarterly, 53,* 2–13.

Trusty, J., Niles, S. G., & Carney, J. V. (2005). Education-career planning and middle school counselors. *Professional School Counseling, 9,* 136–143.

Ttofi, M. M., & Farrington, D. P. (2011). Effectiveness of school-based programs to reduce bullying: A systematic and meta-analytic review. *Journal of Experimental Criminology, 7,* 27–56.

Tynan, W. (2006). *Conduct disorder.* Retrieved from www.emedicine.com/ped/TOPIC2793.htm

Tynan, W. (2008). *Oppositional defiant disorder.* Retrieved from www.emedicine.com/ped/TOPIC2791.htm

U.S. Department of Education. (2002). *No Child Left Behind.* Retrieved from www.ed.gov/nclb/landing.jhtml?src5pb

U.S. Department of Education. (2005a). *Digest of educational statistics.* Washington, DC: Author.

U.S. Department of Education. (2005b, February). *FY 2006 program performance plan.* Washington, DC: Author.

U.S. Department of Education. (2012, August). *Race to the top-district executive summary.* Retrieved from http://www2.ed.gov /programs/racetothetop-district/2012-executive-summary.pdf

U. S. Department of Education, National Center for Educational Statistics. (2012). *The condition of education 2012 (NCES 2012-045) Indicator 33.* Retrieved from http://www.nces.ed .gov/fastfacts/display.asp?id=16

U.S. Department of Education, Office for Civil Rights. (2005). *Regulations enforced by the Office for Civil Rights (Section 504).* Retrieved from www.ed.gov/policy/rights/reg/ocr/index.html

U.S. Department of Education, Office of Educational Research and Improvement. (2008). *Reaching all families: Creating family friendly schools.* Washington, DC: Author.

U. S. Department of Education, Office of Special Education and Rehabilitative Services. (2010, November). *Thirty-five years of progress in educating children with disabilities through IDEA.* Washington, DC: Author.

U. S. Department of Education, Office of Special Education and Rehabilitative Services, Office of Special Education Programs. (2012, November). *31st annual report to Congress on the implementation of the Individuals with Disabilities Education Act, 2009.* Retrieved from http://www2.ed.gov/about/reports /annual/osep/2009/parts-b-c/31st-idea-arc.pdf

U.S. Department of Education, Office of Special Education Programs. (2005). *IDEA 2004 resources.* Retrieved from www .ed.gov/policy/speced/guid/idea/idea2004.html

U.S. Department of Health and Human Services. (2006). *Your rights under Section 504 of the Rehabilitation Act.* Retrieved from http://www.hhs.gov/ocr/civilrights/resources/factsheets/504.pdf

U. S. Department of Health and Human Services (2008). *What challenges are boys facing, and what opportunities exist to address those challenges? Fact sheet: Mental health.* Retrieved from http://aspe.hhs.gov/hsp/08/boys/factsheets/mh/index.shtml

U.S. Department of Health and Human Services, U.S. Public Health Service, Office of Surgeon General. (2001). *Youth violence: A report of the surgeon general.* Washington, DC: Author.

U.S. Department of Labor, Bureau of Labor Statistics. (1949). *Occupational outlook handbook.* Washington, DC: Author.

U.S. Department of Labor, National Occupational Information Coordinating Committee (NOICC). (1992). *The national career development guidelines project.* Washington, DC: Author.

Vela-Gude, L., Cavazos, J., Johnson, M. B., Fielding, C., Cavazos, A. G., Campos, L., & Rodriguez, I. (2009). "My counselors were never there": Perceptions from Latino college students. *Professional School Counseling, 12,* 272–279.

Vélez, C. E., Wolchik, S. A., Tein, J. Y., & Sandler, I. (2011). Protecting children from the consequences of divorce: A longitudinal study of the effects of parenting on children's coping processes. *Child Development, 82,* 244–257. doi: 10.1111/ j.1467-8624.2010.01553.x

Vernon, A. (2004). Working with children, adolescents, and their parents: Practical application of developmental theory. In A. Vernon (Ed.), *Counseling children and adolescents* (4th ed., pp. 1–34). Denver, CO: Love.

Vernon, A., & Erford, B. T. (2014). Lifespan development. In B. T. Erford (Ed.), *Orientation to the counseling profession* (2nd ed). Columbus, OH: Pearson Merrill

Vontress, C. E. (1970). Counseling blacks. *Personnel and Guidance Journal, 48,* 713–719.

Vontress, C. E. (1988). An existential approach to cross-cultural counseling. *Journal of Multicultural Counseling and Development, 16,* 73–83.

Walsh, M. E., Barrett, J. G., & DePaul, J. (2007). Day-to-day activities of school counselors: Alignment with new directions in the field and the ASCA national model. *Professional School Counseling, 10,* 370–378.

Walter, J. L., & Peller, J. E. (1992). *Becoming solution-focused in brief therapy.* New York, NY: Brunner/Mazel.

Watson, M., & McMahon, M. (2005). Children's career development: A research review from a learning perspective. *Journal of Vocational Behavior, 67,* 119–132. doi: 10.1016/j.jvb.2004.08.011

Watson, S., Watson, T., & Weaver, A. (2010). Direct behavioral consultation: An effective method for conducting school collaboration. In B. T. Erford (Ed.), *Professional school counseling: A handbook of theories, programs & practices* (2nd ed., pp. 295–302). Austin, TX: PRO-ED.

Webb, L. D., Brigman, G. A., & Campbell, C. (2005). Linking school counselors and student success: A replication of the Student Success Skills approach targeting the academic and social competence of students. *Professional School Counseling, 8,* 407–413.

Webster-Stratton, C., & Taylor, T. (2001). Nipping early risk factors in the bud: Preventing substance abuse, delinquency, and violence in adolescence through interventions targeted at young children (0–8 years). *Prevention Science, 2*(3), 165–192.

Wechsler, D. (2001). *Wechsler Intelligence Scale for Children–4th edition.* San Antonio, TX: Psychological Corporation.

Wehmeyer, M. L., Shogren, K. A., Palmer, S. B., Williams-Diehm, K. L., Little, T. D., & Boulton, A. (2012). The impact of the self-determined learning model of instruction on student self-determination. *Exceptional Children, 78,* 135–153.

Wehrly, B. (1995). *Pathways to multicultural counseling competence: A developmental journey.* Pacific Grove, CA: Brooks/Cole.

Weiss, C. (1998). *Evaluation* (2nd ed.). Upper Saddle River, NJ: Prentice Hall.

Wessler, S. L., & Preble, W. (2003). *The respectful school: How educators and students can conquer hate and harassment.* Alexandria, VA: Association for Supervision and Curriculum Development.

Whaley, A., & Davis, K. (2007). Cultural competence and evidence-based practice in mental health services: A complementary perspective. *American Psychologist, 62,* 563–574.

Wheeler, A. M., & Bertram, B. (2012). *The counselor and the law: A guide to legal and ethical practice* (6th ed.). Alexandria, VA: American Counseling Association.

Whiston, S. C. (2002). Response to the past, present, and future of school counseling: Raising some issues. *Professional School Counseling, 5,* 148–155.

Whiston, S. C., Brecheisen, B. K., & Stephens, J. (2003). Does treatment modality affect career counseling effectiveness? *Journal of Vocational Behavior, 62,* 390–410.

Whiston, S. C., & Oliver, L. (2005). Career counseling process and outcome. In W. B. Walsh & M. Savickas (Eds.), *Handbook of vocational psychology* (3rd ed., pp. 155–194). Hillsdale, NJ: Erlbaum.

Whiston, S. C., & Rahardja, D. (2008). Vocational counseling process and outcome. In S. D. Brown & R. W. Lent (Eds.), *Handbook of counseling psychology* (4th ed., pp. 444–461). New York, NY: Wiley.

Whiston, S. C., Tai, W. L., Rahardja, D., & Eder, K. (2011). School counseling outcome: A meta-analytic examination of interventions. *Journal of Counseling & Development, 89,* 37–55.

Whiston, S. C., & Sexton, T. L. (1998). A review of school counseling outcome research: Implications for practice. *Journal of Counseling and Development, 76,* 412–426.

Whiston, S. C., Sexton, T. L., & Lasoff, D. L. (1998). Career intervention outcome: A replication and extension. *Journal of Counseling Psychology, 45,* 150–165.

Whiston, S. C., & Wachter, C. (2008). *School counseling, student achievement, and dropout rates: Student outcome research in the state of Indiana* (Special Report). Indianapolis, IN: Indiana State Department of Education.

White, K. R., Taylor, M. J., & Moss, V. T. (1992). Does research support claims about the benefits of involving parents in early intervention programs? *Review of Educational Research, 62,* 91–125.

White, S. W., & Kelly, F. D. (2010). The school counselor's role in school dropout prevention. *Journal of Counseling & Development, 88,* 227–235.

Wicks-Nelson, R., & Israel, A. C. (2003). *Behavior disorders of childhood.* Upper Saddle River, NJ: Prentice Hall.

Williams, G. T., & Wehrman, J. D. (2008). Career assessment portfolios: Documentation and accountability empowering transformed professional school counselors. In G. T. Eliason & J. Patrick (Eds.), *Career development in the schools* (pp. 205–216). Charlotte, NC: Information Age Publishing, Inc.

Williamson, E. G. (1965). *Vocational counseling: Some historical, philosophical, and theoretical perspectives.* New York, NY: McGraw-Hill.

Wilson, F. R. (2004, September). *Assessing violence risk: An ecological analysis.* Paper presented at the Association for Assessment in Counseling 2004 National Assessment Conference, Charleston, SC.

Wilson, S. J., Lipsey, M. W., & Derzon, J. H. (2003). The effects of school-based intervention programs on aggressive behavior: A meta-analysis. *Journal of Consulting and Clinical Psychology, 71,* 136–149.

Wood Dunn, N. A., & Baker, S. B. (2002). Readiness to serve students with disabilities: A survey of elementary school counselors. *Professional School Counseling, 5,* 277–284.

Worden, J. W. (2009). *Grief counseling and grief therapy: A handbook for the mental health practitioner* (4th ed.). New York, NY: Springer Publishing Company.

Wright, K., & Stegelin, D. A. (2003). *Building school and community partnerships through parent involvement* (2nd ed.). Upper Saddle River, NJ: Merrill/Prentice Hall.

Wu, P., Hoven, C. W., Liu, X., Cohen, P., Fuller, C. J., & Shaffer, D. (2004). Substance use, suicidal ideation and attempts in children and adolescents. *Suicide and Life-Threatening Behavior, 34,* 408–420.

Wyman, P. A., Brown, C. H., Inman, J., Cross, W., Schmeelk-Cone, K., Guo, J., & Pena, J. B. (2008). Randomized trial of a gatekeeper program for suicide prevention: One-year impact on secondary school staff. *Journal of Consulting and Clinical Psychology, 76*(1), 104–114.

Yalom, I. D., & Leszcz, M. (2005). *The theory and practice of group psychotherapy* (5th ed.). New York, NY: Basic Books.

Yaremko, S. K., & Lawson, K. L. (2007). Gender, internalization of expressive traits, and expectations of parenting. *Sex Roles, 57,* 675–687. doi: 10.1007/s11199-007-9301-6

Yip, T., Seaton, E. K., & Sellers, R. M. (2006). African American ethnic identity across the lifespan: A cluster analysis of identity status, identity content and depression among adolescents, emerging adults and adults. *Child Development, 77,* 1504–1517.

Young, A. R., & Beitchman, J. H. (2002). Reading and other specific learning difficulties. In P. Howlin, & O. Udwin (Eds.), *Outcomes in neurodevelopmental and genetic disorders* (pp. 405–438). New York, NY: Cambridge University Press.

Young, D. S. (2005). Today's lesson by . . . Roosevelt? The use of character portrayal in classroom guidance. *Professional School Counselor, 8,* 366–371.

Young, I. M. (2011). *Justice and the politics of difference.* Princeton, NJ: Princeton University Press.

Young, R. A., Marshall, S. K., & Valach, L. (2007). Making career theories more culturally sensitive: Implications for counseling. *The Career Development Quarterly, 56*(1), 4–18. doi: 10.1002/j.2161-0045.2007.tb00016.x

Zahn-Waxler, C., Shirtcliff, E. A., & Maraceau, K. (2008). Disorders of childhood and adolescence: Gender and psychopathology. *Annual Review of Clinical Psychology, 4,* 275–303.

Zimmerman, M. A. (2000). Empowerment theory: Psychological, organizational and community levels of analysis. In J. Rappaport, & E. Seidman (Eds.), *Handbook of community psychology* (pp. 43–64). New York, NY: Plenum.

Zinn, H. (2003). *A people's history of the United States: 1492–present* (Rev. ed.). New York, NY: Perennial Classics.

NAME INDEX

A

Abell, A., 142
Abram, K. M., 410
Achenbach, T. M., 369
Adams, S. J., 393
Adelman, C., 255
Adler, Alfred, 227
Agras, W. S., 406
Airasian, P., 137
Akos, P., 142, 268, 287, 288, 293, 301
Alegría, M., 390
Aleman, N. M., 195
Alexander, C. M., 178
Alexander, K. P., 272
Allan, S. D., 234
Amato, P. R., 340
Amundson, N. E., 259, 260
Ananiadou, K., 139
Anastopoulos, A. D., 402
Ancis, J. R., 179
Andersen, E. M., 403
Anderson, C. R., 134
Anderson, D., 182
Anderson, R., 175
Angelou, Maya, 57
Angold, A., 395, 396
Aoyagi, M., 271
Arnold, M. S., 177, 202, 204
Arredondo, P., 10, 178, 179, 188
Arumi, A. M., 54
Asarnow, J. R., 411
Aseltine, R. H., 140
Ash, M. J., 138
Asner-Self, K. K., 182
Atha, H., 140
Athar, N., 184
Auger, R. W., 265
Azrin, N. H., 403

B

Baba, M. L., 176
Bailey, D. F., 184, 194
Baker, B. L., 398
Baker, S. B., 271, 272, 399
Balfanz, R., 180
Bambara, L. M., 374
Bandura, A., 260
Banks, C. A. M., 174
Banks, J. A., 174

Bardick, A. D., 261
Barnes, P. E., 400
Barona, A., 393, 394, 396, 416
Barrett, J. G., 143
Barrett, Kenneth, 224
Barry, C., 256
Bartholomew, A., 383
Barton, P. E., 176
Barton, Pat, 303
Baskin, T. W., 134, 139
Bauman, S., 139, 295, 301
Baumberger, J. P., 242
Baumeister, A. A., 398
Beale, A. V., 139
Beck, A. T., 334
Beegle, G., 322
Beeler, L. M., 267
Beitchman, J. H., 399, 400
Bell, A., 175
Bellordre, C. A., 403
Bemak, F., 201, 205, 206, 211, 228, 229, 349, 395, 396
Bennett, K. J., 405
Benson, F., 321
Berg, I. K., 289
Bergan, J., 305
Berger, E. H., 322
Bergin, J. J., 293, 298
Berglund, P. A., 393, 394
Berk, L., 281
Bernes, K. B., 261
Berthelson, D., 321
Bertram, B., 160, 161
Biederman, J., 403, 411
Bierman, K. L., 405
Blackhurst, A. E., 265
Blair, M., 143
Bloom, B. S., 232
Bloomfield, M., 4
Blue-Banning, M., 322
Blustein, D. L., 276
Bögels, S. M., 414
Bolman, L. G., 197
Borders, L. D., 133, 141, 220, 222
Borum, R., 335
Bouffard, S., 249
Boulton, A., 386
Boyd, R. C., 413
Boyer, E. L., 20
Boyle, C. L., 141

SUBJECT INDEX